More praise for *Hellfire Nation*

"In a beautifully written book, Morone has integrated the history of American political thought with a perceptive study of religion's role in our public life. May *Hellfire Nation* encourage Americans to discover (or rediscover) the 'moral dreams that built a nation.'"—**E. J. Dionne,** syndicated columnist and author of *Why Americans Hate Politics* and *They Only Look Dead*

"This is a remarkably broad, sweeping account, written with verve and passion."—**James T. Patterson,** author of *Brown v. Board of Education: A Civil Rights Milestone and Its Troubled Legacy*

"Morone is an exciting writer. Rich in documentation and eloquent in purpose, *Hellfire Nation* couldn't be more timely."—**Tom D'Evelyn,** *Providence Journal*

"*Hellfire Nation* offers convincing evidence that no political advance has ever taken place in the United States without a moral awakening flushed with notions about what the Lord would have us do. It's enough to make a secular leftist gag—and then grudgingly acknowledge the power of prayer."—**Michael Kazin,** *Nation*

"This book's provocative thesis, ambitious scope, and brisk prose ensure that it will appeal to a broad readership."—*Harvard Law Review*

"[Morone] has written a book for people with no special training in American cultural history. His aim seems to be to meditate on the long history of Christian-based political movements. He wants to encourage people to rethink the possibilities and limitations of the American tendency to conflate religion and politics. Morone has succeeded in meeting these worthwhile goals, and he has done so through a set of engrossing narratives. *Hellfire Nation* . . . is actually fun to read."—**David Harrington Watt,** *Christian Century*

Abolitionists are gathered to condemn slavery and denounce the Constitution as a "covenant with death and an agreement with hell" when a police-led mob bursts into the hall. The intruders stop black men from "promiscuously" preaching to white ladies. ("Expulsion of Negroes and Abolitionists from Tremont Temple, Boston, Massachusetts," *Harper's Weekly,* December 15, 1860)

Hellfire Nation

THE POLITICS OF SIN
IN AMERICAN HISTORY

JAMES A. MORONE

Yale University Press   New Haven & London

Anything Goes, by Cole Porter
© 1934 (Renewed) Warner Bros. Inc.
All Rights Reserved. Used by Permission.
Warner Bros. Publications U.S. Inc., Miami, FL, 33014

Subterranean Homesick Blues
Copyright © 1965 by Warner Bros. Inc. Copyright renewed 1993 by Special Rider Music.
All rights reserved. International copyright secured.
Reprinted by permission.

Designed by James J. Johnson and set in Adobe Caslon type by The Composing Room of Michigan, Inc. Printed in the United States of America by R. R. Donnelley & Sons.

Library of Congress Cataloging-in-Publication Data

Morone, James A., 1951–
   Hellfire nation : the politics of sin in American history / James A. Morone.
      p. cm.
Includes bibliographical references and index.
   ISBN 0-300-09484-1 (cloth : alk. paper)
   ISBN 0-300-10517-7 (pbk. : alk. paper)

   1. United States—Politics and government.   2. Religion and politics—United States—History.   3. United States—Moral conditions.   4. United States—Social conditions. I. Title.
E183 .M873 2002
973—dc21   2002007541

A catalogue record for this book is available from the British Library.

The paper in this book meets the guidelines for permanence and durability of the Committee on Production Guidelines for Book Longevity of the Council on Library Resources.

10 9 8 7 6 5 4 3 2

For my parents,
JIM AND STASIA MORONE

Contents

PART IV

The Social Gospel at High Tide (1932–1973)

PART V

The Puritans Roar Again

Preface

The idea for this book came to me while I was in an upscale supermarket picking out salad greens. Near me, a man suddenly went into a deep, wrenching cough. All around, people stopped what they were doing and looked up with concern. He was a wiry black man, about sixty years old. His clothes and hair were flecked with white dust—he looked as though he had spent the day plastering. Suddenly, a smartly dressed woman, an expensive scarf draped over her shoulder, marched up to him, waved a finger two inches from his face, and said, "I hope you don't smoke." "Oh, no, ma'am," he responded, still recovering from his coughing fit. "No, ma'am, I don't smoke." She apparently didn't believe him and launched into a lecture about the hazards of tobacco.

She was flat-out rude, I thought. But everyone else seemed to approve. Another shopper murmured, "Good for you." They would not normally have tolerated such aggressive behavior—and toward the only black person in the place. I began to wonder about the righteous streak that ran through these polite, well-dressed liberals shopping for health food. This is just how the Prohibitionists must have sounded, I mused.

When I got back home to New Hampshire, I told the story to my neighbor. Yorrick Hurd, age eighty, lives half a mile up the dirt road from here—Hurd Road, as it happens. His family has been in the same house since 1777. I was expecting Yorrick to blurt out a rock-solid bit of New Hampshire Live Free or Die—something like "Smoking and drinking are your own damn business." I was wrong. Turns out that Grandmother Hurd had organized the local Women's Christian Temperance Union. Once a month the women of Lempster gathered at the Hurd farm and plotted the demise of demon rum. What's more, Yorrick still supports Prohibition and laments the day it was repealed. "But Yorrick," I reminded him, "you subscribe to good lefty magazines like the *Nation* and *American Prospect*." "Sure," he agreed cheerfully, but "liquor is different."

Morality is different. I began tugging on a simple question: What happens when our pragmatic, commonsense, split-the-difference American politics turns righteous? And I started with a simple answer: What happens are Puritans, lynchings, witch-hunts, and a thousand angry thou-shalt-nots. But, as you'll see, the moral story is a lot more complicated. Even the Puritans weren't entirely puritanical. I did find plenty of witch-hunts, of course. But I also discovered what Lincoln (speaking of moralists) called the "better angels of our nature." This book, about the two faces of sin, is very different from the jeremiad against Jeremiahs that I set out to write.

I *am* righteous about one cause, however. I have tried to write a book that will appeal to general readers as well as to my colleagues. The style and tone are a kind of manifesto to my companions in the social sciences: it is time to reclaim our place in the public conversation (in academia, we call this honoring the narrative).

Incidentally, I am a political scientist, which gives me a slightly different approach to history. Historians usually look for what is unique in every event; they dig into the details and keep a close eye on the story line. In contrast, we social scientists earn our merit badges for finding the common themes, which gets us searching for abstractions, generalizations, and theories. Today, innovative scholars in both disciplines are crossing the old boundaries, searching out both the unique and the universal in every era. That's my goal: I look for the threads running through the past and try to see the patterns they make in our own time.

A book like this is a community enterprise. And when the subject is sin, everyone's an expert. My friends, neighbors, colleagues, and family all listened patiently to *Hellfire* stories with good cheer and great suggestions.

First, my deep thanks to the friends who brainstormed, read, questioned, commented, and corrected. May the karma flow directly into your own work, Peter Andreas, Jason Barnosky, Tim Bartlett, David Bennett, Don Brand, Ross Cheit, Jonathan Cohn, Tony Dell'Aera, Andy Dunham, Thomas Faist, Dan Gitterman, Marie Gottschalk, Brian Glenn (who wrote a small tome on the manuscript), Richard John (who wrote a long one), Larry Jacobs, Ira Katznelson, Rogan Kersh, Beth Kilbreth, Bob Kuttner, Ted Marmor (a defiant sinner who is ferocious in his scorn for neo-Puritans), Sid Milkis, Peter Morone, Michael Nebblo, Karen Orren, Jim Patterson, Mark Peterson, Jill Quadango, David Robertson, Nancy Rosenblum, Lynn Sanders, Mark Schlesinger, Steve Skowronek, Rogers Smith, Tom Sugrue, Steve Teles (who cheerfully stalked my project, popping up with commentaries when I least expected them), John Tomasi, Rick Valelly, and Gordon Wood. Larry Brown scribbled me a note in the middle of a seminar that put my whole argument into context. Theda Skocpol saw, long before I did, that there are two sides to the moral coin. Leo Weigman rethought the outline. And Jessica Stone skipped her homework to read the final draft.

Every time I presented a version of *Hellfire* I came back with a head full of new questions and ideas—I wish I could thank every person who raised a hand and came up with something disruptive at the Universities of Chicago, Toronto, Virginia, and Bremen; Harvard, Yale (several times), Syracuse, Rutgers, Stanford, Brandeis, and New York Universities; Boston and Middlebury Colleges; the Minnesota Historical Society; and a host of conferences.

The Robert Wood Johnson Foundation's Investigator Award gave me the gift of time. It also provided a wonderful network of companions who asked simple questions that took years to answer. Robin Osborne, Sol Levine, Barbara Krimgold, Al Tarlov, Dave Mechanic, and Lynn Rogut were, each in a different way, mentors, cheerleaders, and companions.

John Covell had his eye on this book before I knew what it was about and signed it for Yale University Press. When John left the Press, Lara Heimert inherited the project, "got it" immediately, and guided it with terrific skill and grace. Heidi Downey was a wonderful manuscript editor—with sharp eyes and good ideas. Special thanks to my agent, Rafe Sagalyn, who is wise about books and shaped this one in important ways.

My deepest gratitude goes to the assistants who've cheerfully worked with me over the *Hellfire* years: Pam Paul, Leah Pratt, Eric Evans, Kelley Turner, and Kelli Auerbach. Among many other things, Kelli tracked down the wonderful illustrations in the book.

Many thanks also to the skillful librarians at the John Hay Library (at Brown University) and the John Carter Brown Library—especially Jean Rainwater (a sensational literary sleuth) and Richard Ring. People in the business will understand what a deeply religious experience it was for me to stand before first editions of some ninety works by Cotton Mather.

And a sad word about my lost companions. Eric Nordlinger and Martin Kessler listened cheerfully to my earliest rambles. Steve Stone saw the final draft—I see from his notes that he got as far as abolition. And the spirit of my teacher, David Greenstone, stirs on every page. I would give anything to have just one more conversation with each of these wonderful friends.

I've dedicated *Hellfire Nation* to my parents, and, given the topic, I'd better say a word about why. My dad reads voraciously and never seems to forget a detail. I'm not sure whether his real love is history or politics, but he's my first colleague in both fields. My mom taught me always to look for the other side. In fifth grade, when the nuns at St. Joseph's Hill Academy were teaching us about the Protestant Revolution, she smuggled me a biography of Martin Luther—turns out some people called it a Reformation. Reading two completely different versions of the ninety-five theses opened a door that eventually led to a world of asking questions. I never forget that the pleasure I get from prowling the library or tapping at my computer comes straight from my parents.

Finally, everyone has a special author—someone who writes so beautifully that you can't wait to read the next piece. I have the joy of living with mine. (If you've been missing out, go pick up something by Deborah Anne Stone, and you'll see what I mean.) Our idea of fun is to sit in the old farmhouse, click-clack away on our computers, and then savor each other's words over a rich red wine from Cahors (sorry, Yorrick!). There's too much to say to Deborah (and never mind that it's a long book on sin), so I'll just say thanks for everything and make a wish for many more years of books and talks and laughter.

HELLFIRE
NATION

Introduction
A Nation with the Soul of a Church

TEN thousand people filled the Holt Street Baptist Church and spilled out into the Montgomery evening. The young minister, Martin Luther King, Jr., slowly worked his way through the crowd. When he finally reached the pulpit and began to preach, loudspeakers carried his message to the black men and women standing outside. King called on them to rise in protest. "There comes a time," he roared over shouts and amens, "when the people get tired of being trampled over by the iron feet of oppression." Then he pointed down a celebrated path. "I want it to be known throughout . . . this nation that we are a Christian people. The only weapon in our hand is the weapon of protest." King capped the first great sermon of the civil rights era with one of his favorite quotations. "We are determined, here in Montgomery, to work and fight until justice runs down like water and righteousness like a mighty stream." King took the passage from the Old Testament's Book of Amos, which is harsher than the preacher let on. "Woe unto you," warns Amos in a passage King never touched, "wailing shall be in all the streets." Why? Because you turned your back on Joseph when he was sold into bondage by his brothers.

The civil rights movement poured out of Holt Street Baptist on that December night in 1955. The activists put aside a traditional black jeremiad about God's wrath toward those who oppressed His children. Instead, they latched onto Christian nonviolence and, in the next decade, transformed the United States. So did the implacable segregationists who stormed back at the marchers with their own twisted moral arguments. Both sides called on God to witness the cause. Today Americans honor King and skip over the segregationist violence, the great shame of the 1960s. The civil rights crusade embodied an ancient political tradition: across American time, nothing rallies the people or expands their government like a pulpit-thumping crusade against social injustice.

Panic spread across the nation. Dangerous young men prowled the countryside. They lured girls into ice cream parlors, wooed them, whisked them off to the cities, and sold them into sexual slavery. By 1910, experts reported, sixty thousand women a year were perishing in the brothels. Heartbreaking screams for help echoed, unanswered, in the urban night. Popular tracts warned young women away from Italian fruit stands, Chinese laundries, German skating rinks, and—most dangerous of all—the Eastern European Jews who had masterminded the sordid business. President William Howard Taft demanded action against the traffic in stolen girls. Congress normally left law enforcement to the states, but how could it ignore white slavery? Taking a woman across state lines for immoral purposes became a federal crime in 1910, and enforcement fell to the tiny Bureau of Investigation. The agency expanded, opened a branch office, and eventually changed its name to the Federal Bureau of Investigation.

When the moral champions finally marched into the sex districts, the enslaved maidens laughed at them. There were no iron bars on the brothels, no Jews skulking behind the doors, no sixty thousand perishing country girls. Still, the panic—and the call for federal action—sprang from real anxiety. The next census would certify the United States as an urban nation, and the rising cities frightened decent rural folks. Political machines prospered. Vice boomed. Cities filled with foreigners who changed American habits, changed America itself. Popular anxiety turned social and economic change into moral crises, fingered a villain, and called the cops. Fearful Americans did not have to make much of a leap to turn their qualms into a white slave panic. Stolen or not, country girls flocked to the cities, where they saw and did things they never saw or did back home. And even if the foreigners—Jews, Chinese, Italians—were not exactly stealing American girls, they were bringing strange ways to the United States. They seemed to threaten hardy Anglo-Saxon virtues. Even the label "white slavery" emits a racial jolt.

The white slave episode offers a variation on an American epic: our innocents fall into demonic hands. Savage Indians, satanic witches, Irish priests, Mormon polygamists, slave traders, saloon keepers, smut peddlers, drug pushers, Internet providers, and generations of black men would all take their turn as a menace to the nation's innocent white women or children.

Even phantom fears provoke real political action. Leaders rallied Americans to defend their civilization from the foreign white slavers and their bestial practices. Congress responded with legislation. The annual Baptist convention cheered the law and pushed the administration to expand its moral mission (fu-

ture social scientists would have said that the Baptists captured the policy).
Even without stolen farm girls, enforcement agencies like the FBI found
plenty of villains to nab. Panics and witch-hunts are an American classic: nothing stirs the people or grows their government like a pulpit-thumping moral
crusade against malevolent dastards.

A new nation, drawn from many tribes and races, always faces the primal
question, Who are we? In this book I trace an all-American answer back to the
Puritans: a godly people, a model for the world, a city on a hill. Moral dreams
define the nation's ideals; they inspire crusades at home and abroad—from the
revolution of 1776 to the war on terror more than two centuries later.

If moral fervor stirs our better angels, moral fever spurs our demons.
Frightening changes—a new economy, booming cities, still more strangers—
rouse fears of decline. Every generation blames a slack-virtued, un-American
"them." At every turn another Jew or Chinese man steals (we used to say
"shanghais") our daughters or corrupts our land. Efforts to convert or control
the dangerous "them" snap across the culture and remake the regime.

Hellfire Nation presents the American story as a moral tale. Political life
constantly gets entangled in two vital urges—redeeming "us" and reforming
"them." The moral perspective revises all kinds of standard stories. From this
angle, the United States is a lot more than a nation of shopkeepers. Take, for
example, that old political science favorite: the United States operates a weak
state, almost no state at all. True enough if you're looking for national health insurance. But turn to moral control and you'll find a powerful government pushing deep into American society. What kind of weak state would outlaw liquor
sales from coast to coast? What kind of weak state enters the twenty-first century with 3 percent of its population in jail or prison, on parole, or under probation? Only a powerful and intrusive regime could get that many people under
its criminal justice thumb.

Why do morals play such a crucial role? For starters, Americans believe in
God. In other nations, a handful of stable faiths claim a fixed social place; in the
United States, religions restlessly shift, split, and spread in a kind of ecclesiastical uproar. The nation develops not from religious to secular but from revival to
revival. The moral fervor mixes with the American social chaos: new people
keep arriving, and each new immigration stirs fears of moral decline. Wide-
open political rules invite some into the political fray and push others out. Economic mobility—down as well as up—generates plenty of status anxiety. Race
relations constantly get renegotiated. Ditto gender—that battle began in 1636.
All those blurry lines between us and them, privileged and repressed, strong
and weak, keep getting rewritten as the boundaries between good and evil. The

recipe for discrimination is simple: paint them bad. We strip moral inferiors—witches, slaves, drinkers, crackheads—of their rights. To win back those rights, simply reverse the process: cry out that good people face injustice.

Morality operates in different ways. Sometimes it simply reflects displaced anxiety. A gust of modernity—a changing economy or a new technology—threatens traditional communities. Our institutions—a synod of ministers, a congressional committee, religion, law—channel the fear toward a familiar demon. At other times, a moral idea catches on. The ideas themselves matter—they rouse mass movements, raise new political possibilities, reverberate against powerful organizations, and rattle the status quo. We will see both kinds of moral outburst. Each transforms the American way.

The moral cacophony filters into every nook and cranny of our common lives. It sounds so familiar that Americans often fail to hear it. But foreign visitors notice as soon as they step ashore. "Religion never intervenes directly in the government of American society," wrote Alexis de Tocqueville in 1835, but it "should be considered the first of their political institutions. . . . Christianity reigns, without any obstacles, the universal faith." A century later, G. K. Chesterton arrived from England with a more acid pen. The Americans have the queer idea, wrote Chesterton, that almost everything involves virtue. One afternoon he politely offered a cigar to a reporter who had come to interview him; to Chesterton's wonder, the man stiffened and coldly declined. "He could not have conveyed more clearly that I had attempted to corrupt an honourable man." It was as though, Chesterton went on, I had been "offering him the hashish that would turn him into an assassin." Later, Chesterton offered another interviewer a smoke. The second reporter slyly looked about to make sure they were alone. Then, snatching the proffered cigar, the newsman hissed apologetically, "Well, Mr. Chesterton, I'm afraid I have the habit." Chesterton could not imagine, he wrote, how these people had managed to convert his cigars into instruments of vice and virtue. He famously summed up the United States as a nation with the soul of a church. Decades later, Gunnar Myrdal arrived from Sweden to study American race relations and promptly tagged the United States the most "moralistic and moral conscious . . . branch of Western Civilization." In contrast to Chesterton, Myrdal cheered. American moralism, he wrote, crowned the "glory of the nation" and might even prove the "salvation of mankind."[1]

In this book I explore the moral urge at the heart of American politics and society. In a nation made by immigrants, marked by social mobility, and home to a thousand religions, morality is dynamite. Visions of vice and virtue define the American community. They designate the worthy "us" (jammed into a

Montgomery church) and finger the dangerous "them" (running brothels in the wicked cities). Moral fevers unleash our witch-hunts and racial panics. They inspire the dreamers who turn the nation upside-down in the name of social justice.

American Stories

The standard portrait of American government—political theorists call it liberalism—has little to do with morals. As James Madison put it, "If men were angels, no government would be necessary." The founders drafted a government that would require virtue from neither rulers nor citizens. Raw self-interest did not have to be suppressed because it could be harnessed. The celebrated system of checks and balances would use my ambition to counter yours. Men and women could chase their own selfish interests—flunking the classic test of virtue—and still produce perfectly good government. When Alexander Hamilton was asked why the Constitution did not even mention God he is said to have replied sarcastically, "We forgot." Today, Americans do not pray in public schools and can barely manage Christmas decorations on the courthouse lawn.[2]

The rival American story pictures a kind of Rotarian nation, a people primed to sign up for any communal effort. The community impulse can look either bright (town meetings, bowling leagues, Bible study groups) or bleak (the Ku Klux Klan, militia groups).

Let's look at these two classics—the liberal and the communitarian—before introducing a hellfire alternative. Each perspective tells us important things about who we are. But while the traditional stories fill our libraries, the American moral epic has been pushed to the side—sometimes analyzed (often masterfully) but rarely explored as a mainspring of American politics and culture.

Liberalism

Liberalism comes with its own Genesis: in the beginning, Americans sailed away from old world tyranny and settled a vast, unpopulated land—the place almost thrust freedom on them. The settlers did not need to push aside barons or bishops to get ahead. Instead, as Tocqueville put it, "Americans were born equal instead of becoming so." Men (and maybe women; the old myth gets a bit shaky here) faced extraordinary opportunities. The land and its riches awaited—all it took was a little capital and a lot of work.

Unabashed individualism became the irresistible consequence. Free to make their own fortunes amid the new world bounty, Americans developed their celebrated faith—you might even call it a cult: free economic markets, limited government, and a firm commitment to individual rights. The Constitution nailed "Don't tread on me" to the mast of a pragmatic, secular regime that Americans now hawk in every corner of the globe.[3]

The theory behind all this, classical liberalism, emerged from Europe's terrible religious wars. Weary of the bloodshed, liberal theorists urged governments to turn a blind eye to people's personal views. Theorists use the term "liberal" to mean something quite different from its ordinary meaning. At the heart of the theory stands an inviolate line between private and public realms. Pick your own values; your private sphere is protected by rights that bar any public authority from meddling in what you think or say. "However strange it may seem," wrote John Locke in 1689, "the lawgiver hath nothing to do with moral virtues and vices." Citizens draw on their private desires or values and then charge into the public, the political, realm to advance their interests. In the patois of economics, every agent maximizes her own utilities.[4]

Liberalism's great American debate turns on precisely where to draw the line between public and private spheres. Americans are famous for their pinched public sector; just protect the basic rights, they say, especially property, and leave people alone to compete in free economic markets—free, that is, from government meddling. Sure enough, many Americans greet new public programs by storming against socialism and grumbling about taxes. In this world view, your ideas, your property, and, oddly, your firearms sit securely in the private sphere.

Occasionally, Americans get carried away. After the Civil War, for example, President Andrew Johnson illustrated how harsh a raw market view could get when he mused about mass black annihilation: if the former slaves "fail and perish away, let us be careful that the failure shall not be attributable to any denial of justice." But hold on. It was 1865. The freemen had no property, no capital, little education, and few rights. They could not vote or, in many cases, move about freely. They lived with the threat of violence and the scars of slavery. It is hard to imagine a more deeply biased political economy. Yet here was the president coolly informing America that the former slaves would swim or sink alongside everyone else (while he vetoed laws that might have given them a decent chance to swim). President Johnson had gone too far in drawing his limits on the public sector. He overlooked the need for a government that protects the basics—the right to vote, to speak, to move around safely—before people start competing in private sector markets. He also offers an extreme reminder that every system is tilted by its political rules and institutions.[5]

And that opens the door to a far more generous—what we'd commonly call a more liberal—theory of liberalism. The state ought to guarantee that every-one has the basics—food, housing, education, health care. As Daniel Webster put it, people are not free to read till we teach them how. Market competition is unfair, say people in this camp, if we don't ensure that everyone begins with a certain minimum—like breakfast.[6]

Liberal theorists became extraordinarily active in the 1990s. From both the left and the right they introduce new variations on the basic theoretical model. Some theorists see a robust moral sense as an aid to liberal citizenship, a kind of prerequisite for good politics; others resist such political incursions into the private sphere. In either case, the liberal paradigm—with its division between private and public—makes it easy to overlook the politics of our private lives. The liberal framework leads analysts to minimize moral movements as anom-alies—peripheral, exceptional, odd. Liberal political history underestimates the roaring moral fervor at the soul of American politics.

Community

During the 1980s, critics began growing uneasy about unabashed self-interest and untrammeled markets. What happens to the common good when every-one pushes only for number one? Back to early America trooped the social the-orists. There they discovered a robust collective life. If a barn burned down, the townsfolk got together and raised another. If iron pots were dear, families shared them with the neighbors—household inventories commonly list a por-tion of a pot or skillet.

The communal story sparks enthusiasm across the political spectrum. Here, argue proponents, lies firm ground on which to imagine a renewed civic culture. Americans are not just celebrants of self but partners in a shared public life, not just individualists but communitarians. A focus on our common life of-fers a counter to the voracious market. Conservatives focus on restoring tradi-tional values; progressives stress our obligations to one another.[7]

It all sounds fine. But draw closer, and the idylls of community get hazy. What precisely is a community, anyway? Champions range from New Left militants in the 1960s to hard-right militias in the 1990s. Jefferson imagined communities of small, rural landowners; at the other extreme Lincoln conjured up a grand national community bound together by "mystic chords of memory, stretching . . . to every heart and hearthstone all over this broad land." The community ideal gets so slippery because it mixes shared interests, solid geog-raphy, and romantic myth. Still, our common life gets invoked so often because real-world communities exist. Members share strong ties. Those local ties combine to bind the great, imaginary community called the United States.[8]

Laying down communal boundaries kicks up a more troubling question.

Defining "us" also designates "them." In fact, the United States long ago patented a quite distinctive other, the un-American. *Life* magazine (January 29, 1951) neatly posed the American difference: "While Americans have no doubt that to be a Communist is un-American, millions of Frenchmen do not consider it un-French. How can this be so?" *Life* never found an answer—the question was a lot larger than the editors imagined. The American others, the un-Americans, stretch all the way back to the early colonies.

Scholars recently have focused on the American urge to reject entire groups. The official American story, symbolized by the congenial melting pot, imagines a nation constantly cooking up a richer democracy with thicker rights. The unofficial alternative counters with a less cheerful story: many Americans have faced repression simply for their ascriptive traits—their race, gender, ethnicity, or religion. Generous visions of inclusion face off against hard prejudices. The two impulses are evenly matched, in this more skeptical view, Manichean twins wrestling for control of each historical moment. As William Carlos Williams put it in 1925, always poised against the *Mayflower* sails a slave ship. American political development offers no clear historical trajectory, no inevitable march of rights, no irresistible triumphs of rights and freedom.[9]

The dark side of the American spirit raises a host of questions. Just who gets attacked? When? Why? And how does prejudice sneak past the vaunted Bill of Rights? If anything, each generation seems to enlarge the roster of citizenship rights—some critics charge the nation with being practically drunk on personal rights and liberties. How do Americans get around all their constitutional safeguards and repress rivals, strangers, and scary others? Morality. We are bound to honor our fellow citizens and their rights, unless the neighbors turn out to be bad. Then they can be—and often are—stripped of their lives, their liberty, and their legally acquired property.

The communal perspective captures an important part of the American spirit. So does the liberal story (though many historians fiercely dispute the idea that it goes all the way back to the colonial era). When we go back and read about early America, we find early stirrings of liberal capitalism and plenty of emphasis on enduring community. But what leaps out, loudest and clearest, is the search for eternal salvation through Christ's grace. Morality mattered most in early America. It still matters—enormously—today.[10]

Morality

Morality politics comes with its own foundation myth. "It seems to me," wrote Tocqueville, "that I can see the entire destiny of America contained in the first

Puritan who came ashore." Those early settlers confronted a question that would echo across the years: Who are we? Back home, the crown had provided the answer by persecuting Puritans. "But New England's peace and plenty . . . breeds strange security," warned minister Thomas Shepherd in 1636. Here "there are no enemies to hunt you to heaven."[11]

Who were they? The Puritans concocted a celebrated solution. They were the community of saints. Leadership, in both church and state, fell to men pre-ordained for salvation by their Calvinist God. They calibrated their ranks with fine moral distinctions—the saints even dreamed up a category for people admitted "half-way" into their church congregations. Virtue distinguished leaders from followers, voters from nonvoters, us from them.[12]

As they founded their towns, the colonists signed covenants pledging "mutual love." The members of these tight communities promised to watch over and assist one another. In the fine print they also vowed, as the Dedham, Massachusetts, covenant put it, "to keep off from us such as are contrary minded." The boundary between the saints and the contrary minded quickly grew hot. The Puritans slaughtered Native Americans (agents of Satan), hanged witches (carnal knowers of Satan), and sent heretics packing to Rhode Island ("the latrina of New England," even then). In his Puritan histories, Cotton Mather portrayed a New England under constant siege; waves of satanic malice crashed down on the good community. "It was time for the devil to take alarm" and "attack a plantation so contrary to his interests," wrote Mather about the first Indian wars against the Pequot people. "A horrible army of devils is broke in . . . upon the people of God," he commented about the witch frenzy in Salem Village. Each enemy clarified the settlers' identity by demonstrating what they were not, what they must never become.[13]

One last leap marked the Puritans and their legacy. They arrived with a mission—redeeming the Protestant reformation. In the old world, Anglican corruption eroded Calvin's ideals. Here the settlers would start fresh, organize a Christian commonwealth, and perhaps set a model for the rest of the world. Even before they reached land, John Winthrop delivered his beautiful sermon. "We shall be as a city on a hill, the eyes of all people are upon us." The stakes were huge. "If the Lord shall be pleased . . . He shall make us a praise and a glory." This odd idea stuck and spread. The Calvinist culture burst out of New England on gusts of religious revival led by the purer Puritans, the Baptists.[14]

The Puritan trope lives on. The essential vision—a community of model citizens—continues to denote the American us. Finely calibrated moral distinctions still run across the ranks—today's bottom, for example, includes the virtuous working poor, the undeserving poor (with their welfare queens, no less), and an underclass (routinely described as morally depraved.) "Horrible armies of devils" keep breaking loose and threatening the good people. And the stakes remain high, for the city still stands up there on a hill. Americans constantly return to the heady image of a providential task, a great experiment unfolding in the United States, while the rest of the world looks and learns. The precise content of the American lesson evolves—faith, freedom, free markets—but 350 years after Winthrop's sermon, one scholar describes his "astonishment, as a Canadian immigrant, at learning about the prophetic history of America." Here was "a population that despite its bewildering mixture of race and creed could believe in something called the American mission and could invest that patent fiction with all the emotional, spiritual, and intellectual appeal of a religious quest."[15]

All this has plenty of roots outside Puritan New England: The southern colonies (which I explore in Part II), Quaker Philadelphia, the Spanish regions in the south and west, and the wild borderlands that mixed native, French, and English cultures. However, I start with the New England Puritans because they incubated and spread such a potent American morality.[16]

The idea of a redeemer nation still drives American politics. At first glance it appears to foster precisely the opposite of classical liberalism: moral politics rush into the private sphere, denying the boundary between public and private. The lawgiver suddenly has everything to do with vice and virtue. Private behavior becomes a public problem.

Moreover, moral politics transform the political process itself. They draw fierce partisans into the fray and blow right past the usual checks and balances, deals and compromises. Who logrolls with evil-doers? Steal our country daughters for white slaves and Congress tosses aside its strict limits on federal police powers. Shine the moral light on segregation and—after almost a century of looking the other way—progressives run South to join the revolution. Moral trumpets call up deep-seated, bare-knuckle fights. Rights evaporate. Nobody compensated slaveholders or saloon keepers (or tobacco companies?) as the nation stripped them of their constitutionally protected but deeply immoral property.

Each moral storm is unique. But across the crusading generations a rough cycle has evolved. First, groups spring up and try to convert the sinners they face. Take the long, hard battle against drink, for example. Reformers pleaded with drinkers to take the pledge to abstain; going dry would eradicate slums, end poverty, and—in the really hot sermons—"rent hell forever." But the stubborn sinners refused to repent. They harmed themselves, abused their wives, ruined their kids, and diminished America. The second phase begins as reformers give up trying to persuade the incorrigibles. Instead, they turn to government and demand prohibitions. The holy warriors put aside other goals—prohibitionists had been fighting for a living wage, comparable pay for women, and sexual purity from men—and focus on eradicating the one big evil. They scoff at politics as usual, they will not compromise. After all, they see a nation teetering between right and wrong, salvation and perdition. Third, when moral campaigns break through and win, they leave their mark on the way government works. We'll trace this powerful, overlooked form of state-building all the way back to the great religious revivals that helped organize the American Revolution. Even if the fervor springs from a passing panic (like the white slave scare) or if the prohibition collapses (like liquor Prohibition), the campaigns leave deep legacies: they lead us to rewrite laws, reinterpret the Constitution, reshape the political culture, and create new public agencies. We find exactly the same cycle—persuasion, prohibition, and state powers—in the campaigns against slavery or segregation or nineteenth-century abortionists. We'll watch the process develop as each era adds its variations to the moral cycle.

Though they may look like opposites, moral politics conspires with liberalism. Locke may have thought that the lawmaker had nothing to do with vice and virtue, but a whole army of revisionist liberal theorists ponder the moral preconditions of civic life. A liberal democracy, they argue, requires virtue from its citizenry; checks and balances are not enough if citizens do not respect common rules and one another's rights. Even Locke himself slipped back around looking for virtue: education and people's desire for public esteem, he suggested, might nurture the moral foundations of liberal governance.[17]

The idea of molding virtuous citizens sounds uncontroversial. Who would oppose moral rectitude? But morality helps Americans answer those subversive questions at the heart of every community: Who are we? Who belongs? Here's where liberalism, community, and morality reach their American symbiosis. Moral images set the boundaries around the liberal political process, around the American "us."

After all, not everyone can belong to the community. In liberal lingo, not everyone can be a full, rights-bearing member. Children are not ready for many rights. A whole race, wrote John Stuart Mill in 1859, "could be considered as in nonage"—treated like children. This is precisely what the slaveholders and the segregationists said. Aliens get some rights (jury trials), but not others (suffrage). In early America, most women could not vote, and once they married they became "dead in the law." White men without property could not vote either; as they came into suffrage they pushed out free black property holders. Convicted felons lose their freedom; in some states, they cannot vote or bear arms even after they've done their time. Every society draws these kinds of boundaries all over the political system. In the United States, the lines get drawn and justified, ripped and razed by moral judgments. The search for moral citizens—so prudent-sounding in the abstract—grows a keen double edge every time another "horrible army of devils" breaks loose and threatens the good people. Are they really sinners poised to drag us down? Or is the convulsion just another racial difference read as moral depravity? Calls for better morals keep rebounding hard against people on the margins. There's always a group who seem a dubious us, who endanger our special status as a city on a hill.[18]

Of course, every nation thrashes out criteria by which to determine members, dispense rights, and distinguish strangers. Every culture constructs "us" and "them." How is the American way different? Compare Germany, in some ways the cultural opposite. German politicians insist that, unlike the United States, Germany is not an immigrant nation. Yet between the end of World War II (1945) and the eve of unification (1990), almost 15 million people immigrated to the Federal Republic and became citizens—that added up to one out of four West Germans by 1990. Count foreign workers (another 4.3 million) and the number of people born abroad leaps to one in three. The United States never saw that many foreigners—not even close. Yet we are the immigrant nation and Germany is not. Why? Because the Germans simply did not view most of those postwar newcomers as immigrants. They were "Germans" returning home after generations—even centuries—of living abroad. The cultural concept of a German is particularly robust—Germans returning from Romania after a century or two are not foreigners; people born in Hamburg of Turkish parents are not real Germans. The Germans have developed their own vivid sense of us and them—of just who is a genuine compatriot. And so, of course, have Americans.[19]

Unlike the Germans, Americans have no enduring sense of pure blood or culture (despite endless efforts to assert one). The United States is so susceptible to moral combustions—to witch-hunts, moral panics, crime wars, and prohibitions—precisely because it is such an open and fluid society. Every immigrant generation changes the face of the nation; every shift in suffrage threatens the political order. Without a stable cultural archetype to determine who belongs, Americans measure one another by a vaguely delineated, highly moralistic code of conduct. Flunk and you're un-American. A society on full boil keeps stirring up the same deep tribal fears: These others do not share our values. They do not understand our religious traditions. They will subvert the virtues that made us rise and prosper. What happens to the city on a hill when it yields power to Irish-Catholics or Chinese-Heathens or Mexican-Americans or former slaves or Muslims? What happens to us if they convert (or marry!) our daughters?

In a vibrant, changing nation, popular images of us and them stay in almost constant motion. They set the agenda, spark social movements, shape the political debate. When the stereotypes shift, the politics change. We'll see entire groups wrench themselves out of one moral frame and into another. They get transformed—or they transform themselves—from a dangerous class into good people who got a raw deal, pushed down by bigotry or bad luck or big business. That's just what Martin Luther King, Jr., was doing that December night at the Holt Street Baptist Church. Some generations treat poor people to sharp sermons about sloth; when political leaders transform those poor people into good neighbors who've fallen on hard times, the sermons give way to social services. Or take liquor. Today, the executive who drinks too much is sick and gets help; a century ago, the immigrant who drank at all was a sinner and caught hell.

From this perspective, the most telling contemporary social metric is the booming prison population. The number of Americans in jail passed the 2 million mark in 2000 despite ten years of falling crime (the murder rate had plunged below its 1915 level). The incarceration rate is the highest in the world, five times the rate of most industrial democracies. Add those on probation and parole to those in prison and the total hits 6.3 million. Turn the focus to black people, and the criminal justice system claims almost one in ten. Do they all really belong there? We will explore that controversy in the final chapter (I stand with the skeptics). But no matter how you read the crime tables, a powerful conclusion leaps out of the record: running up those kinds of numbers—literally clearing our cities of young black men—requires a very low tolerance for mischief and a formidable sense of us versus them.[20]

In short, us, them, and the shifting lines that run between them get drawn, disputed, and dissolved in moral terms. For better and for worse, moral conflicts made America. *Hellfire Nation* shows exactly how and why.

Moral Traditions: Them and Us

The Puritans bequeathed America two different answers to that moral bottom line: Who do we blame for trouble, the sinner or the society? The Puritans believed in blaming both. Salvation and perdition fell on individual souls; however, the Puritan covenants held the entire community responsible. In time, the two halves of that equation—the individual and the community—split. One moral tradition touts personal responsibility. Sinners impoverish themselves and diminish their community. The good society offers firm discipline; it preaches virtue and prosecutes vice. Ironically, the tough love approach passed into popular culture as the Puritanical attitude. (That makes historians wince, for the Puritans also took the opposite approach, but everyone is familiar with "ranting Puritans.") The alternative tradition, the social gospel, shifts the emphasis from the sinner to the system. Poverty, hunger, segregation, racism, sexism, and despair all push good people into corners—into crime, broken marriages, addiction. Social gospel solutions reverse the focus: rather than redeem the individual, reform the political economy.

The two traditions got cast into their modern forms by Victorian preachers in the late nineteenth century. Each emphasizes an entirely different social project. Each attracts intense partisans who tag the other side narrow-minded or naive. The two have alternated, over the past century, as the dominant moral paradigm. And though each side finds the other hard to take, both run deep in the American psyche.

The New Puritans

Moral alarms inspire the essential American literary form, the jeremiad (a lament that the people have fallen into sinful ways and face ruin unless they swiftly reform). A synod of Puritan ministers met in 1679, reviewed stacks of contemporary sermons, and published the classic of the genre: the ancient tenets and taboos were all cracking, reported the ministers. They saw sloth, heavy drinking, bastardy, and rampant sexuality (naked arms and, worse, naked breasts). Public schools were failing, businesses ruthlessly chased profits, and lawsuits had gotten out of hand. These sins all sprang from even deeper trouble: permissive parents and their pampered kids. The evils that afflict our society, summed up the synod, flow from "defects as to family government."[21]

The jeremiads have been doing a brisk business every since. Each generation fears decline, frets over spoiled kids, and scolds its sinners—usually poor people. Benjamin Franklin weighed in with his own jeremiad in 1752. The state of Pennsylvania, he lamented,

> will in a few years be a German colony. Instead of their learning our language, we must learn theirs, or live as in a foreign country. Already the English begin to quit particular Neighborhoods, surrounded by Dutch [that is, Deutch, or German], being made uneasy by the disagreeableness of Dissonant Manners; and, in Time, Numbers will probably quit the Province. . . . Besides, the Dutch under-live, and are thereby enabled to under-work and under-sell the English; who are thereby extremely incommoded and consequently disgusted, so there can be no cordial Affection or Unity.[22]

Here is an early version of what we now call the underclass—right down to the link between hard work and good citizenship. The Puritans had read financial success as a divine seal of approval. That notion blossomed into the Protestant work ethic, which was perfectly embodied by Franklin himself, as Max Weber would point out. Franklin soon recanted, but his pessimism touches points that remain tender to this day: alarm over "our language," anxiety about swarms of lazy foreigners, predictions of middle-class flight, and those mildly ominous "dissonant manners." A fundamental question about American community lurks in the details: Can we be a single—special—people? With *them?* Or will their lax values undermine our virtuous community?23

New groups replaced the Germans in the eye of the storm, but tribal anxiety lived on. A long string of people did not have the right moral stuff to become true Americans. Some, for example, professed the wrong faith. The United States and Protestantism had both been born in rebellion against arbitrary authority; patriotism and piety reinforced each other. Then along came the Catholics, practically bred for tyranny—bound to a foreign pope, bossed by a medieval clergy, and blind to the Bible. How could such sheep become republican citizens? Religious differences melted into moral panics. Pornographic rumors about priests who snatched innocent girls for their nunneries inspired tracts, sermons, and patriotic mobs (who burned an occasional convent to cinders). And if the Catholics posed a menace, what about the Chinese? "All attempts to make an effective Christian out of John Chinaman will remain abortive," wrote social reformer Jacob Riis. "Ages of senseless idolatry, a mere grub worship," leave him incapable of "appreciating the gentle teachings of a faith whose motive and unselfish spirit are alike beyond his grasp."24

The largest immigration to the United States, early in the twentieth century, provoked the most baroque backlash. Edward Alsworth Ross, President Theodore Roosevelt's mentor on the issue, warned about the new American generation in 1913: "That the Mediterranean peoples are morally below the races of northern Europe is as certain as any social fact. . . . William does not leave as many children as Tonio because he will not huddle his family in one room [or] eat macaroni off a bare board." (There were no tablecloths in the shameless tenements.) The Southern Europeans were "selfish" and lived "like pigs." Jews were "moral cripples" with "dwarfed souls"—even their social workers despise them. "Millions of immigrants [are] bred in the coarse peasant philosophy of sex," continued Ross. They "deprave [native] tastes and lower the intelligence of the community." "Avaricious" and "degenerate" "defectives," they come to America with their "sugar loaf heads, moon faces, slit mouths" and "endanger the very Christian conception of womanhood." Any race that opens its door to such flawed humans "deserves the extinction that surely awaits it."25

The registries of moral flaws fall into a distinctive analytic pattern. Every group brought its own corruptions, of course; sins would arise, disappear, and evolve. But to a remarkable extent, each dangerous other threatened us—

threatens us—with variations of the same four sins. Abolitionists pinned them on slaveholders, nativists on the Irish, and contemporary Jeremiahs on our own underclass.

First, the un-Americans are lazy. They just don't get the Puritan work ethic. That explains poverty in the land of plenty and constructs a moral frame for debating social justice. Why assist the have-nots if they are slothful? We've just heard Franklin sniff about underworkers. That attitude would echo through the years. Henry Ward Beecher, a celebrated nineteenth-century Congregational minister, served up perhaps the most muscular version : "No man in this land suffers from poverty unless it be more than his fault—unless it be his *sin*. If men have not enough it is from want of provident care, and foresight, and industry, and frugality." America's bounty offered riches for anyone with a strong back and a bit of pluck. Some scholars read America's late and comparatively stingy social welfare pensions as a sign of a timid state unable to push its way into the robust economy. But what held the tight-fisted line firmly in place was the moral iconography that surrounded poor Americans—sloth, waste, underwork, *sin*. Different approaches would come only when policy makers found alternative pictures of the needy—Civil War veterans, hard workers caught in a bad economy, or unhappy victims of ruthless capitalists. Despite a long line of challengers, Henry Ward Beecher's unflinching standard would mark the poor, on and off, to the present day.[26]

Second, they drink. Or take drugs. This sin did not develop till the early nineteenth century (the colonists guzzled like fish). However, after the religious revivals of the second Great Awakening, the war on rum swelled into the longest and most ardent moral crusade in American history. Substance abuse renders the underclass more frightening. They are not just wicked, but also insensate, irrational, out of control. There is no reasoning with them. Worse, they spread their poison to us, they threaten our innocents. The bad companion lures a decent boy into the saloon, the cunning Chinese offers a white girl his opium pipe, the black field hand gets drunk and grows delirious at the sight of a white woman, the drug pusher stalks the school yard. These addicts (real and imaginary) menace women and children with physical harm; worse, they rob innocent souls, as the Victorians put it, by ensnaring others in their addictions. Substance abuse poses undeniable problems in every community. The Puritan tradition pins those problems on bad behavior, pure and simple. The policy prescription follows directly: get tough, or the depravity will spread.

Third, they threaten violence. Native Americans creep out of the forest, witches skulk through New England villages, slaveholders use branding irons, and predators lurk on urban streets. The violence—it can be real, exaggerated, or imaginary—always seems especially depraved in the dangerous city. The frontispiece of one celebrated Victorian manual, *Traps for the Young,* pictures street urchins cheering a murderous knife fight; "Cut his heart out, Jimmy" shouts one of the youngsters (see fig. 8.1). An often-quoted contemporary update gets just as graphic. "We are terrified by the prospect of . . . being gunned down at random, . . . by youngsters who afterwards show us the blank, unremorseful faces of seemingly feral, pre-social beings." Violent men and women have always roamed through America. Panics pump up honest fears and project them onto entire groups. Suddenly, good people face a race of monsters. Cotton Mather's army of devils rises again.[27]

All these lusts—sloth, drink, violence—are just shadows of the most powerful sin: sex. Here lies the central moral theme and the most unsettling bundle of questions. For starters, sexuality challenges the fundamental Puritan precept: control thyself. Carnality marked the savages; the great danger was always that our people would fall into the same depravity. Sexual politics got more complicated when it became entangled with gender roles. Furious contests have turned on the politics of gender rights, birth control, abortion, marriage, rape, divorce, and homosexuality. When the larger political economy grows tumultuous, some Americans try to find order by asserting control over the "little commonwealth." The well-regulated family, in turn, brings us straight back to the synod of 1679 and the problem at the bottom of all our troubles: the kids. Each generation frets about delinquents running wild, and small wonder. If virtue makes us special, then the nursery becomes the crucible of our civic future. Poor parenting bodes big trouble down the line. Finally, sex and marriage mark the intimate frontier between us and them. The Eve narrative—she succumbed to the Tempter and lost Eden—always waxes loudest around the race line. No American issue ever ignited as much fire as amalgamation, mixing races. We'll see the women's movement, in both the nineteenth and twentieth centuries, get embroiled in apartheid's worries. In short, neo-Puritans have always saved the hottest jeremiads for pelvic matters—carnality, gender roles, the well-regulated family, and the sex-race tangle.

The focus on sinners—not to say, predators—powerfully tilts the political debate. It sinks the communal urge by eroding our sense of common values and shared fate. Instead, the policy problem turns to protecting us and controlling them. The standard solutions run to pledges (for example, temperance, or virginity till marriage), prohibitions (on liquor, abortions, bad books), restrictions (on birth control, sexual partners, curfews), regulations (drug tests, welfare rules that require good morals), more prisons, and tougher laws. As the fear of others rises, every cranny of the regime seems to echo with the fundamental neo-Puritan maxim, "Thou shall not!"

Of course, all societies impose all sorts of controls. Every community has to maintain order and keep the traffic flowing. The political key lies in the emphasis on discipline, in the balance between neo-Puritan policies and their social gospel alternatives. I saw a vivid example of the difference while debating a Republican senator about the Clinton national health insurance proposals in 1994.

The senator opposed the plan. Toward the end of our debate, he abruptly turned to face me. His body language said, "Okay, let's quit kidding around." And here's what followed: "Look, Professor, you can't expect the hard-working people of suburban Cook County to go into the same health care alliance [a kind of insurance pool] as the crackheads in the city of Chicago." The punchline came when I turned to face the audience, all set to joke aside this fatuous dichotomy. Instead, I saw a room full of suddenly sobered liberals. "Yes," they were thinking, "that is a problem." Our imagined community, struggling together over a troubled health care system, had vanished. Now, it was a hardworking us versus a drug-abusing them. "Hey," I yelped, "those uninsured people in the city of Chicago are college students and hard-working nurses and taxi drivers doing double shifts and single moms holding down two jobs . . ." No dice. In fact, it only got worse. Crackheads and single moms.

The Social Gospel

The forgotten Puritans lived in tight communities whose members took responsibility for one another. The heirs of that Puritan tradition flip all the old jeremiads. Rather than blame individual sinners for social problems, blame social pressures for people's sins.

Walter Rauschenbusch made the classic statement of the Social Gospel in 1907. "During the great industrial crisis of the '90s, I could hear virtue cracking and crumbling all around." It was the "industrial machine"—low pay and raw need—that pushed good people into bad behavior. "If anyone has a sound reason for taking the competitive system by the throat in righteous wrath," concluded Rauschenbusch, "it is the unmarried woman and mother with girls." Jane Addams told the same story through the eyes of poor women in Chicago. Many struggled to support their families on miserable wages; hard circumstances and cold neighbors pushed some all the way down to prostitution. Frances Willard, the dynamic president of the Women's Christian Temperance Union, said the same about intemperance: poverty drove people to drink as much a drinking drove them into poverty.[28]

The biblical jeremiads had nothing to do with little vices like drinking and sex, insisted Rauschenbusch. Instead, the prophets spent their wrath on "injustice and oppression." Real sin lay in abusing power, ignoring injustice, or squeezing workers; real virtue lay in constructing a just social order, a good community. The Social Gospel called preachers to engage the world and capitalists to embrace the common good; it wrote down laissez-faire as a dubious moral principle. Once again, the lawgiver—and, now, the business mogul—hath everything to do with vice and virtue. But in the Social Gospel variation, they must answer for the poor and the weak.

The Social Gospel completely revised the four Puritan sins. In a campaign address that he dubbed his Sunday sermon, Franklin Roosevelt recast poverty from a sin to a public health problem. When a modern civilization faces a disease epidemic, said Roosevelt, we find and attack the source of contagion. Just as public health efforts eradicate the causes of disease, public policies should address the causes of poverty. Forget lazy individuals or us versus them. Poverty, like any contagion, threatened the entire community, and the enlightened society addressed it systematically.[29]

The entire roster of personal sins morphed into communal health troubles. Drink would turn acceptable, drunkenness into an illness. Likewise, illegal drugs would pit visions of vice against a diagnosis of disease; contemporary public health advocates are leading the charge against a drug war that they put down as "incarcerating addiction." Sexuality calls up the same public health prescriptions: education, safe practices, birth control, and social supports might nurture stronger families and lasting relationships. The Social Gospel even reinterprets crime; rather than focus on bad individuals, look to the causes— poverty, discrimination, despair.

Historians usually reserve the term Social Gospel for a small group of intellectuals writing at the end of the nineteenth century. But the heart of the Social Gospel—a communal view of vice and virtue—lived on. It came to power in the 1930s, reached its high tide in the 1960s, and was expressed most beautifully by Martin Luther King, Jr. For forty years it served as an often implicit assumption in American policy making.

Always standing against the Social Gospel is robust American faith in individual good and evil. Today the neo-Puritans have roared back in many aspects of communal life. Few political leaders explain poverty or drug abuse or teen pregnancy by pointing to "under privilege" or "poor socioeconomic conditions." That kind of thinking got buried in the backwash of the sixties.

Still, unabashed neo-Puritan moralizing always runs up against the same uneasy problem: the race line. After all, blacks and Latinos are the ones who crowd the courts and jail cells. As one black churchwoman asked plaintively in 1907, "Do Negroes constitute a race of criminals?" Or are the jeremiads and crime wars somehow biased hard against minorities? For most of the past three centuries the answer is inescapable: They were deeply biased. Indeed, downright racist. And today? The race question always raises the most pointed questions about American community, about us and them.[30]

Race

Race troubles kept subverting the high-flying idea of a city on a hill. "I hate slavery," said Abraham Lincoln in 1854, "because it deprives our republican example of its just influence in the world." Enemies of free institutions "taunt us as hypocrites." We are the "scoff of infidel nations," agreed abolitionist Congressman Joshua Giddings (quoting Jefferson). "Reproach has been cast on the . . . Government of the United States," grumped President Martin Van Buren. "The American suffers cruelly," summed up Tocqueville's traveling companion, Gustave de Beaumont, "because in the opinion of other nations, slavery has besmirched his country."[31]

Flash forward a hundred years, and Americans were still squirming. As southern governors furiously stood up for segregation, President Eisenhower kept reminding them what it looked like to the neighbors. "It would be difficult to exaggerate the harm that is being done to the prestige and influence . . . of our nation." Around the world, "our enemies are gloating," and everywhere they are "misrepresent[ing] . . . a system of government based on human rights."[32]

Is there an end to American race trouble? Many observers think that justice is finally at hand: "The economic position of African Americans has improved faster than any other group in American social history—or in the social history of any other country." Here, cheer the optimists, is nothing less than the "greatest social transformation in world history." They deliver the cheerful news with reams of data: before World War II, only one in twenty black families reached middle-class incomes, now it is more than twelve in twenty. And look at popular culture. At midcentury the media completely segregated America—black Americans appeared mainly as victims or as criminals. Twenty-five years later, the popular culture reflects a diverse and pluralistic people.[33]

Still, all that happy data comes half buried in bad news. Nearly a third of African American households remain poor—the rate is nearly two out five for children (that's twice the rate of white kids). And while black Americans were achieving the "greatest social transformation in world history," what was playing in *Time* magazine or the nightly news? Crime, drugs, and the underclass. Andrew Hacker's book title sums up the pessimistic side of the contemporary picture: *Two Nations: Black and White, Separate, Hostile, Unequal.*[34]

How do we reconcile such different pictures? One popular approach does it the old-fashioned way: inequity has nothing to do with race. African Americans who work hard do well. The rest have only themselves—their culture, their attitudes, their morals—to blame. And with that we are back on familiar ground. All the ancient stigmas glint through contemporary stereotypes about crime, welfare, teen pregnancy, drug abuse, violence. Why are people poor? Bad culture, flawed morals. Look closer and you will find the same old set of sins pinned onto every underclass since colonial days. American race politics bristled with prefabricated pictures of "them" from the very start.

American cities have always gathered toughs of every nationality and color. The images of immorality regularly spill onto an entire people—today, the black underclass. One author blurts out what most of his colleagues just imply: it is entirely rational for city dwellers to treat all black men as threatening members of an immoral and predatory underclass. For "taxi-drivers, storekeepers and women, prejudice is warranted. In this context, a bigot is simply a sociologist without credentials." Finally, "discrimination today is . . . based more on reality than illusion." The formula goes back to long before the American Revolution. Project moral fears onto an entire group and do something to control them.[35]

All the optimistic racial stories evaporate in an instant: the quip "sociologist without credentials" is just the latest note in the long, mean chorus of racism in America. Every generation of black writers describes the consequences. Frederick Douglass put it in a mournful letter during a tour of England. Here in England, he wrote, "no delicate nose grows deformed in my presence. . . . I am seated beside white people . . . and no one is offended." Douglass contrasted this with life back home. "I remember attending a revival meeting . . . in New Bedford. . . . I was met by a good deacon who told me, in a pious tone, 'We don't allow niggers here!' " Traveling by steamer from New York to Boston on a chilly December night, continued Douglass, "I went into the cabin to get a little warm. I was soon touched upon the shoulder and told, 'We don't allow niggers here!' " At the eating house, the meetinghouse, the Lyceum, the omnibus, the gentleman's home, and the menagerie on the Boston Common—"we don't allow your people here."[36]

Long past? The worst is over, certainly. But contemporary variations remain sadly familiar. Cornel West writes about nine taxis refusing him, then a tenth. "My blood began to boil," he writes, and "ugly racial memories . . . flashed through my mind." While driving to Williams College, "I was stopped on fake charges of trafficking cocaine. When I told the police officer I was a professor of religion, he replied, 'Yeh, and I'm the flying nun. Let's go, nigger!' I was stopped three times in my first day in Princeton for driving too slowly on a residential street with a speed limit of 25." His fifteen-year-old son, says West, already has similar memories.[37]

As I write this, my friend and research assistant goes off to Boston College Law School. "I'm sorry," the real estate agent tells him, "but there are some neighborhoods that I just can't show you."

Many readers can add their own stories. The hard daily encounters offer a sobering commentary on the American color line. *Hellfire Nation* is not about race. It is about the United States and how we divide our society into friends and enemies. At every historical turn we will find racial oppression embedded in a moralizing frame. But always balancing that painful theme lies its opposite, every bit as strong. Americans keep leaping into crusades for civil rights and social justice. For every witch-hunt stands a Rosa Parks, launching a revolution. Or, flipping around William Carlos Williams, always poised against the slave ship sails the *Mayflower*. Every chapter yields the same lesson: the most successful counter to repression lies in moral calls for rights and justice.

Moral Trends

A close look at morality politics challenges assumptions that usually slip by without notice. Take a closer look at two trends we usually take for granted: the inexorable drift toward a more secular society, and the rise of an active federal government. A moral frame transforms the standard wisdom in both cases.

Secular Drift?

A pocket sociology blames modernity for slowly, surely eroding the bulwarks of belief. "Western intellectual life," intones *U.S. News and World Report*, "has been shedding its links to religion since at least as far back as the 16th century." By now, there's hardly any solid cultural ground left for the virtuous to stand on. "When ordinary men and women . . . wish to make moral judgments," writes James Q. Wilson, they must do so privately and in whispers. Gertrude Himmelfarb wonders "whether the million purchasers of William Bennett's *Book of Virtues* had to overcome their initial embarrassment in order to utter that word." The authors offer sophisticated variations of a familiar lament: we have lost the morals that guided us to our glory days. From across the political spectrum, writers entreat us to take good and bad more seriously. Stephen Carter expresses his distress about the rising culture of disbelief by borrowing from playwright Tom Stoppard. "There came a calendar date—a moment—when the onus of proof passed from the atheist to the believer, when quite suddenly, the noes had it."[38]

Well, if they ever really had it, the "noes" did not keep it for long. They never do in the United States. The secular ground keeps getting buried by the latest spiritual wave. Back to the 1690s, every rationalist moment only provokes another religious revival. Today, Americans worship with a gusto unmatched in the western world. Almost everyone believes in God (95 percent)—in distinct contrast to, say, Britain (76 percent), France (62 percent), or Sweden (52 percent). More than three out of four Americans belong to a church, 40 percent attended services last week, and almost one in ten claims to go "several times a week." One out of four citizens owns five Bibles. The United

States also beats every European nation in the rectitude polls. Eighty-seven percent of Americans say adultery is "always wrong," for example, compared to just 48 percent of French.[39]

The balance of power between secular and pious has shifted decisively in the past half-century—back to more ardent and conservative faiths. At mid-century, with the Social Gospel riding high, fundamentalists looked like cultural dinosaurs on the verge of extinction; religion in the 1950s looks flabby next to the fire-eating faiths that came before and after. To mark the social distance we've traveled, consider the tone of a sociology classic circa 1963. Efforts to outlaw drink, wrote Joseph Gusfield in his estimable *Symbolic Politics,* seem "naive, intolerant, saintly and silly. . . . In an easy going, affluent society, the ant [is] a fool and the grasshopper a hero. . . . People must learn to have fun and be good mixers if they are to achieve respect. . . . The fundamentalist . . . is part of the rear guard with which small town America fights their losing battle . . . a delaying action . . . of the doomed classes. Increasingly [the fundamentalist] fights alone. Churches, schools, and public officials are disdainful of 'rigid' attitudes and doctrines."[40]

What a difference a couple of decades make. More recent editions dash to catch up to the times. "A new underclass, as much feared as the old," writes Gusfield in 1986, helps restore an increasingly hard line on sins like alcohol abuse. The fundamentalists roared back from the cultural margins. Schools or public officials disdain rigid attitudes? That's how it looked during the high tide of the Social Gospel; the crime war has long since swept those soft attitudes right out of the culture. Zero-tolerance policies now thrust rigid, in-your-face moral codes on even the youngest miscreants. Gusfield's rear guard fighting a losing battle in 1963 could plausibly claim to be a moral majority two decades later.

Jerry Falwell once jibed that a fundamentalist is an "evangelical who is mad about something." No joke. But the angry fundamentalists no longer fight alone. An army of preachers, philosophers, and pundits warns about moral decline. The contemporary jeremiad echoes from hot evangelical tracts to dense theoretical tomes. The alarm makes strong politics, moral fears mobilize the neo-Puritan urge to enforce good behavior. On the other side, progressives have been ducking their own formidable moral legacy (or, in some cases, simply offering up soft versions of the sermons about making bad people behave). The contrast makes all the political difference. We'll see contemporary public policies turn decisively toward the neo-Puritan—at least when it comes to poor people's sins.[41]

The long view offers worried citizens a soothing prospect. We'll trace the uproar about rising immorality back to the seventeenth century. For raw sexual depravity, nothing in our own culture matches the antebellum debate over raping slaves. Or the Victorian outcry over abortion clinics. And for the fury against a generation of wealthy self-seekers, nothing heard today is as hard as Franklin Roosevelt's indictments. Three hundred fifty years of morality fevers add up to a reassuring message: Americans have survived their own unprecedented wickedness. Many times.

State-Building

We usually read the rise of American government as a secular story. Wars, armies, veterans, recessions, depressions, capitalists, labor unions, political parties, popular uprisings, public officials, racial fears, and social welfare programs tumble against one another and slowly, inexorably produce an American state. All these themes appear in the pages that follow—all play major roles in the American story. But in this book I focus on a different trajectory: government grew through recurring bids to improve the people. "Thou shalt nots" pushed public power into private lives; dreams of social justice tugged the state into new ventures. Each reform runs the cycle I describe above—persuasion, prohibition, and lingering institutional power. Moral campaigns are not, by any means, the only spur to American government, but they are surely the most often overlooked.[42]

Reframe an issue as a moral cause and supporters begin breaking down old rules and building up new ones. After all, a higher good lies in the balance. The United States coalesced this way in the first place. Colonial society had condemned strife and unabashed self-interest; good communities pulled together and deferred to their big men. Of course, the reality never quite lived up to the theory—the colonists brawled more or less constantly. But, as they kept hearing from the pulpits, they sinned when they flew into "heats and controversies." Then a religious revival, the Great Awakening, shook up American communities. Churches split between New Lights (the revivalists) and Old Lights. People had to choose. Stick with the old congregation, or come out with the rebels? Colonial institutions—the tax codes, for example—shaped the revival; the revivals, in turn, spilled into politics and reshaped existing institutions. Universities and legislatures broke along the same religious lines as the churches. Citizens defied the old taboo—they organized self-conscious factions and pushed their self-interests—in God's name. Religious ardor led the colonists to disrupt the old political norms of deference; it gave them organizational forms through which to plunge into conflicting factions. And all just in time for the greater revolution against the crown.

Each chapter of this book follows another moralizing outburst. Americans invoking a higher good shake up the old rules and organizations. Of course, the dynamics of vice and virtue intersect with the more familiar secular politics.

We'll watch an intricate play—moral hopes and fears spur the growth of government, the growth of government stirs moral hopes and fears. The nineteenth-century Post Office illustrates just how.

In the 1820s, the postal service introduced Sunday mail delivery. The innovation shook the ministers' grip on the village Sabbath, especially in New England. Suddenly the mail coach was barging into town, bringing news, noise, and a ride to the next village. Community leaders organized a great campaign to stop the Sabbath deliveries. They raised funds, held rallies, published tracts, signed petitions, and failed to dent the infidels (or Democrats) in Washington. The congressional committee rudely snubbed the Sabbatarians. But the political movement, now up and running, shifted its attention to a larger moral cause—abolishing slavery.[43]

Unwelcome mail deliveries soon rattled the South. Northern groups mailed great piles of abolitionist propaganda to the slave states. Here, apoplectic southerners told one another, was nothing less than an effort to foment a bloody slave rebellion. In Charleston, South Carolina, a carefully organized mob raided the Post Office, grabbed the offending pamphlets, and fed them to a bonfire. President Andrew Jackson and his postmaster general cheered the rioters for their patriotism. But the abolitionists had lit the greater fire.

The United States was integrating a far-flung and diverse society. The Post Office formed a kind of central nervous system, buzzing with unsettling notions that challenged the old guard. The Post Office was perfectly secular; but the mail forced local leaders, North and the South, to confront distant moral challenges. The postal service fostered private-interest groups (abolitionists, pro-slavery parties), which began crossing swords with rising fury. A stable society might have managed the tensions, but the rush westward kept forcing the slavery issue. Would the new territory be slave or free? Ultimately, both westward growth and national integration defeated every effort to duck the age-old American question: Who are we? In both North and South, activists offered high moral answers that slowly, surely dragged in their reluctant neighbors.

After the Civil War a new moral storm burst around the postal service. Victorian civic leaders found new dangers circulating through the mails. Abolitionist tracts mailed to gullible slaves now gave way to smutty books mailed to innocent children. As usual, Americans faced a broad social tumult. Booming cities full of foreigners and free blacks looked like pure danger. The old elites sought control. Congress complied by clamping down on the mails. Postal regulations banned interstate commerce in obscenity, birth control, and materials related to abortion (abortion had been both legal and common till the 1870s). Courts read the bans broadly enough to nab feminists and free thinkers along with smut peddlers and abortionists. Note the underlying pattern: private groups had pushed federal legislation that vested quasi-police authority in the largest federal agency, the Post Office; the federal legislation, in turn, inspired state laws; and both federal and state action empowered the private vice societies that backed up an increasingly formidable Post Office. Together, the government and its private sector allies lined the cultural barricades against dirty hearts and minds, against threats to established elites and mores. As a result, James Joyce, Upton Sinclair, and Lillian Smith would all be banned in Boston well into the twentieth century.[44]

Rereading the United States through its moral campaigns produces a different historical arc and pushes us into unusual historical crannies. Perhaps the least familiar political terrain lies along the road to "big government." The important milestone usually gets put in the early Franklin Roosevelt administrations (1933–1941) or during the First World War (1914–1918) or among the Progressive reformations (1900–1916). We usually skim right past the 1920s. But in the fifteen years before Roosevelt's New Deal, the United States pursued an extraordinary project: forbidding liquor sales. Prohibition (1920–1933) yielded sprawling police powers, inspired new legal rules (the overcrowded courts popularized plea bargaining, for example), shook up the civil service, and changed the leisure habits of millions of Americans (workers drank a lot less, swells a little more). In many ways Prohibition prepared the cultural ground for the active government of the New Deal. In fact, wet conservatives roasted Prohibition as the greatest government grab of private property in American history (excepting emancipation), then recycled the same arguments against the Democrats throughout the 1930s. We remember the Roosevelt administration for organizing the modern welfare state; we forget how Prohibition poured the institutional foundation for our contemporary war on drugs.

The rise of Prohibition illustrates all the classic political themes—from Post Office politics to interest-group pluralism. Fifteen years later, most of the same factors rearranged themselves and pushed Prohibition aside. (Until the Great Depression wiped out the Hoover administration, no one dreamed that the amendment would fall.) But both the rise and the fall of the dry regime turned, as much as anything else, on shifting images of us and them. Prohibition gathered support as immigration peaked; the program would thrust Anglo-Saxon discipline onto the lax Europeans. Prohibition sank partially because the nativist itch against Europeans faded—immigration had declined for fifteen years before getting almost shut down by the National Origins Act (1926). The accompanying photo, taken in the mid-1930s, illustrates precisely the kind of image that breaks our prohibitions.[45]

A group of gentlemen enjoy a bit of fresh air. They have just eaten a big

1.1. After lunch at Bessie's.

meal at an Italian restaurant called Bessie's on Staten Island. Who are they? The New York branch managers of the Metropolitan Life Insurance Company. And they are all sons of immigrants. The group includes an Irishman, two Jews, three Italians, and—sitting second from right—their boss, a Bulgarian. A generation earlier, sociologists and eugenics texts were warning America about lazy low-lifes from precisely these inferior nations. The men's fathers had all arrived from the "slums of Europe." These were the immigrants who would wreck the nation—eating off bare boards, indulging depraved tastes, and yielding to those peasant philosophies of sex. Now, twenty-five years after the anti-immigrant jeremiads, no one would consider these well-dressed, hard-working men a threat to—well, anything.

Here is America, 1935: the dream of upward mobility has sprung to life and gone to lunch. The men have polished off quite a bit of wine with their meal, and now they are smoking. One of them is slouching. That amounts to two sins and one small lapse in propriety. But these men are not a scary them. They are us. Their small vices hold no dangers for the nation. Let them enjoy their smoke.

I know so much about this group because the jovial-looking man at the far left is my grandfather Joseph Morone.

My cheerful story comes with an alternate ending. Imagine a different group. Turn the men into, say, African Americans. Add a couple of guys from Puerto Rico. Dress them less formally. Do the smokes and wine now carry a more ominous message? Perhaps the need for discipline bubbles up? Sure enough, new prohibitions would rise to greet the next generation of "disruptive others." A drug war would revisit all the trouble of the drink war: corruption, clogged courts, violence, a rising prison population, wrecked lives, and ruined communities.

The lunch at Bessie's taps three very different American generations: the depraved European immigrants of recent memory (circa 1905); the successful branch managers in the photo itself (1935); and our imagined people of color a generation later. The story of American integration has been told many different ways—as national triumph, as looming tragedy, and as almost everything in between. Put a bottle of wine on the table and a powerful moral debate immediately gusts up. In a sense, every chapter follows that bottle of wine as it passes to another generation of drinkers. In each era we will focus on a different moral campaign, explore how it bisects other political issues, and try to understand—across more than 350 years—just what makes this hellfire nation tick.

PART I

The Puritan Foundations of Morality Politics (1630–1776)

We must consider that we shall be as a city upon a hill, the eyes of all people are upon us; so that if we shall deal falsely with our God in this work we have undertaken . . . we shall surely perish out of the good land [which] we pass over the vast sea to possess.

—GOVERNOR JOHN WINTHROP, 1630

You can and you can't . . .
You will and you won't . . .
You will be damned if you do
And you will be damned if you don't.

—Preacher Lorenzo Dow on Calvinism, 1814

IN June 1630, four hundred English Puritans arrived in Salem, Massachusetts. There they found a squalid collection of shacks and tents, but what Governor John Winthrop reported in his journal was the good beer they drank with supper. (So much for the Puritan as teetotaler—but that's a story for a different chapter.) These were the first boatloads in a great migration—twenty thousand people followed over the next twelve years. By 1640, the New England Puritans made up more than half the European population in what would become the original United States.[1]

From the start, these immigrants grappled with the perpetual American question: Who are we? In their search for answers, the Puritans wrote covenants that look something like modern constitutions, introduced political rules that roughly anticipate representative democracy, bore holes through Quaker tongues, whipped women for running naked through their villages, hanged the witches they found lurking in their midst, and prepared themselves for the millennial coming of Jesus to His new Israel.

This pious band of immigrants, living somewhere between the medieval and modern worlds, founded American moral politics. The Puritans articulated attitudes and organized institutions that—in constantly evolving ways—reach across American time. Exploring the Puritans and their legacy offers a new frame for old questions about American political identity.

Historians and literary critics will find this hard to swallow. The New England Puritans have already generated more scholarship, writes Gordon Wood, than "any similar small community in the history of the world." The studies have dug up details "far beyond anything the Puritans themselves could have coped with" (Bernard Bailyn), far beyond anything "sane men should want to know" (Edmund Morgan). Could we possibly have overlooked anything about these settlers?[2]

Political scientists have overlooked almost everything about them. We generally start the American story with the Constitutional Convention of 1787—as if the United States sprang, fully formed, from James Madison's Enlightenment brain. But when you begin the story in 1630, a very different picture of America and its political culture snaps into view. Great bouts of moral fervor (from the second Great Awakening that roared through the country in the early nineteenth century to the culture wars rushing through it today) look less like anomalies and more like the soul of American politics.

In the traditional political story, the Puritans play unwitting colonial stagehands who set the scene for what we now call modern liberalism. Their view of work (a calling) and success (divine favor) would evolve into a great capitalist work ethic: work is virtuous, success smacks of salvation, poverty insinuates moral failure. The Puritan covenants would develop into secular constitutions. The elections by which the Puritans selected their leaders (who by election received a mandate from God) built the framework for modern elections and the mandate of the people.

Modernity, continues the usual story, began tugging on the Puritans almost from the start. Before they had been in America for a decade, Roger Williams insisted on separating church and state while Anne Hutchinson scorched colonial leaders over something vaguely like the rights of conscience. With time, Puritan religious forms and righteous fervor drained away, leaving the foundations of a profoundly liberal society. The result—liberal individualism—is both cheered and deplored. But, good or bad, it is said to drive off almost every other political possibility; liberalism seems to tower over American politics, culture, and institutions.

In this book I recast the story at the start of all that. American liberalism is tangled up in a very different story: the search for God, the moral urge. The trajectory of this alternate story does not run from religious to secular. Rather, American politics developed from revival to revival. The Puritan search for God organized all those pre-liberal institutions; piety drove them toward their modern forms.

Although the Puritan establishment grew rigid and zeal waned, fresh bouts of moral fervor remade the society. Rebels like Roger Williams and Anne Hutchinson shook up that establishment by demanding a more intense religious experience—Williams separated church and state, for example, to protect the church from worldly corruption. A full century later, a fiery religious revival in the meetinghouses reorganized colonial politics and primed the colonists to challenge authority—even to defy the crown.

The Puritans constructed their society around a crusading religious spirit. They identified a mission: saving the world. Leaders used faith to impose order; renegades seized the religious spirit and fomented trouble. Still, the Puritan self proved exasperatingly elusive. Identity and solidarity had been a lot simpler back home in England. There, enemies defined the saints by persecuting them. Thomas Shepherd posed the ironic problem in 1636: "When men are persecuted by enemies, driven . . . six miles off to . . . hear a sermon . . . then men thought, if one Sabbath here [is] so sweet . . . in the midst of enemies, O how sweet to enjoy them all among saints, among friends. But New England's peace and plenty breeds . . . strange security. There are no enemies to hunt you to heaven."[3]

What to do? The Puritans groped back to the tried and true—they found terrible new enemies to define them. The saints constructed their "us" against a vivid series of immoral "them": heretics, Indians, witches. Each enemy clarified the Puritan identity.[4]

Both sides of the Puritan vision would echo through the American experience. Religious revivals would reheat the old fervor and send it racing across the colonies. The little band of Rhode Island Baptists—boosted, as we'll see, by the tax code—rose up and spread. By the Revolution, three out of four Americans were professing some variation of the Puritan faith. The bulwarks of their regime—the grand mission, the special covenant, the tireless jeremiads—would all outlive the Puritans themselves. On the other side, a steady procession of dangerous others would continue to defy—and define—the American us.

Chapter 1
Us: The City on a Hill

HISTORY gives us two different pictures of the Puritans. On the one side, Nathaniel Hawthorne described them as "black browed, witchunters [who] so darkened the national visage" that "all subsequent years have not sufficed to clear it up." "How narrow and cold was their prison," added Vernon Parrington. Their society was "bred up . . . in aristocratic contempt for the sodden mass of the people" and "long lingered out a harsh existence, grotesque and illiberal to the last." They were intent, chimed in popular historian James Truslow Adams, "on making the wilderness blossom like a thistle instead of a rose." Or, as H. L. Mencken famously cracked, the Puritan attitude boils down to that haunting fear that someone, somewhere, might be happy. More recently, J. Hillis Miller recalled the gloomy Puritans in a presidential address to the Modern Language Association: "They knew only to keep their eyes blinded [and] their ears stopped by the monotony of their hymns. The tragedy of American history is that the Puritan attitude has triumphed everywhere."[1]

The alternative view is more generous. The Puritan clergy, wrote Richard Hofstadter, was "as close to being an intellectual ruling class as America has ever had." Six years after sailing into Salem harbor the Puritans had established Harvard College; the Bay Colony required every town of more than fifty families to organize a school. "My attitude toward seventeenth century Puritanism," wrote Samuel Eliot Morison, "has passed through scorn and boredom to a warm interest and respect. The ways of the Puritans are not my ways, and their faith is not my faith; nevertheless, they appear to me a courageous, humane, brave and significant people." Recent historians generally see early modern settlers struggling to define tightly knit communities.[2]

So, which is it? Well, a bit of both. Those early colonists left us plenty of legacies to ponder.

The Mission

No aspect of the Puritan world is more often recalled than the notion of a mission, an errand in the wilderness sealed by a covenant with God. John Winthrop ran through the details in a sermon delivered aboard the *Arbella*, the flagship of the first Puritan fleet in the great migration: "Thus stands the cause between God and us. We are entered into a covenant with Him for this work. . . . That which most churches maintain as a truth in profession only, we must bring into familiar and constant practice."[3]

The mission charged the people to stay above conflict: "We must be knit together in this work as one man, we must entertain each other in brotherly affection . . . we must delight in each other." To make this happen, the members would each have to play their own divinely appointed roles, for "God almighty . . . hath so disposed of the condition of mankind as in all times, some must be rich, some poor, some high and eminent in power and dignity, others mean and in subjugation." Each rank had its mandate. "The rich and mighty should not eat up the poor nor the poor and despised rise up . . . and shake off their yoke." Winthrop and the Puritan leaders would constantly return to the theme of proper order, urging the people not to "murmur and oppose and be always striving to shake off that yoke." Men must defer to their leaders, servants to masters, women to men.[4]

Finally, the stakes were huge: "If the lord shall be pleased . . . he shall make us a praise and glory. For we must consider that we shall be as a city upon a hill, the eyes of all people are upon us; so that if we shall deal falsely with our God in this work we have undertaken . . . we shall be made a story and a byword through all the world."[5]

Future generations would keep coming back to the heady dream of an American mission, a great experiment unfolding in the colonies while the rest of the world—all eyes—waited on the outcome. Later observers would sometimes take the image for a thumping, imperialist, manifest destiny. Winthrop's city on the hill seems to foretell the great thrust of the American narrative—the rush across the North American continent, the slaughter of the Native Americans, the crusades to save the world from pirates, kaisers, Nazis, Communists, or terrorists.[6]

But none of this is in Winthrop's text. Rather, putting the sermon back into its original context suggests a more subtle message. The key to the mission lay in making the society—the domestic, Puritan society—operate in a godly fashion. This meant proper hierarchy (for God deems some "eminent" and others "mean"). Success lay in deference and harmony. This mission was all about authority and order at home. Success had nothing to do with any direct role Americans might play in the world. Rather, their contribution to "all people" would be what the Puritans made of themselves. The city on a hill would be the exemplar, the model to be copied. If New England (and, later, the United States) got its society right, others would see the great success and want to emulate it.[7]

Here lies an almost primal call for public moralizing: New England would succeed and be saved if it got all its citizens to behave. The covenant with God—and the eyes of the world—positively pushed the early Americans to meddle in the behavior of their neighbors. Over the years, few things would shake up American politics quite like our worries about what the rest of the world might think.

Why did the world need a model in 1630? And just where did the Puritans come up with theirs? The Puritan mission sprang from the chaos of the English Reformation. For a century and half, England lurched back and forth—Catholic, Anglican, and (briefly) Calvinist. Henry VIII broke with Rome (1534), Mary Tudor returned the state to Catholicism (1553–1558), Elizabeth restored the Church of England (1559). However, Elizabeth's Protestant church retained many Roman features and the compromises outraged some Englishmen. They demanded religious purity—the term "Puritan" was a jeer that stuck. The Puritans challenged the English church in three ways.

First, it was too Roman, too corrupt. Strip away the vestments, ornaments, miters, and statuary, demanded the Puritans. Clean out the ministry. The Puritans wanted fervor. Instead, they got dissolute clergy and lackluster preaching—sermons no better than "sharp shitting on a frosty morning," as one villager put it. The Puritans published lists of clerical drunkards and fornicators.[8]

Second, Anglicans believed the church offered a road to salvation. Like good Calvinists, the Puritans vehemently disputed this. How could a sinner possibly force the hand of God? Nothing anybody did could wring redeeming grace from the almighty. The gap between God and sinner could not be bridged by prayers or by piety. Salvation came only when God chose to pour His grace into an open and willing soul. What exactly counted as open and willing would turn out to be a very significant rub. But the spiritual bolt from heaven would live on and turn political—more than 350 years later, American political candidates routinely assure the nation that they have, certainly, been born again.

Third, the Anglicans took all comers—saved, damned, or uncertain. Many Puritans limited the church to men and women who could demonstrate God's grace moving within them. The visible church (those who joined the congregation) would be as close as possible to the invisible church (those elected by God for salvation). In the New World, the Puritans would construct elaborate rituals to sort out just whom God had selected. The city on a hill would be run, literally, by saints.

Like many rebels, the Puritans splintered into sects. Alas, said Voltaire about the ensuing tumult, "the English have a hundred religions but only one sauce." The mission in New England flowed directly from the saints' position within the dissenters' ranks.[9]

At one end of the Puritan spectrum, closest to the Church of England, stood the Presbyterians. They would purify the current mess. But Presbyterians advocated a hierarchical national church (with a system of ascending church courts called synods and presbyteries). And while they would limit church leadership to the manifestly elect, they would not impose that requirement on the rank-and-pew members.

In the middle stood the New England Way. These reformers would restrict church membership to God's elect. They condemned all church hierarchy. Each congregation should operate independently; the Bible offered all the higher authority anyone needed. Despite its harsh and steady criticism, the New England faction did not break from the Church of England. As Kai Erikson put it, the New England Puritans insisted that the Anglican church was the true church, "save only that it had the wrong organization, the wrong ceremonies, the wrong members and the wrong ministry." How to negotiate such an extensive overhaul from within? That's precisely what they were doing in New England. Free to organize themselves properly in the New World, the Puritans would display a Christian commonwealth so exquisitely ordered, so godly, that the corrupted English Protestants would be inspired (or shamed) into reform.[10]

Further down the Puritan spectrum lay factions that simply broke with the Church of England. The Pilgrims at Plymouth plantation founded in 1620 were separatists. So were the Baptists who followed Roger Williams to Rhode Island. Williams was ferocious on the subject—he left Plymouth because it had not slammed the door on the Church of England hard enough. (Some members, for example, unapologetically attended the corrupted Anglican services when they visited England.)[11]

The city on a hill had pitched its model precariously close to the edge of paradox—in fact, multiple paradoxes: Here were incessant critics who insisted on their loyalty to the Church of England. They organized a society around their faith but condemned the idea of salvation through church efforts. Their biblical commonwealth was to be an international model, but they rejected the central authority that might coordinate what the different congregations said and did. Each tension would land them in trouble.

It was not the logic of the New England Way, however, that soon imperiled the mission. Rather, a little more than a decade after the sermon on the *Arbella,* the city on a hill was shaken by events in England. In 1642, Oliver Cromwell and the Puritans took the field against Charles I. But the English Puritans were deeply split. Moderates in Parliament, along with the rising merchant classes, clustered toward the Presbyterian view (though they would eventually get purged from Parliament). Cromwell's army tended toward an independent or congregational approach akin to the New England Way. Facing their own bitter divisions, the victorious Puritans imposed tolerance.

"New England did not lie," exaggerates Perry Miller. It "did not falter; it made good everything Winthrop demanded—wonderfully good—and then found that the lesson was rejected by those choice spirits for whom the exertion had been made." Cromwell's new army, in the moment of victory, proclaimed the "fantastic notion" that "once it captured the state, it would recognize the right of dissenters to disagree, to have their own worship, to hold their own opinions." And that, concludes Miller, marked the end of the sacred mission. "Amid the shambles, the errand of New England collapsed. There was nobody left at headquarters to whom reports could be sent." The Puritans had "failed to rivet the eyes of the world upon their city on a hill." Now, "they were left alone with America."[12]

"No!" says Sacvan Bercovitch. The English Puritans might have turned their backs on New England. In fact, it was even worse: the English brethren were chastising the New Englanders for intolerance. But the New World Puritans never abandoned their vision. "And the fact is," writes Bercovitch, "that the vision survived—from colony to province and from province to nation." The Puritans simply would not acknowledge the mistake. They continued to thump their errand. They convinced themselves that the errand had nothing to do with the English church. They declared it to others—and convinced them too. The sermons and jeremiads did not flag. They continued, as Samuel Danforth attested in 1671, "to excite and stir us all up to attend and prosecute our errand into the wilderness."[13]

Here is an odd twist to one of the primal American legends—the one about fleeing religious tyranny in the old world for religious freedom in the new. Back in the 1640s, it was old, feudal England that began pushing religious toleration down reluctant colonial throats. Over the next fifty years the crown would force New England to quit hanging Quakers and to open church doors to the Anglicans. The New England reality got a lot more complicated than the cheerful myths about new world freedom. The colonies mixed unprecedented opportunity with bursts of fierce repression. And both those impulses got pitched against the same soaring rhetorical conceit—the providential mission that all people would see and want to emulate.

The American mission would be constantly rediscovered, reinterpreted, rewritten—from colony to nation, from eighteenth-century republic to twentieth-century superpower. The content of the mission would change, but, just as in John Winthrop's original version, the emphasis would always fall on the domestic order. The city on a hill would become an increasingly self-conscious exemplar for the world. Different generations would promote different American values: Christian hierarchy, economic opportunity, equality, liberty, or free capitalist markets. In every case, the lesson for the world lay in the organization and operation of American society. They would all be watching us, drawing hope and inspiration from what they saw.

The Covenant

The Puritans helped establish American reverence toward a written constitution by organizing their system around a stunning idea: God was offering them a deal, a contract. The idea, worked out in the late sixteenth and early seventeenth centuries, transformed Calvin's God. That God had been awe-inspiring, incomprehensible, unpredictable—pure blazing will. Calvin's God saved a handful and damned everybody else. The Puritans saw God as more predictable. Through the covenant, as Thomas Shepard put it in 1651, "we see with open face God's secret purpose . . . the Covenant being nothing else but His purposes revealed."[14]

The covenant bargain was this. Rather than strike without warning, God promised redemption for His special people. The people, in turn, promise simple faith. Of course, the power of faith itself comes from God. God agrees to supply them with faith, to infuse their souls with grace. For their part, God's people must be ready to embrace the gift, to accept God's grace when He chooses to reveal Himself. Since no one can predict that moment of revelation, Christians must be always prepared.[15]

It is impossible, comments Perry Miller, to fully express so intricate a vision in modern terms. The Puritans were enmeshed "in the coils of their doctrine." They were "desperately striving to vaunt the power of the human intellect without losing the sense of divine transcendence." Their Anglican opponents greeted the whole idea with incredulity. It is a "fantastic conceit," wrote William Lucy, that God might have a contracted "an Obligation and Bond" toward mortal men and women. The very idea, concurs Miller, would have had Calvin spinning in his grave.[16]

Still, the Puritans insisted they had biblical warrant for their covenants. Had not God made a covenant with Noah, abjuring His own power to destroy the earth by flood? And God had also made a covenant with Abraham, creating a special relationship with a chosen people, just as He now did with the Puritan settlers.[17]

The covenant vision nudged the Puritans toward modernity. The very idea draws on biblical precedent to break with medieval thought. There was no place, in the great medieval chain of being, for negotiating contracts with superiors. The foot did not bargain with the head. For the Puritans, argues Michael Walzer, the "freely negotiated contract" emerges "as the highest human bond." It connects God and man, minister and church, husband and wife. The Puritans rejected hierarchical relations as given and rewrote them as mutual agreements.[18]

The covenant linked personal salvation with communal life. Even though the Puritans restricted their church to elected saints, the deal with God included everyone. Glorious success or terrible punishment would rain down on saint and sinner alike. Consequently, the quest for individual perfection turned outward and became political. The saint's temporal fate was tied to the behavior of the whole community.[19]

As the Puritans spread across New England, each town wrote a covenant that was drawn up and signed by the first saints on the scene—the Pilgrims' Mayflower Compact is the most famous. In contrast to so much of the Puritan apparatus, these documents are simple ("plain, sweet, promise[s] of obedience to God and aid to one another," as one nineteenth-century theologian put it). The covenant for Charlestown-Boston is typical:

> We whose names are hereunder written, being by His most wise and good Providence brought together in this part of America and desirous to unite our selves into one Congregation, or Church, under the Lord Jesus Christ our Head, in such sort as becometh all those whom he hath Redeemed, and Sanctifyed to Himselfe, do hereby solemnly and religously . . . Promisse and bind o(r)selves, to walke in all our ways according to the Rule of the Gospell and in all sincere conformity to his holy Ordinaunces and in mutuall love, and respect each to other, so neere as God shall give us grace.[20]

The covenant for the town of Dedham, Massachusetts, draws one Puritan implication to the surface. After the typical promise of mutual love and respect, the covenant avers: "we shall by all means labor to keep off from us such as are contrary minded." The Salem covenant, signed in 1629, would get an anti-Quaker amendment, warning about a doctrine "as bad or worse than that of the Pharisees." Always the two sides of the Puritan quest: mutual love within the community, expulsion for anybody who might be contrary minded.[21]

The Puritan covenant would develop into a pillar of the American regime. For one thing, once the covenant idea takes root, even a king can be accused of violating it. More important, covenants were forerunners of constitutions. As Kenneth Wald points out, the American Constitution not only reflects the covenant tradition but echoes its biblical form. The Constitution explicitly abjures power: anything not clearly enumerated as a federal power is left to the states. The first biblical covenant operates precisely the same way: God's deal with Noah relinquishes power—no more floods. For that matter, Americans approach their Constitution with a kind of piety that mimics the biblical fealty. The parchment itself, says Wald, is a holy relic, displayed in a shrine, honored by generations of republican pilgrims.[22]

The legacy of Puritan covenants goes beyond the documents, of course. Winthrop had warned that if God "ratified this covenant" then He would "expect a strickt performance of the Articles contained within." The good people of Dedham might, alternately, seek to uplift wayward neighbors or drive them off as "contrary minded." In either case, the people's morals were everybody's concern, as all would bear the consequences of bad behavior.

Throughout American history, the covenant language would return, always aspiring to consensus about societal morals. What was planted by seventeenth-century Puritans, writes David Greenstone, would be "reworked through out the eighteenth and nineteenth centuries, by Great Awakening preachers and founding fathers, by party tacticians and moral reformers." They would all conjure up different versions of the American mission, sealed by covenant pledges. Even today, American statesmen reaching for something grandiloquent dig up a "new" or "special" covenant with the people. On the other side, the saints would stumble upon twisted, godless covenants—we'll soon see the witches' covenant with Satan and, 150 years later, the Constitution's "Covenant with death and agreement with hell." Through the years, covenant violations both large and small would unleash a distinctive kind of rhetorical lashing: the American jeremiad.[23]

Jeremiad

God punished New England when it violated His covenant. The Puritans took every sort of trouble as "evidence that God hath a controversy with his people." There were "fearful desolations of the earth"—fires, droughts, bugs, crop failures, cold spells, heat waves, diseases. There were "damnable heresies" and "abominable idolatries"—antinomians, Baptists, Quakers, and vague rumors of Jesuits. There were "barbarous heathens" who made devastating war on the colonists. These, and many more, were all the work of God, "chastizing us with his rods" and "inflicting upon us many judgments."[24]

The jeremiads offered a ritualized rhetorical form through which leaders could admonish and exhort. The jeremiads followed a formula: these hard times are God's punishment, and unless He sees some serious reform, worse is coming. Michael Wigglesworth distilled the message in his great rhyming jeremiad (written in 1662, during a drought).

> Beware, oh sinful land, beware
> And Do not think it strange
> That sorer judgments are at hand
> Unless thou Quickly change.[25]

The jeremiads were often perfectly explicit about the crimes that had provoked God. For example, in 1675 a native leader (Metacom) organized the Indians and led a very bloody revolt against the New England settlers. King Philip's war (as the colonists called it) raged from 1675 to 1678 with catastrophic casualties on both sides. In 1679 the ministers met in synod and pinpointed the cause of the suffering: "Children and servants . . . are not kept in due subjugation, their masters and parents especially being sinfully indulgent towards them. . . . In this respect, Christians in this land have become too like unto the Indians, and then we need not wonder if the Lord has afflicted us by them. Sometimes a sin is discerned by the instrument that Providence doth punish with."[26]

That synod of 1679 has become celebrated for its leering inventory of Puritan sins. Even a partial list touches all the classic jeremiad themes: pride, strange apparel, and ornaments ("the poorest sort of people are notoriously guilty in this matter"); sleeping in church; spoiled children ("most of the evils that abound amongst us, proceed from defects as to family government"); sinful heats and hatreds; drinking, debauchery, heinous breaches of the Seventh Commandment (adultery), and fornication; false hair, naked necks, naked arms, and ("more abominable") naked breasts; dancing, gaming, sinful company, idleness; high prices. And it went on: declining public schools, soaring lawsuits, greedy business practices. The recitation of sins came with an inevitable reminder about the Puritan mission: "We have been forgetting the errand upon which the Lord sent us hither." And all of it was wrapped around the standard warning that "we are a perishing people if we reform not."[27]

But why? Why should the Puritans so energetically preach jeremiads? After all, they were flourishing. God's covenants with both Noah and Abraham had ordered the men to "be fruitful and multiply and replenish the earth." The

Puritans were doing so at a rate unparalleled in the English colonies. For all of God's "rods," they suffered much lower rates of disease and death than Virginia or North Carolina or even England itself. So why such unabashed wallowing in their own iniquity? The answer lies in the tension between their religious ideals and the social reality.[28]

The contradiction began with Puritan economics. God had created a hierarchical society and given each person a rank ("some eminent," "others mean," as Winthrop had put it). People were meant to mind their place. "It transgressed the laws of God and man" when people pushed "above their estates and degrees."

From this, godly economic rules could be deduced. It is false principle, preached John Cotton in 1639, "that a man might sell as dear as he can, and buy as cheap as he can." Or "that a man may take advantage of his own skill or ability" at the expense of "another's ignorance or necessity." Cotton preached his sermon after a Boston merchant, Robert Keayne, had tried to argue his way out of stiff fines for charging excessive rates. Forty years later, the synod of 1679 was especially sharp about "covetousness" and "excessive rates," though by then these crimes were no longer punished. When the synod condemned flashy clothes among the meaner sort, it was criticizing yet another indicator of breaking ranks.[29]

Inconveniently, the saints were also expected to work hard to make the most of their talents. After all, God called people to their occupations. "God . . . gives a man gifts" with which to pursue a calling, wrote Cotton, and "He would have His best gifts improved to best advantage." Worldly success signaled God's favor and failure His punishment; idleness had gotten Sodom burned to cinders.[30]

The Puritans faced a dilemma. Ministers pushed people to work hard. And the incentives to do so were certainly compelling—your fortune here offered a pretty strong hint about your fate in the hereafter. But hard work produced social mobility. Poor men did well. Low families (like the Brattles and the Whartons) forged ahead. And, alas, sometimes the high-born fell. The social order, fixed by God, kept coming unfixed. Puritan piety exalted hard work; Puritan preaching excoriated the inevitable results—rising and falling saints.

Politics offered another variation of the same trap for Puritans. Each town covenant dutifully included a holy promise of "mutual love" (Boston-Charlestown) or "mutual tenderness" (Salem) or "mutual encouragement" (Dedham). Strife and contention were sinful. The city on the hill was supposed to be "knit together . . . as one man," to operate by consensus, deference, and natural hierarchy (which is why the synod of 1679 would see lawsuits as a sign of trouble).[31]

A developing political economy generated plenty of differences, however.

Even pious men and women found their interests clashing with their neighbors'. A new society—constantly, inevitably—faced choices that advantaged some people over others: merchants versus farmers, the mighty versus the middling, town centers versus the periphery, newcomers versus old-timers, Boston versus everyone. Deference and mutual love kept evaporating into "sinful heats and hatreds."

Some political tensions went deeper than self-interest. The new society had to thrash out fundamental questions of political organization and governing philosophy. And the big questions inevitably came up as part of a row. Strife bubbled to the surface as the colonists designed institutions, drafted rules, and debated policies. But the city on a hill was not meant to suffer growing pains or political disputes. The polity was supposed to stand outside historical time. After all, the whole point was to demonstrate the superiority of a biblical commonwealth—Bible truths did not change or bend to circumstances.

The covenants pledged order and harmony; the new world produced disorder and discord. Jeremiads mediated the differences. New England's spiritual leaders may have had a solid religious reason for all those scoldings, but on a deeper level they were lamenting the irrevocable gap between aspiration and reality. After all, the Puritans were reaching for utopia.

The jeremiads reached beyond chiding and cautions. They also reaffirmed the moral quest. And foretold success. After—or sprinkled between—all the terrible warnings came triumphant promises. Even in the synod of 1679: "There is reason to hope that it shall be better with us than at our beginnings" (and by 1679, the preachers had inflated the Puritan "beginnings" into a second Eden). Intimations of "plenty and prosperity" sprout up between the prophesies of doom. Or as the voluble Cotton Mather put it during the Salem Village witch trials: "If we get well through" this attempt on us, "we shall soon Enjoy Halcyon Days with all the Vultures of Hell Trodden under our Feet."[32]

Just beyond this moral crisis, if it can be negotiated, glimmers the success of the mission, national glory, even the biblical millennium. Old Testament punishments mingled, in some jeremiads, with apocalyptic promises of Christ's thousand-year reign on earth. New England would become "the new heaven and the new earth wherein dwells righteousness," as John Cotton put it. Cotton Mather scribbled down timetables for the Second Coming of Jesus—1697, 1716, 1736. He watched the first two dates come and go but insisted, "All that has been foretold . . . as what must come to pass before the Coming . . . is as far as we understand fulfill'd: I say ALL FULFLL'D." And fulfill'd right here on the "American strand." As if the old mission had not been enough, the city on the hill would become the capital of Christ's millennial kingdom, foretold in the Book of Revelation.[33]

Jonathan Edwards kept a journal to track events presaging the apocalypse. "The latter day glory," long foretold in scripture, wrote Edwards, would rise from the west, from America—more precisely, from New England. "What is now seen," he wrote as the Great Awakening began around him, "may prove the dawn of that glorious day, . . . the forerunner of something vastly great. . . . How much it behooves us to . . . promote this work, and how dangerous it will be to forebear to do so." Back and forth went Edwards, between gleams of glory and portents of punishment.[34]

Some contemporaries blasted Edwards's logic. But the apocalyptic version of the new world mission sprang up with each religious revival through the Puritan century and beyond: from John Cotton (in the first generation) to Increase Mather (the second) to Cotton Mather (third) to Jonathan Edwards and, with the Great Awakening, across the colonies and into American history.

In short, the jeremiad begins by holding up communal norms rooted in the scriptures. Then it condemns the sorry state of the community. And finally it works up to a prophetic dream of future glory—even the Second Coming of Jesus. In this way, the American jeremiad came to terms with the inexorable progress of progress. It set aside the static God-given hierarchy and peered eagerly into the future. It scolded the people for moral backsliding, dazzled them with their historical duty, and invested their mission with an immodest goal: redeem the world.[35]

The jeremiad became a kind of American anthem. Revolutionary era ministers drew the religious message into the secular realm, embracing liberty as part of the sacred teleology. The jeremiad rhetoric would return, swell, and dominate American political discourse as the nation rushed to its civil war.[36]

The jeremiad survived into the twentieth century, a trusty feature of the rhetorical landscape. In fact, some of the same sins still flourish. Checking back on the synod's 1679 inventory, for example, we find public schools still languishing, the pursuit of profit even more insatiable, the explosion of lawsuits still completely out of hand. Children are still "not kept in due subjugation," and a broad coalition of reformers insist that "most of the evils that abound amongst us, proceed from defects as to family government." To be sure, the words do not carry quite the same meanings; back then, due subjugation ran to whipping incorrigible children, and the millennium was the real thing from the Book of Revelation. But the rhetorical trajectory lives on: lamentations about decline, warnings of doom, and promises of future glory (if we just get our act together and, recalling Cotton Mather, get well through this attempt on us).

Jeremiads continue to reconcile the tensions between stability and change. America keeps evolving: new people, new mores, and new problems. The flux stirs up echoes of the ancient Puritan warning—our Eden fades into history, and we are not what we used to be. Andrew Delbanco suggests that what the Puritans called declension future generations would call assimilation.[37]

But assimilation looks benign only after it is complete. During the process,

old settlers see terrible decline written all over the poor, huddled masses yearning to remake the American us. New generations of preachers keep turning the
old jeremiads against the latest marginal group: these would-be Americans do
not understand the mission or they do not share our values or they do not work
hard enough to stave off national diminution. This jeremiad is one of the great
themes of American political development, one of the keys to American political culture.

And what about that millennium? That prophesy of glory glinting through
the lamentations of decline? The Puritan apocalypse would also ring across the
American centuries. Evangelical fervor for Christ's Second Coming led the
way to both revolution and civil war; it ran deep in nineteenth-century black
religion and reached its soaring apotheosis in Abraham Lincoln's Second Inaugural Address. And if the millennial prospect never seemed quite as immediate—as biblically inspired—as it did during the Civil War, Americans would
keep launching their crusades to redeem the world—sometimes by reforming
the city on a hill, sometimes, as President John F. Kennedy put it in his Inaugural Address, by going out into the world and bearing any burden or fighting
any foe.

Religion and Politics in the Real World

Jeremiads offered dreams. The hard part lay in organizing real-world institutions to bring those dreams to life. Constructing both church and state thrust
the Puritans into distinctly unpuritanical conflicts. At issue were the political
perennials: How should the saints balance communal autonomy with central
power? Or weigh elite authority against popular participation? Or cull the
saved from the damned?

Religion

The church formed the central Puritan institution. Founding a congregation of visible saints required sifting out God's elect. But how? The first settlers
earnestly examined one another for hints of grace. Those who passed moral
muster signed church covenants, elected officers, and began pondering their
neighbors' souls.[38]

Within a decade New England had hammered out a much more formal
conversion ritual. The path to salvation now ran through multiple stages. Ministers prepared aspirants to receive God's grace if and when He offered it. Candidates who thought they felt the spirit underwent tests. They delivered a spiritual autobiography (or conversion narrative), answered questions, and faced
the congregation's judgment. The intricate theological hermeneutic was de-

signed to separate true conversions, souls truly infused by God, from the "false assurance" of the merely pious.[39]

The rigor of the process varied by congregation. In Massachusetts, about 48 percent of the males were full church members by 1647. Was this too many or too few? The saints aired strong views on both sides. "You are so strict in admission to new members of your church," wrote one English critic to John Winthrop, "that more than one halfe are out of membership in all your congregations." Thomas Hooker quietly agreed. He took his followers to Connecticut, where requirements were less exacting. On the other side, purists like Roger Williams thought the criteria far too lax; Williams kept restricting the circle of saints, clucked Winthrop, until he ended up taking communion with nobody but his wife.[40]

The candidates themselves often waited anxiously to feel God's grace stirring. John Winthrop described a Boston woman who was "in much trouble about her spiritual estate." Finally, she snapped and put an end to the suspense. "She took her little infant and threw it into a well." Now, "she was sure she would be damned, for she had drowned her child." (A neighbor actually managed to rescue the baby.) In Weymouth, a man suddenly cried out one night, " 'Art thou come, Lord Jesus?' and with that leaped out of his bed" and "breaking from his wife, leaped out a high window into the snow and ran about seven miles off." They found him dead the next morning, his tracks marking the many spots where he had dropped to his knees. We'll see another spectacular case of conversion-despair a century later in the middle of Jonathan Edwards's revival. Joseph Hawley, a leading Northampton citizen, slit his own throat after long nights of "mediating terror" over the condition of his soul.[41]

The powerful conversion experience drew an important line across communities. Liberalism's great American dream (read back through Tocqueville and projected onto the "first Puritan who came ashore") imagined a society that cast aside ascriptive distinctions between the settlers. A new world of opportunity overwhelmed old hereditary privileges—as the jeremiads testified, no one ever seemed to stay in rank. But in most New England communities, the boundary separating a privileged us from a less reliable them would not evaporate. That line got constructed not simply out of birth and rank but out of convictions about grace, about moral superiority.

The quest for personal salvation got mixed up with images of America and its mission. In an analysis of fifty-one conversion narratives, Patricia Caldwell found a dramatic theme running through the new world spiritual autobiographies. "No one during the first thirty years of the colony ever had a dream at all—excepting, of course, the one publicly permitted dream, the dream of America." The fact of America was a "central, even obsessive concern of the imagination, and one that is inextricably bound up with each person's notion of . . . his or her own experience of salvation."[42]

The internal conversion experience was recast in political terms. Visions of personal salvation merged with images of the nation and its mission. Here lay the essential moral politics: as a future generation would put it, the personal had become political. In Massachusetts and New Haven (but not Connecticut) there was a more direct political consequence. Only church members could vote.[43]

A broad mix of Puritan notions ran together to define status within the community, at least through the first Puritan generation: traditional rank, worldly success, clerical preparation, eternal salvation, and the idea of America. The result was a distinctive New England caste. Church members had demonstrated grace; they walked in virtue. The members of the new world us were righteous; those who failed to measure up were probably depraved and marked for damnation. That division would evolve, of course, but even today we're sifting out the hearts of others with every welfare reform.

The Puritans expected everyone to attend church service and profit from the sermons. But only the elect shared communion, baptized their children, or participated in church decisions.

In the early years, the congregations wielded real power. The minister answered to the assembly—they elected him, they could send him packing. Northampton even fired Jonathan Edwards, the most formidable churchman in the colonies. More typically, angry congregations withheld the minister's salary. "It is high injustice and oppression, yea a sin that cryes in the Lords ear for judgement, when wages is withheld," charged the synod of 1679. "The Lords Ministers have been forced to neglect the House of God, and goe every one into the field." It only got worse. Over the next six decades (1680–1740), some 12 percent of the New England clergy got into serious financial scraps with their congregations. A pastor in Hartford, Connecticut, summed up what he saw in his saints: "fierce and wrathful people." Still, the churchmen were influential. They governed the conversion process and disciplined drifting saints. A censure before the congregation was humiliating, and excommunication worse.[44]

Congregations did not answer to higher authority. After all, the Puritans were revolting against English church hierarchy. Puritan congregations were meant to be strictly autonomous. However, autonomy in no way licensed diversity. In theory, each congregation would follow the Bible to the same eternal truth.

In practice, it did not work that way. Intimations of heresy constantly rippled through New England. Each cranked up the tension between communal autonomy and central authority. Ministerial synods could advise on doctrine and criticize errors. The civil authorities could protect the faith by banishing heretics or sinners. However, the principle of congregational autonomy made such operations extremely delicate as long as the congregation rallied around its wayward Puritan. When local churches held fast, heresy charges could set off pyrotechnic politics (see Chapter 2). Trouble ran along an early version of the classic political fault line: the principle of congregational autonomy clashed with the state's covenanted responsibility to protect the faith and punish heresy. Local autonomy resisted central control.[45]

The picture of early Puritan tensions can be exaggerated. Some communities avoided trouble for years. Kenneth Lockridge describes Dedham as an idyllic, God-fearing farm community where membership in the congregation essentially overlapped membership in the town—80 percent of the children were baptized. "The life of the utopian commune" lasted "longer than anyone had a right to expect." America, concludes Lockridge, "is the place where utopias are put into practice." And where, inevitably, they get "found impracticable."[46]

Even in Dedham, spiritual decline had set in by the second generation. And never mind the raucous saints in places like Boston. By the 1660s, the Puritans had compromised away their two great principles—the church of visible saints and congregational autonomy.

First, the careful limits on church membership created trouble. The children of the original settlers did not share the religious ardor that had brought their parents to the new world. People drifted from church membership—by 1662, Dedham had not had a single conversion in five years. Men in particular lost the faith. After 1650, women made up between 60 and 70 percent of all new church members.[47]

The grandchildren of the original saints brought the problem to a head. The first generation had baptized its children expecting that they would become full church members. But many of those children had never gone through the conversion ritual. Because they were not full church members, they were not entitled to baptize their own children. With the church ranks dwindling, the Puritans faced a choice between their doctrine and their dominion. They went for the latter. The synod of 1662 propounded a "half way covenant." Yes, those third-generation children could be baptized, so long as their parents were "sound in the faith and not scandalous in life." That made the parents partial (or half-way) church members—they could baptize their children but not share in communion or vote for church officials. This cut it too fine for many congregations. Some simply flung their doors open to all who came forward; others bitterly hewed to the old rules. Churches divided over the issue in Hartford, Windsor, and Stratford, Connecticut. Dedham resisted the half-way covenant for three decades and relented only when sticking to the old way made it impossible to recruit a minister. The fine theological distinction—a half-way member—makes a wonderful, lost icon. American politics would reverberate with careful distinctions between morally worthy and unworthy, between devout and degenerate. Future generations would continue to reckon moral worth in the same meticulously calibrated terms as the Puritans reckoned their covenant membership.[48]

The synod became emblematic of a second great concession. Religious authority slowly drained from independent congregations to the ministers as a group. Public officials had always asked the churchmen for advice and biblical interpretation. With time, the clerical judgments took on more weight. Synods increasingly set policy and provided leadership for the congregations.[49]

The Puritans constantly struggled with the problem of membership. Who belonged? Whom to embrace? Whom to expel as dangerous or contrary minded? And how should the autonomous communities fit together into their shared covenant? The Puritans bequeathed all those ambiguities to America.

That Puritan gray area around congregational independence looks particularly familiar. Three centuries of American politics would never fully resolve the tension between local autonomy and central authority. The principles at stake have radically evolved, of course. Today, local diversity is celebrated. Even so, local differences are bounded by the neo-covenantal Constitution. Never mind celebrating diversity, communities may not pray in public places, harm endangered species, interfere with a woman's right to an abortion, or keep mum about sulfites in the local wine. To be sure, there are multiple sources for this enduring American conflict. But none stretches back further than the Puritan tension between congregational autonomy and colonial authority.

Government

Organizing a government injected more turbulence into the New England Way. Dangers lurked at each extreme—arbitrary government (their memory of English persecution) on the one hand, disorder (pronounced "democracy") on the other. Proponents of godly hierarchy kept fighting what they saw as a steady leveling danger. That dialectic played out against the dominant political question: How should a biblical commonwealth, loosely bound to England, govern itself?

The royal charter authorizing Massachusetts Bay offered little guidance. It actually sanctioned a commercial company managed by a governor and eighteen assistants chosen by stockholders, with quarterly meetings open to investors. Oddly, the charter never specified the headquarters. The Puritans simply transferred their company to Boston. Then they transformed the governor of the company into the governor of the colony, the commercial assistants into colonial magistrates, and the stockholders into freemen. The quarterly stockholders' meetings became sessions of the General Court. Here's another Puritan symbol for the ages: these early Americans hammered their political institutions out of a business charter, then passed the vote from stockholders to proven saints.

Within a year, church members were voting for both their religious and their political leaders. (The two did not overlap as ministers did not hold political office.) By the standards of the time, the franchise was extremely broad. Still, no one mistook it for democracy. Rather, election was a way to bind the covenanted people together and to call their most eminent to office.

Across New England, on both local and provincial levels, voters elected and reelected the same knot of relatively prosperous men. In Dedham, for example, just ten men dominated the board of selectmen from 1639 to 1687; they averaged twenty terms each. Boston and Salem saw even less turnover. Nor did the spirit of liberalism stir much over time. A century later (1740–1749) seven of the nine selectmen in Northampton were sons of selectmen whose fathers had averaged nine terms each.[50]

Leaders were always wary about the decline toward democracy. When the freemen first started voting for governor (in 1632), Magistrate Roger Ludlow "grew into a passion" about the rush to anarchy. "Then we should have no government," shouted Ludlow, but "every man might do what he pleased."[51]

Winthrop fostered the broad franchise. But he was ferocious about the balance between authority and liberty. In July 1645 he offered a dramatic statement of his view before a furious audience: "The great questions that trouble the country are about the authority of the magistrates and the liberty of the people. It is you yourselves who have called us to this office, and being called by you, we have our authority from God."[52]

Real or civil liberty, continued Winthrop, is not the wild liberty of the beast. "It is maintained and exercised in . . . subjugation to authority." Winthrop compared elections to the liberty with which people approach Christ or the way a woman approaches the man she has chosen for a husband.

> Being so chosen, he is her lord, and she is to be subject to him, yet in a way of liberty, not of bondage; and a true wife accounts her subjugation her honor and freedom and would not think her condition safe and free but in her subjugation to her husband's authority.
>
> If through . . . wantonness, she shake . . . off [the yoke], she is at no rest in spirit, until she take it up again; and whether her lord smiles upon her, and embraceth her in his arms, or whether he frowns, or rebukes, or smites her, she apprehends the sweetness of his love in all and is refreshed, supported, and instructed by every dispensation of his authority over her.[53]

Winthrop's sermon would echo long and loud, a strong statement of traditional hierarchy. Proponents of the biblical family still repeat the point (citing the same New Testament texts). Winthrop's plea for hierarchy and deference echoes passages of his *Arbella* sermon, given fifteen years earlier. But his tone had turned dark and fretful—those "questions that trouble the country" (at the start of the quotation) loom over the rest of the speech. And Winthrop was putting it mildly. The general court was in an uproar. Representatives of the public had gotten so angry at Winthrop that they had put him on trial for abusing his authority. As soon as Winthrop was acquitted, he rose and delivered this implacable lecture. Once elected, said Winthrop, the magistrates answer to God, not to the people or their representatives. On the contrary, like the good wife, Winthrop's accusers would be "refreshed" by taking up the yoke of proper subjugation.

The roots of this pandemonium went almost all the way back to the Puritans' first days in New England. In 1632 the residents of Watertown briefly fussed over taxation without representation—yes, that goes all the way back too. To head off the trouble, the elected magistrates (the Charter specified eighteen for the colony) had ordered each town to send representatives to the General Court. Over the next decade these delegates from the towns began to think of themselves as voting members of the government. There were, of course, no clear rules on the matter. The delegates demanded voting rights, the magistrates resisted, and both cited biblical warrant to back their view.[54]

The delegates represented a rising political class, a lesser gentry articulating local interests. They posed a political threat, for they outnumbered the more eminent magistrates. The delegates repeatedly criticized "arbitrary government." The magistrates, in their turn, charged the lesser gentry with fomenting democracy—though it never occurred to anyone to vote out the big men. An occasional hothead ratcheted up the rhetoric by declaring that he would "die at the sword's point, if he might not have the choice of his own officers." Or that the vote of the people "would bear them out in what was past and what was to come."[55]

Never mind mutual love, Puritan politics got positively bare-knuckled. At one point, Winthrop was reduced to denying that his supporters were plotting to murder Richard Saltonstall, a magistrate who sided with the delegates. At the end of another raucous General Court session, Winthrop introduced a motion affirming that despite all their differences, the members were "united in Love and affection." The General Court rudely voted it down. "Let us no longer professe the Gospell of Jesus Christ, but take up the rules of Matchiavell," scribbled a furious Winthrop.[56]

The relationship between magistrates and delegates was resolved during a truly bizarre fight. A woman accused Robert Keayne (the same man who was fined for his "unjust prices" in 1639) of stealing her sow. Keayne was acquitted for lack of evidence, though many people thought him guilty. He then sued the woman for libel, and won. This wealthy character—of "ill report in the country for hard dealing"—was squeezing money from a poor woman, possibly after stealing her pig. The very idea got the public and its delegates into an uproar.[57]

Most delegates voted to reverse the court. The magistrates regretted the irony but thought the evidence of theft flimsy; most voted to let the libel judgment stand. Counting all the votes together would have reversed the judgment. However, the magistrates argued that they had a negative veto—they could block any action of the General Court with a majority of their own number. After months of angry exchanges, the ministers were called in to adjudicate. Both sides, ruled the ministers, had a negative veto. This was a victory for the magistrates; the delegates were more numerous and did not need a veto. Defeated, the delegates stalked off to a separate chamber: Massachusetts bicameralism— the result of a lost or stolen pig.[58]

Below all the thrashing lay a fundamental political question. How should the colony balance government authority and popular representation? For answers, the Puritans thumbed through their Bibles and turned to their clergymen. Winthrop's sermons—both in 1630 and 1645—remain classic statements of orthodox hierarchy. But he constantly had to fight to protect his godly order from the popular ferment that kept crashing against it.

One hundred fifty years later, an assembly of Enlightenment rationalists gathered in Philadelphia to draft a Constitution. They could not have been more different from the General Court in Boston bickering toward bicameralism. Yet both groups faced the same job: framing a government. And the first days of the Constitutional Convention turned on precisely the same question that had roiled Winthrop and his rivals—the balance between proper authority and the "danger of the leveling spirit," as Elbridge Gerry would put it in Philadelphia.

During the Constitutional Convention, James Wilson made a celebrated analogy: the federal pyramid, he said, should be raised to a considerable altitude above the people and therefore ought to be given a broad electoral base. Wilson revisited John Winthrop's approach. The Philadelphia delegates constructed a dramatically new governing frame, but it was a direct intellectual descendant of the Puritans' struggle to balance broad suffrage and high deference.[59]

The covenants called for mutual love. The reality often yielded "fierce and wrathful" people. The philosophy called for the sweet yoke of authority—

woman to man, man to magistrate, and all to God. In reality, the General Court kept breaking out into uproars, heavy with petitions and suits, charges and counter-charges. In places like Dedham, the Puritan dream may have flourished for a time. But everywhere economic pressures and political interests subverted the Puritan idyll.

The Puritans mixed religious utopianism, political struggle, and a restless quest for their own elusive self-identity. In many ways, however, the search for Puritan identity could be answered more directly in the negative—by looking to see who they were not.

Chapter 2
Them: Heretic, Heathen, and Witch

A long string of enemies defined the Puritans. Each foe illuminated a different corner of the Puritan culture, every battle illustrated another pattern in the enduring politics of us and them.

Gender War and the Antinomian Heresy

It sounds boring. Rebels attack the Puritan establishment with cries of Arminianism. The establishment slashes back with countercharges of antinomianism. The sides are eager to fight, but about what? "Few could see where the difference was," wrote John Winthrop. In fact, the clash raised the real issues: power, conscience, the woman's role, and the road to hell. The first great intellectual conflict in the English colonies defined the Puritan establishment. It still stands as a prototype for America's culture wars.

The story begins with minister John Cotton's arrival in Boston in 1633. Cotton quickly made his mark. The Boston church elected him teacher, and his preaching sparked a wave of conversions. (Congregational church officers included a minister and a teacher.) Cotton Mather would later write, "Boston oweth its name and being to him more than any one person in the world." (A Puritan jest: Cotton Mather, born in 1639, is the one who owes his name to John Cotton.) Roger Williams added his own tart testimonial: the people "could scarcely believe that God would suffer Mr. Cotton to err."[1]

A year later, Anne Hutchinson followed John Cotton to Boston. She developed a reputation as a midwife. She was "not only skilful and helpfull" at childbirth, Cotton would later testify, but "readily fell into good discourse with the women about their spiritual estates." Members of the Boston congregation began visiting the Hutchinson house, which soon developed into something of a theo-

2.1. Anne Hutchinson would become an American icon—for religious freedom, for feminism, for trouble. Howard Pyle's dramatic painting (circa 1901) shows Hutchinson preaching in her house in Boston. Pyle imagined men and women at the same meeting, a shocking practice that Hutchinson firmly denied. (Brown County Library, Green Bay, Wisconsin)

logical salon. Sixty, sometimes eighty women packed the house while Hutchinson discussed Cotton's sermons. Men came too, though they met separately.[2]

Fourscore women talking theology might have made the Puritan authorities nervous in any case. But the content of Hutchinson's meetings was pure trouble. Hutchinson followed Cotton back to Calvinist basics: Salvation is entirely and absolutely in God's hands. There is nothing people can do to influence divine judgment. Nor can human behavior offer any clues about whether God has touched a person with grace. Forget about reading piety or prosperity or spiritual autobiographies as signs of anything. In the baroque Protestant idiom, "sanctification" (living a good, pure life) was no evidence of "justification" (being elected by God).[3]

Just as the churchmen were developing their elaborate membership rituals, along came Anne Hutchinson, who—plausibly citing John Cotton, one of the most influential men in town—announced that the entire effort was useless. Worse than useless, in fact: raw heresy. Hutchinson bluntly accused the New England ministry of preaching a "covenant of works." That is, they were spreading the idea that men and women could help determine their own eternal fate—could force the hand of God—through "works" like praying or piety or working diligently. The Protestant reformation had rejected this route to salvation. Putting human endeavor over God's grace was an error called Arminianism. (Even Winthrop would later admit that New England's drift toward stressing works "took me in as drowsy a condition as I have been in these twenty years.")[4]

But if nothing anybody did affected (or demonstrated) his or her salvation, what were the ministers supposed to be doing? If the Holy Ghost directly infused the elect—a flash of spiritual lightning—then there was no point to all the spiritual flagellation that the saints were undergoing to prepare themselves. The jeremiads, the elaborate Puritan rules of conduct, the entire framework of the holy commonwealth were all useless, even heretical. Perry Miller sums up the Hutchinson challenge: "With what face could the ministers blame sinful people for afflictions?" Or hector them about salvation and perdition? In short, Hutchinson challenged the whole Puritan apparatus.[5]

The authorities did not suffer the assault quietly. Hutchinson, they countered, preached rank antinomianism. The term itself derives from *anti* (against) and *nomos* (law). That, argued the Puritan establishment, is exactly where Hutchinson's thought led. A synod met during the crisis (in August 1637) and identified "unsafe" and "unsavory" antinomian speeches from Hutchinson and her followers. The inventory of reckless talk included, "If I be holy I am never the better accepted of God. If I am unholy, I am never the worse." And what *was* worse, "If Christ will let me sinne, let him looke to it, upon his honour be it." And, getting to the bottom Puritan line, "I may know I am Christ's, not because I doe crucifie the lusts of the flesh but because I doe not crucify them." Rather, "Christ . . . crucified my lusts for me." Winthrop drove home the ministers' great objection: "Most of her new tenets tended to slothfulness, and quench all indevour." Historian Edmund Morgan piled on with the Puritan fathers: what Hutchinson was promoting was the "17th century equivalent of nihilism."[6]

At stake were starkly different visions of the Puritan faith. On the one side, New England elites were busy transforming what had been a mechanism of protest into the official faith of a powerful establishment. They were organizing the machinery of authority. Now, the New England covenant called for loyalty, discipline, and attention to the behavior of the whole community. The ministers fostered "indevour" and "striving." They backed them up with social controls vested in both church and state. And, yes, it all certainly smacked of "works."

On the other side, Anne Hutchinson was searching for the intense personal experience of the old Puritanism. She called for an evangelical ministry. She and her followers longed to feel the unmediated power of the Holy Ghost stir their souls. They would break free from the constant anxieties of the New England conversion process for, in their view, the Holy Ghost filled the soul with absolute certainty. "I seeke not for graces, but for Christ, . . . I seek not for sanctification but for Christ, tell not me of meditation and duties, but tell me of Christ." Hutchinson's vision of grace was personal, immediate, revolutionary. If this was the seventeenth-century equivalent of nihilism, it reflected the powerful aspirations originally embedded in that philosophy—call it the seventeenth-century equivalent of romantic individualism.[7]

In short, this is a clash between the old evangelical faith and a new orthodoxy. On a more general level, the tension reflected the enduring antinomies of religious yearning: on the one hand, the urge to abandon oneself entirely in the overwhelming power of God; on the other, the striving toward heaven through the human struggle to live a moral life. The Puritan story is the story of faith that keeps drifting to the latter, toward an emphasis on works, punctuated by great evangelical bouts that throw people back before the awesome and unmediated power of God. This tension eventually would evolve into the great dialectic of American religion. A moral orthodoxy offers guides, demands discipline, and damns deviants. Religious rebels would keep disrupting the establishment with intense outbursts of reforming evangelism. Hutchinson and her followers were the first in a long American line.[8]

In trying to pin down Hutchinson's sin, the churchmen expounded the eternal Puritan complaint. Down through the centuries moralists would point at sinners and echo the synod of 1637: those people refuse to "crucifie the lusts of the flesh."

The Conflict

There was at least one great difference between Anne Hutchinson and John Cotton. She "was more sharply censorious of other men's spiritual estates and hearts." Hutchinson was blunt: every minister in New England preached heresy. There were just two exceptions, John Cotton and John Wheelwright.[9]

In October 1636, Hutchinson and her followers voted to have Wheel-

wright join the Boston ministry as a teacher. They would then have in their
pulpit the two men they admired. But Cotton already shared the pulpit with
John Wilson, a stern opponent of the antinomian faction. By drafting Wheelwright, the rebels were disparaging Wilson. John Winthrop stopped the appointment (selecting ministers required unanimity), antagonizing his already
disgruntled fellow congregants.[10]

Blocked in Boston, the center of antinomian agitation, Wheelwright took
a position in a new church formed at Mount Wollaston (now Braintree, Massachusetts). His frustrated supporters began to spread the antinomian word to
the outlying congregations. The Boston faithful confronted rival ministers
with sharp questions and objections during church services—basically, they
heckled the heretic clergy. This, of course, infuriated the other congregations.
"It began to be as common here to distinguish men, by being under a covenant
of grace or a covenant of works," wrote Winthrop, "as in other countries between protestants and papists." When Boston raised a militia to fight the Pequots, the men almost refused to march because John Wilson, the chaplain,
was under a covenant of works.[11]

The leaders of the factions met in December 1636 to resolve the differences. But no one budged. Each side charged the other with breaching the covenant, for which everybody would suffer. Officials responded to the impasse by
declaring a day of fast and humiliation in January. During the fast-day services,
Wheelwright returned to Boston. Cotton invited him into the pulpit and Wheelwright preached a red-hot sermon. Those who were under a covenant of works,
said Wheelwright, are "Enymeys to the Lord, not only paganish but anti-
christian. . . . We must lay load upon them, we must kill them with the word of
the Lord," and "breake them in peeces as shivered with a rod of iron." Awfully
strong words. And they are even harsher in their Old Testament context:
"They . . . have transgressed the covenant," "The company of priests murder in
the way of consent," "They commit lewdness," and "There is whoredom in
Ehraim, Israel is defiled."[12]

Wheelwright was indicted for sedition. In early 1637, a divided General
Court convicted him amid "much heat . . . between the opposing parties."
Representatives from Boston promptly introduced a petition from the congregation supporting Wheelwright. Treading gingerly, the anti-Boston majority
tabled further action, and the uproar was adjourned till the next session of the
General Court in May. Then, to diminish Boston's influence, the magistrates
changed the venue of the May meeting from Boston to Cambridge—a difficult trip in the seventeenth century.[13]

Elections were held during the May meeting of the General Court.
Sure enough, the antinomian faction—which had included Governor Henry

Vane—got swept out of office. Winthrop himself had been passed over for the preceding three years (1734–1736). Now he got voted back in. Winthrop immediately moved against the antinomians.

The General Court rejected the Boston petition supporting Wheelwright. In fact, the signatories themselves now faced disciplinary action. The court once again deferred sentencing Wheelwright, but it did pass a restriction to keep like-minded English settlers from swelling the antinomian ranks. That law, the very first American limit on immigration, set an enduring pattern by addressing both the politics and the morals of potential newcomers.[14]

In August and September, the ministers met in synod. They identified and confuted ninety errors and nine unsavory speeches of the antinomians. They cracked down on the practices that had led to mischief—questioning ministers during the service, holding meetings like Hutchinson's. Essentially, they tightened their own grip on the church and cobbled together an orthodoxy that the rebels could now be accused of violating. A month later the court punished Wheelwright by banishing him from the colony; it then turned to the main event, the trial of Anne Hutchinson.[15]

This trial was extraordinary. It is the closest we ever get to a record of Hutchinson's own words. And Hutchinson proved a match for Governor Winthrop, the magistrates, and the assembled divines. This was an action of the General Court, so there was no jury; the ministers came from across New England to serve as witnesses. John Winthrop, John Endicott (the deputy governor), various magistrates, and some of the ministers all flung questions at Hutchinson, disputed her answers, and offered testimony against her.

Hutchinson defeated her interrogators in one exchange after another. The magistrates petulantly acknowledged her parries: "We are your judges and not you ours"; "I deny it because I have brought more arguments than you have"; "Why this is not to be suffered." Edmund Morgan neatly sums up most twentieth-century readings of the transcript: "It might have been better for the reputation of her judges had they simply banished her unheard."[16]

The magistrates started at a disadvantage: they did not have a strong charge against Hutchinson. They made do with three rather indirect accusations. Though Hutchinson had not signed the petition supporting Wheelwright, she had encouraged his followers in their sedition (thus violating the Fifth Commandment, "Honor thy father and mother"). She had held those meetings, not "comely in the sight of God or fitting for her sex." And finally, the real gripe, she had "disparaged all our ministers in the land."[17]

Right up to the end, Hutchinson made it difficult for the court. Take the complaint about her meetings. Hutchinson points out that such meetings were "in practice before I came [to Boston]." In fact, by not attending "they said I was proud and did despise all ordinances."[18]

> *Governor Winthrop:* "By what warrant do you continue such a course?"
>
> Hutchinson is ready with a biblical warrant: "I conceive there lyes a clear rule in Titus, that the older women should instruct the younger" (Titus II, 3– 5). Moments later, Hutchinson offers a second authority: "Aquila and Priscilla tooke upon them to instruct Apollo" (Acts XVIII, 26).
>
> Winthrop tries sarcasm: "Priscilla with her husband, tooke Apollo home to instruct him privately, therefore Mrs. Hutchinson without her husband may teach sixty or eighty. . . . Yet you show us not the rule."
>
> *Hutchinson:* "I have given you two places in scripture."
>
> *The court:* "But neither of them will suite your practice."
>
> Hutchinson has a withering return: "Must I show you my name written therein?"[19]

On the second day, Hutchinson hits on a brilliant strategy. John Wilson, the Boston minister, had testified against her the previous day. Reviewing her notes that night, Hutchinson found a discrepancy between Wilson's testimony and previous statements he had made. The next morning, Hutchinson asks that the testimony be under oath. This throws the prosecution into real confusion. Taking an oath means taking God's name. Uttering something that is not exactly true under oath is a serious sin. And the ministers are not confident about what precisely they have said over the long, hot year. They spend much of the morning going in circles, trying to avoid swearing an oath.[20]

Finally, the master compromiser John Cotton is called. True to form, he denies that Hutchinson really disparaged the ministers. Now what? It looks as though the entire case against her is going to fall apart.

Then, suddenly, Hutchinson launches into a long statement in which she claims to get her revelations directly from God. What, they ask her, what does this mean? "How [did] shee know that it was God . . . and not Satan?" The same way Abraham knew, says Hutchinson, "that it was the voyce of God . . . command[ing] him to sacrifice his sonne." Finally! Pay dirt. This, they all agree, is raw heresy—the idea that God speaks directly to the saint rather than through the Bible. Now they have a solid reason to expel her. "I desire to know wherefore I am banished," she asks when it is over. Say no more, they crow, "the court knows wherefore and is satisfied."[21]

Why did Hutchinson speak out so forcefully when she had the court all tied up? There has been plenty of speculation. Sheer exhaustion? Exuberance? A prophetic urge? Hysteria, as some early historians suggested?

Perhaps the mistake lies in reading the speech as a blunder in the first place.

Rather, Hutchinson had vividly crystallized the difference between the emerging, still unarticulated Puritan orthodoxy and her antinomian revivalism. She was expressing just what the rebels had been after in the first place—the soul's immediate, intense, direct relation to Christ. John Cotton had the same urge for immediacy (the major difference between him and his colleagues). Even Hutchinson's enemies (like Thomas Hooker) had once preached in the rhetoric of direct revelation. "Shall I tell you what God told me?" asked Thomas Hooker in "The Danger of Desertion," a sermon delivered in England in 1629. "What if I should tell you what God told me yesternight?" Now, declaring Hutchinson guilty, the General Court and the New England clergy drew a curtain on Puritan revivalism and replaced it with a more formal faith.[22]

The rest is anticlimax. The court banished Hutchinson from Massachusetts, disarmed seventy-five of her followers, and dismissed two Boston deputies. Hutchinson recanted (too late) and was excommunicated from the Boston congregation. She went to Rhode Island with a handful of followers, then moved on to New York. Six years after the trial she and most of her family were killed by Indians.

Sex and Power

The Puritan fathers gave the antinomian affair a dramatic gender spin—both at the trial and after. The issue roiled largely implicit, only occasionally breaking to the surface, while Hutchinson was still in town. Later, Puritan leaders would reframe the affair with almost obsessive, overtly sexual revulsion.

We have already seen Winthrop's view of the wife's role—it was part of God's strict social hierarchy. Women submitted to men, men to their betters, all to God. Men or women wandered from their proper place at great peril. Winthrop's best-known pronouncement is his comment on Ann Yale Hopkins, who lost "her understanding and reason . . . by giving herself wholly to reading and writing . . . many books. If she had attended her household affairs and such things as belong to a women, and not gone out of her way and calling to meddle in such things as are proper for men, she had kept her wits and might have improved them usefully and honorably in the place that God has set her."[23]

This view of women's proper sphere regularly comes into focus during Hutchinson's trial. The meetings at the Hutchinson house were "not tolerable . . . or fitting for your sex." In frustration, Winthrop snaps, "We do not mean to discourse with those of your sex." In the exchange over instructing younger women, the governor is clear on the recommended curriculum he finds in Titus II: "to love their husbands and to not make them to clash."[24]

But afterward, after Hutchinson was found guilty and sent away, the affair's gender motif looms far more prominent. It is almost as if the Puritan writers

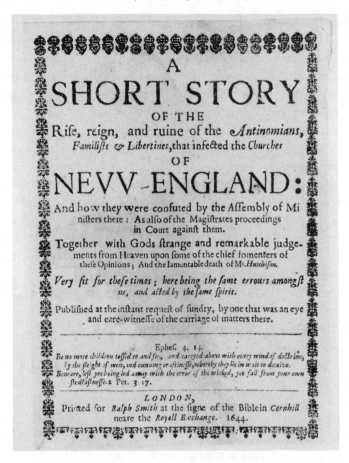

A

SHORT STORY

OF THE

Rife, reign, and ruine of the *Antinomians,*
Familifts & Libertines, that infected the *Churches*

OF

NEVV-ENGLAND:

And how they were confuted by the Affembly of Mi
nifters there : As alfo of the Magiftrates proceedings
in Court againft them.

Together with Gods ftrange and remarkable judge-
ments from Heaven upon fome of the chief fomenters of
thefe Opinions ; And the lamentable death of M*r.Hutchifon.*

Very fit for thefe times ; here being the fame errours amongſt
us, and acted by the fame ſpirit.

Publifhed at the inftant requeft of fundry, by one that was an eye
and eare-witneffe of the carriage of matters there.

Ephef. 4. 14.
Be no more children toffed to and fro, and carryed about with every wind of doctrine,
by the ſleight of men, and cunning craftineffe, whereby they lie in wait to deceive.
Beware, leſt yee being led away with the error of the wicked, yee fall from your own
*ſtedfaſtneſſe.*2 Pet. 3. 17.

LONDON,
Printed for *Ralph Smith* at the figne of the Bible in *Cornhill*
neare the *Royall Exchange.* 1644.

2.2. John Winthrop's account of the rise, reign, and ruine of Anne Hutchinson and her followers—a sustained attack on the people who would not "crucifie the lusts of the flesh." By 1644, Hutchinson was gone, but the lessons remained "Very fit for these times." (John Carter Brown Library at Brown University)

were trying to explain the episode by reconstructing it as sexual drama. In a preface to Winthrop's account of the events ("A Short Story of the Rise, Reign, and Ruine of the Antinomians, Familists and Libertines") Thomas Weld wrote that "carnal and vile persons . . . commonly . . . worke first upon women, being the weaker to resist . . . and if they could winde in them, they hoped by them, as by Eve, to catch their husbands also."[25]

By the time Cotton Mather gets to the story, seventy years later, the Eve construction is the central point of the conflict. "It is the mark of seducers that they lead silly women. . . . Like their father the devil, the old first seducer, they usually have a special design upon the weaker sex." Seducers prey on women because they "are more easily gained themselves and then are fit instruments for the gaining of their husbands." Mather could construct this into a general rule: "There are few controversies where a woman is not at the bottom of them." The language in the pages that follow is full of sexual turns: Hutchinson seduced the servants of the lord, bewitched minds, besotted the people.[26]

Beyond domesticity, vulnerability, and seduction lies procreation. The story told by Winthrop and embellished by Mather reduces Hutchinson to the merely sexual, merely vaginal. During the trial Hutchinson had been pregnant. Afterward, she miscarried. The metamorphosis of Anne Hutchinson is accomplished through vivid accounts of her "monstrous" miscarriage. Cotton Mather put it this way: "The erroneous gentlewoman her self, convicted of holding about thirty monstrous opinions, growing big with child . . . was delivered of about thirty monstrous births at once; thereof some were bigger, some were lesser . . . none of any humane shape."[27]

The antinomian ideas get mixed up with puns about stillborn monsters: "It is frequent for women laboring under false conceptions to reproduce . . . monstrous births." And "most of the errors then crawling like vipers around the country were hatched at [Hutchinson's] meetings."[28]

Again, Mather was following Winthrop, who had expanded the discussion to include one of Hutchinson's followers: "God Himself was pleased to step in with his casting voice . . . in causing the two fomenting women . . . to produce out of their wombs, as before they had out of their brains, such monstrous births as no chronicle . . . hardly ever recorded the like." (Or, in Mather's version, "as hideous a monster as the sun ever lookt upon.")[29]

The other woman is Mary Dyer, a follower of Hutchinson who was "infected," says Mather, "with her heresies." The horrors of this second stillborn "monster" are chronicled in detail. It is a female with no head (which, needless to say, means no brain). The face is upon the breast; the navel, belly, and distinction of sex are all where the hips should be. And—striking coincidence— they discovered Mary Dyer's stillborn monster, already dead and secretly buried, the very day Anne Hutchinson was thrown out of the church.[30]

Finally, that "casting voice" turns out to be not God's but Satan's. For a further description makes clear in Dyer's case and strongly implies in Hutchinson's that there is witchcraft afoot. It is a devil that dies, shuddering, within Mary Dyer two hours before her miscarriage. Dyer's own midwife (Jane Hawkins), also a follower of Anne Hutchinson, would be banished for witchcraft in 1641. As for Hutchinson, her thirty monsters suggest not just thirty false religious conceptions but the satanic imps that were an important part of witchcraft.[31]

In the end, the Puritan histories do not for a moment acknowledge their worthy adversary. The religious rebellion sprang from the weakness of Eve, the vulnerable feminine link in man's struggle with evil. The religious ideas themselves are reconstructed into creatures that spring not so much from the woman's brain as from her womb. Mather spills far more ink on the monstrous fetus than on the issues at stake.

From our twenty-first-century perspective, it is a stunning diminution. But the insistent focus on gender, sexuality, and monsters illuminates the Puritan fears. Hutchinson and her eighty female followers were fomenting what Ben Barker-Benfield describes as a "revolution of the Eves." They were inverting Puritan hierarchy—threatening the godly subordination of woman to man, of man to ministers, of the people to their magistrates.

On a still more fundamental level, they threatened the Puritan emphasis on self-control. They refused—as the synod of 1637 put it—to "crucifie the lusts of the flesh." Like the Indians (the Puritans were slaughtering Pequots at precisely the same moment), the antinomians refused to subordinate their own passions. Puritan leaders saw both groups as uncontrolled, degenerate, frightening. Each group, in its own way, posed a threat of "lustful, anarchic eruption."[32]

In contrast, Puritan society was organized for control, for godly hierarchy. The authority of both church and state were designed to master carnal impulses. Lust and sexuality were turned relentlessly into descriptions of the religious experience. Examples are everywhere in the Puritan texts: converts were brides of Christ, the union with Jesus was marriage (consummated to produce the fruit of a new birth), the true believer was wedded to God. Public worship was the bed of loves, church leaders were nursing fathers, idolatry was adultery, the Roman church was a whore. As Edmund Morgan sums it up, it is not that "the Christianity of the Puritans was merely a sublimation of filial or sexual impulses, but there was a large element of sublimation in it."[33]

Puritan leaders rejected the "sloth" of the antinomian surrender to the naked Christ. They thrashed out the details of their alternative in direct opposition to Hutchinson and her allies. Man and God would work together toward salvation. Only God could offer grace, but His people must be rigorously prepared to embrace it. If election could come at any moment, saints had to be ready at all times. In contrast to antinomian assurance, the Puritan orthodoxy emphasized constant uncertainty, constant striving.

And at the center of the endeavor stood the minister. He would prepare the sinner for God's grace. He would determine when and whether God had justified her. Knowledge that for antinomians lay within each individual now became externalized; it became a professional judgment made by carefully trained ministers. The clerical establishment's victory was so crushing, concludes Perry Miller, that the preparation Hutchinson had scorned was inflated to the "peculiar badge of New England theology." By the late 1630s, the minister held the keys to both kingdoms—election to the church and full citizenship (at least in Massachusetts). In the fight against Anne Hutchinson, the nursing fathers had worked out their perspective and fixed it firmly on New England.[34]

Antinomian Echoes

Anne Hutchinson and her followers made an especially perplexing kind of enemy because they were members of the covenant community, they were part of the Puritan us. Winthrop tried to make sense of it with a biblical parallel. Hutchinson was the latest incarnation of Eve, he suggested. She seduced her followers, "quenching all indeavor" and inducing them to cast off their self-control. She threatened to unleash immorality, even moral anarchy. She disrupted the godly order by refusing to stay in her place—she would not be subordinate, silent, or domestic.

Hutchinson challenged Puritan leaders with an early gender revolution, posing what would prove to be an enduring dilemma. Organizing relations between the sexes is basic to any society; rebellions over gender roles pit members of the same community against one another. How do elites manage such internal, even intimate, tensions? The Puritan mechanisms are still familiar.

First, Puritan leaders affirmed the importance of self-control. Saints would crucify their lusts—no more fussing about whether this was a covenant of works. Strict social mores (as we now call them) set moral standards and gender norms. Backsliding, then as now, set off the sermons about decline. This defense against misbehavior would be inculcated in children and reflected in social expectations. Over the years, people who got it right would be called different things—pious, proper, or well socialized. But by any name, social norms remain the crucial—always evolving, always contested—mechanisms of gender control.

Second, the Puritans backed up self-control with institutional power. The church would teach, censure, and save; the state would root out and punish sinners. Through the years, American government would remain in the business of moral discipline. Forget secular liberalism. Future generations would forbid interracial marriage, ban birth control, outlaw homosexual acts, and jail men who crossed state lines with immoral fancies. When present-day policy specialists recommend backing off the war on drugs, they hear a familiar retort: the state must send a strong moral message to our children.

Finally, there was banishment. But here the Eve narrative collapses. Members of the same covenanted community are responsible for one another. They suffer a shared fate—Adam was driven out of Eden, too. Segregation works a lot better against threats from outside the community. Rank heresy would re-cast people as outsiders—just what the Puritan fathers lucked into during the trial (though Hutchinson had not been accused of heresy beforehand). The subsequent Puritan apologists find something even better: they drop the Gen-esis story and spin Anne Hutchinson into a witch. Witches are profoundly other. They spurn godly covenant. Like Native Americans, they can be driven off without fouling up the logic of Puritan community.

The Puritans defeated Anne Hutchinson. But her kind would be back. We will see many long, hot battles over the same moral territory. On the one side, the moral rules reinforce civic order, social status, and political power. On the other, a faith stirring within individuals inspires them to attack the status quo.

Hutchinson and Winthrop also raised a more subtle antinomy. Today, the-orists call the clashing moral views the orthodox and the progressive. The or-thodox see immutable laws that fix good and evil in a divinely appointed frame. They mix Winthrop's hard, fast hierarchy with Hutchinson's evangelical ec-stasy. The progressives carry on one part of the Hutchinson legacy: they find grace (though usually not the Holy Ghost) turning on personal, subjective, ethical norms. The two perspectives have each taken turns as the establishment and the rebellious.[35]

You can still hear the Puritan echoes in contemporary moral debates. The orthodox still accuse their progressive rivals of spiritual sloth, though they now call it "permissiveness." Once again, orthodox activists echo the synod of 1637; they urge moral endeavor and choke with fury at those who fail to crucify lusts. Once again, the orthodox insist on divinely appointed gender roles and rules, now known as the biblical family. Once again, they sound urgent jeremiad warnings about moral decline. And, most dramatic of all, the orthodox once again focus both their rhetoric and their rage on monstrous images of dead fe-tuses.

Quakers

In 1656 two Quaker missionaries sailed into Boston harbor. The Puritan au-thorities were ready. They seized the women, threw them into jail, boarded up the windows, burned their books, and roughly probed their bodies for the tell-tale signs of witchcraft. One of the women, Mary Fisher, would later say the in-spection had been more painful than giving birth. When the women were ex-pelled, five weeks later, they sailed past another band of Quaker missionaries coming into Boston. The Puritans plunged into another conflict with a dis-senting group.[36]

The Quakers were sailing into a very different Boston than the one that

had cast out Anne Hutchinson two decades earlier. The founders were gone—
John Winthrop died in 1649, John Cotton in 1652. Now, John Endicott was
governor. Brooks Adams famously described Endicott as a "grim Puritan soldier . . . almost heroic in his ferocious bigotry and daring—a perfect champion
of the church." Across New England the intense piety of the first generation
was evaporating. "New England was no longer a reformation," writes Perry
Miller, "it was an administration."[37]

While they fought the Quakers, Puritan leaders were also wrestling with
their own dwindling church (they approved the halfway covenant in 1657 and
ratified the decision in 1662). Meanwhile, back in England, Cromwell died in
1658, and after two years of chaos Parliament invited Charles Stuart to the
throne (Stuart was crowned Charles II in 1661). With the king flaunting a long
string of mistresses and the Anglicans in control of Parliament, the New England Puritans finally broke with the national church. For the saints, the tide of
history was running the wrong way. New England now faced a secular (hell, a
downright ribald) English regime that would be distinctly skeptical about
righteous intolerance.

These troubles produced the golden age of the New England jeremiad. The
Puritans now confronted an identity problem. Kai Erikson has them asking
themselves, "Who are we? . . . Who the devil are we?" More or less on cue, the
Quakers sailed in on the soul-searching and, at least briefly, helped the Puritans
figure out who they were not.[38]

The Challenge

In many ways, this fight looks like the antinomian controversy warmed
over at a higher temperature. The Quakers preached an "inner light" that infused men and women and linked them directly to God. George Fox ("a shoemaker," sneered Cotton Mather, who "became the grand apostle of the Quakers") put it this way: "I was sent . . . to direct people . . . up to Christ and
God. . . . The grace of God, which brings salvation . . . was given to every-
man." The Quakers' inner light looked very much like the antinomians' Holy
Ghost. Once again, a zealous revival promised certainty, salvation, and an intense personal experience of God's grace.[39]

The inner light swept aside any need for ministers, sermons, intricate
canons, and "old mouldy books." What people needed to know lay within
themselves. Even learning—so prized by the Puritans—was just another im-
position of external authority. God's pure inner light would guide even the least
educated. Any man or (horrors) woman could read the Bible, preach, and
prophesy.[40]

The Quakers also challenged civil authority. They "teach doctrines that break the relation of subjects to their magistrates," charged an English critic. And they did so with gusto. The Quakers called "rulers, judges, lawyers and constables—'a tree that must be cut down for the light to shine,'" complained Cotton Mather. They stood "against all earthy powers." "They preached not Jesus Christ but themselves," exaggerated Roger Williams, "yea they preached the Lord Jesus to be themselves."[41]

Like the antinomians, Quakers upset the Puritan idea of godly order. Permitting women to preach was bad enough. But Quakers subverted the authority of husbands over wives, parents over children, servants over masters. What was a Puritan to make of Margaret Brewster, on trial for disrupting church services in Boston?

> *Gov* [magistrate]: Did your husband give Consent to your coming?
> *MB:* Yea, he did.
> *Gov:* Have you anything to shew under his Hand?
> *MB:* . . . This Service was of God and he durst not withstand it.[42]

He durst not withstand it? In Puritan New England, the service of God operated through the husband. This was twisting John Winthrop's "refreshing yoke" inside out. And the Quakers went beyond subverting gender roles. They provoked accusations of sexual misconduct. "Whorish and monstrous, unnatural and brutish," cried Roger Williams. Religious enthusiasts routinely stirred up such whispers. But Quaker maidens got those tongues wagging by running stark naked up the aisles and down the streets.[43]

If the antinomians tended toward "sloth" and "quenched indevour," what could you say about the Quakers? Anne Hutchinson never directly preached her own sermons or taunted the magistrates quite like Margaret Brewster did. However, the Quakers went beyond earlier revivals in a far more important way. They began to press for what we would now call social justice.

The logic of the inner light pushed its adherents to broad tolerance. Of course, they challenged the Puritans' religious intolerance. They also came to criticize New England's treatment of the Native Americans. Cotton Mather was incensed by Thomas Maule's pamphlet, "wherein he sets himself to defend the Indians in their bloody villainies." Ironically, Maule's indictment distinctly echoes the clergy's own jeremiad sermons: "God hath well rewarded the inhabitants of New England for their unrighteous dealings towards the native Indians, whom, now the Lord hath suffered to reward the inhabitants with a double measure of blood, by fire and sword." We'll see the New England ministers say precisely the same thing.[44]

Some Quakers also began questioning slavery. In 1671, George Fox proposed freeing slaves after a fixed period of bondage. By 1676, William Edmundson, a Quaker missionary, took the next step and asked why anyone should suffer slavery at all. In 1688, four Germantown Quakers would quietly draw up the first formal group resolution condemning American slavery: "If this is done well, what shall we say is . . . evil?" A stream of anti-slavery pamphlets, books, and resolutions would follow. Still, this aspect of the Quaker philosophy was just beginning to emerge and was easily obscured in the tumult of the 1650s and '60s.[45]

The Conflict

The behavior on all sides was almost rococo in its excess. The General Court denounced the "damnable heresies" and "abominable idolatrys" which were promoted "to the scandall of religion, hazard of souls, and provocation of divine jealousie against this people." Examine them, warned Roger Williams, and you "will see the cheat, the equivocation, the iniquity" in their teachings. Never to be outdone, Cotton Mather saw in Quakerism "the vomit cast out in by-past ages . . . licked up again for a new digestion, and once more exposed for the poisoning of mankind." It was the "most venomous of all to the churches of America."[46]

Puritan authority matched strong talk with action. In October 1656 the General Court authorized fines, whippings, and banishment for persons who "revile the . . . magistrates or ministers, as is usual with the Quakers." A year later, the law got tough: banished male Quakers would have an ear cut off the first time they returned, then the other ear for the second offense; women would be whipped. Third offenders of either sex would have their tongues bored through with a hot iron. Three ears were sliced off in pursuit of this rough justice. In 1658 the General Court went the rest of the way and instituted banishment on pain of death.[47]

Quaker candidates for holy punishment, writes Kai Erikson, "rushed toward the arena from every corner of New England." One group, banished on pain of death, marched back with an entourage carrying linens with which to wrap the martyrs. On October 27, 1659, three Quakers went to the gallows, including Mary Dyer, the Hutchinson supporter with the stillborn monster. She was pardoned at the last moment but defied the court yet again; she won her martyrdom the following June.[48]

The Quakers self-consciously inverted the Puritan punishment rituals. Executions normally featured a formal reconciliation between criminal and community; condemned people confessed, ministers warned that they all shared the sinners' depravity, everybody prayed for salvation. The Quakers would have none of that. They turned the execution sermons back on the magistrates and clergy, "mad-drunk with blood." They uttered holy (and, more important, widely publicized) curses from the scaffold. The Quaker narratives of Mary Dyer's death had her crying, "The blood of the Innocent is upon you; Wo will be to you for evermore, except you Repent." The Quaker tracts described the terrible results of the holy curses—Endicott, they reported, stank to death (in 1665).[49]

Only four Quakers died on the gallows; at least two more were whipped to death. But the dissenters had other ways to shake up the establishment. The most dramatic was public nakedness. Isaiah had loosed the sackcloth from his loins and walked naked to symbolize the captivity of Ethiopia and Egypt. The Quakers did so to signal wickedness. They walked through town naked, crying woe to the governments that persecuted them. Cromwell's Commonwealth, the Stuart restoration, and the Massachusetts oligarchs all got the treatment. In 1669, Deborah Wilson walked naked through Salem. The authorities tied her to a cart and whipped her as both her mother and sister, bound alongside her, counseled future modesty. Lydia Wardell went naked into Newberry meeting-house to protest ignorance and persecution. She also was severely whipped.

Only a bit less dramatically, Quakers blackened their faces, dressed in sack-cloth and ashes, and burst in on church services making, as the court in Boston put it, a "horrible disturbance and affrigting the people." The Quakers smashed bottles in the middle of service—testifying that the ministers were empty vessels or warning "so shall you be dashed to pieces." (That's the same passage from Psalms that had gotten John Wheelwright into such hot water after his fast-day sermon back in 1636.)[50]

The Quakers were particularly effective at propaganda. They wrote lurid descriptions of Puritan savagery. These torture chronicles are still a major source for scholars describing New England's Quaker wars. Here's a taste of what William Brend ("a man of years") is said to have gotten for running a Quaker meeting in Salem. The jailer seized a tarred rope and beat him "over his back and arms, with as much force as he could drive so that with the fierceness of the blows the rope [broke]. He gave him in all one hundred and seventeen blows . . . so that his flesh was beaten black as in a jelly, and under his arms the bruised flesh and blood hung down, clodded as it were in baggs, and so [fiercely] was it beaten that the sign of a particular blow could not be seen."[51]

The torment runs on for four pages. The Quaker descriptions worked—they provoked an outcry on both sides of the Atlantic. What followed was an elaborate political intrigue between champions of tolerance (led by the crown) and advocates of discipline. In September 1661, a year after Mary Dyer's hanging, King Charles II demanded an end to corporal punishment. Punishment stopped. In June 1662 the king went further and demanded broad religious toleration, excepting Quakers. The New Englanders ignored the call for tolerance, but they took the Quaker exception as an invitation to resume flogging, jailing, and banishment (sullenly, says Perry Miller, they quit hanging Quakers). In 1664 a crown commission intervened. The worst was over, though persecution flared up again in the mid-1670s.

The Quaker conflict ended ironically. Once the Puritan authorities called off the punishment, the Quakers lost interest in haunting them. In the end, argued Cotton Mather, New England would have been better off to just ignore them. Or shame them. "They were madmen. . . . A Bethlehem [a lunatic hospital] seems to have been fitter for them than a gallows."[52]

The Quakers may have sounded like antinomians, but there were important differences. As Erikson points out, the antinomians were looking back to the Puritanism they had known in England. The Quakers pointed forward, toward religious toleration and the slow abandonment of God's fixed social hierarchy. Moreover, the Quakers outlasted their persecutors and fought New England to at least a draw. By the time the episode was over, the New England Puritans had a looser grip on power; toleration was creeping in. Still, neither Charles II nor the mid-century Quakers would live to see a genuinely new order in New England.[53]

The Quakers in American Culture

The Quakers took up where the antinomians had left off. They arrived in New England with hints of what we'd now call individual conscience and glimmers of social justice. At the time, these urges remained inchoate and tenuous, obscured by sackcloth, nudity, and their quest for martyrdom. Even so, the seventeenth-century Quakers offer an early glimpse of reformers who flout convention, challenge authority, and invoke a higher morality in the name of social reform. That moral urge would swell into a heroic American reform tradition.

But the other side is just as American. The Puritan establishment unsheathed its own moral arguments to reinforce convention; it shored up its communal boundaries by rejecting these unusual challengers. Moral righteousness would continue to help Americans figure out they are, who threatens them, who they ought to be driving off.

But look what the Quaker story does to that cherished founding myth. Remember Tocqueville? The Americans fled old world feudal and clerical oppressions. They were supposed to be born equal without having to become so. What we find here is just the reverse: mid-century New England howls over the prospect of enduring Quakers. And who is thrusting that specter of tolerance on them? The king of England. The old world pushed tolerance while New England resisted. This case inverts one of the most basic myths about American political culture.

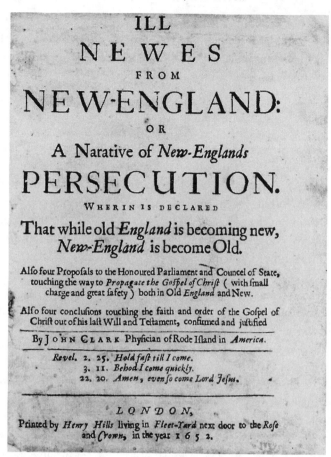

ILL
NEWES
FROM
NEW·ENGLAND:
OR
A Narative of *New-Englands*
PERSECUTION.
WHERIN IS DECLARED
That while old *England* is becoming new,
New-England is become Old.

Alſo four Propoſals to the Honoured Parliament and Councel of State,
touching the way to *Propagate the Goſpel of Chriſt* (with ſmall
charge and great ſafety) both in Old *England* and New.

Alſo four concluſions touching the faith and order of the Goſpel of
Chriſt out of his laſt Will and Teſtament, confirmed and juſtified

By J OHN CLARK Phyſician of Rode Iſland in *America*.

Revel. 2. 25. *Hold faſt till I come.*
3. 11. *Behod I come quickly.*
22. 20. *Amen, even ſo come Lord Jeſus.*

LONDON,
Printed by *Henry Hills* living in *Fleet-Yard* next door to the *Roſe*
and *Crown*, in the year 1 6 5 2.

2.3. Tolerance and intolerance in the wrong place. Writing in Rhode Island in 1652, John Clark cheers England's tolerance and laments New England's intolerance. Within a decade, Old England would lapse back into persecution. (John Carter Brown Library at Brown University)

Not that any simple countermyth—a Puritan tyranny, for example—ought to be extracted. Rather, this is a story of clashing American impulses: inclusion and exclusion, internal grace and external force, toleration and repression. The question posed by the Quaker persecution goes directly to the heart of the American moral legacy: What is the balance between these two impulses as they develop over American history?

Each generation faced the same question, and each wrestled with the same moral antinomy. Rights and freedom do not inevitably spring out of the early American experience. Never mind Tocqueville, the first Puritans brought neither a liberal nor a communitarian destiny with them when they stepped ashore. Each American generation would fight new battles over inclusion and social justice. Those ideals would be won and lost—again and again— throughout American history.

Amerindians

The Native Americans posed a far simpler challenge. No tricky philosophico-juristic riddles about Puritan dogma pop up for this battle. The Indians offered English colonists an irreducible, satanic other—perfect for defining the Christian community. What was most terrifying about the natives was not anything they actually did but the possibility that, deep in the American wilderness, the differences between the tribes would begin to dissolve. If they were not vigilant, the saints might morph into pagans.

Hellish Sorcerers of the New World

Englishmen already had a mental category for the natives they encountered in the new world (as well as those in Africa): heathens. The natives were not simply a different color or an alien culture. They were non-Christian—savage, uncivilized, and unsaved.[54]

In the Puritan prehistory of the new world, Satan ruled. The "barbarous Indians and infidels" served him. "Their whole religion," explained Cotton Mather, "was the most explicit sort of devil worship." Their "chief sagamores are well known . . . to have been horrid sorcerers and hellish conjurers and such as conversed with demons." The English migration set off an epic contest between Satan and Jesus as heathens and Christians fought for control of America.[55]

This picture of Satan and his native legions organized Puritan narratives of every sort. Captain John Underhill served up the conventional view in describing the outbreak of the Pequot war in 1636: "The old serpent . . . stirred [the Pequots] against the Church of Christ in . . . a furious manner. . . . Like the divell, their commander, they runne up and down as roaring lyons, seeking whom they might devour." Or, to switch literary genres, take a typical snippet from Mary Rowlandson's description of her Indian captivity (a best seller published in 1682). "Oh, the roaring and singing and dancing and yelling of those black creatures in the night made the place a lively resemblance of hell." The Puritan thesaurus for "Indian" reads like a demonic menagerie: devils, witches, imps, dragons, lyons, vipers, serpents, wolves, dogs, kennels of cruelty.[56]

To the colonists, the Indians seemed a negative reflection of Puritan norms. They were wild, slothful, ungoverned, and free. Family discipline, so prized by men like John Winthrop, seemed nonexistent. They were "affection-ate" and "indulgent out of measure" in their child rearing. "This extreme affec-tion," wrote Roger Williams, makes their children "saucie, bold, and unduti-ful." Their kinship systems seemed anarchic and polygamous to the Puritans.[57]

Worse, the Indians were lustful. New England Indians had no taboo against sex between unmarried people. The stricture against fornication applied only to married women. They dissolved marriages simply by the consent of both partners. This, of course, was all a long way from the Puritan ideal, and the set-tlers could not find enough derogatories like "whoredoms" and "uncleanness" to describe native behavior. Even worse, Indians seemed to violate fundamen-tal taboos against cannibalism, blood lust, and savagery.[58]

The most dangerous aspect of all this alleged Indian depravity was the lin-gering dread that the saints themselves were sinking into precisely the same immoral state. "Defects in family government" were a jeremiad staple. And sex? Fornication and adultery filled the New England court dockets; it was by far the most common transgression (though most modern analysts find the rates relatively low). When it came to savagery and blood lust, fingers were soon pointing at the Christian soldiers who shocked the natives with their Eu-ropean ways of killing (details in a moment). And although the natives might "range up and downe" like "wild beasts" through the forests, Englishmen were also being lured into the same wilderness, seeking "elbow room" beyond the reach of church or state.[59]

Some English settlers actually became Indians. While captivity narratives like Rowlandson's celebrated redemption from Indian bondage, some captives refused rescue. Minister John Williams was redeemed after almost three years in captivity; but his daughter, Eunice, would not return despite envoys, en-treaties, and promises of land. Minister Increase Mather (Cotton's father) in-credulously described a "wretched English man that apostatized to the hea-then, and fought with them against his own country men." A partial inventory of Indian captivities lists sixty New Englanders who became tribe members. Here was a victory for Satan. Christians were slipping into devil-worship.[60]

That slip fell neatly into the Calvinist picture: Everyone stood on the razor edge of perdition. New England was full of unconverted settlers. Their spiritual estate was no better than the savages'. The threat of impiety surrounded the Puritans and endangered everyone. The natives' presence constantly reminded the saints of the lustful, uncontrolled, pagan depravity that could overwhelm any Englishman. Decades after the most powerful Native Americans had been subjugated, Cotton Mather kept right on warning the colonists: "Our Indian wars are not over yet. We have too far degenerated into Indian vices. . . . We have shamefully Indianized in . . . abominable things."[61]

God's Word

What should Puritans do about the menacing Indians? The original plan called for saving them: "The first planters of this colony did (as in the patent expressed) come into this land with a design to convert the heathen unto Christ." But Puritan orthodoxy complicated the job. The promiscuous French papists might drag anyone who could sign the cross into their church; but membership in the New England congregations was limited to visible saints. Even Englishmen found it difficult to prove their election and enter the communion of saints. The barriers to Native American conversion were formidable.[62]

Nor would the Puritans compromise their faith to accommodate what we would now call an alien culture. On the contrary, they added steps to the conversion ritual. Native Americans had to make several public professions of faith (before distinctly skeptical ministers). Christian Indians had to enter "praying villages" where they wore European clothes and tilled fields in European fashion.

Despite heroic efforts by individual missionaries, the English neighbors harassed the natives. Even Dedham—that utopian, God-fearing community—mistreated an adjacent praying village. "When good land was at stake and the other party was savage," comments Kenneth Lockridge, "the spirit of the covenant could be set aside." As time went by, it got worse. In Maine, "rude, wild ungovernable English did . . . rashly provoke the Indians," reported Cotton Mather. In Boston, mobs would try to lynch the praying Indians when war broke out in 1675.[63]

With so many barriers to success, it is not surprising that the missionary impulse was haphazard and usually half-hearted. The same could not be said about the Indian wars.

God's Sword

Satanic imagery infused the Puritan war narratives. "It was time for the devil to take alarum," wrote Cotton Mather, and "oppose the possession [of New England] which the Lord Jesus Christ was going to have." The colonists inflated their battles into epic contests, Christians fighting for God. God Himself sanctioned the European attacks—and pitched in with horrific epidemics—to "sweep [the savages] hence" and give His people space. Even the Indian allies who fought alongside the Puritans did not fog up the plot line—good versus evil. The friendly Indians, explained Cotton Mather, were simply a "division in the kingdom of Satan against itself."[64]

Within this moral framework, natives could never be trusted. In 1623 some Englishmen had stolen corn from the Massachusetts Indians. Rumor had it that the Indians were planning retaliation. Miles Standish led an armed party from Plymouth colony. They killed eight Indians, decapitated their sachem (Wituwamet), and impaled his head atop the Plymouth blockhouse as a "warning and terror."[65]

In 1636 a more important conflict broke out between the Puritans and the Pequot tribe of Connecticut. It began with the murder of two English captains: John Stone (with his crew of seven) in 1634, and John Oldam in 1636. (Stone had been a notorious troublemaker who had attempted both murder and kidnapping.) It was never clear just what happened in either case. But firm action—again, "warning and terror"—always seemed important against devil worshippers. The Reverend John Higginson wrote to Winthrop from Connecticut, "If some serious and very speedie course not be taken to tame the pride and take down the insolency of these now insulting Pequots . . . we are likely to have all the Indians in the country about our ears."[66]

The traditional story casts the Pequots as particularly ferocious. They had pushed into the lower Connecticut River valley, frightened the other tribes (who allied with the colonists), and left "no Englishman's life safe anywhere upon the river or the sound." John Endicott led an expedition to Block Island to kill the Indians ostensibly responsible for Oldham's death; the natives eluded him. Then the expedition turned to Connecticut to punish the Pequots and avenge Stone.[67]

One of the eyewitness accounts, however, promptly subverts the tale of Pequot ferocity. When the Indians spied the English vessel, they "came running in multitudes along the water side, crying, 'what cheere Englishmen, what cheere, what doe you come for?' They not thinking we intended warre went on cheerfully." The Pequots expected to trade. But the ominous silence from the Puritan vessels made the Indians uneasy. They began to cry "'What Englishman . . . are you angry, will you kill us, and doe you come to fight?'"[68]

In the most detailed recent analysis of the conflict, Alfred Cave suggests that "there is no evidence the Pequots were guilty of any hostility toward the English." They were not imperialistic newcomers to Connecticut, they were not a particularly fierce tribe, and they neither desired nor anticipated war with the Puritans.[69]

In the decisive battle, in May 1637, the English attacked Fort Mystic, a Pequot village enclosed by a palisade. The English struck at both ends of the fort. When the going got difficult, they set the enclosure ablaze, withdrew, and surrounded the burning fort. Cotton Mather gives the standard account of what followed.

The fire . . . carried all before it; and such horrible confusion overwhelmed the savages, that many were broiled unto death in the revenging flames; many of them, climbing to the tops of the pallizadoz, were a fair mark for the mortiferous bullets there; many of them . . . were slain by the English that stood ready to bid 'em welcome. . . . In a little more than one hour, five or six hundred of these barbarians were dismissed from a world that was burdened with them.[70]

In Captain John Underhill's eyewitness account of the battle, a rare note creeps into the narrative: admiration for Indian bravery. "Many couragious fellowes . . . fought most desperately through the palisadoes. As they were scorched and burnt with the flame [they] were deprived of their arms, [for] the fire burnt their very bowstrings, and so [they] perished valiantly: mercy they did deserve for their valour, could we have had opportunitie to have bestowed it; many were burnt . . . men, women, and children."

But Underhill's account does not turn sentimental. Those who came running out of the flames were "entertained with the point of the sword; downe fell men, women, and children . . . great and dolefull was the bloudy fight to the view of young souldiers that never had been in warre, to see so many soules lie gasping on the ground, so thicke in some places that you could hardly passe along."[71]

Surviving men and women were rounded up, killed, drowned, or sold into slavery. Many Puritan accounts linger on the slaughter, then explain it as a sacrificial offering to God. William Bradford repeats Underhill's description of the battle, then adds: "It was a fearfull sight to see them thus frying in the fire, and the streams of blood quenching the same, and horrible was the stinck; but the victory seemed a sweet sacrifice . . . to God."[72] Cotton Mather dwells on "the bodies of so many [natives] barbikew'd, where the English had been doing a good morning's work." After the battle, additional Pequot tribesmen came upon the ashes of their kinsmen and "they howl'd, they roar'd, they stamp'd and were the pictures of so many devils in desperation." To all this, remarks Mather, "Heaven smiled."[73]

But what happened to the Puritan theme of civilization versus savagery? Blood lust was supposed to be a heathen trait. When Underhill notes the hesitation of the younger soldiers, he adds defensively, "It may be demanded, why should you be so furious (as some have said)? Should not Christians have more mercy and compassion?" After some half-hearted discussion of scriptural warrant, he sidesteps the matter with "but we will not dispute it now."[74]

The Puritans' Indian allies, the Narragansett, protested the slaughter: "It is naught, it is naught, because it is too furious and slaies too many men." The natives had a very different conception of battle. After watching their Indian allies enter the battle to cover the English retreat back to their ships, Captain Underhill jeers. "They might fight seven yeares and not kill seven men: they came not neere one another but shot remote, and not point blanke. . . . This fight is more for pastime than to conquer and subdue enemies." The accounts invert the Puritan portrait of Christian and heathen. The savagery comes from the wrong side, and so do the calls for moderation. As Underhill acknowledges, criticism rose up immediately.[75]

John Robinson, the Pilgrims' minister back in Holland, condemned the violence as soon as it began with Miles Standish's raid: The "necessitie . . . of killing so many . . . of those poor Indians . . . I see not." It is "a thing more glorious in men's eyes than pleasing in God's . . . for Christians, to be a terrour to poor barbarous people." Robinson suggests that if the power relations had been reversed, the Indians would not have killed as many Englishmen. "How happy . . . if you had converted some, before you killed any; where bloud is once begune to shed, it is seldome stanched of a long time after."[76]

Roger Williams joined the critics. Williams had been distinctly solicitous of the Native Americans in Rhode Island. He had learned the Narragansett language and won over the tribe to the Puritan side in the war with the Pequots. Now, he wrote Winthrop, I "fear that some innocent blood cryes at Connecticut." He challenged the harsh treatment of Pequot captives and pointed Winthrop back to the Bible: "The children of the murderers he slew not . . . every man shall be put to death for his own sin."[77]

Four decades later, as another bloody Indian war convulsed New England, the Quakers jumped in with the critics. "Our officers," wrote Edward Wharton in 1675, "are like men in a maze, not knowing what to do. But the priests spur them on, telling them the Indians are ordained for destruction, bidding them go forth to warr." The Puritan officers "complain and say with tears, they see not God go along with them." Wharton reverses the Puritan conception of piety versus savagery. In his account, the natives "tell the English Warriors that God is against them and for the Indians; and that the English shall (for their unrighteousness) fall into Indian hands." To be sure, this is Quaker propaganda. But Wharton, like Thomas Maule and other Quakers, was joining a small but growing group of contemporary critics attacking the colonists for their brutality and challenging the basic Puritan account of civilization and savagery.[78]

Historians still debate the issue of Puritan savagery. Many observers see racial genocide behind the mask of religious piety. From this perspective, the colonists turned aside Indian friendship and attacked Native Americans whenever it suited their purpose. Some analyses read the Pequot war as a scramble for economic advantage, opening up the Connecticut River valley to the Puritans. Others see the assertion of white hegemony over New England. Whatever the underlying explanation, the revisionists all agree: The Puritan attacks were horrific—even their own "heroic" war narratives convict the settlers.[79]

Others defend the Puritans. The saints meted out tough justice on both settlers and natives, often punishing Englishmen for crimes against the natives.[80] But the Puritan apologists have steadily given ground. Perhaps the foremost proponent of the Puritan perspective, Alden Vaughan, once assigned blame "more heavily upon the Pequots than the Puritans." Now, he acknowledges, "I am less sure than I was . . . that the Pequots deserve their burden of the blame." The defense of the Puritans has shrunk to this: "a brief but notable effort to avoid the violent confrontations that characterized most other 17th century colonies." Eventually, the Puritans failed, and in large measure because they would not respect the Indians, could not break out of the "heathen" mindset. By the 1670s, concedes Vaughan, the Puritans were indistinguishable from any other English colony: fighting the Indians along an advancing frontier, confining the defeated natives to reservations, slavery, and debasement.[81]

But these accounts all read the conflict only through European eyes. The Native Americans were hardly passive. Alfred Cave suggests that the entire Pequot war might be rewritten from the perspective of Native American politics and the balance of power among the tribes. From this angle, the war grew out of ambitions between rival clans, some of which were more deft at manipulating the Europeans. It is perfectly possible, suggests Cave, that it was the Mohegan, Narragansett, and River Indian sachems who engineered the downfall of the Pequots.[82]

If so, the tribes miscalculated. The Puritans were too powerful and used the war to subordinate native allies as well as enemies. The result was Puritan hegemony over lower New England. A lucrative (to the Puritans) system of tribute forced the Native Americans to finance the expansion of European settlement. Viewed this way, the Puritans took a petty Indian squabble, ended it with a terrible slaughter, turned it to their own geopolitical advantage, and then passed it through a propaganda machine that projected a meta-historical romance in which the people of God triumphed over satanic savages. The Puritan leap would evolve into a familiar national trait. Every American war would take on the same cast: an idealistic moral crusade against a satanic foe.[83]

God's Punishment

After the Pequot war, native grievances gradually accumulated. These finally burst into sustained violence in the summer of 1675, when Metacom (known to the settlers as King Philip) organized a broad alliance of New England tribes and led them against the English. By this time the Indians had adopted European technology and worked out effective guerrilla tactics. Metacom and his allies threw New England into a panic. Of the ninety Puritan towns, fifty-two were attacked, thirteen destroyed, six partially burned. By the following spring Indian forces were fighting within seventeen miles of Boston. The seaboard cities were packed with refugees. English military superiority seemed to vanish in this bloody series of Indian ambushes.[84]

By winter, the contest had turned into a war of attrition and the tide turned. The Indians in southern New England capitulated by the end of 1676 (Metacom himself was killed in August). Fighting continued on the northern frontier till 1678. The losses were catastrophic. The casualty rate for the English is generally put at 10 percent of draft-eligible males—the highest rate for any war in American history. The Puritans would not fully reclaim all the territory they lost for another forty years. "The dreadful Indian war," summed up Cotton Mather, "has so nipt the growth of [the country], that its latter progress hath held no proportion with what was from the beginning." For the Indians, casualty rates were much worse. The war ravaged the New England tribes.[85]

There would be more bloodshed (King William's war broke out in New England in 1689). Metacom's war, however, was the last great domestic clash between Native Americans and Puritans. Afterward the Indians would ally with the French. For the next seventy years New England's Indian wars would be tangled up in old world power conflicts.

By the time of Metacom's war, the Puritans had changed their central Indian narrative. The holy war narrative had faded. God no longer operated through valiant saints in a battle with Satan over the fate of the new world. Now, in the golden age of the jeremiad, the Indians became instruments by which God punished his people. Even when the "English had the better of it," wrote Increase Mather, it was "not without solemn and humbling rebukes of Providence." Again and again the clergy explained what was really happening: God unleashed Indian wars—with all their misery and devastation—because His people had become too much like the heathens.[86]

Indian Echoes

On the theological surface, Amerindian sins look rather like the antinomian sins. Both tribes were lustful, undisciplined, and rebellious. But the sinners themselves were completely different. The Indians lived outside Puritan society—vividly and irresistibly other. Identifying their heresies would not require convoluted cross-examinations before the General Court.

Here was the new world's great social divide. American society never sustained the great European class divisions. Despite all Winthrop's talk about deference and order, the Puritan community was relatively homogenous. But the gap between Christian and heathen loomed larger than any social differences back in Europe. The Indians and, as we shall see, the slaves marked the limits of colonial society. They were the essential American outsiders.

The Puritans did not originally see the natives in racial terms. Rather, the cleavage that divided them was moral and cultural. More than anything else, the Indians provoked Puritan anxiety about virtue: a God-fearing European community resisted dangerous people—irrefutably different, impossible to assimilate—who were always threatening to drag the pious community down into lustful savagery. The Puritans spiced up these moral dangers with frightening narratives about women and children cast into Indian bondage.

With time, the Indian difference grew racial. (In fact, Native Americans, struggling to survive behind the New England frontier, married blacks in substantial numbers.) By the end of the seventeenth century, moral and racial lines began blurring. Racial and moral fears would keep overlapping and soon yield the most potent cleavage in American political culture.[87]

In the end, the Puritans' Indian wars offer one prototype for American race politics: this other could be kept apart—segregated on the frontier, steered into special villages, or sold into slavery. Europeans enforced the segregation by violence and justified it by imagining moral danger to a God-fearing people. This time, a vividly different tribe defined the Puritan community by showing its members what they must avoid becoming. That boundary, built of race and morals, would always haunt the United States. The people who found themselves by segregating others would prove to be America at its most illiberal, Americans at their most deeply un-American.

Witches

In 1692 a fantastic army of witches struck Salem Village. "The houses of the good people," wrote Cotton Mather, were "filled with the doleful shrieks of their children and servants, tormented by invisible hands . . . altogether preternatural." Witches were the most terrifying enemy. Invisible and powerful, they lurked everywhere. Indians could be segregated, even slaughtered, without disrupting Puritan communities; but witches were neighbors, wives, and sisters. The Salem villagers panicked, tossed aside their own standards of justice, and plunged into a "blind man's buffet . . . hotly and madly mauling one another in the dark." The worst danger posed by invisible enemies is always that hot, mad, buffeting that the afflicted society turns on itself.[88]

What happened in Salem Village? A dynamic society outgrew its social and political institutions. The witchcraft frenzy came, in part, from an urge to force secular problems into a moral frame. But this time the Puritans chose an unreliable enemy. Puritans would not rediscover themselves by hunting witches; they would not win even a brief illusion of control. Instead, this crusade against Satan left the Puritan moral framework in shambles.[89] Some colonists began to sneer at the ministers.[90]

Future generations would repeat the witch-hunters' delusion. They would also try to pin social tensions on hidden, immoral villains. They, too, would abandon their own inconvenient legal norms in a clumsy rush for justice. Witch-hunts would wreck plenty of communities.

None of this began with Salem Village or New England, or with the Puritans. Witch-hunts convulsed towns in Germany, Switzerland, Scotland, and England. In two and a half centuries, the British alone burned or hanged some 30,000 witches (beginning in 1479). The most stunning fact about these pogroms—in both the old world and New England—is that both the alleged villains and their victims were mostly women.[91]

The New England witch-hunts seem trivial compared with those in Europe. But John Putnam Demos calculates that, given the smaller population and shorter period, New Englanders prosecuted their witches at least as vigorously as the English. New England accused at least 123 witches and executed 16 between 1647 and 1691—before the panic in Salem Village. But nothing in New England ever approached the scope of the Salem Village trials—144 accused, 19 hanged, 4 dead in prison, 1 pressed to death with stones.[92]

The Setting

By 1692 the city on a hill faced political chaos, war, disease, and religious toleration. The crown had revoked the New England charters. In 1686, James II pushed the colonies into the sprawling Dominion of New England, a political district that eventually stretched from Maine to New Jersey. The dominion's governor, Edmund Andros, seized town land, eliminated representative government, levied unpopular taxes, and held Anglican services in Boston's Old South Church. Rebellions toppled both Governor Andros and King James in 1689. The dominion collapsed, but there was no going back. The Massachusetts Bay Colony no longer existed (Connecticut had hid its charter in a legendary oak tree and was eventually permitted to restore it). When the witches burst in on Salem Village, the people of Massachusetts were in political limbo, waiting for both a charter and a new royal governor.

Meanwhile, there was more bloody war. Native Americans, now allied with the Canadians and French, demolished Schenectady, Salmon Falls (New Hampshire), Casco (later Portland, Maine), and York (Maine). A failed military expedition against Quebec limped back into Boston with heavy casualties, big debts, and bitter recriminations. Alongside war came pestilence. A smallpox epidemic rippled out from Boston.

Salem Village had its own troubles. It was part of Salem town—a larger, richer, more urban community about five miles away. By the 1670s, the village was straining against the limits of its political institutions. The villagers had a long list of complaints. Men had to walk up to ten miles carrying a heavy weapon for their turn on the night watch in Salem town. Worse, villagers had no infrastructure for settling local controversies—tensions multiplied and festered. They wanted to form their own town, elect their own officers, and gather their own congregation.[93]

Salem dismissed the talk of independence. At one town meeting, the moderator ruled complaining villagers out of order. The entire Puritan covenant system was rooted in a tight communal bond. Besides, why shrink the tax base?

But the traditional Puritan communities were passing into history. Salem Village was caught between old covenant logic and new communal needs. The village did secure a parish in 1672 and a proper congregation in 1689. (A parish was a kind of religious clinic; it held services but did not house a congregation.) Without political institutions to sort out their conflicts, villagers kept thrusting their ministers into the hot seat. The parish became the lightning rod for local tensions. After sixteen years, Salem Village was on its fourth minister. Poor Reverend George Burroughs (minister number two) had an especially nasty time. The village stopped paying him and he left town. Freeholders called a meeting to settle things but as soon as Burroughs showed up, one of the flock had him arrested for debt.

Here was fertile ground for social upheaval: political vacuum, war, pestilence, and unresolved local conflicts. But why witches? And what does Salem's crisis tell us about the generations of witch-hunters down through the years?

Witchcraft

Trouble first broke out in Minister Samuel Parris's house. His nine-year-old daughter, Elizabeth, and her eleven-year-old cousin, Abigail Williams, "tampered with the devil's tools." They used an egg and a looking glass to "find their future husband's calling." When they looked into that rude crystal ball they saw a "spectre in the likeness of a coffin." The girls got hysterical. Soon, they were being "bitten and pinch'd by invisible agents." One moment they would make piteous cries, the next "they were taken dumb, their mouths stopp'd, their limbs rack'd and tormented."[94]

The alarming fits spread. Afflicted girls ran wild, shrieked, and interrupted sermons. Deodat Lawson (Salem Village minister number three, now back for a visit) recorded the howls that greeted him as he rose to preach: "Now, there is enough of that" and "Look where Goodwife C. sits on the beam suckling her yellow bird."[95]

Before the year was out, at least forty-three villagers would be officially diagnosed as afflicted, almost all of them young women. But panics are social constructions. If the young women suffered hysteria, it was the adults around them who decided why. The Salem villagers and the larger Puritan establishment channeled the screaming fits into an army of witches.[96]

Diagnosing witchcraft meant ignoring at least two alternatives. First, as Paul Boyer and Stephen Nissenbaum point out, it never occurred to anyone in Salem Village that the girls had been swept up in a religious frenzy. After all, the same symptoms marked the outpouring of God's grace during great religious revivals. In a different time and place, the paroxysms and hysteria would mark sinners in the throes of conversion, the terrors would reflect a great struggle within the soul, the wild speeches a Pentecostal gift of tongues. For future generations, behavior like this smacked of salvation rather than Satan.[97]

Or perhaps the girls were possessed? As Increase Mather explained, "The devil can (by Divine Permission) . . . vex men in Body and Estate, without the Instrumentality of Witches." Why would God give Satan the green light? To punish sinners. This diagnosis pushed the blame firmly back onto the victims. And onto Minister Parris, since he was responsible for the due subjugation of the children in his household. There were hints about possession during the trials—several of the accused tried to shift the onus back onto the shrieking girls. When it was all over, possession would figure prominently in the post-mortems. But in early 1692, New England diagnosed witchcraft.[98]

In the 1690s, witches were real. Societies that believed in witchcraft recruited witches. Sorcery was part of seventeenth-century life. When beer went bad, butter soured, a boat sank, the cow took sick, a man became impotent, a woman miscarried, or a baby died, people looked over their shoulders for spells cast by malevolent neighbors.[99]

There were two distinct attitudes about the dark world. The official Puritan line was simple: saints prayed; they supplicated God. In sinful contrast, "cunning people" mastered supernatural forces. "They obtained an ability to do or know things," wrote Cotton Mather, that they could not possibly do or know "by their own humane abilities." These special abilities could be obtained, in the official view, only from Satan. They were witchcraft. Even children messing around with an egg and a glass could open the door to hell.[100]

But most New Englanders were not correct Puritans all the time. Many drew a commonsense distinction between harmful witchcraft and useful sorcery, between "black" and "white" magic. New England had both kinds. Midwives knew about strange potions. Cunning people foretold the future. People read almanacs, wore amulets for luck, and protected themselves from witch malice with countermagic. They boiled nails and pins in the urine of the be-

2.4. Once the panic began, townspeople saw witch's imps and demons all over town. (Courtesy Peabody Essex Museum)

witched, flinging the spell back onto the person who cast it; they flogged possessed animals and expected to see the scars on the witch.[101]

In Salem Village, the hysterical girls immediately prompted both popular and orthodox responses. One townswoman, Mary Sibley, went to get countermagic from Reverend Parris's slaves, Tituba and John. They mixed the possessed girl's urine into a rye cake and fed it to the Parris family dog (a suspected satanic agent). The idea was to discover just who had cast the spells on Elizabeth. When the Reverend Parris heard, he furiously preached the official view. Witchcraft was witchcraft. Countermagic was simply "going to the devil for help against the devil."[102]

If witchcraft was the popular diagnosis, it was backed up by Puritan authorities. Ministers pressed witches into the jeremiad formula and added this latest affliction to the moral dangers that swirled around the saints. "They swarm about us, like the Frogs of Egypt," warned Cotton Mather, even "in the most retired of our chambers." "Are we at our Boards? There will be Devils to Tempt us into Sensuality; Are we in our Beds? There will be devils to Tempt us unto Carnality." Deodat Lawson, preaching in Salem Village early in the crisis, echoed Mather's warnings: "The devil is come down in great wrath." Salem was now the "first seat of Satan's tyranny" and the "rendezvous of devils." He drove home the standard jeremiad punch line, a desperate plea for Puritan virtue: "Awake, awake then, I beseech you."[103]

The Wonders of the Invisible World.

OBSERVATIONS

As well *Historical* as *Theological*, upon the NATURE, the NUMBER, and the OPERATIONS of the

DEVILS.

Accompany'd with,

I. Some Accounts of the Grievous Molestations, by DÆ-MONS and WITCHCRAFTS, which have lately annoy'd the Countrey; and the Trials of some eminent *Malefactors* Executed upon occasion thereof: with several Remarkable *Curiosities* therein occurring.

II. Some Counsils, Directing a due Improvement of the terrible things, lately done, by the Unusual & Amazing Range of EVIL SPIRITS, in Our Neighbourhood: & the methods to prevent the *Wrongs* which those *Evil Angels* may intend against all sorts of people among us; especially in Accusations of the Innocent.

III. Some Conjectures upon the great EVENTS, likely to befall, the WORLD in General, and NEW-EN-GLAND in Particular; as also upon the Advances of the TIME, when we shall see BETTER DAYES.

IV A short Narrative of a late Outrage committed by a knot of WITCHES in *Swedeland*, very much Resembling, and so far Explaining, *That* under which our parts of *America* have laboured!

V. THE DEVIL DISCOVERED: In a Brief Discourse upon those TEMPTATIONS, which are the more Ordinary *Devices* of the Wicked One.

By Cotton Mather.

Boston Printed, and Sold by *Benjamin Harris*, 1693.

2.5. Cotton Mather's *Wonders of the Invisible World*—his description of the horrible army of devils and demons that descended on the people of Salem Village. (John Carter Brown Library at Brown University)

The witches offered the Puritan leaders exactly what every other looming enemy offered them—a shared identity, a renewed mission for a floundering people. The jeremiads constructed the usual apocalyptic clash with Satan, who was now using his witches and "making one last attempt on us." As usual, the jeremiads balanced pleas and warnings with millennial glimmerings: if the people could just summon up the old Puritan virtues, they would "enjoy halcyon days with all the vultures of hell trodden under their feet."[104]

This enemy was particularly repulsive. Witches reversed the holy covenant with God and entered into a perverted covenant with Satan. They signed the devil's book, they had sex with the devil, they seduced others into satanic service, and they received demonic imps who ran nefarious errands.

People began to see and hear the satanic imps all over town. Witnesses described seeing unusual birds, dogs, cats, misshapen children, snakes, and even hogs. A witch suckled her imps on special teats (yes, witches' teats). The first order of business with any suspect was to search the body for telltale protuberances. Examinations could get brutal. One committee reported finding "on her secret parts, growing within the lip of the same, a loose piece of skin and when pulled it is near an inch long." Another committee discovered one of George Jacob's teats in his mouth—and large enough "to run a pinn through." Recall how Mary Fisher, the Quaker missionary, got the treatment in 1656. The descriptions of Anne Hutchinson's stillborn monsters also clearly implied satanic imps.[105]

Salem Village, it turned out, was crawling with both witches and demonic imps. There was good reason to be fearful. Critics would later let the churchmen have it for their role in stirring up the villagers. "The people stood on panic's brink," wrote the great Puritan-basher Brooks Adams, and "their pastors lashed them on."[106]

But the witch explanation was in the rye cakes as much as the jeremiads, for it rippled up from the people as much as down from the pulpit. The Boston clergy wanted it both ways—a peril without the panic. But rallying the people against an evil empire generally provokes a nasty campaign against the evildoers. The ministers worried about precisely that. Even as they called for witch trials they warned that "all proceedings be managed with an exceeding tenderness towards those that may be complained of." They cautioned about being too harsh on "persons formerly of an unblemished reputation," though that suggestion positively invited trouble for the usual suspects. And sure enough, the usual suspects were the first to be dragged forward.[107]

Witch Trials

On February 29, 1692, the fits and shrieks finally produced arrest warrants against three women, Sarah Good, Sarah Osborne, and Tituba. The next day, two magistrates, John Hawthorn and Jonathan Corwin, made the journey from Salem town. They interrogated Sarah Good first. She is usually described as the perfect stereotype of a witch—a quarrelsome, pipe-smoking hag. Another modern stereotype might fit even better—"welfare mother." Sarah Good was a beggar, she had no fixed residence, she was pregnant, and she dragged her five-year-old daughter around with her.

Good vehemently denied everything, full of contempt for the entire hearing—"I scorn it," she testified repeatedly. But when the afflicted were instructed to look on her, they were all immediately tormented. When pressed to explain the shrieking fits she had obviously provoked, Good passed the blame to her fellow suspect: "It is Grandma [Sarah] Osborne that doth afflict the children."[108]

Good's denial did not impress the magistrates. "Her answers were in a very wicked and spitfull manner," reads the transcript of the hearing. And her denials were promptly undercut by her own husband, who announced that she "either was a witch or would be one very quickly," adding, "shee is an enemy to all good."[109]

Later in the same day, Tituba was called to the stand. Tituba was a South American Indian (most likely Arawak). Parris had purchased her in Barbados and brought her to Salem Village. In the Puritan mind, her background predisposed her to devil worship. And, sure enough, she and her husband had baked the witch cake and fed it to the Parrises' dog.

Witchcraft accusations would ripple up, touching ever more important people till they finally reached the governor's wife. But fingers first pointed toward women who were emblematic of every witch-hunt: the poor, the deviant, the member of a foreign tribe.

Tituba proved the star witness. Her testimony evolved from flat denials to defensive and apologetic admissions that essentially acquiesced to the questions. "Why did you hurt the children?" Because "if I do not hurt the children [the other witches] will hurt me"; they would "do worse to me." But Tituba said she was sorry—"I will hurt them no more." Before long, however, Tituba was taking the questions as clues and confessing in extraordinary, even exuberant, detail.

Yes, she testified, the devil was about. And plenty of imps: yellow birds, black dogs, cats, a strange creature with hairy face and long nose. Yes, she had flown to Boston on a stick. When questioning resumed on the second day, Tituba released her great blockbuster: Oh yes, she had seen the devil's book. And there were "a great many marks in it." How many? "Nine." Nine witches! At least seven remained at large. The hunt was on in earnest.[110]

Elaine Breslaw suggests that Tituba upset the normal power relations and restructured the witch trials. By describing a Boston witch wearing a white silk hood under a black silk hood, Tituba turned the prosecutors toward wealthy people. And a wizard in black clothes also seemed to signal a gentleman, possibly a cleric (perhaps a deft swipe at her owner, Minister Parris himself). Charges poured out from the afflicted. Warrants and arrests followed—four in March, twenty-four in April, thirty-eight in May.[111]

Martha Corey had scoffed at the idea of witches. She had tried to prevent her husband from attending the first hearings by hiding his saddle. Now Mrs. Corey was dragged in and roughly questioned. When she bit her lip, the bewitched girls howled. When she moved her fingers, they felt pinches. When she leaned her breast against the bar they felt as if their bowels were being ripped out. While she was on the stand, two of the afflicted saw the specter of a black man whispering in her ear. Corey denied everything. But how to explain the effects she had on the victims? Bathshaa Pope, one of the oldest of the tormented women, expressed the fury coursing through Salem Village. She threw her muff at Corey and, when that missed, "she got off her shoe, and hit goodwife C. on the head with it." Corey's husband, Giles, lined right up to testify against his wife.[112]

On March 23, the magistrates questioned Sarah Good's five-year-old daughter. It turned out even she had suckled an imp, a little snake that had left a very visible mark on her finger, rather like a flea bite. Where did she get a satanic agent? From her mother. Little Dorcas Good quickly joined her mother in the Boston jail.[113]

The trial of Susanna Martin on April 30 brought an often implicit theme to the surface. Of the first twenty people accused, seventeen were women. Was there a sexual subtext to all this? Listen to Bernard Peach testifying against Martin: "Being in bed on a lords day night he . . . saw Susana Martin come in at the window. . . . Shee was in . . . the same dress that shee was in before at meeting the same day. . . . Shee was coming up toward this deponent's face but turned back to his feet and took hold of them and drew up his body into a hoope and Lay upon him about an hour and half . . . in all which time this deponent coold not stir nor speake."[114]

Martin's spectral image also visited Jarvis Ring and lay on him at night. He could not move or speak either. But Martin bit his finger and it would not heal. She dove into Robert Downer's bed in the likeness of a cat and "lay hard upon him a considerable time." Martin had previously been accused of both witchcraft and sexual crimes with men. In fact, Carol Karlsen reports that twenty-three accused New England witches were also charged with sexual crimes. What to make of these—apparitions? fantasies? fears? We'll return to the fornication angle after we round up a few more of the witches.[115]

The circle of suspects began to reach beyond Salem Village. In April, Ann Putnam was racked and choked by the apparition of George Burroughs, the former Salem Village minister (with the salary troubles). In May, apparitions of his first two wives appeared, testified that Burroughs had murdered them, and cried for vengeance. Burroughs was dragged back from his new parish in Maine. His appearance at the meetinghouse set off such fits and tortures that the afflicted had to be removed from the room.[116]

In May, accusations reached a prosperous woman from Charlestown, Mrs. Nathaniel Cary. On May 24, she and her husband headed to Salem Village to clear things up—after all, Mrs. Cary did not even know her accusers. By lunchtime, the girls had learned the stranger's name, and, along with John Indian (Tituba's husband), they were "tumbling down like Swine," rolling frantic on the ground, screaming "Cary." In short order, Magistrate Hawthorn was sternly cross-examining this latest suspect as two officers held her hands (lest she pinch her victims). Captain Cary described standing alongside his wife, wiping "the tears from her eyes and the sweat from her face." They soon clamped Mrs. Cary in heavy irons.[117]

The jail in Boston was getting packed, but the judicial system was paralyzed. Without a charter, the magistrates did not have the authority to punish the witches. On May 14, a new governor, Sir William Phips, sailed into Boston with the new charter. Increase Mather—lobbying in London—had influenced the crown's gubernatorial selection; Phips was a member of Mather's Boston congregation. The new governor had sailed back from England ready for a war against the French and Indians. Instead, he ran into this extraordinary battalion of devils. Phips asked the church ministers what to do about all the witches.

The ministers recommended "speedy and vigorous prosecution." But they also sent the court clear instructions in demonology and due process: "a daemon may . . . appear . . . in the shape of an innocent, yea, and a vertuous Man." Those specters of Susanna Martin lying hard on Robert Downer's bed or George Burroughs pinching Ann Putnam proved nothing about Martin or Burroughs. Even before the ministers formally submitted their advice, Phips had authorized a court of oyer and terminer (to hear and determine).[118]

The newly empowered court got straight down to business and started clearing out the Boston jail. The court met on June 2 and hanged its first witch eight days later. Five more were hanged in July, another five in August. In those three months, the court tracked down thirty-nine new suspects and imprisoned at least thirty-five of them. The court blithely ignored the ministerial warning that specters could not be trusted and should not be held as evidence against the accused.

Sarah Good was hanged, defiant to the end. When the Reverend Nicholas Noyes urged her to confess from the gallows, she shot back her famous final words: "I am no more a witch than you are a wizard, and if you take my life, God will give you my blood to drink." Sarah Osborne died in jail. Little Dorcas Good languished in jail for some seven months; her father later charged that she never recovered. Susanna Martin was hanged in July, Martha Corey in September. Her husband, Giles Corey, was accused of being a wizard. He mysteriously refused to answer questions. For two days "much pains was used" to get him to talk by piling rocks on his body. Toward the end, the sheriff used a stick to poke the dying man's tongue back into his mouth. Corey was crushed to death, but he kept his silence.[119]

Minister Burroughs never made it back to Maine. From the gallows, he made a dramatic declaration of innocence and concluded with a flawless recitation of the Lord's Prayer. In the popular imagination, witches and wizards could not repeat the prayer without stumbling because they recited it backwards at their own satanic rituals. Burroughs provoked an uproar in the crowd. Some wept, others seemed ready to hinder the execution. But Cotton Mather, mounted on a horse, reminded the people that the devil could transform himself into an "angel of light," that this death sentence was righteous. The story sounds like one of those romantic flourishes that have sprung up around the witch trials—a Puritan on a high horse urging on the hangman. But at least two eyewitness accounts agree on the details. In any case, the hangman did his job.[120]

Nathaniel Cary helped his wife escape, first to Rhode Island, then New York. Tituba revealed the other way out—those who confessed to witchcraft escaped hanging. This inverted the normal Puritan punishment ritual: confession, warnings of shared depravity, communal reconciliation, and inevitably— just punishment.

Clearly, something had gone wrong. Condemned witches talked of God and conscience—and refused to confess. Even as they faced the Almighty they kept insisting they were innocent. "Knowing my own innocencye," wrote Mary Easty in September, "I petition your honors not for my own life for I know I must die . . . but if it be possible no more innocent blood may be shed." Meanwhile, those who confessed to witchcraft somehow escaped capital punishment despite the biblical commandment to kill witches. In the first seven weeks, only Tituba admitted her sin. As soon as the hanging began, however, witchcraft confessions poured out—almost fifty between July and September.[121]

Other problems nagged observers. First was the sheer number of the accused. How could "so many in so small a compass of land . . . so abominably leap into the devil's lap all at once"? Moreover, the status of the accused kept rising—right up to the new governor's wife, Lady Phips. By the time the cries reached her, there was "ground to suspect some mistake." And worst of all, the court was relying on spectral evidence. Even Cotton Mather, who long defended the trials, acknowledged that the devil could take the shape of perfectly innocent people.[122]

Finally, in October, Increase Mather circulated a tract, *Cases of Conscience Concerning Evil Spirits Personating Men,* detailing precisely why spectral evidence was unreliable. Toss out all that testimony about the specters whispering, pinching, or jumping into beds, and the legal case against many witches collapsed. Increase Mather underlined the conclusion: "Better that ten suspected witches should escape, than that one innocent person should be condemned."

Fourteen ministers endorsed the book. (Avoiding controversy like a good Puritan, Mather lamely insisted that he was not implying that the "wise and good" court at Salem was actually *using* spectral evidence.)[123]

Governor Phips immediately called off the hunt. He organized a new court, gave clear instructions about specters, and ordered the judges to swiftly clear the backlog. The court stubbornly chalked up some additional convictions, but Phips countered with reprieves. The last witch-hunt in the English world soon ended. Most of the judges repented, most of the afflicted recovered, most confessed witches recanted, and most witchcraft convictions were reversed. The chosen people were left to try to make sense of what they had done.

The Logic of the Witch-Hunt

Three centuries after the last hanging, witch-hunts remain fresh in the glossary of American politics. Do recent witch-hunts actually have anything in common with the Salem Village original? And what, finally, should we make of the seventeenth-century convulsion? Consider the witch question from three angles.

Economic Development as Moral Crisis

Cotton Mather thought that the devil was making a last attempt to hold on to New England. In fact, it was the Puritan establishment that was trying to hang on by forcing an emerging society into the jeremiad framework. Put abstractly, the great witch-hunt took social and economic tensions and transformed them into a moral crisis.

The covenants had envisioned peaceful, static, orderly communities marked by mutual love and deference to authority. That utopian dream faded as the society grew diverse and the economy complex. Boyer and Nissenbaum locate people who represented both the old ways and the new on the Salem Village map. Those who lived closer to Salem generally embraced the town's merchant economy, cosmopolitan outlook, and worldly comforts. On the other side of the village, rural yeomen clung to the traditional, communal norms. Put crudely, emerging capitalists squared off against faithful Puritans. Boyer and Nissenbaum draw a line, north to south, through the middle of the village. They then take a sample of the witches and their accusers. Almost every accused witch (12 of 14) lived in the eastern part of town, closer to Salem. Almost every accuser (30 of 32) lived in the rural, western side of the village.[124]

When the young women started shrieking, the more orthodox west villagers reached for a traditional explanation. Witchcraft did not simply explain the bizarre fits. It also channeled the anxieties and harnessed the anger that these villagers felt toward their modernizing neighbors. And witchcraft is a perfect emblem of modernity. For better or worse (or both), people develop the "ability to do [and] know things" they could not have done or known before.

Salem Village was enmeshed in what contemporary social scientists would call a development crisis—a historical moment when social and economic changes outstrip the political order. The changes subvert traditional authorities and political institutions. All developing societies face these jolts. The lag between socioeconomic change and the construction of new political organizations, comments Samuel Huntington, is the "primary problem of politics."[125]

It was the underlying problem in 1692. Salem politics was organized for a tight, nuclear community, not a far-flung and diverse society. Greater Salem had outgrown its institutional forms. The Salem villagers knew it and had begged for independent organizations. Salem rebuffed them with outmoded covenant logic.

The entire Puritan federal structure faced precisely the same contradiction. The society had grown too big, too rich, and too complex for its governing philosophy. The orthodoxy flatly condemned controversies while the society was groping for institutions through which people could raise, debate, and settle conflicts. The leaders offered witches as proof of God's displeasure. The people seized those witches and used them to articulate their fears and fight their fights.

In 1692, the moral diagnosis of social trouble boomeranged right back onto the ministers. If a new political order was not yet visible, the witchcraft hysteria is a plausible place to mark the end of the classical Puritan regime. Never again, sums up Perry Miller, would a "governor of Massachusetts, in an hour of hesitation, formally and officially ask advice of the churches."[126]

Respectable citizens used the witchcraft embarrassment to fling Enlightenment notions into the ministers' faces. Thomas Brattle, an influential Boston merchant (and "no small admirer of the Cartesian philosophy") put it directly: "Salem superstition and sorcery" was "not fit to be named in a land of such light as New England is." The "ages will not wear off that reproach and those stains" that the "ignorance," "folly," and "barbarous methods" of Salem Village justice "leave . . . on our land."[127]

Robert Calef was harsher. His sustained refutation of the witch-hunt is best remembered for a single outrageous scene. In 1693, Cotton and Increase Mather both attended Margaret Rule when she began to suffer fits. Calef was part of a crowd that pushed in the door to watch the divines at work. He described their bedside manner: Cotton "brushed her on the face" and "rubb'd her stomach (her breasts not covered with the Bed-clothes) and bid others do so too." When she had another fit, "he again rub'd her breast" and "put his hand on her breast and belly" and that "moved the father also to feel."[128]

"It carries the face of a lie contrived . . . to make people believe a smutty thing of me," responded a furious Cotton Mather. Suddenly, the Mathers found themselves surrounded by demons of a different sort. From one side, Enlightenment lectures from an enthusiastic Cartesian. From the other, pornographic lampoons of the once heroic conflict with Satan.[129]

This time, the jeremiad sermons had exposed only a crumbling Puritan cosmos. The covenant framework was out of joint with the society. Moral solution would not meet New England's institutional needs. Still, the Puritan preachers set an important pattern. The jeremiad response would persist, an enduring American political reflex. The urge to read socioeconomic forces as moral failures runs down the years and still stands, as fresh and powerful as any social movement on the contemporary American scene.

Gender

The brute fact about witch-hunting violence is that it was mainly spent on women—both in the old world and the new. All told, four out of five accused New England witches were women. Even in Salem Village, 70 percent of the accused were women.[130]

Gender bias had been vivid in European witch lore. The great witch-hunter's guide, *Malleus Maleficarum*, sponsored by Pope Innocent VIII in 1484, warned: "Women are chiefly addicted to evil [witch] superstitions." Why? Because "all witchcraft comes from carnal lust, which is in women insatiable." Worse, "for the sake of fulfilling their lusts they consort even with devils." The text puts considerable emphasis on the Eve narrative: Adam "was tempted by Eve, not the devil, therefor she [woman] is more bitter than death."[131]

The raw misogyny of *Malleus* is rare in Puritan writing. On the contrary, Puritan writers resisted the notion of women as inherently evil. But they did keep returning to Eve, paragon of women's moral vulnerability. And Puritan thinking was ferocious on hierarchy and deference—woman must be subject to man. By 1692 the whole godly hierarchy was slipping away. In many ways, the struggle to shore it up set witchcraft's gendered dynamic into play.

Witches disrupted the natural order. Across time and place, the accused were women who had slipped out of their proper roles. Many witches were past menopause (though how far past remains in dispute). They had lost that defining role, procreation. In place of the real thing, witchcraft concocted a nightmare parody. Witches suckled their own misshapen demonic imps while they harmed the neighbors' children.

Carol Karlsen identifies a more subtle form of slipping roles. New England organized inheritance through males—widows did not control the disposition of their own cooking pots, much less their houses. But not all families had male offspring. Most of New England's witches, argues Karlsen, were women who had inherited estates, disrupting the "orderly transmission of property from one generation of males to another." And as women of independent means, they upset the sexual hierarchy.[132]

Midwives were another constant threat. These women managed the great mysteries of life and death, and there was always the danger they would invoke supernatural forces. Stillbirths, sickly infants, preternatural events (did the house shake?), or even unexpected recoveries could prompt questions about the attendants. At least twenty-two accused witches were midwives—Anne Hutchinson and her own midwife, Jane Hawkins, were notorious cases that we met above.[133]

Finally, there is no avoiding the sexual subtext. We saw Susanna Martin's specter lying atop Bernard Peach, Jarvis Ring, and Robert Downer. Hers was not an unusual case. Some confessed witches were perfectly explicit about fornicating with Satan. (*Malleus Maleficarum* speculates about just how they managed that "venereal delectation.") Suckling familiars, often on teats near their private areas, offered another round of almost hard-core sexual images. One sure sign of witchcraft, warned Cotton Mather, was a "lewd and naughty kind of life."[134]

The picture that emerges from the transcripts goes beyond fantasy or fear of fornication. There is a dread of uncontrolled carnality in women: suckling imps, jumping into strange beds and lying hard on men, living "lewd and naughty" kinds of lives. Ultimately, the witch's sin goes beyond sex and raises the danger of lost self-control, of social disorder. And that threat returns us to every Puritan enemy we have encountered. Antinomians, Quakers, and Amerindians all failed to crucify their lusts. They all challenged God and His agents, the Puritan fathers, by failing to control themselves.

Perhaps women who seemed to lose control became a greater menace as Puritan leaders lost their grip on the larger social world. Leaders rooted out the witches as if, somehow, patching up the little commonwealth—family hierarchy, gender relations—might restore traditional order from the chaos. We'll see this pattern again and again.

Some observers think the gender issues were muddled because women filled the ranks of both accuser and accused. But underlying anxieties—about gender roles, internal control, carnality, and social order—would operate on women as much as men, perhaps even more (after all, most church members were women). The gender issue cannot be read, simply, as men against women—either then or now. Still, the churchmen and magistrates were the ones who enforced, judged, and punished. They organized the system.

Why do witches disappear after Salem? Many scholars suggest that changing feminine ideals made the witch irrelevant. By the early eighteenth century, they argue, the middle-class woman had become the desexed, domesticated paragon of bourgeois virtue. Perhaps witches became less scary as women evolved into embodiments of moral purity.[135]

But disruptive sexuality lived on, especially outside the moralizing bourgeoisie. Working-class and black women would inherit the stereotypes—seductive, uncontrolled, carnal. We shall return to the stigma that marked these dangerous women, that marks some of them still. For now, note a final irony. As images of the subversive woman evolved, so did the descriptions of Salem's first confessing witch, Tituba. Although described as an Indian in every original document, she slowly turned black as scholars read their nineteenth- and twentieth-century stereotypes back into history. By the 1940s, John Indian had become a winking, common-law "so called husband." Americans gradually rewrote the Puritan stereotypes, transforming a devil-worshiping heathen into an African American with loose morals.[136]

Enemies

The Puritans split plenty of theological hairs, but, to them, one enemy was a lot like another. Perdition was perdition. Anne Hutchinson was both a heretic and (probably) a witch, Amerindians were both lustful and hellish. However, a good social policy analyst could have told them that the witches were different in a crucial way.

You could not miss Indians or Quakers. Witches were hidden. They could be anyone, anywhere. The distinctive feature about witch-hunts—then, later, and now—is the search for invisible enemies within the community.

The Salem Village panic set the standard. Witch-hunts plunge societies into social convulsions, into Cotton Mather's "blind man's buffet." In the panic, everybody becomes a potential suspect; friends dissolve lifelong ties, husbands testify against wives. The normal standards of justice—today we'd call them civil liberties—get tossed aside in the stampede. In 1692 the ministers all knew that spectral evidence was unreliable; but even Increase Mather sat through the Reverend George Burrough's trial without demurring.

The witch metaphor—scary, hidden subversives—would remain a political perennial. We will see plenty of examples: The panic over urban white slavers seducing and stealing country girls in the waning of the Victorian era. Attorney General A. Mitchell Palmer's roundup of foreign-born radicals after World War I. The red scares following World War II—the attack against Communists ended up chasing homosexuals out of government offices. Many readers will recall the great wave of AIDS hysteria, when frightened Americans dreamed up all sorts of ways to keep unidentified homosexuals from slipping "their" disease into mainstream culture. Like the Salem Village original, each bout involves widespread fear, uncertain (often invisible) enemies, lapses in due process, and a frightening sexuality running just under the official text.

Of course, people face real dangers: Communists sent secrets to the Soviet Union. Terrorists plant bombs on planes. For that matter, witches cast spells in early New England. Real dangers require firm action. It is not the witches who make a witch-hunt. What does? At least three factors: fears spread far and wide, a whole class of people falls under suspicion, due process evaporates. There is also usually a trace of self-interest—some group thinks the frenzy will serves its purpose. It rarely does.

The witches keep returning, but they make unreliable enemies. Hunting them does not effectively rally a community. Witches are too difficult to iden-tify. They provoke too much uncertainty, and—most important—they subvert the very norms the community rises up to defend. Hunts against invisible oth-ers lurking in our midst are always difficult to control. Just about anybody might be fingered as a hidden subversive. In 1692 they named Lady Phips a witch, in 1954 they called the United States Army soft on reds.

The Amerindians proved a far better foe for rallying saints. Some colonies found a similar "other" in race slavery. White Christians could easily define themselves against such visible and unchanging opposites. In contrast, witch-hunts just keep bouncing right back at the hunters. They convulse the society, harm the community, and ruin the reputation of every generation that launches one.

The Puritans forged their own identity against three very different kinds of enemies. As analytic types, each remains familiar. Anne Hutchinson and her followers threatened the social order from within. They insinuated anarchy, re-bellion ("disparaging all our ministers"), lost self-control ("quenching all in-deavor"), and sexual disruption. The Quakers offered a variation of the same internal, moral rebellion. To this day we call people Puritans when they grow obsessed about making the neighbors toe the line; the "Puritan" watchword never changes: thou shalt "crucifie the lusts of the flesh."

The Amerindians provoked the fear of a different tribe. Outsiders threat-ened the city on a hill. The Puritans responded with warnings about falling to the native's low moral level—this other was lustful, savage, and ungodly. The great peril was that we would become like them. The settlers' defense against this enemy set the pattern for racial and ethnic conflicts; fear of mixing— blood and morals—would fire the nation's most bitter conflicts. An immigrant nation built partially on slavery would experience a constant political uproar about the boundaries between the tribes. There's another way to read the Indian conflicts, a different precedent for future American generations. The Puritan-Indian wars were like conflicts with a foreign power. Some ministers—we would probably call them the doves—preached peace, religious conversion, and even a kind of integration (at least into the praying villages). But the official epic imagined conflict between God and Satan, good and evil. The colonists marched and fought as agents of goodness, as the soldiers of God. The pattern, of course, reaches back to the Crusades. What is distinctively American may be the ambiguity of the crusade, the flight of both doves and hawks, the debate about whether to integrate—or fight. Recall the Pequot cries as the boats approached them: Are you here for trade or for war?

Finally, witches offer the frightening combination of both enemies: outsiders posing as members. They live within the good community, they are friends and neighbors. Yet they plot our destruction. And the good people can never be sure exactly who they are.

The Salem Village trials offer a common place to put the period on the Puritan story. But the demise of an old order brings the rise of a new one. The Puritans came in moral fervor. They built a society around a utopian quest for close-knit communities inspired by God. Eventually, Puritan fervor turned dry, and intimations of Enlightenment rationalism seeped in. However, the colonists would leave their Puritan era precisely as they had entered it: with great new gusts of moral fervor. A powerful religious revival sent the mission and the millennium bursting out of New England and across the colonies. The Great Awakening would renew the faith, revise the institutional framework, and tug Americans toward their greater revolution for the "sacred cause of liberty."

Chapter 3
The Puritans Become America

HORRIBLE noises, shrieks, trances, and young women rolling around on the church floors—it could have been another witch frenzy. But this hysteria marked a "mighty exultation of the soul," as Jonathan Edwards put it. In the 1730s and '40s, New Englanders stormed toward heaven and, amid the religious convulsions, remade their society.[1]

The Great Awakening was an early burst of American populism. A surging people walked out of the churches for revivals in the fields and on the commons. The mobbing had wide institutional consequences: new churches, new schools, and a new politics bearing the first traces of unabashed, un-Calvinist, self-interest. The Awakeners shifted the bias—the political tilt—of colonial politics. A century after the *Arbella* landed, New Englanders let go of the Puritan civic ideal. The covenant communities, bound tightly together in mutual charity and immutable congregation, sank into history.

The revival was most powerful in New England, but it flared across the colonies. This first trans-American experience rekindled the divine mission in the new world. The biblical millennium, it seemed, loomed just ahead. Before it was over, the Great Awakening—with its mobs, revivals, reforms, and intimations of the Second Coming—had propelled the colonists toward the revolution of 1776.[2]

Back in England, working-class evangelicals produced an anodyne alternative to radical labor politics. American revivals were different. Here evangelical challenges led directly to political upheaval and social change. The contrast with Europe returns us to the old romance about early American politics: colonists fled old world religious oppression; in the new world they found religious freedom and eventually forged a barrier between the sacred and the secular. We have seen a more complicated early American story. The king of England forced toleration on his obstinate Puritans subjects (who, after all, were trying to enforce a rival to the national church). Now, eighteenth-century Americans inherited the consequence: a growing profusion of competing sects sprang up and entangled religion in politics—but with a new world difference. In Europe, the old faiths bucked up the established order. In America, a kind of religious kaleidoscope inspired every political side. Rebels invoked God when they pushed for change. Reactionaries prayed with equal fervor as they pushed back.

What makes the United States distinctive? There are plenty of celebrated views, but most ignore the restless American quest for heaven. The search for God brought the Puritans to the new world in the first place. In the mid-seventeenth century, religious fervor remade colonial institutions and primed the colonists for their revolution. In the nineteenth century still another evangelical wave would hurl Americans past a secular Constitution and into their religious crusade of a civil war.

The Great Awakening marks the end of Puritan New England and the first stirring of Puritan America. The revival introduced one arc of American political change—moral unrest shakes up the old order and introduces a new one. The quest for salvation remakes politics and society. There are plenty of other paths to the future, of course, but nothing in American political history is quite as exceptional—as unusual—as this recurring moral dream and its powerful political consequences.

The Great Awakening

Born Again!

In the 1730s, New Englanders began complaining. Their religion was mired in "extraordinary dullness." "Dead men" preached to "dead congregations." Stale faith offered no bulwark against fading morals. The people "frequented taverns," indulged in "lewd frolics," and "exceedingly corrupted" one another. Then, in 1734, a religious revival swept through Northampton, Massachusetts. Two people had died unexpectedly, and the townspeople were in terror over the "dreadful pollution . . . and perverseness of their hearts." They grew obsessed with salvation; talk about anything else "would scarcely be tolerated."[3]

Jonathan Edwards, the local pastor, fired up this "Little Awakening" and made it famous with his vivid dispatches from the front. Edwards and the revivalists who followed him rejected the standard sermon of the period, a careful exegesis of biblical text. Men already "abound in light," wrote Edwards; the problem is that they "have no heat." Instead of filling their heads, we ought to touch their hearts. He aimed to "harvest souls" with immediate conversions."[4]

Edwards delivered his sermons in a low voice, scarcely making eye contact. First, he shook off the people's lethargy by describing what lay ahead for the damned. "The devil is waiting for them, hell is gaping for them, the flames gather and flash about them . . . they have no refuge, nothing to take hold of; all that preserves them every moment is the . . . uncovenanted, unobliged forbearance of an incensed God." At the height of the Northampton revival his listeners shrieked, rolled on the floor, and rushed to the pulpit crying for mercy.[5]

Edwards ignored the tumult and turned to God's saving grace. "You have an extraordinary opportunity," preached Edwards. "Christ has thrown the door of mercy wide open and stands crying with a loud voice." God is "gathering in his elect. . . . Awake and fly from the wrath to come . . . fly out of Sodom and look not behind you." The people roared. They spoke in tongues. They laughed and cried and sang. One after another, the people felt God's grace entering their souls. They were born again.[6]

The Northampton revival ended by late 1735. Edwards's uncle, Joseph Hawley, sobered up the town by committing suicide in despair over his own failure to feel God's grace. The main evangelical event soon followed. George Whitefield, a celebrated English itinerant preacher, made a triumphant tour of New England in 1740. Whitefield arrived with a giant reputation (this was his third American tour). An often-repeated story told of a Pennsylvania woman who walked forty miles to hear him preach. Afterward she told her friends that she had never been so spiritually awakened—and this was a German woman who spoke no English. Whitefield's voice and presence had been enough.[7]

Whitefield lived up to his reputation, provoking religious frenzy across New England. "He was strangely flocked after by all sorts of persons," conceded Charles Chauncy, the president of Harvard University and an arch-critic of the revival movement. "It was dangerous to mention his name without saying something in commendation." In Boston, the meetinghouse was packed so tightly that five people died in the crush. "Thousands cried out," reported Whitefield of another sermon, "so that they almost drowned my voice. Some fainted; and when they had got a little strength, they would hear and faint again. Others cried out in a manner as if they were in the sharpest agonies of death." At the end of his tour, Whitefield's farewell sermon drew twenty thousand people to the Boston Common—some four thousand more than the city's population.[8]

At first, the Boston establishment embraced the preacher. The governor of Massachusetts was "most affectionate," and the clergy welcomed him into their pulpits. After all, the rush of conversions seemed to be in everyone's interest. "I never saw so little scoffing," mused Whitefield, "and never had so little opposition."[9]

But the revival carried a powerful subversive current. The evangelical faith did not fit easily into the Puritan hierarchy. There were no preparation, no careful study, and no ministerial tests for aspiring saints. This version of salvation did not even require a proper minister or a regular congregation. Redemption came in a rush, even among mobs congregating on the commons. A blinding flash of light—a sudden circumcision of the heart, as St. Paul had put it—got the ecstatic sinners flying from the pews or fainting in the pastures.

The revival threw Salvation back onto pure faith. God's grace was everything. Whitefield spoke extempore. He urged other preachers to toss aside their texts and trust in God to inspire the words. "Oh what thoughts and words did God put in my heart!" wrote the preacher after a sermon in May 1740. Roughly the same sentiment had gotten Anne Hutchinson banished from Boston.

Nor did Whitefield pay any attention to sects. Anglican, Dutch, Congregational—he scorned the doctrinal differences and preached from any pulpit. If local churches refused him, he and his followers trooped into the fields. "He . . . prayed most excellently," reported the *New England Weekly Journal,* describing a camp meeting in New York, "in the same manner . . . that the first Ministers of the Christian Church prayed before they were shackled by Forms."[10]

And there lay the rub. Whitefield disparaged the clergy's work, their organizations, the "forms" that "shackled" them. And—crucially—he offered a simple alternative to the established churches: the itinerant, preaching in the fields. Who qualified to preach? Anyone who could draw and hold a crowd. Whitefield recruited itinerants (often university graduates without posts), and before long several dozen of these preachers were working New England.

On the surface, the theological differences seemed substantial. The New Lights (as the revivalists were known in New England) recalled Anne Hutchinson and the antinomians: God's grace was everything, the regenerate could feel the Holy Spirit moving within their souls, the line between saved and damned was sharp and palpable. They rejected tepid compromises like halfway covenants. On the other side, Old Light clergy scorned the evangelical tumult and held up the traditional alternative: Bible study, preparation, hard work, piety, and reason.

Still, the doctrinal lines often blurred. Established clergymen began preaching for conversions, and some preached (more or less) extempore. Like many establishments under siege, the New England clerical regime absorbed the challengers' reforms. But the angriest difference between Old and New Lights could not be finessed. What really rankled the Boston establishment this time was precisely what had really rankled it a century earlier: the revivalists disparaged all the ministers.

Breaking Our Congregations to Pieces

The raw challenge burst to the surface with the itinerants who followed Whitefield. Gilbert Tennent, for example, scorched the "unsaved" and "unconverted" ministry. The New England clergy were "Pharisee-Teachers," with "no experience of the Holy Ghost upon their souls." Their "prayers were cold," their sermons "lukewarm"—with "nothing of the savour of Christ." Tennent exhorted his listeners to "go a few miles further than ordinary" and hear preachers who could lift them toward Jesus. Ministers who bound people to local congregations were "like cruel pharaoh"; they "infringed on Christian liberty."[11]

Here was a direct assault on two fundamental principles: ministerial authority and the covenant community organized around a congregation. Itinerancy offered both rebellious talk and a subversive format. And the itinerants made no apologies if, as Tennent put it, the result was "to break our congregations to pieces."

Old Lights vigorously denounced these threats to their authority—and to their peace. "What can be expected but Confusion," asked Chauncy, "when church members will forsake their own pastors for every wandering stranger," when congregations forget their own Duty to "those set over them" and, instead, treat their pastors with "anger and wrath, if not with contempt and insult"? At the heart of itinerancy, he charged, lay "uncomfortable heats, animosities and contentions."[12]

The original Puritans had stressed the gulf between the elect and the unregenerate. Over time, a growing emphasis on rationalism fortified the social distinctions between the groups—the most eminent were the saints. Now rebels restored the evangelical heart and flipped the social implications. The high and mighty were "dead." Ordinary folks, tramping into the fields after the itinerants, felt their souls fill with grace. While the revivals began as broad religious movements, in many places they became distinctly class-based events. Itinerant preachers drew followers who were poor, landless, or politically unconnected. People of all ranks had been saved, wrote the Reverend William Cooper, but "more of the low and poor."[13]

The class tensions were most vivid in James Davenport's bizarre revivals. Davenport was no outsider—he had been a top graduate of Yale. Now he dropped in on local clerics, examined their souls, and broadcast his usually unhappy diagnoses. His sermons were wild, angry, and emotional. He plunged into the crowd and interrupted sermons with songs that he pressed the people to repeat over and over. He led singing mobs into the streets, disrupting or waking up the towns. The whole business was almost calculated to offend the local powers (and never mind the clergy—better to drink rat poison than to listen to them). In New London, Connecticut, Davenport lit a bonfire and urged the people to burn their vanities. Books went in first, then cloaks, then—as the prayer and psalm and hymn frenzy grew—the preacher stripped off his own trousers. A colleague intervened—and just in time, said a critic, or the preacher would have had to "strutt about bare-arsed." A Connecticut court found Davenport insane and threw him out of the colony.[14]

The preacher had exposed the class animosities running under the revivals. His "wild, frantik, and extraordinary" activity, reported one correspondent, aroused "idle or ignorant persons, and those of the lowest rank." All the itinerants were "admired by the vulgar," added Chauncy, but Davenport was the "wildest enthusiast" with "the wildest manner; and yet, he is vindicated . . . in all his extravagancies." Repeatedly, critics fumed about low rank and loud riots.[15]

The critics stated the class issue most directly in their constant complaint that the revivals interfered with labor. Hay went uncut in the fields while all hands flocked to hear Davenport. Servants carried their religions "abroad 'till late in the night," then came home "unfit for the services of the following day." The people were "perpetually hearing sermons to the neglect of all other business." Fretting about lost work spread through the colonies. The Southern Anglican hierarchy criticized preachers "for holding forth on working days" and subverting the "religion of labor." In Pennsylvania, "idle visions" of salvation lured people away from their farms and workshops. And in Boston, "poor deluded tradesmen and laborers" forgot their work to the "private detriment of their families and great damage to the public."[16]

Jonathan Edwards acknowledged the critics but did not yield a bit. "None objects against injuring one temporal affair for the sake of another of much greater importance." Well, "eternal things" are of "infinitely greater importance." To clinch the argument, Edwards whipped up a bit of cost-benefit analysis: "probably five times as much has been saved" from "frolicking, tavern haunting, [and] idleness" than has lately "been spent in extraordinary . . . religious meetings."[17]

Beyond all the shirking lay a still more disturbing specter: "anarchy, leveling and dissolution." Revival enthusiasm led to "republican and mobbish principles and practices." "What has been the effect," asked Chauncy, but the people "running wild"? The precedents sent up a terrible warning. Inspired by similar "visions, raptures and revelations" at the start of the Protestant Reformation, the mobs in Germany "took up arms against the lawful authority and were destry'd, at one time and another, to the number of an HUNDRED THOUSAND."[18]

The two great American faiths had come into conflict: the Puritan work ethic (read down to the rabble by employers worried about stability) clashed with the tumult of evangelical revival. The liberal tradition in America ran up against morality. This time, the hellfire roused a social movement. And by imagining an alternative to a major social institution—the New England churches—it posed a threat to the established order.

Jeremiads (Sex, Again)

The warnings about political chaos mixed with the usual anxiety over discipline. Once again the people were talking back. "Raw, illiterate, . . . conceited young Men or lads" and even "women, yea, girls" spoke out in church. They interrupted sermons with rude questions, they exhorted one another to experience Jesus. They boldly breached St. Paul's admonition that "for women to speak in the church . . . is a shame." Conservatives could not imagine how anyone would mistake the uproar for God's grace. Instead, they saw that primal Puritan sin—loss of control.[19]

Sure enough, a sexual subtext emerged this time, too. Chauncy blasted the "infinite evil," an "abomination" of making "all things in common, wives as well as goods." Whitefield was "running from Place to Place," moving "the Passions of the younger . . . Females." A cartoon (published in 1760) had one comely young woman responding to Whitefield's sermon: "I wish his Spirit was in my Flesh," while another calls on the preacher to "lift up ye Horn of thy Salvation unto us."[20]

But the most sustained attention to the danger came not from critics but from Jonathan Edwards himself. "Natural love to the opposite sex," he warned, "may degenerate . . . till it issues in that which is criminal and gross." The "Christian love and holy kisses" can turn into "unclean and brutish lust." Edwards fretted that young people would seize on the revival "to consort together in couples." All this religiosity, cracks Perry Miller, "increased the number of bastards . . . where there were already too many."[21]

The fear of lost control and sexuality kept haunting the Puritan mind. From antinomian fetuses to Native American lusts, from spectral witches lying hard on men to those holy kisses sinking into brutish lust—it all provoked deep anxiety about authority, control, and hierarchy. Every time social turmoil hit, the same charge sprang up: someone was not crucifying her lusts.

Beyond the Puritan era and all the way down to the contemporary American culture war, anxious sermons echo the 1679 jeremiad: "the evils that abound among us" always seem to "proceed from defects as to family government." Social disorder, rapid change, and cultural confusion all provoke the ancient quest for the "biblical family," for godly male authority.

Millennium

Each generation invents its jeremiad. By 1740, the Old Light fulminations are most dramatic for what (or rather, whom) they leave out. The attacks are

3.1. A bawdy English satire of George Whitefield, 1760. One young woman comments, "I wish his Spirit was in my Flesh," while another suggests that Whitefield "lift up ye Horn of thy Salvation unto us." A third woman cries out, "His poor eye sparkles with holy zeal"— Whitefield was distinctly cross-eyed. (© Copyright The British Museum)

hot, but they scarcely mention hellfire or Satan. Chauncy's writings, in particular, read more like agitated clinical reports than partisan religious tracts. Revivalists are deluded or mad more often than they are bedeviled or bound for hell. Even as they thundered against their challengers, many Old Lights exposed their Enlightenment attitudes, which the evangelicals now scorned as "modern notions" and "polite religion."[22]

It was the evangelical preachers—simultaneously revolutionary and conservative—who saw devils and damnation all around. During the Awakening, however, they emphasized the other side of the Puritan jeremiad: millennial glory. Fiery terrors were just backdrop to the extraordinary work of God, "hastily gathering in his elect." Surely, they kept telling one another, something miraculous was at hand. "Some great things seem to be on the anvil," wrote one observer from South Carolina, "some big prophecy at birth." In figuring out just what, the revivalists could draw on a full century of millennial Puritan thought.[23]

"What is now seen in America, and especially in New England," wrote Jonathan Edwards in 1742, "may prove the dawn of the glorious day . . . so often foretold in scripture." God intends this "uncommon and wonderful [revival] . . . as the beginning of something vastly great." No wonder there was such commotion. With elaborate metaphors and syllogisms (which drove Chauncy to distraction), Edwards demonstrated just why God had chosen New England for the "first fruits of that glorious day." The following year, some seventy New England ministers signed a manifesto; the Awakening, they declared, showed that the kingdom of God was imminent. Never mind the old errand of saving Christianity. Now the Americans had a greater mission—preparing for the Second Coming.[24]

In the analytic framework of contemporary social science, this was a "moment of madness"—a revolutionary, romantic moment when an entire society seems to be up for grabs. In these moments, fundamental change appears irresistible; for a brief moment, "all seems possible, all within reach." Across time, people who get swept up in a moment of madness imagine that their own "radiant vision" is at hand: a workers' paradise, a grassroots democracy, *fraternité-égalité-liberté*, or the Second Coming of Jesus. The utopian imagination is—suddenly, powerfully, briefly—inflamed by the immediate prospect of radical change, by visions of an apocalypse now.[25]

Moments of madness burn themselves out quickly. By mid-decade, the New England revival moment had passed. (Northampton would dismiss Jonathan Edwards by 1751.) Even so, most latter-day observers see an enduring legacy in the revival. In fact, many historians find nothing less than the "key to the American Revolution" in the Great Awakening. The Revolution too, writes William McLoughlin, was a movement infused with religious devotion, propelled by a millennial faith and fought with the conviction that God had ordained the result. Revival mobs in the 1740s prepared the way for the revolutionary mobs of the 1770s.[26]

The Key to the Revolution?

But always the pesky question: How could a movement that had grown cold by 1745 combust into a revolution that did not begin for decades? Does anything actually link the rebellions? The answer lies both in the mindset fostered by the revival (the usual answer) and in the institutions that it left behind.

Primed for Conflict

The revivals exploded the old covenant communities. Awakeners challenged clerical authority and split religious congregations. The differences quickly spilled into politics. In God's name, all sides tossed aside the old taboo against fomenting controversy.

Clerical authority was the first casualty. Deference had never come easy in New England. Now, judgment about salvation passed from the religious professionals to their flock. Preachers who refused to speak in the vernacular were blasted as enemies to "lowly preaching." The people began measuring church covenants by their own spiritual progress. "By covenant I am not held here," explained a Norwich woman, "any longer than I am edified." John Winthrop would have launched a mighty sermon: "The covenant . . . is the oath you have taken . . . that we shall govern you and judge your causes." Now, a century later, an entirely different idea floated in the New England air. Even humble people (even "women, yea, girls") would judge their own causes.[27]

The itinerants backed up the idea of religious discretion with concrete choices. When Gilbert Tennent urged people to go a "few miles further than ordinary" for their preaching, he was cracking the geographic boundaries of the covenant communities. (He sounded just like the first Puritan generation, with its rosy memories of walking "six miles off . . . to hear a sermon," back before the great migration.) Now people faced the local congregations with radical new options: exit and voice as well as loyalty.

Congregations split over the revival. Recall how Salem Village had struggled to break free from the covenant embrace of Salem. Now, New Lights walked out of congregations all over New England. In fact, Salem Village finally broke free and became the town of Danvers in 1752. Some forty congregations split in Connecticut, thirty more in Massachusetts.

Old Lights struggled to defend the traditional community and its mores.

The conflict flowed into politics. Some colonies prohibited itinerant preachers—Connecticut did so in 1742, Virginia in 1747. More important, both Connecticut and Massachusetts refused to recognize the separatist congregations. Would-be rebels would have to keep paying taxes to support the established Congregational church. Never mind the great religious principles, separatists were prosecuted as common tax delinquents.

Of the seventy-seven New England congregations that separated by 1750, only twenty-three were still around in 1765. However, the political rules gave disgruntled New Lights other alternatives. The crown had long ago pushed toleration for other sects—New England recognized Baptists, Anglicans, and Quakers.[28]

Born-again New Englanders rushed to the Baptists, who had always been the purer Puritans. In 1740, at the start of the Great Awakening, there were three Baptist congregations in Connecticut and eleven in Massachusetts. By 1770, the numbers had jumped to thirty-six and thirty, respectively. Thirty years later there were 312 Baptist congregations in New England (the population had only doubled). The Baptists had originally criticized the revivals; now they sent missionaries to other colonies with stunning success.[29]

Insurgents established schools that fed their insurgency. In 1746, New Lights founded the College of New Jersey, later named Princeton. Jonathan Edwards was very briefly president of the college before dying from a smallpox inoculation in 1758. In 1764, Rhode Island chartered a Baptist school, eventually named Brown University, where I teach. Moors Indian Charity School (later Dartmouth College) and Queens College (Rutgers University) also emerged during the revivals. The new schools graduated a steady cadre of young men looking for jobs ministering to the different sects.

The religious effervescence—Separatists, Baptists, Anglicans, New Light Presbyterians—rendered unworkable the whole notion of an official (or established) church. Americans would soon ratify the inevitable: no faith would get official sanction, though some would be distinctly more welcome than others.

In some places, religious differences yielded political factions. The struggle for faith overwhelmed the taboo on fomenting controversies. By 1755, Old Lights and New Lights were publicly attacking each other in Connecticut. John Woodward, a vehement Connecticut New Light, took the next, great step. He urged freemen to cast aside the venerable electoral standard and vote—not for the most eminent men but for those "firmly attached to your civil and religious interests." Elections ought to make officials "tender to all your rights and privileges." Virginia heard the same wild talk. A block of religious dissenters "extracted bonds from candidates to serve and stand by their interests before they should suffer them to be elected." This was rank partisan

3.2. "The Wicked Statesman, or the Traitor to His Country, at the Hour of DEATH," a cover illustration from the *Massachusetts Calendar; or An Almanack for . . . 1774*. The attack on Governor Thomas Hutchinson features the devil with a list of crimes and hellfire roaring up from the underworld. On the desk sits Machiavelli (amoral lust for power) alongside Hutchinson's controversial crown salary. (Rare Books Division, The New York Public Library, Astor, Lenox and Tilden Foundations)

spirit. Opponents ripped the "most unjustifiable and unprecedented" innovation.[30]

New Lights gathered political power and turned to secular issues. In Connecticut they splintered into factions and wrestled over matters ranging from paper money to settlements in the Susquehanna Valley (claimed by Connecticut in what is now Pennsylvania). By the 1760s, New Lights controlled the Assembly. Voters still deferred to big men when it came to higher office; Old

Lights held the Upper House and the governor's office. Then, in 1765, the Stamp Act hit the colonies. Governor Thomas Fitch, supported by the Upper House, reluctantly did the proper thing—at least by his traditional lights. He prepared to swear the required oath to faithfully collect the tax. New Lights refused to go along and spurned the oath. They had been challenging authority for two decades. Now they withdrew from the legislature rather than countenance the stamp tax. In the spring of 1766 they met in convention to nominate acceptable (anti-tax) candidates—another "pernicious precedent," previously "unknown" and "unpracticed." More precedents were broken the following month when the rebels swept into office. In May 1766, Governor Fitch was voted out and the New Lights won control of both Connecticut chambers.[31]

In short, the revivals remade communal boundaries and reorganized colonial politics. Congregational churches lost (or were losing) their status as the integrating mechanism of New England communities. Religious groups became political factions and stumbled into the rhetoric of "civil interests," "rights," and "privileges." The scope of the religious revival hinted at a trans-colonial American identity. But the Great Awakening pointed to the great Revolution in a more concrete way.

One of the trustiest political aphorisms has it that "all organization is the mobilization of bias." Organizations mobilize some fights into politics and shut other fights out of the system. The Great Awakening negotiated a critical shift in the bias of colonial institutions. The revivals legitimated conflict; the religious fervor mobilized challenges to authority into the political process. When the crown finally took a sustained interest in colonial affairs it discovered a politics biased toward resisting authority.

Calvin's Populists

The standard conclusion is simple: the Great Awakening allowed individuals to take control of their own spiritual yearnings. Shepherds had to compete for the allegiance of their flocks. Focusing strictly on individuals overlooks another big story, however: the revivals were powered by collective action. Breaking with a traditional congregation was a profoundly communal act. So, for that matter, was rallying around the minister when others walked out. New preachers elbowed their way to prominence by attracting crowds; the Baptists roared through the colonies with an early form of community organizing.

The revivals bore what would prove to be the classic features of American populism. In *The Democratic Wish* I tell the story of popular participation—grand democratic aspirations keep yielding unresponsive institutions. At the time I thought that I was starting the story at its beginning—in the 1770s. Any historian of the Great Awakening could have told me that I had jumped in at the middle.[32]

Populists begin by rejecting torpid institutions. Never mind piecemeal reform; they would replace unresponsive organizations with direct participation by the people. The eighteenth-century revivals offer the essential image: mobs walking out of the meetinghouses seeking salvation in the fields or on the commons. A generation later the colonists would walk out of the legislatures and courts. Like the itinerants before them, the rebels would take their business to the town commons and the open fields. "Liberty," proclaimed the revolutionaries of the 1760s, lies "out-of-doors." (A full two centuries later, Students for a Democratic Society would announce, "Democracy is in the streets.")

But neither politics nor religion can operate out-of-doors—outside an institutional framework—for very long. The struggle for popular participation inevitably introduces new organizations and transforms old ones. In the 1740s, revivals in the fields eventually yielded separatist congregations, a Baptist boom, and Congregationalists preaching extempore. In places like Connecticut and Virginia, it produced unapologetic, un-Puritan political factions just itching to resist the high and mighty.

As the people trickle back indoors, populist fervor turns to organizational maintenance. Damnation and redemption give way to tax disputes. American populism—ironically, inadvertently—ends up reconstructing the institutions it rejected. Over time, successive outbursts leave behind layers of reform (each designed to restore power to the people). The changes accumulate in an incoherent jumble. In politics, the result would be the inchoate American state; in religion, it is the extraordinary American profusion of faiths, sects, and movements. The messy outcomes set up the conditions for the next crusade.

Every angry generation is of course angry in its own way. But the underlying dynamic—rebellion, mobbing, institutional reform, organizational maintenance—runs faithfully across the years.

American populism is unusual in its urge to renounce powerful institutions and replace them with direct popular participation. The mobs in England, France, and Belgium would confront their states (and their churches) more directly. In different ways, each would try to seize the power of the state and wield it in the people's name. Americans would try to seize that power and somehow vest it directly in the people; in the religious sphere they would walk out of the old churches and find God's amazing grace stirring in the souls of the mob.

The contrasts return us to the great question about American difference. Every nation is unique, of course. But what is it that's different about this one?

The eighteenth-century revivals offer a twist on the familiar answers about American exceptionalism.

America's Puritan Legacy

The Great Awakening began in England then leaped to the colonies. On both sides of the Atlantic, evangelical fires burned hottest among the poor. In both places commoners found more comfort in revivals than in cold Enlightenment rationalism. But alongside the similarities lay great contrasts.

In England, the Great Awakening did not challenge the established order. Instead, writes E. P. Thompson, workers picked between religious revivals and political radicalism; revivals were built on the ruins of labor's political aspirations. English elites eventually figured out the connection and funded missions to steady the dangerous classes. Preachers condemned political radicalism; even John Wesley, the great revivalist, scheduled his open-air meetings to avoid conflicts with Anglican services. In a sense, the preachers were in the same business as the police and the workhouses—shoring up power, soothing disruptive workers.[33]

Across Europe and through the eighteenth century, adds Eric Hobsbawm, there was no significant working-class Christian socialism. Most radicals were ardently anticlerical. Religious revivals were more likely to kindle hot defenses of ancien regimes. Germany's Protestant Awakening rallied orthodox Calvinism. In France, ultramontane clergy renewed the cult of the Virgin Mary. The French Revolution set an implacable, conservative religious backlash rolling across Europe.[34]

Anti-Jacobin mobs summed up the reactionary piety as they ran through the streets of Naples singing:

> This tree without roots,
> This cap without a head,
> The Republic of Naples is gone
> Here's an end to equality
> Here's an end to liberty
> Long Live God and His majesty.[35]

In the new world, the Great Awakening ran in the opposite political direction. The revivals rattled New England with radical, millenarian politics. Moral populism provoked disrespect, disruption, and disorder. Revivals aggravated the political violence on the streets of Boston, set off a bonfire of the vanities in New London, and inspired slaves to rise up in the South. Meanwhile, the American old guard fretted over the consequences: sleepy servants, hay rotting in the fields, workers misbehaving, women speaking shamelessly in the churches, and (a little later) slaves rising up and slaying their masters. When mysterious fires broke out in New York in 1741, the authorities ruthlessly rounded up black people, burned or hanged more than thirty, and blamed the entire incident on Whitefield for preaching to the Africans.[36]

In Europe revivals inspired reaction; in America they roused rebellion. Moral upheaval spilled into the political realm and transformed colonial politics. Why was the new world different? What channeled its populist fervor into moral revival? Consider two explanations.

First, colonial populism simply followed the path of least institutional resistance. The English church was bound to a powerful central state; reformers faced a potent alliance of clergy and gentry. In contrast, New England religious elites were renegade Congregationalists who put their faith in local autonomy. Of course, the rules—right down to the tax code—propped up the New England Puritans; but this was the official denomination only when no one back in London was paying attention. The Boston Anglicans were the ones praying in the national church. The contradiction could be finessed only as long as the people stuck to their covenant congregations—precisely why itinerants and separatists posed such threats to the standing moral order.[37]

When the community boundaries were broken and the people began choosing among competing sects, religious success (and power) would be reckoned by the size of the crowd that gathered around a preacher. Once the religious flux went into motion it stayed in motion. Without state authority to prop up the religious status quo, populist agitation could remake American religion. The pulpits or the tree stumps or the airwaves would stay open to any preacher who wanted to challenge the "polite religion" of the day.

Still, open institutional space explains the supply of preachers but not the demand for their services. Why did the people respond? And why did religious fervor turn into political furor? A second explanation for the new world difference gets deeper into the American way. The sacred sphere lay at the heart of New England politics. Faith called the Puritans to the New World in the first place; it shaped the mission, organized the institutions, and launched the jeremiads. A growing majority may have failed to muster in as full-blown members of the Congregational elect. But—as the weeping, fainting, born-again Awakeners testify—many people continued to cast their aspirations and their anxieties in religious terms. These populists followed a path broken by a century of Puritan life. Religion mattered. Deep convictions and wide-open institutional space would prove a formidable recipe for igniting social movements.

This is not, of course, the entire story of American Puritanism or American populism or American political development. The people would chase plenty of visions, but salvation may be the most important; it is certainly the most often overlooked. The eighteenth-century mix of class effervescence and religious fervor had deep consequences: new churches, new universities, new communities, new factions, and new political fights. And that was just the start. The next Great Awakening would race across the United States and pick up where the first revival left off.

Puritans All

The United States rings with Puritan metaphors. The city remains on a hill, its citizens still fancy the eyes of all people upon them, the grand mission flourishes. Moral lines still run between us and them. When those lines get hot, we still call the results a witch-hunt.

Puritan economics seems to offer its own intimations of the future. The first settlers managed to squeeze their political institutions out of a commercial charter—then granted broad suffrage to proven saints. Reading salvation and perdition into wealth and poverty eventually merged with the idea of a national mission and produced the nation's unabashed—almost imperial—drive toward capitalism. From this angle, the Puritans help explain the primal energy of American liberalism. Of course, economics are just half the story.

The Puritans stepped ashore in the new world searching for a purer faith. They remade their society, a century later, still reaching for a more intense religious experience. They bequeathed their restless faith to future generations. To this day the American sacred sphere stands apart—at least in the industrial world—for its breadth, its depth, and its vibrant chaos. Bursts of fervor keep right on rippling across the United States.

The Puritans left America a religious tradition for every political side. With Winthrop, religion stands for order, stability, conformity, and control. With Anne Hutchinson, it inspires rebels who fight the system in heaven's name. In the next section, we'll see both slaves and slave-holders invoke the Bible to justify their cause.

For all the vast differences running across the American narrative, the moral urge inspires every generation. The United States develops, its people change. And yet, in many ways, we remain Puritans all.

PART II

The Abolitionist Crusade
(1800–1865)

PART II

The Albigensian Crusade

(1840–1850?)

America stepped forward in the first blossoming of the modern age and added . . . a vision of democratic self-government. What an idea and what an area for its realization—endless land of richest fertility, a population infinite in variety . . . self reliant pioneers, unafraid of man or devil. . . .

And then some unjust God leaned, laughing, over the ramparts of heaven and dropped a black man in the midst. . . .

It transformed the world.

—W. E .B. Du Bois, 1935

GUSTAVE de Beaumont traveled around the United States in the early 1830s with Alexis de Tocqueville. When he got back to France he cast about for a way to explain America to his countrymen. I believe, he wrote in the introduction to his book, I should describe the first time I attended the theater in the United States. "I was surprised at the careful distinction made between the white spectators and the [rest of] the audience. In the first balcony were whites; in the second, mulattoes; in the third, Negroes. An American, beside whom I was sitting, informed me that the dignity of the white blood demanded these distinctions."

Beaumont soon spied among the outcasts a "young woman of dazzling beauty, whose complexion, of perfect whiteness, proclaimed the purest European blood." What's that about, he wonders? His companion tries to explain.

"That woman . . . is colored."
"What? Colored? She is whiter than a lily!"
"She is colored," he repeated coldly; "local tradition has established her ancestry and everyone knows that she has a mulatto among her forebears."

Next, Beaumont sees a "very dark" woman brazenly seated in the section reserved for whites. The men repeat their routine.

"The woman who has attracted your attention is white."
"What? White! She is the same color as the mulattoes."
"She is white. Local tradition affirms that the blood which flows in her veins is Spanish."[1]

Americans have been furiously assigning one another to balconies since the seventeenth century. We sort each other by religion, ethnicity, gender, and bank account. But nothing marks American differences quite like race. And every time racial politics heats up, skin color seems to turn into a code for moral difference.

Three decades after the United States declared independence, people began thumping Bibles again. Another religious revival swept the country. Evangelicals rattled the new nation; born-again Americans launched swarms of crusades to save the world. By the 1830s—the "age of Jackson"—the moral reformers began converging on a single issue: American slavery.

Once upon a time, the age of Jackson was an intoxicating democratic epic. The people got control of presidential elections in 1828. They swiftly tore down old economic privileges, built up mass parties, booted the tired New England gentry out of federal office, exuberantly smashed the White House china, rushed into the open western territories, and scrambled to get ahead in their fluid, raucous, rising economy. The United States constructed the world's first mass democracy—80 percent of the voters voted (today, we're lucky to lift turnout above 50 percent). That was the time, beams Samuel Huntington, when the American dream got closest to the American reality.[2]

Abraham Lincoln described a very different Jacksonian age: "Outrages committed by . . . the worse than savage . . . mobs form the every-day news of the times." In Mississippi they lynched black men (suspected of insurrection) and white men (suspected of collaborating). "Dead men were . . . dangling from the boughs of trees upon every roadside," wrote Lincoln. A "wild and furious . . . disregard for law" pervaded the entire country. Why? Because radical abolition had worked the nation into a lather. Anti-abolition riots convulsed northern cities, workers in Philadelphia went "hunting for nigs," gentlemen threw rocks at women's rallies, southern crowds burned abolitionist mail, and President Jackson cheered the rock-throwers and mail-burners. Northern states banned black voting, western states banished black people, and congressional deliberations ran to fists, knives, canes, and guns. Through it all, Jacksonian Democrats pushed a frankly genocidal Indian war and celebrated the mighty Anglo-Saxon race.[3]

Rogers Smith sums up the paradox. Jacksonian Democrats were "more militantly republican" and "more radically libertarian" than any party in U.S. history. They were also "more openly racist." In this section we will see that the Jacksonian urges were deeply interconnected: rising democracy unleashed racial demons.[4]

Americans had opened up their politics, their economy, and their borders. Immigrants poured into the East, settlers pushed out to the West. The upheaval provoked those anxious questions: Who are we? Who counts as a full member of our community? Expanding the community meant fixing new boundaries, and that brought those airy all-men-are-created-equal generalizations down to earth with a thud. Should Irishmen or slaves or women or Cherokees share our rights? Become our political equals? Our economic rivals? Simply posing the question hints at why democratic changes stirred such "wild and furious" backlashes.

When abolitionists attacked slavery they were not just running down southern labor economics. They were condemning the American system of racial control. That is why abolition terrified most northerners. What was supposed to happen to those 2 million slaves? They would grab white jobs—and work practically for "slave wages." They would marry white women—and goodbye, mighty Anglo-Saxon race.

Right on cue, pious American women waded into the slavery debate. Abolition set off what one historian calls the "greatest organization and mobilization of women in American history." Women began lecturing on abolition (this was touchy). Some lectured men (immoral!). And in New England, women attacked the laws that forbade interracial marriage (which got gentlemen throwing bricks and choking about a "degraded race of wooly-headed mulattoes"). Each new whisper of abolition unleashed fresh jeremiads about the looming racial catastrophe.[5]

Now that slavery was being challenged, southerners swiftly worked out their defense. "Instead of an evil," they insisted, slavery was "a good—a positive good." Speaking before the Senate in 1837, John Calhoun laid out a famous argument. Slavery uplifted slaves. It uplifted the white race. It was the "most solid and durable foundation [for] free . . . political institutions." Besides, abolition did not mean race mixing, as northerners feared. It meant race war. "Slavery . . . cannot be subverted without drenching the country in blood and extirpating one or the other of the races."[6]

Against southern defiance and northern dread, black activists struggled to keep the focus on abolishing slavery. White reformers kept getting distracted. They fought bitterly over whether women ought to be in on the fight. Their own cause got tangled up with others: nativism, temperance, free-labor capitalism. Some frustrated abolitionists eventually renounced the United States to keep themselves pure from the sin of slavery. The Anti-Slavery Society "started to free the slaves," lamented Frederick Douglass. "It ends by leaving the slave to free himself." In a way, we'll watch the slaves doing just that—their race for the Union lines would finally force the hand of policy makers hesitating over emancipation.[7]

For thirty years abolitionists and slaveholders pushed rival notions of the regime. America's greatest moral crusade faced off against the nation's most sustained anti-liberal project. What does their clash tell us about our political culture?

For starters, we'll watch it sink one classic story. Americans are supposed to be state-bashing, welfare-begrudging individualists because they were "born equal," free to rise or fail in the new world. Yet the South, with its quasi-feudal racial legacy, ends up becoming the most resistant to government programs. On the other side, the northern land of free labor (which can at least spin a plausible myth about individuals escaping old world oppression and rising or falling on their own merits) would go on to develop a taste for relatively more government, almost European-style social welfare programs. More freedom back then did not foster a more anti-governmental political culture now. Just the reverse.

Then what makes for that infamous American political culture? The answer sits in Gustave de Beaumont's balconies. Social distinctions—in this section, race—get read as moral differences. The need to contain the dangerous them drives American politics, policies, and organizations. Moral fears cut just as deep as Tocqueville's escape from feudalism.

Across the details of this section runs an extraordinary story: a small band of radicals touched off an argument that—through a long and convoluted series of actions and reactions—transformed America. One key to the nation's big bang, its civil war, lies in the way we rigged the national divide: the virtuous versus the vicious. That great national antinomy always gets hottest when the moral lines are drawn in black and white.

Chapter 4
The Wrath of God in
Black and White

THE first African slave stepped onto North American shores in 1619. More than two centuries later, Americans began brawling over abolition. What heated up the argument after all that time? Another religious revival. Evangelical fervor rolled across the United States for three decades, peaking in the early 1830s. If the First Great Awakening primed Americans for their Revolution, the Second lit the long fuse to the Civil War.[1]

Political scientists usually focus on the democratic ferment that shook both sides of the Atlantic in the early nineteenth century. But nothing struck the young United States with the force of the Second Great Awakening. People who were barred from party politics—like women and slaves—flung themselves into the business of salvation.[2]

By 1830 the Awakeners had organized a network of institutions designed to rival political parties, save the nation, and redeem the world. Once again, evangelical fervor seemed to nurture every political side. Religion repressed slaves and inspired them to rebellion; it stabilized Jacksonian political parties and organized their ruin. The quest for God set America on a corkscrew path toward abolition, civil war, and black liberation.[3]

Lightning Round the World Shall Fly:
The Evangelical Roots of Abolition

In many ways, the Second Great Awakening looks like another bare-knuckle class fight. People flocked to camp meetings and night lectures, "as in Mother Hutchinson's time." "Illiterate sailors" were preaching. So were women. And for a fleeting evangelical moment, white sinners could be seen prostrating themselves in the dust before black preachers. Western revivals were vulgar "hot beds of unrestrained freedom" exalting religious ecstasy.[4]

The most famous revival met at Cane Ridge, Kentucky, in the summer of 1801. Baptist and Methodist missionaries gathered between 10,000 and 25,000 people (about one out of ten people in the state). The born-again frenzy lasted almost a week. Here's what one preacher saw in his corner of the tumult:

> The noise was like the roar of Niagara. I counted seven ministers, all preaching at one time, some on stumps, others in wagons. . . . People were singing, others praying, some crying for mercy in the most piteous accents while others were shouting most vociferously. . . . A strange supernatural power seemed to pervade the entire mass. . . . At one time I saw at least five hundred swept down in a moment, as if a battery of a thousand guns had been opened upon them, and then immediately followed shrieks and shouts that rent the very heavens.[5]

No one embodied the frontier's raucous evangelical spirit quite like Lorenzo Dow. A bearded, manic Methodist itinerant, Dow boasted about walking 10,000 miles and preaching to more than 500 camp meetings in 1804 alone. Dow's revivals featured "jerking exercises"—an irresistible rush of the spirit that left sinners flopping uncontrollably on the ground. The jerks might give way to the "dancing exercise," the "barking exercise," the "singing exercise," or the "running exercise." Dow mixed religious frenzy with radical Jeffersonian ideas. He flung acid sermons at the "purse proud" elites. Virtue stirred in ordinary people, he said, not in puffed-up hypocrites. "Ye men of self importance," preached Dow, "if you ever obtain the religion of Jesus Christ, you must obtain it on the same principles with publicans and harlots . . . a truth which I expect you bitterly hate." Over and over he repeated his democratic punch line: "You may support your distinction and feed your pride, but in a religious point of view, all men are on a level."[6]

Methodist itinerants like Dow tramped across the nation organizing a kind of people's church. They preached, gathered new congregations, and enlisted local lay leaders and exhorters. Then they moved off while their recruits continued preaching. The yield was stunning: 14,000 American Methodists in 1784 grew to 250,000 by 1820 and to more than 1 million by 1844. Baptists organized their own people's church—they were even more democratic, thanks to the Puritan faith in congregational autonomy—and their growth almost kept pace with the Methodists'. Anyone who heard the call could get a license and begin saving the neighbors.[7]

Meanwhile, back East, church leaders presided over a completely different revival. Lyman Beecher—Presbyterian, Whig, Yankee—embodied the sober Awakening. Think of him as a nineteenth-century Jonathan Edwards lacking

4.1. Lorenzo Dow and the jerking exercise. "At the religious gatherings, persons would be suddenly taken with irresistible spasms, inciting them to the most strange and extravagant performances." From Samuel Goodrich, *Recollections of a Lifetime*, 1857.

the fire and brimstone. When Beecher's congregants got swept up in religious excitement he sent them home to calm down. In trusty Puritan fashion, Beecher kept explaining how God-given "inequality of condition" made for the "best possible constitution of society" (the Presbyterians always were the hierarchical Puritans). Egalitarian fevers, mass political parties, factions, Sabbath-breaking, and rum-selling all threatened to drown the American paradise in a "poor, uneducated, reckless mass of infuriated animalism." The mob would "leave behind an utter desolation," Beecher warned. Every nation of antiquity had lost its liberty in the corruption of the lower classes; America too would "perish by anarchy" unless the masses could be "imbued with knowledge and virtue."[8]

The eastern churchmen deployed their moral forces like the politicians organizing wards. They launched benevolent organizations to fight sin. They distributed Bibles (through the American Bible Society, formed in 1816), handed out moralizing pamphlets (through the American Tract Society), organized Sunday schools (through the American Sunday School Union), and sent missionaries far and wide (through domestic and foreign missionary societies). The churchmen and their organizations raised funds, signed petitions, held rallies, and indefatigably organized still more uplift societies.[9]

Beecher pushed for ecumenical cooperation against the rising tide of infidelity. But those vulgar western itinerants sorely provoked the establishment clerics. "They demand a seven year apprenticeship for . . . learning to make a shoe or an axe," fumed Yale University's Timothy Dwight, but "they suppose the system of Providence . . . may all be comprehended without learning labour." Where there is "great excitement and little knowledge," agreed Lyman Beecher, "lasting . . . odium [is] attached to the revivals." Others put it more pungently. When a celebrated itinerant Baptist preached before a joint session of Congress, Representative Manasseh Cutler (Federalist, Massachusetts) blew up: "Such a farango, bawled with horrid tone [and] frightful grimaces," such a "poor, ignorant, illiterate, clownish . . . cheesemonger," "such an outrage upon religion and common decency."[10]

Yet beneath the sharp class differences lay profound similarities. The screaming western itinerants and the grave Yale divines were unwitting partners in a grand American project: bringing a kind of liberal individualism to the nation's religious life. Together the different preachers pushed the same four moral innovations, which added up to religious democracy.

First, they threw aside old-time Calvinism. Forget predestination with its little band of God's elect. Nobody was irredeemably depraved. The very idea was "odious" and "twisted," wrote Beecher. As usual, Lorenzo Dow served up the spiciest version of the new creed. "Christ gave himself for ALL . . . and

A-double-L does not spell SOME nor FEW but . . . ALL." Dow bore down on that old Protestant heresy: Could a sinner work her way to heaven by good works? Now, the answer was an unambiguous yes. Anyone who opened her heart would win salvation. A heckler once challenged Dow to explain Calvin's doctrine. Dow shot back with a sarcastic rendition of the old Credo's tension between faith and works:

> You can and you can't . . .
> You will and you won't . . .
> You will be damned if you do
> And you will be damned if you don't.[11]

Second, people were responsible for their own souls. No frowning clergy-man would render judgments about God's intentions. Now the clerics scrambled for business against a swarm of competitors. Gordon Wood illustrates the explosion of sects by simply drawing up an inventory of Baptist factions: General Baptists, Regular Baptists, Free Will Baptists, Separate Baptists, Dutch River Baptists, Permanent Baptists, and Two-Seed-in-the-Spirit Baptists— and all these before nine southern states formed the pro-slavery Southern Baptist Convention in 1845. Other denominations splintered into just as many pieces. Religious choices fell, willy-nilly, to the customer.[12]

Third, the Great Awakening pushed religion into the vernacular. Rousing gospel songs thrust aside formal church music. Western revivalists scorned the "dry science" of boring, Latinate sermons—"all hic haec hoc and no God in it," scoffed Charles Finney. Finney led a roaring evangelical revival in Rochester, New York. He prayed for the conversion of the damned—by name—and pioneered that revival classic, testimony from sinners who had seen the light. Even Beecher caved in and called for zestier preaching.[13]

Finally, preachers on every side pushed the personal disciplines of sobriety, piety, and hard work. The new benevolent societies steadied individuals in their battle with sin. And just in time, note labor historians, to negotiate the transition to industrial capitalism. Inculcating personal virtues helped break the inefficient habits of an artisan and farm economy—the lunchtime rum, the spontaneous vacations, the afternoon off. Christian discipline would bend workers to the regulated, clock-driven monotony of mill and factory.[14] Urban workers often resisted the change, cursing the bluenoses for meddling in their private lives. However, entrepreneurs and ambitious young professional men eagerly signed up with the benevolent societies. This aspect of the revival— some historians dub it the "shopkeeper's millennium"—served stability and the rising industrial order.[15]

The revivals reorganized American morals for a new era of broad markets and mass democracy—a religious bulwark for Jacksonian liberalism. Individuals would make their own spiritual way, without waiting for ministers or church elders or the inscrutable motion of the Holy Spirit. And in the true spirit of the era, the preachers began to brawl over just where to draw the boundaries. Who qualified for a full role in the new church order? The oldest American controversy—the woman's proper sphere—split the eastern and western revivalists. Was it still a shame for a woman to speak in church? "What absurdity!" fumed Lorenzo Dow. "You would apprehend no danger [if she participated] in a ball or a barbecue." When the evangelical factions met to negotiate a truce in 1827, their conference exploded over the gender question. Beecher (leading the conservative eastern forces) furiously warned Charles Finney (leading the more open westerners) to stay off his New England turf. When the leaders later reconciled, they tactfully stayed mum about women.[16]

The race boundary proved even harder to negotiate. In 1832, Beecher became president of Lane Theological Seminary, a Presbyterian school in Cincinnati. When the students began treating a black classmate as an equal, the townspeople threatened to riot. The school's trustees tried to rein in these intimations of amalgamation before violence erupted. Most of the first-year class (led by Theodore Dwight Weld and joined by Charles Finney) bolted and founded Oberlin College. In the ensuing uproar, President Beecher found himself on trial for heresy.[17]

All of this—from budding individualism to frank racism—neatly reflects the spirit of the Jackson Democrats. However, one final twist of faith would eventually bring down the entire Jacksonian paradigm. The Second Great Awakening rekindled sublime visions of America's mission. The United States would redeem the Book of Revelation and usher in the Second Coming of Jesus. Lurking in the millennial glory lay a great subversive catch.

Millennium!

Jonathan Edwards had been right after all. Perpetual glory would rise—was rising—in the west. God had selected America for the "moral and political emancipation of the world." When talk turned to the Second Coming, even Lyman Beecher began gushing: "Nation after nation, cheered by our example, will follow in our footsteps till the whole earth is freed." America's "character and destiny would be stereotyped forever." Dow parsed Revelation, verse by verse, and reached the same conclusion. Forget Europe, he wrote, the prophesies were "perfectly fulfilled under American government." Charles Finney challenged his listeners to come forward, dedicate their lives to Jesus, and bring on the millennium right then and there in Rochester.[18]

The drama came from the way American evangelicals were reading the key passage in Revelation: "And they lived and reigned with Christ a thousand years." A pre-millennial reading (popular today) expects Christ to abruptly return, bringing His thousand years of peace and justice. In contrast, most nineteenth-century revivalists were post-millennialists. Jesus would appear only after humanity had achieved the thousand years of peace and justice. Men and women would be the central agents in the cosmic pageant; the coming of the Lord awaited their moral triumph. The millennial visions reflected the rest of the Second Great Awakening: destiny had passed from divine volition to the people's free will.[19]

The preachers recast history and prophesy into a distinctly American idiom. A great teleological arc ran from 1517 (Martin Luther) to 1642 (Cromwell) to 1688 (the Glorious Revolution) and soared toward its millennial culmination in 1776. Now, fulfilling the scriptures required spreading three reforms to all humanity. First, those who tilled the soil must own it—universal land reform. Second, representative government must triumph over kings and tyrants. Third, the rights of conscience must prevail over religious despotism. For guidance in all these matters, the world had only to study the United States—Americans were back in business as God's chosen people.[20]

Right on millennial cue, great revolutions and reformations rushed across the globe. Naples (1820), Greece (1821), Brazil (1822), Spanish South America (by 1822), France (1830), Belgium (1830), Poland (1830–31), England (where the reforms of 1832 tripled the electorate). On and on ran the roll of rebellions—some successful, others harbingers of future freedom, all reaching (as the American evangelicals saw it) for the same liberty that flourished here in God's redeemer nation.

The millennial project helped remake the American view of history itself. The original city on the hill stood outside time. John Winthrop's commonwealth had aimed for eternal biblical harmony and godly order. Thomas Jefferson's republican yeoman—so different from Winthrop's saints—also participated in an unchanging society. For these American idylls, change meant corruption, development marked decline. Now the scriptures offered an escape into time—a robust new teleology for the American way. Change meant progress toward the redemption of Bible prophesy.

The fresh millennial imperative laid a heavy burden on godly men and women. If America was really going to reform the world, virtue had to triumph on every level of society. Americans had to prove themselves to be worthy exemplars. The millennial day waited for social vices to "abate their violence," preached the Reverend Gilbert Haven. "Intemperance, Sabbath breaking and infidelity" would have to be "replaced by the graces of Christianity." Personal salvation was not enough. America's destiny fired up that old Puritan reflex—improving the neighbors.[21]

Wherever the revivals flourished, uplift movements followed. "What a fertility of projects for the salvation of the world," gibed Ralph Waldo Emerson. Missionaries, pacifists, sabbatarians, anti-pauperism groups, Bible societies, purity advocates, temperance reformers, and on and on—no doubt, wrote Emerson, a "society for the protection of ground worms, slugs and mosquitoes" would be next.[22]

But all the high moralizing eventually had to face up to American slavery. Was this not a sin? How could Americans offer humankind a vision of liberty—universal land reform, no less—when they held 2 million humans (almost one in six Americans) in bondage? As the Great Awakening rushed toward its peak, millennial dreams began turning into anti-slavery jeremiads. In the moral hothouse of antebellum America, a righteous blow against slavery began to attract believers. Abolish slavery—immediately. Inconveniently for the redeemer nation, tired old England showed the way by abolishing slavery in 1833.

The moral agitation developed much of its political muscle from its organization. As we just saw, men like Lyman Beecher pushed a whole network of sin-fighting institutions—an evangelical "benevolent empire." Each moral cause sprouted central organizations and local chapters. For example, Connecticut organized a temperance society in 1829; within a year its members managed 172 local branches and claimed 22,000 members. A similar organization enabled the American Bible Society to hand out 6 million Bibles by 1849. The benevolent empire drew many women—moral uplift seemed an appropriately feminine enterprise. "What door would be rudely closed against female loveliness?" purred the Baltimore Bible Society in 1822. "What heart so hard, as to be insensible to the soft, imploring tones of her voice?"[23]

In short, the millennial search for God was changing American society in two very different ways. On the one hand, the revival fostered individualism, egalitarianism, and a faith in historical progress. It seized moral authority from the pulpit and invested it in ordinary men and women. All this powerfully reinforced the rising spirit of American liberalism. On the other hand, the revival kindled that hoary—nonliberal, anti-Jacksonian—American passion for uplifting the neighbors. Sin was collective, retribution would be shared, redemption must include everyone. If Americans were going to fulfill the Bible prophesies, sinners had to be converted or convinced or cast out. By the 1830s, slavery began to eclipse all of Satan's other works. For the next three decades Americans broadcast millennial dreams and blasted jeremiad warnings at one another with more gusto than they had ever worked up before or ever would muster again.

Abolition societies began organizing in towns and cities outside the South. As the abolitionists gathered and called for an immediate and unconditional end to slavery, all hell broke loose. The religious context explains the force with which immediate abolition burst onto the scene—driven by an evangelical tide, dreaming millennial dreams, and delivering a distinctly unwelcome message through the benevolent empire's efficient organizational network. Still, the abolitionist call would not have rattled the nation quite the way it did if it had not echoed the religious revivals in the black communities.

Call Me By the Thunder: African American Religion

The Great Awakening moved black communities in two very different ways.[24] Religion taught submission and justified slavery. But religion also stirred moral outrage, inspired slave rebellions, and fostered the first network of black institutions in the United States. Today, scholars like to play up the moral militancy, but both aspects played important roles. This dialectic between compliance and defiance transformed black communities. Then the black communities helped change America.[25]

On the surface, the revivals appeared to prop up slavery. Methodists and Baptist preachers had come into the black communities with the best intentions. The Methodists had formally denounced slavery, ordained black preachers, and recruited "exhorters"—a useful loophole in places that barred black preachers. Baptists had often burst into town with the same wide-open racial attitudes. Both sects had encouraged charismatic preaching, ecstatic services, chants, and songs that dimly recalled African spiritual traditions.

The egalitarian spirit, however, put evangelicals at a disadvantage. "The masters are afraid of . . . our principles," complained Methodist Bishop Francis Asbury. "We are defrauded of great numbers by the pains [they] take to keep the blacks from us." By 1804 the condemnation of slavery had quietly slipped out of the Methodist *Discipline*. Baptist congregations began establishing their own racial restrictions—pushing black people up into separate balconies, for example. Evangelicals tried to get onto the plantations by promising slave owners that conversion would make the slaves better; and that, writes Albert Raboteau, "was easily transposed into making 'better slaves.'" As a missionary association in Georgia put it, "Judicious religious instruction . . . will effectually counteract evil influences . . . [on] our colored population." Christianity would keep the slaves submissive, humble, obedient, and long suffering.[26]

Evangelical churches—even some black churches—appointed watchmen to keep an eye on unruly slaves. The African Gillfield Baptist church (Virginia) expelled slave members who had run away from their masters. Frederick Douglass reported the general result: "Many good, religious colored people . . . were under the delusion that God required them to submit to slavery and to wear their chains with meekness and humility." Or as a bitter antebellum blues riff summed it up,

> White man use whip
> white man use trigger
> But the Bible and Jesus
> Made a slave of the Nigger.[27]

The passive, otherworldly logic of Christianity leaked into abolitionist texts. Harriet Beecher Stowe drew her Uncle Tom as a Jesus figure, a redeeming exemplar of Christian virtue. But it is not hard to see why even some of her contemporaries jibed at his attitude—or, rather, his lack of attitude.

> O Mas'r, when I was sold away from my old woman and the children, I was jest a most broke up. . . . And then the good Lord, He stood by me and He says "Fear not, Tom" and he bring joy into a poor feller's soul . . . and I'se so happy, and loves everybody.[28]

A southern variation of the benevolent empire began pushing for a Christian clergyman on every plantation, "deriving his entire support from the master." The slaves "are yours—wholly yours," wrote one clergyman to the slaveholders, "and no one has, according to the teachings of heaven, and the laws of men, any right to interfere in the smallest degree with you or them." He smuggled in just one exception to the masters' ironclad authority: no one may interfere save the minister.[29]

The churchmen thumbed through their Bibles to construct elaborate justifications of slavery. Again and again they cited the same passages as God's warrant for bondage: "Cursed be Canaan; a servant of servants shall he be." "Both thy bondmen and thy bondmaids, which thou shalt have, shall be of the heathen that are round about you." "Servants be obedient to . . . your masters . . . with fear and trembling." With an elaborate "display of exegesis," writes Randy Sparks, "the churchmen became the chief defenders of the South's most cherished institution."[30]

Frederick Douglass, deeply inspired by his own religious experience, wrote bitterly about what happened when faith fell into the wrong hands. "Religion in the South is a mere covering for the most horrid crimes—a justifier of the most appalling barbarity. . . . Of all the slaveholders I have ever met, religious slaveholders are the worst." "The man who wields the blood clotted cowskin during the week" wakes up on Sunday and "claims to be the minister of the meek and lowly Jesus."[31]

The combination of ministers and masters looks vaguely like the European feudal structure. The lord and the priest prop up the established order—and one another's power. But, as usual, there was an American difference. Here, faith mobilized both sides. Religion also offered black communities a network of organizations and a biblical narrative of rebellion.

Toward the end of the eighteenth century, black preachers began organizing black churches. White evangelicals unwittingly encouraged the effort by pushing black ministers from their pulpits and black worshippers from their pews. The most famous confrontation took place in 1794 during the service in St. George Methodist Church of Philadelphia. The church had just been renovated with contributions from both white and black members. "We came in," as the black clergyman Richard Allen later described the event, "and took our seats over the ones we formerly occupied, not knowing any better." Suddenly, just as the elder was saying "let us pray," a loud scuffle broke out. One of the trustees (a white man) began pulling up the Reverend Absalom Jones (an African American) by the elbows and telling him, "You must get up, you must not kneel here." Jones responded, "Wait till the prayer is over," which only provoked the trustee to call for reinforcements. "We all went out of that church in a body," concluded Allen, "and they were not more plagued with us in the church." The black exodus from St. George is known as America's first freedom march.

Allen organized his own church, limited to "descendants of the African race," then spent decades battling a hostile Methodist establishment—both in the church aisles (when officials tried to shut down his services) and in the state courts (where they tried to sink his church). Other black preachers formed African congregations—mainly Baptist and Methodist—across the nation. In Philadelphia alone, blacks built fourteen churches in the first third of the nineteenth century. As black men and women came out of the increasingly hostile white churches, they developed the first network of black institutions in the United States. By 1816, Allen and other black churchmen combined to form the African Methodist Episcopal Church—still the "greatest Negro organization in the world," wrote W. E. B. Du Bois more than eighty years later.[32]

The churches became the political and cultural heart of the black community. The network of churches summoned a cadre of black leaders—the preacher, wrote Du Bois, became "a politician, an orator, a boss, an intriguer, an idealist"—holding the black community together and offering promises of salvation, redemption, and freedom.[33]

Evangelical religion gave African Americans the Exodus narrative to counter the Anglo-Saxon city on a hill. The true Children of Israel had not yet been delivered; they languished in cruel captivity. Oh, yes, the millennium was at hand and the world would be Christianized; but God would work His will through the special people He had chosen and tested. Faith surged into the political dream of abolition. Du Bois put it famously: "That which was a radical fad in the white north, and an anarchist plot in the white south, had become a religion to the black world."[34]

African Americans seized the Bible back from the slaveholders and used it to frame warnings about God's righteous wrath. David Walker, a black store-keeper living in Boston (and a member of the Methodist congregation), wrote what may be the most tooth-rattling jeremiad in American history, published in 1829.

> Do you think that our blood is hidden from the Lord because you can hide it from the rest of the world by sending out missionaries and by your charitable deeds . . . ? O Americans! Americans!! I warn you in the name of the Lord . . . I call God—I call Angels—I call men to witness, that your destruction is at hand and will be speedily consummated unless you repent. . . .
>
> Unless you speedily alter your course, you and your country are gone!!! For God almighty will tear up the very face of the earth!![35]

A great African American jeremiad developed over the ensuing decades. The Reverend Henry Highland Garnet revisited Walker's themes in 1843: "Slavery sets all [the scriptures] at nought and hurls defiance in the face of Jehovah." Garland looked hopefully at the old world, "moving in the great cause of universal freedom," and, like Walker, called on the slaves to rebel. "If you must bleed, let it come all at once—rather die freemen than live to be the slaves." And the warnings always reinforced the idea of the "righteous retribu-tion of an indignant God." Frederick Douglass ended his autobiography, two years later, with the same warning, drawn directly from Jeremiah. "'Shall I not visit for these things?' Saith the Lord. 'Shall not my soul be avenged on such a nation as this?'" All the talk of blood and vengeance appalled some white abo-litionists. Others, like William Lloyd Garrison, exuberantly picked up the black biblical jeremiad. By 1865 this terrible black poetry was soaring through Abraham Lincoln's last, great, mournful speech.[36]

The black jeremiad soon got everybody's attention—not because of the moral imperative or the biblical prose but rather through a rash of slave rebel-lions. In contrast to the large and frequent slave uprisings in Jamaica, the Guianas, and Brazil, there were relatively few in the United States. But the threat seemed greater here because black and white lives were more fully inter-twined.

The American rebellions were organized by church members, inspired by Bible metaphors, and followed by white efforts to suppress black religion. When Gabriel Prosser planned a rebellion against Richmond, Virginia (in 1800), he recruited at religious meetings; his brother, a preacher, reminded the conspira-tors how God had promised the Israelites that "five of you shall conquer a

hundred and a hundred a thousand of our enemies." When the plan was discovered, both South Carolina and Virginia passed laws forbidding Negroes to
assemble at night for religious worship. Denmark Vesey, a Methodist exhorter
in Charleston, South Carolina, also recruited church members and read to
them from the scriptures (in 1822). When his plot was crushed, the large First
African Methodist Church was demolished in retribution.[37]

Nat Turner's rebellion, in August 1831, ignited the abolitionists' big bang.
Turner's uprising killed some sixty white people in rural Virginia. He then terrified the region by remaining at large for two months. Militia units, vigilante
groups, and (briefly) federal troops poured into the county to hunt down
Turner. He was finally captured, swiftly tried, and killed. Turner's *Confession*
(actually written by Thomas Grey, a white lawyer) narrates the rebellion in
prophetic Old Testament terms. "As I was praying one day at my plough, the
spirit spoke to me saying, 'Seek ye the Kingdom of Heaven.'" What spirit?
"The spirit that spoke to the prophets in former days. I was greatly astonished,
and for two years prayed continually." Another revelation then "confirmed me
in the impression that I was ordained for some great purpose in the hands of
the Almighty."[38]

What alarmed white southerners was not just the bloodshed but the conspiracy. Turner revolted two years after David Walker published his *Appeal,* just
eight months after William Lloyd Garrison began publishing the *Liberator.*
Black preachers were reading these tracts from the pulpits before "large assem-
blages of Negroes," claimed Virginia Governor John Floyd. The conspiracy
was huge. "I am fully convinced that every black preacher in the whole country
east of the Blue Ridge was in the secret."[39]

The root of the problem, argued Governor Floyd, lay in the notion of
"making them religious." Naive females "thought it was piety to teach Negroes
to read." Before long the slaves were reading scriptures and religious tracts.
Then preachers started "telling blacks [that] God was no respecter of persons"
and "that all men were born free and equal." It followed that "the black man was
as good as the white." Pretty soon they had all the slaves thinking "that they
cannot serve two masters." And their conclusion was that blacks had a right to
rebel for freedom, just as the whites had rebelled.[40]

White southerners swiftly addressed their problem in the usual ways. Virginia forbade black people from preaching, conducting religious meetings, or
even attending prayers without the master's direct supervision. North Carolina
ordered thirty-nine lashes for those who taught slaves to read, and outlawed
prayer meetings for slaves from more than a single family.

Black writers described the harsh days that followed. Harriet Jacobs vividly
pictured the white thugs who burst in on her North Carolina town looking for

Nat Turner. They "committed the most shocking outrages . . . with perfect impunity." When searchers found letters in her house, they called for the thirty-
nine lashes (a white acquaintance intervened). Jacobs sadly describes the implementation of North Carolina's new religious policy: The slaves "had a little
church in the woods, with their burying ground around it. It was built by colored people and they had no higher happiness than to meet there and sing
hymns together and to pour out their hearts in spontaneous prayer. . . . The
slaves begged the privilege of again meeting at their church. . . . Their request
was denied and the church was demolished."[41]

Still, black Americans kept the faith, and black Christianity survived and
flourished. Secret meetings "in the quarters, groves and hush harbors" became,
in themselves, acts of Christian rebellion against bondage.[42]

David Walker died in suspicious circumstances before Turner's rebellion.
Poison? The city records say consumption. But William Lloyd Garrison picked
up the red-hot racial jeremiad. Like Walker, he had warned the slave owners of
the bloodshed to come. Now he rubbed it in: "What we have so long predicted . . . has commenced its fulfillment. . . . The first drops of blood are but
the prelude to a deluge." You may have quelled Nat Turner's rebellion, he wrote,
but "you have seen . . . but the beginning of your sorrows. . . . Wo to this guilty
land, unless she speedily repent of her evil doings! The blood of millions . . .
cries aloud for redress! Immediate Emancipation can alone save her from the
vengeance of heaven and cancel the debt of ages."[43]

Here, panicked southerners told one another, was terrible mischief. Northern abolitionists were calling for southern blood. Black preachers fanned trouble by spreading the abolitionist message. And two million slaves walked among
three and a half million white southerners. Before the end of the year, reports
began to circulate about a massive slave rebellion in Jamaica.

The Virginia legislature met the following winter and confronted the question that Nat Turner had pushed on them: What role would slavery—and
black people—play in the commonwealth? Stray bits of liberalism cropped up
for the last time in antebellum southern race debates. Might the black man
"mount upward in the scale of civilization and rights, to an equality with
whites?" asked Thomas Dew, who chronicled the Virginia discussion. Governor Floyd submitted a more popular proposal: drive all free Negroes from the
state. Some Assembly members proposed calling on the Colonization Society
for help in shipping them off to Africa. A few members mused aloud about
seeking federal help to "extirpate the curse of slavery from the land." By the
time they finished, the legislators had defined the South's non-negotiable bottom line for the next thirty years. Before we explore the South's view (in Chapter 6), let's look at the abolitionist challenge. First, colonization—today, we

might call it "abolition lite"—then the radical moral crusade for immediate and unconditional abolition.[44]

White Dreams, Black Colonies

The American Colonization Society, founded in 1816 by the Reverend Robert Finley, oozed with the benevolent empire's missionary piety. Americans would disdain power or plunder and use their colonies to push along the grand millennial pageant. Centuries ago, Europeans had plucked up Africans "immersed in barbarism and heathenish darkness." Providence "permitted . . . these people . . . to be dragged into bondage" so that America could tutor them. Now we would return them "with the light of civilization and the blessings of Christianity." The black colonists would become our missionaries in Africa; they would lift up the entire continent.[45]

In its most high-minded variation, the colonization plans would end slavery. Slaves would be bought, freed, equipped, and sent off to create new communities in Africa. Whisking black people away might simplify manumission by sparing white America the fearful aftershocks of freedom—race war, race mingling, black people demanding equality, or black people doing anything at all.

The missionary dream quietly endured. Lincoln kept musing about the "moral fitness in the idea of returning to Africa her children." The idea would even come to inspire black nationalism: an eastward-looking Manifest Destiny calling African people back to their ancestral home. But black nationalist dreams lay decades away. The Colonization Society itself was rapidly becoming dominated by an entirely different spirit.[46]

Alongside missionary dreams lay hard white fears and calculations. The colonial idea underscored slavery's importance as a form of race control. Reasonable people might negotiate the economics of liberating slaves; the specter of all those free African Americans, however, compelled more heroic schemes. "We heartily wish success to the colonization project," ran one editorial in the *Niles Weekly Register.* "We especially encourage send[ing] out young females. The annual emigration of about 15,000 girls, would keep the whole mighty mass of the black population in check." It might even "exterminate the color, in a few generations, in all the states north of the Potomac . . . and so make room for a free white laboring population."[47]

The Democratic newspaper was casting its anxieties in the timeless language of racial economics. The "mighty mass" menaced white labor. Free black men and women heard about it all the time. Frederick Douglass reported watching white carpenters throw down their tools rather than work with black freemen: "If free colored carpenters were encouraged, they would soon take the trade into their own hands, and poor white men would be thrown out of employment." The talk rapidly turned to "niggers taking over the country." The motif is as fresh as the contemporary arguments about affirmative action, as old as Benjamin Franklin's fears about the Dutch "underliving" and "underselling" the English. The poor others always arrive with insidious advantages that threaten the white working guys.[48]

But intimations of black freedom also aroused more visceral anxieties. Antebellum race talk compulsively leaped to race mingling or amalgamation. Black freedom meant black husbands. Colonization advocates kept citing Thomas Jefferson's tortured reflections on emancipation. "Roman emancipation required but one effort. The slave, when made free, might mix . . . without staining the blood of his master." But in the United States, emancipation was going to need a second step, unknown to history. "When freed, [the slave] is to be removed beyond the reach of mixture." Why was mixture so inevitable? In perhaps the most chilling lines he ever wrote, Jefferson dredged up a twisted bit of natural history: Black men have a preference for white women over black women "as uniformly as . . . the preference of the Oran-utan for the black woman over those of his own species." African Americans protested, but the miserable image was out and running loose through antebellum race debates.[49]

Race mixing became a metaphor for national perdition. "A darkened nation," writes Winthrop Jordan, "would present incontrovertible evidence that sheer animal sex was governing the American destiny and that the great experiment in the wilderness had failed." Nineteenth-century authors insisted that black freedom meant intermarriage and intermarriage meant decline, failure, and extinction. Patrick Henry (anti-slavery, pro-colonies) summed it up: "Our country will be peopled. The question is shall it be with Europeans or with Africans?" Even Lincoln: "The separation of the races is the only perfect preventive of amalgamation," and "such separation, if ever effected at all, must be effected by colonization."[50]

Colonization advocates knew that their discussion brimmed with bigotry. But what could they do? Black freemen lived impoverished lives on the periphery of the American political economy. They were not slaves, yet they were not permitted to live fully free. The feeling against them was ferocious—"Invincible," said Henry Clay, "too deep to be eradicated." As Lincoln sadly told one group of freemen, "Your race suffers very greatly . . . by living among us, while ours suffers from your presence." In such a harsh context, said the colonization advocates, emigration was best for everyone.[51]

African Americans disagreed. Even as the Colonization Society was getting organized, three thousand black Philadelphians packed into Richard Allen's Bethel Church and unanimously rejected the entire business. They

voted down colonization again the following year (1818) and the year after that
(1819). Much as some of us might enjoy becoming "presidents, governors and
principals," read one of their statements, "the people of color of Philadelphia
proclaim their solemn protest against the contemplated colony on the shores of
Africa." Between 1830 and 1832 alone, free people of color rejected the idea in
twenty-two northern cities. "We now inform the colonization society," wrote
the black people of Pittsburgh, "that should our reason forsake us, then we may
desire to remove. We will apprise them of this change in due season." "America
is as much our country as yours," added David Walker. "We have enriched it
with our blood and tears." Walker offered a simple alternative. "Treat us like
men and there is no danger."[52]

At first the black community was largely united in its opposition. Paul Cuffee, a black shipbuilder from Massachusetts, famously pushed colonization and
put his own money down to help African Americans emigrate; but he was an
exception that underscored the general rule. "Let us not hasten to condemn,"
prayed Peter Williams at Cuffee's funeral in 1817. "Let us suspend our judgment." Decades later, as the abolition crusade waned and the American race
regime grew harsher, weary black leaders would begin to turn to the prospect of
racial justice abroad. The idea would eventually nourish messianic dreams of
black nationalism; the true Christians—black Americans—would quit this
cruel country and fulfill their divinely ordained destiny in their ancestral lands.
But until the 1850s, people of color fought hard against the colonizer's all-
white American fantasy.[53]

Most people finally heard the protests when William Lloyd Garrison
launched his ferocious assault on colonization in the early 1830s: "The friends
of colonization may be summed up in a single sentence: they have an antipathy
against blacks. . . . They can love . . . them 4,000 miles off, but never at home."
When the colonizers insisted that American racial hostility was implacable,
Garrison told them, "Then we had better burn our Bible and our Declaration
of Independence and acknowledge ourselves to be incorrigible tyrants and
heathens." Garrison hurled volumes of invective at colonization, never stinting
on the exclamation points. "O cursed combination full of subtlety! . . . The
mocker of God and man! The complication of all evil! The masterpiece of all
the contrivances of the devil!"[54]

Garrison was part of the broad new reform wave that swept the United
States at the height of the religious revivals in the early 1830s. The new spirit
cast aside wary Calvinist efforts to uplift the dangerous mob. Instead, born-
again Americans now dreamed their ambitious dreams of millennial perfection. Colonization rapidly lost support and money to more radical abolitionism.

Many southerners had been attracted to colonization—of the 233 local societies, 136 were in the South. When Nat Turner rebelled, Governor Floyd's first reflex was colonization. Could Virginia get rid of its free black people? How about deporting them all, slave or free? Prudence had restrained Virginia from really tackling the question of slavery in the past, reported Thomas Dew in his description of the legislative debate. Now that Turner (and the radical abolitionists who were stirring up the slaves) had forced the issue, the Virginia legislators took a long, hard look and returned their finding: "Emancipation and deportation is . . . totally impracticable." The bill would run to $900 million (total federal government revenues in 1831 were $28.5 million). But it was not the money. "Every principle of expedience, morality and religion" drove them to reject the notion of "abandoning" their slaves. On the contrary, they would henceforth start proclaiming the virtues of slavery. The colonial illusion—leaping out of slavery by disappearing all the black people—would evaporate in the South. In its place came a truculent defense of slavery.[55]

The Jackson administration, with its laissez-faire animosity to active government, hammered another nail into the Colonization Society's coffin. The idea of paying for black colonies was just one more Whiggish "internal improvement," ripe for presidential veto. This government would remove Indians but not slaves.

By the early 1830s, northern radicals were blasting colonization; southern politicians had rejected it, and the Jackson Administration had ruled out government assistance. But the shifting political tides did not really make much difference—colonization was not going anywhere. After more than a decade, the colonizers had managed a paltry exodus. With great fanfare, little knots of black people—just three thousand in thirteen years—departed for Africa. Garrison made hay over the trickle. To put that number in context, Tocqueville pointed out that 700,000 black people were born in the United States during the same years. For all the support it gathered, colonization was more significant as racial fantasy than as social policy.[56]

Still, the idea lingered. Lincoln kept coming back to it, leaping over the manifest difficulties by turning to Exodus: the Children of Israel "went out of Egyptian bondage in a body." Lincoln would even pencil in a line about black colonization when he drafted the Emancipation Proclamation. Secretary of State William Seward promptly illustrated the barriers by scribbling a couple of tough qualifiers into the draft (which I have emphasized here): "The effort to colonize persons of African descent *with their consent,* upon this continent or elsewhere, *with the previously obtained consent of the governments existing there,* will be continued." By the final draft, all mention of colonies had vanished.[57]

Colonization took an especially weird turn when it became entangled in white Manifest Destiny. By 1850 the United States had developed a new, bluntly racial strain of millennial thought. The *American Review* published a typical example: "No nation on the face of the earth or in the record of history" had such a "Providential origin," such a "sublime destiny," or such a "wondrous future." But this was not the same old city on a hill. God had a "consummate and glorious plan involving the interest, not of a nation but of a race." Mexico and South America "will speak the English tongue and submit to the civilization, laws and religion, of the Anglo-Saxon race." On and on it would roll, the "great civilized and Christian nation" moving to the "glorious destiny [of] our race in the New World."[58]

Both sides of the slavery debate concocted elaborate new colonization plans in the spirit of this Manifest Destiny. Slavery's champions, hemmed in at home, imagined colonies in Cuba, the West Indies, Mexico, the Amazon Basin. Here lay elbowroom for southern plantation culture. Black slaves, guided by their Anglo-Saxon masters, would colonize, dominate, and uplift. "The African [has] his mission," wrote slavery apologist Gilmore Simms. But freedom was no longer part of the colonial deal. The slave, "designed as an implement," would become the "destined agent for the civilization of all the states of Mexico and all the [South] American states beyond."[59]

The pro-slavery colonizers managed to squeeze a missionary angle into their self-interested plans. Latin America lay in ruins—wrecked by (what else?) amalgamation. "The great race . . . of Spaniards parted with their own superiority," wrote the ardent white supremacist J. H. Van Evrie. The United States was the last hope "for the rapidly perishing civilization of the great tropical center of the continent." Naval scientist Matthew Maury imagined a great American slave colony in the Amazon forests: "Shall it be peopled . . . by a go-ahead race that has energy and enterprise?" Or "with an imbecile and indolent people?"[60]

The anti-slavery Republicans also dreamed up their own colonies to the south. In their version, free black people would get a suitable new homeland. More important, black colonies would ring the southern United States and create a "wall of fire" against the spread of slavery. Destiny would surely smile upon this colonizing variation. After all, argued supporters, black Americans had become a "vastly superior" race to the "dwarfed and imbecile natives" of Central and South America. These were complicated racial currents for anti-slavery colonizers: Slavery was wrong, of course. But the freed slaves were not worthy of joining the American (that is, the Anglo-Saxon) us; and yet they were far superior to the amalgamated, enervated Latin American them.[61]

Nothing ever came of the Latin colonies. For one thing, the Manifest Destiny crowd was hoist on its own arguments. The United States, argued John Calhoun, had never "incorporated into the union any but the Caucasian race. . . . Ours is a government of the white man." America would swallow the less populated parts of Mexico—but not the entire nation, much less Central America or the Amazon basin.[62]

By 1850, colonization operated mostly as a grand metaphor, an almost millennial mirage that dissolved racial troubles into Anglo-Saxon fantasies. While the competing bands of would-be colonizers fought bitterly over slavery, they shared a vision of America as a white nation. The urge to ship an entire race off in boats may seem a bizarre bit of nineteenth-century cultural flotsam. But what the colonizers were after is not so foreign: colonization would segregate the races, close the American community, and keep the established racial hierarchies—economic, social, political, sexual—firmly intact.

Ultimately, the colonization metaphor stood for the race lines that already existed in antebellum America. White Americans did not need boats or colonies to push black people to the social margins. The hard lives of the freemen testified that the social and economic rules could be powerfully rigged along the color line. Eventually, white Americans would find simpler ways to separate from their black countrymen. But at what price to their own principles?

Today, social scientists tirelessly debate the motor of historical change. Is the organization of political institutions the key? Do ideas matter? Does culture play a role? And what about the morals that I emphasize here? The experience of the early nineteenth century offers a clear answer for at least one era: They were all operating. And together they produced political dynamite.

The Second Great Awakening reorganized the civic culture. It restored an early American vision—the city on a hill, a mission to the entire world. Reformers mixed the biblical millennium with republican ferment: the Second Coming awaited land reform and representative government. The moral dreams inspired what we would now call a powerful social movement with vast institutional consequences. Religions spread and changed. A network of reform organizations sprang up and set out to save the world—or at least the nation. The new institutions recruited new kinds of activists from the margins of public life: women were perfect for light duties, like distributing Bibles; black religious leaders formed churches, preached the gospel, and called for freedom. Before long, the new social network—benevolent societies, women's clubs, black churches—began questioning the political order.

Abolition was radical because it challenged the entire American racial regime. Nat Turner—the abolitionist jeremiad sprung to life—focused everyone's attention on what the radicals were saying. And just when the racial order began to rattle loose, women started questioning sexual hierarchies. In the

1830s the abolitionists pushed Americans into a kind of national existentialist crisis. It was not just about slavery but about the role—the nature, really—of black people in society. And, quite suddenly, about the role of women in politics and society. And then, inevitably, about the nature of the United States and its most fundamental principles.

Chapter 5
Abolition!

WILLIAM Lloyd Garrison's newspaper, the *Liberator*, often gets the credit for whipping up the abolitionist fracas. But why? Calls for immediate abolition had been popping up for years before the paper was founded, in 1831. And as Boston Mayor Harrison Gray Otis reported eight months after the *Liberator* went into business, nobody "of my acquaintance had ever heard of the publication." The mayor eventually "ferreted out the paper and its editor." He was not impressed. Garrison's office was an "obscure hole, his only visible auxiliary a Negro boy, and his supporters a very few insignificant persons of all colors." Garrison's enemies were the important people. Otis was responding to letters from Governor John Floyd (Virginia) and Senator Robert Hayne (South Carolina), who both were seething over Garrison's alleged role in stirring up Nat Turner's rebellion. Southern wrath, followed shortly by northern wrath, is what trained the limelight on Garrison and the abolitionists.[1]

On a deeper level, the Second Great Awakening launched the movement. The abolitionists simply redirected all that moral energy by lifting the fight against slavery above the crowd of righteous causes. They transformed slavery into the nation's greatest mortal sin, the "bellwether of America's fidelity to its covenant with God," as Robert Abzug puts it. Garrison himself was a volcano of Old Testament cries and curses. For better and worse, he never shied away from the celebrated promise he printed in the first edition of the *Liberator:* "I will be harsh as truth and uncompromising as justice. . . . I do not wish to think, or speak, or write, with moderation. . . . I will not equivocate—I will not excuse—I will not retreat a single inch—AND I WILL BE HEARD."[2]

In the early 1830s, joining the abolitionists became a kind of religious conversion. True believers were born again and would rerun many of the familiar revival routines. Like religious enthusiasts back to 1636, some reformers (Stephen Foster, Garrison's printer at the *Liberator*, was notorious) disrupted services at churches that refused to condemn slavery. They exhorted the surprised worshippers to "come out" and save themselves by joining uncorrupted fellowships.[3]

Taking the abolition pledge was serious business—it could bring on violence and ruin reputations. The reform networks buzzed with gossip about just who would be next. "Fear of his popularity," wrote abolitionist James G. Birney about a colleague, "keeps him from coming out." All that ardor could get tiring. Lydia Maria Child, herself a prolific abolitionist, mocked the fetish for breaking every possible tie with slavery: "The come-outers talked to him till the tower of Babel seemed falling about his ears and his brain was all on fire. One told him to come out of one thing, and another out of another, till the whole earth seemed slipping away under his feet and the heavens rolling off overhead."[4]

Differences swiftly tore the abolitionists into factions. Should they compromise their principles for political progress? (Never, said Garrison.) What role, if any, should women play in the freedom movement? (As usual, that was a tough one.) How about African Americans? (Garrison and Frederick Douglass eventually came to loggerheads over this question.) Should black Americans get full civil rights? (Only radicals would go that far.) How about black men marrying white women? (You can imagine.) Like every American moral crusade, this one specialized in exposing terrible sinners. The hottest abolitionist jeremiad laid into the evil men who were tormenting the innocent and threatening the nation.

The Slaveholders' Sins

The abolitionists developed a picture of slaveholders that still stands as the classic construction of an immoral American other. Of course, the details of their attack were all rooted in the time. But from a more analytic angle, the abolitionists charged the slaveholders with the four great American trespasses: violence, intoxication, laziness, and sexual depravity.

Violence

The abolitionists vividly described the slave's physical suffering. Theodore Weld wrote the classic of the genre, *American Slavery As It Is: Testimony of a Thousand Witnesses*. The book culled newspapers and collected southern "narratives" to tell the ugly story. The cool reporting style and the simple accumulation of data gave the book a powerful impact. It remains painful reading more than 150 years later. In one section, for example, Weld simply reprinted advertisements for runaway slaves; each ad featured the telltale physical marks by which the owners identified the runaways: "a woman much scarred by whipping"; "a Negro boy . . . much marked with the whip"; "I burnt her with a hot iron on the left side of her face . . . to make the letter M." The book was an anti-slavery sensation—it sold 22,000 copies in its first four months.[5]

Weld's roster of cruelties became a standard on the abolitionist lecture circuit. Slaves were beaten, overworked, underfed, underclothed, and deprived of sleep. Frederick Douglass's autobiography (another anti-slavery sensation) went over the same ground in more depth and with more anger; he, too, described whippings, beatings, and killings. He also emphasized smaller, equally abusive violations. Douglas was often cold. As a child, he said, "I was kept almost naked—nothing but a coarse linen shirt reaching only to my knees." He often went hungry. "Our food was coarse corn meal boiled." This mush "was put in a large wooden . . . trough, set down upon the ground"; then the children were called, "like so many pigs, to devour the mush."[6]

The debate spilled into all sorts of nooks and crannies. For example, slavery apologists often wrote that the insensible slaves needed very little sleep. The abolitionists directly challenged this myth. The slaves often lacked beds, they argued, and never had enough time to sleep. After a long day in the fields, wrote Douglass, the slaves had "washing, mending, and cooking to do," and all without the "ordinary facilities for doing these." Douglass emphasized the relentless pace of slave time—the long workday, the chores at night, the driver's horn in the early morning, another hard day in the fields. And "there must be no halting," for the "large hickory stick and heavy cowskin" were always waiting for laggards. Like many features of the slavery debate, the image of sleepless black Americans would stick. Decades later the Progressives would embellish a kind of up-all-night black-vampire myth. And in the early 1990s, social welfare skeptics killed one spending measure, saying they would not sanction "midnight basketball in the ghettos." The theme had multiple morals: the black people were different, they were irresponsible, they were immoral, they were scary.[7]

Back in the 1830s, the violence narrative grabbed public attention. But, in the abolitionist calculus, the deeper consequence was worse. All that violence stripped slaves of moral agency over their own lives. Slavery annulled that great evangelical standard: a person's free will to choose God, to choose good. Hannah Johnson, a free black woman, put it this way in a letter to Lincoln: "Robbing the colored people of their labor is but a small part of the robbery. Their souls are almost taken, they are made bruits of often." The image of the pious

slave, kneeling in prayer, became an abolitionist icon—stamped on books, poems, cards, pamphlets, and sheet music.[8]

Abolitionists warned that all this cruelty would boomerang right back on
the masters. Slaveholders corrupted themselves by the power they wielded over
other human beings. Drawing on a classical republican critique of tyranny,
abolitionists pictured the slaveholders as men and women racked by their own
lust for power. They would endure all kinds of horrors, wrote Lydia Maria
Child, "rather than relinquish . . . despotic control." Like emperors or sultans,
"they had rather live in constant fear of . . . the midnight dagger than . . . give
up the pleasant exercise of tyranny."[9]

Intemperance

Puritan New England had long charged the self-indulgent South with
heavy drinking. The slavers, they said, were just like the Indians—children of
immediate passions. The critique was part of the Puritan obsession with mas-
tering all lusts, with moral self-control. The alcoholism charge runs through
the anti-slavery literature as both a metaphor and a scandal.[10]

The metaphor was ubiquitous: "Arbitrary power is to the mind what alcohol is to the body," wrote William Weld. "It intoxicates." "Alas," wrote Frederick Douglass about a sympathetic new owner, "the fatal poison of irresponsible
power was already in her hands, and soon commenced its infernal work." Precisely like alcohol, bondage subverted the masters. "That cheerful eye, under
the influence of slavery, soon became red with rage . . . that angelic face gave
place to a demon." Temperance crusaders worked the same analogy from the
other side—Lyman Beecher preached long sermons about the eternal "middle
passage and darkness and chains and disease and death" that came from drink.
Intemperance, said Beecher, must arouse in all Americans the same horrors as
slavery—intemperance was slavery.[11]

But the drinking charge went beyond analogy. Many of the abolitionists
had gotten their crusading start as temperance preachers, and they knew all
about the debauched southerners. The South had been hard territory for the
anti-drinking reformers even before temperance advocates got mixed up with
abolition. In 1831 the region had managed just 15 percent of the local temperance societies and a scant 8 percent of all pledges to stop drinking—a poor
showing for a region with 44 percent of the American population.[12]

Tracts, sermons, and lectures reported the "Terrible Parallel Between Intemperance and the Slave-Trade." The literature of anti-slavery made a stock
character of the drunken slaver. The crueler the master, the more he drank.
Harriet Beecher Stowe's Simon Legree—the epitome of the rapacious slave-

5.1. The Pious Slave, frontispiece to Lydia Maria Child, *An Appeal in Favor of the Class of Americans Called Africans* (1833). The slave kneeling in prayer was a popular image in the abolitionist press. The figures look noble (and often rather Caucasian), a distinct contrast to the grotesque racial distortions in the anti-abolitionist press. Compare figure 7.4. (Brown University Library)

holder—is never far from his brandy. Worse, the masters did not just indulge themselves, they pushed liquor on their slaves to degrade and more fully enslave them. The holiday binge became a standard feature of slave narratives and abolitionist propaganda. Legree forces drink down his enslaved mistresses till they cannot live without it.[13]

The intoxication narrative returned the abolitionists to a stock jeremiad warning: anyone might slip. Slaveholding was unspeakably sinful, but there was nothing morally unique about those southerners. The intoxicated slaveholder responded as any man or women would after falling under the influence—of liquor, of power, of any lust. Like Cotton Mather, warning his own people about becoming like the Indians, reformers knew how northern debauchery sanctioned southern depravity.

Finally, intemperance rendered slaveholders irrational, even demonic. They had fallen under the influence of a lower power. Here lay the greatest irony: slaveholders had not merely robbed the slaves of free moral will, they also abandoned moral control over their own lives.

Laziness

By relying on slaves, the whole South had grown enervated, backward, and poor. Those people did not seem to grasp what one social reformer called the "severe, Puritanic, Saxon . . . religion . . . of work." With this argument, the abolitionists hit paydirt in the North. Travelers kept returning from the South with stories of a dilapidated, underdeveloped region. The image of lounging masters explained the lagging southern economy.[14]

A young Henry Adams visited Virginia with his father in 1850. The older Adams saw the "pest of slavery visible everywhere" in the "sluggish and antiquated habits of the people." But it was young Henry who drew the concrete lesson: "To the New England mind . . . roads, schools, clothes, and a clean face were connected as part of the law of order or divine system. Bad roads meant bad morals." The implication of the rough Virginia journey was not hard for the Adams to puzzle through: "Slavery was wicked, and slavery was the cause of this road's badness which amounted to a social crime."[15]

Many northerners who scorned abolitionism accepted this picture of southern lassitude, even corruption. The *New York Daily Times* explained to the irate southerners "Why we meddle with your slavery" (in 1857): "Whatever impedes the advance or interferes with the prosperity of the Nation, of the United States as a grand consolidated empire, will excite the attention and invite upon itself the indignation of the northern states." The slave system violated the American gospel of work. This part of the attack on slavery swept far beyond the small band of abolitionists, but it rested on two grand Puritan themes: hard work and national mission. Slavery, concluded the *Times*, endangers "our prosperity and our destiny."[16]

Sex

Sexuality was dangerous territory for the abolitionists. When they called for freedom, opponents—North and South—heard racial mixing. Nor does it take any fancy textual deconstructing to find the sexuality. Sex was the reflexive, rhetorical counter every time Americans got a whiff of abolition.

Denials did not work. Lydia Maria Child wrote a painstakingly moderate catechism of anti-slavery. In it she put the question directly, then floundered about, searching for an answer that would not offend anyone.

> Q: You know that abolitionists are universally accused of wishing to promote the amalgamation of colored and white people.
> A: This is a false charge . . . a bugbear to increase the prejudices of the community . . . [a] silly and unfounded objection . . . trust Providence to take care of the matter. It is a poor compliment to the white young men to be so afraid that . . . the girls will all be running after the . . . colored ones.[17]

The abolitionists did a lot better with a direct attack. They said, essentially, look who's talking. "Can the slaveholder use the word amalgamation without a blush?" The slaveholders were the ones crossing that color line and fathering interracial children. The southern legal regime pandered to the slaver's lust, for children born of slave mothers were slaves. That, said Frederick Douglass, makes a "gratification of their desires, profitable as well as pleasurable." (Douglass himself wondered about "the whisper that my master was my father.")[18]

The result, wrote Harriet Jacobs in her narrative of a slave's life, was "all-pervading corruption." "The slave girl is reared in an atmosphere of licentiousness and fear." Forget the "religious principles inculcated by some pious mother, or grandmother, or good mistress." When the slave girl is fourteen or fifteen, the owner or his sons or his overseers start in with little bribes and presents; if those don't work, she gets lashed and starved. Resistance is futile. "My master was, to my knowledge, the father of eleven slaves," wrote Jacobs.[19]

The abolitionists spun all kinds of moral tales out of the southerners' debauchery: in one classic, the father anguishes over the fate of his own enslaved flesh and blood. The most gothic variety pictures the man, fallen into debt or hard times, selling his own son—an ironic moral counterpoint to the biblical Abraham, who would sacrifice his son, but not for lust or avarice. Another sensational Victorian story tsked about the inexorable medical consequences of southern profligacy; the unbridled carnality ravaged both the slaver and his sons. Still another variation featured white daughters who violated the ultimate taboo: "I myself have seen the master of such a household whose head was bowed down in shame," reported Harriet Jacobs, because everyone knew that "his daughter had selected one of the meanest slaves." The consequences of such unions were predictably sensational—lashed slaves, smothered babies, and a lifetime of shame for both the young woman and her parents. But these familiar parables were all flourishes around the central abolitionist theme: moral contagion spread like poison through the entire slave system. Lust lay at the very heart of slavery.[20]

"A slave country," wrote Unitarian minister William Ellery Channing, "is

5.2. The lust-inspired whipping was a standard in the abolitionist press. Like the elaborate descriptions of the slaveholders' debauchery, some depictions had a distinctly prurient flavor. (Manuscripts, Archives & Rare Books Division, Schomburg Center for Research in Black Culture, The New York Public Library, Astor, Lenox and Tilden Foundations)

reeking with licentiousness. It is tainted with a deadlier pestilence than the plagues. . . . Among the pollutions of heathenism, I know nothing worse than this." James Thome, who had grown up in slaveholding Kentucky and later joined the student rebels at Lane Theological Seminary, added his own pew-rattling rendition of the moral turpitude sermon: "This great system of licentiousness. Pollution, pollution! Young men of talents and respectability, fathers, professors of religion, ministers, all classes! Overwhelming pollution! I have facts; but I forbear to state them; facts . . . startling enough to arouse the moral indignation of the community." On it went—degraded, profligate, sinful. "The slave states are Sodoms and almost every village family is a brothel."[21]

5.3. T. S. Noble, *The Price of Blood*, 1868. The wealthy slaveholder has fallen into debt and is forced to sell his own mulatto son. The planter waits impatiently, drumming his fingers on the table. The handsome son looks angrily away. The slave trader, oblivious to all the emotional drama, carefully rereads the contract before turning over the gold coins stacked on the table. On the wall, to the right, Abraham is about to sacrifice his son. Two unfinished glasses of liquor add another sin to the terrible scene. (Morris Museum of Art, Augusta, Georgia)

Anti-slavery advocates pictured an erotic society without moral scruples or social checks. The analogies piled up: a Sodom, a Turkish harem, a brothel, a moral lazarhouse. One theme connected these depravities from all corners of the globe, argues Ronald Walters. In all these places—as on the plantations— men were free to indulge their worst erotic impulses with impunity.[22]

The image of rapacious slaveholders blurred into a wider picture of lascivi- ous southern society. Temptation was everywhere. In taverns, boardinghouses, and private homes, "boys and girls verging on maturity, altogether unclothed, wait upon ladies and gentleman, without exciting even the suffusion of blush on the face of the young females." Even women sank into slavery's depravity, their vaunted purity and virtue degenerating into a "mere boast and sham."[23]

Amid the sex scandal glinted an old theme that would later haunt race re- formers. One source of contagion, said abolitionists like James Thome, wafted up from the lower castes. The slaves (cut off from normal family life) passed the evenings in obscene merriment. "When the night is far spent, reported Thome, they "crown the scene with indiscriminate debauchery." Then, danger strikes. Smutty knowledge trickles from wild slave to innocent mistress—for they gos- sip together without any shame or sense of propriety. "The courtezan feats of the over-night are whispered into the ear of the unsuspecting girl, to poison her youthful mind." Thome safely pushed the corruption narrative in an abolition- ist frame. "This pollution is the offspring of slavery; it springs, not from the character of the negro, but from the condition of the slave."[24]

But once slavery was finally gone, the familiar image would be twisted back around to impeach black Americans struggling to make a new life. White lead- ers, snatching back their racial hegemony, found a familiar foundation on which to build their story. The slaves had always corrupted innocent girls. The danger had lain in the character of the Negro all along. All this lay decades off. But some abolitionists were building the foundations for future prejudices even as they thundered about the depravity of the slave masters.

Still, the abolitionists directed most of their fire at the legally protected slaveholding rapists, the true American amalgamists. This is the abolitionist theme that struck home in the South. Slavery's most ardent defenders con- ceded the point even as they pummeled the hated abolitionists.

Senator Benjamin Leigh, for example, took the Senate floor and roasted slavery's critics. But he began with one admission. There are "men of depraved, cruel, ruthless hearts in the slaveholding states." Sex with slaves? Well, "such facts . . . may have occurred." And in sharp contrast to the thumping denials with which he met every other abolitionist charge, Leigh managed just a weak—a downright milksop—defense on this one. "It is . . . wonderful how little amalgamation has taken place in the course of two centuries." "Particular instances of intemperate and shameless debauchery," allowed South Carolina's William Harper, "may perhaps be true." "There is one painful chapter," concurred W. Gilmore Simms. There are "too many cases . . . of illicit and foul conduct; some among us . . . make their slaves the victims and the instruments of the most licentious passions." Here—and only here—do the southern apologists offer concessions and excuses.[25]

The abolitionist hit can easily be exaggerated. As we shall see, men like Harper and Simms worked out aggressive justifications for all that "foul" and "illicit" conduct. Even raping black women played its role in uplifting white southern society. What the apologists could never concede was the blasphemy that southern white women were anything less than pure. Why, slavery and the "availability" of black women protected pure white women from male lust.

The most anguished cry on the whole subject of masters, slaves, and sex came from a prominent southern white woman. In three feverish sections of her Civil War diary, Mary Chesnut furiously (and famously) reflected on the southern double standard.

> God forgive us, but ours is a *monstrous* system and wrong and iniquity. . . . Our men live all in one house with their wives and their concubines, and the mulattoes one sees in every family exactly resemble the white children—and every lady tells you who is the father of all the mulatto children in everybody's household, but those in her own she seems to think drop from the clouds. . . . My disgust sometimes is boiling over. . . .
>
> Bad books are not allowed house room. But bad women, if they are not white or only in a menial capacity may swarm the house unmolested. The ostrich game is thought a Christian act. . . .
>
> I hate slavery. . . . What do you say to this? A magnate who runs a hideous black harem with its consequences under the same roof with his lovely white wife and his beautiful daughters. He . . . poses as a model of all human virtues to these poor women whom God and the laws have given him. . . . You see, Mrs. Stowe did not hit the sorest spot. She makes Legree a bachelor.[26]

Historians are still trying to pin down the sexual dynamics of slavery. The incidents of rape were probably diminishing as the argument over slavery was heating up. Winthrop Jordan suggests that race mixing was probably more prevalent in the eighteenth century than in the nineteenth. And Robert William Fogel and Stanley L. Engerman go further; not only did the miscegenation taboo grow stronger, they say, the whole rape narrative was vastly exaggerated. The latter argument, in turn, has provoked furious rejoinders. Catherine Clinton, for example, insists that we should not focus on counting up the interracial babies but on the larger social consequences of the slave regime: "emasculated male slaves, dehumanized female slaves and desexualized . . . plantation mistress[es]." The most jarring indictments on the sex and slavery issue, however, flow directly from the defenders of the system (see Chapter 6).[27]

Sexual stereotypes would be perpetuated, disputed, exaggerated, excused, defended, and dismissed right up to the Civil War. After the war, the race-mixing story itself would be reconstructed. White southerners turned rape into the "foul daughter of reconstruction." They rewrote all the old roles. They switched the villainous white master for the dangerous black freeman; they replaced the enslaved black victim with innocent white daughters. The new sex narrative permitted renewed racial brutality—justified in flowery moral language as the protection of white innocence. But one theme from the antebellum race wars survived intact: fear of race mixing. White Americans, both southerners and northerners, would find new ways to keep the old taboos in place, to hold a black "them" apart from a white "us."

With all their sex talk, the abolitionists managed to be both revolutionary and conservative. They attacked an entrenched order that showed little sign of succumbing. They preached revolution in American race relations. They broadcast the most scandalous kinds of accusations (back when it was completely impolite to do so). In many ways the abolitionists were genuine American radicals.

On the other hand, the picture of the lustful and uncontrolled South reinforced the charge that the Congregational synod first threw at the antinomians in 1637: these people did not control themselves, they did not conquer their cravings, they would not "crucify their lusts." The abolitionists revived the perennial Puritan charge.

Uncle Tom's Virtue

Where in all this propaganda were the African Americans? The answer takes us to another weird corner of the antebellum story. The abolitionists, along with most other white Americans, dreamed up elaborate stories about black people. Stereotypes are nothing unusual, of course; but antebellum United States may have been the golden age of stereotyping. African Americans ran a long moral gamut—from a degraded underclass to Christlike redeemers of all humankind. The sheer range of stereotypes highlights the key political point: every image gives the racial agenda a different twist. The depraved underclass provokes curfews, jails, and jeremiads; decent people who face unfair treatment get allies marching for social justice.

In the 1830s, the stereotyping began on familiar ground: Free African Americans lived in squalor and deprivation. They faced deep prejudice everywhere they turned. Even the jails discriminated; a reform school director told Alexis de Tocqueville that "it would be degrading to the white children to associate them with beings given up to public scorn." "Let us not flatter ourselves that we are in reality any better than our brethren in the South," wrote Lydia Maria Child. "The *form* of slavery does not exist among us; but the very *spirit* of the hateful and mischievous thing is here in all its strength."[28]

However, few white abolitionists appreciated the scope and depth of American racial animosity. Nor did they grasp how it was escalating amid that explosive Jacksonian mix: equality, economic competition, status uncertainty, and hints of black freedom. Most abolitionists simply bought the stereotypical view of African Americans as "degraded." Even Garrison: "What do we see? . . . Confessedly the most vicious, degraded, and dangerous portion . . . of the American people." And it went downhill from Garrison. All the underclass sins got pinned on free black people: "idleness," "indolence," "pauperism," "frolicking," "looseness of manners," "drunkenness," "intemperance," "vice," "crime," and so on. "Enlightened" whites were the ones who believed that environmental factors—racism, repression, exclusion—explained black sins.[29]

The facts could have supported a different story. Black Americans struggled against enormous odds. They sought comfort in their congregations (more than half the African Americans in Philadelphia, for example, were church members). They scraped together substantial piles of cash to buy relatives out of slavery—a quiet, hard-won route to liberty that proved, for all the abolitionist thunder, the most successful path until the Civil War. One survey in Cincinnati found that almost 75 percent of some 3,000 African Americans had "worked out their freedom" through the efforts of their families and friends. Here was solid material for building an entirely different kind of racial image.[30]

Instead, the abolitionists leaped over these real struggles and conjured up a more glorious racial rhapsody. White Americans had their aggressive Anglo-Saxon Manifest Destiny myths; some abolitionists cast black Americans in a kind of countermyth. The African race incarnated Christian virtue. "The Negro," preached Gilbert Haven, "has the most of Christ, he is the nearest to God." Historian George Fredrickson dug up this antebellum fantasy and termed it "romantic racialism."[31]

It all began with the image of the loyal, affectionate slave. Even the proslavers bought that one. As William Sullivan, an ardent Boston anti-abolitionist, put it, "The first recollections of my infancy are associated with Negro kindness and faithfulness. . . . The Negro, by disposition, is good-natured, obliging, and affectionate." Romantic racialists seized on the "kindly Negro" cliché, inflated it into an innate racial trait, and set it onto the stage of world history.[32]

Africa joined America as midwife to the looming millennium. Alexander Kinmont, an Ohio schoolmaster, explained the phenomenon in a series of celebrated lectures (1837–38). It is the "effect of a particular Providence, or to speak in the dialect of science, an express law of nature, that each peculiar race of men should occupy their own limits." The present age, said Kinmont, belonged to the Caucasian race, with its quick, hard, acquisitive, intellectual energy. But soon a "more advanced and millennial stage" of humanity would reflect the "softer attributes of divine . . . mercy and benevolence." Those "milder and gentler virtues" were the virtues of Africa.[33]

This Christian fantasy sprang from an abolitionist cry against the Jacksonian scramble for money, votes and land. The romantic African offered abolitionists a quixotic leap out of the crude, materialistic, manifestly destined braggart of a nation that increasingly sneered at the waning evangelical crusades. Black Christian virtues would lead humanity to its new age, to the millennium itself. The new era would be "sweet" and "mellow," and brimming with "innate love of goodness"—just like the black people everyone knew and loved.[34]

Throughout the 1840s, abolitionists embellished the romantic motif. They celebrated the black gift to America: an "infusion of gentler and less selfish qualities," such as "self-denial," "self sacrifice," and "meek, long-suffering, and loving virtue." The alleged black characteristics added up to a perfect description of Jesus and His teachings. White abolitionists had taken their all-American "underclass" and imagined it into the world's redeemer race.[35]

The theme reached its apotheosis in *Uncle Tom's Cabin*. Throughout the book Harriet Beecher Stowe described her millennial vision. "The Anglo Saxon race had been entrusted [with] the destinies of the world during its pioneer period of struggle and conflict." The stern, inflexible, energetic Anglo-Saxons were good at that. "But as a Christian I look for another era to arise." The great arc of history now turned to a different race.

> Come it must . . . [Africa's] turn to figure in the great drama of human improvement. . . .
>
> In that far off mystic land of gold and gems . . . and waving palms . . . the Negro race, no longer despised and trodden down, will . . . show forth . . . the most magnificent revelations of human life. Certainly . . . in their gentleness, their lowly docility of heart, their childlike simplicity of affection and facility for forgiveness . . . they will exhibit the highest form of the peculiarly Christian life. Perhaps . . . God . . . hath chosen Africa . . . to make her the highest and noblest . . . when every other kingdom has been tried and failed.[36]

Sometimes in her own voice, sometimes through her characters, Stowe revived the millennial dream and located it in black Christian heroism. And what a Christian martyr she conjured up to make her point. By sheer passive Christian love, Uncle Tom converts masters and slaves; he wins liberty for everyone else on the old plantation, though—like Christ—he gives up his own life to do so.

Stowe's book landed in the nation's drawing rooms with fantastic force. *Uncle Tom's Cabin* sold a million copies (there were 25 million people in the United States). The characters from the book immediately scampered into every corner of the American literary scene—even pro-slavery writing was soon crawling with Uncle Tom, Simon Legree, Little Eva, and the rest. At an especially parlous moment in the fight against slavery (the Fugitive Slave Act now implicated the whole nation in the chase for runaway slaves—see Chapter 7), the book refreshed the reforming spirit. Stowe reinforced the anti-slavery crusade as a fundamentally feminine exercise. As Jane Tompkins points out, *Uncle Tom's Cabin* is a book written by a woman, for women, about feminine virtue. Take another look at all those qualities that romantic racialism projected onto African Americans: they were loving, patient, meek, virtuous, Christian—precisely what supposedly characterized antebellum women.[37]

That soft, meek side of Christian virtue goaded the critics of *Uncle Tom's Cabin*. The Reverend J. B. Smith, a black minister, thought moral virtue called for a bit less patience and a lot more Christian militancy. William Lloyd Garrison's review of the novel took precisely the same line. Garrison went straight for the racial assumptions. The slaves "ought to shed no blood," "be obedient to their masters," wait for peaceful deliverance, and "abstain from all insurrectionary movements." Why? "BECAUSE THE VICTIMS ARE BLACK." Oppressed white men take up arms to vindicate their rights. Like the American revolutionaries, "they return blow for blow" to "the destruction of the oppressors." But blacks must submit and talk of nonresistance. How does Christ justify rebellion in the one and not the other, asked Garrison. "Are there two Christs?"[38]

Stowe herself eventually picked up the militant theme (her novel first appeared as a serial). For all its lush romanticism, *Uncle Tom's Cabin* ends in classic jeremiad: "And is America safe? . . . Can you forget . . . the day of vengeance? . . . Both North and South have been guilty before God. . . . Injustice and cruelty shall bring on . . . the wrath of Almighty God!" Four years later, Stowe returned to the "scenes and incidents of the slaveholding states," and put that Old Testament wrath at the center of her work. In a far bleaker novel, *Dred: A Tale of the Great Dismal Swamp*, Stowe tells a story based on Nat Turner's rebellion.[39]

Uncle Tom and Nat Turner loomed over the black experience, symbols of the contrasting approaches to white oppression—Christian virtue and righteous militancy. These alternatives, writes Wilson Jeremiah Moses, would pose the essential antinomy of black nationalism for the next century. On the one hand, the black community clung to biblical images of providential mission, moral superiority, and the idea of being "chosen." On the other hand, it scorned submission and longed to rise up and seize justice—angry, rebellious, and separate. For every Martin Luther King there would be a Malcolm X. Marcus Garvey would sardonically touch both sides of the equation when he cracked, "The black man has a kind heart and no one knows it more than the white man on the North American continent."[40]

The pictures of the black community—from Christlike Uncle Tom to vengeful Nat Turner—remind us that stereotypes are constantly contested. African Americans were scrambling to set the record straight, answer critics, correct allies, and urge virtue on one another. But it was never easy to challenge the propaganda about who they were, how they acted, and what the white majority ought to do about them.

Nothing illustrates the sheer capriciousness of these cultural pictures more than the romantic racialism dreamed up by well-intentioned allies. With a great leap, abolitionists rewrote black America from downtrodden underclass to redeeming Christians. The images of black America would not end there, of course. A long line of stereotypes—old and new, celebratory and disparaging—followed the antebellum images.

The romantic racialists unwittingly set up future racial stigma. Their watchwords for black America—"childlike," "simple," "humble"—radiated condescension. The old underclass stereotypes had dismissed black Americans as too lowly for the rough and tumble American economy; now the romantic racialists told them that they were too high and spiritual for it. Those Anglo-Saxons might be cruel in blood, but they would compete, acquire, and win. The Christian redeemers, on the other hand, were just not equipped for success. They were bound to fail, destined for poverty—at least until the dawn of the next millennial age. As George Fredrickson points out, no one told the Anglo-Saxons to toss their own purported racial traits and emulate those of the morally superior Africans.[41]

Even worse, the cause of their inevitable failure lay in their African genes. Romantic racialists acquiesced to the notion of innate racial types. The question became, simply, which stereotypes were most accurate? Just asking the question opened the white mind to all the vicious racial stories floating through the culture. With the best intentions, the romantics gave away the firmest ground from which to resist racism: the universal rights ostensibly written into the American creed.

Women and Their Promiscuous Assemblies

Women embodied the Christian virtues, too. Victorians gushed about feminine goodness. Women uplifted men and turned the family into the "very cen-

5.4. *Sweet Content.* The good wife radiates beneficence over her domestic sphere—
her grace falls on the children, the dog, and even the plow horse. When Father returns
from the hard, manly sphere, the feminine touch will soothe and uplift him, too. From
T. DeWitt Talmage, *The Pathway of Life.*

ter of earthly bliss"—"hearth" and "home" usually figured into the enthusiasm
as well. Romantic reformers saw the family as the key to transforming society;
social perfection meant spreading domestic virtues across the nation.[42]

Woman as moral paragon reflected the general lines of the African as ultimate Christian. Lydia Maria Child listed the warm and fuzzy similarities: both
woman and Negro were affectionate, spiritual, sentimental, religious, and submissive. And "both have been kept in subjection by physical force and considered rather in the light of property than as individuals." The abolition movement itself demonstrated the point. Women signed up for the fight against
slavery. Within a decade they found the entire abolitionist movement had
split—not over fighting slavery but over the women in the ranks. Once again,
gender turmoil lay at the very heart of the challenge to the standing order.[43]

It all began innocently. Anti-slavery reformers appealed to women's spiritual sensibilities. Since women were the "ministers of Christian love," they
could understand—they could feel—the cruelties of slavery. They especially
felt the crimes against women. Women's groups flaunted treacly gender plati-
tudes as their special qualification for pushing the cause. "Suffer us, we pray

you . . . as wives, as mothers, and as daughters" began the most popular of the anti-slavery petitions that buried Congress beginning in 1835. "We should be less than women, if the nameless, unnumbered wrongs of which the slaves of our sex are made the defenseless victims, did not fill us with horror." "When woman's heart is bleeding," added the Lynn (Massachusetts) Female Anti-Slavery Society, "shall woman's voice be hushed?"[44]

Buried among those "nameless unnumbered wrongs" lay the first moral trap. The slavery-rape narrative depicted a woman's horror. But what did the genteel white woman know about rape? Or, more accurately, what could she properly say about it in public? Lydia Maria Child tiptoed up to the topic in 1833: "The Negro woman is unprotected by law or public opinion." "Those who know human nature" might "conjecture," she wrote, about the "unavoidable result, even if it were not betrayed by the amount of mixed population."[45]

The abolitionists were not so delicate for very long. By the time Susan B. Anthony tackled the topic, three decades later, there was no need to mess with the little winks and nudges. "Mothers, I appeal to you. Half the slaves are women, helpless, defenseless creatures with no law, no religion, no public sentiment to shield them from the sensual Legrees who hunt them."[46]

Abolitionist women stirred up trouble in three different ways. First, beginning in 1835, they deluged Congress with petitions pleading for an end to slavery in Washington, D.C. The southern states would not abolish slavery, reasoned the petitioners, but Congress could wipe it out in the district. The sight of slave pens in the shadow of the Capitol became a great badge of American sin. As the petitions poured in, Congressman James Henry Hammond of South Carolina rose to propose that they be rudely rejected. Congress had never rejected public petitions, and the idea set off a month of ferocious debate and years of political fireworks.[47]

Some women's groups, especially in Massachusetts, took a second step. How could the North rip slavery when it tolerated its own invidious race laws, they asked. They petitioned against all discriminatory statutes. Naturally, they set off a holy furor—to put it mildly—when they condemned the bars on interracial marriage. Well, too bad if such a stand shocked the white menfolk, retorted the activists; northerners would have to accept that "the colored man is a man" (exactly what worried the white menfolk). Lydia Maria Child explained why it mattered: "This legalized contempt of color in Massachusetts . . . [directly] sustains slavery in the South, and is publicly quoted for that purpose." (The charge proved prophetic; the Dred Scott decision would go directly to this point.) Child went on to poke the commonwealth about its own peculiar heritage on women's issues: "Posterity will look back with as much wonder to the excited discussion on the subject as we do now to the proceedings of learned lawyers and judges who hung witches for raising a storm." By 1839, thirteen hundred women had signed petitions against the Massachusetts anti-amalgamation laws even before the legislature convened. They faced the inevitable mockery. "Sir," said one legislator, "I don't believe there is a virtuous woman among them." Another promised that he would not stop any lady who wished "to take to her embraces some gay Othello."[48]

Finally, some women went beyond essays and petitions. In the mid-1830s women began to lecture on abolition. They rattled the standards of the day by speaking before mixed groups of men and women—"promiscuous assemblies." The first American woman to lecture "promiscuously" about slavery was twenty-nine-year-old Maria Stewart, a black Bostonian. Stewart blended early feminism, standard antebellum gender views, and exhortations that black listeners improve themselves. Talking promiscuously was scandalous, she knew, but "it is no use for us to wait for a generation of well educated men to arise." "We have never had the opportunity of displaying our talents," she told the black women in the audience, "therefore, the world thinks we know nothing."[49]

Stewart was on the lecture circuit for less than a year. She was followed by Sarah and Angelina Grimké, sisters from a South Carolina slave-owning family. The Grimkés became the first female agents for the American Anti-Slavery Society and began to work the sewing circles and parlor meetings. Unfortunately for genteel moral strictures, they proved extremely effective speakers. Men began to filter into their lectures; at first the men stood in back, but soon—typical males—they boldly took seats right up front. Suddenly, promiscuous groups were assembling all over the place.

By 1838 thousands of people were gathering in large halls to lectures by women like Angelina Grimké, Lucretia Mott (a Quaker minister who had run the meetings where the Grimkés first spoke out), and Abby Kelley Foster (a Quaker from Lynn, Massachusetts). In May 1838, all three spoke before some three thousand people in the grand salon of Philadelphia's new Pennsylvania Hall, the reformers' marble temple to free speech. When Grimké rose to speak, a large mob outside began to smash the windows with stones and brickbats. As William Lloyd Garrison described the scene, the tumult only kindled her eloquence. "Her eye flashed, and her cheeks glowed, as she devoutly thanked the Lord that the stupid repose of that city had been disturbed by the force of truth." Grimké gave an extraordinary speech—for more than an hour she spoke over the roaring mob and the crashing glass.[50]

The rioters finally shouted down the convention and then burned the building to the ground—a pretty accurate measure of how most Americans felt about promiscuous assemblies and abolition societies. Philip Hone, an aristocratic Philadelphian, wrote unsympathetically in his diary: "A large portion of the abolitionists assembled in the hall were females, of whom several ha-rangued the meeting and were foremost in braving the excited populace." What really got the mob stoked, reported Hone, was the shocking spectacle "of white men and women walking arm in arm, with blacks . . . in the public streets." Where would it end? "This dreadful subject gains importance every day and reflecting men see in it the seeds of the destruction of our institutions."[51]

The very idea of women getting mixed up in politics became one of the most familiar objections to abolition itself. It is a rare anti-abolition tract that does not deplore the females. The critics all returned to the same two themes: proper gender roles and improper sexual partners. The women had fallen from their God-given place; conservatives wrung their hands over gender "spheres" and "orbs." Alongside the fretting over proper spheres came the racialist expressions of sexual disgust. James K. Paulding, a northern Democrat angling for a post in the Van Buren administration, touched on both themes in the standard anti-abolition style.

> From various notices we have seen of abolition meetings in Boston and else-where, it would appear that the abolition societies consist principally of fe-males. . . . We would take this occasion to remind them that the appropriate sphere of women is their home and their appropriate duties at the cradle or the fireside.
>
> Surely they cannot be aware of the direct inference which must and will be drawn from their support of the disgusting doctrine of amalgamation, namely, that they stand ready and willing to surrender themselves to the embraces of ig-norance and barbarity, and to become the mothers of a degraded race of wooly-headed mulattoes. . . . Gracious heaven! what prostitution![52]

Opponents went straight to the terror of that "degraded race." Of course, when the issue was repealing the amalgamation statutes, the sex angle was out there—swift, loud, and predictable. Repeal the marriage law, warned one newspaper, and the "real Anglo-Saxon blood" of Massachusetts would vanish. The *Boston Morning Post* snidely drew the standard inference: "Perhaps some of these ladies despair of having a white offer and so are willing to try the colored race." And what, asked the critics, "was the condition of the gentlemen whose wives' names appeared on the petitions?" It was a rhetorical question, of course, because the answer was obvious: the wives wanted black men instead of their feeble husbands.[53]

Even when the issue turned away from marriage or amalgamation, sexuality remained at the center of the storm. In 1833, for example, Prudence Crandall opened a school for black girls in Canterbury, Connecticut. Garrison nosed around the area incognito and reported what the local folks were saying.

One "poor fellow was horrified at the thought of intermarriages between the whites and the blacks." Another declared "if he had a sister who should marry a nigger he would put a ball into his (the nigger's) heart in a moment." Of course, marriage was hardly involved when a white woman ran a school for young black girls. No matter, the townspeople condemned, harassed, sued, and mobbed the school. The state legislature did its part by outlawing such schools. Together, they soon drove Crandall and her radical notions right out of town.[54]

When the critics finally got beyond amalgamation, they started in on the horrors of the promiscuous assemblies. The fuss may seem silly today, but reformers were subverting the whole antebellum gender view. Instead of "cheering the family hearth" and "radiating social virtues," women were crashing out of their sphere and "rushing into the fierce (read: male) struggles of political life." "Woman moving calmly in her own sphere, is as lovely as the evening star," wrote William Sullivan. However, "it is as unbecoming to her to appear in the world *dis-robed,* as unattired." Even some activists grew queasy. "Is it not very difficult to draw the boundary line?" asked one female abolitionist. "On the one hand, we are in danger of servile submission to the . . . other sex," on the other of "losing that modesty, & instinctive delicacy . . . which our Creator has given us as a safeguard."[55]

The Congregational clergy of Massachusetts brought the crisis to a boil in 1837. The New England fathers did not care for women sermonizing any more than they had when Anne Hutchinson led her meetings two centuries earlier—though Hutchinson had stoutly denied ever mixing men and women. Now the clergy issued a sharp pastoral letter: "The power of woman is in her dependence, flowing from . . . the weakness which God has given her for her protection. . . . When she assumes the place and tone of a man as public reformer" she thwarts God's plan that men care for and protect her. The clergy hauled out those familiar scraps of St. Paul—for a woman to speak in church is a shame. They warned of danger to the family. And they pleaded with the women to consider common custom and propriety.[56] The Grimké sisters did not back off a bit. Common custom and propriety? That's what the slavers were saying. And wasn't slavery the real sin? God had called on them to testify. How could they walk away?

The clergy's attack forced a tactical question. How should the abolitionist women respond? Many abolitionists begged the women to just stop (actually, most *demanded* that they stop). It detracted from anti-slavery; women could still be involved, they said. They could form their own societies, they could go back to the sewing circles. Others, like Lydia Child, urged a middle position. "It is best not to talk about our rights but simply go forward and do what we deem our duty." That is, politely ignore the fuss and keep preaching. Garrison would have no pusillanimous little compromises. He showered contempt on the pious clergymen who turned a blind eye to slavery—which licensed rape while it barred marriage—and then had the face (said Garrison) to rebuke the women who spoke out against this terrible sin.[57]

The gender issue eventually split the abolition movement. In 1840 the annual meeting of the American Anti-Slavery Society elected Abby Kelley Foster to the executive committee over the furious objection of a large minority (the vote was 557 to 451). Philanthropist Lewis Tappan denounced the selection, judging it "immoral for a lady to sit behind closed doors with gentlemen." He led hundreds of delegates out of the meeting room and into a rival organization. "The split was . . . chiefly because Garrison and his party . . . foisted upon the American Anti-Slave Society the women question," scribbled Tappan in a note to Weld. "All have a right to be *members* but the *business* to be conducted by the men." The women made such a fuss that "the slave has been lost sight of."[58]

Traditional scholars bought Tappan's argument. The radicals had forced a fringe idea onto a respectable moral cause. They may have been ahead of their time, but back then they could only bring scorn on abolition. Today the women's side gets a more generous hearing. No one "forced" gender issues on abolition societies. Reformers recruited a talented group of women with fine words about nobody having "the right to make property of another man." Then, as Lydia Child put it, the husbands and brothers and ministers who had recruited them began to shout, " 'Stop there!' " Do not sign those petitions, do not speak before men, do not "publicly gush of a sister's sympathy." But the women were not about to stop. Like the sorcerer's apprentice, the men "who urged women to become missionaries and form tract societies . . . have changed the household utensil to a living, energetic being; and they have no spell to turn it into a broom again."[59]

Amid the chorus of nay-saying, reported Child, "a new and agitating Idea took shape. . . . Why has a women nothing to do with politics?" One agitating idea led to another. Next came what Susan B. Anthony described as the "grand idea of pecuniary and personal independence. Woman must have a *purse* of her own and how can this be, so long as the 'wife' is denied the right to her . . . earnings?" The slippery slope led directly to nineteenth-century feminism: the urge to speak out against slavery fostered an "agitating Idea" of political rights followed by the "grand idea" of economic independence. And all these subversive reflections fostered an attack on the basic principle that married women gave up their legal rights, that they were "dead in the law."[60]

The Seneca Falls Convention (July 1848), the first American political meeting focused on women's rights, illustrates the push that the abolitionists' resistance gave to gender rights. The convention's organizers, Lucretia Mott and Elizabeth Cady Stanton, met at an abolition convention in London in 1840; leaders at that meeting rejected the credentials of women from American anti-slavery societies and shuffled them off to the visitor's galleries. "We have good cause to be grateful to the slave," summed up Abby Kelley Foster. "In striving to strike *his* chains off, we found, most surely, that *we* were manacled ourselves."[61]

Civil rights campaigns would mix race and gender right through the next century. Ironically, the two causes seesawed as the "unrealistic" reform. In antebellum America, abolitionists pleaded against the rash, lewd gender agitation. The United States was choking on slavery. What point was there in throwing sexual equality onto the reformer's plate as well? Even Frederick Douglass, a strong advocate of gender equality, lamented the new focus. Douglass wrote almost lyrically about Abby Kelley Foster. Her simple beauty, "large knowledge and great logical power bore down all opposition. . . . She was the most successful of any of us." Still, added Douglass, how "beautiful" it would have been if she had turned down that nomination to the executive committee, saying, "I can for the slave's sake forgo the privilege . . . the slave's cause [is] already too heavily laden."[62]

Sixty years later, reformers made precisely the opposite argument. What reform might the Progressive-era United States agree to swallow? Women's rights. Proponents would hush reformers pushing racial equality. They read Frederick Douglass's lament back the other way: the women's cause is already too heavily laden; raising the race issue would be too unpopular, it would drive the South crazy, it would doom women's suffrage altogether. Still another half-century later, liberals fighting for the Civil Rights Act of 1964 would shift the charges of "unrealistic" back to gender; feminist issues—like banning gender discrimination in the workplace—threatened the racial cause that seemed "already too heavily laden."

Once again, the sex question lay beneath a moral conflict. My biggest surprise in surveying American moral crusades is how regularly sex wars run through them. The gender turmoil around the abolitionists looks like the gender turmoil among the early Puritans. Once again women were preaching, instructing men, and challenging the ministers; once again everyone heard all about St. Paul, godly order, and roles "fitting" for their gender. In the 1830s, each side taunted the other with historical analogies. "A Quaker woman had been known publickly to walk through the streets of Salem, *naked as she was born*," reported a New Haven minister. "Miss Grimké [has] not made such an exhibition of herself *yet*." Abolitionist James Birney opposed promiscuous assemblies, but he cut the clergyman, twice, over this foul language and proudly broadcast the details of their spat. On the other side, abolitionists like Lydia Maria Child scored their own Puritan points with analogies to despotic witch-hunting fools.[63]

Beneath the squabbles lay a profound challenge to the social order. The abolitionist women were testing both the race line and traditional gender controls. Each issue brought trouble, and mixing the two was dynamite.

Take the gender issue. Activists were raising questions about the role of women in contemporary society. What was the women's sphere? What, for that matter, was the nature of the family? The basic demographics were already moving fast. The American fertility rate fell 12 percent between 1840 and 1850 alone—it dropped even further in New England. The economic logic of the family was also shifting; farming gave way to urban, industrial capitalism. Where did the changes leave gender roles? As we have seen, the alternatives on the American social agenda covered a vast range—from romantic gush about moral guardians in their domestic sphere to the radical rights championed at Seneca Falls. Antebellum society wrestled over its most basic social institution. Today we would call it a culture war.[64]

In this anarchic social context, radicals seemed intent on razing American racial controls. What that meant, in the nineteenth century, was amalgamation. The din grew as each political side blamed someone else—the slaveholders were ruthlessly mixing, the abolitionists were eager to mix, the abolitionist women were incredibly naive about mixing. Smack in the middle of the storm, women assailed traditional barriers—even the bars to interracial marriage. All the talk about crashing orbs and spheres stood for something serious: women ultimately controlled the race line. Those who plunged into abolitionist politics seemed to break with all the traditional social controls—both racial and gender norms.

The charge against Anne Hutchinson echoed back on a new generation of disorderly women. The Puritan histories had accused Hutchinson of bearing "false conceptions." The phrase had two meanings. She promoted dangerous ideas; she fornicated with devils and conceived stillborn monsters. The Puritan pun neatly summed up the fears provoked by female abolitionists. Their ideas were alarming. And sleeping with the wrong people (the harsher Anglo-Saxons would say sleeping with the devil) endangered the entire Anglo-Saxon destiny. The racialist texts could not howl loud or long enough about a national fate of monstrous "wooly-headed mulattoes."

Sin is about losing control, about failing to "crucify lusts." That's why sex always figures into the underclass. But the sharp point of the gender fear was the way "they" threatened to melt into "us." Controlling any dangerous them—Indians, Africans, poor people, immigrants—ultimately rests on regulating sexual relations. On controlling "our" women.

Jacksonian America was open, egalitarian, tumultuous, and frightening. All that flux sparked another debate about the boundaries of American liberalism, about the nature of America itself. Who ranked where? Abolitionist women plunged into the political fray with a moral challenge to the most basic American social boundaries. The raw animosity they met—raw eggs and brickbats and arson—welled up from the deep threat they posed to the social status quo. Even in the fluid age of Jackson—especially in the fluid age of Jackson—the radical women frightened many Americans who were not ready to reconsider their basic race and gender boundaries. Once again the Eve narrative went to the heart of American cultural conflict. The Genesis parable seemed right on the mark. Women carried the disruptive power of letting the other take a place in the American Eden. What a mess that would make of the ancient tribal question: Who are we? Abolitionists set off a storm across America with their deeply troubling answers.

Chapter 6
South:
The Pro-Slavery Argument

Afull-scale attack on bondage shook the political scene. Starting in the early 1830s, abolitionists organized, Britain abolished slavery, the women's petitions hit Congress, and anti-slavery pamphlets started reaching the South. Under the barrage, white southerners tossed aside the airy African-colonization schemes and developed a full-blown pro-slavery argument. The Virginia legislature, frightened by Nat Turner's rebellion, took one last heated look at the alternatives (in 1831–32). Beginning with Thomas Dew's review of that debate, southerners portrayed slavery as a "positive good" and as the "cornerstone" of southern civilization.

From a distance, the pro-slavery argument looks like the fiercest attack on liberalism in American intellectual history. Southern theorists lined up to blast Jefferson's idea that all men are created equal: "ridiculously absurd" (Governor Henry Hammond); a "sentimental phrase . . . palpably false" (William Harper); "sentimental French philosophy" destined to drown all France in blood (W. Gilmore Simms); the "architect of ruin . . . useless, if not dangerous" (George Fitzhugh). These southerners appeared to construct an alternative America based on systematic repression.[1]

The pro-slavery project makes for painful reading. One scholar calls it a "wild," "weird" "mass of agonies," "well nigh berserk." The arguments appear to echo from a distant, happily buried past. But they pivot around a familiar American theme: race. Slavery's defenders literally defined their society by the black men and women at its bottom, by their "mud-sill" class. Many defenders built their racial arguments on moral claims: slavery uplifted slaves; it made white women more virtuous and white men more responsible. All stressed the need to control moral inferiors. And with that, we're right back to an especially ugly variation of the main Puritan theme: controlling the immoral other.[2]

The pro-slavery argument (violently) underscores a story that ran through the Puritan history: The efforts to control the immoral other do the work which Americans (and their favorite visitors like Alexis de Tocqueville) have long ascribed to the liberal tradition. The imperatives of sorting us from them, moral from immoral, and—in this chapter—black from white, give American politics its distinctive frame, its focus, and its furies.

It's Good for Them

The pro-slavery forces did not attack just Jefferson and the Declaration of Independence. They rejected the very idea of a society based on a social contract. The southern apologists of the 1830s turned from John Locke to Edmund Burke. Societies, they argued, develop slowly through the ages. Revolutionary changes bring blood and terror. Slavery was rooted deep in southern society and immediate abolition would yield nothing but annihilation. "Be it good or bad," repeated the apologists, slavery is so "interwoven in our society and institutions" that "to destroy it is to destroy us as a people." But, they all added hastily, slavery was a noble achievement that improved everyone.[3]

Moral Stewards

The southerners met abolitionist moralizing with pro-slavery moralizing. Slavery was God's plan. It rescued the African, said William Gilmore Simms, from a land where "he was destined . . . to eat his fellow or be eaten by him." The slaves arrived here, John Calhoun told the Senate, "in a low, degraded and savage condition." The stewardship of the southern masters had lifted them up. "Never before has the black race attained a condition so civilized and so improved . . . physically, morally, and intellectually." The slave, echoed John H. Van Evrie, a New York physician, is in the "best moral condition possible *for him.*" Slavery was part of a "divine plan for promoting the general progress of civilization and elevating . . . humanity."[4]

Simms, a South Carolina novelist and one-term Congressman, explained God's deal with the masters: "The slaveholders of the south, having the moral and physical guardianship of an ignorant and irresponsible people under their control, are the great moral conservators. . . . *Providence has placed [the slave] in our hands, for his good, and has paid us from his labor for our guardianship.*"[5]

The moral guardian theme runs through the literature. The urge to enslave is part of God's natural order, wrote William Harper. However, the enslaver carries the "highest moral responsibility and is most guilty if he wantonly inflicts misery or privation on beings more capable of . . . suffering than brutes, without . . . any view to the greater good which is to result."[6]

What "greater good" is he talking about? The slaves' own moral improvement, of course—the answer to all that ignorant abolitionist propaganda about cruelty. Take the "blows" and "stripes" that "drive" the slave to labor. "Such punishment would be degrading to a freeman," explained Harper. "It is not degrading to a slave." Simms clinched the point with a swipe at another degraded race: "Pity it is that the lousy and lounging lazzaroni of Italy cannot be made to labor in the fields under the whip of a severe task-master!" (The *lazzaroni* were homeless beggars in Naples.) "They would then be . . . a much nobler animal then we could possibly esteem them now."[7]

The happy men and women flourishing under slavery's moral tutelage contrasted with their lurid shadow—black people who had slipped out from under the stewardship of the white slave driver. Again and again writers pictured the horrors of emancipation in Latin America. Colombia and Guatemala blundered into emancipation, wrote Thomas Dew. The results were "a lazzaroni in rags and filth, a colored population drunken and revengeful, her females licentious and her males shameless." Both men and women carried knives, and the murder rate ran to one a day (five on holidays). Emancipation inexorably brought "relapse into darkness, thick and full of horrors."[8]

J. K. Paulding reported more of the same in Jamaica. After England abolished slavery, the streets of Kingston rang with "drunken debauchery, Negro drumming, and dancing. Jamaica promises to become [a] pestiferous sink of vice and corruption." Worse, the whole island was one big "apprentice[ship] for laziness." For Santo Domingo or Haiti, just stir in a few additional depravities and repeat. (Like a proper northerner, Paulding lingered indignantly on the sin of laziness.)

Despite Paulding's intent, a very different story glimmers between his lines. Jamaican licentiousness spilled out "under the mask of preaching and singing at the evening conventicles"—the dissenters' religious services. Religion? Wouldn't religious fervor make a hash of the moral degradation story? Worse, Paulding frets about all the time being lost from work for religious service—an ancient lament that generations of preachers (from Jonathan Edwards to Lorenzo Dow) delighted in slamming. Paulding eventually scrambles off to a trustier outrage, the dangers of amalgamation.[9]

On its face, the slavery argument is sui generis. It is difficult to imagine a crueler story. But read abstractly, a familiar fear leaps out from the pro-slavery tracts. A dangerous class is incapable of self-control, so the virtuous people must impose control. The dangers that allegedly loom when black people break free ring perfectly familiar: violence, drunkenness, laziness, and a dozen synonyms for sexual depravity. Here is the very paradigm of the dangerous American other. Left to its natural inclinations, this group would threaten good people, ruin our culture, and endanger the United States itself—just as it debauched the once idyllic Caribbean.

The Limits of Moral Stewardship

The stewardship argument eventually hit a snag. If African Americans were flourishing under all this tutelage, what was to stop them from rising till they were fit for freedom? W. Gilmore Simms got all tangled up in this issue. "Taught by our schools and made strong by our training, the Negroes of our southern states may arrive at [a] . . . condition . . . such as would enable [them] to go forth out of bondage." (The original version of the piece had been even stronger; Simms had "doubted not . . . that the time will come.") In a remarkable admission Simms wondered if perhaps, "like Pharaoh, we too shall prove unwilling to give up our bondmen." Simms sounds like a black preacher parsing Exodus. But by the end of a very long paragraph he has scrambled back to safety: "I do not believe that he will ever be other than a slave."[10]

For a moment Simms had almost twisted the racial discussion back into the framework of all-American individualism. Even in the thick of the repressive pro-slavery project, a flash of liberal rights glimmered briefly. The trouble lay in the apologists' urge to celebrate Christian stewardship. Steady training, hard work, and moral guidance might yield what? Success? Mobility? Freedom? Nothing but endless generations of slavery?

The Puritans had run aground on precisely the same work-ethic shoals. Puritans were supposed to work hard while somehow remaining in the social niche God had selected for them. Unfortunately for Puritan theology, New England economics rewarded the striving bounders. Slavery ruled out that prospect. But many of its defenders found themselves ensnared in the same contradiction: they insisted on a fixed social order but could not resist the language of upward (moral) mobility. They morally lifted up their slaves—higher than Native Americans or Mexicans or Colombians—but never high enough for freedom.

One vicious solution to these ambiguities simply slammed the door on the slaves by denying their humanity. Josiah Nott, an Alabama physician, used scientific ethnography to "deny the unity of the human species." (Privately, he called his skull-measuring studies "niggerology.") Nott dismissed Africans as subhuman. Others picked up the motif. In 1853, Van Evrie "strip[ped] off the skin of the Negro" to demonstrate that "he is not a black white man, or a man merely with a black skin, but a different and inferior species of man." Van Evrie was particularly distressed by the images of noble black men and women in *Uncle Tom's Cabin*. He trotted out allegedly scientific data—skull measurements again—and concluded that the racial difference "is radical and total" and would stand "as long as the present order of creation itself lasts." Van Evrie placed African people "somewhere between the 'Ouran Outan' and the Caucasian, though somewhat closer to the former." Well, that theory took care of any upward mobility or fanciful dreams of freedom. And by reducing people to beasts, it shrugged off cruelty.[11]

The allegedly scientific argument came at too high a price for many southerners. Asserting separate origins challenged the scriptures. What about Genesis? How about Adam and Eve? Worse, the scientific argument threatened the influential southern churchmen. Nott's reputation grew tarnished in a long brawl with the clergy. And all for what? The Bible—as white southerners read it—sanctioned slavery loud and clear. The very first human record of slavery, reported minister Thorton Stringfellow, was right there in Genesis. Noah's youngest son, Ham, had gaped at his father while the old man lay drunk and naked. When Noah sobered up he cursed Ham's son: "Cursed be Canaan, a servant of servants shall he be unto his brethren." Through a tendentious bit of Old Testament exegesis, Ham became the progenitor of Africans. The curse of Canaan clung to them through all time.[12]

The pro-slavery argument, writes Stephen Jay Gould, constitutes the last time that scriptures would definitively trump science in the service of racism. But the raw politics of racial difference gathered steam in the 1850s. Jefferson Davis, then the Secretary of War, described Van Evrie's ravings about Africans as an inferior species as an "able and manly exposure of a fallacy which . . . has disturbed the tranquility of our people." Darwin's *On the Origin of Species* (1859) burst onto the scientific scene at the end of the decade and offered a whole new framework for debating race.[13]

On the surface, the slavery apologists fenced with one another about the true nature of the slaves. In practice, the schools overlapped. Both pictured African Americans as brutes, but they disagreed over just why this was so. Both defended whipping, but one side fancied it a moral education. Both stressed the dangers of losing control over black people. Both sensationalized the horrors of emancipation. And they all went on and on about the moral and political importance of slavery to white society.

Good for Us

Southerners often called slavery the cornerstone of their civilization. Alexander Stephens, the newly elected vice president of the Confederate States, made the metaphor famous in 1861. Both the old southern society and the new Confederate government, said Stephens, laid its cornerstone "upon the great truth that the Negro is not equal to the white man." Whether "by nature or by curse against Canaan" (this politician did not have to pick sides in that fight), "subordination is his place."[14]

The cornerstone rested on another architectural metaphor, the mud-sill—a foundation timber placed directly on the ground. James Henry Hammond, in a speech to the Senate in 1858, explained that a society's lowest-ranking group, "constitutes the . . . mud-sill." Slavery gave the South a mud-sill class. The entire social edifice rested on the group bound to the bottom. "If there are sordid, servile, and laborious offices to be performed," asked William Harper, "is it not better that there should be sordid, servile, and laborious beings to perform them?" Conveniently, this "inferior and servile" caste is "infallibly marked"; its members can be cast into slavery at birth.[15]

Women and Purity

When it came to their women, the antebellum southerners outgushed everyone. They pushed the "higher," "gentler," "more spiritual" gender story to new heights. Woman is weak. Her sexual organs, wrote Thomas Dew, render her domestic, timid, and long-suffering. Precisely because she cannot push herself forward we can calibrate a civilization's virtue by her "elevation in society." And what most elevates the women? Why, slavery. The labor of slaves directly substitutes for women's work. "She ceases to be a mere beast of burthen." She instead becomes the "cheerful animating centre of the family circle." The usual bounty follows: "reflection," "the cultivation of all those mild virtues," "charm and delight around our homes and firesides." The blessings flow to everyone. She soothes the male temper and lifts the slave to greater happiness. The pro-slavery literature repeatedly celebrated this picture of feminine perfection.[16]

In actual practice, the virtuous woman propaganda simply imposed new limits on what was already a hard life. Plantation women oversaw a complicated domestic economy—household management, food production, and all that uplifting of the slaves and the menfolk. Life was even more difficult for women on the small, hardscrabble upcountry farms. As Stephanie McCurry describes it, the small farmer's proud political independence rested on the women's relentless work. White women and (sometimes) slaves "grew, raised, preserved and cooked" almost everything the household ate; the women "spun and wove, dyed and sewed" practically everything they wore. The hard work in both kitchen and field, on both great plantation and yeoman farm, never made it into the southern gender romances.[17]

Instead, the tracts focus on a theme that the abolitionists were trumpeting—sex. At the heart of the southern gender narrative lay purity. And the image of white purity came at the price of what might be called the sexual mud-sill—an almost gothic blend of misogyny and racism.

The abolitionist lust attacks got under the skin of slavery's defenders. "It might be supposed," huffed William Harper, "that a slaveholding country was one wide stew for the indulgence of unbridled lust." There indeed might be "particular instances" of "brutes and shameless debauchees," but those exist in every country. Vice in the South, however, did not "debase the civilized." As W. Gilmore Simms explained, the Negro and the colored woman in the South filled the place that white girls filled in the North. Consequently, male lust affects only a race that has no "consciousness of degradation." It (that is, rape—a lot of pronouns sidestep the ugly reality in these tracts) "scarcely affects the mind of the Negro and does not materially affect his [her!] social status." In fact, reports Harper, the female slave feels no more shame than she would over some "venal impropriety." Her fall "has done no great injustice to herself."[18]

But think of the benefits. In the South there is no divorce, almost no adultery, and no court actions for "criminal conversation" with another man's wife. The purity of the southern woman comes from the "existence of an enslaved class of relaxed morals." Raping slaves leaves white women—and society as a whole—free from all the complications of sex, lust, and the messy social repercussions of pelvic sins.[19]

On the other side, the white male might give in to lust, but he will feel "repulsion" and "something of degradation in the act." He is not going to become fascinated by a slave; he is not going to get entangled in her "allurements" to the destruction of "his principle, worth and vigor." And there is no danger about "bewildered . . . moral feelings" that confuse the "boundaries of virtue and vice." The sex is completely safe—for white society. Men and women of the same class do not fall into "social licentiousness" with one another. Slavery makes white women pure and white men manly.[20]

The slavery defense ends with a counterattack. While southerners carefully protect their white women and their marriages, look what the North does to its daughters. Up there, the harsh, cold market capitalists throw the women to their terrible, anonymous perdition. Prostitutes huddle in the cities; women abandon the babies they cannot afford or never wanted; moral reformers open homes for "fallen girls" (unheard of in the South). And it gets worse: divorce, rape, sexual assault, and feminism. All these violations of the natural order are unknown in the South.

Today, academic commentaries often seem dulled to slavery's horror. One historian speculates that at least some owners must have fallen in love with beautiful slave mistresses—and the slaves with their masters. Others write that the frequency of rape has been exaggerated; that such incidents diminished over time; that adult slaves were generally well fed and decently cared for. The most eloquent responses to such cold speculation lie in the defense of slavery itself. In tract after tract, on page after page, defenders of slavery begin by justifying the system and end up cataloguing the most brutal attitudes and terrifying practices. Reading them is like walking through a chamber of horrors.[21]

Men and Politics

With slaves doing the hard labor, southern men had time for the chivalrous pursuits of gentlemen—"constant exercise with weapons and on horseback," for example. And, of course, they had time for politics. Even the lower-class whites, wrote Hammond, "are higher toned," thanks to the social status that lifts them above the mud-sill class. "However high or low, rich or poor," argued Vice President Stephens in his "cornerstone" address, white men all enjoy equality in the eyes of the law.[22]

The writers were explicit about slavery as a solution to the old Republican conundrum: How do we combine universal suffrage with stability and deference? As Hammond and many others argued, the poorest and most ignorant half of the population was, in the South, simply ruled out of politics. That still left poor, uneducated white voters, of course; but they would be more deeply invested "in preserving a stable and well ordered government than the same class in any other country."[23]

What the slaveholders managed was one solution to the classic problem of political order and stability. We've seen Winthrop's Puritan view. James Madison devised a more familiar alternative in *Federalist* no. 10. Madison's plan protected the (presumably wealthy) minority by expanding the scope of government and letting the great pluralism of interests check one another so that no group trampled the rights of any other. A half-century after the slavery debate, Chancellor Otto Von Bismarck would confront the same political problem, now known as working-class unrest, and hit upon a very different solution—buying worker loyalty with social welfare programs. The slavery regime produced its own formula for stabilizing society and controlling the non-slaveholding majority. Slavery offered white men social rank and invested them in the status quo.

Treating the pro-slavery argument as a terrible aberration makes it easy to overlook the broader applications of this southern recipe for social stability. W. E. B. Du Bois found the same spirit in poor white workers after the Civil War and called it the "wages of whiteness"—a kind of psychic wage, said Du Bois, that protected the social order. Even disadvantaged white mobs knew they would lose their "wage" if radicals leveled society and disrupted the racial hierarchy.[24]

Social scientists normally find pluralism at every twist in the American political story. What explains American politics? Ultimately, in this view, the flux of groups, the ideology that celebrates the pursuit of self-interest, and the constitutional structure that frames and regulates the scramble for advantage. These add up to remarkable political stability. They account for why Americans never developed a full-blown Bismarck-style welfare state. The classic liberal perspective—individualism, self-interest, hostility to government—sums up our politics.

The southern argument introduces an alternative. The mud-sill construction pictures a poor white majority ardently invested in the social order. It will defend that order, even at a very high cost. Radical white Democrats were the most ferocious about maintaining the bottom—the racial mud-sill made it possible to level the rest of society. Regardless of their political orientation, white southerners organized their social theories around the powerful psychic wage, around whiteness.

Here is an alternative explanation for that distinctive American combination of broad early suffrage, political stability, and relatively stingy social welfare programs. It is an unusual place to look for the soul of American politics. But the political implications of the southern argument reach far beyond the southern story. Throughout history, the poor white majority would often be reluctant to cast its many votes for radical social change. Their alarm over losing racial status forms an often-overlooked bedrock to American political development.

The Two Pro-Slavery Schools: Same Differences

Southern writers developed two different views of slaveholding society as a whole. On the one side were genuinely conservative writers, who pushed a cavalier social hierarchy; on the other lay what George Fredrickson calls the *Herrenvolk* democracy, an egalitarian view that insisted on the equality of white men. Both schools attacked the claim that all men are created equal. Paternalists emphasized the many ranks in every society. Herrenvolk Democrats thought that all white men were, indeed, free and equal but—to take a typically spiteful comment—that "all men, niggers, and monkey's ain't."[25]

The distinction between paternalists and racial Democrats is useful but easy to overstate—there is plenty of overlap in the pro-slavery fine print. After all, alongside the theorizing ran hard political calculation—elites needed the support of the poor white majority. In the end, the real pro-slavery kicker

comes at the point where the two views converge: keeping black people enslaved and white women under tight control.

Paternalists

These apologists began with that old conservative standard: a society in
which everyone knows his or her proper place. "Each one should remain in society in the condition in which he has been born and trained," wrote Thomas
Dew in 1832, "and not mount too fast without preparation." Stick a crude slave
overseer in a drawing room with polished gentlemen, and the poor man will be
"perfectly miserable" and "soon sigh for the fields" and his rough buddies.
Every society, added James Henry Hammond, "has the rich and the poor, the
educated and the ignorant."[26]

The paternalists generally drew their white hierarchy in vague strokes.
Though they often announced conservative principles, American individualism kept barging into their essay—recall how Simms almost blundered into
blessing the slaves with the prospect of liberty. All white males got constant
scraps of deference. Take that unpolished overseer squirming in the drawing
room; Thomas Dew asserts he cannot rise without preparation. Just thirty
pages later the guy is back. This time he gets lunch: "The man to the north will
not shake hands familiarly with his servant, and converse, and laugh and dine
with him . . . but go South and you will find that no white man feels such inferiority of rank as to be unworthy of association. . . . Color alone is here the
badge of distinction, the true mark of aristocracy."[27]

A genuinely conservative pro-slavery argument—one that emphasized
hard class lines and stable social ranks—would look quite different. We do not
have to guess about the details, for the South produced a bona fide neo-feudal,
pro-slavery theorist. George Fitzhugh tried to leap past race and defend slavery
as an abstract socioeconomic system. His extremism neatly demonstrates the
general rule: most pro-slavery writers were fixated on slavery as race control,
not on slavery as a theoretical way to organize the political economy.

Fitzhugh, on the other hand, boiled every trace of liberal individualism out
of southern apologetics. Proper society is hierarchic and stable, he wrote. Slavery is the best—the kindest, the most Christian—way to organize the social
bottom. And not just for black people. Fitzhugh prescribed southern medicine
for the "toil worn, half fed, pauperized population of England." The only way
to "remedy [their] complicated evils, would be to ENSLAVE the whole of the
people of England who have not property."[28]

Other writers tossed off occasional zingers about how lounging Italian lazzaroni would profit from the whip. But Fitzhugh really pushed slavery for the
masses—white and black, American and English. Southern slavery was gen-

tler than "free" northern labor, insisted Fitzhugh. The slaveholders fed and clothed and kept their workers; capitalists in Boston or London simply threw men and women out of work with every dip in the market. The North was more prosperous only because its capitalists wrung more money out of their "wage slaves." In the end, said Fitzhugh, slavery and freedom formed a false dichotomy. The few always flourished from the hard work of the many. Whether they lived off the toil of black slaves or white mill workers, the top dogs were "cannibals all."[29]

What about black people? Fitzhugh insisted that slavery was not just a system of race control. "As an abstract question, Negro slavery has no . . . claims over other forms of slavery." It was just an empirical fact that "almost all Negroes require masters, whilst only the children, the women, [and] the very weak, poor, ignorant . . . whites need such protective relation."[30]

Fitzhugh's argument landed him right in the middle of a northern economic controversy. Some northerners were blasting capitalism with precisely the same arguments—wage slavery was just as bad, they said, as race slavery. Their opponents, free labor advocates like Abraham Lincoln, used Fitzhugh's extreme views to undercut the critics. Lincoln sent Fitzhugh's clippings to the newspapers just to make his political rivals squirm. Southerners felt a lot less ambivalence—Fitzhugh's book *Cannibals All!* provoked howls of protest. Race was the only true basis for slavery, and everything followed from that "fact."

Fitzhugh faced so much southern heat that he soon had to eat his words. He eventually dropped the slavery for white workers routine. In a review of Van Evrie's book, in 1861, Fitzhugh capitulated. "The Negro is physically, morally, and intellectually a different being from the white man." He always would be. Africans were the natural slaves.[31]

Herrenvolk Democrats

The alternative tradition furiously denied any hierarchy or class distinctions among white men. This school invoked "Andrew Jackson, the slaveholder" and built its world view on two simple ideas. As William Yancey from Alabama put them to a sympathetic northern audience in 1860, "the first is that the white race is the master race and the white man is the equal of every other white man. The second idea is that the Negro is the inferior race."[32]

Members of the Herrenvolk school pushed both themes hard. They were ferocious in their assertion of white equality. "The poorest meet the richest as an equal," wrote Thomas Cobb and "sits at the table with him." All this equality, they insisted, rested on the existence of the black slaves.[33]

The Herrenvolk school flung Adam and Eve aside and embraced the idea that Africans were a "different and inferior" species. The missionary justifications of writers like Dew, Harper, and Hammond evaporated in the raw racism of Nott, Cobb, and Van Evrie. The latter sneered at all the fuss over stewardship or uplift or improvement. In my own reading, the bare-knuckled racism of the Herrenvolk school began to eclipse the pious racism of the paternalists during the 1850s, though this is still in dispute among historians.

Some scholars emphasize the division between the paternalists and the Herrenvolk. They see aristocrats versus levelers, seaboard elites versus western yeomen. Still, the two traditions were working different angles on the same pro-slavery project. Ultimately, they put their accents in different places. The Herrenvolk writers were far more democratic when it came to white males. However, as we have seen, a leveling trace also seeps through the paternalists' writings—paternalists too were (sometimes) ready to dine with any white man. And the schools agreed over what elevated the whites: standing above a black slave caste. Both schools emphasized the danger of emancipation. Both imagined an immoral black threat to civilization. The Herrenvolk tossed aside the moral up side of slavery for black people, but they shared the paternalists' terror of a great fall for the Anglo-Saxons.

The two schools took very different views about the "true nature" of African people. But from the black perspective, the differences must have seemed trivial. Both insisted that the racial mud-sill class was the basis of southern society. Both justified brutality. The difference was that the Herrenvolk school did not confuse violence with moral improvement.

Finally, shifting the focus to the white women's separate place in society blends the entire pro-slavery literature into a single argument. Paternalists and Herrenvolk agreed that abolition and racial equality made as much sense as sexual equality or freedom for children. Even Fitzhugh stands out only in his tireless efforts to shock the reader.

Almost nothing seemed to offend southern writers more than the active roles played by abolitionist women. The pro-slavery advocates could not cite the bizarre evidence often enough: women entering politics, women lecturing men, even women bossing men around. These were perversions of the natural order. "Husbands, whom nature places at the head of the household," wrote Van Evrie, stand behind [the women's] chairs, to receive their orders, thus outraging common sense as much as nature herself." Women's rights and abolition flourish together in this unnatural soil where the "laws of nature are violated and reason trampled under foot."[34]

At the other end of the pro-slavery spectrum, Fitzhugh hammered the same theme. What abolition is really after, he wrote, is "free love," "free women," "free Negroes," and "free children." (For readers who might have missed those shockers the first time, Fitzhugh repeats them in a later chapter.) "The terminus of all abolition is . . . the total overthrow" of the family. Feminism was grotesque; it perverted nature. "Even the hens who loiter about," cackled Fitzhugh, "have caught the infection of Woman's Rights. . . . Madame hen was strutting about in as large a liberty as any wise woman of the north." Meanwhile, the Shanghai cock stayed home with a brood of chicks.[35]

The pro-slavery ranks were united on the race and gender tangle: on the place for white women, on the importance of keeping blacks on the social bottom, and—finally, inevitably—on the rigidity with which the color line had to be maintained. "The Anglo-American [race], with that high instinct of superiority that so remarkably distinguishes it," wrote Van Evrie, "utterly refuses all admixture with aboriginals." This great fact—not Puritan jeremiads or northern economic power—explained American superiority. When confronted with another race, boasted Virginia Senator Benjamin Leigh, Anglo-Saxons know only three alternatives: "exterminate," "enslave," or "abandon the country."[36]

Ultimately, this debate was not about paternalism or social order or slavery as an economic proposition. (Though, for a while, Fitzhugh tried to make it about all three.) Rather, the arguments repeatedly landed on race with both feet. The authors—paternalist and Democrat—filled their pages with racial hopes and promises and threats and fears. Controlling the race line, in turn, prompted that picture of southern ladies who always knew their place. As we have seen, abolitionist women were prolific writers, editors, and speakers. The pro-slavery response came from men.

American Exceptionalism

The pro-slavery story makes a mess of the traditional theories about American political culture. The literature may be, as Louis Hartz said, "well nigh berserk." But a closer look hints at an alternate way to read America.

First, remember the classic story. Americans leaped out of feudalism into a new world where everyone was born equal—success or failure lay in one's own hands. That bred a nation of ardent individualists. In time, Americans developed their famously liberal regime marked by broad suffrage, a celebration of markets, a suspicion of state action, and a puny administrative apparatus—any European would be "disgusted" at the state's incoherence, commented Tocqueville. The escape from feudalism led to a nation that celebrated the private sphere and deprecated its own government.

Slavery introduces a problem. The American region with the closest thing to a semi-feudal heritage ends up with the most ardent government bashers, union-busters, and welfare skeptics. Something about the South seemed to incubate that anti-welfare American culture. But what?

Well, it is not "feudalism." Read the pro-slavery argument carefully and you catch even the paternalists shoving their neo-feudalism to the side. Of course, hierarchy and bits of southern chivalry stuck out all over their writing; but almost none of the southern theorists really stuck to the class-based story. Their writings drifted toward liberal-sounding notions about "improvement" and "elevation"—at least in theory, white men from every rank shook hands and did lunch.

What the pro-slavery argument writers really cared about was race. Hightoned South Carolina gentlemen and fire-eating Mississippi Democrats offered different justifications and honored different social ideals. But the real force of their writing comes to a single point: they would keep African Americans enslaved. Liberating them would be scary, it would destroy southern society, and it would unleash a terrible perdition. One after another the writers pictured a kind of immoral apocalypse.

Southerners arguing about social theory agreed on two points: Black people down on the bottom. And—just to be safe about keeping the tribes apart—women up on the pedestal. Even poor whites were vested in southern society by their racial status.

We've seen the general formula: Some immoral group threatens "our" society. It is incapable of abiding by the values that the rest of us share. It must be controlled—for everyone's good. At least one version of the pro-slavery argument adds a new twist: everyone is uplifted by the social controls. Male voters become more responsible, female virtue grows among white women, and the happy mud-sill people prosper under Christian tutelage.

The struggle to curb dangerous others—clamping on our own controls rather than (as Tocqueville thought) escaping from European controls—shapes American political thought and culture in every era. Enforcing the lines between us and them turns American policies into their distinctive forms: a first-world laggard in traditional social welfare programs, an international leader in government efforts to control (or improve or uplift) its people. That is how we get 2 million Americans—overwhelmingly black and Latino—stuffed into prisons and jails.

Chapter 7
North: The Ragged Chorus of the Union

THE abolitionists created an uproar in the North, too. "A few thousand crazy blockheads," reported the *New York Herald*, "have actually frightened 15 million people out of their senses." While the South developed a party line in the early 1830s, the North remained up for grabs. Ultimately, both regions faced the same tribal question: Who are we? Each found its answers in a tangle of economics and morals, in both liberalism and hellfire.[1]

Race Riots

Southerners imagined a North united in an anti-slavery frenzy. There was plenty of frenzy, but most of it came from mobs routing the abolitionists. In 1835, President Jackson applauded the riots. "It is fortunate for the country that the good sense, the generous feeling and the deep rooted attachment of the people of the non-slaveholding states . . . to their fellow citizens of the same blood in the South have given so strong and impressive a tone . . . against the . . . wicked attempts . . . to produce all the horrors of servile war."[2]

Just how did the "generous" people express that "strong and impressive" tone? They smashed printing presses, threw rocks at women's meetings, looted homes, beat up abolitionists, burned churches, and ran wild through the black parts of town. Racial violence spread quickly: one riot in 1832, four in 1833, twenty in 1834, fifty-three in 1835 (when President Jackson applauded them), and sixteen in 1836. Rumors circulated about bounties on abolitionists' heads—rewards allegedly ranged from $100,000 in New Orleans to $100 in Boston (where the supply was so much greater). "We have managed," wrote Lydia Maria Child in 1835, "to get along in safety so far; but I have . . . at times . . . trembled and wept like a very child. . . . Tis like the times of the

French Revolution when no man dared trust his neighbor." The mobs led Lincoln to his famous warning: "If destruction be our lot we must ourselves be its author."[3]

But why such frenzy? We can get a pretty good idea by looking at one of the most celebrated mobbings, the Boston riot of October 1835. The Boston Female Anti-Slavery Society had invited an Englishman, George Thompson, to address its first anniversary meeting. (Think of Thompson as Garrison with an English accent.) Some three thousand men—"gentlemen of property and standing from all parts of the city," sneered the *Liberator*—were waiting outside the society's office. Thompson got wind of the trouble and did not show up. The mob clogged the stairway leading to the meeting room, howling insults and drowning out the speakers. Mayor Theodore Lyman and his constables finally appeared and ordered the women to break up their meeting. After some argument, the Anti-Slavery Society voted to adjourn and left the hall to the "taunts, hisses and cheers of mobocratic triumph." The mayor tried to break up the crowd, but he got nowhere. Instead, the mob tore the society's sign off the building and smashed it to splinters. Then the shout went up that Garrison himself was about—working late in the society's office. The mob cornered him in the second floor of a nearby carpentry shop.[4]

Garrison faced the mob, bowed, and descended a ladder that materialized out of the crowd. He was seized by a couple of muscular men who—surprise—pushed him through the throng shouting, "He shan't be hurt. You shan't hurt him." This excited the sympathy of others. They took up the cry, "He shan't be hurt." Others screamed for tar or for hanging Garrison on the Boston Common. The rowdy, bickering procession wound its way to the Common and then to City Hall, where Garrison was shoved through a guarded door. The mayor finally protected Garrison by locking him in jail.

Perhaps those strong men saved his life. But even in Garrison's account there was not very much violence. The episode reads like the elaborate public ritual of an eighteenth-century crowd enforcing communal norms. Garrison himself shot down the most dramatic rumors: No, the crowd never tied a rope around his neck; no, nobody stole his watch or his pocket book; and NO! he was NOT "frightened" or "pale" or "pallid"![5]

Anti-abolition crowds across the North repeated this highly ritualized kind of mobbing. As long as the rioters did not run into black people, the violence was usually limited. *Niles Weekly Register* tallied up the consequences of another incident: "an alarming riot . . . eventuated in the loss of a little blood and much reputation."[6]

Why the surge in riots? The Boston episode offers three major clues: the Englishman, the women, and the shattered sign.

First, the Englishman. Many northerners saw abolition as a foreign conspiracy. Just as the United States was rising to meet its Manifest Destiny, rival nations instigated this treacherous project, which was designed to drive southerners to disunion. Any idiot could tote up the costs and benefits to liberty. "No beneficial consequences to any class of mankind, or to the whole universe," wrote J. K. Paulding, "can counterbalance the evils that will result . . . from the dissolution of the Union." By threatening America, abolition threatened liberty itself.[7]

And who was behind this abolitionist plot? Foreigners. Monarchs. Tyrants. The despots of Europe, wrote the anti-abolitionists, "affect a marvelous regard to the rights of one colour, while withholding the rights from another." What about the misery they brought to Ireland? What about the "half-fed" and "pauperized" working classes in England?[8]

In the mid-1830s, Americans did not have to settle for vague abstractions about foreign villainy. They had George Thompson right at hand. Thompson's name was plastered all over the anti-abolitionist project. Andrew Jackson was referring to Thompson when he declared open season on the "emissaries from foreign parts who have dared to interfere" in American affairs. William Sullivan, the ardent New Hampshire anti-abolitionist, endorsed the "torrent of indignant contempt" pouring down on this meddling "foreign emissary" who would "rashly apply to [our] peace the fire of DISUNION." In New York, a hundred lodgers in the boardinghouse where Thompson was staying delivered an ultimatum: if the "foreign emissary" and his family stayed, they would all go. A mob in Concord, New Hampshire, threw stones and eggs as Thompson addressed a women's meeting; a crowd in Lynn, Massachusetts, repeated the performance; the men of Boston were primed and waiting. This English meddler symbolized abolition as a foreign invention, as a European tyrant's plot.[9]

Abolition stands in a long line of foreign contagions that washed up on the shores of liberty. From the first days in the new world, Europe was the source of corruption—of heresy, tyranny, immorality. The city on a hill had lit a beacon for Europe; but the incorrigible old world kept threatening to extinguish the American experiment. In actual practice, we keep running into moral reforms that flow stubbornly in the wrong direction. In the seventeenth century, we saw the king of England push religious tolerance on the reluctant Puritans—he forbade Quaker hangings and opened church doors to Anglicans. Now, in the mid-nineteenth century, English abolition inspired the American anti-slavery movement. An act of Parliament phased out slavery in England's Caribbean colonies (1833–1838). Why, asked American abolitionists in the 1830s, couldn't Congress just do the same? They soon found out: moral lessons from abroad rarely go down easily in the United States. American pride, commented Gustave de Beaumont, "will not admit the superiority of any other."[10]

Second, the Boston men mobbed a female society. Abolition, they felt, had insinuated itself in the United States thanks to the most gullible Americans—credulous women. Shifts in the "little commonwealth" of "hearth and home" always kindle powerful moral backlashes. Antebellum feminists and their promiscuous assemblies challenged the racial and sexual order. As we have seen, they provoked a feverish reaction. The women were naive, irresponsible, immoral—male critics never seemed to know whether to condescend or howl.

One trusty measure of every culture war is the outrage over what the other side is teaching the children. The abolitionists published little homilies, poems, and primers. The anti-abolitionists pounced on this preaching to the "kiddies." An abolitionist alphabet primer—"'A' is an Abolitionist"—came in for particular criticism. Political agitation by women evolved into agitation by "women and children," mocking the very idea of women in politics. "Would any sensible man who loves truth and reason," asked William Sullivan, "follow the guidance of women and children?" The entire social order was being rattled by confused naifs.[11]

Third, that Boston mob smashed the sign identifying the Boston Female Anti-Slavery Society. Local leaders across the North fiercely opposed the new abolitionist groups. The riots usually broke out when the societies arrived in town—the uproars peaked between 1834 and 1836, just as the societies got organized. The old guard saw local abolitionist groups as the benevolent empire turned political and run amok. "Here is a declaration of war against the entire frame of society as it exists in the United States," wrote Paulding.[12]

The new organizations raised all kinds of hell: They recruited women and black people. They promoted radical ideas, like racial justice and feminism. They brought in outside preachers and agitators. They were well funded, thanks to philanthropists like Arthur Tappan of New York. And they were extraordinary propagandists. New printing technology enabled abolition groups to churn out vast piles of cheap pamphlets, which they mailed far and wide. The sheer volume stunned opponents: 122,000 anti-slavery mailings in 1834, 1.1 million in 1835. Part of this torrent flowed into the South, setting off the caterwaul about bloody Nat Turners.

President Jackson led the condemnation. "Attempts to circulate through the mails inflammatory appeals addressed to the passions of the slaves" produced "painful excitement in the south." Jackson called for prohibitions and "severe penalties" against mailing such "incendiary material." And incendiary was just the word. A group of men in Charleston, South Carolina—more "gen-

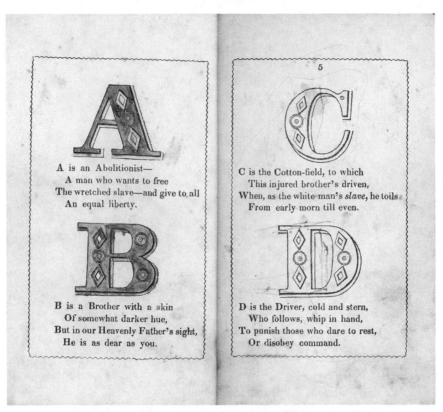

A is an Abolitionist—
A man who wants to free
The wretched slave—and give to all
An equal liberty.

B is a Brother with a skin
Of somewhat darker hue,
But in our Heavenly Father's sight,
He is as dear as you.

C is the Cotton-field, to which
This injured brother's driven,
When, as the white man's *slave*, he toils
From early morn till even.

D is the Driver, cold and stern,
Who follows, whip in hand,
To punish those who dare to rest,
Or disobey command.

7.1. *The Anti-Slavery Alphabet* (1847), primers like this one infuriated anti-abolitionists by taking political argument into the nursery. Critics charged that politics had left its proper sphere when women and children were involved. A child partially colored in this copy. (Brown University Library)

tlemen of property and standing"—hauled the offensive mail from the post office and lit a bonfire. The local postmaster wrote to his New York counterpart, Samuel Gouverneur, and advised him not to send any more of the stuff. Gouverneur agreed. Jackson's postmaster general, Amos Kendall, announced that in blocking this sort of mailing Gouverneur was certainly "justified before your country and all mankind."[13]

The fight over the mail was a battle for the soul of a powerful new federal machine. The Post Office sat at the heart of the emerging Jacksonian state; it held 80 percent of all the federal jobs and grew as the country expanded. The Post Office tripled in size during the thirty years before the Civil War. Nor was this some distant leviathan—every village had a postmaster. This far-flung agency was the first great national bureaucracy.

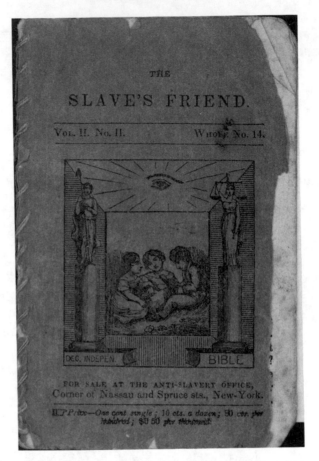

7.2. *The Slave's Friend*, published by the New York Anti-Slavery Society, 1836–1837. The penny pamphlets caused an uproar. They were written simply so that an uneducated slave might understand. The title page of this one explains the scene on the cover: "You will see three little abolitionists are sitting down while one of them is reading to the others." The real hint of disruption lies in the fine print on the bottom of the cover: the pamphlet is priced for purchase by the thousand. Shown actual size. (Brown University Library)

Here stood a frightening symbiotic relation between private organizations and federal machinery. The abolitionists constructed a national organization and set up local societies in every northern town and village. They spread their word through the national postal bureaucracy, which itself had branches in every town and village. Together the two organizations penetrated deep into society.[14]

All this might have sensibly frightened the many who opposed abolition— except for one detail. The ardently anti-abolitionist Democrats were running the government. They checked the abolitionists at every level. On the street, they disrupted the abolitionist mail with impunity. On the local level, postmasters from Charleston and New York pledged to bar the abolitionist material. On the national level, the postmaster general cheerfully acknowledged the mail tampering and gave it his blessing; the president applauded the mobs, endorsed the postmasters, ripped the abolitionists, and called for stricter penalties to protect America from the anti-slavery menace. The fate of the pamphlets seems to illustrate nothing but the power of abolition's enemies.

But in a deeper sense, a brave new world jolted every political side with the shock of diversity. The new institutional machinery—public bureaucracy and private organizations—was integrating a diverse, sprawling nation. Even small towns had to face up to unfamiliar ideas and attitudes.

The abolitionists themselves had resisted the growing federal regime—in fact, that's what got many of them into politics in the first place. As we saw earlier, northeastern Puritans had campaigned against Sunday mail service because the mail coaches had unsettled their village Sabbaths. The Sabbatarian campaign (1828–1832) failed to stop the Sabbath deliveries. The Democratic majority in Congress did not bother to disguise its contempt for the effort. The battle did, however, recruit moral reformers and give them their political baptism—historian Bertram Wyatt-Brown calls the Sabbatarian campaign the "prelude to abolition." Richard John adds that it was, in many ways, successful: it not only mobilized moral reformers, it stimulated attention to the Sabbath itself.[15]

Americans were integrating their far-flung, diverse society. Everywhere the results challenged the old guard. People in both the North and the South saw distant moral villains poised to subvert the social order. The threat helps explain why "gentlemen of property and standing from every part of the city" would organize mobs and plunge into riots. The anti-abolitionist crowds indulged one of the trustiest American reflexes: they saw frightening social change as moral villainy.

Once the anti-abolitionist mobs took to the streets, a new concern elbowed slavery almost entirely out of the fight. "The great question to be settled," screamed Garrison after his mobbing, "is not whether 2,500,000 slaves in our land shall be either immediately or gradually emancipated . . . for that is now a subordinate point." Subordinate to what? Why, Garrison's own rights. The prime question, wrote Garrison, has become "whether freedom is with us— THE PEOPLE OF THE U.S.—a reality or a mockery." Would it be "liberty of speech and press" or "padlocks . . . upon our lips," "gags in our mouths," and "shackles upon that great palladium of human rights, the press"?[16]

Garrison had finally hit a note that played well. Even people who loathed the abolitionists began fretting about their liberties. Philip Hone, for example, thought the anti-slavery pamphlets were far less dangerous than the response to them. "The people are to be governed by law just so long as it suits them," wrote Hone in his diary. "Every party postmaster in the country is made the judge of the cases which justify his interposition"—now, any party hack could break into the mail. When Congress rejected the anti-slavery petitions it provoked more fretting about the petitioners' rights. The central issue moved from the slaves' liberty to the abolitionists' civil rights. The new focus may have contributed to the steep drop in mob violence after 1836.[17]

The shifting political subject reminds us what was at stake. Americans were fighting over their identity: new organizations, new forms of government, women in politics, and—sometimes barely audible above the uproar—slavery. These were all confusing matters. But when it came to maintaining the race line, most white Americans remained implacable. That point became clear through a very different kind of riot.

When the mobs turned from white abolitionists to black Americans, the riots got much uglier, and talk of civil liberties vanished. Contrast the Garrison mob with the New York race riot of the previous year. In July 1834, a white man published a notice announcing his engagement to a black woman. That twisted race tension into white rage. For three days and nights a mob ran through the sixth ward, a poor and racially mixed neighborhood. In a grotesque parody of Exodus, the rioters warned citizens to light candles in their windows and stand before them. White faces were "passed over," black faces or dark windows attacked. The crowd vandalized six black churches, torched more than sixty homes, and destroyed five brothels (disgusting emblems of amalgamation). As the crowd set whole areas ablaze, the militia mobilized, then stood by—torn, thought one foreign observer, between horror at the violence and sympathy with its purpose. There were five New York race riots in nine months.[18]

The following month, August 1834, a Philadelphia mob replayed the violence. The crowd ran through Moyamensing, a poor neighborhood, destroying, pillaging, looting, and "hunting the nigs." Black churches were again singled out. So were buildings where blacks and whites congregated together (like grog shops). The crowd ignored the homes of poorer blacks and focused on those of the well-to-do African Americans. One black man was beaten to death, and another drowned trying to get away from the mob. Seven riots shook black Philadelphia between 1834 and 1838. Some rioters boasted about pushing African Americans out of Philadelphia altogether. But a local newspaper got to the real heart of the matter in its analysis of the riot: "The law of this state has not, it is true, affixed many disabilities to the black man, but public opinion and universal custom require that his place in society should be inferior to that of the least favored white man."[19]

There was little talk in the North about mud-sills or cornerstones. But "public opinion" and "universal custom" pushed black Americans to the social bottom. White men fought to keep them there. When abolitionists questioned the race hierarchy, they unleashed racial demons. As Americans expanded suffrage to white men, they pushed black people out of public life. By the 1850s, the racist Herrenvolk spirit was stirring through the North as well as the South.

The abolitionists spread fast—there were 328 societies by 1835 and 1,350 (claiming 250,000 members) by 1838. But the cause never commanded the influence its opponents feared it might. Funds dried up after a financial panic in 1837. The anti-slave society had splintered by 1841. When abolitionist James Birney ran in the presidential election of 1844, he managed just 2 percent of the popular vote. By the mid-1840s American abolitionists were divided, dispirited, and despised. Yet within fifteen years slavery would sink the Whigs, divide the Democrats, and set off a civil war. How? Two other mass movements swept the nation and got mixed into the anti-slavery cause: nativism and free labor. All three movements were monumental disputes about the nature of the United States. Americans still live with the legacies of each.

Nativism

Immigrants had been coming to America all along—15,000 a year in the 1820s, 57,000 a year through the 1830s. However, in 1845 a towering wave of "pauperism, ignorance and degradation" (as Elizabeth Cady Stanton described it) crashed ashore. Three million foreigners arrived in a decade. Suddenly, strangers—first Irish, then German—seemed to be everywhere. By 1850 almost 1 in 10 Americans had been born abroad; it was 1 in 7 by 1860.[20]

The foreigners provoked that familiar reflex—a terrible moral crisis was threatening the nation. A new underclass wallowed in the same old sins: they were lazy, violent, soaked in whiskey, and promiscuous. They were worse than promiscuous, they were depraved—they stashed virgins in convents that American patriots occasionally burned to the ground.

Even the reasonable Lydia Maria Child lost it on the Irish. Don't bother talking reform to them, she wrote. "Their moral and intellectual state is such that [one] might about as well attempt to call the dogs together for reform. . . . Voting and beating are the [only] moral agencies they have any idea of." Moral uplifters looked on in horror while godless Jacksonians embraced this rabble and bought their votes. As the reformers saw it, the Irish got drunk, voted proslavery (Democratic), and then celebrated by beating up abolitionists. Fighting slavery soon got tangled up in fending off immigrants.[21]

A more charitable onlooker might have seen the hardship. Back in Ireland there was awful poverty. There were too many people, and rents kept rising.

Most farmers scratched out only the most meager living. Then a fungus destroyed the potato crop. In the next ten years as many as 1.5 million people starved to death (in a nation of 8 million). Two million others fled, mostly to America. The Irish left their small, hungry communities and landed in the middle of the American antebellum frenzy. If ever there was a poor, huddled mass, this was it.

Nativists saw only immoral un-Americans. For starters, the Irish were Roman Catholics, and Catholics would destroy the nation's republican virtue. Liberty flourished in Protestant soil. Both the American Revolution and the Protestant Reformation had been rebellions of conscience against tyrannical autocracies—against king and pope. Protestant yeomen read the Bible, struggled with conscience, awaited God's grace, and ran their own congregations. In frightening contrast, the Roman Catholics clung to feudal hierarchy. A corrupt foreign leviathan—popes, bishops, priests—ruled passive congregations.[22]

Beyond the moral dangers of Catholicism lurked the usual iniquities. Some were grounded in genuine cultural differences—yes, the Irish and Germans drank unapologetically. Others were odd bits of bigotry—no, the convents were not harems. Let's look at this latest underclass, one sin at a time.

The Immigrant Sins

First, immigrants were lazy. No matter how many packed into the neighborhood, Americans always dominated the economy. Why? Because Yankees valued "discipline, sobriety, and reliability." The "spirit of achievement" was foreign to the immigrants. Instead of working harder, they crowded onto the paupers' lists. By 1856, Samuel Busey counted ten foreign-born paupers for every native one. In New York, the indigent rolls grew fivefold between 1850 and 1855 alone. There was no escaping the conclusion, wrote Busey, that the "source of pauperism in this country is immigration." In Europe, the pauper count ran between 15 and 25 percent of the population. Indolence stretched down through the generations; laziness lay deep in their bones.[23]

Nativists focused on the Irish and the Germans—especially the Irish, who were poorer and more Catholic. But Chinese immigrants began arriving in the mid-1850s (13,000 in 1854), and they would eventually get the "beast of burden" label. "The cheap servile labor pulls down the more manly toil to its level," announced Senator James Blaine (R-Maine). The free white laborer could never compete with the slave labor in the South. "In the Chinaman, the white laborer only finds another form of servile competition—in some aspects, more revolting and corrupting than African slavery."[24]

Both laziness and brute insensibility cut people out of the economic competition for the American dream. The lazy would not work hard enough; the servile worked too hard—an unfair advantage enjoyed by lower races. A recurring tribal urge would fight to protect "manly toil" from outsiders (who must have been the opposite of manly—unmanly? feminine? not quite human?). We saw the impulse in Ben Franklin's lament about Philadelphia Germans (in 1752) and in Frederick Douglass's description of the shipyard strike against free black workers. Labor markets, local communities, even the American dream itself all had racial boundaries.

Ironically, when black Americans broke free from slavery, they were stuck with both stereotypes—they were lazy yet somehow would snatch jobs away from hard-working whites. The Irish faced a less complicated stereotype: they were just lazy.

Second, there was the liquor. The Germans, for example, introduced lager beer and commercial breweries into American life—Anheuser-Busch and Miller were both antebellum brewers. "Nine-tenths of all the dram shops in the city of New York," reported *American Protestant Magazine*, "are kept by foreigners. . . . They bring the grog shops like the frogs of Egypt among us." Perhaps tippling immigrants actually fostered temperance among Americans looking to mark their superior social status, as sociologist Joseph Gusfield suggests. In any case, moral reformers ranked temperance right up there with abolition as crucial to purifying America.[25]

Drinking—even a little bit of drinking—lectured Lyman Beecher, "paralyzes the power of conscience, hardens the heart, and turns out upon society a sordid, selfish, ferocious animal." As we saw above, reformers often drew the analogy between drinking and slavery—the two harshest forms of human bondage. Go to the jails and you will not find "a single inmate" who "has entirely abstained from intoxicating drinks," reported Rufus Clark in 1853. Alcohol, sounded another alarmist, is what drives so many Catholics "to prison and almshouse, to reformatory and orphanage, to dive and brothel."[26]

Third, the immigrants were violent. By the 1830s, gang fighting was a staple of urban life, especially during election season. Philip Hone kept jotting variations of the same entry in his journal: "Dreadful riots between the Irish and the Americans have again disturbed the peace." The culprits always seemed to be "Irishmen armed with clubs." "We have already had one frightful battle" between the Irish and the Americans, added Lydia Maria Child, and "everyone expects a worse one election week." The violence brought European feuds crashing in on American cities—the Irish and the English, the Catholics and the Orangemen. Old world troubles seemed to roil America's peace and endanger its character.[27]

The urban violence was undeniable. However, it sometimes swelled, in the anti-immigrant imagination, into a vast, free-floating epidemic. Dangerous foreigners lurked in every American shadow—servants ready to poison their masters, foreign workers with violent (even revolutionary) fancies, common thieves and drunken murderers set to pounce on the innocent. Rufus Clark estimated "about one murder every day" from these dangerous foreigners. Anne Norton brings antebellum American fears back to the anxious, almost subconscious, fears about Roman Catholicism itself: "The Catholic church was the realm of death and sex, of intemperate attitudes and unrestrained appetites."[28]

Which brings us to sex. The Irish could not control themselves, as their large families testified. If wealth consisted in children, snickered the *New York Independent*, "the Irish would be rich people."[29]

The anti-Catholic sex story featured variations on the lurid abolitionist tales about plantation life. Maria Monk's sensational best seller, *The Awful Disclosures . . .*, claimed to expose clerical life. Virgin nuns forswore marriage and entered convents; they pledged obedience, but to Monk's "utter astonishment and horror," obedience led straight to "criminal intercourse" with the priests. The children of these unions? Immediately baptized and strangled. Nuns who balked? Murdered—stomped to death by other nuns, no less. "To put a nun's veil on a girl," declared another book of *Startling Disclosures,* is "to expose her to public prostitution." "Monasteries and nunneries under control of Jesuits," added a third writer in 1859, are "vast Sodoms" where "every confessor has a concubine." Most Jesuits enjoyed several. *Awful Disclosures* sold more copies than any American book before *Uncle Tom's Cabin*.[30]

The most famous anti-Catholic riot offered a live variation of these startling disclosures. In 1834, Boston newspapers repeated a wild rumor that a music teacher, Elizabeth Harrison, had tried to escape from the Ursuline convent school in Charlestown, Massachusetts. The convent was a prominent school for girls from wealthy families. In anti-Catholic lore, convents were full of captive women—flagellated and abused. Now, rumors flew about the city. Harrison had been lured back to the convent; she was being held in one of the secret basement dungeons; she had disappeared without a trace; her father was frantic. A working-class mob—more than a thousand people—gathered in front of the convent. Although briefly stymied by a formidable nun, they eventually broke into the building. The crowd searched the place (no captives, no dungeons), then looted it and burned it to the ground. The patriots capped their triumph by marching around town brandishing weapons, burning the occasional Irish house, and roaring deprecations at the papists. Mayor Lyman called meetings to condemn the violence, but no rioters were punished.

Lyman Beecher was in Charlestown, raising funds for his Theological Seminary in Cincinnati by scorching papists—he preached on "the Devil and the Pope of Rome" the night before the riot. Some recent historians try to absolve Beecher from directly fomenting the riot (he spoke to a higher-toned crowd, argues Daniel Walker Howe), but a distinct whiff of nativist violence clings to him to this day.[31]

Anti-Catholicism, commented Richard Hofstadter, has always been the pornography of the Puritan. In fact, every Puritan enemy—Quakers, Indians, witches, slaveholders, antinomians, priests and nuns—has stirred up pornographic fancies. Some consorted with Satan. None ever crucified their lusts.[32]

The anti-Catholic itch mirrors many of the dynamics we saw in the witchcraft panics. There is the horrific congress with the priests (if not with Satan). There are the young girls in terrible danger (kidnapped and disappeared, if not possessed). There is the horror of dead babies (this time strangled newborns rather than monstrous fetuses). There are the young women making wild accusations (like the possessed girls in Salem Village, a young woman told stories about the Charlestown convent.) Finally, there are distinguished members of the clergy—Cotton Mather, Lyman Beecher—inflaming the people, getting tangled in the panic, and sullying their own reputations.

But it was not just the sex. Like previous panics, this one was about the role and control of women. Once again the soft lures of the undisciplined natural state endangered family hierarchy. The Indians had posed the same danger. Recall how the early New England settlers had agonized about women and children who fell into Indian hands, how they warned about Puritan society sliding down to the lustful and undisciplined moral level of the natives. Abolitionist women and their promiscuous assemblies posed a similar danger. Now the Romans offered still another variation of the fall. Those Catholics were shamelessly spreading their faith, and any girl might be converted, perhaps even lured into a convent. Catholicism, writes Anne Norton, "destroyed the family by permitting wives and daughters to evade the authority of husband and father." Free women were once again the weak link in the moral conflict against others. Here lies yet another a version of the Eve narrative. The men might stand strong and virtuous, brawling against vicious job-stealing Catholics. But it was all for nothing if the weaker sex fell, if she gave in to the Tempter.[33]

Immigrants before the Civil War stood in a long line of groups struggling at the American social bottom. Of course each group posed its own dangers to civic society, each frightened the neighbors in a different way. Still, Americans found variations of the familiar underclass sins in the immigrants. And they read those low morals in the usual way: deeply ingrained racial traits threatening to leech from the dangerous other and stain the virtuous American character.

Northern Herrenvolk

The Irish and the blacks faced the same miserable bigotry. The Irish were "simian," "wild," "sensual," "bestial," and "savage." Cartoonists routinely portrayed the Irish as apes or ape-like. Writers compared "Southern cuffee" to "Northern Paddy"—and "Paddy" often weighed in lower on the social scale. The racial boundary between the groups was ambiguous—the Irish were not yet white.[34]

The two groups lived in the same poor neighborhoods and competed for the same low-wage jobs. At first many employers resisted the turbulent Irish. Want ads specified "any color or country except Irish." As their population grew, the Irish began squeezing out free blacks on the wharves, on the railroads, in the coaches, and in the servants' quarters.[35]

Life was hard for everyone on the economic bottom—competition kept the wages low. The Irish channeled their frustration into a visceral racism. They seized on white supremacy, deflecting anti-Irish bigotry by violently emphasizing the color line. Irish men filled the anti-abolition mobs and plunged into race riots with jarring ferocity. As Frederick Douglass put it, the Irish are "warm hearted, generous, and sympathiz[e] with the oppressed everywhere when they stand up on their own green island." But when they set foot on this Christian country, "they are instantly taught . . . to hate and despise the colored people. They are taught to believe that we eat the bread which . . . belongs to them." What they learn, added a sharper tongue, is that it is always fashionable "to give Jim a whack."[36]

The emphasis on color made the Irish boil at even hints of amalgamation. Democrats playing that theme could always count on a hot reaction. One celebrated example came during the 1864 presidential election. In an effort to pump up the anti-Lincoln vote, David Croly published a pamphlet titled *Miscegenation*, a word he invented. The document pretended to be a Republican argument in favor of race mixing. Croly knew just which chains to yank for a big reaction: "The white Irishwoman loves the black man," he wrote, and "they will be the first to mingle." The bitterness and tension between the blacks and Irish are only the "fusion of kindred electricities."[37]

African American leaders tried to emphasize their people's respectability. They contrasted their own behavior with that of their immigrant neighbors. Black mobs built railroads, they said; Irish mobs rioted and visited beer gardens. But it was no use. In both North and South, free black people kept getting pushed down as "depraved."[38]

Democrats supported the urge. They enlarged white democracy while explicitly restricting the franchise for African Americans. When New York expanded suffrage to every male citizen, it disenfranchised most black men; in

7.3. *Harper's Weekly.* "Southern cuffee" versus "northern paddy" balancing each other on the scales of American civilization. (Brown University Library)

Pennsylvania, a state constitutional convention (in 1837) extended white suffrage and flatly banned black voting. Many northern Democrats—no less than the southern Democrats—acted as if an egalitarian society could be built only when the common man had racial inferiors to stand above. Democrats bitterly resisted any innovation that might threaten that "universal custom" that placed black people below the "least favored white man" (as the Philadelphia newspapers had put it after the 1834 riot).[39]

Why have American workers not been more radical? Before the Civil War, radical working-class politics sprang up in many northern cities. But even with relatively few black people around, Americans on the economic bottom developed a violent legacy of racial division. Jackson Democrats in the North shared the racial reflex celebrated by Herrenvolk Democrats in the South. As W. E. B. Du Bois argued, the racial hierarchy permitted elites in both regions to expand their democracy with less fear of social instability. Even very poor white people would remain deeply invested in the standing social order.

The democracy in the North developed with two great stabilizers. The regime reinforced intense racial divisions; at the same time, it offered white males grand opportunities. Expanding American markets left white men room to rise; the open western spaces gave them room to roam; and the party machinery gave ambitious men a way up through the political system. The white man's republic organized a lower class to fear and plenty of higher opportunities to grasp for.

Know-Nothings

If Irish Democrats forged their American identity in the heat of race hatred, some moral uplifters organized their own repressive impulse around bashing foreigners. In the 1850s, the anti-immigrant urge coalesced into a political movement that shot—briefly, brilliantly—across the political sky. The American (or Know-Nothing) Party defined the United States as a moral Protestant nation. The Know-Nothings articulated a bundle of grievances. They generally condemned slavery, touted temperance, denounced corrupt political parties, profited from discontent with the Whigs, and—their political signature—pushed for curbs on immigrant politics. They would stem the tide of "rum, Romanism, and slavery" that menaced America.[40]

The Know-Nothings bolted out of nowhere to astonishing political success. In 1854 they carried the entire Massachusetts congressional delegation and almost all four hundred Assembly seats. They won nine of eleven congressional districts in Indiana, eleven in New York, and up to seventeen out of twenty-five in Pennsylvania (because this was a secret order, it was not always clear just who belonged). The Know-Nothings grabbed majorities in six state legislatures and ran strong in a dozen others.[41]

This looked like a movement with a future. Without press or power or prestige, the Know-Nothings had flattened the other political parties. The Democrats lost seventy-six (or almost half) their seats in the House of Representatives. The Whigs vanished entirely. What next? The American Party, wrote George Templeton Strong in his diary, will probably "rule a future Congress and may carry in a President on its wave."[42]

Abraham Lincoln worried about the same thing: "As a nation we began by declaring that 'all men are created equal.' We now practically read 'all men are created equal except Negroes.' When the Know-Nothings get control, it will read 'all men are created equal except Negroes, and foreigners and Catholics.' At that point, I should prefer emigrating to some country where they make no pretense of loving liberty, . . . where despotism can be taken pure, and without the base alloy of hypocrisy."[43]

But the Know-Nothing tide ran out just as fast as it had come in. For one thing, the party began to define itself. In 1854 it had struck different themes in different states. In New York, for example, the Know-Nothings played down anti-slavery and temperance; they did the same thing in the South, of course. Millard Fillmore, the party's presidential candidate, tried to build a national base by ducking slavery and disparaging immigrants. That lost northern support without gaining southern ground. Opportunists who had jumped onto the bandwagon in 1854 now began jumping off. Fillmore polled just 21 percent in 1856.[44]

In Massachusetts, the nativist government had promised a twenty-one-year delay before immigrants could be naturalized and allowed to vote; by the time that pledge became a law, the waiting period had dwindled to two years. Even that infuriated Democrats across America—especially because fugitive slaves had to wait only a year in Massachusetts. Democrats in California penned an angry condemnation: "Massachusetts degrade[s] the foreign white man below the level of the Negro and the mulatto and we, the Democracy of California, utterly repudiate such infamous doctrine." The Know-Nothings were fading while American racial divisions held fast.[45]

By 1859, the American Party was gone. Enough of its voters turned to Abraham Lincoln to make the difference in 1860. (Historians have a lively debate going about whether Republicans made nativist concessions to get those votes.) In either case, the nation's moral hopes and fears kept growing louder. The North brimmed with angry factions: abolitionists (with their splinter groups bitterly laying into one another), anti-abolitionists, Jackson Democrats, nativists, feminists, and black nationalists. Each mobilized over a different outrage until the country buzzed with jeremiads and moral causes.

Ultimately, the crosscutting northern battles sorted themselves into two radically different visions of the American millennium. On one side, the heirs of New England Puritanism imagined America reaching for its biblical destiny. Their post-millennial agenda ran to freedom for the slaves, sobriety in the masses, and Bibles to the Catholics. Along the way, some of the high moralizers fell for the lure of nativism. After all, the immigrants mocked everything the reformers believed in; they drank, debauched American politics, and—worst of all—defended slavery. Still, the latter-day Puritans preached one of America's grand moral visions.

On the other side, Democrats dreamed up their own Manifest Destiny. They resented all the moralizing and uplifting. Meddling with slavery posed a profound danger to America's providential mission. Abolitionist folly threatened to break the union and bury Anglo-Saxon glory. The abolitionists would destroy the country, perpetrate feminism, and mingle white blood with that of other races.

A focus on the Democrats makes the age of Jackson look just the way traditional historians pictured it: a time of political democracy, economic liberalism, and—adding recent revisionists—racial troubles. Take a wider view of the political scene—include abolitionists, blacks, and women—and the era begins to whirl with moral fights and millennial fancies. But the spiritual conflicts gathered real velocity when they ran alongside hard economics. North and South would find their differences finally, flatly irreconcilable when they could no longer duck the labor question.

Free Labor?

Southerners had been slamming northern economics. The idea of free workers was an "empty and delusional mockery," hooted George Fitzhugh. Northern workers were free to work hard for a pittance, free to get fired, free to scramble for work, free to starve if they failed to find it. Markets were harsher than slavery. Capitalism was the cruelest master.[46]

Some northerners had been saying pretty much the same thing: wage slavery was as oppressive as race slavery. Free men and women, they insisted, did not work under others. In a republic, men should work as equals; in traditional shops, each craftsman labored at his own pace, paused for a mid-morning whiskey, and sometimes took the afternoon off to fight fires or go fishing. But the mills and factories imposed a harsh new work regime—bosses, clocks, rules, discipline, and no whiskey—on or off the job. Freedom vanished in the new American workplace. "Wages is a cunning device of the devil," wrote the radical editor Orestes Brownson, "for the benefit of tender consciences, who would retain all the advantages of the slave system, without the expense, trouble and odium of being slave-holders."[47] Where did such tyranny spring from?

Despotic England. English cities—clogged with paupers, choking on factory smoke—had bred still another menace to American liberty.[48]

In the 1850s the Republicans came up with their famous rejoinder. Where the critics were wrong, said Abraham Lincoln, was in assuming that the northern wage laborers were "fatally fixed in that condition for life." Among us, he said, nobody languishes permanently in the "mud-sill class." "The man who labored for another last year, this year labors for himself, and next year he will hire others to labor for himself." Any man, repeated Lincoln throughout the late 1850s, who is "industrious," "honest," "sober," and "prudent" will soon enjoy his own capital and be in a position to hire others to do his labor for him.[49]

The free labor creed reached back to the Puritan ideals—hard work praised God, success marked salvation. Now people like Lincoln filtered old Calvinist sermons through Jacksonian dreams about upward mobility. The new American faith celebrated a dynamic free people racing to success. Anybody could make it. The belief in free labor and upward mobility took root at the heart of Republican Party ideology (where it still flourishes). Most northern Democrats shared the faith. Free labor, wrote Lincoln in 1856, fosters "intelligent power in the masses"; it is the true "bulwark of free institutions."[50]

But what about those pestiferous northern cities? Irish immigrants or black workers or village girls sweating in the mills were not going to cash in on Lincoln's boasts about hiring others—much less next year. The free labor rejoinder came straight from Calvin: falling short meant moral failure. Lincoln put it lightly, in the fine print of his speeches—the prudent would prosper, he said. Others pounded home the down-side of the homily. The poor would be rich, preached Horace Greeley, "if they would make the needful sacrifices of ease and mortifications of appetite." They left the mills or the shops and plunged straight into "the groggery, the cigar store, the gambling den, or some other haunt of vileness." They simpered about their poverty but could "afford to smoke and drink freely." In every social class, wrote Greeley, "inordinate expenditure is the cause . . . of crime and . . . misery."[51]

The *Chicago Press and Tribune* estimated that nine-tenths of the pauperism in the West came from drunkenness and laziness. "Lock[ing] up every gaming house, theater and brothel" would render "prisons and almshouses and poor-laws almost unnecessary." Even great economic panics sprang from moral corruption, "ruinous extravagance," and "riotous living." Simplicity and sobriety could always set America right. Opportunity beckoned every free person. Poverty, dependence, and failure were the wages of sloth or immorality. After all, sniffed the free labor advocates, just look who populated those urban masses—immigrants, Irishmen, and sinners of every kind.[52]

All sides agreed that poverty was a moral problem. Where they differed was on just whom to blame. Republicans admonished dissolute individuals to work harder and save more. Radicals like Brownson pointed to the corrupt system. Don't blame workers; wage slavery (or race slavery, for that matter) wrecked innocent lives. Brownson attacked the mills and factories. "The great mass wear out their health, spirits and morals without becoming one whit better off then when they started. . . . Few of . . . the poor girls . . . ever marry; fewer still will return to their native places with reputations unimpaired."[53]

The free labor perspective eventually triumphed. (Ironically, the great war fought partially for the free labor ideal undermined its logic by incubating great capital, massive organizations, and armies of wage earners.) However, the radical critique kept coming back to challenge American economics. A long line of moral critics would follow Orestes Brownson: late nineteenth-century populists, the social gospel movement after the turn of the century, the New Dealers in the 1930s, and the new left in the 1960s would each push variations of the same moral cry against industrial capitalism. The result might be called the dialectic of economic blame: the dominant tradition blames individuals for their poverty; on the other side, increasingly self-conscious social critics blame the system for keeping good people down. Each view taps a different side of the Puritan covenant, the individual and the collective. The clashing moral economies sprang up in the early republic, took full flight in the late nineteenth century, and have wrestled over American wealth and poverty to the present day.

Before the Civil War, free labor advocates clinched their case by looking West. No one had to stay in the crowded cities, wrote men like Greeley. Open land (once the Army had cleared out the natives) beckoned anyone with pluck and industry. The frontier promised freedom, wealth, and a second chance—all without class conflict or labor controversy. Free soil guaranteed the free labor premise: striving would win success.

There was just one problem. The American rush westward thrust the most perplexing question directly onto the political agenda. Would the new land go to free men or to slaves? In the thinking of the time, there could be no middle way. Wherever slavery took root, said Andrew Johnson, "the white man was excluded from employment" and "the foreign immigrant turned away." Who could compete with slaves?[54]

Tempers ran so high because each region needed western land to keep the peace back home. Southern leaders thought that slavery would not survive if it did not expand. They tantalized the poor white majority with the prospect of rising into the planter class; that dream required new land and lots of it. But the westward rush might yield more free states, which would capture the Senate (equally balanced between slave and free states) and strangle the South.[55]

Northerners needed the western territories to underwrite their rags-to-riches ideology. The battle for the West roiled every political party. Northern Democrats tried to hang on to their southern partners by dancing around the slavery question. They kept deferring the question—to the states, to the people in the territories, to the future. Each move further entangled them. Ultimately, the Jacksonian vision itself—Manifest Destiny, Indian removal, and expansion into the grand empire for liberty—forced the question that the Democrats kept trying to duck. The trail west ran straight into the slavery issue.

Slavery had tripped up the Know-Nothings and buried the Whigs. When the Republicans emerged, in the mid-1850s, they bluntly opposed slavery in the West. The Republicans drew together an odd anti-slavery coalition—from radicals pushing abolition to racists promoting apartheid. In 1846, for example, Congressman David Wilmot (originally a Pennsylvania Democrat) attached an amendment to a spending bill; his Wilmot Proviso forbade slavery in any territory won during the Mexican war. The House passed the measure and fourteen state legislatures endorsed it. "Anti-slavery is marching forward with irresistible power," exulted Garrison. But Wilmot himself described his proposal as "the White Man's Proviso"; he aimed to snatch up the new territory for the "sons of toil of my own race and own color." As they "marched forward," many members of the anti-slavery legion kept serving up variations of the same nasty attitude: "I want to have nothing to do, either with the free Negro or the slave Negro. We wish to settle the territories with free white men."[56]

Western settlers generally resisted slavery. But they did not stop with anti-slavery. They also rejected all black people. For example, those who rushed to California looking for gold bitterly complained about the handful of black miners (slave and free) in their midst; they called it degrading "to swing a pick by side with the Negro." Negrophobia from the mining regions pushed members of the California Constitutional Convention (1849) to ban slavery. Other states were more direct and banned all black people. Illinois (1848), Indiana (1851), and Oregon (1857) added constitutional provisions barring African Americans from entering.[57]

The Oregon Territory notoriously ordered all black people out. When it applied for statehood, Oregon's constitution forbade slavery and refused residency to free African Americans. Sixty-five percent of the voters approved the provision against slavery, eighty-five percent the proscription on blacks. Other states required African Americans to post large bonds guaranteeing good behavior. Men and women who violated these provisions could be expelled, whipped, or (under an Illinois law of 1853) sold at public auction.[58]

The restrictions were generally ignored, but they licensed mischief when race tensions rose. Ohio had required a $500 bond since 1804. In 1829, officials in Cincinnati announced that the old provision would be enforced—black citizens had thirty days to pay up or get out. The black community negotiated an extension while its members looked for new homes. The foot-dragging moved white mobs to attack black neighborhoods. Eventually, half of Cincinnati's black people left for Canada. Then white leaders voiced a new complaint. The most industrious had gone and left behind the "idle, indolent and profligate"; the black community now lacked the moral restraint formerly provided by community leaders.[59]

The western clashes may seem odd—race prejudice spread in areas with almost no black people. But, as Tocqueville pointed out, unsettled social orders often produced the rawest prejudice. When the boundaries between us and them—and winners and losers—go up for grabs, status anxieties rise and racial tensions rush to the political surface.[60]

Back in the East, some Republicans also mixed sharp opposition to slavery's expansion with fierce hostility toward African Americans. The full blast of racial animosity could be startling. Take James Pike, an influential Republican columnist for the *Herald Tribune* in New York. As the sectional crisis deepened, Pike feverishly cast about for a way to reconcile the North and the South. The only enduring solution, he wrote in 1860, lay in the "elimination of the Negro from our controversy. But how is he to be got out?"

> The free states should confine the Negro to the smallest possible area. Hem him in. Coop him up. Slough him off. . . . The immediate purpose and duty of the Republican party is . . . to inexorably limit the area of African slavery. . . . Let its next aim be to get rid of the Negro population entirely . . . by massing it within its present limits. This is to be the result in the end, and it is just as well to recognize the fact and thus aid in accelerating the period of our final deliverance from the great burden and nuisance and crime.[61]

Perhaps there were different ways to meet Pike's aims. But the chilling upshot seems clear enough. Pike imagined an American harmony built on free labor, free soil, and slow racial genocide.[62]

Buried deep in Pike's free soil vision lies the analytic strand that connected North to South. Each region and every era struggled for ways to separate us from the undesirable them. On the surface, of course, slavery was completely and implacably different. No other American institution ever pinned people so harshly into place; men and women who broke free from it were exhilarated to work at even the most menial jobs. Even so, every region had its race line.

Racial biases worked their way deep into the North's free labor markets. However, even where markets are terribly skewed—by laws or norms or neighborhood toughs—the prejudice is hard to see, much less overcome. It seeps into the societal machinery. Horace Greeley made no exceptions for bigots or race riots when he traced poverty to "inordinate expenditure." Worse, in a system organized to blame failure on indolence or self-indulgence, there is always a blurry line between social injustice and sour grapes. Slavery (or segregation) stands out; it is unmistakable and unjust. Unfair free labor markets raise the old, subtle question about whom to blame—is it an unfair system, or lazy individuals?

Immediately after the Civil War, President Andrew Johnson would blithely wave aside all the disadvantages and injustices that faced the freemen. They had no property, little education, no right to vote, and—in some places—could not even move around freely. Yet Johnson was in no mood to lend a hand: "Their future prosperity and industry must rest mainly on themselves." If they "fail and perish away," said Johnson in 1865, "let us be careful that the failure shall not be attributable to any denial of justice." The market—even American history's most profoundly unjust market—allowed him to pin responsibility for success and failure on black individuals, regardless of their impossible situation.[63]

The extreme case illustrates the larger point. Markets are always embedded in a social and political context. Biases sneak in. Reformers were so committed to their free labor premise that some even failed to see the barriers facing the freemen. Legal emancipation would take an army. What would genuine economic opportunity require? Constitutional amendments guaranteeing equal protection of the laws? (The Fourteenth Amendment would be ratified in 1868.) An occupying army in the South? Land reform? Forty acres and a mule? The postwar conundrum is an early ancestor of today's disputes about affirmative action. Once again, Americans wrestle over how to address the market's biases—indeed, whether they exist and, if so, how deep they go.

Slavery and free labor were stark antinomies in almost every way. Slavery was the bluntest social control mechanism in American history. Rigged labor markets have been the most subtle. But each in its own way clamped down hard on the racial other. Each came with elaborate stories to explain inequality between the races. Southerners defended slavery as a moral venture; free labor advocates traced class differences to moral flaws—people were poor because they had been lazy, profligate, or incompetent. For all the enormous contrasts, the North and South each eventually found a way to melt the economic gap between the races into questions of vice and virtue.

Shifting Racial Images

Of course, the saints and the sinners keep shifting. Americans constantly redefine their communal boundaries. How? By challenging old moral stories and spinning new ones. The resulting images define some people as virtuous and others as vicious. The cultural pictures frame the political agenda and focus policy debates. The process never ends. But antebellum politics produced an especially fantastic string of stories as Americans vigorously constructed and reconstructed black Americans. Each new picture arrived with urgent moral instructions.

First, recall some of the stories we have already seen. The black clergy pictured African Americans as God's special people—cruelly enslaved, bound for freedom, and awaiting His terrible day of reckoning against their oppressors. Slaveholders pictured them as moral inferiors—happy as slaves, depraved in freedom, dangerous near abolition. Most northern whites imagined a degraded underclass. Early abolitionists saw "bleeding humanity"; later, they inflated African Americans into Christlike agents of the millennium.

In the 1850s, a dramatic new racial image burst onto the American scene. The Fugitive Slave Act—one piece of the rickety Compromise of 1850—sent federal commissioners chasing after runaway slaves.[64] The commissioners (they got $10 per returnee) needed only an affidavit from the alleged owner; the accused received no trial, no rights, and no chance to testify. Often, wrote Greeley, the "first notice the alleged fugitive had of his peril was given him by a blow on the head . . . with a heavy club." The fugitive slaves, wrote W. E. B. Du Bois, became the greatest piece of abolitionist propaganda. They stood on northern soil and said, " 'I have been owned like an oxe, I stole my own body and now I am hunted . . . to be made an oxe again.' " Northern whites felt sympathy, said Du Bois. However, they never forgot that behind this trickle of fugitives loomed 4 million slaves who would swamp every hope for a decent wage.[65]

The fugitives could be read as heroic, pathetic, or threatening, but they suddenly drew the north into the once-distant slave regime. Boston, in particular, became embroiled in the most dramatic cases. Federal agents decided to make that abolitionist hotbed a showcase for the Fugitive Slave Act. What they generated instead was an anti-slavery spectacle. When deputies nabbed Shadrach Minkins (in February 1851), a band of black Bostonians burst into the courthouse and rescued him. By the time federal agents seized Anthony Burns, in May 1854, it took an army with cannons to keep 20,000 protesters at bay.[66]

The specter of federal bounty hunters prowling northern streets did wonders for the anti-slavery cause. The Fugitive Slave Act inspired *Uncle Tom's Cabin* (chapters started running in an anti-slavery newspaper in 1851). The aftershocks of the Burns case toppled the government of Massachusetts—historian Albert Von Frank calls the consequences a "pocket revolution." And it gave

Garrison still another opportunity to make headlines and shock his country-men.[67]

A July 4 "counter demonstration," organized to protest the Burns seizure, included a long line of important speakers—Garrison, Henry David Thoreau, Abby Kelley Foster, Sojourner Truth, Wendell Phillips. When Garrison rose, he read the Fugitive Slave Act aloud, set a copy on fire, and, following a formula from Deuteronomy, called out, "And let the people say 'Amen.'" The crowd responded. He repeated the procedure with papers from Burns's hearing. Then Garrison held up a copy of the Constitution, read the pro-slavery passages, denounced this "Covenant with death" and "agreement with hell" (quoting Isaiah), set alight the Constitution, and prayed: "So perish all compromises with Tyranny! . . . And let all the people say, 'Amen!'" Shocked cries and hisses were overwhelmed by the great mob of abolitionists roaring back, "Amen."[68]

Four months later, in November 1854, the new Republican Party snapped up 108 congressional seats and the majority in the House of Representatives; the largely anti-slavery Know-Nothings took forty-three seats. The Democrats lost almost half their number in the House, though they gained two seats in the Senate (still chosen by state legislatures). Southerners had plenty of reasons to get the wrong idea: they imagined the whole North rising up in anti-slavery fury.

The changing images of black America came to a head in the Supreme Court in 1857. A slave named Dred Scott sued for freedom; Scott tried three different arguments as his case wound through state and federal courts: his owners had taken him to live in a free state, they had taken him into free territories, and they had sold him to a New Yorker.

The courts rebuffed each claim. By the time the case reached the Supreme Court, a simple ruling stared the justices in the face: because Scott lived in the slave state of Missouri, he was a slave and had no business in court. Instead, Chief Justice Taney—egged on by President James Buchanan—took on the entire slavery controversy.

Dred Scott v. Sandford is a hopeless tangle. Eight judges wrote separate opinions, two of them dissenting. At the heart of all that jurisprudence sits Chief Justice Taney's majority opinion, an implacable picture of black men and their place in the American regime.

A Negro, wrote Taney, could "not be a citizen in the sense in which that word is used in the Constitution of the United States." A state might grant black people rights, he acknowledged, but such prerogatives applied only in that state—they were meaningless anywhere else and never entitled black people to the rights and privileges of the federal Constitution. The founders had never intended such a thing. When the Declaration of Independence and the

Constitution were framed, the founders plainly regarded black people as "beings of an inferior order, and altogether unfit to associate with the white race, either in social or political relations; and so far inferior, that they had no rights which the white man was bound to respect."[69]

The founders, argued Taney, did not give black people political rights. On the contrary, early Americans enslaved blacks for their own good—"an axiom in morals as well as in politics which no one thought of disputing." At the time Taney wrote his opinion, most states still rejected black political rights. To clinch the case, Taney pointed to the most savagely guarded feature of the race line. If there was any doubt about black inferiority, why was intermarriage regarded as "unnatural and immoral and punished as crimes"? Laws against intermarriage marked the "stigma, of the deepest degradation, fixed upon the whole race."[70]

On the surface, the case addressed a simple but explosive question: Who could interfere with slavery? Taney supplied a clear answer: only a sovereign state, and only within its own borders (and even that might not survive Taney's next visit to the issue, said Lincoln). The federal government could never interfere with slavery. Forget the Missouri Compromise (which ruled out slavery in the northern territories), the Compromise of 1850 (with its popular sovereignty in the Utah and New Mexico territories), or even the very idea of popular sovereignty itself—no one had the authority to restrict slavery in any territory.

Taney rested this reading of the Constitution on a picture of black people as different, inferior, irredeemably "them," held apart from white America by the most basic laws and norms. Here was a defiant statement of American community: no political rights for moral inferiors, no equality for people who could never marry your daughters. Lydia Maria Child had been exactly right in her attack on laws barring marriage across the race line: the "legalized contempt of color," she had said back in 1839, "sustain[s] slavery." Now the laws against amalgamation stood at the heart of the *Dred Scott* decision—striking down the Missouri Compromise, spiking the free soil argument, and snatching American citizenship away from all black people.

In dissent, Justice Benjamin Curtis of Massachusetts exposed Taney's argument as bad history. The founding generation had been *more* liberal with black rights. Back then, five states—including North Carolina—permitted free black people to vote. By 1857, only Massachusetts and New Hampshire still granted full suffrage. Abraham Lincoln echoed Curtis's dissent, then went straight to the sexual powder keg. "The very Dred Scott case affords a strong test to which party most favors amalgamation. . . . Slavery is the greatest source of amalgamation; and next to it, not the elevation but the degeneration of the free blacks." The Democrats—Justice Taney, President James Buchanan, Senator Stephen Douglas—who defended slavery were the ones who promoted racial mixing.[71]

But this was treacherous ground. Only the wildest abolitionists tolerated mixing Anglo with African. During their debates, Stephen Douglas kept taunting Lincoln over the race and sex tangle: "He goes out and draws from [my] speech," jibed Lincoln, "this tendency of mine to set the Negroes and white people to marrying with one another." Douglas took special delight in mocking Lincoln by snickering at Frederick Douglass and the white ladies. "The last time I came here . . . I saw a carriage . . . with a beautiful young lady on the front seat . . . and Fred. Douglass, the Negro on the back seat. All I have to say is this, if you Black Republicans think the Negro ought to be on a social equality with young wives and daughters, and ride in the carriage with the wife while the master of the carriage drives the team, you have a perfect right to do so." In a debate a month later, "Fred. Douglass, the Negro," has the "white lady and her daughter in the carriage sitting by his side" while the poor fool of a husband has "the honor to drive the coach to convey the Negro."[72]

In response, Lincoln jockeyed, joked, and jumped back to free labor. First, he sidestepped the "counterfeit logic that, because I do not want a black woman for a slave I must necessarily want her for a wife. I need not have her for either. I can just leave her alone." Next, he taunted the Democrats right back about lust across the color line: "I . . . never had the least apprehension that I or my friends would marry Negroes if there was no law to keep them from it, but . . . Douglas and his friends seem to be under great apprehension that they might if there was no law to keep them from it." And, in the end, Lincoln always scrambled back to his free labor message. "In some respects she certainly is not my equal . . . but in her natural right to eat the bread she earns with her own hands without asking leave of anyone else, she is my equal and the equal of all others."[73]

But all of Lincoln's quips and commentaries did not add up to a solid alternative to slavery. Could African Americans be "us"? In 1858, the answer was still no. Republicans resisted the spread of slavery but were not ready to embrace black America. Rather, Lincoln stuck to the familiar anti-slavery critique; rapacious slaveholders were the ones mixing bloodlines. He clung to colonization; the "separation of the races is the only perfect preventive of amalgamation." Lincoln covered the raw implausibility of his solution with a wave at the scriptures. The Children of Israel marched out of Egypt together, "in such numbers as to include 400,000 fighting men." But Exodus itself hinted at the problem: black America would have to replay the Moses epic with more than five times as many Israelites.[74]

Grand Bobalition of Slavery .

Grand and most helligunt Selebrashum of de Bobalition of Slabery in de Nited Tate ob Neu Englunt, and commonwet of Bosson in de country of Massa-chuse-it.

7.4. Changing images of black America. "The Grand Bobalition of Slavery." This broadside (date uncertain) mocks a black abolitionist band, celebrating "African day" by beating drums and carrying spears. The grossly exaggerated racial features—typical of anti-abolitionist imagery—suggest a savage people. (Brown University Library)

Even as northerners marched toward the Civil War they had no design for freeing slaves and no desire to live with black people. In his First Inaugural Address, Lincoln rejected any lawful right to "directly or indirectly interfere with the institution of slavery in the states where it exists." Instead, the president pleaded with the South: "We are not enemies, but friends. We must not be enemies." Southerners were not impressed. "The flimsy jests of a harlequin," wrote the editor of the *Richmond Examiner,* "proposed to cozen the South by cheap sentimentalism." On the other side, the abolitionists were just as skeptical. As the war broke, Frederick Douglass noted that both armies were fighting for slavery. "The South was fighting to take slavery out of the union, and the North was fighting to keep it in." For many northerners, the urge to keep all those black people contained in Dixie never flagged.[75]

THE ESCAPED SLAVE IN THE UNION ARMY.—[See Page 427.]

7.5. Heroic military service helped turn sneering images of subhuman Africans into frankly admiring military portraits. *Harper's Weekly,* July 2, 1864.

The war itself transformed northern aims. Lincoln moved slowly, reluctantly. He clung to colonization. He pondered a gradual emancipation—stretching the process out for thirty-seven years. The slaves themselves forced the issue. They ran toward freedom. Thousands set out for the Union lines. "Always there was the embarrassed and reluctant dragon of emancipation," wrote C. Vann Woodward, "the invading Union army." Slowly the fight for the Union turned into the crusade for freedom.[76]

As the war's purpose evolved, a radical new racial image took shape. The northern army mustered 180,000 black troops—by the end of the fighting a third of them would suffer casualties. In their first major battle, at Port Hudson on the Mississippi in May 1863, two regiments of black troops from Louisiana advanced bravely—they were "heroic" and "daring," ran the dispatch from the front—across open ground and despite withering enemy artillery fire. The *New York Times* cast its verdict two weeks later: "It is no longer possible to doubt the bravery and steadiness of the colored race when rightly led."[77]

"It was their demeanor under arms that shamed the nation into recognizing them as men," wrote Thomas Wentworth Higginson, who commanded a black regiment. The Negro soldier, added Union General Ben Butler, "opened new fields of freedom, liberty and equality . . . with his bayonet." Lincoln put it more sharply. When peace arrives, "there will be some black men who can remember that, with silent tongue and clenched teeth and steady eye and well poised bayonet, they have helped mankind on this great consummation; while . . . there will be some white [men] unable to forget that, with malignant heart, and deceitful speech, they have strove to hinder it." In the last desperate days of war, even the Confederate Congress would call for 300,000 recruits, "irrespective of color."[78]

The northern iconography of black men took a sharp turn for the better: cartoonists had been scornfully depicting buffoons—one pictured a black man putting on airs before the barnyard animals with the nasty caption, "Cutting His Old Associates." Another imagined the abolitionist's bestial black army. Before the war was over, those sarcastic pictures had—at least in some hands—evolved into respectful, even gallant, military portraits. Here was a whole new picture for white Americans to ponder: their black countrymen as war heroes.

Sadly, the racial spinning would not end there. The sneering images of black America flourished right alongside the heroic pictures of men and women battling for their freedom. Even reports of black military heroism came with nasty questions: Could they "be kept to the limits of civilized warfare," or would they fight "in the wild Indian style, with unrestrained barbarity"? The liberating Union soldiers often mistreated the slaves they met. They sometimes plundered slave quarters, abused black people, and tarred comrades who talked about marrying black women. The New York City draft riot of July 1863 took northern racial violence to horrifying new levels: miserable whites (mainly Irish)—suffering from poverty, inflation, and competition for jobs—turned on their black neighbors. The mobs hunted down, killed, and mutilated black New Yorkers, then fought bloody battles with federal troops. At the time, fearful commentaries pegged the number of dead at more than a thousand. (We now estimate the figure at just over 100—awful enough.) A "volcano" of race fear and class antagonism seemed to be running under the city and across the land—a portent of future troubles. But those race troubles would not begin to obscure "mankind's great consummation" till after the war.[79]

In an era rich with moral crusades and millennial dreams, the Civil War itself became the long-awaited American apocalypse. Decades earlier, Lorenzo Dow had parsed the Book of Revelation, line by line, and pronounced the moment of prophesy at hand. Preachers across the American spectrum—from Charles Finney to Lyman Beecher (and, before them, from Cotton Mather to Jonathan Edwards)—had all prepared America for millennial glory. Now the moment seemed to be at hand. Julia Ward Howe reflected the apocalyptic fervor when she reworked passages of the millennial scriptures into "The Battle Hymn of the Republic." Writing in a Union army camp, Howe gave the biblical images their now familiar form: "And the angel . . . gathered the vine of the earth, and cast it into the great wine press of the wrath of God" (Revelation 14:19) became "He is trampling out the vintage where the grapes of wrath are stored." And "I saw a great white throne and him that sat on it. . . . And I saw the dead stand before God . . . and they were judged every man" (20:12–13) became "He is sifting out the hearts of men before the judgment seat." On it went, four stanzas and a chorus from the Book of Revelation. The Bible's most seething and delirious images summing up the Final Holy Battle—long prophesied, now come at last.[80]

They marched to battle, wrote W. E. B. Du Bois, "singing the noblest war song of the ages." Since Cromwell's time, added Thomas Wentworth Higginson, there had never been soldiers "in whom the religious element held such a place." This was a "religious army," a "gospel army," always "mingling . . . the warlike and the pious."[81]

In the moral turbulence two great jeremiad traditions, the African American and the Puritan, finally converged. At the heart of the African American religious experience lay Exodus. God's chosen people had languished in captivity; but in His time, the Almighty would bring them to the Promised Land and punish their iniquitous captors. As Lincoln moved toward emancipation he poured the content of this African faith into the mold of the Puritan jeremiad—lamentations over the broken covenant (all men *were* created equal), warnings about God's just wrath, hints of forgiveness, and glimmers of future glory.[82]

Lincoln preached this grand synthesis most vividly in his Second Inaugural Address, the most beautiful jeremiad in American history. Lincoln placed his trusty free labor image at the center of the shattered covenant with God: "It may seem strange that any man should dare ask God's assistance in wringing their bread from the sweat of other men's faces." He filled the address with allusions to providential fury: "'Woe to that man by whom the offenses cometh,'" and "fervently do we pray that this scourge of war may pass away." Then, going straight to the heart of the African jeremiad, Lincoln acknowledged God's righteous anger over His children's bondage. "If God wills that . . . the scourge of war . . . continue, until all the wealth piled by the bondsmen's two hundred and fifty years of unrequited toil shall be sunk, until every drop of blood drawn with the lash, shall be paid by another drawn with the sword . . . so . . . it must be said, 'the judgments of the Lord are true and righteous altogether.'"

Finally, every jeremiad returns to the dream of redemption. America restores its covenant with God, the people resolve to deal righteously with one another and return to their great errand: "With malice towards none; with charity for all; with firmness in the right, as God gives us to see the right . . . let us strive on to . . . do all which may achieve and cherish a just and a lasting peace among ourselves, and with all nations."

With Lincoln's grand sermon, the Puritan jeremiad reaches its apotheosis. John Winthrop's "Model of Christian Charity" grows into Lincoln's sadder, modern vision. The millennial dream—the literal, biblical faith in America's redeeming national character—would never sweep America in the hot, broad, fervent way it did during the Great Awakenings or the Civil War. The imperatives of efficiency in the age of industrial organization would eclipse the romance of biblical perfection. The American millennium would live on as powerful metaphor, as a patriotic faith in American destiny, and as a bleak strain of fundamentalism warning about the end of days. But it would not survive—at least not in the cultural mainstream—as the belief in a literal post-millennial American redemption of biblical prophesy.

Still, the city would remain up there on the hill for all to emulate. Americans would cling to their soaring sense of self: a chosen people with a great errand in the world. The endless conflict over just who counts as a member of that special American us—along with the agonizing over whether this race or that group spelled decline—would keep thrusting images of vice and virtue to the heart of American politics. The eyes of the world—sometimes imagined, often real—would keep American attention keenly fixed on the moral order at home.

Now what? Amid the devastation in the South, some Americans reached hopefully toward civil rights. Slave families joyfully reunited. African Americans formed communities, organized around churches, participated in politics, and demanded respect from their former owners. Free blacks came to the South to participate and teach. They met ferocious resistance. Moral fervor had helped bury slavery; moral fury slowly built a new racial apartheid.

Political scientists usually chart the decline from racial justice with a half-century of gloomy institutional milestones: Congress pulled the federal troops (in 1877) and repealed the laws that implemented the Civil War amendments (1893); the Supreme Court accepted segregation (with *Plessy v. Ferguson*, 1896); the southern states held conventions that clamped Jim Crow laws into place (1895–1905). What is less often observed is how these maneuvers rested on moral stigma. By the end of the century, a savage white narrative remade the racial story: black men had not been ready for freedom. They drank, fought, refused to work, and roamed the countryside looking for white women to rape. They sank the political system in corruption. Freeing the slaves had unleashed a wave of crime and rape. White southern violence—perpetrated by the Ku Klux Klan, for example—finally restored order and saved society. The story eventually blotted out the hard struggle for freedom and dignity that marked the decades following the war. Liberals and conservatives, mainstream scholarship and popular culture, North and South all bought the white southern revision—at least till the civil rights movement jarred historians into taking another look.

Another century of race troubles only underscores the remarkable story: a jeremiad dream about banishing slavery—radical, unconventional, almost crazy—gathered velocity and strength as it rumbled down the nineteenth century. Historians have explored all kinds of issues in the effort to understand the Civil War. But something extraordinary runs alongside the many careful discoveries: a powerful moral idea—a religious obsession, a black jeremiad—revolutionized America.

PART III

The Victorian Quest for Virtue

(1870–1929)

Syphilis and gonorrhea are . . . very common among the Negroes in the south. This is a real menace to our white boys and through them, after marriage, to our innocent daughters.

—*American Journal of Public Health,* 1915

Every generation of youth is sent out into the world as sheep in the midst of wolves. The danger, however, is not that they will be devoured . . . but that they will be transformed into wolves.

—Anthony Comstock, *Traps for the Young,* 1883

IN the half-century following the Civil War, farmers stormed into politics, labor fought bitterly with capitalists, the South roiled over race, women reached for suffrage, and a new administrative state broke free of political parties and embarked on all kinds of projects—regulating railroads, inspecting meat, busting trusts.

At the same time, a new generation of Jeremiahs began warning about disorder in the family. Reformers pushed into the private sphere, pledging to restore America's "hearthstone values." The new abolitionists, as they fancied themselves, drew the state into a great quest for Victorian virtue. The moral campaign attracted all kinds of voices. For every woman who joined a suffrage group, ten signed up for the "home protection" sponsored by the Women's Christian Temperance Union. The personal grew profoundly political.

During their fifty-year crusade, moral reformers banned bad books, barred birth control, outlawed abortion (which was common after the Civil War), raised the age of sexual consent, demolished red-light districts, prosecuted dangerous anti-family ideas, forbade men with immoral fancies from crossing state lines, and—at the high tide of virtue politics—outlawed the sale of alcohol. The swelling list of prohibitions expanded government authority, inspired fresh reform groups, and cracked down on dangerous races. In the tumult, the United States constructed a virtue regime that stood for almost a century. The laws governing sex and reproduction did not fully fall till 1973; the rules guiding the vice police laid the foundations for our own drug warriors.

The moral uproar went beyond thou-shalt-nots. While some reformers sought to control women, many others fought to empower them. Together, they stirred up a fierce debate—and in many ways a small revolution—in American gender roles.

There were plenty of reasons to feel anxious about morals. A nation born in the country was rushing to town. When the Civil War began, in 1861, four out of five people lived in rural districts; sixty years later, the census found an urban nation. As they roared ahead, the cities seemed—as Englishman James Bryce put it—"mountains . . . of corruption, . . . the one conspicuous failure of the United States." The Reverend T. DeWitt Talmage, one of the lions of the Presbyterian ministry, took famous "midnight explorations" into Brooklyn's "inferno of vice" and regaled the nation with lush stories about the sins he saw. New York City practically called out to the countryside, wrote Talmage, "Send us more men and women to . . . grind up. Give us more homes to crush, give us more parental hearts to pulverize."[1]

At the bottom of all that depravity stood the immigrants. More than 10 million came ashore between 1905 and 1914 alone (there were just 83 million people in the United States in 1905). "It would be a paying investment for some showman to catch and preserve a pure American," wrote a Michigan physician. In fifty years there would be none left.[2]

Worse, the Anglo-Saxon middle class had grown feeble—it married late and raised fewer children with every generation. Horatio Robinson Storer, a vice president of the American Medical Association and formidable anti-abortion crusader, summed up the sexual stakes: "The great territories of the far West . . . offer homes for countless million yet unborn. Shall they be filled by our own children or by those of aliens? This is a question that our own women must answer; upon their loins depends the future destiny of the nation."[3]

Some reformers tried to rouse Americans about the dangers posed by foreigners. The immigrants drank, indulged in casual sex, spread venereal disease, and had only the loosest idea about family responsibility. The most depraved Mediterranean races raped their own daughters—they would soon be raping ours. "The pagan ideas . . . mingle in our air with the ideas that shaped the men at Plymouth Rock and Valley Forge." Like Cotton Mather warning the early settlers about growing "indianized," Victorian preachers warned their countrymen about adopting slack immigrant attitudes. The white South turned a bare-knuckled variation of the Victorian sermons on their black neighbors.[4]

By the turn of the century many reformers found another voice. The Social Gospel movement pushed Christian duty toward public service rather than personal salvation. Love thy neighbor meant lift the poor. Believers denounced economic exploitation and cutthroat capitalism. The economic system—not personal depravity—spawned saloons and brothels.

Two very different moral visions developed and, for a time, overlapped. The dominant view, as we'll see in this section, blamed social problems on individual sinners. Public policy set out to control the wolves and cultivate virtuous citizens. In time, the alternative grew more urgent: responsibility lay with the whole community. Forget prohibitions. Real morality calls for higher wages, better working conditions, and more personal rights. As the Victorian impulse receded, the Social Gospel alternative would start to swell. The competing moral visions would grow increasingly distinct and wrestle for control through the twentieth century.

Chapter 8
Purity and the Woman's Sphere

IN the 1870s, one wishful free thinker imagined a genuinely liberal society: "Morality in its very nature is voluntary. Its appeal . . . should be to the conscience . . . alone." That is an almost perfect description of what the late Victorian era was not. Instead, the politics of private lives—of purity and virtue—went decidedly public. The great clashes over sexual purity do not fit a traditional reading of American politics. We usually imagine a formidable division between the public sector and the private sphere. Men confer in the polis. They compete in the market. The bedroom? That's the ultimate private space. But as feminists have been pointing out since the Civil War, it reverberates with politics.[1]

Sexual Politics

American gender wars keep returning to the same four battles: the women's role in society, lust, dangerous people at the gate (with bad blood and low morals), and moral traps for the children. The Victorians fought bitterly over all these issues. By 1900, virtue reformers had constructed a sex and birth control regime that did not fully collapse until the early 1970s.

Women's Role

There was hell to pay whenever women ventured from the private sphere into the public (or male) realm. Recall how Anne Hutchinson (1636) or the Grimké sisters (1830s) provoked thunder for crossing the line. The Puritan family had been a patriarchy, a "little commonweal" with the husband as economic and moral leader. The bourgeois Victorians developed a vision of "separate spheres." Men struggled over politics and commerce. Women reigned over the moral and domestic realms; they ran the household, raised the children, regulated the family's religious life, and signed up for light missionary work aiding the less fortunate.[2]

Women's suffrage was radical precisely because it broke free from the domestic sphere. Employment posed the same problem—and some women even fancied careers. The men wrestled long and hard, in tracts, sermons, and the ubiquitous Victorian advice books, over which professions might be suitable for a lady. Physician Nicholas Francis Cooke thought medicine was just the thing. "It rests upon the knowledge of individuals [and] . . . who can surpass a woman in these powers?" Others disagreed. Horatio Storer "emphatically condemned . . . the experiment . . . of females attempting to practice medicine." "I am no advocate for unwomanly women," declared Storer. "I would not transplant them from their proper and God-given sphere."[3]

At least Cooke and Storer could agree about women in politics: "fatal or useless or ridiculous." And college? "Great mental exertion," cautioned one popular health manual, "is injurious . . . to the reproductive power." College produced a generation of women who were "functionally castrated" and "sexual incompetents" with "monstrous brains and puny bodies." And what was the point? "Why spoil a good mother by making an ordinary grammarian?" No, concluded many advicemongers, the women's sphere lay before the warm Victorian hearth doing her "high and sacred duty, . . . the duty of the mother."[4]

The Victorians exalted motherhood. And yet, for all the romantic gush, the birthrate was falling fast. Why? In 1881, the editors of the *New York Times* hit upon the answer. The problem with women was shopping. "The awful prevalence of the vice of shopping among women is one of those signs of the time which lead the thoughtful patriot almost to despair of the future of our country. Few people have any idea of the extent to which our women are addicted to this purse destroying vice." The *Times* had the data to back that up. "Out of every thousand women between the ages of 18 and 45, no less than 963 are habitual shoppers." And what were the women actually buying? "Ribbons." Of course, like all addicts, "she soon craves a stronger stimulus" and moves on to "trimmings." The depravity reached all the way down to the nursery, where girls under ten got involved in the "ghastly mockery [of] play[ing] store." Shopping dwarfed whiskey for sheer social waste. "Promiscuous and unrestrained shopping" ruined husbands, desolated homes, and pushed an entire nation toward the economic abyss.[5]

The *Journal of the American Medical Association* also pinned the falling birthrate to this female madness: "The man does not marry young because the woman puts on too much style and he cannot afford it on a small salary, hence marriage is deferred until later in life." (The average marriage age was, in fact,

higher in 1890 than it has been at any point since.) The problem was aggravated, wrote one minister, by "poorer classes imitating the richer—especially in
the matter of female dress. The young man's dear wife often becomes *too dear*."
Even Frances Willard warned that fancy French dolls "may unduly foster [the]
love of finery which is one of woman's greatest temptations." But unlike the
others, Willard hit upon a radical alternative—give girls and boys the same
toys and training.[6]

Beneath this odd jeremiad lay a great transformation. An economy of local
producers was turning into a national market of consumers. The new age would
soon produce those grand temples of consumption, the downtown department
stores.

New cities, new economies, new mores. As the Jacksonian mechanic faded
into memory, observers kept reaching for the trusty Republican sermon. All
the talk about shopping as a vice was simply the latest variation of Horace
Greeley's famous analysis: "inordinate expenditure" caused poverty, misery, and
crime. And, yes, back in 1850, Horace Greeley had blamed greedy and profligate wives for hounding their husbands to ruin. After all, grumbled Greeley,
"what man can stand the April shower of feminine sorrow" when "all he wants
[is] quiet at home."[7]

The fuss over shopping exposed a contradiction at the heart of the women's
sphere. As Carroll Smith-Rosenberg puts it, the Victorian woman was supposed to be "domestic, docile and reproductive"; at the same time, she was expected to affirm her husband's class status and to aid the less fortunate. When
she worked to enhance his bourgeois status—through shopping!—critics
blasted her for having too many baubles and not enough babies. When she
joined women's charity organizations, she developed skills that edged dangerously toward that boundary of the public (the male) sphere. Here was the
catch-22 of the Victorian woman: the Bourgeois Matron developed skills unbecoming of a Good Wife and Mother.[8]

How to reconcile the two? Radicals disparaged motherhood and the whole
sphere of domesticity. I would rather face "solitary confinement in prison,"
wrote Lizzie Nesbett to her husband in 1864, than face the "doom" of bearing
a child every other year. In one of her most eloquent speeches, Elizabeth Cady
Stanton declared that a woman's rights sprang from four sources: her individu-
ality, her citizenship, her gender (for she was "an equal factor in civilization")
and, only incidentally, the relationships—mother, wife, daughter—that defined the female sphere.[9]

A more popular response invoked religion to reconcile the clashing roles.
God gave woman a more spiritual nature. Pursuing her moral duty—her wom-
anly role—required honing skills that lay outside the realm of domesticity.

With that move beyond the domestic, comments Smith-Rosenberg, the "good wife" started to become a "dangerous social phenomenon." Here, once again, is a formula for revolution that stretches back to the first Great Awakening: grab people by the conscience, then watch them arise and challenge the old norms. We'll see women like Frances Willard seize the shibboleths of domesticity to rally their followers; Willard launched a mass movement by appealing to moral female duty. Even conservative women began demanding sexual purity from men, votes for women, and sobriety for everyone. Victorian morals challenged the Victorian gender roles.[10]

Sex

The old gender images had spun around lust. The European witch frenzy fed on fears of woman's carnality. Back in 1484, Pope Innocent VIII's advisors summed up the danger in *Malleus Mallificum,* the definitive witch-hunter's guide: "All witchcraft comes from carnal lust which is in women insatiable."

The Victorians turned that classical misogyny inside out. Women became pure, spiritual beings, wafting above gross carnality. They were "innocent of the faintest ray of sexual pleasure," reported one physician. They "do not feel any great sexual tendencies," agreed Horatio Storer. "Many married women never become sexually awakened," never feel "physical pleasure" or "yearning." Again and again, writers drew the same gender conclusion: "It is an insult to the sex when men treat women . . . as though they were as sensually minded as themselves." The Victorians kept celebrating this virtuous paragon. But every angel comes with its demonic counter—in this case, the fallen woman.[11]

One slip and a woman lost every claim to virtue. She became an outcast, an untouchable. But how could so many women fall—prostitutes clogged the city streets—if women were asexual? Women may have been the better angels of the Victorians' nature, but—as the sermons and the medical journals all stressed—their high, moral way was littered with snares.[12]

Which brings us to the other half of the Victorian sexual universe: boys will be boys. Nineteenth-century manhood celebrated conquest—political, economic, and sexual. Men were expected to be sexually active; even physicians often agreed that abstinence posed a threat to male health. The whole nineteenth-century sexual ideology revolved around a jarring double standard.[13]

Men were sexual, women spiritual. Something would have to give. The late nineteenth century offered two very different solutions, and each raised an uproar. First, red-light districts sprang up in most cities. These were not the furtive brothels of modern times but explicit, often celebrated, sexual districts: Storyville in New Orleans, the Levee (Chicago), Happy Hollow (Houston), and The Alley (Boise, Idaho). In New York, tourist books offered guidance:

"This is a quiet safe and respectable house," reads the description of Mrs. Everett's establishment, "conducted on true Southern principles. . . . Gentlemen from the South and West are confidently recommended." After the Civil War, many men—politicians, physicians, and civic leaders—defended the districts as a necessary evil. But reformers like Susan B. Anthony began objecting. They condemned the districts, the men who winked (and prospered), and society's double standard.[14]

The alternative demanded that men return to the Puritan virtues: purity and self-control. In the late nineteenth century, this sermon came packaged as health counsel. Advice manuals attacked the old fable about needing sex. Just the contrary, warned one manual after another: "Vice prostrates the whole nervous system." Promiscuity would wreck a man's constitution, and if the dissipated wretch somehow managed to father children, it would wreck their nervous systems too.[15]

J. H. Kellogg (a health reformer and father of the famous cereal) drew vivid pictures of "excess indulgence." People saw a broken husk of a man and muttered "overwork" or "hereditary predisposition." But any medical man could see the problem: "Too frequent emissions of the life-giving fluid and too frequent excitement of the nervous system"—the fast track to destruction. Nor did marriage repeal the iron law of moderation. The married man who fell into excessive sexual congress would "suffer as certainly and as seriously as the unmarried debauchee." Well, how much was safe? The medical books hemmed and hawed and qualified before announcing: "once to thrice a month." If you were young and healthy.[16]

All nature delivered the same lesson: sex was for reproduction. That might result in "less sensual enjoyment," conceded Kellogg, but the reward was "more elevated joy." Another writer summed up the rising ethical stance: "Self control is the root of all virtues." For mother—the "angel spirit of the house"—this discipline came naturally. Father might have more difficulty. But the stakes stretched far beyond the individual. How could America prosper if its people could not control themselves?[17]

By the turn of the century, the purity legions had turned the single sexual standard—self-control and continence—into the bourgeois norm (if not necessarily the practice). This, they told one another, was one way they distinguished themselves from the dirty immigrants and the dangerous classes.

More important, the new standard empowered women. All that talk about asexuality actually conveyed a blunt message: men must not force themselves on their wives. Morals permitted "neither violence nor suffering" in the marriage act. Some physicians were brutally direct; others tiptoed around marital violence. But the sheer repetition of the theme suggests a frightening reality. Celebrating continence and control meant that a woman might say no.

For a time, feminist speeches rang out against marital violence. "I have seen the most damning misery," cried Victoria Woodhull. "Thousands of poor, weak, unresisting wives . . . imploring humanity to . . . bring out into the fair daylight all the blackened, sickening deformities" now hidden by "sham morality." Elizabeth Cady Stanton echoed Woodhull, denouncing "the husband's right of property in his wife," which only protects bloody deeds with the "old common laws of the barbarous ages." The marriage vows sanctioned rape. By the early 1870s, however, that kind of talk violated the obscenity laws. The moral classes cheered the single sexual standard, but running down Sacred Marriage was going too far.[18]

Buried deep in the purity reform lay a contradiction. On the one hand, a cry went up for continence and self-control. The good couple abstained and rose to a higher—a feminine—spiritual level. On the other hand, the middle-class birthrate was plummeting, and high-minded self-control only made things worse. The lascivious lower castes were making big families. Their wild children plagued the cities. A new Puritan generation faced the same old danger: a sinister, foreign them seemed poised to overrun our country.

Them

Good Americans were surrounded by savage, lustful, immoral people. We have already seen the panics provoked by the Indians, Africans, and Irish. Now, along came the Italians, Chinese, Russians, and Jews. Their numbers grew, their dirty habits and attitudes insinuated themselves, their youth mingled with ours, their "private" diseases infected us. These people, reported those who knew them, would have sex in a crowded tenement without a second thought for the kids milling about—small wonder the street urchins were so familiar with the "immoral side of life." Across all the purity proposals and panics ran the familiar theme: a God-fearing nation is threatened by hordes of strangers who just don't get the values that define us.[19]

The new urban setting scrambled the small-town norms. Even in the best hotels, wrote one scandalized preacher, gamblers passed for gentlemen and harlots posed as virtuous wives. They might fool anyone (they had fooled him, he warned his readers). Daily newspapers proliferated and filled their pages with terrible stories and dirty advertisements—for abortionists, contraceptives, and who knew what else. Publishers peddled romances that filled young minds with impossibly wicked images. Urban America seemed to be constructed out of lax rules and low races. Surely the demoralization of our society was at hand.

The others endangered American innocents in two ways. First, they stirred the old amalgamation fears. Black rapists, Chinese opium smokers, and Jewish flesh peddlers all provoked panics. Without a broad middle-class movement militating for racial justice (like the radical abolitionists), the Victorians came down hard on immigrants and blacks.

Second, the shadowy other posed a threat to the good family. Fears about national decline—going all the way back to the synod of 1679—invariably push the family to the forefront of our culture conflicts. After the Civil War, American reform circles began to buzz with warnings. Strangers—Irish, blacks, Jews, foreigners—were out to seduce and ruin young America. Reformers launched a purity campaign to protect the children. Their movement rapidly escalated into a tumult over sexual politics and policies.

Defending the community produced a distinctive political cycle: Moral dangers hit town. Good people push for tough laws and regulations. Cautious second thoughts (civil liberties or states' rights) get trampled in fear and haste. Once in place, the new policies take on a vigorous life of their own.

Comstockery

In 1872 the Young Men's Christian Association decided to fight the filth. It was a formidable crew—millionaires, gentlemen, captains of industry, men listed in the *Social Register*. They organized the New York Society for the Suppression of Vice. The idea came from England (where a society had been formed in 1802), but the New Yorkers found a quintessential American Puritan to lead their charge.[20]

Anthony Comstock was a bull-necked twenty-eight-year-old dry-goods clerk from Connecticut brimming with righteous fervor. During the war Comstock had been shocked to see fellow soldiers drink, smoke, swear, gamble, and frolic with women. He prayed and preached: "Touch not. Taste not. Handle not." His comrades, he said, "twitted" him and ran him down. But Anthony never wavered. By the time the Society for the Suppression of Vice called on Comstock, he was haunted by a single idea: "Our youth are in danger."[21]

The Comstock Law
Comstock charged down to Washington wielding the clout of his YMCA patrons. Before long his distinctive literary style—high moral dudgeon about imperiled youth—began to flow from every side. Representative Clinton L. Merriam of New York carried the message to Congress: "The outraged manhood of our age . . . condemns . . . the low brutality which threatens to destroy the future of the Republic by making merchandise of the morals of our youth." We have all been bewildered, said Merriam, by the "crime and depravity in this our day." But now we know the cause: a smut pandemic. Comstock had

brought before Congress 15,000 letters "written by our students of both sexes . . . ordering obscene literature."[22]

The *New York Times* took the same distinctly Comstockean tone: "It is disgusting even for a hardened man of the world to see the circulars and books which are sent by post to the girls and boys in our schools." Thankfully, gushed the *Times,* Mr. Comstock had already seized "ten tons . . . of the most loathsome printed matter ever sent into the world to do the devil's work."[23]

Before the Civil War, reformers had tried to persuade the sinners; now they backed up their sermons by proposing tough purity laws. Comstock's obscenity legislation came before an exhausted House of Representatives in the final minutes of a congressional session that had been marred by the Credit-Mobilier financial scandal. Congressman William Niblack (from Indiana) rose to complain: "Some members are sleepy and others object to further action . . . at this late hour." He pointed out that it was "now Sunday morning" and that "members are not [even] listening to what is said." The chair waved aside the objections, and the weary representatives slogged on to Comstock's bill. There was no debate. However, just before the final vote, an effort to bury the legislation back in committee fell short by 7 votes. The obscenity bill then glided through (100 to 37), and President Grant signed it without a word, alongside 117 other bits of legislation.[24]

The law—which actually revised postal regulations—erected a framework for controlling obscenity: smut, bad thoughts, birth control, abortion, and "immoral articles." It would stand for a century. The nation's great public bureaucracy stood in the thick of yet another nineteenth-century moral campaign; forty years earlier, postal battles had helped to shape abolition campaigns. Now they opened the political door to the domestic sphere. The key passage reads:

> That no obscene lewd or lascivious book, pamphlet, picture, paper, print or other publication of an indecent character or any article or thing designed . . . for the prevention of conception or procuring of abortion, nor any article or thing intended or adopted for any indecent immoral use or nature nor any written or printed card, circular, book, pamphlet, advertisement or notice of any kind giving information directly or indirectly, where, or how, or of whom, or by what means, either of the things before mentioned may be obtained or made . . . shall be carried in the mail.[25]

There. That would cover just about anything. The penalty for violating the Comstock Act ran to $5,000 and from one to ten years at hard labor. State legislatures used the federal act as a model for their own obscenity laws, known as Little Comstock Acts.

The law was silent on implementation. Instead, Congress anointed Anthony Comstock a postal inspector and set him loose. He was a master at self-promotion, constantly tabulating his smut-fighting score. By the time he was done, more than forty years later, Comstock had bagged fifty tons of books and four million pictures. He boasted four thousand arrests and more than fifteen suicides. Comstock never flinched; he treated the suicides as just one more roster of victories over "bloody," "gross," and "vicious" lives.[26]

Others rallied to fight for purity, though none with Comstock's genius for self-promotion or bureaucratic infighting. The New York Society for the Suppression of Vice was his silent partner, approving each case before Comstock pursued it. The Western Society for Suppression of Vice worked to clean up Cincinnati, St. Louis, and Chicago. The New England Society for the Suppression of Vice (renamed the Watch and Ward Society in 1890) made "banned in Boston" a byword of American censorship. Joseph and Deborah Leeds tackled Philadelphia. Each of these—and many others—used the revised postal code and the new state obscenity laws to hunt down the miscreants who would ravage our children and ruin the country.

The law covered a lot of sins—obscenity, radical ideas, birth control, abortion. Each set a different political dynamic into play.

The Comstock Sociology

The law's direct object was "obscene, lewd, or lascivious reading." The legislation came surrounded by extravagant warnings about threats to children. The "warfare with passion" was long and strenuous. One glance, one whisper, one slip, and a child could be lost. The mania about smut sprang from a ferocious attitude toward "self-pollution." The Victorian advice manuals went on and on: masturbation was the "most dangerous," the most beastly, the most "doubly abominable" of all sins against nature (except sodomy).[27]

The experts hectored parents to watch for telltale signs of the solitary sin: bashfulness, boldness, acne, round shoulders, bitten fingernails, lassitude, sleeplessness, sadness, the loss of vermilion from the lips or whiteness from the teeth, a desire to be alone, chewing pencils, taking tobacco, or—that sure-fire giveaway—an inability to argue clearly.[28]

Masturbation led to insanity, consumption, epilepsy, imbecility, a life of crime, even death. Anthony Comstock tracked down a thirteen-year-old girl who had gotten entangled in an obscenity ring at school. When he questioned her, "she went to a bureau drawer and brought . . . the most debasing and foul-worded matter." Soon "the child was . . . dying." Nicholas Cooke, a physician, wallowed in the clinical details. A young man started abusing himself and before long he could not stop. Here lay the ultimate in lost self-control. "The spasm . . . had become habitual and often seized him without apparent cause." The author visited the poor wreck and found a "corpse groaning from the straw ... a constant slime flowed from the mouth ... excrements on his bed ... continual spermatic flux." "In the presence of my God," stormed T. DeWitt Talmage, "I warn you of the fact that your children are threatened." Youth were "falling on every side." "The secret sin," added another physician, "is all but ruining the whole race."[29]

What turned smut and masturbation into political dynamite was the malevolence behind the plague. Sinister characters were preying on American children. Who? Behind the rhetorical melodrama—"secret agencies" of "evil men" serving "their satanic master"—lurked the usual suspects. Foreign nurse-maids and servant girls (right there in the good family's household) taught children the abominable crime so the kids would lie quietly once they were put to bed. "The vileness that would lead a person to thus rob a childhood of its innocence, and blast its prospects for this life and the next, is base enough for the commission of almost any crime. Indeed, the crime could hardly have been worse had the nurse ... in cold blood cut the throats of those innocent children; it might have been better for the children."[30]

Comstock publicized piles of villainy. "The beautiful girl not quite fourteen" is "approached by a miscreant" who hands her a paper parcel that contains "the most abominable matter ... shock[ing] beyond expression." The boy at the boarding school finds a parcel, "breaks the seal, and lets the monster loose." The black man in livery descends from an "elegant carriage" and enters a "leading high school" bearing "fifteen handsomely addressed envelopes purporting to be wedding cards." They contain, instead, the "most obscene matter" designed to "ruin the students body and soul."[31]

Every feature of these dramas—nurses, nannies, boarding schools—coded the villains and their victims by class. In contrast to the small town, the city tossed strangers together. The dangerous classes, sometimes in disguise (you could never be entirely sure), were everywhere. The false servant in livery was a variation of the gambler or strumpet passing for respectable in the best hotels.

The proper Victorians were almost frantic at the corrosive touch of the dangerous classes. Every story offered another helping of the same sociology—the boundaries between us and them were leaking. Loose, foreign, low sexual morals were trickling into the better classes. Perils lay all around. Enlightened parents worried about the serving girl, the nanny, the hired man, the immigrant, the rough workers, the bad characters—the whole booming urban experience. The smut and masturbation stories riveted all that free-floating class anxiety onto the children. The endless fretting about "blasted prospects" eloquently voiced Victorian fears about America itself—here, after all, were decline, corruption, and lost control.[32]

The trouble stretched beyond dirty stories. The media of the day seemed to

foster cynicism and glorify evil. Comstock scribbled down long lists of repugnant themes: hired assassins, Indian massacres, villains resisting arrest, explo-
sions, romances, oaths, easy money, irreverence to the law, disrespect for God,
beautiful women seducing men, men seducing beautiful women. They all
taught youth to "sneer at religion," they all "nourish[ed] wrongdoing." Cheap
urban amusements like the dime museums lured boys with "blood and thunder
dramas full of powder smoke and western bravadoes." All this corrosive immorality was driven by a ferocious chase after a quick buck. The sin merchants
seemed animated by an almost willful depravity—they were cold, cruel, cal-
lous.[33]

Despite all their bawling about childhood in peril, moral reformers took a
decidedly ambivalent view of the kids themselves. Lower-class children threatened everyone, of course. But their insolence was contagious. "Every new generation of youth is sent out into the world as sheep in the midst of wolves,"
wrote the Reverend James Buckley in his foreword to Comstock's book. "The
danger, however, is not that they will be devoured by them, but that they will be
transformed into wolves."[34]

Today the medical alarms—death by masturbation, no less—sound silly.
But the deeper fears are alive and well. Young people are still vulnerable sheep
surrounded by wolves. They face drugs on the playground, smut on the internet, violence on television, guns on the street, divorce at home, sexual depravity
everywhere. Today's purity crusaders still roast the popular media for mocking
traditional values, fostering cynicism, and glorifying evil. Contemporary writers precisely echo Comstock: our culture, reports one dispatch in the *Atlantic
Monthly*, "has contrived over the past few decades to transform sin into a positive." The Victorian "sinks of iniquity" produced "the shrugged shoulder, the
tossed head, the curled lip"; our postmodern society promotes the same bad attitude: "Cruel is cool."[35]

The filth still threatens to transform innocent children into nihilist wolves.
Each generation hears variations of the warnings. The frontispiece of Comstock's book illustrates the "modern newsstand and its results": knives, guns, arson, robbery, and murder. The list needs almost no updating. The street urchins
are now "super predatory" teenagers who come out of bad neighborhoods and
broken homes to prey on the rest of us.

Members of Comstock's generation lamented the loss of all-American values. They lashed out at genuine problems, at imaginary monsters, at innocent
victims. Today's moralizing generation ponders media that again seem out of
control. Shouldn't we find a way to rein in the filth? The yes comes from many
political sides. Some feminists would ban pornography for its violence against
women; conservative policy analysts propose subjecting free speech to cost-

8.1. THE MODERN NEWS STAND AND ITS RESULTS, frontispiece to Anthony Comstock's *Traps for the Young* (1872). The media of the day corrupts young minds and leads them into horrible crimes—robbery at gunpoint, arson, deadly knife fights, depravity ("Cut his heart out, Johnny," screams one little predator). In the background the public school offers these urban toughs an opportunity they ignore.

benefit analyses; communitarians suggest we give shame a chance. The Victorians vividly illustrated the dilemma that faces censors in every age: Where does one draw the line?

American Censorship
One Great Society for the Suppression of Vice

Crushing the demons—implementing the Comstock laws—passed into the hands of the vice crusaders themselves. First they had to define the crime. At least three different groups struggled over the meaning of obscenity—today, social scientists would call it a contest over issue definition. Radicals opposed marriage in its Victorian form; they had utopian dreams about free love unencumbered by legal shackles or double standards. Feminists put the focus on marital violence and male dominion. Finally, purity crusaders took an expansive view of the obscenity—it included provocative ideas. They defended Sacred Marriage and, eventually, used the radicals and the feminists to extend the reach of the Comstock Acts.

The battle warmed when Comstock went after Ezra Heywood for a pamphlet entitled *Cupid's Yokes*. Heywood was a socialist, a pacifist, a free thinker, a Brown University graduate, and a proponent of free love. Comstock could not contain his revulsion for *Cupid's Yokes:* "A most obscene and loathsome book, too foul for description." He viewed the author and his many followers as "disgusting" and "vile" "free lusters." "What license has done for the Turks [i.e., "crushed out common decency"] this doctrine is doing for America."[36]

In reality, *Cupid's Yokes* is an earnest (actually, boring) treatise about love and sexuality. Both must flow from free choice, argues Heywood. Marriage shackles couples and fosters repression, even violence. "When a man seeks to enjoy a woman's person at her cost . . . he is a libertine and she a martyr." Forget the legal forms, urges Heywood. Love alone should guide the relationship between man and woman. Love would regulate sexuality far more effectively than marriage laws that enslave, fornication statutes that repress, and vice laws that promote deceit.[37]

A handful of feminists made similar arguments. Victoria Woodhull was the most flamboyant. Woodhull was the first woman to address a congressional committee (in 1871 she argued that the Fourteenth and Fifteenth Amendments made no reference to gender and so applied to everyone); she was the first woman to run for president (in 1872, with Frederick Douglass as running mate). Woodhull made a fortune trading stocks and won international fame for communing with departed souls. However, her free-love lectures scandalized almost everyone: "The courts hold if the law solemnly pronounce two [people] married that they are married, whether love is present or not." An enlightened age, said Woodhull, would recognize this as legalized prostitution. "Love is what determines marriage." When love fades, the marriage is over. Even her friends winced at this radical talk, but Woodhull was fearless: "I will tell the world so long as I have a tongue and the strength to move it, of all the infernal misery hidden behind this horrible thing called marriage, though the YMCA sentence me to prison a year for every word."[38]

Elizabeth Cady Stanton boldly supported Woodhull (brushing aside her friend's notoriety) and emphasized one feature of the free-love argument: "There is no other human slavery that knows such depths of degradations as a wife chained to a man whom she neither loves nor respects." And in another lecture: "It is a sin against nature, the family, [and] the state for a man or woman to live together in the marriage relation in continual antagonism, indifference, disgust." The solution, said Stanton, lay in reforming divorce laws so that women could flee from abusive husbands. Susan B. Anthony supported the idea but always emphasized that without economic reform—without "her own purse"—easy divorces would not help women.[39]

The women's views proved prophetic. As women slowly won economic power, divorce became more popular. Already the divorce rate was rising: it grew fifteenfold between 1870 and 1920. Still, Stanton's position never won much of a following. Even most feminists were more interested in fixing marriages than in filing divorces. They wanted rights for women and manners from the men.

One especially powerful theme connected Heywood, Woodhull, Stanton, Anthony, and many others: the terror faced by a married woman. Her husband could coerce her, beat her, rape her—all with complete legal impunity. Husbands had "right of property in the wife." Even the "bloated drunkard" or "diseased libertine" could play the tyrant. She could not enter a contract or claim her own property. She could not even claim her own body. Like a slave, said Stanton, the wife cannot testify against her husband—nor escape from him. Even the conservative physicians repeated the charges. "Though the crime may be unrecognized . . . by law," wrote Horatio Storer, "many a married man has . . . virtually committed rape upon his wife." In fact, almost every Victorian advice book I have read urged men to be less bestial in their marital relations.[40]

The purity advocates were not impressed. They denounced all this "liberal obscenity mongering." In 1877, Comstock seized Heywood at a public rally and dragged him before the circuit court in Boston. Judge Daniel Clark ruled *Cupid's Yokes* too "obscene, lewd, and lascivious" to be entered into the court record. Clark ruled that the jury did not have to judge the pamphlet as a whole work—just look at the lewd bits. In his instructions to the jury, he pointed out that Heywood's ideas would make Massachusetts a vast house of prostitution.

8.2. Thomas Nast, "GET THEE BEHIND ME (MRS.) SATAN." Victoria Woodhull as the devil tempting the good wife with free love. The virtuous woman turns her back on this false salvation and treads the hard marital road. She carries a drunken husband and three children. The cartoon appeared in *Harper's Weekly* (1872). (Collection of the New-York Historical Society)

The jury found Heywood guilty. However, President Hayes foiled the censors and pardoned Heywood in late 1878; the attorney general had trouble finding anything lascivious in *Cupid's Yokes*.[41]

Undaunted, the Society for the Suppression of Vice went after Heywood's friend, DeRobigne Mortimer Bennet. Comstock had already unsuccessfully seized Bennet for a fiercely anti-religious pamphlet, "An Open Letter to Jesus Christ." ("Have you ever doubted whether your first miracle, changing water into wine, at the wedding in Cana was well advised, especially as the guests were already drunk?") Now, Bennet was back in the dock for defiantly advertising obscene material in his newspaper, the *Truth Seeker*. The offensive ad promoted—surprise—*Cupid's Yokes*.

Judge Samuel Blatchford produced a landmark decision in the Bennet case. He drew on English case law to propound a definition of obscenity: "whether the tendency of the matter charged as obscenity is to deprave and corrupt those whose minds are open to immoral influences and into whose hands [the] publication . . . may fall." The decision permitted a judgment on the basis of isolated passages, ruled the social value of the work irrelevant, and upheld the Heywood precedent of prohibiting any discussion of the obscene material in court. The court also upheld the Comstock standard: obscenity was stuff that would stir libidinous fancies in the "young and inexperienced." That hazy and circular norm—"tends to deprave those whose minds are open to [depravity]"—became the basis for American obscenity law. It was not fully overturned till 1973, when Chief Justice Warren Burger ruled that literary works must be judged in their entirety rather than on isolated passages.[42]

Bennet got thirteen months. Once again, supporters rallied for a presidential pardon (which had a certain logic, since President Hayes had pardoned the author of the pamphlet that Bennet now stood convicted of advertising). But Comstock, flourishing indiscreet letters that Bennet allegedly had written, managed to thwart the pardon. Bennet, already in poor health, died shortly after his release from prison. Comstock would convict (and ruin) Victoria Woodhull and, after years of trying, Ezra Heywood. Free-love arguments had never been popular; now they were obscene. Elizabeth Stanton continued to denounce male domination in marriage, but wife abuse slipped quietly from her lectures. Around the country states repealed the liberal divorce laws that feminists had won before the Civil War.[43]

In closing his argument against Bennet, the prosecutor turned a famous phrase. "Now gentlemen, this case is not entitled Anthony Comstock against D. M. Bennet; this case is not entitled The Society for the Suppression of Vice against D. S. Bennet. It is the United States against D. M. Bennet, and the United States is one great society for the suppression of vice." He meant it as a statement about American virtue and culture. But the little court speech neatly describes the legal machinery of the anti-obscenity campaign.[44]

The anti-vice societies had written the law. They then lobbied Congress and the states. Comstock's words found their way into the *Congressional Record* and the *New York Times*. The political authorities, federal and state, passed the laws and then promptly ceded the new public authority back to the vice-fighting organizations. Men like Comstock selected the cases, made the arrests, prepared the prosecutions. Even some allies grew queasy at placing so much public power in private hands: "Our voluntary associations for the prevention of various evils," reported the *New York Times* in 1875, "resemble vigilance committees, regulators or lynch policeman."

By the end of the decade, the purity advocates had gained still more power; the courts took up highly controversial cases and, in deciding them, tilted the law sharply toward convictions—Comstock would be successful in 90 percent

8.3. "Your Honor, this woman gave birth to a naked child!" an Anti-Comstock classic, from *The Masses* (1915). (Brown University Library)

of his cases. When the state began to grow in earnest, social scientists would charge that private interests often "captured" government power. As the purity case suggests, the political reality involved a more intricate public-private partnership.[45]

The Comstock regime illustrates the great cycle of modern moral legislation. Panic hits. Obscenity laws get pushed into place amid fears about immigrants, cities, and sliding values. The moral interest groups, legislatures, and courts work together to shape a legal framework and build an enforcement bureaucracy. Comstock's purity campaigns placed the growing power of the post office in a network of formidable private groups. Once the enforcement mechanisms started ticking, they proved difficult to stop. Allies gathered and demanded more. The institutions fighting the crime remain running long after the fears that prompted them fade into history. Comstock was still racking up legal victories into the 1910s, long after obscenity had given way to entirely different kinds of panics.

A Liberty Above Any Price

Public opinion on fighting vice was complicated. The flourishing vice societies flowed along the broader current of urban philanthropy. Comstock marched with plenty of allies. He got a respectful hearing from the Women's Christian Temperance Union (in 1884) and the National Mother's Congress (1897). The purity reformers endlessly compared their own aspirations to those of the abolitionist crusaders.[46]

On the other side, the censors faced opposition, almost from the start. The National Liberal League, founded in 1876, fought to "roll back the wave of intolerance, bigotry, and ignorance which threatens . . . our cherished liberties." Members rapidly gathered fifty thousand signatures calling for reform of the obscenity statutes. Most accepted the principle of obscenity legislation but protested the ambiguities that "permit the prosecution of . . . honest men." They furiously objected to the vice societies' wide discretion and power. League politics got especially hot over the Heywood and Bennet prosecutions.[47]

Workers were still quicker to blast the virtue mongers. They sweated long hours at monotonous jobs, then went home to crowded tenements. On days off, the working classes thronged to public amusements—dance halls, public concerts, movie houses, and amusement parks. The moralizers did not think this suitable. They gave these promiscuous entertainments—unmarried couples dancing and drinking without chaperones?—their full-throated condemnation. When New York enacted the Saturday Half-Holiday Act, even vice reformers who supported the idea fretted about the likely consequences—"dancing, carousing, low behavior, rioting, shooting, and murder."

When Comstock complained that concerts in the park violated the Sabbath (in 1884), *Life* magazine put a new spin on the working-class jeers. The editors sarcastically apologized for the "vulgar amusement of those horrid people who have to work all the week." As a compromise, the magazine suggested a polar expedition so that "injured saints" might find a place to take their Sabbath undisturbed. *Life* organized a "Comstock polar fund." The contributions appeared in the next issue: a lead nickel, a white plug hat, the proceeds from a lame joke ($.003), a fourteen-hundred-pound Henry James manuscript. Among the ribbing came the inevitable from Anthony Comstock himself: "LIFE: Suspend your subscription. . . . I do not wish to go." "That's all right, Mr. Comstock," replied the editors, "this is one of those honors which the public are anxious to thrust upon you. So pack up."[48]

By the end of his long career Comstock was being derided on almost every side. Cartoonists loved to mock him—the most famous depiction is of a fat and clueless Comstock dragging a poor, worn-out woman into court by the scruff of her neck and announcing her crime to the scowling puritanical-looking judge: "Your Honor, this woman gave birth to a naked child!" Nor did Comstock much help his own cause. In 1905 censors challenged George Bernard Shaw for *Mrs. Warren's Profession.* Though Comstock was not involved in the case, he had Shaw's number: "this Irish smut dealer," "this foreign writer of filth." "Englishmen and Irishmen—I have destroyed their stuff by the tons." Well, actually, he admitted to the *New York Times,* he had never read any of Shaw's stuff. In response, Shaw coined a term that stuck: "Comstockery: the world's standing joke at the expense of the United States!" As the *New Republic* (which was generally sympathetic to Comstock) would admit, the man often "conspicuously made an ass out of himself."[49]

By the end of Comstock's career, the long Puritan swing was winding down. "Comstockery" decidedly lost the war. Shaw taunted his censors: "It confirms the deep seated [European] conviction that . . . America is . . . a second rate country-town civilization after all." Shaw got it at least partially right. Many Americans did cling to their "country-town" heritage, but that world was vanishing into the new urban civilization. By the 1920s, Upton Sinclair could still get banned in Boston (the Watch and Ward remained on smut patrol). But Sinclair's scorn reflected the spirit of the times: "I . . . never told a smutty story in [my] life." Yet, a "Boston police magistrate has decreed that my last [book] manifestly tends to corrupt youth." Sinclair's punch line might stand as Comstock's epitaph: "Every time you get a censor you get a fool, and worse yet, a knave, pretending to be a guardian of morality while acting as a guardian of class greed."[50]

Comstock's career offers a vivid warning to would-be censors. In the moving preface to her book on Comstock, Anna Louise Bates explains how she picked her subject: because pornography degrades women, she thought it should be banned. But studying Comstock, writes Bates, turned into a painful exercise. The obscenity campaigners' harassed, jailed, and destroyed a long line of people. Perhaps some deserved the punishment, but the archives and court records are packed with cries from honest intellectuals. Why, asks Bates, "would any man willingly force such suffering on his fellow human beings?"[51]

Comstock answered that question again and again: they were evil, they threatened our children, God wanted them crushed. Like so many others fighting against sin, Comstock did not truck with either due process or undue pity: "Hunt these men as you hunt rats, without mercy." By the end of her own project, concludes Bates, she had grown powerfully committed to free speech, a "liberty above [any] price." It is hard to read Anthony Comstock and not come away cherishing that freedom.[52]

Many sensible people worried about obscenity. They supported legislation. Then they went back to their lives. The zealots remained on patrol; they enforced the laws and hammered out the legal guidelines. By the time they were through, the process did not distinguish between smut, social criticism, and sociology. Comstock's crusade against immoral "rats" echoes back to the early Puritans (how could any people slaughter Native Americans so furiously?) and down to the present day (2 million people in jail?). Morality crusades mobilize Americans to fight for their soaring principles—see Abraham Lincoln. But mix morals with fears and strangers, and those high-flying principles get trampled in righteous indignation. American values melt into Comstockery.

Feminists

Feminists blended radical ideas with orthodox gender norms. They focused on the wife's right to refuse both undesired sex and unwanted children. The idea became known as "voluntary motherhood." Giving women control of their own bodies—over having sex and bearing children—may seem to us like the most basic human right. But in the nineteenth century it was a bold position that challenged both law and practice. As Pauline Davis bitterly noted in 1871, the husband's "right of property in his wife" made sexual submission an "obligation" and maternity "compulsory." Critics promptly demonstrated her point by tagging Davis a free-lover for even raising the issue. In the 1870s, writes Linda Gordon, voluntary motherhood became the feminist key to birth control, family size, and personal integrity.[53]

The subversive proposal overlapped the standard pieties. Voluntary motherhood rang with Victorian religious sentiment: women were morally superior, they rose above carnal lust. Now, feminists, preachers, and physicians were all urging men up to the same spiritual level. Men should relinquish their double standard, renounce sexuality outside marriage, and rein in their lust at home.

Frances Willard's Social Movement

In the mid-1870s, Frances Willard burst into the debate and reframed the whole issue of sex and politics. In the process, she mobilized women like no one had done before. Willard was a charismatic leader, an inspirational lecturer, and one of the most influential evangelical reformers in American history. One colleague, Kate Sanborn, described the first time she heard Willard lecture. Sanborn was also scheduled to speak and had braced herself to share the podium with a crusading temperance fanatic. Instead, Willard was "beautiful" and "impressive." Sanborn was so moved that she sneaked out of the room rather than follow Willard to the podium. "When my name was called, and my little speech expected, I was walking up Fifth Avenue thinking about her and her grand work."[54]

Willard called on women to rally round and defend their special sphere. She exhorted them to protect themselves, their children, and their homes from male violence. The first step was temperance, since liquor turned men brutish. Women would also fight against impurity. And if women were going to defend America's homes, they would need the vote. Once they had won a role in American politics, mothers could protect their families, uplift their communities, and inspire the nation. Women would triumph through the power of "mother love." Over and over Willard reminded her audiences that "mother love" would always "vanquish brute force."

Willard ferociously attacked male violence. "I see fair women in beautiful robes . . . in fine social surroundings." And the men around them? "Puffing tobacco smoke into their face and eyes." Willard tarred male behavior as a vestige of "past savagery and debasement and immolation of women." Willard roasted the swaggering males—all attitude, alcohol, and assault. "Every day," she said, "two hundred fifty thousand saloons" disgorged mobs of men with "inflamed natures" to prey upon "weak and unarmed women" who "attract their savage glances" or are "bound to them by the sacred tie of wife." Violence seemed to permeate every aspect of male life. She sardonically challenged elite American men in 1894: "Why not debate the following? Resolved—the differences between Harvard and Yale be settled by arbitration, without resort to football."[55]

Willard built the first mass women's movement. She became president of the Women's Christian Temperance Union (WCTU) in 1879 and held the post till 1898. When she took office the organization had 27,000 members (and the National American Woman Suffrage Association, 13,000). Within a decade, the WCTU counted almost 200,000 women in its ranks. In small towns and villages across America, conservative women joined up. They met, distributed WCTU pamphlets, sent petitions to their congressional delegations, and discussed ways to elevate their communities. Frances Willard's portrait hung in countless American parlors—her vivid blue eyes staring out, practically exuding temperance and purity. [56]

Home protection led the WCTU to champion a "white life for two." Members emphasized purity for both men and women; they insisted on the "respectful treatment of women." In 1886, the Episcopalian bishops introduced the White Cross Army (originally an English church organization) and turned the purity ideal into a national movement. The WCTU jumped into the crusade. Willard toured the nation, addressing big crowds in large cities. Respectable men came forward and took the pledge: "I will maintain the law of purity as equally binding upon men and women . . . and I will use every means to fulfill the sacred command, 'Keep thyself pure.'" Upright men and women sported white lapel ribbons.[57]

The White Cross (and its White Shield sister organization) gave the women's movement a terrific boost. All kinds of allies began signing up for the single standard. Educated young men pledged to champion the new egalitarian sexual ideal. The Protestant clergy overcame its fear of sexual politics and pushed the cause. Even the YMCA joined with the gender reformers.[58]

Frances Willard managed to sell the same arguments that Elizabeth Stanton, Susan Anthony, and even Ezra Heywood had been pushing. She insisted on a single sexual standard, pushed voluntary motherhood, demanded respect for women, ripped male violence (in and out of marriage), called for woman suffrage, and eventually demanded an equal living wage for men and women. Willard stopped short of demanding divorces (like Stanton) or denouncing marriage (like Heywood). When Paulina Wright Davis condemned marital violence and compulsory motherhood she was dubbed a "free lover." But for Frances Willard even preachers like T. DeWitt Talmage stood up and cheered (though Talmage could not stifle that trace of masculine condescension): "God bless the White Cross Movement" and "its ablest advocate on this side of the sea, the talented Miss Frances Willard."[59]

How did Willard reframe the politics? By subordinating radical means to conventional moral ends. Stanton and her colleagues reached for rights by challenging the status quo; Willard called for the same rights in order to defend it. Conservative nineteenth-century women followed Willard to a bold pro-

gram—votes for women, continence for men—in order to protect their domestic sphere and extend the influence of mother love. Stanton rallied people
with a vision of human rights, Willard with Christian duty. Once again, religious fervor mobilized people. The WCTU jolted America with a familiar
recipe for social upheaval: old-fashioned values, moral outrage, and fears of the
violent them.[60]

Still, Willard was a moralizer with a difference. She placed the fight for
virtue in a larger social and economic framework. "Poverty causes intemperance," she declared in 1893, as well as the other way round. That idea challenged the central pillar of Victorian moralizing—that social ills come from
personal failings. Willard did not deny personal responsibility (intemperance
did cause poverty); but she fixed it in a larger political economy (poverty
spawned sins, too). "Father absence" also plagued poor families—then as now.
Willard rounded up the usual solutions: close the saloons and preach male responsibility. Then she pushed further: win an eight-hour workday and pay a
living wage. Willard allied with the Knights of Labor (which professed the
same faith) and kept a photo of its chief, Terrence Powderly, on her desk. Powderly may have been the moderate leader of a moderate union, but Willard was
urging the coalition with workers in an epoch of bitter conflict. Her "Christian" politics led the WCTU to the left on social and economic issues.[61]

Willard's social morality reflected the Social Gospel movement that swept
America at the turn of the century. The movement always balanced personal
responsibility with societal conditions. Like Willard, proponents of the Social
Gospel movement blamed the socioeconomic system for spawning intemperance, father absence, poverty, impurity—for all kinds of apparently personal
vices. This reform impulse echoes the radical economics espoused by Orestes
Brownson. Its legacy would run through the twentieth century, wrestling with
its more robust twin—the urge to pin vice and virtue on individuals.

In theory, the two perspectives build different moral worlds—Victorians
pinned immorality on individuals, the Social Gospel blamed society and the
political economy. The difference would grow increasingly vivid and self-conscious. However, in nineteenth-century practice, the difference blurred. Social
Gospel preachers condemned sinners with all the brio of Calvinist preachers.
We can see that urge in full flight by turning to minister Charles Sheldon's romantic novel *In His Steps*. The book, which sold 30 million copies, imagined a
city transformed when the community leaders settled every question by asking
"What would Jesus do?"

Well, one thing he would do, decided a local minister, would be to take the
White Cross crusade directly into the heart of the slum—"a vile, dirty,
drunken, impure, besotted, bleary mass of humanity." The reformers promptly

pitched the purity crusade's tent in the impoverished "Quadrangle." But when the minister rose to speak he could not control the "jeers, oaths, impurity and heavy drinking of the debauched slum dwellers." What to do? The minister turned to the pure, spiritual, beautiful Rachel and asked her to sing.

Immediately the brutal neighborhood "stirred itself into a new life" as the pure song floated out into the vile surroundings. Before long the wild people were hushed, reverent, timid. Even the men loudly quarrelling inside a saloon stopped and listened. The "dirty, drunken, impure humanity . . . trembled and wept and grew strangely, sadly thoughtful, under the touch of the divine ministry of this beautiful young woman." By the end, the slum "lay like some wild beast at her feet."[62]

Purity triumphs. Touched by the good virgin, those people cast off their debauchery. In Sheldon's moral daydream, they will take the White Cross pledge, embrace temperance, boot out the nasty machine politicians, rise and prosper. The dream of virtue leaps over the gritty reality of cities bursting with newcomers, racial brawls, economic busts, epidemics, and the bitter contest between workers and capital. Blink away the complex problems, see only individual sins, and the solutions become alluringly simple: Repent. Pledge temperance. Promise purity. Pin on the White Cross. Vote for municipal reform.

The easy answer comes with a high price. When virtue campaigns drift from social and economic moorings, they erode support for more substantive reform by dividing society into the virtuous and the vicious. The pejoratives that Sheldon attached to the slum dwellers pack a powerful, inadvertent message: Why fight for social and economic justice, for a living wage or an eight-hour day or unemployment insurance? Those people are incorrigible. Their sins drive them into poverty. And, despite all the big-hearted missionary efforts, they refuse to repent, reform, and rise.

Worse, everyone knows just who the sinners are. The vicious men and women typify entire races—Irish, Italians, African Americans. Their worst problems lay in their stubborn sins, such as liquor, sex, and violence. Moral reforms became the solution. This critique—resting on individual behavior—turns reformers away from more fundamental social and economic change.

Race always offers the acid test for Social Gospel urges. Even Frances Willard lapsed into hurtful moralizing when the talk turned to black and white. After all, the "white life for two" buzzed with racial ambiguity. The slogan sounded its call to gender justice and the single sexual standard; but the "white life" also distinguished the comfortable Anglo-Saxons (marching forward with ribbons pinned on their lapels) from the "gross" races who supposedly drank, fornicated, bred big families, and didn't even sport lapels—never mind the ribbons.

The "white life" erupted into racial controversy toward the end of Willard's life, when she gave in to the rising racism and nativism of the 1880s and 1890s. Ida B. Wells-Barnett, campaigning heroically against southern lynch mobs, pleaded for Willard's help. The WCTU crusade against violence, said Wells-Barnett, might have embraced our "oppressed people," who ask only for "a fair . . . trial" and "protection from butchery." Most lynching had nothing to do with sexual violence, said Wells. Only one-fifth of the victims were even accused of rape, and those cases included black men and white women in "voluntary, clandestine, and illicit relations."

This went too far for Willard. By suggesting that "white women have taken the initiative in nameless acts between the races, [Miss Ida B. Wells-Barnett] has put an imputation upon half the white race in this country that is unjust and save in the rarest exceptional instances wholly without foundation." Willard would not hear of white women seducing black men, would not accept black men as victims. Besides, to court southern allies she busily flattered her southern sisters. In the process, charged Wells-Barnett, Willard was condoning racial repression.[63]

After a southern tour Willard got involved in a discussion of the alleged epidemic of black rape that provoked the terrible wave of lynching. "The grogshop," Willard told one reporter, "is the Negro's center of power. Better whiskey and more of it is the rallying cry of great dark faced mobs." Returning from another tour of the South, she commented on the denial of black voting rights. We "irreparably wronged ourselves" by letting "alien illiterates" vote in the North; we have wronged the South by "pushing the vote onto the Plantation Negro, who can neither read nor write, whose ideas are bounded by the fence of his own field."[64]

When Frederick Douglass denounced lynching, he provoked a roar of protest. White southerners justified their racial reign of terror by imagining an epidemic of black rapists. One ex-governor of South Carolina blustered, "As you value your own good fame and safety as a race, stamp out the infamous crime." But what stung him most, said Douglass, was Frances Willard's "sweet voice." She wrote Douglass, "I pity the Southerners. . . . The colored race multiplies like the locusts of Egypt. The safety of woman, of childhood, of the home is menaced in a thousand localities at this moment, so that men dare not go beyond the sight of their own roof-tree."[65]

The WCTU put the same thing more politely with a flaccid anti-lynching resolution of 1894 (written by a southern delegation). "No human being should be condemned without due process of law." So far, so good. Then the organization added a "prayer" that the "unspeakable outrages which have so often pro-voked such lawlessness" would soon be "banished from the world," so that "childhood, maidenhood, and womanhood shall no more be the victims of atrocities worse than death." While black men and women were fighting for their lives, said Frederick Douglass, this kind of talk was designed "to blast and ruin the Negro's character as a man and a citizen. . . . It has cooled his friends; it has heated his enemies and [it has] arrested . . . the generous efforts that good men were wont to make for his improvement and elevation." Wells-Bar-nett was harsher. She said that Frances Willard and the WCTU condoned "fraud, violence, murder, shooting, hanging and burning."[66]

Once again we find a profound ambivalence in American moralizing. Willard managed an extraordinary grass-roots mobilization. No one else had ever stirred up a women's movement like this one. But in the process she di-vided the community into us and them. Mother-love drew power by trading in fear—fear of violent men, fear of drunken foreigners, fear of black rapists.

Even when middle-class reformers honestly struggle to uplift social mor-als, the charges of immorality rush straight to the weak groups at the fringes. The swarming, incorrigible poor are impure, cruel, drunken, and sinful. They have only themselves to blame for their poverty. Even Frances Willard—who keenly saw the deeper social dilemmas, who kept a labor leader's photograph on her desk, who pushed her woman's army toward Christian socialism—could not resist the moralizing tide. In the end, she too justified the lynch-mobs in the South and jeered the immigrants in the North.

Morality's Double Edge

Even the most urgent moral reforms could get tangled up in social divi-sions. In the 1880s the WCTU campaigned across the states to raise the age when a woman may legally consent to sex. At the time, most states set the legal standard at ten; Delaware had it at seven.

The deep South clung to ten as the legal norm; once the fuss began, Mis-sissippi actually lowered its age from twelve. Other states raised the age of con-sent only to drop it back down. The conflict always gusted around the same touchy questions: When was a woman old enough for sex? How long should the government protect girls? Most states agreed that ten was too young. On the other hand, the purity advocates pushed for twenty-one—that would cer-tainly rein in the kids. States resisted going that high. Between 1886 and 1895, thirty-five states raised the age. At the same time, authorities imposed new controls on teen-agers. Four thousand local governments introduced curfews. Some barred youths without chaperones from morally dubious places—like skating rinks and dance halls. Of course, the young working people who relied on public amusements chafed at the restrictions. A blurry line separated moral protection and unfair restraints.[67]

The real devil lurked in the implementation details. Mary Odem examined the age of consent in California and discovered a sharp racial bias in the punishments. White men convicted of sex with a minor generally got probation. Sometimes the court blamed the victim; it would take a strong man, said Superior Court Judge Frank Ogden, to escape the traps set by the young lady before him in one case. On the other hand, every black man in Odem's sample got jail time.[68]

One case sums up the racial rhythms. Raymond Thompson was a black man living with a fifteen-year-old black runaway. Thompson's lawyer argued that his client had a good job as a barber, that he planned to marry the young woman, and that most similar cases (more than 60 percent, calculates Odem) had resulted in probation. The prosecution countered with a familiar line: "It is about time that we should educate these colored people and tell them that they should obey the laws." The court agreed. Thompson got ten years.

The fate of immigrant men is less clear (murky records), but the same urge to teach them a lesson came up at least some of the time: "I realize that in some foreign countries, the same code of morals is not present," Judge Ogden lectured an Italian immigrant. "In some countries today a man can forcibly take [a] woman that . . . he wants, but of course we don't call those countries civilized. . . . If we permit [their] customs to prevail upon this soil, instead of having the higher code of ethics, we would descend to the code of ethics and the morals of [these] other communities."[69]

The age of consent dispute illustrates another variation of the same old moral snarl. On its face, the reform is undeniably important. In its struggle to raise the age, the WCTU won some of its most unambiguous victories for home protection. Yet, once again, the results cut two ways. Some reformers pushed for unrealistic, even stifling, ages of consent; in some places, they piled restrictions on young people. And once the moralizing alarm went off, Americans began to worry about "descending to the code of ethics" of the benighted and dangerous other. High moral aspirations met waves of strangers and ambivalent visions of young women. The volatile mix yielded important protection and new ways to discriminate. Once again the call to virtue rallied Americans to important reforms even while it also subverted social justice.

Birth Control

The Comstock Act took a firm stance against two increasingly visible reproductive technologies—contraceptives and abortion. The purity crusaders marched into this battle alongside two of their bitter rivals. Most feminists and many free-love advocates also opposed birth control, fearing that it would further license male promiscuity and even sexual aggression. When it came to abortion, the vice regulators enjoyed an even more powerful ally, the American Medical Association. Together these groups constructed a legal birth regime—bars on birth control and bans on abortion—that would stand for a century. The conflicts surrounding reproductive politics summed up all the gender issues: the woman's role in society, sexuality, and the nature of the family. Political conflict—the legislatures, the courts, even the postal bureaucracy—reached into the very heart of the private sphere.

Contraceptives

Condoms had cost five dollars a dozen before the Civil War; by the 1870s they went for six cents apiece, diaphragms for a dollar. Even workers could afford them. Advertisements spread across the newspapers and almanacs. As more people started using contraceptives, sermons began to flow. However, this time the preachers mixed their thunder with diffidence. "To even mention these . . . accessories of evil," wrote Kellogg, "would be too great a breach of propriety." Cooke had the same problem, but he still managed to get all the usual adjectives lined up: "disgusting, beastly, positively wrongful, unnatural and physically injurious." Dr. Horatio Storer blended medical opinion with male prejudice: "Willful interference with the laws of nature [causes] vast amounts of disease." Worse, the spread of contraceptives explained what every thinking man "must miss in this generation of women . . . the loss of beauty, of expression, and [of] sweet maternal charm." The physicians all concluded by longing for the great big households of the good old days.[70]

The Comstock laws offered relief by forbidding any "article or thing designed . . . for the prevention of conception." Nor could you give anyone information about how to get them. Comstock enthusiastically raided purveyors; he wrote for advice about birth control, then nabbed physicians who mailed him a response. After just two years the Comstock ticker stood at 60,300 rubber articles seized and destroyed.[71]

Couples trying to avoid pregnancy found alternatives to those wicked rubber articles. Some men simply withdrew before orgasm. Nicholas Cooke thought withdrawal had become "so universal it might well be termed a national vice." But its popularity did not diminish the sin. Victorian moralists lustily condemned the practice they called the Sin of Onan. "Onan spilled his seed upon the ground, lest children should be born"; this was so "detestable" that the Lord immediately slew him. The advice books roll through their lists of gory medical consequences—from cancer to infidelity. But this time the

preachers remain oddly defensive; one acknowledges that readers "might be in-
clined to smile and charge us with exaggeration." Comstock spent his last years
furiously trying to fend off artificial birth control. That battle would race
through the twentieth century, drawing feminists, eugenicists, physicians, civil
liberties groups, and many others into the fray.[72]

Abortion

In the first part of the nineteenth century, abortions were widely available.
They were legal as long as they were done before "quickening," before the fetus
first stirred (around the end of the fourth month). Even abortions done later
were not high crimes or serious sins. Neither politics nor morality defined
abortion as a problem. After the Civil War the first anti-abortion movement
swept across the states. The fetal politics covered a lot of ground: the social role
of women, cross-pressures on male identity, the status of the medical profession, the falling birthrate, America's racial character, and the question of just
when life begins. By the time it was over, the reformers had managed a sensational social transformation: they turned a common practice into a terrible
crime.[73]

Before the fight began, effective abortion techniques were easy to find—
and so were quack prescriptions and procedures. On balance, writes historian
James Mohr, a nineteenth-century abortion posed roughly the same danger as
a live birth. Still, descriptions are not for the faint-hearted. As late as the 1870s,
for example, many abortionists pulled out a healthy tooth on the theory that
the pain would induce a miscarriage.[74]

The great shift in attitudes began, like so many moral itches, in the wicked
city. Abortion providers rose out of the domestic realm of wives and midwives,
as Carroll Smith-Rosenberg puts it, and entered the world of commerce.
Abortionists proliferated and developed their practices into sophisticated commercial operations with multiple clinics. Their advertisements appeared in city
newspapers. The commercial drug industry pushed the abortion business.
And, of course, providers found a ready market in a bourgeoisie eager to limit
family size. "A rare and secret occurrence," reported one physician, has become
"frequent and bold." Sure enough, between 1800 and 1830 there had been one
abortion for every thirty live births; by mid-century the pace had leaped to one
for every six.[75]

Storer led the charge. We have heard from Storer on such issues as who
would populate the vast American plains (Americans or aliens?) and why his
generation of women were such losers (contraception). But his life's work lay in
suppressing abortion. Physicians already knew that popular talk about quickening was medical myth. Those first kicks that a woman felt in her womb did

not mark any particular stage of gestation—much less the start of life. But if quickening was not the beginning of life, what was? Roused by Storer, the doctors took their stand: "The very moment of conception." With that point established, physicians rose up on their expertise and howled at couples looking to abort. When a professor asked Nicholas Cooke for help with an abortion ("before life or animation has commenced"), Cooke launched into an angry lecture. "You must base your teachings upon the clearly determined facts of science." And from a scientific perspective, it would be the same to "murder the infant six months or a year after birth." Or better yet, snorted Cooke, do the easy thing—"murder your present child and let the other come."[76]

Induced abortions were a "crime against life," railed Storer. They were so terrible that soliciting one should "almost be looked upon as a proof of insanity." He rallied the American Medical Association (the AMA, formed in 1847) into fighting the crime. At its 1859 annual meeting, the AMA committed itself to publicly "protest against the unwarrantable destruction of human life" and to urge the "legislative assemblies of the union" to revise their abortion laws. After the Civil War the state organizations threw themselves into the effort. On both the state and the national level the doctors flattened the opposition. Their campaign may have been the most successful political operation ever run by an organization that would become legendary for its political conquests.[77]

The AMA led a large army of allies. Scandal sheets like the *New York Police Gazette* puffed up and popularized fetal horrors. Abortionists were selling dead babies to the medical schools. Abortionists botched operations and hid the women's bodies from their husbands. The *Police Gazette*'s nightmare tales generally featured middle-class women trapped in an urban hell. In one of the period's most famous sketches, the *Gazette* printed an image of the "female abortionist," a sad-looking woman with a monstrous, infant-devouring bat-creature in place of a womb. At the other end of the literary spectrum, the *New York Times* was calling abortions "nefarious," "odious," and the "Evil of the Age." And, of course, the Anthony Comstocks around the country poured out their high dudgeon about the road to hell.[78]

Between 1866 and 1877 the anti-abortion forces won thirty new state prohibitions. At the national center of all this action stood the Comstock Act. The law proscribed "any article or medicine for causing an abortion except on a prescription of a physician in good standing"—the closest the federal government has ever come to outlawing abortion, comments Mohr. Once the statutes were in place, the purity activists went after the miscreants.[79]

The most celebrated case involved Madame Restell, an English immigrant whose real name was Ann Lohman. Restell ran one of the most visible and successful abortion organizations; she had clinics in New York, Philadelphia, and

8.4. "The Female Abortionist," from the racy *National Police Gazette*. A bat-like, child-devouring monster has replaced the abortionist's womb. (Rare Books Division, The New York Public Library, Astor, Lenox and Tilden Foundations)

Boston—and an ostentatious house on Fifth Avenue, reported the *New York Times*, that made "the finest Avenue in the City odious by her presence." The *Police Gazette* reportedly used Lohman's face for its female abortionist cartoon. In 1878, Comstock tricked Restell into selling an abortifacient preparation and promptly arrested her. The story was a national sensation. It became really huge the day before the trial, when Madame Restell slit her own throat with a kitchen knife. The virtuous positively crowed. "Driven to desperation at last by the public opinion she had so long defied," exulted the *New York Times* on page 1. "A bloody end to a bloody life," scribbled Comstock in the ledger of the Committee for the Suppression of Vice. The dramatic case marked the end of abortion as a commercial enterprise in the United States till the 1970s.[80]

The American Medical Association had organized an enormous shift in both law and culture. But why? Three different goals moved the doctors. First, personal conviction. Once they saw that quickening was meaningless, the doctors needed an alternative. The vast majority found it in the same mix of science, faith, and instinct that runs through all the Victorian medical tracts. At first, some physicians demurred; one complained that Horatio Storer "seems to have thrown out of all consideration the life of the mother." When they saw themselves in a despised minority, however, the protesters quickly shut up.[81]

Second, physicians were reaching for professional authority. They had not yet won their place at the center of American healing. Rivals flourished on all sides. Botanic doctors blended herbal medicines (often mixing in radical politics). Homeopaths offered a hands-on drug-based therapy that replaced the disease with a milder ailment that the patient's body could defeat. But the largest and most ancient challenge came from midwives. "Every neighborhood or small village has its old woman, of one sex or another, who is known for her ability," complained one Detroit physician. And now those village women, dispensing folk wisdom about birth and death, were morphing into an urban industry.[82]

Flaunting both their science and their scruples, the medical societies prodded state governments into wiping out the competition. In a sense, the medical profession organized itself in counterpoint to these professional others. The medical journals practically gagged over all the undereducated "quacks," "irregulars," and "doctresses" who cluttered their field. In truth, obstetrics and gynecology did not yet offer much of a scientific alternative; its members would not fully work out the menstrual cycle till the 1920s—a half-century away.[83]

The physicians' search for status went beyond their role as healers. By standing up for Science, God, and Country, they were stepping into the role of civic leaders. "Physicians alone," they told one another, "can rectify public opinion." Oh, sure, theologians and parents were important. But only the doctors could draw on science to present the subject in a way that guided legislators trying to frame "suitable laws"; only doctors could teach women the "value of the foetus." The doctors simultaneously cleared away their fraudulent rivals and posed as moral pillars of the community.[84]

Third, the doctors shared class anxieties about all those strangers. Abortion was "infinitely more frequent among Protestant women than among Catholic," warned Storer. The great war had already torn "gaps in our population." Now, the better classes shirked their childbearing responsibilities. In Massachusetts the population growth came entirely from the foreigners. Across the country, Storer's colleagues broadcast the same alarm. The "ignorant, the low lived and the alien" were swamping American society. The true Americans—along with their peerless moral character—would be bred right out of the nation. "The annual destruction of foetuses is [so] truly appalling," wrote one physician in 1874, that "the Puritanic blood of '76 will be but sparingly represented in the approaching centenary."[85]

In the end, the AMA's abortion campaign landed squarely on a villain: the wealthy bourgeois matron. "Abortion is demanded . . . merely because of the annoyance of pregnancy and the duties involved by the new-born helpless child," wrote physician Walter Channing. "Is self indulgence the only thing to be sought in this life?" asked another doctor. "Is there no such thing as duty?" In 1871, the AMA Committee on Criminal Abortion expressed the doctors' severe rebuke: "She yields to pleasures—but shirks from the pains and responsibilities of maternity; destitute of all delicacy and refinement, [she] resigns herself, body and soul, into the hands of . . . wicked men."

Naive husbands were easily fooled by such hedonists. "Let not the husband of such a wife flatter himself that he possesses her affection. Nor can she ever merit the respect of a virtuous husband." The medical men worked themselves into a fine misogynist dander: "She sinks into old age like a withered tree, stripped of its foliage; with the stain of blood upon her soul, she dies without the hand of affection to smooth her pillow." And beneath all the shirked duties lay the whisper of "women's rights."[86]

The sermons about gratifying lusts and shunning duty were firmly rooted in the classic Puritan jeremiad. But beyond all that lay a distinctly modern fear. Childbearing had become unfashionable. Horatio Storer spun a bitter variation of shopping as female vice: "Ladies boast to each other of the impunity with which they have aborted as they do of their expenditures, of their dress, of their success in society." The Victorian woman had stepped out into society and gotten distracted from her true role. The folly had grown into the "tide of fashion—for it [is] fast becoming the way of the world to bear no children." Today, few women dare "publicly or privately to acknowledge it the . . . first, highest, and . . . holiest duty of her sex to bring forth living children."[87]

The physicians did not entirely get away with their attitude toward women. Frances Willard opposed abortion too. But she had choice words for the groaning "accumulation of books written by men to teach women the immeasurable iniquity of arresting . . . a new life, but not one of these volumes contains the remotest suggestion that this responsibility should be at least equally divided between himself and herself." The men were clueless. The "most hopeless feature," thought Willard, was the "utter unconsciousness" with which the men flaunted their biases and blamed women for abortion.[88]

Two great organizations fighting for purity found precisely opposite villains. The doctors defined their profession partially through a great attack on middle-class women. As the AMA saw it, Victorian women were drunk on women's rights and fashionable pleasures. They recklessly threw off all controls (meaning male authority), aborted their babies, and ducked both motherhood and duty. You can clearly hear the aggrieved echo of John Winthrop about not "crucifying lusts." And you can also hear the fury—even the arguments—that surround abortion politics today. Opponents still blast "abortions of convenience" and unwittingly echo Storer, who was himself looking back wistfully to still "earlier times," when raising children was every woman's "universal lot."

The Women's Christian Temperance Union pointed right back—at oppressive, lustful men and the laws that permitted them to use and abuse their wives. Those very same bourgeois women were pinning white ribbons on their husbands and working hard to reform them. And what were the women fighting for? Mother love! Home protection! The women were under no illusion about getting much help from even middle-class men who still vibrated with "past savagery" and the present "immolation" of their wives. The WCTU used the wayward husband to help forge an image of his spiritual counter, the wife and mother.

Each group used the dangers it attacked to define its political agenda, to define itself and its members. Still, for all the differences between the doctors and the mothers, the same deep anxiety galvanized both into action. Like every faction in the great purity army, these middle-class groups fretted about the rapidly breeding others. They knew that the immigrants threatened us with their low morals and vicious habits. The active loins of the Italians or the Germans or worse were threatening to populate those American plains—and fill the cities—with aliens.

The anti-abortion campaign managed something exceedingly rare. It discovered a terrible new sin. Once the doctors and their allies put the issue into political play, abortion would always be either banned or bitterly contested. The issue is so powerful because it wraps murder charges around the three irresistible themes of American sexual politics. First, abortions offer women a way to elide motherhood—dredging up the deepest questions about gender roles and obligations. In the mid-nineteenth century, motherhood ranged, in different hands, from the blessed salvation of society to "worse than solitary confinement." Second, abortions conjure up images of sex without consequences, of women who fail to crucify their lusts. We've followed that perennial all the way back to 1636. Finally, gender wars always gather velocity when hazardous others stand on the threshold of the American Eden. The strangers keep threatening to breed their way in and bastardize the race—the panic over black men sprang from the fear of miscegenation. The immigrants added another variation. They threatened to swamp us with their children. They bred too quickly for the upright middle class. Aborting white babies only hastened the alien triumph over America's special people.

Victorian reformers evoked the old-fashioned family and its values. Even medical journals indulged in idylls about the "young mated couple" of the olden days, setting up their lares and penates" and "working out life's problems together." Every American jeremiad mourns the lost moral family. Sins such as abortion, birth control, and small families go back a century; the danger of bad influence and loose discipline go back much further. Each nervous generation echoes that 1679 synod's bottom line: our woes all flow from "defects as to family government."[89]

For the Victorians, fading Anglo-Saxons only focused attention on the immigrants who never shared (or even understood) American values. Worse, with the complicity of the media, those people put dangerous thoughts into our children's heads and threatened to transform those innocents into a generation of wolves. The fate of the nation rested then—as it rests today—with the good family gathered around the hearthside or the parlor or the kitchen table, resisting a corrosive media culture, inculcating the ancient values. Forget the liberal distinctions between private and public. In every generation the family is ground zero of the culture wars.

Chapter 9
White Slaves and the Modern Witch-Hunt

AT the wicked heart of the city stood the fallen woman selling sex. All the purity crusades—all the White Cross pledges and confiscated books—scarcely touched the flourishing red-light districts. The prostitutes created a medical problem, a moral peril, and a mass panic.

The medical problem remains familiar: sexually transmitted diseases. Urbanization, large-scale immigration, and widespread dislocation appeared—then as now—to exacerbate the contagion. By the turn of the century, many physicians were warning of a plague with no cure available. The medical problem inevitably got entangled in moral danger. After all, doctors believed that the health risk ran—through vice, through sex—from the respectable bourgeoisie to the dangerous classes. Male promiscuity seemed to connect even the best families to unclean hordes. Physicians echoed Comstock's sociology: sexual danger filtered up from them to us.

In 1910 the fear became panic. Once again, complex social pressures produced furious efforts to chase the enemies lurking among the good people. The witch-hunt rallied the nation against shadowy foreigners selling American girls into prostitution. This panic took a distinctive twentieth-century form: calls for action produced legislation, administrative rules, judicial precedents, and a bureaucratic agency in search of a mission. The government, lobbied hard by morality groups, rapidly expanded its mission from saving stolen girls to stopping immoral men. In the uproar, policy makers laid down the institutional foundation for federal crime-fighting.

The high moral tide that rolled in as Americans mobilized for World War I eventually swept away the sex districts. But prostitution got away. The grain of truth at the heart of the panic—the exploitation of sex workers—outlasted the reformers. So did the old tangle of anxieties that ran so vividly through the sex war: America faced terrible decline, moral ruin, and "race suicide." By the twentieth century these had become matters for federal government action.

Venereal Swamps

The modern battle over brothels went back to the 1870s, when St. Louis adopted a French public health measure. In Paris, physicians operating under police authority examined sex workers for venereal disease every week. In the United States, the notion set off roars of protest. Critics blasted the amoral state. Public officials, they said, would be implicitly condoning prostitution every time they handed a woman her health certificate. The government itself would be luring young men into dangerous habits with an illusion of safety. (Medicine could not even offer an effective diagnostic procedure till the Wassermann test in 1906.)

Feminists joined the protest. Frances Willard, who had studied in Paris, described terrible wagons, shrouded in black, ferrying the miserable prostitutes to their weekly examinations. "Those awful wagons seemed to me . . . the most heart-breaking procession that ever Christian woman watched." That memory drew her into politics. "If I were asked why there has come about such a revolution in public thought," said Willard many years later, "how I gained the courage to speak of things once unlawful to be told . . . my answer would be: 'Because the law-makers tried to import the black wagons of Paris . . . and Anglo-Saxon women rose in swift rebellion.'" Purity groups—members fancied themselves the new abolitionists—mobilized against the brothel bills; their organizations outlived the issue and helped spur the broad gender agitation of the late nineteenth century.[1]

As the Progressive movement gathered force at the turn of the century, physicians joined the women and purity crusaders in a fight against the red-light districts. The stance reflected the doctors' rising status. "If there is a lower, more contemptible role that could be played by a medical man than that of official inspector of bawds," testified one doctor, "I do not know what it is." The physicians' attack on prostitution reverberated with all the features of crusading Progressivism—science, idealism, moralizing, muckraking, and racism.[2]

The doctors focused the moral and gender agitation on a precise medical target: sexually transmitted diseases. The consequences of these diseases, reported one physician in the *Journal of the American Medical Association*, were "relentless . . . suffering and mutilation and slaughter of innocents." Disease threatened the whole family. Any foolish man who wandered down to the Levee (in Chicago) or Storyville (New Orleans) risked bringing home some terrible illness. There is more venereal disease among virtuous wives than among prostitutes, announced Dr. Prince Morrow, who chaired a 1901 investigation sponsored by the New York County Medical Society. Up to 80 percent of the men in New York City had been infected with gonorrhea at one time or another, he reported. Almost one in five were currently suffering from syphilis. By 1910 the U.S. Army would report the same number—just under 20 percent of its recruits suffered from venereal disease. Another physician drove home the main worry: "The ban placed by venereal diseases on fetal life outrivals the criminal interference with the products of contraception as a cause of race suicide."[3]

The danger came from a familiar source. "Degenerate racial stocks" furnished the bulk of American prostitutes. They made the red-light districts "culture beds" of venereal disease, wrote one physician, just as surely as the swamps were breeding grounds of malaria. That malaria swamp was a popular Progressive analogy. But what bred most quickly was anxiety about the immoral strangers multiplying in the urban quagmires.[4]

The fear of venereal disease spread from the sex districts to the foreign population as a whole. One physician summed up the "sad state of affairs": "The immigrants . . . bring their foreign ideas here, commit acts which are considered criminal in this country, but which, in their native lands, would be looked upon with indifference." We heard a Superior Court judge express precisely the same worry in Chapter 8. Now, serious concerns about disease combined with old fears of moral contagion and metastasized into a pandemic.[5]

The physicians responded with a "social hygiene movement." In his wonderful analysis Allan Brandt points out that the very label—social hygiene—implies an effort to cleanse society. The sexually transmitted diseases became a kind of dirt that spread from them to us, from the festering swamps of the poor to the high ground of the upright middle class.

There was good reason to panic: no one could control the virus that circulated among the classes. In the new industrial city, there was no sealing off the ubiquitous poor. "The personal services of the poor must daily invade our doors and penetrate every nook in our houses," wrote one physician. "Think of the countless currents flowing daily in our cities from the . . . poorest into those of the richest." Those currents would "equalize the distribution of morality and disease." The foreign, the poor, and the immoral were driving America toward disaster. Worst of all, they now threatened us not through the gullibility of children but through the lax morals of our men.[6]

In the South, a large public health literature kept returning to the urtext of all American moralizing—the danger posed to a white us by allegedly promiscuous African Americans. L. C. Allen, a physician writing in a special issue of the *American Journal of Public Health*, offered the standard analysis, his race and gender double standards both flying at full mast: "Syphilis and gonorrhea are . . . very common among the Negroes in the south. . . . This is a real menace to our white boys and through them, after marriage, to our innocent daughters also. For despite the best efforts, many boys are going to sow their wild oats." Even as a lynching holocaust murdered thousands of black men for allegedly imagining sex with white women, Allen breezily condones the white exploitation of black women. Meanwhile, our own emblems of purity—white women, innocent daughters—were imperiled by the loathsome disease oozing from the classes and races below.[7]

The social hygiene movement introduced a new cast of physician-activists. But they still sported the older generation's reflex—they blamed women. The doctors leaped right past the Victorian romance of innocent prostitutes trapped by cold men or cruel mores. Instead, they saw prostitutes as venereal bogs, as the mechanism by which the poor, foreign, black transmitted loathsome maladies and low morals to the better classes.

Physicians almost feverishly publicized the dangers of venereal disease. They called for education and public health protection—like blood tests before marriage. Their concern spread to policy makers and formed a public health backdrop for the era. But right in the middle of the earnest medical efforts, one last imaginative leap recast the villain and whipped the public into one of the nation's most unusual frenzies.[8]

Panic

Suddenly, the remorseless white slaver stalked onto the scene. Foreign devils snatched innocent daughters off the family farm, dragged them to the dangerous city, and chained them in brothels till they perished. The old fear of endangered innocents—this time, fresh country girls—roared back into the popular imagination.

For God's Sake, Do Something!

McClure's magazine broke the story in 1909: New Yorkers had seized control of the world's flesh trade. "Out of the racial slum of Europe [Russia, Austria, and Hungary] has come for unnumbered years the Jewish *kaftan*, leading the miserable Jewish girl to her doom." The governments of Paris and Buenos Aires had thrown out this scum. Now, continued George Kibbe Turner, the cruel flesh peddlers were pouring into America. The "debauched" politicians who ran American cities welcomed the white slavers into their vice districts. The Jews "opened the eyes of the . . . politician . . . to the tremendous financial field." Then Tammany took over. The adroit machine politicians thrived by exploiting white slaves. "Thus our American cities become dumps for the outcast filth of Paris."9

It got worse. The Jews "cruised" New England and Pennsylvania—sometimes "in the garb of a priest"—and lured innocent country girls into slavery. The prostitution rings had developed into a "closely organized machine," a white slave trust every bit as inexorable as the steel or railroad or copper trusts. Decent Jews "slashed the lapels of their clothing . . . and went through the ancient ceremonial for the dead" the moment their daughters disappeared. They knew the white slavers' cruelty. The French and the Chinese also did brisk business in stolen girls.10

The two *McClure's* articles sparked a national sensation. Turner had named names and delivered details. His description fit familiar anxieties—dangerous cities, corrupt machines, greedy trusts, and scary foreigners. It took less than a month for the outcry to reach the White House. President Howard William Howard Taft met with political leaders about the "startling . . . traffic in young girls [being] enticed away from their homes in the country to [the] large cities." A month later, in his first Annual Message, Taft described the "urgent necessity for additional legislation and greater executive activity to suppress the recruiting . . . of prostitutes." He was ready to allocate $50,000 to fight "the White Slave Trade."11

Turner's real aim had been to expose Tammany. The respectable press jumped all over the machine connection. They turned the heat high enough that Tammany's candidate for mayor, J. Galvin, offered $30,000 to anyone with proof of Turner's allegation. George Washington Plunkett, the colorful Tammany politician, once said admiringly off his boss's unquestioned clout—"You never heard of Charlie Murphy delivering a speech did you?" Well, Murphy gave plenty of speeches once the Turner article broke. His ardent denials were echoed by the Jewish community, which refuted the false charges about "kaftans" and, slightly later, organized to fight the traffic in white slaves.12

But there was no calming this storm. The lurid tale grew more melodramatic as the story spun along. Turner's prostitutes had been mainly poor foreign girls who "knew nothing of American life." But he pictured "cadets" combing the countryside for fresh girls—and that part of the story struck a nerve. In fact, President Taft focused right in on the "country girls" dragged off to the city. Turner's story rearranged itself around a simpler plot: foreigners stole young American girls with a wink and a bribe to big-city politicians.

The horror stories took a dramatic narrative line: Fancy young men fanned through the rural districts. They boarded in the best hotels. With smooth manners and plenty of cash, they courted the naive country girls. The girls were easy pickings. "There was never a time . . . when it was so simple for even well reared girls to begin a promiscuous acquaintance." Only yesterday, young men courted at her parents' house; they sat in the front parlor and ate dinner with the family. Now unmarried couples ran off alone—to the "ice cream parlor," the "public dance," the "German skating rink," the "moving picture arcades," and even "fruit stores largely run by foreigners." Any young man could glide into a community and "meet the very best class of girls."[13]

The remorseless young man lured his prey to the city. Perhaps he even staged a fake wedding. Then he took her to a ladies' boardinghouse with some fanciful story about preparing the family mansion. Suddenly she finds herself behind locked door and barred window. No point calling for help, for the police are part of the business. So is the corrupt city government. Preachers walking through the depraved districts reported hearing midnight shrieks. "My God, if only I could get out of here!"[14]

But there is no escape. Eventually the doomed girl gives in and tumbles down the reformers' checklist to perdition: "She drinks the wine that is constantly offered her." Next, "she smokes the cigarette with its opium and tobacco." Everyone knew the sad conclusion of this terrible story. As a letter to the *New York Times* put it in 1910, "This horrible crime leads to death in five years."[15]

Reformers packaged their sensational revelations for maximum impact. A banner across the cover of one popular book blares "For God's Sake, Do Something!" Another banner is splashed along the bottom: "The Greatest Crime In the World's History." Pictured in the center, an innocent, long-haired maiden prays tearfully behind the brothel's bars. The cover of another best seller pictures Mother, her arm protectively around Daughter, staring at the want ad from hell: "Sixty thousand innocent girls WANTED to take the place of 60,000 white slaves who will die this year."

The white slave panic offers one variation on an American epic: innocent girls fall into demonic hands. The Puritan captivity narratives organized the genre. Wild Indians captured young Christian maidens and carried them into pagan savagery. The natives, in those Puritan stories, were lustful and brutal. Some of the young women fell all the way and became Indians themselves. Recall the maxim in Anthony Comstock's preface: the danger for every generation "is not that they will be devoured" but "that they will be transformed into wolves."

Another variation of the female in moral peril came from the "true disclosures" of life in the Catholic convents. Women were stolen, locked in barred rooms, and sexually abused by foreigners, by Roman Catholics. The Victorians made a similar story out of Mormon polygamy; tyrannical men imprisoned women and forced them to serve as sex slaves. The abolitionist slave narratives

9.1. *Fighting the Traffic in Young Girls.* The cover of a popular exposé. The innocent girl, locked in a brothel, cries, "My God, if only I could get out of here," while a shadowy man stands behind her. The title page promises to tell worried parents "How to combat this hideous monster. How to save YOUR GIRL. How to save YOUR BOY."

offered another less fanciful turn on the same theme—rapacious men, innocent women, bondage, lust, and violence. Now, the endangered American virgin returned.

The white slave delirium sounds silly, but the exaggerations expressed profound fears about rapid change. Consider, for example, just one technology and
the social changes it brought: 8,000 automobiles in 1900 had become 2.5 million by 1915. The accelerating trend gave critics a glimpse of the future—a nation of car owners sounded like social chaos. "The car destroyed the cornerstone of American morality," quipped Frederick Lewis Allen. "The difficulty of
finding a suitable locale for misconduct."[16]

In fact, American sexual mores were moving fast. Tired old Anthony Comstock now faced Margaret Sanger, who explicitly championed birth control for
women—not even Elizabeth Cady Stanton or that free luster, Ezra Heywood,
had been so bold. Meanwhile, the wicked city became America. The 1910 census would be the last to show more people living in the country than the city.
Maybe it wasn't exactly the Jewish "cadets," but something was dragging the
neighbor's daughter to town.

Worse, the white slave threat came from an irresistible flesh trust. The
American economy of independent entrepreneurs had been obliterated by
massive economic combinations. Now those clever Jews had figured out an efficient way to steal our daughters and turn a profit on them. The district attorney general in Chicago, Edwin Sims (the most ardent crusader against the
menace), vigorously played up this shadowy business machine, though it would
be the first part of the panic to be exposed as a fable.

Like the other robber barons, the white slavers enjoyed the blessing of machine politicians. The sexual panic offered reformers another way to lambaste
the "filthy officials of Tammany" and their police minions. That's what George
Kibbe Turner had been muckraking for in the first place. A decade earlier, the
Reverend Charles Parkhurst had blasted the police for "enticing prostitutes
from other cities to come to New York." Parkhurst focused on police corruption: "From top down they are the dirtiest, crookedest and ugliest lot of men
ever combined in semi-military array outside of Japan or Turkey." When the
white slave story hit, no one was surprised to find the cops in on the deal.[17]

Finally, of course, this was an immigrant peril. "Jew traders" and "typical
Jew pimps" littered the news dispatches and congressional investigations.
Women were warned never to go into Chinese laundries without an escort. A
congressional committee summed up the danger in 1911: depraved men
brought the "vilest practices . . . here from continental Europe." Over there,
"the feeling regarding sexual immorality is much less pronounced than in the
United States, the women have not the consciousness of degradation from

their fallen condition that . . . causes the American girl her keenest suffering."[18]

The white slave tracts struggled to rouse the morally lethargic American people. "Shall we defend our American civilization, or lower our flag to the most despicable foreigners—French, Irish, Italians, Jews and Mongolians?" "Energetic war upon the red light districts" was the only way to redeem the United States from "oriental brothel slavery," "Parisian white slavery," and "Jew traders." The war against prostitution would rally the nation into reclaiming its fading virtue.[19]

On the surface, the white slave narratives read like trashy soap operas. But the underlying pattern reflects an important national reflex. The scare turned social change into a moral crisis. Fearful Americans might very well sum up those frightening trends and get something quite close to phantom strangers dragging farm girls from the countryside: the sudden loss of America's innocence.

Transporting Women for Any Immoral Purposes

Representative James Mann of Illinois had a plan. He grabbed jurisdiction over the crisis for the Committee on Foreign and Interstate Commerce (which he chaired). With Edwin Sims, Mann drafted legislation to combat the "startling traffic in white girls." Whispers of new federal power often raised political storms. Sure enough, the southern Democrats immediately fretted about state's rights; if this bill became law, said Representative William Richardson from Alabama, "there are no limits to which the Federal Government might not go . . . to regulate the morals of the state." Others denounced Mann for using interstate commerce as the opening wedge for a federal police authority. But the critics never gained much traction. Who was going to defend debauched white slavers? Dangerous Jews and Chinese trumped the dread of federal power.[20]

Still, the sponsors rushed to reassure potential critics. The congressional committee had just one objective, they said: to rescue "women who are literally slaves—women who are owned and held as property and chattels—whose lives are lives of involuntary servitude." The bill's proponents, pandering to delicate southern sensibilities, jumped up to declaim how this kind of slavery was much worse than that other kind. The white slave traffic, said Mann, "while not so extensive, is much more horrible than any black-slave traffic ever was in the history of the world." Representative Coy of Indiana upped the rhetorical ante: "A thousand times worse and more degrading in its consequences on humanity than any species of human slavery that ever existed in this country." The bill sailed through Congress, and President Taft signed it in June 1910.[21]

The legislation famously identifies the criminal: "Any person who knowingly transport[s] . . . in interstate commerce . . . any woman or girl for the purpose of prostitution or debauchery, or for any other immoral purpose, or with the intent . . . to induce, entice or compel such a woman or girl to become a prostitute or give herself up to debauchery or engage in any other immoral practice."

The sponsors kept insisting that they were limiting the bill to white slavery. But they drafted broad and vague language to plug loopholes—the intent to engage in any immoral practice covered a lot of sins. Eventually, that phrase would make the Mann Act famous.

Back in 1873, Congress had handed the Comstock Act right back to Comstock and his allies. As a creation of the Progressive Era, the Mann Act took a longer route back into the moralizers' hands. This time there would be an independent federal agency. Congress turned over enforcement to the fledgling Bureau of Investigation—a small agency, twenty-three agents strong, that had been chasing down anti-trust and postal violations. The war against foreign pimps gave the agency a new mission. The bureau established a special commissioner for the Suppression of the White Slave Traffic, opened a field office, and began recruiting deputies in major cities. The agency would eventually change its name to the Federal Bureau of Investigation—today's FBI got its big organizational break from the white slave panic.[22]

Congress gave the attorney general and the bureau clear instructions: stop the "pernicious traffic in women." But the ambiguously worded law was on the books, tantalizing moral activists and district attorneys across the nation. Anybody could plainly read that the law forbade "interstate commerce . . . for any . . . immoral purpose." Why limit prosecution to white slavers? The "libertine" was also a "dangerous miscreant." Church groups began to clamor for a literal reading of the legal text. The 1913 Baptist Convention wrote President Wilson that "this great law is . . . increasingly needed in the work of protecting our youth and our homes against the social evil." Preachers scoffed at the distinction between "greed and lust," between stolen women and stolen kisses.[23]

At first, federal officials defended the law's original goal of prosecuting men who forced or tricked women into prostitution. As a result, reported the *New York Times,* an avalanche of criticism, "toppled . . . upon the administration." Newspapers hectored the government about reducing the scope of the law: Would the politicians apologize for "going too far in protecting the daughters of decent households from the evil machinations of the . . . young men about town"? Preachers began asking why the feds would want to protect lust, seduction, and adultery. The administration capitulated; the Mann Act became an "anti-lust statute." After four years of enforcement, the department had racked up only seventy-five convictions (14 percent of its successful prosecutions) that fit the popular picture of white slavery. Most arrests and convictions came, instead, from fornication, adultery, or men transporting perfectly willing women who had been prostitutes for years. As most political scientists would predict, the law had been "captured" by the moralizers.[24]

The broad interpretation of the Mann Act got written into the law by the Supreme Court in *Caminetti v. United States* (1917). Young Drew Caminetti had gone from California to Nevada with his mistress. There was no question of coercion or prostitution, but the defendant had crossed state lines with an immoral purpose. The defendant's father was President Woodrow Wilson's commissioner of immigration, which guaranteed front-page coverage (the couple had actually fled to Reno to escape the media storm over their adulterous affair). Republicans gleefully called for vigorous prosecution. The Supreme Court faced a clear choice between the congressional intent (stopping forced prostitution) or a "plain reading" of the statute (immoral purposes). A 5–3 majority dismissed the original meaning (well documented in the record, complained the dissenters) and vastly expanded the scope of the Mann Act. Young Caminetti himself got eighteen months in prison.

Why did the court expand the Mann Act? Historian David Langum points to fear, expressed by the lower court: "society was paying the price" for the "laxity of social conditions and the lack of parental control." The social hygiene movement had publicized the VD epidemic; the numbers appeared to be growing more alarming. There would be more than 5 million cars on the road by the end of the year. And religious groups had gotten their fight against immorality on the political agenda.[25]

After *Caminetti* the feds turned serious about enforcement—the FBI would investigate 50,500 allegations of "immorality purpose" in sixteen years. Even so, the Mann Act practically begged for arbitrary enforcement. The crime, as redefined by the Supreme Court, was common; sentences varied from $50 slaps on the wrist to five years in the penitentiary. Public officials often used the law to go after troublemakers—like black men who dated white women.

The most notorious case involved Jack Johnson. Johnson crossed the color line in professional boxing in 1908 and shocked white America by knocking out Canadian Tommy Burns and becoming the first black heavyweight champion. A cry went up for the former champion, Jim Jeffries, to return from retirement and, as the *New York Herald* put it, "remove that golden smile from Jack Johnson's face." On July 4, 1910, Johnson knocked out Jeffries in Reno. Riots followed. *Life* magazine captured the reaction among working-class whites with its cartoon of a great apelike Johnson mashing the noble Anglo-Saxon into the dirt—an ironic halo encircles Johnson's head.[26]

To make matters worse, Johnson unapologetically consorted with white women. Federal prosecutors searched for a way to bring him down. In 1912 they arrested him for violating the Mann Act with a prostitute named Lucille Cameron. She refused to implicate Johnson, however, and the case did not stick. Undeterred, the Bureau of Investigation went out and found another woman. Chicago crowds chanted for a lynching, and the district attorney called for a tough sentence "to set an example to Johnson's race." The governor of South Carolina weighed in with free counsel: "The black brute who lays his hands upon a white woman ought not to have any trial." Johnson fled the country, lost his title in 1915, and eventually returned to serve a year-long prison term in 1920.

Three decades later the law still cut the same way. In 1960, rock and roll star Chuck Berry got three years in jail on a dubious case.

Note the familiar arc: Moral panic hit. A loosely written law rushed through. An enforcement bureaucracy went into place. Activists elbowed into the administrative process and pushed for a more ambitious program. The administration acquiesced. The Supreme Court codified the broad new reading of the act. And a new enforcement regime, led by the FBI, grew through a vigorous morality campaign. The results laid an institutional foundation for federal crime-fighting. Meanwhile, harsh punishments were assigned to people who needed to learn a moral lesson. And—from Jim Johnson to Chuck Berry—the urge to teach lessons tilted toward black men who did not know their place.

Was the whole white slave epidemic just another crazy witch-hunt? Yes and no. Americans frightened one another with imaginary monsters, but beneath the bedlam lurked real villainy.

Just Another Witch Scare?

The Progressives loved their studies. As the panic spread, the reformers ran straight to the brothels and interviewed everyone in sight. They diligently reported the findings, churning out page after page of torpid, quasi-scientific prose. The results surprised them. The women flatly denied that they had been forced into prostitution. No white slaves. No barred windows. No screams in the night.

A New York investigation team carefully interviewed 1,106 women and came up empty. Purity reformers bent on rescuing captive women reported the same frustration. "I have entered at least 2,500 houses of ill-repute and talked face to face with possibly fifteen thousand of these women and I . . . do not hesitate to tell you that they are wedded to their ways and that they laugh and make fun of those who try to help them."[27]

Even worse, the reports reveal a most subversive villain. A major cause of the women's fall turned out to be "neglect and abuse by parents," even the "immorality of different members of the family." Here is a complete inversion of the original white slavery panic. The girl was not being ripped from the bosom of loved ones but escaping from her dysfunctional family.[28]

The studies yield a long list of additional reasons why the women turned to sin: they were lonely, demoralized, ignorant, giddy, subnormal, loveless, childless, rebellious, weak of will, discouraged of heart, poverty stricken, or just plain unhappy. When the reports stopped with the psychological profiles they offered a more potent variation of that old female shopping vice: the women were after money, pleasure, nice clothes, and good times. Some reformers became positively bitter. They had gone out to slay dragons and rescue enslaved maidens; all they found were accomplices in an unsavory enterprise.[29]

A closer look deflated all the wild slavery stories. The brothels did not seize sixty thousand girls a year. The young women did not all perish within five years—one study reported that the majority were still "aggressive in seeking trade" after seven years in the business. That merciless white-flesh conglomerate proved a phantom. Even George Kibbe Turner (who had gotten the panic started with his articles in *McClure's*) debunked the idea and denied ever suggesting it. "In spite of continued representations to the contrary, I never stated . . . there exist . . . trading organizations whose business, as organizations, is to deal in women."[30] In fact, Turner's articles were tame compared to what followed. The exaggerations and innuendoes grew more fantastic as others picked up the story and added their own shockers.[31]

Historians are still sifting through episodes, searching for grains of truth. The reconstruction gets complicated because the champion panic-mongers, District Attorney Edwin Sims and Chicago Prosecutor Clifford Roe, pop up at every turn. For example, more reliable witnesses, such as Jane Addams, also reported white slave stories. Where did Addams get her details about stolen women? Sims and Roe. Who did Congressman Mann turn to for help drafting legislation? Sims and Roe. Here is Sims meeting with President Taft, there he is gazing down from the frontispiece of the most popular white slavery tract, *Fighting the Traffic in Young Girls* (that book featured "special essays" by—who else?—Sims and Roe). In 1933, sociologist Walter Reckless went back to compare Roe's rollicking white slave narratives with court documents. Sure enough, bald exaggeration.[32]

Turner, Sims, Roe, and many others had spun an incredible story. Turner faced immediate critics, and historians later exposed Roe. But people don't panic unless they find the horror stories plausible. And at the time, millions of impoverished foreigners were generating trouble and anxiety. The feverish fantasies offered Americans an allegory for modern times: the nation seemed to shrug off its innocence; cities lured young people; urban society was more, well, wicked; and more than one in seven residents had been born abroad (in 1910). Immigrants were changing the face of the nation like never before or after.[33]

Nor was it all metaphor and illusion. Real prostitutes faced intimidation, exploitation, and violence. Many prostitutes were immigrants—poor, vulnerable, and far from home. Almost 6 million people had arrived in the United States between 1905 and 1910, roughly 70 percent of them men. Mass dislocation, disrupted families, and extensive poverty created an atmosphere for sexual coercion, then as now. The real Eastern European and Asian problem lay not in the danger to our daughters but in the exploitation of theirs.

In California, for example, Asian prostitutes suffered under terrible conditions. In some cases, writes Lucie Cheng Hirata, impoverished Chinese families sold their daughters into American prostitution; women faithfully sent hundreds of dollars back home to help their parents and their families. The women often flabbergasted social workers by refusing to leave their sexual bondage for the Christian missions. Real prostitutes always had more complicated hopes and fears than the mythic creatures the moral reformers went forth to rescue.[34]

The Chinese experience ironically twisted the villainy back to the white majority. Mob violence and complicated legal restrictions kept Chinese families out of the United States; by 1910, the gender ratio stood at ten Chinese males to every woman. White America fostered the conditions that bred prostitution, then indignantly warned respectable women to brave those dangerous Chinese laundries only with an escort.

Native-born women also got trapped by hard times, rough cities, and the perils of the double standard. And prostitution paid. In all their investigating, nothing shook the Progressives quite like the cash to be made in the sex trade. The startled New York commission kept emphasizing the contrast between prostitution and honest wages. Former stenographers made five times as much when they turned to prostitution, servants up to twelve times as much, factory girls up to twenty times more.[35]

The studies exploded an old cliché about women working only for a little pin money. "The roles had changed," wrote Jane Addams, "and the wages of the girl child supported a broken and dissolute father." But she was not paid enough to support herself and her family. City girls "yielded to temptation" when they became "utterly discouraged." Addams chronicled one girl's fall: "When the shoes became too worn to endure a third soling and she possessed but ninety cents towards a new pair, she gave up her struggle; to use her own contemptuous phrase, she sold out for a pair of shoes."[36]

Reformers faced an unexpected (and uncomfortable) dilemma: What were they going to do about the women who had consciously chosen prostitution? Toledo's flamboyant mayor, Samuel "Golden Rule" Jones, rubbed the problem into righteous faces. When a purity group demanded that Jones close the brothels and drive the prostitutes out of town, he let them have it: "Where shall I . . . drive them? They have to go somewhere, you know."[37]

The purity crusaders and Progressive reformers converged on the same larger question: How were single women going to survive? An obvious conclusion leaped out of the red-light districts: improved economic alternatives for working women. Perhaps the real moral problem lay in that extraordinary ratio—twenty to one—between wages in the bordellos and those in the factories. Their encounters with real prostitutes helped push reformers toward the broader Progressive battle for decent wages and working conditions. By 1913, eight states had introduced minimum-wage laws, often over furious protests from the women's employers. Many purity crusaders turned to the more gritty economic conflicts. American reformers run both ways—some turn economic pressures into moral problems while others trace moral problems back to economic roots.

The prostitutes story reveals a deeper social trouble: women had few options. They were poorly paid, faced harsh working conditions, and—despite three generations of feminist struggle—could not protect themselves with basic legal rights. Instead, some women sought money and even a measure of independence in a system of coercion, violence, and exploitation. Innocent white slaves dragged out of the ice cream parlors by nefarious Frenchmen and greedy Jews? No. Sexual exploitation? Yes. And plenty of it.

Smashing the Districts

The red-light districts must have gotten crowded with all the do-gooders passing through. Federal agents posted Mann Act notices in the brothels. Kidnapping and slavery, they announced, were against the law. The agents left stamped, self-addressed envelopes so madams could report rumors of abducted girls. The men took a census of the prostitutes just to keep track.

Outside, the preachers gathered. Rodney Gypsy Smith (who claimed that every $4.92 in his collection basket would turn another soul to Jesus) led 12,000 praying men and women through Chicago's red-light district in October 1909. More crowds came praying through in the following years. Moral vigilantes gathered in front of police stations and bawdy houses. Meanwhile, forty-three cities had vice commissions scrutinizing the situation. Physicians kept warning about venereal plagues. And municipal reformers blasted the districts as yet one more rotten fruit of the political machines. The anti-prostitution forces wrung "red-light abatement" laws from the legislatures (beginning with Iowa in 1909). These statutes permitted any citizen to sue both the brothels and their landlords. If the court found against the owner, it sealed the building. In some states (like New York) the court could also fine the owner. The once lucrative brothel trade might now ruin the real estate speculator. By 1917, thirty-one states had passed red-light abatement laws. Once again, the governments empowered moral vigilantes to sue and shut down immoral businesses.[38]

Property rights (normally the most sacred cow in the nation) did not stop the moral stampede. Nor did second thoughts about what might happen to the women themselves. Prodded by popular protests, state laws, and court rulings, the cities began to shut down their vice districts. In many cases, the local police simply announced the date when the district would be closed. For example, on Thursday, June 14, 1915, sightseers flocked to Houston's Happy Hollow for one last rowdy party. The next day, the moving vans rolled everything away.[39]

World War I finally tipped the scales decisively toward morality. The war largely ended the old red-light districts. It would also bring liquor prohibition. Organized moral campaigns—with clear goals and strategies—found their golden opportunity in the fervent idealism that surrounded military mobilization.

Closing the districts only scattered the prostitutes, turning them into street-walkers and call girls. Chicago's Levee was dead, reported the local vice commission, but its ghosts were "stalking about the streets and alleys of the South side." In some cities, arrests for prostitution rose when the districts shut down. Out on the street, the women became more vulnerable than they had been in the brothels. Male pimps displaced female madams. Violence grew. "We found that the police, if they were brutal enough, could drive the girls off the streets," recalled Mayor Brand Whitlock of Toledo. "Of course, after a while the poor things . . . would come back. Then the police would have to practice their brutalities all over again." A final irony marked the end of the great white slave panic: the crusaders forgot about the women they had mobilized the nation to save.[40]

The moral tide that began rushing in with the Comstock laws crested during World War I. The government—federal, state, and local—harried prostitutes, along with smut peddlers, birth control advocates, abortionists, adulterers, and fornicators (if the man helped a woman cross state lines). The greatest Puritan victory of all, Prohibition, lay just ahead. For all that, the virtuous society seemed to be slipping ever further out of reach.

Theodore Dreiser's first novel, *Sister Carrie* (1900), imagined an entirely different fate for the fallen woman. His heroine, Carrie Meeber, follows the standard route toward perdition. She leaves her honest little hometown, takes the train to wicked Chicago, falls for the first fast-talking, slickly dressed traveling salesman she meets, then uses her sex and her smarts to rise and prosper. Needless to say, that plot line led to trouble. Publishers ducked the book until Doubleday tendered an offer. As Dreiser told the story, Mrs. Frank Doubleday, a "social worker active in moral reform," got a look at the manuscript and immediately tried to quash the book. When the lawyers told the publisher that he could not revoke the contract, Doubleday printed the book but refused to sell a single copy. Dreiser was only slightly exaggerating (the book sold fewer than 700 copies). *Sister Carrie* made Dreiser famous in England long before the book was accepted in the United States. In a way, the white slave scare, the Mann Act, *Caminetti v. United States,* and the FBI prosecutions might be read as an effort to hold off the Carrie Meebers and their new social and sexual norms.[41]

For a time, the double sexual standard, the conspiracy of silence, and the sure ruin of fallen women all remained embedded in the official moral code. In real life, however, the code was cracking. If *Sister Carrie* had been more widely available, Americans could have read something about the future of their sexual mores. There would be no continence for men, no "white life for two." On the contrary, the decline of the double standard brought on bold new ideas about proper feminine conduct.

The neo-Puritans kept winning the political battles while they slowly lost the moral war. By the 1920s, Dreiser's Carrie Meeber sprang to life in a whole generation of young flappers. Even so, fearful citizens found solace when Congress finally slammed the door on immigrants. The moral turbulence of the early twentieth century kept raising the same question. Which was the deeper urge: fostering virtue or fending off dangerous others? It is often difficult to tell the two apart.

Slouching Toward Modernity

Eugenics

The sex wars entered modernity with a chilling new campaign against the dangerous them sponsored by the cocky new science of eugenics.

Cries about "race suicide" began right after the Civil War. The original AMA campaign against abortion had featured the "loins of our women" more or less pitted against the loins of aliens. But no one stormed about cheering for children, lots of children, more ardently than Teddy Roosevelt. While he commanded the bully pulpit, President Roosevelt lavished praise on large families—"Work, fight and breed!" He heaped scorn on those who were not doing their bit. "The man or woman who . . . has a heart so cold . . . and a brain so shallow and selfish as to dislike having children, is in effect a criminal against the race and should be an object of contemptuous abhorrence by all healthy people."[42]

As Roosevelt grew older, his railing against race suicide grew louder. "The American stock is being cursed with the curse of sterility," wrote Roosevelt in 1911. "It is due to coldness and selfishness, to love of ease, to shirking, . . . to an utter and pitiful failure." The race could not survive unless the "average man and woman who are married . . . have a family of four children." (Recall that the average had fallen to 3.56 by 1900.) Race danger was everywhere. Mongolians and Filipinos threatened to swamp the Pacific Rim (Roosevelt used "Chinese" as a slur). The American southwest had to cope with the "lower civilizations" of Latin America. Southern Italians—the "most fecund and least desirable population of Europe"—poured into eastern cities. And in the South, the Negro tended "to go backwards rather than forward." All this riffraff was piled on top of the usual collection of "criminals, shiftless, and worthless people." The danger boiled down to this: the lower races would swamp the higher in the "battle for the cradle."[43]

The furor over race suicide ran straight up against a radical new women's movement led by Margaret Sanger (at the time, a Socialist) and Emma Goldman (a member of the radical International Workers of the World). Sanger and Goldman had discovered vaginal diaphragms in Holland and had brought the idea back to the United States. Lose the old fears about male promiscuity, they argued; here was women's chance to control reproduction. Sanger and Goldman brashly violated the creaky Comstock laws. They organized, handed out leaflets, and opened birth control clinics. Between 1914 and 1918, birth control leagues spread across the large cities. Arrests only fed the movement, generating broad publicity and defiant enthusiasm.

Old Anthony Comstock himself prosecuted one of his last cases against William Sanger, who was charged with distributing his wife's "obscene" booklet *Family Limitation*. The judge suggested that women would be "rendering society a greater service" by "advocating childbearing" instead of "woman suffrage." William got thirty days. Margaret thumbed her nose at Comstock from Europe, and the popularity of the birth control cause continued to grow.[44]

After World War I, however, the United States took a sharp turn to the right. All kinds of reformist dreams foundered in the new political mood. Heady ideas about liberated women sank into darker fears about race suicide. Margaret Sanger, looking for powerful allies, turned to the rising eugenics movement.

Though most eugenicists were ardently antifeminist (women were for breeding), Sanger courted the scientists with virulently racist propositions. In 1930 she recommended the sterilization of entire "disugenic" populations.

E. A. Ross, Theodore Roosevelt's advisor on inferior races, thought that Sanger might be onto something; birth control might just save the world from "hordes of defectives." Eugenicists had been emphasizing getting more children from the fit. "We went back of that," said Sanger, "and sought first to stop the multiplication of the unfit." Early family planners found a common cause in racial eugenics—not because they were racists, comments Linda Gordon, but because they had no tradition of racial justice with which to ground their moral compass or check their mean self-interest.[45]

Eugenics offered a confident, scientific way to protect the nation from criminals, prostitutes, and low races. The textbooks all introduced the new enterprise with the same "natural experiment." More than a century ago, a Revolutionary War soldier named Martin Kallikak had had a fling with a feeble-minded woman named Margaret; Margaret bore Kallikak's bastard. Then Martin settled down with a good wife and produced a normal family. Now, six generations later, the results were in. Margaret's line yielded 143 feeble-minded people (with 291 more in serious doubt), 33 prostitutes, 24 confirmed alcoholics, 8 brothel owners, 36 bastards. In sum, "Margaret, *the mother of criminals*, has left a progeny of some 700 paupers, prostitutes and criminals." They bred recklessly and burdened society with unsavory rabble. Meanwhile, the other side begot nothing but the cream of the community—doctors, lawyers, judges, educators, and (the ambiguous little blemish that adds verisimilitude), one case of "religious mania."[46]

Here, promised the scientists, lay the key to all the troublesome others who had plagued America for so long. The eugenicists went back to take a scientific look at the white slave investigations: "From forty to sixty percent of this class of woman are defectives." Prostitutes, paupers, thieves, murderers, alcoholics, and bootleggers could all be identified in advance—defective people sprang from defective parents. The foreigners pouring in were criminals, prostitutes, and idiots. "To continue to absorb these aliens . . . is nothing short of criminal carelessness." And forget about black Americans. "Only the most worthless and vicious of the white race will . . . mate with the Negro and the result can not but mean deterioration on the whole for either race."[47]

The eugenicists posed as the latest scientific thing. However, their texts have an uncanny echo; they rerun the nativist alarms from the previous century. Back before the Civil War, immigrants had produced nine out of ten paupers. Scholars like Samuel Busey had worked out the numbers by European breed (the Dutch were the worst—one out of five was a pauper or a criminal). The eugenicists wrapped those old original sins in the cloak of science. But they did not tinker with the story line. The defective other—the American sinner—could be identified and controlled. Once again, "our very life blood was at stake." And, of course, "mongrelization of distinctly unrelated races . . . is a great hazard." Mongrelization is the surefire sparkplug for every culture war. And with good reason. It is how the nation changes.

If the diagnosis was familiar, science offered a brand new cure. First, set aside false charity. "The superficially sympathetic man flings a coin to the beggar; the more deeply sympathetic man builds an almshouse for him so that he need no longer beg; but perhaps the most radically sympathetic of all is the man who arranges that the beggar shall not be born." As the eugenics movement took off, general magazines carried more articles on eugenics than on slums, tenements, and living standards combined.[48]

Indiana cashed in first on the promise of science (in 1907). Since heredity "plays a most important part in the transmission of crime, idiocy and imbecility," the institutions that housed the incorrigible would sterilize them. California followed with a forerunner of its "three strikes" program. Convicts committed three times for any crime (twice for sex offenses) would be "asexualized." Any convict who acted like a "moral and sexual pervert" also got the treatment. By 1931, thirty states had passed laws encouraging the sterilization of feeble-minded men and women.[49]

Some lower courts balked. A federal district judge struck down a Nevada eugenics law sterilizing habitual criminals, rapists, and child abusers. He called vasectomies "ignominious," "degrading," and a "brand of infamy." The Indiana Supreme Court overruled the state's law (in 1921), prompting the legislature to redraft the statute (1927, 1931). The U.S. Supreme Court finally weighed in with one of its most inglorious cases, *Buck v. Bell* (1927). The case involved Carrie Buck, an eighteen-year-old "feeble-minded white woman" in a state institution. Her mother was allegedly feeble-minded as well. So was Carrie's daughter. The question was whether Carrie Buck should be sterilized. Justice Holmes practically celebrated the idea. Here was the "radically sympathetic man" sprung from the pages of the eugenics textbook: "It is better for the world, if instead of waiting to execute degenerate offspring for crime, or to let them starve for their imbecility, society can prevent those who are manifestly unfit from continuing their kind. . . . Three generations of imbeciles are enough."[50]

With the Nazi horrors, racial science became emblematic of the totalitarian state and fell into disrepute. The textbooks, laws, and court opinions seem positively sinister. More recent studies indicate that the eugenics scientists faked and cheated. The pictures of depraved Kallikaks, writes Stephen Jay Gould, were clumsily retouched to make them look like imbeciles. The mournful epilogue on *Buck v. Bell* comes from a 1985 article by Paul Lombardo, "Three Generations, No Imbeciles." Lombardo picks up the story following the trial. After Carrie Buck was sterilized, she left the institution and lived with her husband until his death. She was an avid reader, says Lombardo, and lived her life with intelligence and kindness. Her daughter, judged feeble-minded as an infant, made the honor roll in her first two years in school. She died when she was eight.[51]

Eugenics seems to violate the most basic American values. Heredity replaces individual striving, and success (or failure) comes programmed in the DNA. But this was not just a random instance of rogue science. Eugenics drew on the dark side of the moralizing nation. Every American generation finds its own way to sort out the virtuous from the vicious. The eugenicists' great difference reflected their times. They made the old moral distinctions with a chilling modernist faith in white lab coats and objective solutions.

The Patterns of Moral Power

Both the Constitution and the culture tilt against active government. Expanding public authority is usually difficult. Yet Congressman Mann snatched up new federal police powers. His Mann Act and how it grew illuminates a new angle on the growth of government.

How Government Grows

Some southern politicians stuck to the traditional text. They denounced the federal incursion onto state turf. Lower courts were also dubious. Some rejected the way the law stretched federal jurisdiction through the interstate commerce clause. The Supreme Court cautiously picked its way through the thickets of federalism. The court had already upheld interstate bans on obscenity (the Comstock Act), impure drugs, and diseased cattle. In *Hoke v. United States* (1913) it accepted the leap into debauchery and affirmed the Mann Act. But the court set clear limits. Health and morals (often intertwined) were fine till they ran up against business and commerce. In *Hammer v. Dagenhart* (1918) it struck down a ban on the interstate commerce of goods manufactured by children and offered a little homily on federalism: "It must never be forgotten that the Nation is made up of States." Women fell under federal jurisdiction; widgets did not.[52]

But even private property sometimes got flattened in the moral storm. The states passed red-light abatement acts over furious opposition from business; real estate groups denounced the governments for confiscating property. Those complaints would swell into an angry national chorus as Americans turned to alcohol prohibition. Reformers responded with scorn over vice profits. Purity reformers self-consciously mimicked abolition—the grand prototype of righteous politics in the United States. When slaveholders had tried to stand on property rights, abolitionists scalded them for trafficking in human misery. Well, what was prostitution but more traffic in souls? And the saloons? Still more blood money, said moral reformers.

The purity victories revise the old wisdom about how government grows in a system biased against it. The simplest answer is—slowly. State power expands one small step at a time. A more historically nourishing perspective points to epic moments when enormous congressional majorities or terrible crises or powerful social movements (or all three) puncture the political equilibrium. What we have been following is an alternative path to the rise of government. During this era reformers won new public authority—bans on abortion, limits on contraception, control over speech, teen curfews, the Mann Act, red-light abatement laws, and national prohibition—with a politically explosive mix: high-flying aspirations and fears about immoral villains menacing America from the fringes of society. Nothing launches political programs quite like rumors of Jews stealing (never mind selling) country girls.[53]

Moral panics and dreams of virtue enlarge the American state. Governments seize new forms of authority (controlling interstate commerce, confiscating real estate), enter private lives (banning abortions and contraceptives), organize new agencies (like the FBI), and kindle popular expectations ("For God's Sake, Do Something!"). The purity crusaders rolled over formidable barriers—states' rights, southern discomfort, constitutional scruples, private property, business interests, and fears of government power. The traditional liberal view protected private lives from political meddling. But back at the end of the nineteenth century, the people's character seemed like the key to national destiny. Today, a new generation of Victorians still sees it that way.

The Great American Moral Dialectic

By the start of the twentieth century, a great contest had developed about whether to pin the blame for moral trouble on individuals or on society. We saw Frances Willard illustrate the difference when she suggested that poverty leads to drink (solution: more social and economic reforms) as much as drink leads to poverty (solution: push Prohibition and personal responsibility). Winning the battle over whom to blame profoundly shapes the kind of government that emerges from bouts of moral agitation.

On the one side, each generation of moralizers spins its variation on the Puritan gospel of hard work. Recall Horace Greeley insisting that poverty, crime, and misery were the wages of "inordinate expenditures" and profligate wives. Or Henry Ward Beecher delivering the same message after the Civil War: "No man in this land suffers from poverty unless it be more than his fault—unless it be his sin." What follows are the politics of tough love and personal responsibility—curfews, abstinence, jail time.

When the Progressives actually went out into the poor neighborhoods, they sometimes developed a different view. Long lines of poor people cross Jane Addams's pages—freezing widows, desperate old men, abandoned boys. Their many sins are often ways of coping with terrible conditions. A harsh political economy throws up all kinds of adversities—from racial discrimination to miserable wages—and pushes good people into bad behavior.[54]

Laura Clay, who was active in both the Woman Suffrage Association and the WCTU, framed the classic riposte to Comstock's attacks on bad mothers and their incorrigible little wolves. "Statistics show where the dangers lie when they tell us such dreary facts as that half the children die before they attain the age of five years, and that in the city of New York alone 70,000 daily go to school unfed." The Social Gospel movement grappled with the complicated moral patterns of poverty, exclusion, and inequality.[55]

Over time, the neo-Puritan focus on sinners has been the more politically robust American moral ideology. The social gospel comes in waves—powerful, exuberant, and exhausting. Perhaps the political process more easily digests campaigns organized around simple vice and virtue. And why not? Fighting obscenity or prostitution or drunkenness seems perfectly sensible. Why stand against efforts to make people better?

The first hint of trouble lies in the sheer intensity of the campaigns. Take the sex wars. "The passion aroused by commercialized sex appears so intense," muse D'Emilio and Freedman, "that one wonders whether it stood for something more in the minds of the anti-vice crusaders." The extraordinary American temperance movements would raise precisely the same question. The passions run too strong, the stakes seem too high, the reform promises too much.[56]

Translating social troubles into individual sins subverts the social gospel and its policy agenda. If the poor are bad or inferior, what is the point of more programs? That will only weaken them and everyone else. And with that we come back to the political dynamite at the heart of the moral crusades. The struggle against sin keeps devolving into strife against the sinner. How many different ways have we heard Americans deprecate the "vile practices" or the "bestial refinements of depravity" that some other—Irish, Chinese, African, or Jew—threatens to unleash? The fears have always been exacerbated by the American flux: broad and early democracy, wide social mobility, great immigrations, and a thousand religious sects. They add up to hellfire politics.[57]

By the twentieth century, an institutional difference brought new force to the moral cycle. In a simpler time panics swept through the villages, did their social damage, and burned themselves out. Modern panics leave behind rules and agencies open for business; the most intense activists gain the administrators' ears.

The panic over white slavery may look foolish. But the episode had important consequences. The scare took a tangle of complicated issues and transformed them into a dramatic tale of good versus evil. The cheap melodrama—urgent, frightening, outrageous—kicked the political system into action. President Taft demanded a law to sign. Reformers flattened the usual opposition. When Americans took a second look at those fruit vendors, they found nothing nefarious. But by the time panic ended, a new set of laws were on the books, beckoning a new generation of Anthony Comstocks to enforce American virtue. We have seen this cycle before, we will see it again. Temporary social panics leave permanent political legacies.

Chapter 10
Temperance:
Crucible of Race and Class

THE fight against liquor may be the greatest reform movement in American history—only abolition came close. No other social movement lasted as long, promised as much, or stirred up more trouble. Temperance organized modern feminism. It fired progressive imaginations and roused men and women to better themselves. Some historians even score Prohibition a success. Americans may have scrapped the program in 1933 (it took effect in January 1920), but by then Prohibition had shut down the noxious saloons, sobered up the working class, and slashed liquor consumption. Americans did not get back to their pre-Prohibition drinking levels till 1971.[1]

But wait a moment. A great reform? Doesn't Prohibition belong on the cultural scrap heap alongside witch-hunters, book censors, and chaperones for young ladies? Humorist Will Rogers captured the popular temper back in 1919: "The Prohibitionists just seem sore at the world." Say, "Why not settle this Prohibition fifty-fifty? Let the Prohibitionists quit drinking." Later, Richard Hofstadter made the same point in fancier adjectives: "Prohibition was a . . . pinched, parochial substitute for reform which has widespread appeal to . . . the rural Protestant mind." Critics dismiss the whole episode as an uptight, bluenose, "wowser" spasm against modernity and foreigners. (In 1920s slang, "wowsers" were meddling reformers.) Immigration soared in the 1910s. The strangers packed into the cities and careened—as former President Taft put it—from "orgy" to "sodden stupor." A new generation of American Puritans got themselves positively tipsy pondering that combustible urban mixture—sin, spirits, and strangers.[2]

Besides, wasn't Prohibition an awful flop? When President Herbert Hoover cheered the "great social and economic experiment, noble in motive and far reaching in purpose," the *New York World* served up a tangy rejoinder.

> Prohibition is an awful flop.
> We like it.
> It can't stop what it's meant to stop.
> We like it.
> It's left a trail of graft and slime
> It don't prohibit worth a dime
> It's filled our land with vice and crime,
> Nevertheless, we're for it.[3]

Which view gets it right? Prohibition as stirring reform, or just the latest convulsion against modernity? Well, it was both. Temperance stands out in the crowded American field of utopian schemes. Going dry was the city on the hill at its most ambitious. But dry dreams kept getting tangled up in racial fears. The dreams of sobriety kept evolving—from improving people to controlling them, from the pulpits into politics. The fear of others—Irish, German, African American—pushed the moralists toward Prohibition laws, and the whole issue got entangled in the terrible southern racial convulsions. On balance, I'm with the critics.

Prohibition came on in waves, won its great national victory, then faded fast. Conventional wisdom suggests that it just went too far. Even the ardent drys grew increasingly defensive about the efforts. But the cause also lost a powerful bulwark when, shortly after national Prohibition, the United States shut down immigration. As the mobs of strangers dwindled, the prohibitionist itch faded.

The Great Depression finished off the noble experiment and transformed American moralism. President Roosevelt would preach a very different kind of gospel. The long moral swing that began when Anthony Comstock rushed down to Washington to save the children finally collapsed in the frenzy of bootleggers, speakeasies, shootouts, and conservative groups bitterly denouncing Prohibition's dreadful innovation—a big, intrusive federal government.

Prohibition shakes up a lot of standard wisdom. Take that political science classic: the United States has a weak, carefully limited government. But how does a limited government outlaw an entire industry and push so deeply into people's personal lives? The Russian Bolsheviks had outlawed liquor, howled the wets; now here we went, down the slippery slope from liberty.[4]

Or take the picture of Americans as rugged individualists. What kind of liberal individualists embrace such intrusive government? This looks a lot more like the "nanny state" that modern conservatives love to hate. And how about the federalism and local autonomy before the New Deal? Any state (and many counties) could vote itself dry. Most did. Three-quarters of America lived in dry areas by the time national Prohibition went through. But the majority pushed ahead. Sobering up the moral laggards beat local autonomy.

Finally, Prohibition is American government's overlooked growth spurt. The New Deal usually gets tagged as the mother of big government (though recent analyses have uncovered plenty of welfare programs going back to the nineteenth century). But in the fifteen years before the Franklin Roosevelt administration, Americans embarked on an extraordinary public project. Government officials tried to stamp out a major industry and an everyday form of leisure. Reformers used the state to redeem the citizens and their society. Did the New Dealers ever try anything quite as ambitious?

By now, the political dynamic is familiar. Moral fervor sweeps the United States. It rocks the status quo. The spirit eventually fades, but it leaves its imprint. The Comstock craze criminalized abortion. The white slaves fostered the FBI. Prohibition would rewrite American federalism, criminal justice, the courts, civil liberties, crime-fighting, crime families, and national attitudes. Americans still live with its legacy.

The Prohibition Cycle

Historians usually count five American anti-liquor eras. The first banned alcohol in thirteen states by the mid-1850s, then collapsed. A brief history of that first wave illustrates the recurring political features of the cycle.

In early America, drinking was no vice. "Virtually everyone drank," exaggerates one historian, "virtually all the time." Harvest laborers got a daily pint of rum. City artisans broke for toddies. Merchants served their customers, auctioneers their bidders. "I could scarcely visit New York on the most important business without getting drunk," reported a shoe dealer from Newark. President John Adams washed his breakfast down with hard cider, young boys took their rum when they came in from playing, and a southern churchgoer could count himself temperate if he drank only a quart of peach brandy a day. By 1800, the average American adult was draining roughly seven gallons of pure alcohol a year—today, that would be something like 185 bottles of wine per capita.[5]

Americans drank hard spirits—mainly rum, whiskey, brandy, and gin. Beer did not keep and would not pay without a denser population. Coffee and tea were expensive. And water was risky. Manhattan's wells were shallow and unpleasant, Washington, D.C., refused taxes for public water, Mississippi towns got sludge. Moreover, people thought cold water dangerous, especially during summer. Back in 1620 the Pilgrims had complained that "drinking of water would infecte their bodies with sore sickneses and greevous diseases." Almost two centuries later, at the end of the eighteenth century, Philadelphia placed warnings on its water pumps: "death to him who drinks quickly." Best to mix a bit of wine with your water. Liquor was good for you; it would cool, nourish, impart strength, and quench thirst. In reality, of course, liquor dehydrates. Those field hands must have been miserable after a day soaking up sun, sweat, and rum.[6]

All this adds up to a larger point. Every society frames alcohol differently: normal or deviant, the "goodly creature of God" (as the Puritans thought it) or the "demon rum" that haunted Victorians. Rural nations often tolerated a lot more drinking than did crowded industrial countries. Scots and Swedes both drank much like the early Americans. In contrast, English officials had used stiff taxes to push people from spirits to beer.[7]

In the early nineteenth century, the Second Great Awakening swept the nation. With preachers announcing that the millennium lay at hand, men and women began to swear off hard spirits; the yearning for perfection drew them until they were pledging total abstinence. The evangelical American Temperance Society, founded in 1826, swept across the country; at its peak, a decade later, it claimed 8,000 auxiliaries and 1.5 million members—one out of ten Americans.

Proper ministers soon got elbowed aside by a more raucous temperance movement. In the early 1840s, urban workers launched the Washington Movement—an irreligious, irreverent, dry revival. Shaken by the hard times that hit in the late '30s, the Washingtonians preached self-improvement and mutual aid. They launched the first female temperance groups, the Martha Washington Societies. Workers flocked to the rowdy rallies. They shared ribald confessions, sang lusty nondrinking songs, and pledged abstinence. The Washingtonians sponsored revivals without the religion, bashes without the beer.[8]

Like many working-class revivals, this one made elites distinctly queasy. Church leaders blasted the Washingtonians' "infidelity." Employers fretted over disruption, democracy, and the dangers of labor radicalism. The Washington movement faded; its leaders became enmeshed in scandal—a bizarre occupational hazard for revivalists through the years. John Gough, perhaps the movement's most celebrated orator, managed to get caught dead drunk in a bordello. He came up with the classic fallen evangelical's response: I'm unworthy, I've shed "bitter tears of repentance," and I was framed.[9]

As the economy developed, merchants and mill owners also pushed sobriety on their employees. Abstinence would steady the workers and render them more fit for the emerging industrial order. The first annual report of the American Temperance Society offered meticulous calculations: total abstinence among the workers would yield 25 percent more profits. (More than a century and a half later, we are still toting up liquor costs. Today the "total net lifetime cost per heavy drinker is $38,000."[10])

Americans changed their drinking habits remarkably fast. By 1845, Americans averaged about one-quarter of the alcohol they had drunk just fifteen years earlier. People even drank water as the cities improved the supply. In 1842, New York inaugurated an aqueduct from Croton, forty miles away. Temperance advocates proudly became "cold water warriors." Amid religious fervor and technical innovation, Americans cast off their premodern drinking culture.

As drinking declined, the drys got hotter. They turned from preaching to prohibition. Why? In part, liquor had been successfully challenged. And what was even worse than the sin were the sinners. The Irish and the Germans arrived at the same time as temperance. And they ignored the sermons. Something had to be done about these hard-drinking swarms of un-Americans.

Maine went first. Neal Dow, the vain, scrappy mayor of Portland, dedicated his life to fighting liquor. Dow practically burst with braggart tales about how, for example, he had single-handedly disarmed a drunken madman while the police cowered. Now, Dow would fix the drinking danger once and for all. Using the local Washington society as a foil, he maneuvered increasingly stringent controls through the legislature till he won the first statewide prohibition in 1851: no liquor sales in Maine. Dow hit the road to celebrate his contribution to American public policy. In an effort to make the Maine law more respectable—a crucial step in every prohibition surge—he pushed the promiscuous women's issue out of his reform movement.[11]

Nativists latched onto Maine's innovation. Here was just the thing to control the urban mobs. Immigrant politics had been organized around the saloons. Those noxious urban dens financed political careers, operated as political clubs, and even served as polling places. The Irish and Germans drank—openly, unapologetically, even on the Sabbath. Immigrant culture framed liquor differently than did the increasingly dry natives; perhaps the difference made the natives even more ardent in their new convictions. Between 1852 and 1855—precisely during the Know-Nothings' spectacular rise—twelve states followed Maine to prohibition. Despite furious opposition in the degraded cities, the Know-Nothings pushed through liquor laws in every northern state where they won power.[12]

Enforcement was another story. Prohibition kept producing violence. The Father of Prohibition himself got into a bloody scrap. Mayor Neil Dow sold medicinal and industrial alcohol from City Hall. (Supplying these necessities would bedevil every prohibition effort.) Under the strict new law, only an authorized agent could sell the municipal liquor. Dow's enemies caught him on a technicality: the official agent had not yet been appointed. "The mayor of the city has no more right to deal in liquors than any other citizen," they gleefully announced. "Let the lash which Dow has prepared for other backs be applied to his own."

Protesters gathered around the spirits stored in city hall, and the demonstration became a riot. Dow called in two dozen militiamen to help the police. At his order, they began to fire volleys into the rabble. When the smoke cleared, one man lay dead and several others wounded. The coroner called a grand jury to determine whether Dow should be tried for manslaughter or murder.[13]

The jury waived any charges, but the deeper problem stuck. Drink reformers had promised to restore virtue to America. Instead, they plunged the government deeper into urban chaos—riots, shooting, killing. In Chicago, Know-Nothing Mayor Levi D. Boone (Daniel's brother) tried to crack down on Sunday drinking and set off the Chicago Lager riot—one dead, dozens injured. In Philadelphia, Mayor Robert Conrad got so frustrated over lax enforcement that he fired every foreign cop. Unfortunately, he forgot to distinguish between "our" immigrants (Protestants) and "theirs" (Catholics). His Know-Nothing party promptly lost control of the city council.

Everywhere, local populations resisted, courts struck down prohibitions, liquor interests stirred up trouble, and the immigrants kept right on drinking. The Know-Nothings and the temperance reforms both got swept aside in the American maelstrom of the 1860s. Civil War armies revived the culture of drinking. By 1870s, prohibitions had been repealed everywhere except the three states of northern New England, where it was largely ignored.

Those first anti-drink crusaders set the pattern. Each reforming wave would repeat elements of this first prohibition cycle.

First, temperance bubbles up from below as a self-help movement. Prohibition promises some Americans a chance to rise and prosper. This time, the Washingtonians; next time, black leaders reaching for respectability and women seeking home protection (a motif that Mothers Against Drunk Driving would echo in a still later round of anti-alcohol politics). Revisionist historians telling a sympathetic story about the dry crusades can always find underdogs trying to pull themselves up by swearing off liquor.

Second, temperance also comes with a preachy side. Business jumps on the water wagon. Less liquor means more efficient workers. Moreover, drinking seems to explain that nagging American dilemma—poverty in the land of opportunity. The poor are either lazy or drunkards. There's a simple answer to their troubles: take the pledge. In these pragmatic hands, what started as a broad reform movement gets narrowly focused. Dow set the precedent when he ducked the gender issue.

Third, the exhortations gradually turn coercive. Dry preachers call in the government. The crucial ingredient for this change is usually a frightening enemy. Prohibitions emerge amid immigrant fears or race panics. Really successful efforts add a second enemy—the evil industry peddling the poisons. Saloons, dope peddlers, and tobacco companies have all performed brilliantly in the role of heartless villain.

Next, reformers win their prohibitions: thirteen states in the 1850s; seven states during the 1880s (when fourteen others seriously debated the issue), the entire nation in 1920. But, in every case, the efforts fail—or fall, anyway. Prohibitions never last. They keep getting entangled in the very sins they had promised to redeem—violence, corruption, ruined lives, and mean cities.

Finally, panics and mobilizations leave legacies, especially after American politics moved into the bureaucratic era toward the end of the nineteenth century. Here is the same outcome we just saw during the purity wars. Prohibition laws foster political changes—legal precedents, political organizations, cultural consequences. The political changes outlive the moral efforts.

The pattern continues. Exhort people to abstain. Condemn the stubborn drinkers who won't listen—usually the latest underclass. Prohibit. Watch the violence escalate, and then see prohibition collapse, leaving behind a political legacy. Pause and repeat. Through out the process, the dry crusades pivot around the same two trusty American themes, wickedness and economic success. Drinking violates both the Protestant ethos and the spirit of capitalism.

National Prohibition Rising

In December 1873, Diocletian Lewis delivered a temperance sermon in Washington Court House, a prosperous little Ohio town of 2,000 people. Lewis had been preaching for decades, but this time he got an astonishing response. Forty or fifty women grabbed their Bibles and hymnals and went calling on the local saloons. They sang, prayed, and exhorted the saloonkeepers to forswear the evil business. (No hatchets or iron bars—those were back in the 1850s.) When the startled men slammed their doors shut, the women knelt in the snow and prayed for the sinners inside. Within eight days, the women of Washington Court House had vanquished all eleven saloons and the three liquor-plying drug stores (quite a ratio of saloons to citizens). The activists inspired others and protests spread across Ohio, Indiana, and western New York before bursting out all over. Perhaps 100,000 women in more than 900 towns took to the streets. Borrowing the Ohio tactics, the women challenged liquor peddlers by kneeling in front of their establishments.

Popular historians soon gave the story its predictable twists. They patron-

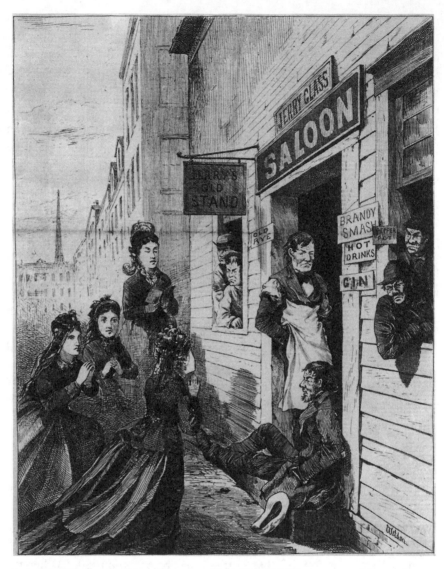

10.1. "The Temperance Crusade—who will win?" (1874). The cartoon celebrates the new women's tactic—praying before the debauched saloon. The German saloon (Jerry's) is full of foreign-looking toughs (including Irish and Chinese). (Library of Congress)

ized the ladies who had "evinced" such "unsuspected powers." And the villains? Here's a typical nineteenth-century description: "The . . . ludicrous . . . proprietor kept running from window to window. 'I dells you,' he wails while his motley customers absorb their beer and pigs' feet, 'I dells you, dem vimins is shoot awful.'" Already savvy in American ways, his first thought runs to property rights. "'I shoost go and see my gounsel.'" But in the end, virtue triumphs and the German throws in his apron. "'Mein Gott! Shentlemens, I quits.'" With a frankly inspiring us and a thoroughly un-American them, the United States began its march toward national prohibition.[14]

The street demonstrations led to the formation of the Women's Christian Temperance Union (the WCTU, founded in November 1874). The new group called the protesters off the sidewalks. Organizations often muffle radical politics—the meetings bury the militancy. But this new organization launched the first mass women's movement in the United States. Frances Willard led the WCTU into all kinds of causes: women's suffrage, equal pay for men and women, day care for children, sexual purity, mine safety, and, of course, temperance. The WCTU served up something to offend almost everyone. Suffrage was bad enough—but equal pay for women?

Almost intoxicated by analogies to the abolitionists, Willard and the WCTU rebuffed every call for moderation. Temperance advocates constructed fantastic parallels with the battle against slavery. They also reached further back and dusted off the ancient Puritan covenant with God: "The evil is a national evil, the sin of perpetuating it is a national sin. God deals with nations as nations and accepts no actions of isolated members as expiation for the nation's sins."

That is precisely what John Winthrop's generation had preached in the 1630s. Collective responsibility for sin lay at the very heart of Puritan morality. Willard and the WCTU self-consciously seized the great American moral tradition—from Puritan covenant to abolitionist jeremiad—and trained its power on the great sins of their time.[15]

Willard pushed the WCTU into an alliance with the radical Prohibitionist Party. Some women chafed over that alliance. Although each WCTU chapter operated autonomously, Willard cracked down at the 1884 convention. The delegates voted to "reaffirm our allegiance" to the political party that rejects the liquor traffic and "recognizes equal suffrage and equal wages for women." Anybody who couldn't go along with that was "declared disloyal to this organization."[16]

Temperance would remain a women's issue right up to national prohibition. By 1918, you could not miss the connection. Women had won full suffrage in thirteen western states; except for notoriously wet California, every one of them voted statewide prohibition, often just after women had won the vote. Novelist Jack London saw the trend. "When the women get the ballot, they will vote for prohibition. . . . It is the wives and sisters and mothers, and they only, who will drive the nails into the coffin of John Barleycorn." The *New York Times* agreed—"Liquor is going out as women suffrage is coming in."[17]

Even so, it was those reluctant WCTU members, "disloyal to this organization" or not, who had more accurately seen the future. A "narrow gauge" faction rose up within the Prohibitionist Party in the 1890s. It would fight only for prohibition. That new spirit produced a powerful new interest group, the Anti-Saloon League (or ASL, founded in 1893). The ASL took the next step in the political cycle: it narrowed the reform.

The ASL also stood in a venerable moral tradition. Moral depravity alone explained our social troubles. Our problems all flowed from the liquor traffic—period. Prohibition would lower taxes since without liquor, the nation could stop pouring money into prisons, poorhouses, and police forces. Prohibition would smash the corrupt machines, alleviate poverty, soothe labor conflict, and shape up the immigrants. Business leaders, church officials, and politicians gratefully latched onto this simple solution to complicated problems. The ASL offered an easy escape from labor legislation or anti-lynching resolutions or votes for the ladies—all particularly unpalatable to southern leaders.

The Anti-Saloon League fit the time. Progressive reformers were fighting corruption by pushing expertise and specialization. The Progressives had managed to pry the system loose from the political parties. But the results did not quite match the reformers' blueprint. Government grew decentralized, fragmented, and chaotic. The future slipped away from the experts and fell to interest groups that focused on single issues and targeted individual politicians. In a classic treatise written about the ASL in 1928, political scientist Peter Odegard discovered a new kind of organization: "the pressure group [which] carries on agitation for . . . projects . . . favorable to its interests." None wielded more political clout, said Odegard, than the Anti-Saloon League. Lincoln Steffens put it more sharply. "How do you do it?" he asked the brilliant, monomaniacal ASL leader, Wayne Wheeler. "Wheeler bent forward and . . . hissed his shrewd, mad answer: 'I do it the way the bosses do it, with minorities.'" He organized intense minorities and made sure they got heard.[18]

The ASL carefully burnished its reputation for power. Led by Wheeler, the organization celebrated each prohibition victory on the state level and skillfully hogged the credit (regardless of its actual involvement.) In its annual reports, the ASL published maps that became famous. Dry counties were white, unredeemed territories black; floating above them all ran the ASL exhortation, "Make the map all white!"

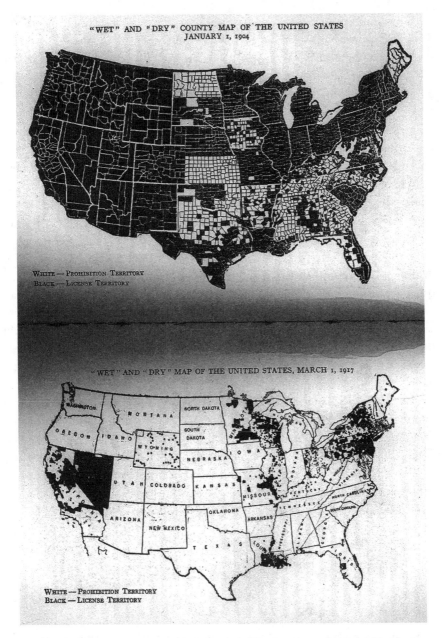

10.2. The Anti-Saloon League published maps of dry America and exhorted "make the map all white." In 1904, most of America is wet, while the South features its checkerboard of wet and dry counties. By 1917, the eve of Prohibition, not much more than the urban centers—and the northeast—remain to be conquered.

The Anti-Saloon League managed to find the perfect villain in beer. The drink had grown popular as cities grew. At the end of the nineteenth century, the industry became fiercely competitive. Breweries multiplied and took over saloons to push the product. The saloons seemed to be practically pouring their beer down the men's throats. The bars offered free lunches—often elaborate meals featuring ethnic eats. And thanks to all that competition, beer was cheap. Temperance reformers loved quoting George Bernard Shaw: "I see enormous capitalist organizations pushing drink under people's noses at every corner and pocketing the price leaving me . . . to pay the colossal damages." The reformers even had a stock melodrama: the little boy looked desperately for his father among the drunks in the back of the saloon. "This town is full of kids that know all about it," says one character in Upton Sinclair's *Wet Parade*, "either you get father home or you don't eat the next day."[19]

American men were not actually guzzling more alcohol. By 1915, they were drinking about a third less hard liquor than they had in 1870. But beer was another story—its consumption tripled in the same period. And beer kept bad company. It was the city drink, the immigrant drink, the worker's drink. Here sat everything the good folks in the declining rural areas loathed. Why should those lazy foreigners ever bother to get a job when the saloons offered a warm stove, free food, and cheap booze? The Anti-Saloon League had a foe almost every upright American could despise.

But how did this jumble of hopes, fears, and eager organizations get us to national prohibition? By 1904, only three states were even nominally dry. Frances Willard was dead. The Prohibition Party had dwindled into a cipher. That ASL map was mainly black outside of the rural South.

The answer lies in the states. Prohibition met local needs. The South went first. Between 1907 and 1915, ten southern states voted Prohibition. As the reform leaped into the western states, southern leaders joined the ASL and charged onto the national level.

Trouble in the New South: Race and Liquor

That ASL slogan—"Make the map all white"—glittered with racial irony. Talk about a "them." Southern prohibition took wing during the bitter racial convulsion around the turn of the century—what African Americans would later call the "nadir" of their status in American society.[20]

To get a feel for the velocity of prohibition across the South, I step back from drinking and explore one of the most terrible moral convulsions in American history. The rise of legal segregation in this period—a vital moral story in itself—set the political stage for southern prohibition.

The Nadir

At the turn of the century, southerners organized their legal apartheid. They had plenty of help getting Jim Crow into place. Congress repealed the laws that implemented the Civil War Amendments (in 1893). The Supreme Court accepted segregation (with *Plessy v. Ferguson* in 1896). State conventions drove black Americans out of politics and into segregation (1890–1905). What social scientists often fail to notice is how all these maneuvers rested on moral stigma as well as racial violence.

In the 1890s, white southerners constructed an image of black men and women who had been morally unprepared for freedom. The white majority essentially rewrote the story of the Civil War and its aftermath—valorizing their own history and twisting the story of the former slaves. The white southerners, they said, had always been patriots. They had been bitterly unhappy firing on their own stars and stripes. Why, any Union army veteran who went south on July 4th would "fail to mark a single sentiment to which, as a patriot, he could take exception." Lincoln understood. He had been magnanimous in victory. But after his murder, bigoted northern radicals punished the South by setting loose the wild black man. Historians now dredged up the hot language of white defiance from the late 1860s and turned it into the official story of the "tragic era": "The white man could not be expected to submit supinely to be ruled and plundered by its former slaves." The white people could not permit the "lapse of Caucasian civilization into African barbarism." "Every white man in the South would rather die than submit to horrors certain to attend Negro ascendancy."[21]

An almost hysterical portrait of black men overran the popular culture at the turn of the century. One scene from Thomas Dixon's best-selling *Leopard's Spots*, set in 1865 but published in 1902, illustrates the revised view of race and Reconstruction. Tom, a heroic Confederate veteran, comes home to discover that his daughter is engaged. The soldier is not sure about this apparently callow bridegroom. "No licker . . . in my house," lectures Tom. "I want you to quit your foolishness and be a man." At the wedding, tragedy strikes. A group of burly black men in federal army uniforms ("their eyes bloodshot with whisky" and all the power of Washington backing their depravity) burst in on the wedding party. They seize the terrified bride and carry her off into the woods. The young bridegroom and his pals now prove their manhood. They grab their guns and shoot the bride in the temple before the black men can do the unspeakable. The father is overwhelmed with gratitude. "You saved my little gal. I want to shake hands with you."[22]

Writers pushed on to their audacious conclusion. Southern white men had redeemed their land from northern mischief and black immorality: "When the Klan began to ride," wrote historian Claude Bowers, "white women felt some sense of security." Dixon went on to portray the Ku Klux Klan as gallant defenders of white virtue in *The Clansman,* published in 1905. A decade later, the images leaped into the movies. D. W. Griffith's celebrated *Birth of a Nation* faithfully recounts the new Dixie narrative. It's the "birth of the nation" because North and South embrace. Now they see what had divided them: the lust-crazed black man. In the triumphant finale—Griffith conjures up cinematic magic to tell his awful story—heroic Klansmen ride (and ride and ride) to rescue the brave white people huddled in a cabin while savage black soldiers in blue uniforms hammer at the door and fire through the windows. President Wilson saw *The Birth of a Nation*—it was the first film to screen in the White House—and announced that he had "seen history written by lightning." (He backed off when the National Association for the Advancement of Colored People protested.) The movie helped revive the Klan.

In the real 1860s and '70s, black men and women had struggled to make new lives for themselves despite poverty, prejudice, and violence. As Eric Foner puts it, "blacks seized the opportunity . . . to establish as much independence as possible in their working lives, to consolidate their families and communities, and stake a claim to equal citizenship." Many black Americans threw themselves into a great education effort. Unpolished teachers taught in crude schools; they aspired to lift up their students and "plant a genuine republicanism in the Southern states." By the turn of the century all that hope and effort was buried by a lurid story featuring fear, chaos, and lust.[23]

Progressive social scientists, their heads stuffed with misapplications of Charles Darwin's theories, repeated and enlarged the unhappy racial stereotypes. Frederick Hoffman, a German-born actuary (and therefore, he avers, without prejudice on racial matters), comes to the following conclusion in his highly influential *Race Traits of the American Negro:* "All of the facts prove that a low standard of sexual morality is the main underlying cause of the low and anti-social condition of the race at the present time." Hoffman finds a remarkable way to measure this low morality: "The rate of increase in lynching may be accepted as representing fairly the increasing tendency of colored men to commit the most frightful of crimes." He concludes with a stern warning: "Intercourse with the white race must absolutely cease."[24]

Hoffman was no marginal figure. A review published by the American Negro Academy called *Race Traits* the most important book on American race relations since *Uncle Tom's Cabin.* As chief statistician (or actuary) for the Prudential Insurance Company of America, Hoffman defined African Americans as uninsurable risks. Two decades later he would help lead the first great fight against national health insurance.

The biased image of black immorality—of a people not ready for freedom—covered the rise of Jim Crow. As one North Carolina congressman explained during the Prohibition debate, "we have disenfranchised the Negro vote" to protect our civilization, our homes, and our peace. "We took away the ballot as the adult takes the pistol from the hand of the child." With only small pockets of resistance, northern opinion acquiesced in the "conclusion that universal Negro suffrage has been a failure," thick with "evils."[25]

The rest of the nation also swallowed perhaps the bleakest episode in American history. The rape narrative justified a wave of lynching that ripped through the South in the 1890s and 1900s. In the past, mobs had murdered whites as well as blacks. Now lynching was turned almost entirely on black men. The terror reached its height alongside the revisionist southern writing (like *The Clansman*) and the rise of Jim Crow. In the fifteen years following 1892, mobs murdered more than 2,050 people, over three-quarters of them black. Nor were these furtive midnight crimes. The people did their killing openly, in broad daylight, while the police maintained order. Afterward, the congregation often posed for pictures: adults and children—surly, defiant, smiling, laughing—gathering around the dangling and often charred black body. The photos were made into postcards to terrify the alleged savages and keep them in line. After seeing a collection of the photos, a *New York Times* reporter got it exactly right: "These images will burn a hole in your heart."[26]

The brutality masqueraded as moral regulation. "No law of God or man can hold back the vengeance of white men," swaggered one Atlanta newspaperman. "We will hang two or three or four of the Negroes nearest to the crime until the crime is no longer done or even feared in all this Southern land we inhabit and love." In reality, the mobs were enforcing the new South's race line. Forget rape. As Ida B. Wells had long pointed out, less than one-quarter of the lynching even involved a rape charge. The victim's sins more often ran to independence, success, self-protection, illicit love, and bad luck.[27]

Black Americans struggled long and hard to set the record straight. They repeatedly heard the White Sermon: as President Theodore Roosevelt put it, "Every colored man should realize that the worst enemy of his race is the Negro criminal . . . who commits the dreadful crime of rape." All Negroes ought to rise up and "help the officers of the law in hunting down . . . every such infamous offender." Ida Joyce Jackson, an official in the National Association of Colored Women, offered a typical rejoinder: black people positively "abhor the brutal piece of humanity . . . who would assault a poor female of any race," she wrote. But the law is no help, she points out, when it so routinely dissolves into the "angry mob [that] strings up the first Negro whom it meets . . . and then tortures his dangling body by shooting it full of bullets."[28]

The bluster about black savagery deflected attention from the real brutality.

10.3. The lynching of Lige Daniels in Center, Texas, August 1920. (Allen-Littlefield collection, Special Collections Division, Robert W. Woodruff Library, Emory University)

Southern whites were perpetrating the very crimes they pinned on black men—and not just mob violence, but rape as well. The forced sex across the race line more often came from white men abusing black women than from black men. Recall the antebellum romance about white women's purity. How did the South manage it? Why, the men had their black women, who did not feel "degradation" from just a bit of sex. The blithe white attitudes—and the exploitation they justified—did not evaporate at Appomattox. Historian Leon Litwack describes a "maxim that enjoyed almost universal acceptance throughout the white south" at the turn of the century: "Black women were naturally licentious, making rape redundant." The *American Journal of Public Health* routinely implied the same attitude. Not surprisingly, the law offered black women little relief. Today, wrote Nannie Burroughs in 1915, the courts view black women's virtue with "amused contempt."[29]

There is a hard, sad tone in the black efforts to talk back, to assert their moral dignity. Ida Joyce Jackson's article ran with the discouraging title, "Do Negroes Constitute a Race of Criminals?" How can one ask this, she wanted to know, about a race that has worked so hard to improve itself? "22,000 churches built, 32,000 schoolteachers in the classroom, and an illiteracy rate that has gone down 45% since Emancipation." "However surprising this may be to some," added the president of a black college in North Carolina, "our race leaders . . . are generally sober, upright and honest."[30]

White southerners never paused. They had convinced themselves—and the rest of the nation—that they faced trouble from African Americans. The white majority slipped the American political rules in the usual fashion: by discovering and decrying moral depravity. They stripped their fellow citizens of the vote and called it removing the gun from the child's hand; they stripped them of human rights and called it protection for our women and children.

Southern Prohibition

Drinking fit smoothly into the story. After the Civil War, recalled one prohibitionist in 1906, "swarms of Negroes, many of them drunk with whisky and all intoxicated with the delirium of newfound liberty, roamed the country." In that terrible time, "every country crossroads had its barroom or 'doggery.'" In order to control the "idle Negroes," southern states had worked out local-option laws. Most rural counties prohibited the sale of all intoxicating liquor. But alcohol remained at the heart of the black depravity narrative—liquor, lust, and lynching all ran together, especially in the dangerous cities.[31]

Again, this was a distorted story. In the 1870s and early '80s, many African Americans joined the temperance cause. The black churches, eager to prove themselves respectable, lined up alongside their white brethren. Each group testified about the ravages of drink. Prohibition rallies explicitly invited everyone, regardless of color. Black and white reformers belonged to separate organizations, of course; but the black leaders sat right up on the platform. And the very things that made the Prohibition Party unpopular in the white South—abolitionist analogies, anti-lynching resolutions—spoke directly to black churchgoers. There were plenty of black voters on the other side. But as historian Edward Ayers puts it, "blacks enjoyed their greatest political activity and visibility in the entire New South Era [after 1877] in the prohibition movement."[32]

The liquor question stirred powerful southern interests on both sides of the issue: liquor dealers, small farmers (with their homemade corn whiskey), preachers, and men looking for patronage plums (such as liquor revenue agents). Since African Americans also fell on both sides of the issue, they often became the crucial swing voters. When it came time to cast ballots in one Atlanta election, black voters were "courted, bribed, feted, and marched to the polls by both wets and drys." Historical analyses of dry counties have not turned up clear racial trends. But black voters in the middle? A recipe for southern trouble.

As one newspaper editor in North Carolina put it with a sneer, "his former owner" now "takes [the Negro] by the hand as a man and a brother" and "labors with him as an equal citizen either for or against Prohibition." The very idea— fellow man and brother—jeopardized the racial fears that lay at the heart of southern Democratic politics. The minority Republicans, always casting around for a racial wedge, found a dynamite issue: Democrats were soft on drunken Negroes.[33]

Nervous politicians applied the standard formula—attack the black population. Black swing voters now became the ignorant, corrupt black mass that kept killing off moral reforms. African American leaders responded furiously. "Negroes . . . supported prohibition in large numbers and repeatedly," declared the NAACP publication *Crisis*. "Colored men," added another black leader, "have been on the side of temperance and fought valiantly for its success." *Crisis* discovered exactly the same editorial that appeared in North Carolina running in Nashville and in Newburyport, Massachusetts, under the headline "The Annoying Negro Vote": "When it is considered that . . . the Prohibition Amendment . . . in the Texas election . . . was defeated by only 5,000 votes out of a total number exceeding 450,000, it will be keenly appreciated how annoying it is for [the Negroes] to hold the balance of power in deciding such a question. They like whiskey and they want it sold where they may purchase it without the least restraint."[34]

The NAACP's magazine challenged the "deliberate lies" about the Negro vote in Texas and then raised pointed questions about identical editorials popping up across the nation—"Who is doing this philanthropic work? Who is paying for it?" And "is it our patriotic duty to sit and sleep" while the "Negro haters in the south . . . foment race strife" and "poison the rest of the nation on race matters?"[35]

But black protests were buried by the harsher tale. "All over the South," ran the emerging history, "the Negroes almost to a man voted for 'free rum' as often as the question came up." A Georgia minister explained why in 1908: "The Negro constitutes a child-people in our population." The reason the country people of Georgia were finally turning to statewide prohibition was simple: "Drunken Negroes had become a contagion among country women." White men grew determined to see "an end to drunken Negro parties . . . return[ing] from nearby towns." Of course, we've already seen Frances Willard's unkindest cut: "The grogshop is the Negro's center of power. Better whiskey and more of it is the rallying cry of great dark faced mobs."[36]

By the 1890s, temperance had become a tool in the effort to strip the vote from black men. As one delegate to Mississippi's disenfranchisement convention put it, "Dry counties are in the white section [of the state] . . . wet counties are mostly in the black belt. . . . What are we here for if not to maintain white supremacy especially when . . . whites stand for a great principle of public morals and public safety. How long is it to be expected that white solidarity can be maintained, if the Negro is to be brought forward to arbitrate this great question?"[37]

There would be no reforms of any kind till the vote was removed. Latter-day Progressives repeated the new wisdom right into the 1960s. Removing the "mass of illiterate and propertyless Negroes from politics," wrote one temperance historian, eliminated corruption and cleared the way for future reform. Only the shameless liquor interests "aligned themselves against the Progressive cause [and] opposed Negro disenfranchisement." White Progressives forgot all about the black temperance movement, and about democratic principles. They rewrote Prohibition into another part of the white supremacy fantasy: the southern majority wisely reasserts control of its immoral black folk.[38]

The liquor revisionists did not stop with the allegations of easily gulled black voters. They cut all the way to the main taboo. Liquor, they said, is what transformed the black male into a rapist. In a multipart article in *Colliers*, Will Irwin told the story. "Is it plain, now—the secret of many and many a lynching and burning in the South? The primitive Negro field hand, a web of strong, sudden impulses, good and bad, comes into the town or settlement on Saturday afternoon and pays his fifty cents for a pint of Mr. Levy's gin." The bottles, on view in every "low Negro dive of the south," brim with pornographic suggestions. "Pictures of naked white women on the label," brand names so obscene they could not be printed in a decent magazine. The black man orders his drink and "absorbs its toxic heat. . . . He sits in the road or in the alley at the height of his debauch, looking at that obscene picture of a white woman on the label, drinking in the invitation which it carries. And then comes—opportunity. There follows the hideous episode of the rope or the stake."[39]

Others picked up and embellished the story. The obscene labels keep reappearing, always with those lascivious "pictures of naked white women," and invariably "sold only to the brutish Negroes." Horrible rapes litter the stories— the murder of Margaret Lear in Shreveport, a man named Johnson nabbed in Chattanooga, a Pickens County Negro "seized for the nameless crime." A bottle always lies near the scene of the crime. What leaps out of the lynching narratives is their offhand concern for evidence: just dark brutes, dirty pictures, heavy drinking, and dreadful crimes. As Irwin delicately puts it, sometimes, the "evidence does not run in a chain so direct." The stories mimic the mob justice they describe—like that call to "hang two or three or four of the Negroes nearest to the crime." Even the courts, in these accounts, took shortcuts to justice. "I have seen the bottles," says judge to jury in one of the gothic southern liquor articles. "Nothing more is necessary."[40]

All the pieces of the new race narrative melded in Atlanta in 1906. Twenty years earlier, black voters had actively participated in the city's vote on prohibition. But by the turn of the century, everything had changed. An eighteen-month disenfranchisement campaign—Georgia was the last southern state to clamp on restrictions—put black sins on the front pages. A play based on Dixon's *Clansman* preached the venomous modern version of Reconstruction. A close primary contest for governor got both candidates race-baiting around the inevitable trio: drinking among blacks, liquor labels with naked white women, and black lust for white innocents. On September 22, an Atlanta newspaper touched off the firestorm with an extra edition that screamed, "THIRD ASSAULT." For the third time, a black man had gotten away with molesting a white woman. Were white men going to protect their women or not? Mobs went searching for blacks to beat and torture. Some 10,000 young white men ran through the streets. They broke into black businesses and dragged out the proprietors; they stopped streetcars and pulled out the black passengers. The riot lasted two days and claimed an unknown number of black lives.[41]

How to explain the horror? The easy answer—the one that let the white elites off the hook—boiled down to the combustion of race and liquor. Dry moralists already had prohibition on the political agenda. Now they were offering it up as a form of race and class control. "In any Southern community with a bar-room a race war is a perilously possible occurrence." Intelligent white people had had enough of the "depraved and criminal Negro," as well as the "irresponsible white man." When the Georgia legislature met in June, it voted statewide liquor prohibition.[42]

The southern states almost all followed Georgia to prohibition—North Carolina and Mississippi went the following year. Prohibition took its place at the heart of the southern political agenda. The 1912 election brought the Democrats back to power in Washington—they controlled both houses of Congress for the first time in eighteen years. The southern delegation (all Democrats, of course) were thrust into power and led the charge toward national prohibition. They would push harder for a constitutional amendment than the representatives from any other region—61 percent of the southern delegation voted for Prohibition, compared with just 28 percent of the congressmen from the northeast.

Not all southerners went along. A minority kept warning about the perilous first step down the slippery slope toward racial equality. "If it is right for the legislatures of 36 states to decide how all 48 states shall deal with the liquor traffic," warned Congressman Edward Pou (North Carolina, Democrat), "it is also right for the legislatures of 36 states to prescribe the qualification of the voters in all the . . . states of the union." Suppose they rammed through an amendment that read as follows: "No state shall deprive any citizen of the right to vote." The southern skeptics began conjuring up terrors that might be lurking behind the Prohibition precedent. "Someone will propose a constitutional amendment against the separate coach laws" (segregated transportation). Or against "separate schools and churches and graveyards." Or, worst of all, someone "will seek an amendment . . . providing that there shall be no state laws against the intermarriage of the races." The southern majority ignored such horror stories about equality and pushed Prohibition.[43]

Wets would soon be blasting the race-crazed "solid south" for its Prohibition mania. "The people of New York are being deprived of their right to the harmless enjoyment of wine and beer," wrote anti-prohibitionist Fabian Franklin, "in order that the Negroes of Alabama and Texas may not get beastly drunk on rotgut whiskey." The New York congressional delegation knew just how to retaliate. "If drastic laws are passed by Congress to enforce the National Prohibition amendment," declared Brooklyn Congressman Reuben Haskell, "equally drastic laws will be advocated to enforce the Fourteenth Amendment, which conferred the right of suffrage on men of the Negro race. . . . If one drastic amendment to the Constitution [like Prohibition] is to be enforced on all sections of the county, then an equally drastic amendment, like the fourteenth, should also be enforced."[44]

Honest moral aspirations led many southerners to fight liquor. Black churchmen embraced Prohibition as a form of racial uplift. White dries reached across the race line for their moral cause. Evangelicals throughout the South had ardently campaigned for this personal and communal salvation. But the crusaders also tapped the dark side.

Moral fictions stripped black America of its most basic rights. Americans slide into bigotry when they think they see savages threatening their good women and children. That fear stretches back to the first Indian slaughters ("God smiled," wrote Cotton Mather). It stretches forward into modern times with *Birth of a Nation*. The central moral image—imperiled white innocents— is what made Griffith's movie so powerful, so persuasive; it turned a frankly bigoted novel into "history written by lightning." Southern politicians came to

Prohibition through the lurid southern race story—marked by religious fervor, racial repression, and lynch laws. But the white South cast its call for Prohibition in the timeless language of American moral fears: the depraved savage endangers us. Put that way, it reverberated across the rest of the nation. Even Haskell, a Democrat who hated Prohibition, conceded the deeper moral point: when it came to African Americans, Fourteenth Amendment voting rights were "drastic" and unreasonable.

Trouble in the North: Immigrants

Meanwhile, the rest of the nation was brawling over strangers. As we have seen, after the turn of the century, immigrants rushed into the United States faster than at any other time in American history, before or since—by 1910, almost 15 percent of the American population had been born abroad.[45]

The new people provoked the old fears. They came from the lowest classes of the lower races. One Baptist missionary manual outlined the Slav's not-so-vital signs: "Low living, low intelligence, low morality, low capacity, low everything." And we've already sampled E. A. Ross, the influential sociologist and advisor to Theodore Roosevelt, on the latest immigrants: they were liars, cheats, selfish, dirty, often insane, mostly dark, and all ugly. Each immigrant group also had its own special flaws: "You can't make boy scouts out of the Jews," reported Ross. "They are absolutely babies." And, of course, the implacable genetic laws would soon be sealing the Nordic Americans' doom. Pretty soon, we would look and act—we would be—just like these inferior races. "Like it or not," wrote the well-known zoologist Madison Grant, "the mixture of two races . . . revert[s] to the lower type. . . . The cross between a white man and a Negro is a Negro, a white man and a Hindu is a Hindu; and the cross between any of the three European races and a Jew is a Jew." Americans faced their decline and fall. The solid, homogeneous, get-ahead nations—like the Norwegians or New Zealanders—pitied our immigrant stew, "a chaos rather than a people."[46]

Most authorities agreed that the gravest danger was these people's loose morals. In previous chapters we caught the immigrants—with their "continental ideas"—fomenting white slave rings, fostering urban machines, and frolicking on the Sabbath. But one sin tied all their depravities together. "By far the most effective instrument for debauching popular morals is the liquor traffic," wrote reformer Josiah Strong. Saloons run by foreigners were the taproot of every urban corruption. The saloons supported gambling, dance halls, and prostitution; they were "mother and nurse of American socialism"; they were the soul of the old machines. No saloonkeeper could hang onto his liquor li-

10.4. "The Recruiting Sergeant for the Army of Crime." This cartoon was an Anti-Saloon League favorite. The saloons were gathering an entire army under the banner of "no discipline, no work, no law, and a life of idleness and indulgence."

cense for long, wrote Ross, "if he fail[ed] to line up his fellow countryman for the local machine." At the rum shops, wrote another critic, people mixed their poison with their politics.[47]

Jacob Riis gloomily toted up the score in the battle between God and the devil. Below New York's 14th Street stood 111 Protestant churches and chapels. And 4,065 saloons. Naturally, the saloons had larger congregations and better-attended services. In 1906, the Baptist Missionary Society analyzed just why the devil was so far ahead in Riis's contest. Visitors to lower New York would find colonies that were "Italian, German, French, African, Spanish, Bohemian, Russian, Jewish"—you get the idea. "The one thing you will ask for in vain in the chief city of America, concluded the Baptists, is a distinctively American community." Three years after Prohibition went into effect, the federal Prohibition commissioner, Roy Haynes, announced that four times as many aliens as citizens violated the liquor laws in New York City. Data? No, they didn't collect it. But Haynes knew it was those people.[48]

When frightened Americans went into full outcry, they could work up a pretty ferocious jeremiad. Temperance advocate Alphonse Alva Hopkins served up a fine specimen:

> Our boast has been that we are a Christian people, with Morality at the center of our civilization . . .
>
> Besodden Europe, worse bescourged than by war, famine and pestilence, sends here her drink-makers, her drunkard makers, and her drunkards, or her more temperate and habitual drinkers, with all their un-American and anti-American ideas of morality and government; they are absorbed into our national life but not assimilated; with no liberty whence they came, they demand unrestricted liberty among us, even to license what we loathe; and through the ballot box, flung wide open to them by foolish statesmanship . . . they dominate our Sabbath, they have set up for us their own moral standards, which are grossly immoral; they govern our great cities, until . . . foreign control or conquest could gain little more through . . . armies and fleets. . . . Foreign . . . conquest is rapidly making us un-Christian, with immorality throned in power.[49]

The drink jeremiads imagined every kind of perversion coiling at the bottom of the glass. But ultimately the dangers boiled down to that most fundamental Puritan lapse: lost self-control. The foreigners were "largely controlled by their appetites." And what better metaphor for people who had lost command of themselves—who would not crucify their lusts—than the drunk lying in the gutter.[50]

The most scary thing about immoral others is always the danger that we will fall to their level. The Puritan ministers lashed the chosen people for becoming like the Indians—all desire, no self-discipline. Now, drink was the way good Americans melted into the foreigners. The standard temperance narrative, repeated in endless variations, told the story of the strong, promising young man who took a sip. And then another. He lost control, wrecked his prospects, and ruined his family. In the last scene, they are usually burying the poor wretch. Drink was the direct route to hell.

The parables of the era lingered on the delusion of moderate drinking. "Each one thinks he will escape," wrote Upton Sinclair. But with every drink "you throw the dice with death." "The moderate drinker," warned *Harper's* in 1921, always "runs the risk of being overpowered by his habit and swept into the abyss of excess." He poses as a sophisticate, but he is just an "ignorant self-poisoner." Jack London wrote a long, nightmarish description of his own tangle with drink. "I should drink it," he kept saying to himself, "but carefully avoid . . . overdrinking." He would chase down John Barleycorn "and hail him as benefactor and friend. And detest and hate him all the time." Eventually he learned the hard lesson: "There is not a devotee but pays for the mad dances John Barleycorn pipes." The writing of the era draws a feverish, frightening portrait of alcohol and its snares.[51]

The peril ran beyond vulnerable individuals to the whole race. Alcohol attacked Nordic people with peculiar intensity, wrote Madison Grant. Rum cost our nation its "most brilliant," "attractive," and "desirable classes." Why? Ross thought he had the answer. Ancient races—Italians, Jews, Greeks—had, over the millennia, weeded out their heavy drinkers. But Northern Europeans were new to this vice. Leave the saloons in business, warned Ross, and a perverse, Darwinian selection would kill off a million drinkers a decade till we had evolved into a race as "resistant to alcoholic beguilement as the Portuguese." (Ross pegged the date at about 2100 AD—actually pretty swift for evolutionary work.)[52]

The signs of moral decline were all around us—just look at the cities. Amid the bedlam, American Protestant churches threw themselves into the campaign to crush the saloon. They organized the greatest American evangelical crusade of the twentieth century. They fought and prayed for Prohibition through the first two decades of the century; once the amendment passed, they fervently supported it. No other program rallied conservative Christians in quite the same way. The sober, God-fearing American legions would prevent their nation from melting into an irresponsible, foreign chaos.

The fight against the saloons would return the United States to its appointed place—up on a hill, moral exemplar for all people. "The whole world is watching America," wrote Haynes as his program got under way. "Watching, hoping, fearing, wondering." Going dry would transform the urban-immigrant debacle into a hopeful beacon for "little people" struggling all over the world.[53]

Former President William Howard Taft took a more benign view of drinking foreigners. He recalled an archbishop named Guidi who visited the United States from Rome. When the archbishop arrived in St. Paul, Minnesota, his colleagues entertained him with "bounteous" hospitality. Except for just one thing. "We had coffee and water for breakfast," recalled Guidi, "water and coffee for luncheon and coffee and water for dinner." Finally, the Roman prelate couldn't stand it. He burst out, "Is this all you drink? I am in the habit of drinking wine. I have a vineyard in the hills of Rome. I have wine for every meal. I do not consider all this water healthy. I have drunk wine since my childhood." The archbishop of St. Paul, a leader in the temperance movement, coldly told his guest, "You will get no wine in my house." Guidi moved on down the road to the Benedictine monastery, where he could at least get some good German beer.[54]

Taft's view implied that maybe innocent differences had been amplified into a kind of cultural war. White temperance ribbons invested old American castes with special moral standing. Americans brandished their values as sure signs of moral superiority. They comfortably, perhaps even smugly, contrasted their virtuous communities with cities teeming with foreigners, crime, corruption, poverty, labor unrest, and that mother of all sorrows, the saloons.

Later, sociologists landed on precisely this idea of cultural difference. Rural, native, Protestant Americans felt their culture slipping away, argues Joseph Gusfield. They shored up their waning sense of power by pushing temperance down urban, immigrant, often Catholic throats. In fact, the great Prohibition victory would come just one year before the census made it official in 1920—the United States had become an urban nation.[55]

The South, where almost the entire population (98 percent in 1910) was born in America, started the prohibitions. The west (82 percent native born) went next. Finally, the East (only 76 percent) slouched reluctantly toward reform. The congressional roll calls reflect the same regional tilts.[56]

Recent historians are distinctly skeptical about dismissing the great moral battle as mere cultural difference. Surely the dry cause offered something more than the rear guard action of a waning rural culture. Or a bald cry against immigration and modernity. Alcoholism was a genuine problem. Frances Willard's army of women were reaching for something more than status when they pleaded for home protection. Finally, say the revisionist scholars, shutting down those noxious drinking holes did everyone—workers, women, America—a lot of good.

Other pictures of saloon life seem to describe a different planet. Theodore Dreiser's salesman saunters into Fitzgerald and Moy's "swell saloon" in Chicago in 1900: "It was ornamented with a blaze of incandescent lights, held in handsome chandeliers. The floors were of brightly coloured tiles, the walls . . . of rich, dark, polished wood which reflected the light . . . and gave the place a sumptuous appearance. The long bar was a blaze of lights, polished wood-work, coloured and cut glassware and many fancy bottles."[57]

Successful men about town—merchants, politicians, actors—gather in saloons like Fitzgerald and Moy's, and they, in turn, draw in all the eager young strivers. We'd call it networking. Of course, working men and immigrants would not haunt such a sumptuous place. But even the shabby dramshops, reported Jacob Riis, "were a poor man's club, his forum, and his haven of rest."

One "investigative committee" (read: wet propaganda) managed a cheerful spin on the immigrant saloon. "About the German beer shops, one observes in them a large consumption of beer and various foods, little visible intoxication and an air of heartiness (Gemuthlickeit) all the Germans' own." The sneers from the other side lingered on the pigs' feet and foreign accents rather than the Gemuthlickeit; but in the clashing images you can see the different American tribes working out their differences. In a detailed study of saloon life, Madelon Powers cheers exactly what the conservative drys were blasting. "Old time saloons were places where union leaders first organized their members, machine politicians cultivated the workingman's vote, and immigrants sought the assistance of their countrymen." Sympathetic portraits of saloon life invariably turn on the same idea: these were clubs for the poor man. The saloon-goers enjoyed being members.[58]

Even the gender bias of saloon-going rested in a more complicated story. After the turn of the century, most (between 63 and 72 percent) immigrants were men. The Census Bureau thought "excess . . . males" one of the most "noteworthy" aspects of the new immigration. The ratio varied from place to place (in Boston, there were actually more foreign women—and lots of saloons). But in many cities, the male haunts reflected the community's basic demographics. Still, as Jon Kingsdale points out, no amount of justification would jibe the idea of the saloon—of sitting around, schmoozing, and drinking—with the American Protestants' Puritan memories and Calvinist faith.[59]

In reading the great saloon debates, I found it difficult not to find some truth on both sides. The saloons reflected the urban, immigrant reality—for better and for worse. Liquor offered a poor escape from the grinding conditions of sweatshops and tenements. The breweries competed, the price of beer fell, and the amount of drinking—and perhaps the number of drunks—rose. But if the temperance crusaders fought real problems, they routinely got carried away. The drinking dangers became evil itself: "If our republic is to be saved, the liquor traffic must be destroyed." And, according to Josiah Strong, "Civilization must destroy the liquor traffic or be destroyed by it. The death struggle is desperate."[60]

The dry millennium also promised too much. America would vault over all the trouble of the emerging industrial order: inequality, poverty, tenements, sweatshops, ill health, and immigration. Temperance offered a simple moral solution that blithely ignored the complications of urban, industrial capitalism. Temperance took social and economic complications and transformed them into individual sins backed by unspeakable corporate greed. The immigrants—like the blacks in the South—were alternately depraved and duped.

Which returns us to the real force driving the campaign against this sin: the fear of the sinner. It is the rare dry tract that fails to huff about the alien sitting in his filthy saloon, or the southern black man staring at the label on his gin bottle.

The alternative is easy to imagine. Frances Willard pushed it throughout her career: poverty caused alcoholism as much as alcoholism caused poverty. Under her leadership, the WCTU organized itself around Willard's controversial double vision. You want temperance? asked Samuel Gompers, echoing Willard. Easy. It can be won by "increasing wages, establishing a shorter work day, affording better aspirations and higher ideals which the better standard of living . . . will bring."[61]

But the more complicated vision proved a tough sell. Willard's claim about poverty as a cause of drinking was always controversial, and the WCTU dropped it soon after she was gone. What is most striking about the American reform tradition is how eradicating poverty never unleashed anywhere near the same prolonged, fervent, millennial reformation as fighting drink.

What if Americans had pursued Willard's Social Gospel with the energy they spent chasing down individual sins? The fight against poverty and exploitation might have been pursued for generations. Resisting sin always seemed to rouse a greater constituency. Why?

Maybe it's the price the nation pays for throwing multiple tribes together, one tumbling in after another. They bump up against one another in a nation racked by racial tension and riveted by its own moral standing. The virtuous constantly rally over that most basic question: Who are we? Woman praying for temperance outside the saloons, settlement house workers in the cities, the women of the Lempster WCTU, protesters in the rallies against the red-light districts, immigrants passing through Ellis Island, and (alas) the lynch mobs were all offering answers to the question. In the 1920s, the old-fashioned Victorian moralists would get one last crack at supplying an answer for the nation.

Prohibition Wins

In 1905, just three states clung to prohibition. By 1917, the Anti-Saloon League map gleamed white from coast to coast. Two-thirds of the states had taken some action. Twenty-seven had gone dry; others offered local governments the option. In Florida, for example, only the area around Tampa smudged the anti-liquor map (see fig. 10.1).

But local efforts often flopped. Drinkers next door plagued dry counties. "If you want good roads leading into town," advised Will Rogers, "vote wet and the surrounding towns will fix up your roads for you." The saloons lured the impious element into town for their toots—recall the huffing about "drunken Negro parties" returning home.[62]

When reformers pushed prohibition up to the state level, they ran into another problem—they had no authority over interstate commerce. Oregon might go dry (in 1914), but the state could not stop those incorrigible Californians from shipping liquor to Oregon drinkers. States could not touch a legitimate business in another state. And the hard-liquor distilleries were concentrated in wet strongholds—Illinois, Kentucky, Ohio, and Pennsylvania. The Constitution, the railroads, and the liquor industry conspired to keep even the driest states at least a bit moist. If state prohibitions were going to really prohibit, the reformers would need help from the federal government.[63]

Preliminaries

Led by the Anti-Saloon League and the Women's Christian Temperance Union, the drys took the crusade to Washington. In 1912 they proposed federal legislation to plug the interstate loophole. Their proposal, the Webb-Kenyon bill, would forbid shipping liquor into a state if doing so violated state law. All sides descended on Washington, and, in the ensuing chaos, agreed on just one thing—their opponents were behaving scandalously. The debate spotlighted a controversial political innovation: pressure group lobbyists. The wets denounced this "sham," "decreed [by] the leaders of the Anti-Saloon League" who had unleashed "salaried agents" who in turn besieged members with "petition, letter, and open threat." These were all backhanded testimonials. The nonpartisan, narrowly focused ASL fit neatly into the emerging political system. The other side caught on almost as fast. Drys hooted about the flood of "voluminous briefs" from "every organization in the liquor business in this country."[64]

The Webb-Kenyon Act passed (February 1913) only to run into President William Howard Taft's veto. Unconstitutional, he said; the states would control interstate commerce every time they voted prohibition up or down. Just in time, the Supreme Court upheld the Mann Act (in *Hoke v. the United States*). Congressman James Mann, representing wet Chicago, explained how the two acts were entirely different. His colleagues shrugged him off and easily overrode Taft's veto. The majority figured if they could ban the transportation of women, they could also bar whiskey.[65]

Flush with success, the ASL went for national prohibition. In December 1913, thousands of prohibitionists marched down Pennsylvania Avenue to the Capitol and delivered a "human petition" to their Democratic champions, Senator Morris Sheppard (D-Texas) and Congressman Richmond Hobson (D-Alabama). A year later the full House got its hands on—or more accurately, its jaws around—an amendment to prohibit the sale (only the sale) of alcohol. They plunged into the longest debate Congress would hold on the issue—"ten mortal hours of speech making."[66]

Representative Hobson did a distinctly rotten job as floor manager for the bill. He was a Navy hero, a hellfire Chautauqua-circuit orator, a diehard dry, and an incompetent parliamentarian. He just could not resist a good brawl. When Mann announced that prohibitions did not prohibit, for example, Hobson leapt to the bait: "We do not propose that the gentleman from Illinois . . . shall proscribe to the . . . moral forces of America how to bring about Prohibition in this country." The scourge of white slavers shot right back: "I have accomplished more . . . for the moral forces of America . . . while the gentleman from Alabama was drawing pay on the Chautauqua circuit than he ever has or ever will. [Applause.]" Hobson waded in for another crack before cooler heads separated the jousting moralizers with points of order.[67]

When they actually focused on drink, the representatives offered a pretty good sample of the rhetoric that would swirl around the question for the next five years.

Prohibition proponents pushed the slavery analogy. Drinkers "have shackles on their wrists, a ball and chain around their ankles." "A few thousand brewers and distillers to-day own 5,000,000 slaves." The drys stressed the saloon's control over the "growing degenerate vote" in the cities, noting that this surely would be curtains for "our free institutions." Liquor, they insisted, caused the bulk of American crime, pauperism, insanity, and industrial accidents. It was hell on business. And it was poison. Representative Willis Hulings (Pennsylvania) announced the death toll: moderate drinkers lost 14.5 years of life and heavy drinkers 30. The representatives especially roasted the drink industry for targeting young boys. How could America stand by watching the "slaughter of the innocents"? Speakers lambasted the liquor industry's ruthless quest for profits. A few tin ears hailed Russia's ban on vodka—the wets would soon leap all over this uninspiring model for the city on the hill.[68]

The other side fixed on states' rights, centralized power, and personal freedom. Representative James Cantril (Kentucky) quoted every Democratic Party platform back to 1856, each flourishing another variation of the Democrat's signature theme: "Local self government . . . will guard the rights of all citizens more securely than any centralized power." The nays also repeated an argument put most deftly (and famously) by William Howard Taft: Prohibition "would much increase the power of the federal government, already too much swollen." Making Prohibition work would take an "army of officials," who might easily be turned to "sinister use." And how about the unanticipated consequences of state prohibitions? Law-breaking, disrespect for authority, and people shifting dangerously "from drink to dope." The wets emphasized personal liberty, warming up arguments that would get a lot louder as Prohibition bore down. And, of course, the southerners talked about "our Negroes."[69]

At the end of the long, loud day, the Sheppard-Hobson proposal scraped together a slim majority (197–190), far short of the two-thirds necessary for a constitutional amendment. Still, a majority in the House had gone on record supporting national prohibition. The ASL promised to take the fight back to the people. The group went after wets with great gusto (and with their knack for taking credit whenever things broke in their direction). After the 1916 election they claimed to have a sure-to-win majority.[70]

Four months later, a cynical wet maneuver boomeranged right into the prohibitionists' laps. In March 1917, the drys stacked a routine post office bill; they wanted to stop the liquor advertisements flowing into dry states. Southerners dusted off their old shockers about gin labels. Suddenly, Senator James Reed (Missouri), a wet curmudgeon with a flair for irony, tossed a jarring dry rider onto the table. His Reed-Randall proposal would ban all transportation of liquor into dry states. This would be a far stronger prohibition than most states had bargained for. Most dry states prohibited saloons to stop the riffraff from public drinking. But decent folks could still import and drink their own liquor. In fact, before 1915, no state had banned all liquor. Now Reed dared his colleagues to turn every Prohibition state "bone dry"—no legal liquor at all. That, he figured, would shame the fanatical hypocrites. Even the ASL's leaders ducked this bomb (vote your conscience, they told their friends). To Reed's shock, the harsh bill sailed right through Congress. President Wilson did not like it one bit, but with the shadow of the European war drawing near, he had to keep the mail moving. Wilson signed.[71]

Under normal circumstances, Americans might now have found themselves with a model of moral federalism. States which voted prohibition for themselves were backed by national regulations and rhetoric. Assuming that the Supreme Court would go along, the Webb-Kenyon and Reed-Randall bills might have produced a political equilibrium. Except for two final political twists. Temperance reformers wanted to save all Americans. And World War I.

Prohibition

By now, the dry movement had gathered powerful momentum. Generations of American reform had preached temperance as the route to national salvation. Conservatives wanted to stop weak individuals from drinking; liberals despised the arrogant liquor industry. The Progressive movement, with all its dreamy ideals, was cresting. Prohibiting liquor looked like one more Progressive social amelioration, blending easily into the movement's disdain for inferior people and corrupt politics.

Progressives did a lot more than just set the mood. Far from the liquor wars, they won two crucial changes in the way the government did its business. Each would clear the way for Prohibition.

First, they introduced a new tax. For years, the largest source of internal revenue had come from liquor taxes. Alcohol money brought in one-third of all government receipts and almost two-thirds of the cash collected at home (that is, excluding customs duties). The national government was hooked on that liquor money. Then the Progressives won their income tax (the Sixteenth Amendment, ratified in 1913). Now the government had an alternative. At first the tax landed on just a handful of wealthy people. But with the advent of World War I, federal tax revenues grew eightfold. Even though liquor revenues doubled, they now made up just 9 percent of the federal take. The liquor money was finally expendable.

A barefaced economic determinist who thought that money explained everything could offer the following reinterpretation of the drive against liquor. Prohibition became possible only after the income tax went into effect and World War I broke the resistance to collecting it from the masses (5.5 million in 1920). Now that the nation had a new source of revenue it could afford to abstain from drinking. Until the federal government had an alternative to the liquor revenue, however, all the WCTU marches from Portland, Maine, to Washington Court House, Ohio, were not going to make a jot of difference.

A second Progressive reform may also have eased the way. The agents who collected the liquor taxes had enjoyed some of the finest plums of the spoils system (the other major positions were postmasters and customs officials). The federal jobs went to party members who then donated part of their salary and much of their time to winning the next election. By the early twentieth century, however, civil service reform had rolled across the federal bureaucracy. A professional civil service meant that party politicians no longer needed those revenue jobs to use as spoils.[72]

The United States entered the war in April 1917, bringing American moral fervor to a full boil. President Wilson warned the nation about the "sacrifice we shall freely make" with "civilization itself seeming to be in the balance." Wilson imagined a moral crusade. The United States would "show the world a new motive in warfare, a heretofore unheard of motive" pursued by a pure, clean, righteous army. The War Department organized "moral zones" around training camps—no liquor and no prostitutes. The military emergency finally brought down the red-light districts (with no noticeable effect on the rates of venereal disease among the servicemen). And it put the whole debate about alcohol in the context of national sacrifice and special virtue.[73]

During graduation exercises that spring, orators extolled the new American purpose. At Princeton the graduates heard about the "just cause" and "sacred mission." At Harvard they listened to exhortations about this brave new army they would soon be joining. "In the long monotonous drudgery that precedes the storm of battle, in the outburst of exultation or depression that follows it, in the short leave of absence . . . in the allurements of a great city," our boys would—must—"preserve their ideals unsullied." They would remain sober and chaste. And how about the men and women who stayed behind? Could they do anything less? President William Faunce of Brown University put it directly to the class of 1917: "Patriotism spells Prohibition."[74]

The war fervor gave the drink debate an urgent new context. A full-page advertisement in the *New York Times,* courtesy of the irrepressible Dr. J. H. Kellogg, illustrated the new rhetorical turn. "Grain sunk by submarines last year was EIGHT MILLION bushels. Grain used by American brewers last year was SIXTY EIGHT MILLION." And down the page a bit: "The brewers of the country used over 3,000,000 tons of coal . . . save the fuel and help win the war." And talk about selfish: "Packages to the boys 'over there' are prevented from being shipped while the brewers use millions for shipping." Finally, in the center of the page, the now ubiquitous punch line: "We are fighting three enemies—Germany, Austria and Drink."[75]

American brewers were hogging materiel, they were subverting the war effort, they were—German! These selfish "hyphenated Americans," as Wilson put it, were not real Americans at all. Congress uncovered links between the brewers' lobby and the German American alliance and revoked the organization's charter. The states eagerly cracked down on all kinds of Hun influences—music, culture, language, subversive educational ideas. Patriots lined up to blast those treacherous Germans: Pabst, Schlitz, Blatz, and Miller.[76]

War fervor also provoked a backlash against radicals. Socialist Eugene Debs had polled 5 percent in the 1912 election. Strikes had been rising fast; from 1,200 in 1914 to 4,450 by 1917. Now American politics took a sharp right turn. The attorney general deported radicals; employers fought unions; states outlawed red (communist) and black (anarchist) flags. The dangerous classes—immigrants and workers—were thought to be fomenting much of this trouble while idling in the saloons. Kellogg's ad told Americans what many of them already believed: "Almost every disturbance in the ranks of organized labor can be traced back to some connection with the saloon." Prohibition would steady working men and women. Sinclair Lewis's infamous conformist,

George Babbitt, hears exactly that from his pal Vergil Gunch: "You don't want to forget prohibition is a mighty good thing for the working classes. Keeps 'em from wasting their money and lowering their productiveness."

Now all the grand issues of Prohibition were boiled down to the far more manageable matter of wartime controls. The emergency centralized enormous authority in federal hands. Federal officials controlled, planned, and rationed across the economy. The drys seized their chance to reframe the liquor question. Using foodstuff to distill alcohol or brew beer was practically treasonous. The newspapers constantly ran articles about "diverting grain used by brewers and distillers to general food consumption." In August 1917—five months into the U.S. war—Congress passed a measure banning the diversion of foodstuff into distilled alcohol. Beer escaped for a time. But the following December, the president lowered the maximum alcohol content of beer to 2.75 percent (roughly what a light beer is today).[77]

Amid the war frenzy, the long-awaited Prohibition amendment practically slipped through Congress. There were no committee hearings. Debates were perfunctory. Wets submitted their old objections rather than bothering to draft new ones. By all accounts, Congress was happy to finally be done with the issue. On December 22, 1917, the House followed the Senate and voted a constitutional amendment. This one was a lot stricter than the version they had debated three years earlier: "The manufacture, transportation or sale of intoxicating liquors. . . . for beverage purposes is hereby prohibited." Bone dry.

The states ratified with what was then the political equivalent of the speed of light. Nebraska put the amendment over the top on January 16, 1919—it took a bit more than a year (many state legislatures met only every other year). One year later—at midnight on January 16, 1920—the Eighteenth Amendment would go into effect. Every state except Rhode Island and Connecticut would ratify the Prohibition amendment.

But victory came with glimmerings of trouble. Right from the start, people sneered about hypocrisy. "They sent around to all the various Bars in Washington," said Will Rogers, "and collected a quorum and voted everyone dry." Nasty Senator James Reed said the same thing without the smile: "The leprosy of hypocrisy has become epidemic. Half drunken legislators enact dry laws and celebrate in moonshine. . . . Washington has become the universal Mecca for human freaks." More important, fourteen states—including almost the entire northeast—had consistently rejected prohibition laws. Now their legislatures went along with the program. But once the war fever passed, how would drinkers respond to the dry regime? The outcry about cherished American values started up immediately. Samuel Gompers, president of the American Federation of Labor, went around warning everyone that this was the sure path to "radicalism" and "bolshevism." And, in a delicious variation on the theme, 250 New York Italian Americans signed a petition lamenting their lost personal liberty: "If the signers could not be permitted to . . . drink the wines which they have always drunk, they would go back to the land of their nativity which, although a kingdom, gives greater personal freedom to its citizens."[78]

Prohibition's opponents managed to claim democracy as another victim of the movement. The storm hit in Ohio. The state had narrowly approved its own state-level prohibition in 1918; at the same time, however, the voters approved an amendment to the state constitution stipulating that all general assembly votes on federal amendments must go before the voters. A year later, the Ohio legislature ratified the Eighteenth amendment. They certified the results and sent them to Washington. The amendment went over the top and got affixed to the U.S. Constitution. And then, the following November (two months before Prohibition took effect) Ohio voters got their direct vote and rejected Prohibition. That gave the drys new hope. Groups in fourteen states started promising referenda. Around the country, many judges caught the popular vote bug. Even in Nebraska, which had come up with that thirty-sixth vote, a district court held that the legislature's vote didn't count till it went before the voters. The Supreme Court eventually ruled that this was all nonsense and that the legislatures had satisfied the Constitution's requirements. Prohibition was here to stay. (*Hawke v. Smith*, decided unanimously.) But the wets salvaged an effective political spin: the people were being hustled into Prohibition even when they voted against it. Everyone quoted Will Rogers, again: "Ohio was voted wet by the people and dry by their misrepresentatives."[79]

But all those intimations of future trouble cannot obscure the extraordinary reform. Americans had amended their Constitution (for just the ninth time since they approved the Bill of Rights in 1791) to keep one another from drinking. On the surface, it sure looks like the amendment—and the political cause—that does not fit. Other amendments all secured rights or reorganized the government. But, in many ways, Prohibition fit right in. In fact, it practically serves as an illustrated guide to American government.

The prohibitions bubbled up from the states. When the federal government got into the act, it began with interstate commerce. We have seen that one before. Congress also got at obscenity, impure drugs, and stolen women with the same constitutional wedge.

The next major federal step, the Reed-Randall postal bill, at first seems like Washington shenanigans at their most bizarre. But take another look at the institution in the middle: the Post Office. We've seen postal skirmishes during every moral crusade back to 1828: The Sabbitarians rose up to protest mail delivery on Sundays. The abolitionists used the mails to drive southern leaders wild. And Anthony Comstock led the great Victorian charge against obscenity in his official capacity as a postal inspector. We have seen hot moral challenges pass from one region to another along what amounted to the nineteenth-century American regime's nervous system.

The private groups buzzing around liquor reform also reflected the changing contours of the government. In the last third of the nineteenth century, the WCTU led the campaign. The women took sides on a range of political causes, but each local union determined which issues it pursued. The WCTU was practically designed to work, hand in white glove, with local political powers. It neatly fit the nineteenth-century establishment, dominated by local party leaders. The Progressives came on, at the turn of the century, promising clean and efficient governance. By the Taft administration, they had managed to impose real limits on the power of the political parties. The WCTU faded as the Anti-Saloon League arose. The new organization was nonpartisan and single-minded. It was based in Washington, D.C., where it deployed its capital lobbyists and lawyers. It fit the emerging political establishment. The people got their first taste of modern interest-group politics; judging by the commentary, they didn't like it any better in 1912 than they do today.[80]

There was another political classic at work in the Prohibition story. Nothing empowers central government power quite like wars—wars build states. After the endless brawls over drinking, wartime mobilization—and war fervor—finally lifted national Prohibitions into place. But there is a twist to this familiar story: world war brought all sorts of administrative innovations to American government. The one wartime innovation to win a place in the Constitution—and one of the few to last through the 1920s—was the war on liquor.

On one level, the Italian wine drinkers seemed exactly right: Americans do not usually empower government in such dramatic ways. Propelled by a war to make the world safe for democracy, the new amendment shut down an enormous, perfectly legal business without any compensation to the capitalists who might be ruined. In all the details about the WCTU and the ASL and the winning majority (in Ohio or in Congress), it is easy to forget how unusual—how illiberal and un-individualistic—the whole thing looks. After all, liberal government is built on rights protected from the passions of the majority. And, in the United States, no right has been protected with more gusto than the right to own property.

The Prohibition story illustrates, once again, the limits of private rights, of liberalism itself. The boundary lies at the moral sphere. Convince the majority that they faced wicked people and the miscreants' rights evaporate. The prohibitionists, like the abolitionists they emulated, pictured an evil empire. The crucial step in alcohol's demise lay in the drys' ability to sell the image of liquor as poison. The same indictment now animates the great charge against tobacco.

Moralizing politics rolls right over the liberal limits—even the staunch American faith in property rights falls aside. But what counts as evil? The answer is contested, changing, constantly up for political grabs. Moral politics in the United States is hotheaded and unstable. In 1825 there were only the vaguest intimations of abolition, largely in the black community; by 1865, slavery was gone. In 1905, you could drink in most places (outside the rural South, at least); fifteen years later, all but two state legislatures agreed that these poisons were not worthy of property rights. Fifteen years after that, the crowds lined up to cheer the return of intoxicating brews.

The politics of good and bad wash across America in powerful waves. Moral reforms spring in part from a deep religious yearning. In part, from the robust image of a nation standing as an exemplar for the rest of the world. And in part from a steady procession of different tribes stirring anxiety about decline. That combination drives American politics in every generation. Prohibition offers us, not a bizarre exception but yet another example of morality politics as a mainspring of the American regime.

Chapter 11
Prohibition and the
Rise of Big Government

MY great-grandfather, Vincenzo Morone, made two barrels of wine every year during Prohibition. He cooked up a pretty good zinfandel for everyday use and a sweet muscatel for company—apparently the guests got pretty dreadful stuff. Vincenzo always insisted that his wine was perfectly legal. Prohibition, he used to say, never forbade homemade wine you drank with friends. Was he right? Or were the Morones another Prohibition-era family on the wrong side of the law? These kinds of details got hammered out in the Volstead Act, the law that implemented the Eighteenth Amendment.

The Volstead Act

Intoxicating

The Volstead Act pressed righteousness against political compromise. Wayne Wheeler, the hard-line leader of the ASL, claimed credit for drafting the bill. Congressman Andrew Volstead, a Republican from Minnesota, insisted he was the real author. They both deserve credit. Plenty of hands marked the measure as it whipped through Congress.

The very first question stirred up trouble. The Eighteenth Amendment prohibited "intoxicating beverages." But just what was intoxicating? The amendment did not say. Many Americans assumed that they would get the wartime status quo; light beer and wines of up to 2.75 percent alcohol. Governor Al Smith assured New Yorkers that light beverages were not "intoxicating." Prohibition aimed to control the hard, degrading stuff that temperance forces had rallied against so long and hard—who needed home protection from light beer?

Congress surprised the moderates. The Volstead Act pegged intoxicating at anything more than 0.5 percent alcohol. The really serious states already had fixed their prohibition laws at this bone-dry level. The victorious drys did not intend to suffer the irony of a prohibition amendment that actually loosened liquor controls in their own strongholds. The hard-line decision offended moderates. Newspapers filled up with reports of campus rallies, sober declarations, and scientific affidavits all attesting that light beverages would not intoxicate. With great fanfare, students at the University of Pennsylvania conducted a public demonstration to show the world that they could not possibly get drunk by guzzling beer with an alcohol content as high as 3.5 percent. Wet labor leaders happily posed as moderates and organized a large Washington demonstration for light wine and beer. Meanwhile, the Northern Baptist Convention appealed to Congress to ignore the fuss and stand firm. Congress did. But by choosing to defend such a hard line, the drys had committed a strategic blunder in the very first sentence of their prohibition law.[1]

There was another jolt lurking in the details. The constitutional amendment had outlawed "manufacture, sale or transportation." Now Congress made it illegal to even "possess." But as the bill worked its way through the process, Congress added two wet twists—both over the furious objections of the ASL. First, Congress allowed Americans to "possess liquors in one's private dwelling," as long as it was really your home (no funny business with warehouses) and the liquor was really for you and your guests. Just to make sure that the home sippers were safe, Congress tacked on another protection: "No search warrant shall issue to search any private dwelling . . . unless it is being used for the unlawful sale of intoxicating liquor." In short, possessing alcohol was illegal. Except at home. And the law promised never to break in on you there.[2]

In one final bit of constituent service, the California wine industry won a clause permitting home manufacture of "non-intoxicating cider and fruit juices exclusively for use at home." The wine makers soon began shipping barrels of grape juice with large and prominent labels along the following lines: "WARNING—Department of Agriculture tests have determined that the contents will turn into wine of 12 percent alcohol if permitted to sit for sixty days." That left home beer makers outside the law while home vintners got a broad legislative wink. They could legally buy wine-making kits. When the grape juice fermented they could legally possess at home. And the law could not bang down the door if they served it to friends and family.[3]

So my great-grandfather was perfectly safe. But was he also perfectly legal? The *New York Daily News* published a list of legal do's and don'ts just before Prohibition took effect: "You cannot manufacture anything above 0.5 percent (liquor strength) in your home." Six months into Prohibition, the enforcers explicitly lifted the ban on home brew. The ambiguous back and forth—involving the courts, Congress, and the administrators—lasted for Prohibition's entire life. As late as 1930 the Supreme Court ruled that the makers of home wine paraphernalia—corks, bottles, and barrels—were subject to punishment. The Prohibition Bureau promptly pronounced them "immune from prosecution." Representative Fiorello La Guardia (New York) cut through the thicket by mailing his constituents the official federal rules for making "non-intoxicating wine"—make whatever you want, winks the congressman, and just call it "non-intoxicating." In short, the Volstead Act itself proscribed my great-grandfather's behavior—and prohibited anyone from prosecuting him for it. The courts were even more ambiguous, while the Prohibition Bureau and some (but by no means all) politicians invited him to go right ahead and make his wine.[4]

Vincenzo was not the only one in the Volstead gray area. Supreme Court Justice Oliver Wendell Holmes was offered a glass of champagne at his eightieth birthday party. What was a justice to do? "The 18th Amendment forbids the manufacture, transportation, and importation," reflected Justice Holmes. "It does not forbid possession or use. If I send it back I shall be guilty of transportation. On the whole, I think, I shall apply the maxi de minimis, and drink it."[5]

As a theoretical matter, the ambiguity about home use reflects a deeper tension. Moral politics cross the line between public policy and private sphere—the government aims to foster personal virtue. But that liberal line (and the majority's liberal instincts) hardly vanished. Even during this ambitious effort to reshape people's everyday habits, Congress balked at actually breaking into private homes. And amid all the moral visions and liberal limits, the California delegation managed some trusty constituent service.

As a practical matter, the ambiguities reflected a fundamental problem at the heart of this amendment. Prohibitions become especially difficult to enforce (even to define) when they proscribe behavior many people consider normal. Moral commandments work best when they are directed at unacceptable behavior, or at a clear and dangerous presence—an enemy. The image of unreliable German workers in a city saloon had worked nicely. But in the real world, drinking took many forms. These shades of gray would return to haunt the drug wars a half-century later.

Enforcement: Who Governs?

Constitutional amendments usually place enforcement with Congress. Prohibition was different. The amendment read, "Congress and the several states shall have concurrent power to enforce this article." That idea shaped (or, more accurately, sealed) the Eighteenth Amendment's fate. Why the ambiguous approach?

The states had always led the fight against drink. They were the laboratories of democracy experimenting with ways to restrict liquor. The federal government had simply plugged the gaps—regulating interstate shipments and shutting down the mails. And it had also made forceful symbolic statements about national values: good Americans stayed sober. Still, each modest federal step had come with strong warnings (usually in southern accents) about how police powers belonged to the states.

National Prohibition forced the issues of federalism and enforcement. Social conservatives were looking for more than mere symbols from their government. Through the next decade they would rally around this law, their law. They dreamed of a great American redemption. But who would make it happen? Criminal justice had always been a state and local enterprise. Even after leaping into battle against white slavers, the federal crime-fighting budget was just 3 percent of local police budgets. Few crimes fell under federal jurisdiction, and the national government did not have much enforcement capacity. Moreover, really drying out America would be an enormous job.

That left the state governments and local officials. They had experience in enforcing laws, but the worst offenders, the northeastern states, were ambivalent about prosecuting Prohibition. In 1921, Wayne Wheeler reviewed the problem: "Ten states have shown their indifference or hostility to prohibition by failing to enact state law enforcement codes." California and Massachusetts had actually voted the codes down. The rest passed laws that were not up to ASL standards. New York and New Jersey brazenly enacted laws permitting the light wine and beer that Volstead forbade. When the Supreme Court struck down these efforts, New York simply repealed its enforcement statute altogether (in 1923)—half nullifying Prohibition. By 1926, the state legislatures across the country were spending eight times more on their fish and game departments than on enforcing Prohibition.[6]

Frustrated conservatives bitterly complained about the lack of zeal. Many called for the federal government to simply take over all enforcement. Henry Ford made headlines when he pleaded for putting Volstead enforcement in the hands of the Army and the Navy. The heroine of Upton Sinclair's fervent 1931 Prohibition novel closes the book with a motto she promises to plaster across every church front and newspaper in the nation: "PROHIBITION HAS NOT FAILED! PROHIBITION HAS NOT BEEN TRIED! TRY IT!" President Warren Harding, a man with no detectable sympathy for Prohibition, suggested that the problem lay with the states' own lax attitudes. Treasury Secretary Andrew Mellon later made the critique more pointed; the law, he said, had vested enforcement exactly where it ought to be: in the local public opinion.[7]

Federalism had made Prohibition possible. Liquor control spread across states that would have never accepted a federal law, then it leaped into the Con-

11.1. "Going into captivity." Alcohol enslaves people in every class. The liquor pluto-crats—distillers, brewers—arrogantly look on as the saloons drive their helpless victims to perdition.

stitution amid war fever. But the legislative path to victory undermined the program's prospects. The southern and western states guarded their own police power against federal incursions while they pushed Prohibition on a reluctant northeast, which cheerfully used the limits on federal power to hobble the pro-hibitionist effort just where it was needed most.

Still, the lack of effort is often exaggerated. Despite the folklore, drinking

From New York *Evening World*

11.2. "Still packing them in." Now it's the dry law sending the people into captivity. The evil liquor interests have been replaced by the faceless and anonymous state.

plummeted. In New York, federal agents made 11,000 arrests in 1922 alone. The federal government mobilized with real results and important consequences. The federal courts were soon choked with liquor cases. The federal prisons overflowed—Prohibition stimulated a minor building boom in penitentiaries. The government faced a monumental task: shutting down an industry—suddenly made criminal—that had been pouring the annual equivalent of two gallons of pure alcohol into every adult in America. The effort would alter the shape and scope of American government.[8]

Jobs!

The Volstead Act had one final wild card to deal. The law placed enforcement in the Treasury Department rather than in the more obvious place, the

Department of Justice. That's because the revenue agents knew the industry inside out. The amount of pure alcohol had determined the size of the liquor tax. (The definition of bone dry as 0.5 percent alcohol content came from the minimum taxable level.) Government agents measured alcohol levels at every stage of the process. Treasury Department officials worked closely with the industry and developed shared interests—more alcohol meant more revenue. Tax collectors had tormented meddling state-level prohibitionists for years. Even in dry states the agents continued to collect liquor taxes (after all, federal tax laws were not affected by state prohibitions). The revenue agents stoutly refused to share any information with the state officials who were trying to shut the industry down. The agents would not release tax receipts or testify in court. When they were finally forced to spill their records they produced documents scribbled in impenetrable codes. And when they confiscated liquor from tax delinquents they insolently auctioned it off from the post office steps—right there on dry territory in broad daylight.[9]

Now Congress handed enforcement over to these experts. The ASL pushed for an exception to the civil service rules so that it could exercise direct control over the Prohibition agents. The dry reformers planned to place their own reliable people in the service; and, after watching federal agents subvert state prohibitions for decades, the reformers wanted the power to sack anyone who got cozy with bootleggers. The ASL quickly got a lesson in political science.

First came the howls from their good-government allies. Civil service reformers had fought long and hard for clean government. Suddenly the "Old Spoils Evil," as the *New York Times* called it, was rearing its slimy head. Even the best intentions did not justify weakening the civil service. Of course, the wets gleefully professed to be shocked—shocked!—by this federal backsliding into the bad old days of bosses and corruption.[10]

Worse, after taking the blame for flouting the civil service rules, the ASL never managed to get control of the agents. Even recent Prohibition histories forget to wonder what Congress might have been thinking. Did the ASL really bully the members into acquiescing? Not likely. It had been roughly twenty years since reformers had fully wrestled the federal bureaucracy into a civil service. Suddenly, Prohibition offered a fat opportunity for booty. Political leaders eyed a fresh and potentially large stock of jobs. Even savvy operators like Wayne Wheeler and the ASL were no match for the true professionals: the politicians and the jobbers. To Wheeler's horror, Prohibition enforcement soon crawled with political appointees. Here's an alternate theory: the politicos grabbed for the plums and left the ASL holding the blame.

Of course, political jobs always come with their own dark lining for the politician who controls them: demand always outruns supply. Thomas Jefferson made the statesman's classic lament. Every appointment, he said, gives me one ingrate and a hundred enemies. Now, Republicans snarled about getting cut out of their share. President Coolidge, for example, got an earful from national leaders who knew there just must be more posts for them to dish out. Why, they fumed, some of the agents were Democrats! Coolidge wised up and eventually folded all those jobs into the civil service.[11]

A decade later, the Democrats would bring the New Deal to Washington. All those alphabet agencies meant another fresh supply of federal jobs. The first appointees included those celebrated eggheads from the universities; but before long, the jobs were going to solid party men—courtesy of a consummate Democratic Party politician, Postmaster James Farley. Both Prohibition in the 1920s and the New Deal in the 1930s dreamed big. In each case the state set out to raise the nation to a higher standard. The two government growth spurts reflected entirely different political and moral visions. But, in both cases, the high-flying dreams generated plenty of good old-fashioned political pork.

Prohibition in Action

The day before Prohibition took effect, a thousand clergymen begged New Yorkers to protect the law. Delegates from fifty nations gathered in the United States to watch and learn. Billy Sunday, a celebrated evangelical preacher, pumped up ten thousand faithful and a national radio audience with one last glimpse of the looming dry millennium: "The reign of tears is over. The slums will soon be a memory. We will turn our prisons into factories and our jails into storehouses and corncribs. Men will walk upright now; women will smile and the children will laugh. Hell will be forever rent." A political advisor would have warned him that this might be a good time to start lowering expectations. But Sunday, like many of the law's champions, were in the salvation business— politics was just their vehicle for the grand American spiritual revival.[12]

Many listened to the Billy Sundays. The law was the law. "Well, that's settled," wrote journalist Herbert Asbury. "There had been a liquor problem. But a Law has been passed." Liquor became harder to obtain, and drinking decreased nationwide—at least by half, and probably by a good deal more. But a new American millennium? Not even close.[13]

Crime!

Prohibitionists had aimed high—rent hell and renew the nation. In more sober moments they would settle for just uplifting Americans a bit. Instead, Prohibition immediately delivered a crime wave. All the dull old news features—ratification and Volstead, pros and cons—got pushed aside by much hotter stuff: raids, arrests, bogus federal agents, protection rackets, more arrests, bigger raids, and thousands of gallons of liquor poured on the snow. Police rounded up druggists, bartenders, and liquor distributors. Every sleazy operator tried a different angle. False federal agents raided more than a hundred New York City "cafes" and vanished with the liquor—in Prohibition's first week. One liquor dealer set a pack of Great Danes on the agents. Another moved a cot into the warehouse and declared it his private residence. And in one delicious story, furious diners attacked a federal marshal for shutting down their restaurant in the middle of supper, only to discover that he was another sham agent looking for a bribe. The pretender got charged with disorderly conduct.[14]

The police themselves seemed to melt before the nation's eyes. The New York department announced, two weeks into Prohibition, that it did not have the manpower to spare for detective work on Volstead violations. That job would have to go to the feds. Two weeks later officials nabbed the first federal agent for taking bribes. Corruption became a Prohibition staple. The jobbers in the Prohibition Bureau were underfunded, understaffed, and underpaid. Eventually, one out of twelve federal agents would get caught lining his pockets.

Enforcement was not really the right word. Two well-organized sides plotted and countered, almost like armies on a battlefield. One critic put it nicely in 1922: "The generals in charge of the campaign decide whether they shall or shall not attack a particular body of the enemy." Their decisions had nothing to do with the usual principles of law enforcement; they did not simply punish the lawbreakers. Instead, like generals, they made "calculations about the chances of victory" with each fresh assault or strategic retreat.[15]

The crime story ran throughout Prohibition. In 1930, for example, the *New York Times* ran more than four hundred crime reports—arrests, indictments, conspiracies, shootings, and deaths. Over time, attention became fixed on the killings. In 1920, one federal agent and one civilian were shot dead. But the toll rose rapidly after that, and conflicting tallies of the carnage trickled in from all directions: 23 Prohibition agents indicted for killing civilians (*Chicago Tribune*, 1928); 61 agents dead, 151 civilians killed by the agents (*New York Times*, 1930); 263 lawmen dead (La Guardia, 1929); a total of 1,360 people killed (*Washington Herald*, 1929).[16]

Different interests squabbled about everything: the "true" toll, whether the numbers should be printed in the *Congressional Record*, what to do next, and how the government ought to respond to what a later generation would call police brutality. Moderates screamed about the Coast Guard's "shoot to kill orders"; the authorities responded that those were mere shots across the bow. As complaints about violence got louder, Prohibition's champions began to taunt sissies and cheer the tough line. When a Washington police officer shot and killed the driver of a "liquor laden auto," the House of Representatives burst into applause. Moderates recoiled. The drys just rubbed it in by announcing that the word "applause" would remain in the *Congressional Record*. Two weeks later the two sides were tangling again, this time over a Virginia college student who was shot and killed by dry agents.[17]

The overall homicide rate had soared long before Prohibition—it rose more than fourfold between 1900 and 1916. (See fig. 15.1.) During Prohibition it spiked up another 30 percent to some of the highest levels in American history. By 1928 almost 8,000 Americans had been murdered; by the end of the noble experiment the toll had reached past 12,000 (or 9.7 murders per 100,000 people). The murder rate would not return to Prohibition-era levels for another half-century. Today it stands roughly a third lower.[18]

The crime numbers sprang to life in that American icon, the Prohibition gangster. George Remus seized on a legal loophole for medicinal whiskey and became the Rockefeller of bootleg liquor. He built an enormous chain of fake drug stores—opening and closing pharmacies just ahead of the law—and funneled liquor through them. At its peak, the business employed 3,000 men and permitted Remus a famously swashbuckling lifestyle. At one house party he gave each woman in attendance (there were about fifty) a new Pontiac.[19]

The murder rate may have been rising at a slower pace in the 1920s, but now shootings could be pinned on colorful characters and spectacular events. Rival gangs fought bloody turf battles. They seemed to finance Chicago—Al Capone once estimated that total liquor payoffs in the city topped $30 million a year. Some eight hundred men were murdered doing business in Chicago. The gangsters refined a "new technique of wholesale murder," wrote Frederick Lewis Allen in 1931, thanks to those fruits of progress—cars and guns. Capone made a special name for himself. He became famous partly for the sheer size of his operation; an often-repeated guess had him grossing $100 million in 1927 alone. And partly it was the brazen violence. The most famous episode took place on Valentine's Day 1929. While seven members of the Bugs Moran gang sat in a North Clark Street garage waiting for a liquor shipment, Capone's men drove up, two of them dressed as cops. They feigned a routine bust, then lined up the Moran boys against a wall and mowed them down with machine guns. One of the victims lived just long enough to wise-mouth the cops one last time—"Nobody shot me," he said. The movies turned the crime into a dark American epic. Stars like James Cagney and Edward G. Robinson specialized in half-romantic gangsters; the St. Valentine's Day massacre became a cinema standard—see the beginning of Billy Wilder's *Some Like It Hot* for a classic example. F. Scott Fitzgerald took the same material and imagined a more brooding, hollow gangster in Jay Gatsby—possibly modeled on George Remus. Devout Americans had imagined a national purification, but the culture delivered violent, dangerous, romanticized criminals.[20]

"The legal revolution occurred," growled Senator James Reed, "but the moral miracle did not come off according to schedule." Prohibition ran up against that old sociology lesson: construct a crime, create a crime wave. The Puritans blundered into this lesson when they condemned the Quakers and threatened harsh punishment if any set foot in Massachusetts; members of the sect responded by running straight to Boston. As Kai Erikson put it, people in every society "choose a deviant style exactly because it offends an important value," because it crosses conventional society. Of course, prohibitionists also lured "deviants" with a more direct inducement—enormous profits.[21]

Through all this trouble, the drys kept their faith. They made excuses: crime waves, said one, always follow wars. They looked on the bright side: "During the first four years [of Prohibition], more than 750,000 individuals who would have been arrested for intoxication under the old order have not been apprehended"—they were now sober and productive. They tried denial: crime was falling. Why, by the end of the first year, the town of Wausaukee, Wisconsin, had sold its empty jail to a fellow who needed a woodshed. And always they tried to rally the old, righteous army: "There is too much awkward . . . silence on the side of decency."[22]

The holy warriors strained to blow life back into the old crusade. Groups still mobilized, for and against; their representatives bickered more than ever. But the politics of Prohibition had changed. Now federal organizations sat at the heart of the debate. Agencies, rules, and procedures set the political pace. The conflicts—even the interest groups—organized themselves around administrative agencies and their judgments.

The Dry State

Crime grabbed the headlines. But a larger story rumbled below the surface. The old states'-righters had warned about the spreading reach of federal authority. Now their fears sprang to life and were codified by the judiciary. "As a direct result of . . . the American government's 'noble experiment,'" wrote legal scholar Forrest Revere Black in 1930, "the relation between the nation and the states is being altered. The old landmarks in the law are crumbling." Prohibition pushed federal power into broad new areas of American life. Enforcement agencies hammered out new procedures, courts reviewed them, and the rulings turned procedures into precedents. Many still stand.[23]

Prohibition swamped the courts. The attorney general was soon pleading for relief from the glut of liquor cases. In response, the federal courts picked up and expanded an old efficiency measure—plea-bargaining. Defendants could negotiate a punishment, plead guilty, and waive their right to a jury trial. The courts and Congress hashed out other innovations in the mechanics of criminal justice. For example, the right to jury trials would apply only when the punishment exceeded six months in jail. The *Yale Law Review* tallied the number of liquor cases that turned on a rule of law. The number mounted from 4 (in 1920) to 220 (by 1926). Prohibition forced Americans to revise a substantial body of criminal justice law.[24]

The liquor wars also forced the government to cope with new crime technologies—like cars and telephones. In one Michigan case, Prohibition agents driving down the road recognized a car coming the other way. The driver was a local bootlegger, obviously running liquor in from Detroit. The agents whipped around, chased down the suspects, and searched the car. Nothing. Then the agents ripped apart the seat cushion and found sixty-eight cases of liquor. They arrested, charged, and convicted the bootleggers. But what about search warrants and probable cause? The Fourth Amendment grants Americans the "right to be secure in persons, houses, papers, and effects against unreasonable searches and seizures." Normally that requires going to court for a search warrant. But how would that work for a fast-moving car? The Michigan case went to the Supreme Court; in *Carroll v. United States* (1925), Chief Justice William Howard Taft ruled that officers may seize a vehicle if they have "reasonable and probable cause for believing that the automobile has contraband liquor therein which is being illegally transported." As the dissenting justices pointed out, the court was expanding the common law of arrest. While the court later backed away somewhat (a seizure did not work in a garage, for example), the precedent was allowed to stand, an important step on the way to contemporary rules on search and seizure.[25]

With cars, trucks, and boats all running liquor into the nation, the court also permitted authorities to seize property that moved the contraband—even if the property belonged to innocent third parties. This Prohibition rule, like the seizure cases, laid legal groundwork for contemporary drug war cases.

Prohibition agents tested another new technology, wiretapping telephones. The most famous case involved Roy Olmstead, once a talented lieutenant on the Seattle police force. Olmstead drew on his law enforcement connections to build an efficient liquor smuggling operation. His organization poured so much whiskey in from Canada that the price in Seattle stabilized at just two dollars a bottle higher than in wet Vancouver. The Prohibition Bureau credited Olmstead with running 1.5 million gallons in 1922 alone. The bureau wiretapped his phone and caught him chatting to the police; in one case, a cop apologized for nabbing one of Olmstead's guys. When they finally charged him,

Olmstead claimed that those wiretaps (he actually had figured it out and had toyed with the agents listening in) violated the Fourth Amendment. Again, Taft ruled for the government. The telephone wires pass outside the home. Wiretapping is not at all the same thing as an agent breaking in and rifling through papers. Wiretaps were neither search nor seizure.[26]

This time, four justices dissented. The Fourth Amendment should be construed, argued Justice Louis Brandeis, as the "right to be left alone—the most comprehensive of rights and the right most valued by civilized men." Brandeis went on to issue his famous warning: "Crime is contagious. If the Government becomes a law breaker, it breeds contempt for the law. . . . It invites anarchy." Oliver Wendell Holmes also dissented, calling the whole thing a "dirty business." The Supreme Court would overturn the Olmstead precedent forty years later (*Katz v. United States,* 1967). On balance, however, the Prohibition regime weathered the 1960s judicial backlash a good deal more successfully than, say, the purity cases—the Supreme Court often qualified the Prohibition cases rather than overturning them.[27]

The dissents went straight to the big question. Brandeis and Holmes were asking about the limits of public incursions into private lives. How far could federal agents go? The majority ruled that the agents might stop your car, listen in on your phone conversations, or seize your boat. And all this during the back-to-normalcy, market-thumping era of Republican Presidents Warren Harding, Calvin Coolidge, and Herbert Hoover. Even the Taft court, famous for striking down government regulations, gave Prohibition and its enforcement agents a great deal of latitude, at least till the late 1920s. Philosophical questions about tradeoffs between personal rights and public safety—about private sphere and public duty—came down to earth with black-and-white judicial rulings about police procedures.

Under cover of moral regulation, the federal authority barged into the everyday lives and habits of American people. Prohibition expanded the public sector: federal agencies developed new skills, the courts explored new doctrines, and the states organized new kinds of enforcement policies. States like New York got all the press for scorning the dry regime. But many places took their Prohibition seriously. By the end of the decade, for example, four-time Volstead offenders in Michigan faced life in jail. The national administration also reorganized and cracked down harder. During the Calvin Coolidge administration federal officials took an extraordinary step—they deputized every state, county, and municipal cop for the purposes of Volstead enforcement. The Herbert Hoover Administration pushed through the Jones Act (in 1929), known as the five and dime law: first time offenders could get up to five years or $10,000. The harsh new steps drew cheers from social and religious conservatives dismayed about the breakdown of authority and order.[28]

Civil liberties groups responded with alarm. As far as they were concerned, Holmes had summed it all up: it was indeed a dirty business. Moral uplift had knocked into personal liberty a bit too hard. Economic conservatives grew increasingly edgy about the rising federal leviathan. If the federal government could get so entangled in American social life, where might it go next? Americans began to agitate against the new statism. The great moral crusade of the Republican 1920s got anti-government conservatives primed to protest even before the Democratic New Deal hit them.

The Fight Over Prohibition

"Repealing the Eighteenth Amendment," wrote the very wet Clarence Darrow in 1926, "is well nigh inconceivable." No constitutional amendment had ever been scrapped, and no one expected Prohibition to be the first. But maybe drinkers could loosen up the Volstead Act—that was just another law. After all, Congress had repealed the statutes implementing the Civil War amendments in 1893.[29]

Prohibition inspired fierce politics throughout the 1920s. Critics thrashed it; supporters hung on. The culture war grew bitter. But with Prohibition up and running, the political terrain had changed. The great expectations had dwindled: there was no more talk about the glorious dry millennium. The apocalypse, if one was coming, would look more like the brooding version of fundamentalism stirring in some Protestant churches. Both wet attack and dry defense drew together strange political coalitions.

The Wet Resistance

One interest evaporated almost immediately. The cruel liquor industry may have enslaved millions, but it did not last long enough to mount a decent counterattack. Instead, the criticism came from conservative business leaders who despised the surge in federal power. The national government, they said, had trampled over the states' role and the people's rights. The Association Against the Prohibition Amendment (AAPA, founded in 1920) opened its campaign by jeering the hubris of a federal regime that dictated people's diets from Louisiana to Alaska (how delicately their "diets" sidestepped the L-word). "If there is one thing in the wide world . . . which naturally belongs to the individual state and not . . . Washington," wrote AAPA member Fabian Franklin, "that thing is the personal conduct and habits of the people of the state." As the uproar continued, the tireless AAPA always seemed to be around to keep the political pot at full boil.[30]

Prohibition's critics cheerfully deplored the eroding respect for law and order. The newspapers reported almost daily sermons about how Prohibition "bred crime and corruption," "brought in an era of lawlessness," incited the "rise of racketeering," and—inevitably—stirred up a "new wave of juvenile delinquency."[31]

Who could respect authority under these conditions? Government hunted down ordinary, decent citizens, wrote Franklin, "by its spies, its arrests, [and] its prosecutions." The campaign trampled old rules and liberties. And for what? Prohibition had forced "men and women to abruptly abandon customs which they thought [neither] immoral or wrong." Eventually the Supreme Court began focusing on civil liberties. In the early 1920s, the court had routinely given Prohibition's prosecutors a green light. By the mid- and late 1920s, the majority grew more cautious, the dissenters more caustic. By 1930, the majority had turned skeptical about the entire enterprise.[32]

Women also turned. For years, gender rights and temperance reform had marched together. "Since our opponents desire the right of [woman] suffrage mainly for the purpose of saddling the yoke of prohibition on our necks," charged a German-language newspaper before either amendment had passed, "we should oppose it with all our might." But women finally broke through and won suffrage, in much the same way as the drys had won Prohibition: through focused, single-issue campaigns that permitted broad alliances, often with strange political partners. The New York suffrage advocates even allied with wet machine politicians (in 1918). Our old friend Charlie Murphy of Tammany Hall got the New York machine casting (or was it stuffing?) ballots for the women's vote.[33]

Of course, many women kept the Prohibition faith. But others made a break. In 1929 the skeptics founded the Women's Organization for National Prohibition Reform (WONPR, another repeal organization with a jawbreaking acronym). WONPR, like its male counterpart (the AAPA), sprang from Republican soil. The women dug up the famous old arguments—home protection, higher morality, the children's fate—and turned them against Volstead. Women from the old Prohibition groups practically gagged: "It is unthinkable that the American woman having achieved her emancipation from this curse will return to the bondage of beer and the humiliation of old Saturday night." WONPR countered with its own variation on the motherhood theme. "Today, in any speakeasy in the United States you can find boys and girls in their teens drinking liquor." Crime, gangsters, speakeasies, contempt for law, and the lure of liquor (mainly to upper-class kids) all added up to WONPR's new twist on that pious classic: "Mothers of this country feel something must be done to protect their children."[34]

The women's group got the usual treatment—bemused contempt. The critics scoffed at the "cocktail sippers," a ladies' auxiliary to the business leaders in the AAPR. These snickers came with class animosity. The Women's Organization for National Prohibition Reform recruited in elite circles—the wealthy women actually posed for *Vogue* in their scarves and pearls ("chic, sincere and temperate"). What could these "Bacchantian maidens" possibly know about alcohol's harms on the working class? Even their fears—the lure of the speakeasy on Junior—spoke in upper-class accents. But the caste conflict did not alter the consequences: gender politics had shaken loose from temperance. Women were divided, just like (almost) everyone else.[35]

The issue of light alcohol gave these critics an easy target: the cranky Puritans who would not abide even harmless light beers. Drys worked hard to celebrate the bone-dry regime. Sociologist E. A. Ross, for example, pictured the modern college campus. Instead of drinking, he enthused, students were now enjoying "'high jinks' unknown to the college of olden times—'rushes' and 'hops,' 'song fests' and 'circuses,' athletic 'meets' and football 'rallies.'" While all that dry "pep" gushed from the professor, the kids were making headlines by calling for light alcohol, demonstrating that they could not get drunk on 3.5 percent beer, running afoul of the law, or modeling their flasks in the magazines. As the decade wore on, children of privilege developed a light, ironic, coed cocktail culture. The college boy in the speakeasy replaced the worker in his saloon. In some circles, drinking became downright fashionable.[36]

Opponents to Prohibition gathered allies, organized, rallied, and delivered marvelous sermons. But so what? Few could see any impact on the dry regime. Even lightening up on the Volstead rules, reported Clarence Darrow, would take a revolution. Or the political equivalent of a giant meteor. Till something came along and changed the political scene, the wets would have to draw their satisfaction from watching the discomfort on the other side.

The Drys Hang On

The Anti-Saloon League lost its way after winning. Part of the problem came from simple political gravity: all causes lose force and shed members after they win their prize. The counter-revolutionaries are the ones who get angry and pay their dues. But the ASL slipped more than most.

The organization—and, in many ways, the whole dry cause—offered critics almost irresistible targets. Take the problem of industrial alcohol. Even a bone-dry nation needs industrial alcohol. The challenge is keeping drinkers away from the stuff. The Volstead Act required manufacturers to render their product unfit to drink. But how thoroughly should they do the job? In 1921, Wayne Wheeler let them have it for pussyfooting around: the process rendering industrial alcohol "unfit for beverage use" simply leaves the "liquid a little less palatable, but does not prevent it from being used as . . . liquor." It may taste awful to normal folks, continued Wheeler, but the "drinker has a different standard." The solution? Poison. Under ASL pressure and government supervision, the industry began dropping toxic chemicals into its brew.[37]

The outrage reverberated across the debate. Senator James Reed's condemnation is a good example:

> Now comes the most inhuman product of Prohibition: the Poison Squad. . . . The saloonkeeper was denounced for selling rotgut, but not even [Wayne] Wheeler ever accused him of deliberately and maliciously putting into his whiskey barrels such death dealing toxins as strychnine, wood alcohol, formaldehyde . . . or mercury. A single dose of Dr. Wheeler's chemical compound has produced blindness and death in fifteen minutes. . . . When an upright citizen gets a dose . . . and is sent to the eternal bar of Judgment . . . the Anti-Saloon League . . . chuckle[s] and declare[s]: "It served him right, he broke our law."[38]

Newspapers tallied the death toll after every holiday weekend. The headlines after Christmas in 1926, for example, reported twenty-three New Yorkers dead and eighty-nine hospitalized from poisoned drink. The medical examiner called the government "morally responsible." A *New York Times* editorial scorched "The State as Poisoner." Senator Edward I. Edwards (D-New Jersey) later chimed in with a denunciation of the "legalized murder." Wheeler piously corrected the senator's error. Drinking denatured alcohol was suicide, not murder, he said. In fact, Wheeler softened this nasty rejoinder and even seemed to call for less drastic ways to denature alcohol. But that was too subtle to fit into the headlines, which left Wheeler bragging like a ghoul about the latest Prohibition "suicides."[39]

The image of the fanatic who would rather poison a fellow than let him drink in peace outlived Prohibition. Richard Hofstadter pungently summed up the standard view in 1955, echoing James Reed's salvo: "Before prohibition became law, the prohibitionists decried alcohol as a form of deadly poison. After prohibition became law, they approved the legal poisoning of industrial alcohol, knowing full well that men would die from drinking it."[40]

Some suggested a different approach. "Instead of crude and wholesale compulsion," asked Fabian Franklin, why not try "regulation," "restriction," and "persuasion?" Even some members of the ASL favored more education and less force. The moderates, led by Ernest Cherrington, had struggled with Wheeler's faction over taking a less confrontational tack. Sympathetic observers to this day wonder how the story of the Eighteenth Amendment might have been different if the more accommodating Cherrington had won the internal contest at the ASL.

But that is precisely the trouble with prohibitions. Gentler methods—education, exhortation, treatments—tend to get trampled in the rush to enforce.

The imperatives of crime fighting elevate the hard-liners in both the interest groups and the government . The political program reshapes public and private forces. We've seen the pattern many times: the most passionate find their place on the front lines while the moderates go back to their lives. After the white slave scare had passed, for example, most people stopped paying attention; but conservative religious groups stuck around, prodding a reluctant Wilson administration into escalating the battle against lust. Forty years before that, we saw Anthony Comstock expand the popular assault on obscenity into a more dubious battle against free thinkers. When prohibitions are approved, the hard-liners—in public and private sectors—generally leap in and take command.

Fundamentalists

Far from all these Washington maneuvers, Protestants fervently supported a dry America. Keeping John Barleycorn in his grave, wrote one religious historian, "became the crusade and the panacea for a whole generation of Protestants." Later, trying to remember just what had hit them in the early 1920s, progressives would lump Prohibition with the attack on Darwin—and dismiss both as spasms of rural religious fanaticism.[41]

In the 1910s, a conservative religious revival had swept the nation. Preachers attacked the nation's slack morals and "creampuff" religions. They poured contempt over the "godless social service nonsense" like the social Gospel movement. "It is a Christian act to give a down and outer a bath, a bed, and a job," conceded Billy Sunday, "but the road into the kingdom of God is not by the bathtub, the university, social service or gymnasium." Instead, the path to heaven ran through a literal reading of the Bible. Modern efforts to jibe the Bible with science infuriated the revival preachers: "When the word of God says one thing and scholarship says another," preached Sunday, "scholarship can go to hell."[42]

Between 1910 and 1915, conservatives published twelve pamphlets that summed up the Christian basics, *The Fundamentals: A Testimony to the Truth*. The message spread rapidly (more than 3 million copies were mailed to Protestant leaders), and a loose alliance of orthodox traditions found a common name—fundamentalists. The Fundamentals included five non-negotiable principles: the deity of Jesus, His virgin birth, His Resurrection, Christ's Second Coming, and the literal truth of the Bible—the infallible word of God, said Sunday, from cover to cover. The movement organized as the World's Christian Fundamentals Association in 1919.

The fundamentalists introduced two particularly controversial items. For one thing, their emphasis on the Second Coming rekindled millennial fevers. One fundamentalist tradition in particular, Dispensational Premillennialists, warned of the impending apocalypse. In contrast to the optimistic nineteenth-century postmillennialists, these were Premillennialists: there would be no thousand years of peace and justice till after Jesus Christ returned. Believers worked out the Return in excruciating detail. First, a long series of increasingly horrible epochs (or "dispensations"); finally, near the end time, an antichrist would rise amid chaos, blood, and tyranny. An angry Jesus would return, call His faithful (who would rise bodily into the sky to meet Him), and unleash the final blood-soaked conflict before ushering in His millennium of peace and justice. As the time draws near, people are helpless to do anything against the gathering storm. Except save themselves.

Science offered one of the signs of the end times. Darwinian evolution denied the very first passage of the scriptures. World war, communists, socialists, labor unrest, godlessness—how could anyone deny that the end was near? From the mainstream Protestant seminaries, the Dispensational Premillennialists looked marginal, even extreme; but they found enthusiastic support at the religious grass roots.

A second, fundamentalist issue became a great emblem of the American culture war. The World's Christian Fundamentals Association helped drag Charles Darwin out of the classroom in five states; another fifteen put anti-evolution bills before the legislature. Then the faithful sat and watched while the moderns descended on Dayton, Tennessee, and hooted through the trial of John Scopes, a young schoolteacher charged with teaching evolution in violation of Tennessee law. The Scopes trial became known as the case that launched 2 million words—almost everyone of them sarcastic. H. L. Mencken spat out some of the most colorful acid in the history of American journalism. "Men quite without taste or imagination, whoopers and shouters, low vulgarians and cads" had set out to lynch Scopes. But they couldn't pull it off, taunted Mencken. "Protestantism in this Great Christian realm is down with a wasting disease. One half of it is moving in the direction of the Harlot of the seven hills; the other is sliding down into voodooism." Mencken rubbed it in with glee: "Every day a new Catholic Church goes up; every day another Presbyterian church is turned into a garage."[43]

Scopes got convicted, of course. Clarence Darrow wrapped up the defense with a tough cross-examination of the prosecutor and fundamentalist champion, Williams Jennings Bryan. To accommodate the mob, the famous exchange took place on the courthouse lawn. Darrow pushed Bryan to concede that maybe some interpretation might be necessary after all. Then, convinced he had won the intellectual argument, Darrow conceded the case—Scopes had never denied his misdemeanor. The point was to get the Supreme Court to overrule the Tennessee law. On appeal, however, those Tennessee whoopers outsmarted Clarence Darrow. The state court reversed the decision on a technicality. No slap on the wrist for John Scopes, no Supreme Court appeal for

Clarence Darrow and the liberals. Despite the Dayton legends, the anti-evolution law survived the slick city sarcastics. Far from the boob-bashing media, Darwin slipped out of the Tennessee textbooks. John Scopes went happily off to graduate school (in geology) at the University of Chicago.

Premillennialism and biblical inerrancy provoked scornful attacks. But at least on one issue, Prohibition, the fundamentalist stood in the political mainstream. Keeping the nation dry lay at the political heart of their revival. These men and women struggled vainly (or so it seemed at the time) on the fringes of onrushing modernity. Prohibition offered them their one link to national authority, the one public commitment to resisting moral decay. They fought long and hard to maintain it.

For the next fifty years, conventional wisdom pegged the Scopes trial and Prohibition as the final twitches of the American fundamentalists. They denied science and were humiliated before the nation at the Scopes trial; they hung on grimly to a Prohibition program that would not last long outside of the culturally backward South. As modernity brushed them aside, the fundamentalists turned sour—"hostile, coercive and nativist," wrote sociologist Joseph Gusfield in 1963—before getting completely buried by the New Deal. "Today, the evolution controversy seems as remote as the Homeric era," wrote Richard Hofstadter in 1955.

Prohibition's fall would signal the end of a long neo-Puritan swing. Beginning in the 1930s—and peaking in the despised 1960s—the Supreme Court would strike down everything the revivalists had built up, including, finally, the creationist laws like the one that John Scopes had violated (in *Epperson v. Arkansas,* dubbed Scopes II by the media, 1968). Still, as the First Great Awakeners informed those dull Boston Cartesians in 1740, polite (or humanistic) faith never entirely captures the American religious spirit. The fundamentalists would be back.

All of a sudden, it seemed, an American president was calling the evangelical stalwarts back into the political limelight. You can't endorse me, twinkled Ronald Reagan in 1981, but I can endorse you. After fifty years in the wilderness, the fundamentalists would flock back onto the national stage. And they would bring new prohibitions, old gender roles, biblical creationism, and a populist premillennialism right back with them.

The Ku Klux Klan

Further to the political right, the Ku Klux Klan mushroomed back to life. W. D. Griffith's epic film *Birth of a Nation* had helped get those "Nordic" juices flowing again. This time, the Klan specialized in lost moral values. Members prowled lover's lanes, denounced kids who had slipped out from under parental authority, and warned about modernity's "harvest of revolution and orgy of anarchism." This Klan—like the last one—got really agitated about sex. The Klansman's manual offered its creepy instructions for the men in shining armor: "The Knight . . . demands reverence for American womanhood and insists that her person shall be respected as sacred, that her chastity be kept inviolate, and that she not be deprived of her right to the glory of an unstained body." A peculiar mix—traditional values, intimations of pornography, and a lynch mob waiting to ignite.[44]

In the 1920s, the Klan broadened its appeal. Women joined an affiliated group. Northern states signed up—Indiana elected at least five Klan-friendly congressmen. At its height, the new Klan had about 4 million members. This time the Klan took a more expansive view. Its anti-Catholic, anti-Semitic, anti-urban side rivaled its raw racism. One thing that tied it all together was the war on liquor. "The single most important bond between Klansmen throughout the nation," writes historian Leonard Moore, was "support for Prohibition."

Drinkers flouted authority, morality, and the law. And who lay behind the crimes? Catholics, aliens, blacks. The harsh side of Prohibition may have appalled the *New York Times,* but the men and women of the Klan stood up and cheered. They watched Prohibition "foundering for lack of adequate public sentiment" and responded with one of the nation's most sustained, and vicious, anti-vice campaigns.[45]

The Klan peaked in 1924–1925 and declined rapidly after that (partially because leaders got embroiled in alcohol and sex scandals). This Klan, say some observers, should be remembered as more than just another hate group. Look at its causes: drink, loose sexual morals, changing gender roles, the slick cities, and other vexing modern notions. But, as Nancy MacLean reminds us, the Klan's moral populism meshed inextricably with its racial bigotry, Jew baiting, and misogyny. The new Klan first announced its presence by lynching an innocent Jewish man, Leo Frank. They accused him, with no real evidence, of raping and murdering a fourteen-year-old girl who worked in his store. Alongside that moral populism gleamed racial malice.[46]

How can anyone read hate and lynching as just another kind of moral urge? The same answer comes back in every chapter of American history. Moral campaigns have deep roots and special standing. When these men and women wrapped themselves in the mantle of morality and stood up for family values like prohibition, it became easy to forget that they did a lot of their business in a lynch mob.

The End of the Aliens

Prohibition tantalized some Americans with the illusion of mastery over the modern chaos. But there was also a more direct solution—do something about all those foreigners. We've watched the long lament develop over the decades. The United States was slipping into the hands of inferior, fast-breeding, left-leaning, ugly-looking strangers. Congress eventually stirred. It had been tacking on immigration limits for a generation—no anarchists (in 1903), no radicals (1917), rough quotas (1921). Now, in 1924, it firmly shut the national door. As the National Origins Bill went through, Albert Johnson exulted from the Senate floor, "The United States is our land." President Calvin Coolidge read from exactly the same script when he signed the bill. "America must be kept American."[47]

The new rules let just 150,000 newcomers trickle in each year. Complicated quotas determined where they would come from based on who had been around in 1890—before that latest, lowest wave of immigrants. Historian Mae M. Ngai calls the quotas a "hierarchy of racial desirability." They tilted toward "Nordics," biased against southern and eastern Europeans, and locked Asians out almost entirely. The secretary of labor, James Davis, offered a nice, clear explanation. "We want the beaver type of man. We want to keep out the rat type." The only way to do that was this careful, unblinking, "selective" immigration.[48]

The law worked. Fewer strangers arrived. More than 10 million newcomers (between 1905 and 1914) had already dropped to 4 million (1915–1924); in the next decade fewer than 2 million landed (1925–1934). The law's impact looks even more dramatic when one turns to, say, the Polish immigration: from 95,000 in 1921 to fewer than 3,600 a decade later—and a further fall after that. The long, loud cry about bad blood began to fade—and so, of course, did those huddled masses yearning to breathe free.

As the danger receded, so did the quest for control. The diehards held on. Plenty of nasty talk continued to rattle around. But the anti-immigrant feeling drifted to the political margins. One of the quiet, gut-deep imperatives pushing America to sobriety began to fade. The receding fear sets the deep background for the next mystery: Why did Prohibition collapse so fast? Sherlock Holmes solved one mystery by noticing that the hounds had not barked. We can use the same clue; the fear of a fast-breeding, uncontrollable, immigrant "them" was one great American hound that had begun to fall silent during the final rounds of the Prohibition debate.

The immigration question would largely disappear till 1965, when, in an almost offhand moment during Lyndon Johnson's Great Society, Congress repealed the quotas. American immigration resumed. Suddenly, you could hear foreign languages in the schools and the cities. Is it just coincidence? Or would the new faces—alongside a civil rights revolution—help resurrect another generation of neo-Puritans and their prohibitions?

Repeal!

The long argument about drinking did not seem to make much of a dent. Repeal? How would you get thirty-five states to go along? Through most of the 1920s, both national parties ducked the issue with pious noise about respect for law. Then, in the 1928 election, the parties each took a strong stand on opposite sides of the issue. The drys won by a landslide—and doomed their program.

The Democrats nominated Al Smith for president. Smith was a popular New York governor who represented everything the heartland drys despised: he was an unvarnished, Roman Catholic, Tammany Hall, immigrant-family, New York City politician. Like so many of his kind, he was an out-and-out wet and did not deny it. In his final campaign stop, in Milwaukee, Smith told the crowd that the Volstead Act should be amended to let the states decide their own drinking rules. "The cure for the ills of democracy is more democracy. Hand this back to the people. Let them decide it." *Life* magazine ran a cover of Al Smith framed by a sardonic variation of a popular New York song, "East Side, Wet Side." Most of the gibes were not so gentle.[49]

On the Republican side, the majority crushed an AAPA effort to concede problems with Prohibition. Instead, candidate Herbert Hoover nailed the dry law to the Republican mast. In his acceptance speech, Hoover made his famous statement: "Our country has deliberately undertaken a great social and economic experiment, noble in motive and far reaching in purpose." Sure, conceded Hoover, there had been "grave abuses." "But it must be worked out constructively." From that day on, Prohibition would be the "noble experiment" and Hoover its champion.[50]

Of course, Prohibition did not decide the election. The Republicans had held power in peace and in boom times. But the Democrats paid the price for running Al Smith. Methodist Bishop James Cannon, running for Top Dry after Wayne Wheeler's death in September 1927, toured the South scorching Smith as a "moral menace" and a tool of Pope Pius XI. (Cannon ended up hurting the dry cause by getting entangled in a series of nasty sex and money scandals shortly after the election.) Speakers lined up to warn the nation about the looming terror of rum and Romanism. Which was worse? "I'd rather see a saloon on every corner," said Bob Jones (an ardent dry evangelical), "than a Catholic in the White House." On the other hand, historian Robert Moats Miller reminds us that "to millions of Protestants, Prohibition was an issue of transcendent importance." Most, he argues, were dry believers rather than religious bigots.[51]

Hoover trounced Smith. Even the solid South abandoned the Democrats. Smith managed just eighty-seven electoral votes, the worst drubbing since

Abraham Lincoln's reelection sixty-four years earlier. And loyal prohibitionists also grabbed the biggest congressional majority they had ever won. The results looked like a crushing defeat for Prohibition's opponents, who were reduced to denying that the election had wrecked all hope of reforming the Volstead Act.[52]

After the election, each party stuck to its position. The new Democratic Party chairman, John Raskob, came from the board of the Association Against the Prohibition Amendment. And when analysts brought out the magnifying glasses, they found new Democratic strength in the wet northern cities. On the other side, Herbert Hoover hailed the noble experiment in his inaugural address and called for vigorous enforcement on every level of government. The tough new enforcement statute, the Jones Act (the five and dime law, described earlier), now sailed through the Republican House, 284 to 90—the most lopsided vote yet on a major liquor issue.

For a golden moment, the economic boom continued. Prohibition had come in with all kinds of promises about improving America. As prosperity spread through the 1920s, drys grabbed for the credit. Explaining the hot economy had become a kind of parlor game. Popular explanations ranged from "advertising" to "electricity." But no one could match the prohibitionists' long history of promising health and wealth. Now they bragged shamelessly about their reform. Prohibition had increased the level of insurance, raised personal savings, lifted real estate value, fostered thrift, put tramps to work (no more free lunch in the saloon), and even made American men more handsome.[53]

The stock market crash in the fall of 1929 flipped everything. As the United States plunged into the Great Depression, Herbert Hoover's embrace turned into a political kiss of death. Prohibition caught even more abuse than the rest of his program, thanks, in part, to a special report prepared by the Wichersham Commission. A blue-ribbon commission normally offers safe haven from controversy. But this one painted an especially nasty picture: courts were clogged, jails overflowing, laws disrespected, states slacking, bootleggers everywhere, and corruption ditto. In standard blue-ribbon style, the commission served up vanilla for formal recommendations, but the commissioners each attached tart individual statements—two called for repeal, six for immediate changes. Herbert Hoover received this dismal inventory with an unpersuasive look on the bright side: "The commission, by a large majority, does not favor repeal." The contrast between the withering review (an official with the AAPA said he could not have put together a better indictment) and the president's upbeat reaction led to rounds of hooting—at Herbert Hoover, at his "noble experiment," at the clueless collection of dry leaders.[54]

The Democrats surged back into power. Four years after their debacle, they gave President Franklin Roosevelt majorities of 193 seats in the House and 25 in the Senate. Poor Herbert Hoover managed to take even fewer electoral votes than Al Smith. In the 1932 elections, eleven states held prohibition votes—every one of them went wet.

All the arguments that had ushered in Prohibition were now turned inside out. Permitting liquor would create thousands of jobs, give local economies a sorely needed boost, and raise tax revenue. Farmers would find markets for their grains and hops. And the nation needed that tax money—the Depression had flattened income tax receipts.

Less than two weeks after taking office Roosevelt sent Congress one of his briefest messages: "I recommend . . . immediate modification of the Volstead Act, in order to legalize the manufacture and sale of [light] beer and other beverages . . . and to provide . . . a proper and much needed revenue for the Government." Two months later, the administration unveiled its National Industrial Recovery Administration, the centerpiece of Roosevelt's economic strategy; funding would come from liquor revenues, just as soon as the states ratified the Twenty-first Amendment repealing the Eighteenth.[55]

Let's bring back that economist who believes that finances explain everything. Prohibition became possible, she told us, after the United States introduced an income tax, which made liquor taxes expendable. A bit more than a decade after Prohibition went into place, the economy crashed. The government needed that money again. Prohibition promptly got tossed.

Congress amended Volstead in three weeks. In states that did not have bone-dry laws on the books, the light beer began to flow. At just after midnight on April 7, 1933, a beer truck rolled up to the White House carrying two cases and a large sign: "President Roosevelt, the first real beer is yours." Hundreds of men and women stood outside the White House and cheered. In the popular imagination, those beers toasted the end of Prohibition. However, full repeal had not yet made its way through the states.

The Twenty-first Amendment went through the lame duck Congress before Roosevelt even took office. Proponents kept repeating a simple argument: look at that landslide. Their amendment turned liquor control back over to the states; you could not ship alcohol into a state that said no (essentially lifting the old Webb-Kenyon legislation into the Constitution). Still, wet leaders worried. State legislatures overrepresented the rural districts, and they might resist the amendment. Now the anti-Prohibition organizations came in handy. They had researched and drafted a model bill calling for state constitutional conventions to ratify the Twenty-first Amendment—the only constitutional amendment to get ratified via state conventions rather than legislatures.[56]

The anti-Prohibition organizations poured their resources into repeal cam-

paigns that already looked unbeatable. The states raced to repeal—eleven acted
in the first month, thirty-nine within four months. For pure speed, no one beat
the taciturn Yankees at the New Hampshire Repeal Convention. They did
their work—from invocation to final farewell—in seventeen minutes.

Alcohol control returned to the states, and many passed the choice back to
their counties. The counties are still sorting it out, prompting only an occasional (often sarcastic) glance from the national press. The *New York Times,* for
example, could not resist handicapping a liquor referendum in—I'm not making this up—Dry Creek, Kentucky (75 of Kentucky's 120 counties remain
dry). The Dry Creek wets called it an "issue of convenience, not morality." The
Reverend David Tucker, pastor of the Sherman Baptist Church, cheerfully demurred and offered up some ancient wisdom: "Progress can be a wild ride."[57]

Legacies

Prohibition gave the American government an extraordinary job to do: change
the way people lived. What ended up changing most may have been the government itself.

Prohibition pushed federal power into the nooks and crannies of American
crime-fighting. The consequences included federal plea-bargaining, a boom in
prison construction, and voluminous legal precedents guiding searches, seizures, wiretaps, judicial process, and more. The dry effort integrated federal,
state, and local law enforcement. And once again it drafted government into
the nation's cultural conflicts. It constructed institutional and legal precedents
for almost every aspect of the war on drugs (still fought, in many ways, by the
same rules). Finally, Prohibition left a more subtle social legacy. Fifteen years of
buzzing over federal policy may have helped fertilize the political culture for
the New Deal.

Of course, Prohibition and the New Deal draw on entirely opposite sides of
the Puritan legacy. The drys campaigned against individual sinners. They fixed
on the underclass vices spilling out from the saloons. Ultimately, drinkers
flunked the essential Puritan test: self-mastery. And the individual sinners were
abetted (or perhaps duped) by an evil empire—distillers, brewers, and saloonkeepers. Ardent drys imagined all the troubles of modernity flowing from this
tangle. Win the liquor war, promised the Billy Sundays, and make a memory of
slums, prisons, jails, and even hell itself.

The 1930s would turn to the other American moral tradition, the Social
Gospel. Morality lay in community service. Ethics—Christian ethics—cried
for social justice, for helping those on the bottom. Instead of kicking lazy bums

out of the warm saloon, this perspective asked why they were there and how the society might help them. Here lies the moral basis for a welfare state.

The Social Gospel vision would dominate the next five decades, cresting in the 1960s. The New Deal, it seemed, had buried that cranky, narrow, prohibitionist mindset. Modern people took a tolerant view. But the focus on individual vice and virtue—given up as hopelessly old-fashioned at midcentury—would roar back. The Social Gospel preachers would, in turn, rediscover the prime lesson of American morals: you never really bury either side of our Puritan tradition.

But let's bring back our economic determinist: don't the shifting moral tides simply reflect economic swings? The fat 1920s pushed an individual view. The lean 1930s pressed Americans toward a more collective vision. Or put more cynically: conditions in the 1920s permitted the majority to deport radicals and discipline sinners; in the 1930s there were too many to punish, so the nation had to buy them off.

Economic conditions mattered. The Great Depression is exactly what defeated Prohibition. But the larger story won't boil down to economics alone. The long moral surge that we have been following lasted fifty years, through good times and bad. The Social Gospel that dominates the next section rose out of the Great Depression and reached high tide in the 1960s, the height of the postwar economic boom. Again, good times and bad. The recurring American moral traditions—the neo-Puritan versus the Social Gospel—operate a more complicated dialectic than our mad economist dreams of.

PART IV

The Social Gospel at High Tide
(1932–1973)

We have always known that heedless self-interest was bad morals. We know now that it is bad economics.
—President Franklin D. Roosevelt, 1937

Our government makes no sense unless it is founded on a deeply held religious faith—and I don't care what it is.
—President Dwight Eisenhower, 1954

Rarely in any time does an issue lay bare the secret heart of America itself. . . . The issue of equal rights for American Negroes is such an issue. And should we defeat every enemy, should we double our wealth and conquer the stars, and still be unequal to this issue, then we will have failed as a people and as a nation.
—President Lyndon Johnson, 1964

"THE stock market crash was almost like a rending of the earth [on] the day of judgment," marveled Edmund Wilson. "The slump was like a flood," an "earthquake" or a "religious conversion." It was exhilarating. The Puritans finally lost their grip on the national culture, concluded Wilson, though there must have been some Puritan afterglow if he saw millennial omens in the stock ticker. Presidential candidate Franklin Roosevelt urged his countrymen to rethink their basic values before the "mental lethargy of a speculative upturn" dulled their moral sense again. Hard times shook free a completely different kind of morality.[1]

The evangelist Billy Sunday caught the changing moral seasons with two versions of a familiar Bible story. In the traditional gospel, explained Sunday, Jesus was preaching to a large crowd when, "like many modern speakers, He overran His time limit." The disciples, seeing that the people were getting hungry, told Him, "'Master, there is nothing to eat in this desert place; dismiss them so they can go into the towns and get food.' Jesus looked around and spied a little boy whose ma had given him five biscuits and a couple of sardines for his lunch." He called the boy over and asked him for the food. Jesus prayed, divided the little lunch, fed five thousand people, and then told the disciples to pack up twelve baskets of leftovers.

However, modern preachers were not satisfied with the Lord's miracle, continued Sunday. They wanted a natural explanation. Now, when the disciples tell Him that the people are hungry, Jesus responds

> "We have some lunch, haven't we?"
> "Yes, but not enough to feed this crowd."
> "Well, let's divide it up and see." So Jesus proceeded to divide his lunch with the hungry crowd.
> An old Jew, seeing Jesus busy, asked, "What's he doing?" "Dividing his lunch." "Huh," grunts this old knocker, "he is the first preacher I've ever seen who practices what he preaches." Shamed by the preacher's example, the old tightwad brought out his lunch basket and began to divide.[2]

Others catch the spirit. They take out their food and split it with strangers. Though the Billy Sundays did not see it, the modern version offers its own miracle—the spirit of sharing that Jesus stirred among the people. Agency has passed back, once again, from heaven to earth; the people learn to minister to one another, and, as a result, everyone has plenty to eat. It is the perfect parable for the New Dealers.

Fundamentalists loathed the secular revision. "Ridiculous"—hissed Sunday—"blasphemy," "spiritual cocaine." But the conservatives had lost their national audience. Sunday himself returned to New York in 1934 and played to small crowds—perhaps a tenth of the audience he had drawn when Prohibition was hot. Now, sniffed *Time* magazine, no amens sounded from the rafters, and almost no one bothered to go forward and shake hands with the old, gray preacher. Evangelical hellfire had become embarrassing. A new age pushed aside biblical inerrancy, Catholic-bashing, Puritan thou-shalt-nots, and the very idea (at the heart of evangelical faith) that salvation turned entirely on repenting sin and relying on grace.[3]

Around the turn of the century, reformers had proposed the Social Gospel alternative. "Morality consists in being a good member of the community," wrote Walter Rauschenbusch, that's the "only thing God cares about." Drop all the harping on individual vices. The biblical prophets hurled their jeremiads at "injustice and oppression," not at "intemperance or unchastity." The 1930s version of this gospel brimmed with social (many would say socialist) commandments: Laissez-faire is a morally dubious principle. Honor the labor movement. Condemn not individual sinners but the economic system that pushes poor people into hard corners. In the Social Gospel view, the community shares responsibility for vice and virtue, for wealth and poverty.[4]

During the Great Depression, the Social Gospel sprang back to life—and into law. Roosevelt preached a vivid version. Over the next forty years, variations of the new social morality dominated American politics. Policy makers blamed the system rather than the sinner. The Victorian regime came down—case by case, law by law, norm by norm. For a bumpy, often interrupted progressive interlude, the focus on social issues—and the soft, sophisticated view of sin—seemed like modernity itself.

Some things, however, did not change. The United States remained a model for the world—now, more than ever. The New Dealers championed "freedom from want" through the 1930s; they turned abroad in the 1940s and promised "freedom from fear." The search for these freedoms produced powerful political establishments—a social welfare state in the 1930s, a military and security state in the 1940s and '50s. Each drew a different political constituency—and offered a different vision of public morals. The social gospel era finally crested in the 1960s with another great awakening—a grand moral revival with all the trimmings.

Chapter 12
The New Deal Call to Alms

A famous cartoon from 1933 pictures two coal miners hard at work, covered with soot. "For gosh sakes," says one of the men, "here comes Mrs. Roosevelt." Another cartoon from the same period looks at the same subject from high above the filthy workers. A knot of men and women in dapper evening clothes stop by the neighboring mansion and propose an evening's entertainment. "Come along," they say to the moneybags next door, "we're going to the Trans-Lux to hiss Roosevelt." In the 1930s, the New Deal recast sin and virtue. Like Mrs. Roosevelt, the state got deeply involved in the social welfare of American workers. The wealthy may have hissed, but they managed to hang on to their mansions. Meanwhile, the government began getting out of the vice business; someone else would have to make the movies clean and wholesome for our cartoon plutocrats. Amid these shifting moral tides stands the great American alternative to Puritan moralists.

Poverty and Morals

Franklin Roosevelt sketched out the new attitude during his 1932 election campaign. In a celebrated speech before business leaders at the San Francisco Commonwealth Club, Roosevelt promised a new "economic constitutional order." Government would no longer meekly serve the "great promoter or the financial Titan," granting him anything he asked for "if only he would build or develop." Instead, enlightened public administration would guide business.[1]

The following week, in Detroit, Roosevelt gave this activist government a righteous mission—winning social justice. Since it was a Sunday, said Roosevelt, he would not be "talking politics" but "preaching a sermon." Good to his word, he packed his homily with religious quotations and allusions. For his text, the candidate reread the classic American moral problem: poverty and its causes.[2]

The early Puritans looked at poverty and detected signs from heaven. Later generations saw sloth, personal extravagance, bad blood, weak will, or criminality. Roosevelt's explanation mixed Social Gospel and modern science. "The causes of poverty . . . are beyond the control of any individual." Economic competition had sunk Americans into "jungle law." "The survival of the so-called fittest" served only the cruel and ruthless. American churches—Protestant, Catholic, and Jewish—all condemned the "unbrotherly . . . distribution of wealth" and the "spirit of mammon" that were routing the "eternal principles of God and justice." What was the alternative? "Community effort." When a modern civilization faces a disease epidemic, said Roosevelt, turning from gospel to science, it "take[s] care of the victims after they are stricken." But it also finds and attacks the source of contagion. Just as public health efforts eradicated the causes of disease, public policy would wipe out the roots of poverty. How? Through modern social programs like workman's compensation and old-age insurance.

The public health analogy gave Roosevelt's program the glow of modernity. And it established a contrast that remains familiar. Moralists blamed a vice like drinking for poverty, slums, and crime. They responded in the obvious ways: preach, pledge, and prohibit. Progressives blamed an illness like alcohol abuse on environmental factors, such as poverty, slums, and stress. They responded in obvious ways: treatment, education, and assistance. The fault line would run right through the rest of the century—vice versus illness, crime versus public health, individual sin versus social responsibility.

Roosevelt brought his Social Gospel down to earth with sad stories about good people. An eighty-nine-year-old neighbor had died while milking the cow—after a blizzard, no less; they had to place his eighty-three-year-old sister in an insane asylum because there was nowhere else to put her. Roosevelt was off and running down a roster of impoverished innocents: "six million . . . public school children who do not have enough to eat," injured workers, sick men and women, crippled children, the unemployed. Each example came with the same political spin: poor people are virtuous neighbors who have fallen on hard times.

There was not a hint about those past icons of depravity—lazy immigrants, undisciplined black men, or drunks lounging about the saloon. Prohibition was still in place, still in political play. But in an earlier address, Roosevelt had pledged to send that sin firmly back to the private sphere. "We have depended too largely upon the power of government instead of . . . the authority of the home and that of the churches." The Democrats flipped the last generation's

12.1. "Come along. We're going to the Trans-Lux to hiss Roosevelt." (Copyright The
New Yorker Collection 1936 Peter Arno from cartoonbank.com. All Rights Reserved.)

moral standards. They promised to wade deep into the American economy to
win social justice. But alcohol? Suddenly, they were pious advocates of limited
government. "The attempt to impose the practice of virtue by mandate," in-
toned Franklin Roosevelt, simply "undermined public authority."[3]

Once the Democrats were in office, conservatives began ripping the new
morals. A Georgia churchman tried to spin Roosevelt's virtuous poor back into
the sinners they used to be: this government, he said, "seems to place a premium
on . . . the shiftless, the mentally, physically, and morally unfit." "I object to the
President's moral liberalism," added a Texas minister, "which has inundated the
country in debauching liquor and brought a high wave of gambling and laxity
in home life." An annual survey of Protestants morosely faced up to the 1932
electoral debacle. "The church bodies maintained their support [for] the eighteenth amendment and the electorate did not heed [our] call."[4]

12.2. "For gosh sakes, here comes Mrs. Roosevelt." (Copyright The New Yorker Collection 1933 Robert Day from cartoonbank.com. All Rights Reserved.)

But a different group was up and cheering for the rising Social Gospel. The Council of Methodist Youth met in 1932 and filled the hall with its take-no-prisoners pledge. "I surrender my life to Christ. I renounce the Capitalist system." "The time is past for mere churchgoing and hymns," a Democratic official told another enthusiastic Methodist gathering. Now, they would "build a society upon the living principles of Christ." As soon as the administration launched its recovery program, a coalition of liberal ministers, priests, and rabbis rallied public support. "The program incorporates into law . . . the social principles which our religious organizations have [long] stood for." Some nervous religious leaders began urging the clerics to tone down their political enthusiasm and "preach from Scriptures rather than on social questions."[5]

Still, for all the rattling in the liberal pews, organized religion languished in the 1930s. Conventional wisdom reported a great decline in churchgoing (though church affiliation at the end of the decade stood roughly where it had been at the start, just under 50 percent). Observers rounded up the usual mod-

ernist suspects: the march of science, the fast pace of the industrial age, the "sec-
ularization of life." Perhaps there was—and is—a secular dynamic within the
Social Gospel urge itself. Keep applying religion to worldly problems and it begins to lose its transcendence, its religiosity. Young New Dealers found more
exciting things to believe in—like the "magic of technocracy," which crackled
with the heady power of modernity. "At the Metropolitan weekend dances," reported a cheeky *New York Times* dispatch, "the stag line is said to have been seriously depleted while the sons of Princeton and Yale forgathered in the smoking rooms" and buzzed about "social, economic and technological trends."[6]

Us and Them Revisited

Roosevelt, however, stuck to his moral rhetoric. Today, it is easy to overlook.
The language sounds like political oil poured over class tensions, chaotic policy
making, and stubborn self-interests. But the rhetoric framed the New Deal's
"three ring circus" in an important way.

At the heart of Roosevelt's moral talk lay his utopian picture of shared
community. Roosevelt constantly pounded the selfish individual. He closed his
first, hard-fought reelection campaign by wearily telling supporters, "I should
like to have it said of my first administration that the forces of selfishness . . .
met their match." Instead, he extolled mutual responsibility. During his second
term, he urged the clergy to "return to the religion as exemplified in the Sermon
on the Mount"—the ultimate statement of what we owe one another, culmi-
nating in the Bible's most lyrical call to alms.[7]

Eventually, Roosevelt's little sermons took a predictable form, almost a formula. First invoke religion; in the next breath, turn to social conditions. Faith
sets up economics. "We have always known that heedless self interest was bad
morals," Roosevelt said in his second inaugural address. "We know now that it
is bad economics." Again, cheering his own first term: "The greatest change
. . . has been the change in the moral climate of America." With this change
came "our rediscovered ability to improve our economic order." Sometimes he
reversed the order: "There is not a social, political, or economic [problem] that
would not find full solution in the fire of a religious awakening."[8]

When a group of Protestant missionaries visited the White House, Roosevelt confessed that he had been skeptical of mission work. What changed his
mind? "I have seen what American church missions have accomplished in
many countries, not only on the religious side"—here comes the familiar Roosevelt twist—"but on the side of health and education." This time, however,
Roosevelt took his sermon one step further. "We call what we have been doing
'human security' and 'social justice.' In the last analysis all of those terms can be

described by one word; and that is 'Christianity.' " The comment could be the defining statement of the 1930s Social Gospel: religious roots, a social payoff, and—that mild clang to our contemporary ear—an occasional tendency to overlook the non-Christians.[9]

Of course, moral rhetoric did not repeal politics as usual. Special interests carved up the New Deal's offerings the moment they were served. Deep social conflicts shaped the programs. Jolts of bigotry snapped across the nation. But for all that, Roosevelt's tone mattered. It explained and justified the surge of social legislation; more important, it submerged the familiar discourse about them and us, about vice and virtue.

We have seen moral politics sanction a long history of cruel stereotypes— German drinkers, unclean women, black rapists, Salem witches. Now, a lot less political energy went into finding an immoral underclass at the root of America's troubles. With fewer sinners stalking the land, the stigmas faded from the political debates.

Biases remained, of course. In fact, they fundamentally shaped the Democrats' program. But without the harsh rhetoric assailing a dangerous underclass, the New Dealers found some negotiating room on the margins of the old conflicts. We can see how social divisions operated in the 1930s by revisiting three familiar fault lines—class, race, and gender. Each operated without the full blast of moralizing images.

Class

The centerpiece of the early New Deal pushed communal dreams implausibly into the industrial realm. The National Recovery Administration (NRA), launched in June 1933, invited industries to get together and design voluntary codes of competition. No more dog eat dog. True to rhetorical form, Roosevelt imagined an "industrial Covenant" that would push aside "selfish interests" and unite Americans in a "great cooperation." Economic competitors would sit down and hammer out deals about wages, work hours, prices, and production levels. Almost any business might work out a code. How many striptease acts should go in a burlesque show? The bump-and-grind moguls negotiated an agreement: four strippers. Companies that stuck to the deals affixed a blue eagle to their merchandise; the little icon sprouted up on White Rock seltzer, Vaseline hair tonic, Bayer aspirin, the *Portland Journal,* and a racy magazine called *Cupid's Capers.* In theory, the American people would shun the shirkers without eagles. In reality, this soaring communal wish passed industrial policy directly into the eager hands of large firms and trade organizations that, for a time, could collude without any trouble from anti-trust laws.[10]

The hand-off to industry came with a potent kicker. The legislation

vaguely invited organized labor to the bargaining table. The law's most controversial passage forbade "interference, restraint or coercion" over workers and
unions—an ambiguous, potentially explosive prohibition lobbed into the middle of America's bitter union-busting history. Just what, exactly, did the law
ban? No one could be quite sure. Congress piled hazy workers' rights onto an
equivocal economic program that no one was going to enforce—and set off one
of the great social movements in American history.[11] John Lewis, the volcanic
president of the United Mine Workers, seized the opportunity. He baldly
exaggerated: "The President wants you join the union!" Working men and
women found a new legal toehold in their long struggle to organize. They
rushed to join. The blue eagle produced marches, strikes, and fistfights. The
upheaval exposed the dream of a covenant community, rattled the National Recovery Administration, and remade the American union movement. Two years
later Congress turned the NRA's vague and controversial nod to labor into the
more definitive Wagner Act. Workers kept mobilizing and eventually became
a major part of the Democratic coalition.[12]

Other class-based movements jolted the New Deal. A California physician
entered the political scene with a simple plan and a genius for organizing.
Dr. Francis Townsend's prescription for depression would give every sixty-
year-old a monthly stipend with just one string attached—spend every penny.
Townsend clubs sprang up around the nation and lobbied for the intrepid economic remedy. The Townsend chorus could be distinctly heard in the background as Congress and the administration negotiated over the Social Security
Act.

Senator Huey Long blew out of Louisiana with his own recovery plan. The
problem was simple, said the Kingfish. The rich had grabbed too much. The
answer was just as easy: share the wealth. Long pushed a jarring property tax;
personal wealth—not just income—reached the 100 percent tax bracket at $8
million. An income tax would confiscate anything over $1 million a year. In-
heritance taxes also took 100 percent after the first $1 million. The government
would gather all that money and give every needy family a household estate of
$5,000, followed by an annual income of between $2,000 and $2,500.

Long seemed poised for a run at the presidency. American elites saw a blus-
tering, populist demagogue who had managed to wipe out most political
checks and balances back in Louisiana. Lots of Kingfish stories made the
rounds; they got nastier, he wrote, as his popularity swelled. In one infamous
episode, a drunken Huey got into a brawl in the men's room of a Long Island
country club. Apparently, in his boozy impatience, Long had marched up to a
urinal that was already in use and tried to relieve himself by aiming between the
legs of the man in front of him. The man's trousers got soaked. Long emerged

with a battered face and a ready explanation: The international bankers from "the house of Morgan" had tried to assassinate him.[13]

For all his backwoods bluster, Huey Long was pointing to the great issue of the day: the concentration of wealth. Long's rhetoric darkly echoed Roosevelt's—in a way, he brought the president's airy generalizations about "the selfish" down to earth with that high-octane economic plan. The speeches about shared community and social action have to be read against these bitter class tensions. Workers organized and fought bloody battles with employers (and sometimes with one another). Townsend clubs formed around the nation. Huey Long became a star for NBC radio. Idylls of unity and calls to social action got interrupted—and the New Dealers found their program pressed—by the bitter class animosities.

The American "them" had passed from the poor failures on the fringe of power to the greedy, who had grabbed too much. Their malevolent influence radiated from the top. "Sometimes a guy'll be a good guy," sums up Tom Joad in Steinbeck's *Grapes of Wrath*, "even if some rich bastard tries to make him [act mean]." The blame for American troubles lay not with the lazy poor but with the irresponsible rich. Political leaders framed the economic crisis in moral terms that reversed the traditional sermonizing about wealth and poverty. And that changed the tone—the assumptions, the agenda—of public policy.[14]

Race

Nothing in American history seems quite as malleable—as up for cultural grabs—as the black image in the white mind. We have seen a long line of racial caricatures infuse a long list of political projects. The New Deal was different. Race politics lay near the center of the action, but this time the Democrats hushed the issue to keep their coalition together.

Back in the 1920s, dry southern Democrats had faced off against wet northern Democrats. Many southerners had even tossed aside their lifelong political habits and voted for a Republican rather than accept Al Smith. When the stock market crash finally wiped out the liquor question, the Democratic coalition gingerly restored itself. Northern liberals supported social programs, and southern Democrats eagerly went along. The Depression had flattened the South, and the region badly needed help. But southerners held tightly to the usual line, welcoming federal programs that posed no threat to racial segregation. Ira Katznelson describes the results with a jarring analogy: the New Deal congressional coalition resembled a marriage between Sweden (northern social democrats) and South Africa (southern racial apartheid).[15]

Roosevelt preached his beautiful sermons, liberal churchmen cheered, populists agitated for action. But nothing went through Congress without first getting past the racial censors. This time, however, race worked quietly. Robert Lieberman makes the point by quoting an exchange between Congressmen Howard Smith (Virginia) and Thomas Jenkins (Ohio).

> *Mr. Smith:* Of course, in the South we have a great many colored people and they are largely of the laboring class . . .
>
> *Mr. Jenkins:* I should like to ask the gentleman . . . whether in this law it is contemplated that there be any loophole by which any State could discriminate. . . .
>
> *Mr. Smith:* No, Sir. . . . You will not find in my remarks any suggestion to that effect. It just so happens that that race is in our state very much of the laboring class. . . . But you will find no suggestion in my remarks of any suggested amendment that would be unconstitutional, if I may use that expression.

Exquisitely polite, nodding and winking around the race question, the ungainly Democratic coalition organized the modern American welfare state. In fact, Smith and Jenkins were in the process of hemming the Social Security Act (1935) to fit southern racial controls. The administration had organized its Old Age Insurance, later known as Social Security, around an insurance metaphor. Working people paid into the program, and their benefits were pegged directly to their contributions; the federal government would send them checks directly from Washington. Retired black workers would win their financial independence right alongside their white colleagues.

But Congress found a loophole. It "exempted" farm workers and domestic servants from the program. As black leaders like Adam Clayton Powell immediately noted, "Most Negroes are employed along these two lines." In fact, Congress had managed to push some 60 percent of black southern workers (and four out of five black women) right out of the Social Security program. The rules also pushed out most Latinos. Three years later a broad campaign to extend Social Security to African Americans came to nothing. The New Dealers expanded the program, but not to them.[16]

The other half of the legislation got cash to the needy. Aid to Dependent Children—"welfare"—fell into this category. The federal government made grants to the states, which matched the funds and ran the program. The states could negotiate their own way through the tangle of race, poverty, and assistance. Many distributed the dole with ambiguous moral stipulations about the "suitability" and "propriety" of the recipients. Keeping control of black beneficiaries was the key. Congress even scratched out a provision calling for a "reasonable subsistence compatible with decency and health." This was "dictatorial power . . . over what the state is permitted to do," explained Senator Harry Bird of Virginia.[17]

On the racial ground, the ugly basics seemed the same. Congress may have turned subtle, but the lynch scourge ran on. In February 1930 a mob seized James Irwin and accused him of raping and murdering a white woman. They cut off his fingers. Then his toes. They jammed a burning hot poker into his throat. And they set him on fire. Crowds went on to lynch at least ninety-four more black men in the next five years—a third more than they had murdered in the previous five years. Southern liberals, fighting hard against the violence, pleaded with the administration for action, for statements, for something, for anything. But the Roosevelt administration—trapped in its coalition—stayed silent.[18]

Even here, however, the New Deal made a difference. Farm subsidies (from the Agriculture Adjustment Administration) pumped money into dirt-poor areas. Slowly—and painfully, for plenty of workers got fired—southern agriculture began to modernize. A more moderate urban middle class had also begun to grow in the South. As the region developed, the murders declined. Getting capital into the communities eased the hard desperation that helped fuel the mobs. And it raised the stakes for business leaders. "We have managed to reduce lynching," said Jessie Daniel Ames, an anti-lynch crusader, "not because we've grown more law abiding or respectable, but because lynching became such bad advertising. . . . A lawless lynch mob population isn't going to attract very much outside capital."[19]

Southern apartheid remained. But in contrast to past progressive generations, northern New Dealers did not repeat the old litanies about sexual depravity or dangerous black drunks or white women afraid to leave the house. On the contrary, national moral sentiment turned the other way: revulsion grew. Reginald Marsh captured the outrage—missing among mainstream white progressives for the past half-century—with a fierce charcoal sketch. Marsh pictured a crowd, bodies savagely contorted, eyes glinting with blood lust. Grandmother holds a young child above the mob and explains to Leering Neighbor, "This is her first lynching." The young girl sits up there and stares, without any expression, learning to see like the grown-ups. The sketch ran in the *New Yorker*, a barometer of shifting upper-middle-class attitudes. At the height of the populist era, even Frances Willard had sided with the bloodthirsty mob. At the height of the Progressive reformation, D. W. Griffith had celebrated the lynch mob in *Birth of a Nation*. Marsh's angry sketch—designed to stir repugnance—marks a turning point. World War II would finally nudge the Roosevelt administration toward long-awaited action against lynching.

President Roosevelt's rhetoric had shaped an image—virtuous poor people. Even the programs sculpted around the race line came without the harsh rhetoric and racial stigma that had fueled the vice wars of past generations. The

12.3. "This is her first lynching." Reginald Marsh's fierce charcoal sketch appeared in the *New Yorker* in 1934. (Copyright The New Yorker Collection 1934 Reginald Marsh from cartoonbank.com. All Rights Reserved.)

changing moral tone gradually began to tell. Winking senators just do not light the same racial fire as outcries about black rapists, drunkards, and depravity.

Gender

The Roosevelt administration broke new ground in hiring women. Frances Perkins, the secretary of labor, was the first woman in the cabinet; Nellie Taloe Ross, the former governor of Colorado, directed the mint; Josephine Roche, a consumer activist, was an assistant secretary in the Treasury Department. The list goes on. Moreover, New Deal programs generally used gender-neutral language—a break from the Progressive Era, which had loud, explicit preferences about proper roles.

Even so, the New Deal programs reflected—and often bolstered—the familiar view of men as breadwinners and women as mothers and wives. "At the basis of American civilization," Princeton economist J. Douglas Brown told the House Ways and Means Committee, "is the concept of the family." For many New Dealers that meant ensuring a "family wage." A man received higher Social Security payments if he had a wife to support. It didn't work the other way; if she had the only Social Security–eligible job, she did not get higher benefits to support him. She could receive widow's benefits; he could not.[20]

Of course, the widow's benefits would not be as high as the husband's pension. Why not? asked a member of the Social Security Advisory Council. Well, responded the chair, because a "single woman can adjust herself to a lower budget. . . . She is used to doing her own housework whereas the single man has to go out to a restaurant." And she could move in with the kids. Grandmother can make herself useful in the home, but grandfather "is the man who sits on the front porch and can't help much."[21]

To some extent, the tilt reflected the attitudes and interests of the New Deal coalition. Union leaders, rural southern Democrats, and urban northerners were mainly men with their own agendas. The trauma of Depression exacerbated the biases. Public officials worried about women taking jobs that might go to unemployed men. Twenty-six states added limits on married women's employment. When federal agencies faced layoffs, they first cut women married to male employees.[22]

And yet these are all relatively quiet discriminations embedded in the machinery of programs and policies. They contrast vividly with the moral fury we've seen running through past gender wars. The 1930s heard less about biblical families or St. Paul's counsel to women or the glory of the submissive wife. There were fewer subversive women, Eve narratives, or witch-hunts. At least in the New Deal mainstream, the gender line remained relatively cool. The next generation would dramatize the point by reviving the old image—woman as a danger to society in the face of our enemies.

Comstockery Cracks

Avez-vous Ulysses?

Lonely Comstocks still manned the moral barricades and won an occasional victory. They fended off James Joyce's *Ulysses,* for example. The vice society challenged the book when a New York literary journal, the *Little Review,* ran it as a serial (Leo Bloom's erotic daydreams about Gertie got him into trouble). In 1921 a bewildered three-judge panel ruled the work obscene (and handed down a bit of judicial literary criticism—the "ravings of a disordered mind"). When the book's first edition arrived, a year later, the Post Office burned all five hundred copies. In 1928 the Customs Court decided the book was still "vile" and "rotten."

Joyce himself saw a silver lining: having enjoyed the "pleasure of being burned while on earth . . . I hope I shall pass through the fires of purgatory as quickly as my patron, S. Aloysius." By the late 1920s, the *New Yorker* was chuckling along: a distinctly unsophisticated matron hisses to a Parisian bookseller standing in the shadows, "Avez-vous *Ulysses?*" In 1929, Will Rogers toasted a publishers' convention: "Since sex stuff came into vogue in recent years, prosperity has been [your] lot." Social mores were shifting.[23]

Random House tested the ban once again. In 1933, U.S. District Court Judge John Woolsey reversed the previous judgment: "In *Ulysses,* I do not detect anywhere the leer of the sensualist." Earlier rulings had plenty to say about the terrible language—Joyce blithely tossed around "fuck" and "arse." "The words which are criticized as dirty are old Saxon words," responded Woolsey, "known to most men and, I venture to say, to many women." Sure, there was sex, but after all, "his locale was Celtic and his season spring." One anticensorship attorney saw the victory as part of a larger social movement: "The New Deal in the law of letters is here." Like the Roosevelt administration, the courts were backing out of the vice business.[24]

On appeal, Judge Augustus Hand rewrote the Victorian obscenity rules. The old test had checked isolated literary bits for a tendency to "deprave and corrupt . . . minds open to immoral influences." Now, ruled Hand, the court would judge the work by its "dominant effect" on the "average reader." Moreover, the literary and artistic merit had to be factored in. Most courts adopted the Hand rule. The same year, 1934, another observer noted the changing social morals, tongue lightly in cheek: "Good Authors, too, who once knew better words / Now only use four letter words / Writing prose / Anything goes."[25]

Still, some courts held out against books that "manifestly tend to corrupt the morals of youth." The Massachusetts Supreme Judicial Court banned Lillian Smith's *Strange Fruit*, a book about interracial love in Georgia. The race-sex tangle still remained off limits, but the cultural tide was running strong the other way. The Customs Bureau virtually gave up confiscating dirty classics. World War II would bring another shift in popular norms. In 1946, the court continued its retreat from Comstockery by striking down a Post Office ban on *Esquire*, at the time a somewhat risqué men's magazine.[26]

The ban on birth control also began slipping. In the 1930s Margaret Sanger offered family planning as a relief measure; both poor Americans and their welfare agencies would benefit from smaller families. Congressional Democrats held hearings, though they eventually ducked the issue—northern Catholics were part of the coalition, too. Sanger's organization got publicity from Congress and action from the courts. At one point, in the early 1930s, sixteen birth control cases were working through the judicial system. The landmark judgment came from the Federal Court of Appeals in 1936. Augustus Hand (again) struck down the 1872 ban on mailing contraceptives. In *United States v. One Package,* Hand ruled that when Congress had passed the Comstock Act, members could not have known what medical science would now say—that contraceptives were safe and that childbearing could be dangerous. Once again, modern science trumped Victorian morality.

The Supreme Court did not rule definitively on birth control till 1965. But during the 1930s, condom use became commonplace. Men of every class could find them. By 1940 the teen-age Malcolm X was getting good entrepreneurial advice from a friend in Boston: "Pick up a couple of dozen rubbers, two bits apiece. Charge a dollar."[27]

The Legion of Decency

As the state retreated from the vice wars, the Catholic church moved in to fight dirty movies. Private action appeared to replace public power; however, we'll see that the two remained interconnected—for a time, the courts braced the Catholic effort.

Cecil B. DeMille's *Sign of the Cross* pushed the church into action. DeMille had managed to pack his pious subject with sex, nudity, hints of homosexuality, murder, orgies, a "lesbian" dance, and a glistening Claudette Colbert luxuriating in a milk bath. The movie cheerfully met Hollywood's languid moral code—do not lower the viewer's moral standards—with the usual formula: six reels of sin, one of salvation.[28]

The church took a dual strategy. First, it mobilized the faithful. The Legion of Decency guided churchgoers by rating the movies: "morally unobjectionable" (or class A), "morally objectionable in part" (class B), and "condemned" (the infamous class C). The legion's first list, published in July 1934, put such classics as *The Thin Man, It Happened One Night,* and *Tarzan and His Mate* into class B. The condemned films ran to *Girls for Sale, Born to Be Bad,* and *It Ain't No Sin.* The legion flourished plenty of thou-shalt-nots for the moviemakers, but *Time* magazine immediately boiled them down to the "demand for less sexy pictures." Most of the statements issued by the legion would focus on sex. Moviemakers dissented. "This violent burst of condemnation is directed against something greater than the motion picture," complained Columbia's vice president, Jack Cohn. This is a "Crusade . . . against the tendencies of the times."29

The legion also negotiated the film industry into developing stronger internal controls. The Hays Office, which had overseen the old codes, got strong teeth and a crusading director, Joe Breen. Breen was an Irish Catholic who had led the charge for stronger codes from within the Hays Office, where he worked. Breen despised the slack Hollywood morals. And he got attention by attacking the Jews who ran the movie industry: "They are simply a rotten bunch of vile people with no respect for anything beyond the making of money," he wrote. "Ninety-five percent of the folks are Jews of an Eastern European lineage. They are, probably, the scum of the earth." Once again, a rally against vice found a "vile" and "rotten" them at the bottom of the trouble.30

The Legion of Decency and the new moral code met extraordinary success. Breen wielded his power (fines of up to $25,000) to oversee every stage of moviemaking—from the original script to the final cut. The Hays Office changed the moral tone of American movies. Nick and Nora Charles (in the "Thin Man" series) found themselves in twin beds. Jane lost her suggestive laughter as Tarzan dragged her up to his treetop. American movie directors snipped out nudity, toned down intimations of lust, and cut back on kissing (apparently, the average kiss fell from 4 seconds to 1.5). Between 1936 and 1943 the legion had to condemn only a single film, Howard Hughes's production of *The Outlaw* starring Jane Russell (1943).

The first serious crack in the legion's power came in 1948. The courts ruled that studios were violating anti-trust laws by owning and operating their own movie theaters. The five major studios had divided the country into spheres of influence (Paramount owned half the theaters in the South, for example), and they shared prices, profits, and plans. Breen's authority had rested on a deal among the studios to keep the pictures clean. When the courts pried the movie houses away from the big companies, they opened up screens for independent filmmakers who were not involved with the Hays Office. Four years later, the Supreme Court struck down New York's ban on a foreign film and, essentially, read First Amendment rights into the movies: "The importance of motion pictures as an organ of public opinion," wrote Justice Tom Clark for the Court, "is not lessened by the fact that they are designed to entertain as well as to inform."[31]

The legion had looked like a private sector affair. But, as it turned out, it was buttressed by public policies—both implicit (anti-trust nondecisions) and explicit (state-level censors). Now the courts began dismantling the public supports around the purity effort.

The Legion of Decency itself marched on, fighting a rising tide of "condemned" and "morally objectionable" films. Before long, starlets like Brigitte Bardot were washing ashore in condemned vehicles like Roger Vadim's *And God Created Woman*. At the time, familiar movies like *Pal Joey, High School Confidential, Three Faces of Eve,* and *I Was a Teen-Age Frankenstein* all looked "morally objectionable in part."

As late as the early 1960s, I remember standing up at Mass, solemnly raising my right hand, and pledging to abjure the forbidden films (an idle gesture on my part, as I was way too young to get in). The pledge itself sounded a call to moral arms that the faithful recited once a year: "I condemn indecent and immoral motion pictures. . . . I promise to do all that I can to strengthen public opinion against the production of indecent and immoral films . . . that are dangerous to my moral life. As a member of the Legion of Decency, I pledge myself to remain away from them."[32]

But the legion was fighting, as Cohn had seen back in 1934, against the tendencies of the day. By the time I was condemning immoral motion pictures, a shocking number of my fellow parishioners were sitting defiantly in their pews. Some shook their heads in silent protest. "They think they should make their own decisions about what's right and wrong," my mother later explained. She had put her finger right on the big issue.

The moral shift in the 1930s involved a profound rethinking of the private and public spheres. It reconfigured American liberalism. The state pushed personal vices into the private sphere. There were, of course, plenty of exceptions. Congress banned marijuana, and Mayor Fiorello La Guardia shut down Times Square burlesque shows. But the general trend was vivid. Governments left the vice field, and they began withdrawing support from private purity campaigns. The secular motion ran right through the Roosevelt administration, Congress, the federal courts, and the special state constitutional conventions of 1933 that buried Prohibition.

The next decades would bring religious revivals, pious presidents, and plenty of talk about the mission God had given America. But the government—led by the courts—would continue to leave personal morality in private hands. People could make their own decisions about right and wrong.

On the other side of the liberal divide, of course, the Democrats profoundly expanded the public sector in social and economic affairs. Self-reliance gave way to "social justice through community action." For a time, competition, if not capitalism itself, developed the vague odor of "bad morals." However, as the administration ended its second term, national attention fixed on another familiar moral tradition. The redeemer nation reluctantly returned to its ancient Puritan mission: saving the world.

The City on a Hill Again

As more nations became involved in World War II, Americans checked their own values. Who were we? Where should the United States stand in world affairs?

American Anthems

Roosevelt framed his American faith in the "Four Freedoms" address, which eventually swelled into a kind of anthem for an entire generation. Delivered in January 1941, eleven months before the attack on Pearl Harbor, the address literally called the United States to arms. Roosevelt warned about foreign peril, announced a military mobilization, and promised to supply the Allies. Deep (sixty paragraphs deep) into his address, Roosevelt turned to his famous theme. "As men do not live by bread alone, they do not fight by armaments alone." What Americans believe, said Roosevelt, rests on four essential freedoms. "The first is the freedom of speech—everywhere in the world. The second is freedom of every person to worship God in his own way." As usual, Roosevelt immediately followed his glance to heaven with a reminder of social responsibilities on earth. "The third is freedom from want"—"economic understandings" that could offer everyone a healthy peacetime life. The whole New Deal Social Gospel would infuse this third freedom; it swelled into a communitarian pledge of shared prosperity. (Originally, Roosevelt had international trade agreements in mind.) "The fourth is freedom from fear," meaning peace and security for everyone. Tyrants around the globe threatened free people "with the crash of a bomb." The United States would fight back with a "greater conception—the moral order" of a "good society." We would win the four freedoms "in our own time and generation," he said. The speech summed up Roosevelt's Social Gospel—and a broad American mission—as it flew out to meet the world.[33]

A more burly call to arms matched the Four Freedoms. The United States, wrote editor Henry R. Luce in *Life* magazine, faced a "manifest duty" to become the "good Samaritan of the entire world." Why? Because Americans are the "inheritors of all the great principles of Western Civilization—Justice, the love of Truth, the ideal of charity." Americans alone could lift "mankind from the level of the beasts to what the Psalmist called a little lower than the angels." "The twentieth century is the American century," he wrote, and the entire world was to be better for it.[34]

After the United States declared war, Luce raised the rhetorical ante. "America must be first in the councils," he announced in 1942, and "first in the policy of the world." Faintly echoing John Winthrop's city on a hill, Luce proclaimed that it was all up to us. We would have to prove "whether or not the great experiment in human liberty . . . can survive . . . not merely for a colonial province or a great nation or even a hemisphere but for the whole world." To redeem liberty, hope, justice, and mankind itself, the United States must act as the entire globe's "elder brother, strong [and] brave."[35]

Before the attack on Pearl Harbor, many Americans resisted the saber rattling. Last time, Progressives had cheered their righteous army (recall those stirring 1917 graduation sermons), then watched their gullible dreams get trampled in the carnage. Now, they went the other way and called for peace. The last war had been a "useless and unholy enterprise," declared an editorial in the *New Republic,* and "the world would have been far better off if we had stayed out of it." Intellectuals drew a clear lesson from recent history and condemned the talk of war.[36]

The isolationist "America First" Committee, led by Charles Lindbergh, put a nativist twist on the pacifist impulse. Lindbergh himself admired the German regime right down to its anti-Semitism. His organization glowered with xenophobia. The America-Firsters chanted a jeering variation of the patriotic World War I song.

> Over there, there's mud and shedding of blood
> And tongues confusing and strange,
> So why lend a hand to an alien band
> Whose dreams we can never change?

As Roosevelt nudged the nation toward mobilization, Lindbergh pummeled the New Dealers. America First quickly disbanded after the attack on Pearl Harbor. But its world view would bounce right back after the war, a truculent counterpoint to the four-freedom idealism. Fear of foreigners—confusing, strange, stubborn, dangerous—would form one strand of the campaign against communism.[37]

Once the war began, anti-war sentiments faded to the political fringe. A rush of books, pamphlets, essays, paintings, murals, and even a symphony (by Robert Russell Bennett) celebrated Roosevelt's Four Freedoms. But no one caught the American imagination quite like Norman Rockwell. His four paintings—still instantly familiar—appeared in successive issues of the *Saturday Evening Post* in 1943, each accompanied by an essay on that week's freedom. Rockwell brought Roosevelt's high-flying speech down to earth by portraying his homespun neighbors in Arlington, Vermont.

In *Freedom of Speech,* a handsome, rough-hewn man stands up at a town meeting. You can tell by his clothes that he is a working man, a gas station attendant. Honest oil stains smudge his jacket. Rockwell bathes the man's face in light and gives him a firm, self-confident gaze. The white-collar neighbors, ties loose, turn and listen respectfully. The tableau is Tocqueville's *Democracy in America* sprung to life. This one was Rockwell's favorite and it shows. In *Freedom of Worship,* men and women crowd the frame. They come, clearly, from different ethnic backgrounds, and they worship in very different ways—clutching a bible, saying a rosary, lost in private thought. They are all fervent, solemn, and intense. In *Freedom from Want* a Thanksgiving table groans with excess. Vice President Henry Wallace thought that freedom from want meant a daily quart of milk for every child in the world; but here, as Rockwell himself admitted, what we see is good old all-American overabundance. The family members—warm, happy, far from want—barely notice the food as they giggle over some bit of small-town gossip. Finally, in the only painting with a hint of war, Mom and Dad tuck in their children, sleeping safe and tight and free from fear. Word of the "Bombing Horror" in London trickles ominously into the Vermont home through Dad's newspaper. But there is no way those bombs are going to harm these sleeping youngsters. "No other paintings ever so caught the American imagination," comments Warren Susman. The paintings toured the country as the central attraction of the "Four Freedoms War Bond Show." Eager American families tacked them up everywhere. You can still find them in many Vermont diners.[38]

The Rockwell paintings told Americans who they were, who they wanted to be. Each delivered the same message: we are fighting for this plain American life, the family and the community. Our strength lies in moral values and deep communal bonds. And the hints of danger tap a familiar theme. Evil—real or imagined—endangers American innocents. Indians drag Christian women into captivity, predatory Legrees whip virtuous slave girls, Irish priests seize unsuspecting women, pornography coils around our youngsters, drunkards assail women, husbands beat wives, and malicious agents snatch 60,000 farm girls and sell them into slavery.

Now, terribly real dangers come from abroad, from the Nazis, the Japanese

OURS...to fight for

Freedom of Speech

Freedom of Worship

Freedom from Want

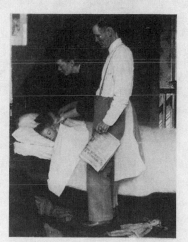

Freedom from Fear

12.4. Norman Rockwell's Four Freedoms appeared in successive issues of the *Saturday Evening Post*, February–March 1943.

navy and, later, the Communists. Two strains in American demonology converge: threatened American innocents meet the corruption of the old world.

Roosevelt, Luce, Lindbergh, and Rockwell each lay down a different American vision. Roosevelt's Social Gospel sent the New Deal out into a world where people are "ill housed, ill clad and ill nourished." In Rockwell's version, the freedoms came back home to archetypal images of innocent America, of family and community. We fight to protect our way of life. Lindbergh's distrust burrows into those Rockwell pictures and turns them sour. The American yeomen stand against the incorrigible "alien band" which can only endanger our way of life. Finally, Luce offered a can-do American alternative. His brawny, triumphal nationalism urges the great country to guide its wayward younger brothers. America would lead, protect, minister, and teach. Luce offered a variation of the white man's burden. The Englishman's sense of duty gets transformed into America's high morals, big purse, and cosmic destiny.

A New American Consensus?

Luce was too much for the left. The *Nation* blasted his "cult of American superiority." Luce's "pompous poppycock" was "no whit less revolting," wrote Freda Kirchwey, "than the Nordic myth that provides moral sanction for Hitler's brutal aggressions." "It can only be done by American ingenuity, American principles, American I-forget-what-all." And the rest of the world "will take it and like it." But we Americans could hardly agree among ourselves. What about the industrial struggles here at home? What about our own running battles between rich and poor? "We are in the thick of that conflict every day of our lives." In fact, our side, in the world war, "is rather a mixed team," concluded Kirchwey, that runs to imperialists, capitalists, trade unions, socialists, and Communists.[39]

The exchange signals two great emerging themes. First, the *Life* editorials assume an American consensus: we agree on our values and fight to give them to our younger, foreign brothers. The *Nation* sees, instead, class conflict raging at home and abroad. This moment, as the United States plunged into the war, marked the turning of the cultural guard. In the 1930s, politics and history seemed just the way the *Nation* described them—bursting with class conflict. The struggle between rich and poor drove history. It explained the Constitutional Convention as persuasively as it predicted the next election (historians dubbed this perspective the Progressive view). *Life* offered the up-and-coming alternative. By the 1950s, the official American ideology had put conflict aside and stressed, instead, a vast consensus. The Declaration of Independence proclaimed this grand harmony, and the Constitution organized it for action. Oh, sure, sometimes we fight with one another. But American fights are mainly efforts to redeem shared ideals. The dream of consensus—forged in world war and polished to a high gloss in the contest against Communism—dominated American thought for two decades. Consensus finally began to flicker out in the mid-1960s, perhaps on that June evening when Stokely Carmichael got out of jail and started leading thousands of angry young black people in the chant: "Black power, black power, black power."

On a second issue, it is the *Nation* that reflects the new era. Across the spectrum of respectable opinion, the racist had become demonic. Unlike the last war, this one did not yield any triumphs of Anglo-Saxon politics. On the contrary, horror at what the Nazis did in the name of racial superiority buried the old nativist arguments.

Franz Boas, the influential anthropologist, had been challenging the racial arguments for a generation. Now his students piled up evidence against innate racial "traits, abilities, and moralities." "Racism has been a travesty of scientific knowledge," concluded Ruth Benedict in 1940, and has "served consistently as special pleading for the supremacy of any group . . . to which the pleader himself belonged." "The White intellect that will unshackle itself from a cultural residue of race myths," added the *New Republic*, "can find ample evidence of the equality of men." The debate about race became a rout. One after another, professional associations—representing anthropologists, geneticists, psychologists, university professors, and others—adopted resolutions condemning theories of racial superiority. They did not simply reject the approach, writes historian David Bennett, they repudiated and reviled it. Racism had become "irrational, destructive, even pathological." The resolutions themselves generally follow the same form: they invoke professional expertise, condemn the Nazis, then reject the science of racial superiority. Alas, as wartime memory faded, scientific racists would begin creeping back toward intellectual respectability.[40]

Political leaders also preached the new racial harmony. In the best-selling book of 1943, Wendell Willkie—the Republican candidate for president in 1940—described his global goodwill tour. There are things that the "white race needs to learn," he reported. "Freedom is an indivisible word. If we want to enjoy it, and fight for it, we must be prepared to extend it to everyone . . . no matter what their race or the color of their skin." Japan is our enemy and China is our friend, said Willkie, and "race has nothing to do with it." Willkie pictured a great international democracy; his conversations with people from Belem to Baghdad offer an elegant rebuttal to Luce's glorious Americanus. Every nation carried its own experiences to the international brotherhood, said Willkie, and we had plenty to learn from every one of them.[41]

Hollywood offered its own variation on the same theme. The war movies drafted every kind of individual into its heroic platoons: the tough Italian kid, the slow-talking redneck, the Irish Catholic, the Jew, and the philosophy teacher. They get thrown together, they bicker, they bond, they fight valiantly, they whip the enemy or they die trying. In some movies, like *Bataan* (1943), the platoon even included a black soldier, though the real army remained segregated. The old melting pot had changed: instead of individuals abandoning their old ways, each brought his own strength to the inevitable American triumph in the final reel. Hollywood was offering America the same message as the resolution of the American Anthropological Association: the old racial divisions were irrelevant; we were all in the big fight together.[42]

Even the traditional race line was beginning to crack. Back in 1940, African Americans had been excluded from the war production industries. Fewer than 300 African Americans got jobs in the industrial mobilization that employed some 100,000 aircraft workers. A. Philip Randolph, a formidable civil rights leader, terrified the Roosevelt administration by organizing a protest march on Washington. The prospect of thousands of angry black Americans descending on the capital (with Germans, Japanese, and everyone else all eyes) prodded the administration to act. Roosevelt slipped past Congress with an executive order banning discrimination in war industries; the order instituted the Fair Employment Practices Commission, which would keep tabs on compliance. By 1944, 1 million African Americans (300,000 of them women) held manufacturing jobs. As the often-repeated black jibe put it, "Hitler got us out of the kitchen." Hitler and their threat to take the fight to the streets.[43]

The Old Lines Linger On

American enemies did get some black Americans out of the kitchen. And through the 1940s and 1950s, ancient biases were reexamined for how they played abroad. Still, foreign peril sometimes boomeranged on American groups. Snapshots from the traditional racial boundaries reveal undeniable racial progress punctuated by spectacular nativist relapses and racial blowups.

Jews. The old anti-immigrant coalition held firm despite rising alarm over the fate of the Jews in Europe, especially after 1938. With American unemployment still over 10 percent, Congress would not budge on quotas for fleeing Jews. Progressive efforts to loosen the immigration limits stirred up such a backlash that sponsors dropped the measures rather than risk even tighter restrictions. English children would be welcome, central Europeans would not. President Roosevelt took cautious steps—hosting meetings (which he did not address) and calling for an international effort (which he did not push). He stayed focused on dragging American public opinion past the isolationists and xenophobes. He resolutely spun all his efforts away from the Jewish question. In 1938, Roosevelt restored the German and Austrian quotas (the Hoover administration had suspended them). But he sternly told a press conference that this did not mean just the Jews. "It means a great many Christians, too, a very large number." The door to fleeing German and Austrians cracked open, and the number of immigrants inched up from 5,200 in 1935 to a high of 33,500, in 1939. As the war raged on, frantic calls for help roused little attention. Journalists like I. F. Stone begged newspaper editors to take up the cause. "The longer we delay the fewer Jews there will be left to rescue," he wrote in 1944. "Between 4 million and 5 million European Jews have been killed since August, 1942." The reasons for the silence go beyond the blunt anti-Semitic opposition to Jewish refugees. Before, during, and even after the war, the Holocaust remained buried in a larger picture of Nazis as pure evil, as menace to everyone. After Victory in Europe, the long, hard prejudice against central European Jews finally began to dissipate. But it would be years before Americans fully confronted the meaning of the Jewish Holocaust—and the way the old nativist instincts had undone the prewar cries for help.[44]

Japanese Americans. The war immediately provoked racial violence. "Misguided mobs beat up a number of slant-eyed citizens, including not a few Chinese," reported *Life* in its first wartime dispatch. "Meanwhile the FBI was making a swift roundup of enemy aliens, by week's end it had some 2,541 in custody. . . . Reporters trying to interview the head of the Japanese school at Seattle were told: 'So solly. No school today. FBI have principal.'" Animosity raced hard across the West Coast. "Local politicians have suddenly remembered the Yellow Peril, a sure-fire political issue," commented the *New Republic.* Some politicians remembered to clothe their rancor in security-speak: "We are at war with the Japanese people. Let's be realistic, all Japanese people look alike." Others did not bother: "Japs live like rats, breed like rats, and act like rats." Magazines tried to sooth the injustice with handy guides for telling our Chinese friends (open, friendly, kindly) from the Japanese (arrogant and supercilious). Amid the racial frenzy, Roosevelt signed an executive order permitting military authorities to round up all Japanese, three-quarters of them American citizens, and deport them to what one congressman described as "inland concentration camps." It would take too long, said military authorities, to check out the potential subversives individually—a textbook case of illiberal thinking.

By all accounts, the camps were miserable. The cold, flimsy barracks offered few amenities and no privacy. Japanese Americans lost their liberty, their jobs, their property, and their bank accounts. Then military authorities arrived in camp and asked the inmates to sign loyalty oaths. Many resisted. They organized strikes, petitions, and mass meetings. Others tried to prove themselves by enlisting in the American army. After the war, Yale law professor Eugene Rostow lamented the roundup as "our worst wartime mistake"—a "sinister" and "reactionary" attack on basic rights that "enlarged the power of the military in relation to civilian authority." Of course, we did not just slip into Asian bashing in the frenzy of the war. The "terrible mistake," muses historian Howard Zinn, followed a long legacy of attacks against Asian Americans. The war just stimulated the old itch.[45]

Mexican Americans. Animosity toward Mexican Americans also surfaced during the war. The Hearst Press dreamed up a Mexican crime wave, splashed details across its front pages, and pummeled local police for their feeble response. National officials (from the Office of War Information) dashed out to the West Coast and reasoned with the publishers: race-baiting looked bad. The papers cheerfully complied with the letter of the message. No more criticizing Mexicans; instead they lashed the "zoot suiters." Eventually, Los Angeles responded. The city outlawed zoot suits in an effort to stamp out crime. The hounding boiled into a riot in the summer of 1943. A newspaper story alleged that a gang of "pauchos"—Mexican toughs—had beaten up a sailor. Thousands of soldiers and sailors poured through Los Angeles, attacking Mexican Americans while Anglo crowds gathered and cheered. The thugs stopped and searched streetcars for men and boys to attack; they ran wild through bars, movie theaters, and Mexican neighborhoods. The next day, the *Los Angeles Times* pictured beaten victims lying naked on the pavement. The police stood by.[46]

African Americans. World War II revolutionized the race line, partially by changing African American attitudes. Black troops fought bravely. Then they returned home to segregation. Walter White, the head of the NAACP, told a story that came in thousands of variations. His brother's family had worked hard so their son could graduate from college and go on to earn a master's degree in economics. The young man volunteered, became a fighter pilot, and was shot down over Anzio Beach. When his broken leg mended, he asked to go back into combat. Like many others, he flew bravely till his fighter was hit over Hungary and burst into flames before he could bail out. The mother and father of this war hero got more than a Purple Heart. They also got to hear men like Senator James Eastland of Mississippi run down black troops as "utter and dismal failures in the combat of Europe." White recalled watching black soldiers, fresh from combat in the Pacific, turn and head for home. "Our own fight for freedom will start," one young man told him, "the day we arrive in San Francisco."[47]

Race riots expressed the frustration. When a white cop shot a black military policeman in the shoulder, a riot erupted in Harlem that left 5 dead and 367 injured. In Detroit, race tension burst into a melee between white and black men. The rage ran out of control for three days, till Roosevelt declared a national emergency and sent in federal troops. The toll came to 34 dead.

During the war, the Roosevelt administration finally began to move against the lynch mobs. In 1942, Cleo Wright had been arrested in Missouri on suspicion of attempting to rape a white woman. In the scuffle with police, he was shot and badly wounded. As he lay dying in a jail cell, a crowd gathered. They weren't going to let him get away without serving as a lesson. The mob took Wright, tied him to a car, and dragged him to his house. There they forced his wife to look. Then, continuing in the familiar way, they forced black people to watch while they burned their victim—the same "terror and warning" that stretched back down the decades. But now, suddenly, the lynching sickness had a worldwide audience. The Japanese allegedly held up Wright's murder as a typical American attitude toward nonwhites. While the United States marched out to save the world, the lynch mobs made us look bad, even hypocritical. Finally—after more than 4,000 lynchings—the Justice Department stepped in and prosecuted the mob leaders. The accused were acquitted. But holding a trial at all marked progress. Things were changing now that the city on a hill had to worry about how it looked abroad.[48]

Each of these groups—Jews, Japanese Americans, Mexican Americans, and African Americans—challenged economic power or social status. In each case, a nation, defined by individual rights, turned on groups that allegedly threatened the good community. Jews came without jobs and threatened to become paupers. Asians remained strange, cruel, and subversive—they'd turn the West Coast over to the emperor (though no one thought the Italians would deliver South Philadelphia to Mussolini). Mexicans threatened violence—and, besides, jobs were scarce. And Cleo Wright had been accused of trying to rape a white woman as African Americans began pressing against the old race barriers.

For all the pain in the stories—and the long legacy that precedes them—the war moment marked another turning point, extending the New Deal's tentative progress. The Justice Department had finally intervened in a lynching case. National attention would soon focus on segregation. African American bravery would get harder to deny—desegregation in the real army would soon catch up to Hollywood's movie platoons. Meanwhile, another federal agency, the Office of War Information, was protesting Latino bashing. "Our worse mistake" would cap a century of virulent anti-Asian racism that now, finally, came to a shameful end (and would soon segue into a whole generation of new stereotypes featuring, among others, the model minority). Postwar quotas for displaced persons opened the American door to tens of thousands of Holocaust survivors. The postwar shifts offered no comfort for millions of victims, of course, but they signaled tectonic shifts in the American iconography of us and them. Polite anti-Semitism became a contradiction in terms. The same, eventually, with polite racism. Constant concern about international opinion profoundly shaped American attitudes toward one another. There would still be sinners and enemies, but postwar America would start looking for witches in very different places.

A New Moral Frame

The 1930s roiled with economic anxiety, class struggle, and New Deal frenzy. In contrast, religion faltered and traditional morality seemed to fade right out of politics. Personal behavior no longer held deep (much less dire) consequences for the republic. The Democrats returned drinking to the private sector—or to the state and local governments. The courts began dismantling the old Comstock sex rules, and they would continue backing out of bedrooms, libraries, and movie theaters for the next forty years. When alarmed Americans called for new controls in the 1950s, they found the courts and government agencies tilted against them—latter-day Comstocks would not find any institutional foothold.

Instead, the old fervor rushed into the public sphere. Economic issues—fairness, inequality, hard times, self-interest—turned moral. The Roosevelt rhetorical formula hailed religion as another foundation for social justice, another call to communal duty. In that context, the ancient political divisions—race, class, gender—briefly lost their moral freight. Roosevelt's rhetoric mixed calls to moral duty with modern medical metaphors; old sins (like laziness) turned into public health problems (like poverty). The new piety demanded public action against private suffering. World War II resurrected the city on a hill. The virtuous people—free from want (thanks to the combined efforts of government and industry) and free from fear (thanks to rising American might)—marched out to save the world. Wartime restored the hard lines between us and them. The new enemy, of course, lurked abroad; but anxiety about subversives seeped into home soil. The fears that first lashed out against Japanese Americans would soon turn on subversive Communists.

Finally, the Roosevelt administrations left behind a powerful moral legacy operating in the institutions that rose (or fell) on its watch: Victorian morality controls disintegrated; a robust, unruly, chaotic social welfare state spread; and a formidable military establishment grew. The next generation of moral crusaders faced a radically new political framework—some sins would fit in a lot more easily than others.

Chapter 13

Manifest Destiny and the
Cold War

THE gates swung open and the GIs from the 442nd Division got a look at the Dachau concentration camp. Men and women, more dead than alive, heads shaved, half starved, and almost skeletons. The American soldiers would tell stories—still hard to fathom more than a half-century later—about warm ovens and neatly stacked chalk bars stamped with numbers. As the troops filtered through the camp, one confused prisoner stopped a GI and asked, skeptically, whether he was really an American. The soldier was Nisei—born in America of Japanese parents and recruited into the Army from an internment camp. He looked at the haggard survivor. "I am an American soldier," he said, "and you are free."[1]

The Nisei became American. So did the children of the European immigrants—they had lost their hyphenated identity by the war's end. America's enemies rewrote "them" and "us." The image behind those Dachau gates—radical evil, sin, holocaust—seeped into the American view of the next foreign peril, Communism. Americans held up their own faith as an inspiration for the rest of the world. A new national motto—"In God We Trust"—now showed everyone the difference between us and them.

As the cold war developed, the fear of hidden enemies struck again. Congress first sounded the alarm and set off a wild, national scramble to expose the Communists in our midst. The United States roiled with rumors of traitors. True to form, the panic ran its course and left behind powerful government organizations—this time, a national security state that grew up alongside the New Deal welfare state. At the same time, an urge to bolster the nation's moral fiber by going back to the old virtues got frustrated by the courts and buried in the popular culture. Instead, the old Social Gospel was drafted for a new job: saving the world for democracy.[2]

Cold War

The fight against Communism settled into the cultural bones. It turned up everywhere. Brewers peddled beer with ads celebrating "this friendly, freedom-loving land." When Macy's department store urged New Yorkers not to hoard goods, the newsweeklies leaped on the story with a whoop for the American business that advised shoppers to buy less: "Wonder what Stalin and company would make of this example of predatory capitalism. . . . Well done, Macy's!" The news from foreign hotspots came with patronizing sermonettes about doing your geography homework: "To most Americans, Kasmir is . . . strange and remote . . . but it should be a matter of very deep concern." Writers plundered history for dire precedents. Two nations go to war across the 38th parallel; a "great democracy, rich in freedom" versus a "powerful police state . . . insulated against the outer world." No, not the United States facing Communists in Korea (where the 38th parallel divides North from South), but Athens fighting Sparta. Athens failed to rally its dithering allies, "lost its nerve and purpose," and perished.[3]

At times, the cold-war angle turned silly. In 1950, an American hustler went off to Europe with two roller derby teams. One represented the United States, the other pretended to be a local team. The Americans cheated like carnival bullies, kicking and punching their ostensibly European rivals. The French practically rioted, reported *Life*, when an "American" stomped on the "French" skater she had maliciously tripped. The State Department rebuked the fast-buck artist for fostering trouble with our allies. What would happen, asked the magazine, if we had to call on France to fight alongside us after the roller derby debacle?

The French particularly perplexed the United States. "While Americans have no doubt that to be a Communist is un-American, millions of Frenchmen do not consider it un-French. How can this be so?" *Life* printed a long story in search of an answer. After the usual exhortations to brush up on civics ("This is necessary for Americans to understand"), the magazine dug up the red mayor of St. Junien for a colorful Gallic shrug: "Let all the systems be tried. It's like cooking—in the end, the people always choose the best dish." Impossible, huffed the magazine—those foolish, facile, French.[4]

Humorist Art Buchwald gave the same story a different spin by telling it through the eyes of an imaginary Frenchman who goes on American TV to explain his nation's views. He immediately gets hit with the obvious question, "Will the French fight?" Before he can answer, the interviewer follows up with "Why are all you Frenchmen Communists?" Before he can deny it, she rattles a string of questions at him: Aren't American women prettier than French women? The men nicer? Soap better? Wine preferable? Seasoning tastier? Fabrics more inspiring? Fruit juice healthier? Floor wax superior? The Frenchman finally gets it—he is just an advertising foil. In the course of a one-page column, our beleaguered Frenchman faces American cultural bombast, Communist bashing, and manic capitalism.[5]

The Moral Contest

The cold war was no place for a genteel marketplace of ideas. The United States was locked in a titanic moral contest between good and evil. Secretary of State John Foster Dulles put it bluntly in 1954: "There can be no coexistence between the free world and the Communist world." Communism was evil, and merely containing it "tantamount to sin." He called China "fanatically hostile," "aggressive," and "treacherous." Dulles plugged right into the Puritan legacy; he was the son of a Presbyterian minister and—as one historian puts it—a "twentieth-century Calvinist carved in the mold of a seventeenth-century English roundhead." Critics tagged his moralizing "dull, duller, Dulles." Even when the secretary went to Congress for a simple increase in foreign economic aid he managed a Sunday sermon: "The American people believe in a moral law and in the concept of the brotherhood of man." A special issue on Christianity offered *Life* magazine a chance to echo the secretary: "It seems pretty clear that Communism is Satan in action, to be resisted by all means at all times." The United States reverberated with covenant, mission, and manifest destiny.[6]

The crusade stirred critics. George Kennan, the best-known strategic thinker of the era, blasted the impulse to read international affairs as right versus wrong. State behavior, he wrote, is not a fit subject for moral judgment. Invoking moral law arouses indignity against law-breakers, and when "indignation spills over into a military contest, it knows no bounds short of . . . total domination." Ironically, "high moral principle . . . makes violence more enduring, more terrible and more destructive to political stability."[7]

Theologians agreed. A Unitarian group reminded Dulles that coexistence with the Soviets was already an established historical fact. Reinhold Niebuhr—a "hawk-nosed, top-flight theologian," according to *Time* magazine—warned Americans not to "identify our particular brand of democracy with the ultimate values of life" or "to give a false and idolatrous religious note to the conflict between democracy and communism." A prestigious generation of religious thinkers—Paul Tillich, Reinhold Niebuhr, Richard Niebuhr—resisted drafting God into our side of the cold war. The strong voices reminded Americans of human frailty and sin. At the heart of their theology, known as neo-orthodoxy, lay a demanding existentialism reverberating with irony, paradox, and historical contingency. Reinhold Niebuhr quoted Søren Kierkegaard to sum up the modern condition: "treading water with 10,000 fathoms beneath us." These theologians were hardly doves or pacifists. Rather, they rewrote the Social Gospel for a cold war marked by institutionalized power and human depravity in every camp. The international struggle, wrote Niebuhr, must proceed with "awe," "modesty," and "contrition." "Human frailties and foibles lie at the foundation of both the enemy's demonry and our own vanities."[8]

But this was hard advice, easily brushed aside. We were on God's side (and vice versa, surely). Soviet blasphemies had been a back-page staple in the press for decades: Moscow silenced its beautiful church bells by sending them to the foundries, commissariats turned children into atheists, Russian peasants burned their icons, Soviet art shoved aside religion. During the 1930s, churchmen seasoned the stories about the Soviets with alarm about our own failing faith. World War II ended those worries.

"The change in a generation is enough to make wiseacres blink," chortled *Time* magazine. Back in the 1930s, the "up to date intellectual was so uninterested in Christianity, that he rarely found it worth while even to be anti-religious." "Today, the Christian faith is back in the center of things." Membership in U.S. churches had risen 70 percent in a generation, and religious identification had reached an all-time high. Not only had the people got religion, but the secularist, the atheist, and the free thinkers had practically vanished from our midst.[9]

The popular religion of the 1950s looked like a free-floating mix of God, patriotism, and the American way. President Eisenhower summed it up perfectly: "Our government makes no sense unless it is founded on a deeply held religious faith—and I don't care what it is." Historians often scoff at such fatuous 1950s piety. But, taken in context, Eisenhower made complete sense. This was no time to be squabbling about Darwin or the pope or the historical Jesus or the Second Coming. The world split into God-fearing good people and godless Communists. Faith of any sort underscored the nation's transcendent goodness in its battle for the world.[10]

The American faith won a flurry of political endorsements. The most popular flashed through Congress in May 1954. It was an eventful month. On May 17 the Supreme Court announced its decision in *Brown v. Board of Education* (striking down segregated schools), which was immediately recognized as one of the most important rulings in American constitutional history. Meanwhile, the saga of Senator Joe McCarthy dominated the front pages as the Army-McCarthy hearings headed toward their climax. Despite all that drama, reported the *New York Times*, Congress was "flooded with mail" on a completely different issue: the Pledge of Allegiance.[11]

The Reverend George Docherty, the pastor of President Eisenhower's Presbyterian church, got the matter rolling when he challenged the pledge. There is nothing American about the Pledge of Allegiance, he said one Sunday. It could be repeated in any nation. Docherty imagined "little Muscovites repeating a similar pledge to their hammer-and-sickle flag." After all, "Russia is also a republic . . . that claims to be indivisible." Let's tell it the American way, he suggested, by adding "under God" to our pledge of allegiance.[12]

Americans loved it. The Senate unanimously pushed through the change. In the House, Representative Louis Rabaut (D-Michigan) elbowed aside fourteen other pledge resolutions and managed to steer his version to a floor vote. Controversy erupted only over whether the Senate sponsor, Homer Ferguson (R-Michigan) would share the credit with Rabaut. The men settled their differences by standing shoulder to shoulder and reciting the new pledge in unison as President Eisenhower signed the bill.[13]

The president cheered the nation's moral rearmament. By reaffirming America's religious faith, he said, we "strengthen those spiritual weapons which forever will be our country's most powerful resource, in peace or in war." The president offered his country a grand moral image: millions of schoolchildren, across America, chanting "One nation, under God" every day of the week.[14]

The Post Office pitched in with a new stamp. Around the Statue of Liberty ran the words "In God We Trust." The stamp, for international mail, was a "postal ambassador" to the rest of the world, flying out at the rate of about 200 million a year. The Post Office launched this moral envoy with what the postmaster general hailed as the "biggest ceremony of its kind in the history of the United States Post Office Department." Just to be sure no one missed the cold-war subtext, President Eisenhower and Secretary of State Dulles spoke at the ceremony, which was carried live on both radio and television.[15]

Sharp eyes might have seen hints of trouble in the city on a hill. The same day Congress approved the new pledge, the Florida Cabinet declared an "emergency" and allocated $10,000 to protect its citizens. This disaster was man-made: the Supreme Court ruling against segregated schools. "Florida is not ready," explained the state attorney general, who planned to spend the emergency funds to protest the *Brown* decision. "One nation, under God, indivisible, with liberty and justice for all" remained a work in progress.[16]

Ironically, the flag-waving actually undermined serious religious fervor. American religion celebrated a kind of patriotic belief in God. In one poll, taken at the height of the revival, the "most significant event in world history" turned out to be Columbus's discovery of America. Jesus Christ's birth and crucifixion (combined) tied for fourteenth place, along with the flight of the *Kitty Hawk* and the discovery of the X-ray. *Life* magazine unwittingly illustrated the same point in its Christianity issue. "Few educated Westerners have taken the Devil seriously for many years," it reported, "but he does exist. Where? In Communism, of course. Getting beyond politics, the magazine could manage only this: "The challenge . . . to Christianity today is the temptation, amid so much health and comfort, to settle for less than . . . (in Paul Tillich's words) 'the inner aim of life.' " The inner aim of life? The magazine had conjured up a modern wimp of a devil.[17]

Of course, many people professed more muscular faiths, but they did so far from the mainstream. The strong stuff did not make a useful emblem for the American Way. When *Life* featured twelve "top" Protestant congregations, it slipped in little asides hinting at more robust religion. Take the peppy description of Bellevue Baptist in Memphis: "Dr. Robert C. Lee, who was born in a log cabin and preaches a hell-fire brand of fundamentalism famous in the South"—after that brief glimpse at evangelical hellfire, *Life*'s sentence scampers cheerfully along—"is also president of the Southern Baptist Convention [and] turns back half his church salary to Bellevue." Real fundamentalists held inconvenient beliefs: they spurned ecumenical calls, wrestled with ferocious devils, and proclaimed just one path to salvation. *Life* played Lee's hellfire fundamentalism as just another touch of southern color. It did not ripple the smooth consensus—God, flag, freedom—that Americans all shared.[18]

Billy Graham rolled into this polite consensus with a gentler evangelicalism perfectly geared for the time. "The hot gospel played a major part in the making of America," revealed *Time*. But "upper crust Christians" had always turned up their noses at the "sweaty urgency of evangelistic Christians." Graham was different. "He always looked immaculately pressed and groomed." The format had not changed since Jonathan Edwards. First, the dire warning: "I am a Western Union boy! I have a death message! I must tell you plainly—you are going to Hell! You listen! Don't you trifle with God! You are a sinner! Your punishment is sure!" And then the promise of grace. "You can leave here with peace and joy and happiness such as you've never known. . . . You can only come to Christ when the Spirit of God is drawing and wooing you." Finally, Graham's trademark call to come forward to say, " 'Billy, tonight I accept Christ.' "[19]

But Graham's Madison Square Garden revivals lay light-years from Lorenzo Dow's Kentucky tree stumps. Graham backed his sermons with a well-oiled organization. When people felt the spirit and came forward, ushers handed them to one of 4,000 counselors who led them backstage, advised them, and filled out a card. (Check a box: "acceptance of Christ as savior," "reaffirmation of faith," "dedication of life.") Then the inspired Christian was smoothly passed on to a local church—roughly a third were new converts.

Graham became immensely popular with his colleagues around the nation. He grew into the dominant figure in the New Evangelicalism—a smoother evangelical form that tolerated minor doctrinal differences and did not come with the low boiling point of the traditional fundamentalists.

With great fanfare, the preacher took his mission abroad. People packed into foreign stadiums—raising their hands, coming forward, accepting this American's version of the lord. In London's Wembley Stadium, Graham drew 120,000 people. "Who knows" what might be the "long-term effect on Britain's anemic religious life?" gushed *Time,* but the "clergy of England are warmly grateful." Graham appeared to be a formidable weapon in the American arsenal, vigorously mixing personal salvation and cold-war politics. "Communism is a religion inspired, directed, and motivated by the Devil himself who has declared war against Almighty God." We would win this war with evil just the way we had won the last one: "God's people prayed."[20]

Graham found critics both abroad and at home. When the crusade got to Nairobi, Sheikh Mubarak Ahmad challenged Graham to a faith-healing contest. Let the world see whose prayers could heal more incurables. Graham let that gauntlet lie. Meanwhile, back home, some Roman Catholics were admonished to pass on Graham's revivals. And intellectuals dismissed Graham as just another evangelical embarrassment. "A hick and a huckster," remembers Richard Wrightman Fox, "whose prime aspiration was to graze with presidents on lush fairways." Serious religion meant wrestling with the moral ironies of Paul Tillich or Reinhold Niebuhr (who scoffed at Graham's fundamentalism, "too simple in any age, but particularly in a nuclear one with its great moral perplexities"). But the New Evangelicals would eventually bury the sophisticated liberals and their struggle—so modern looking back in the 1950s—to sanctify the secular. A full half-century later, one supermarket tabloid splashed a message from the ailing Billy Graham across its front page: his latest vision of the apocalypse is "the most terrifying ever!" And inside, "Jesus is coming sooner than you think!" By the turn of the century, Graham and his evangelical standards had soaked deep into American popular culture. His last millennial prophesies reached back—in style and tone—to the postwar era, when the New World Athens clung to God and fought for its life.[21]

Red Scare

The war for the world stirred deep anxiety. Starting in the late 1940s, Hollywood cranked out hundreds of anti-Communist films. One after another, they pictured an insidious, invisible enemy slipping into the nation. In *The Invasion of the Body Snatchers* (1956), a strange power steals over people—seizes their bodies—and turns them into automatons. In *The Manchurian Candidate*

(1962), the Chinese brainwash the protagonist, who goes into a trance and blindly does whatever he is told whenever he sees the queen of diamonds; it's all a plot (masterminded by his mom) to deliver the United States to the Communists. In these paranoid visions, national victory and defeat pass from the public sphere into the private. The unseen enemy infiltrates American hearts and minds. The nation will endure only if its people stay strong and virtuous. National survival rests on that fundamental Puritan precept: control thyself.[22]

In this setting, good citizenship meant social conformity. Hollywood flirted with gangster romances back in the 1930s. Not any more. Peter Biskind illustrates the breadth of the impulse by comparing three completely different films: *Broken Arrow* (1950) was a western; *Blackboard Jungle* (1955) featured juvenile delinquents; and *On the Waterfront* (1954) told a story about the mob down at the docks. But "whether they were dealing with delinquents, dock workers or Indians, they all set out to solve the same problem: social control." It's up to each man and woman to enforce the rules, to stop his or her own people from subverting a group's values. In *On the Waterfront,* for example, Marlon Brando's Terry Malloy turns from punk to hero by ratting out his corrupt friends. A tough priest pushed him to do the right thing. Director Elia Kazan had himself been before Congress, naming Communist names. Then he made this brilliant parable of a hero who stands up and fights for decency by spilling everything to the authorities. In another era they would have called Malloy a stool pigeon.[23]

Social control demanded the familiar. This was no time for strange, foreign notions. "Did you ever shop for dinner in Paris?" asks a 1951 magazine advertisement pitched to a middle-class audience that surely had not. "Even if you parlay-voo like a native, you get a queer, lost feeling the first time you go marketing in a foreign country." The shelves are filled with strange stuff, "and you haven't the faintest idea which are good, which are so-so and which won't satisfy you at all. And if, by chance, you happen to see a familiar American brand among the strangers—well take our word for it, you embrace it like an old friend! The American system of brand names makes life easier—and safer too."[24]

Strange foreign products might endanger the family. During the New Deal, American housewives were supposed to punish the selfish capitalists who spurned the blue eagle. That housewife still stands guard, but the blue eagle has melted into any "familiar American brand." After all, the French shopkeeper in the beret looks like a jolly fellow. But who could tell? He waves a weird little price sticker at the buyer. What does that number mean? Is he honest? Is it safe? Who knows?

Only strong Americans would resist perilous foreign ideas. "The trouble is inside you," Dr. Miles Bennell tells one woman in *The Invasion of the Body*

→ Did you ever shop for dinner in Paris?

Even if you parlay-voo like a native, you get a queer, lost feeling the first time you go marketing in a foreign country.

You look at the shelves filled with strange goods, and not one of them means anything to you. And you haven't the faintest idea which are good, and which are so-so, and which won't satisfy *you* at all.

And if, by chance, you happen to see a familiar American brand among the strangers—well, take our word for it, you embrace it like an old, old friend!

There's nothing like a little travel to make you realize how our American system of brand names makes life easier and pleasanter—and safer, too.

Here at home, when a manufacturer develops a product

he thinks you'll like, he puts his name on it—big and clear and proud. You try it, and if it doesn't suit you, you know what not to get the next time. And if it does please you, you can buy it again with the certainty that it will be just as good . . . because the manufacturer can't afford to let his brand name down.

Brand names give you the wonderful power of taking it or leaving it alone. And that power—a force as mighty as your right to vote —is what keeps manufacturers vying with each other for your favor . . . making their products better and better . . . offering you more and more for your money.

So make use of your power of choice to get what you want. Know your brands—and study the ads on these pages. That way you will get what pleases you best—again and again and again.

Whenever you buy—
    demand the brand you want

Brand Names Foundation
INCORPORATED
A non-profit educational foundation
37 WEST 57 STREET, NEW YORK 19, N. Y.

103

13.1. A magazine advertisement from 1951 celebrated brand names. Good old familiar American products are a lot safer than the strange stuff in this Parisian store. You had to be careful with foreign goods—and ideas.

Snatchers. It would be a woman. Cold-war anxiety brought ancient gender fears rushing back to the cultural surface. Once again Eve became the weak link. In the past, dangerous races threatened to use American women to insinuate their way into the mainstream, to sneak from them to us. But cold-war danger emanated from distant enemies through their ideologies. Now Eve would subvert the American Eden by making us too weak to resist.

Mothers were the problem. Like the Athenians in *Life*'s decline parable, American men were getting weak, flabby, effeminate. Philip Wylie's *Generation of Vipers*—an offensive, frantically written, barely coherent, highly popular rant—concocted the basic charge: in the old days, "mom had been so busy raising a large family, keeping house [and] doing the chores . . . that she was rarely a problem to her family." But now, modern life leaves her nothing to do. "Every clattering prickamette in the republic survives for an incredible number of years, to stamp and jibber in the midst of man, a noisy neuter . . . all tongue and teat and razzmatazz." With her iron grip she threatens to render every American male a mama's boy, if not a full-fledged homosexual. And yet the culture still worships Mom. She has been elevated alongside the Bible and the flag (no mention of apple pie). Wylie was here to open men's eyes. "Gentlemen," he sums up in *Vipers*, "mom is a jerk." Wylie managed to whip this misogyny into a best seller.[25]

The fear filtered into middle-class discourse. When *Life* did a special issue titled "The American Woman" in 1956, the editors plunged right into momism: "The American woman is often discussed as a problem to herself and others. Has she become too dominant in our society, joylessly raising an infantile breed of men?" Fifteen years later this castrating virago would return, not as mom but as feminist. Looking back to the 1950s, contemporary Americans imagine a golden era of father-knows-best and family values. But, back then, *Life* bluntly summed up a completely different consensus: "In America the family is in special trouble." J. Edgar Hoover, the FBI's director, had offered precisely the same warning earlier in the year. "Unfortunately, the home no longer provides the inspiration for right living," he told a Catholic women's group, "The result is a juvenile jungle." The answer lay in a stronger family life. And better families—*Life* and Hoover agreed—meant more attention to child rearing and more faith in God. Children "need the firm moral backing of . . . a good Christian home," said Hoover. "Strong morals" stand as the "major obstacles in the path of communist progress."[26]

Manliness, family values, Communism, and the "American woman" all got tangled together. During the war many women had taken manufacturing jobs vacated by men. In the 1950s, with a lot less fanfare, many women went back to work, though not to the same jobs. By 1955 the percentage of working females had surpassed the World War II figure; by 1960 the number had reached one in three. But reality did not jibe with the rules. Proper gender roles did not include working women. "If a mother realizes clearly how vital [her] . . . care is to a small child," advised baby doctor Benjamin Spock, "it may make it easier for her to decide that the money she might earn or the satisfaction she might receive from an outside job is not so important at all." Woman felt the stress in silence. The role tensions operated quietly, uncontested. In the next decade, a new wave of feminists would politicize the issue. But in the 1950s the popular analyses ran to hand-wringing editorials about rotten families or to fretting about overbearing moms and their sissy boys. The 1950s jeremiads rang out from movies, magazines, speeches, sermons, and best sellers: flabby men—a morally weak nation—would be easy pickings for the hard, strong Communists.[27]

Witch-Hunt!

Americans fought two different wars against Communism. As historian Robert Wiebe puts it, one confronted the Soviets, the other combated sin. Containing Communism became a moral cause, and the moral cause incited a witch-hunt.[28]

Witch-hunters chase real witches, and the late 1940s was no exception. The Soviet Union bristled with hostility. The Communist Party (CP) in the United States remained dedicated to Moscow; former allies bitterly criticized the CP's unwavering Stalinism. The Communists made things worse by exacting complete secrecy from their members—the perfect strategy for drumming up paranoia.

What turned anti-Communism into hysteria? American witch-hunts generally share four features. First, the hunters violate their own society's norms. They rely on apparitions (in 1691) or hearsay (in 1950); panicked hunters trample the most basic rights as they root out and crush their demons. Second, the boundary between guilt and innocence blurs. The evildoers might be anyone, anywhere. The authorities immediately leap after unpopular groups—and then they keep right on going, chasing ever less plausible miscreants. The delirium breaks after the charges become outrageous. (They call the governor's wife a witch or the U.S. Army soft on reds.) Third, people ascribe setbacks (a stillborn cow, the fall of China) not to a messy real world but to the malice of the neighborhood witch. Finally, buried in the panic glints cold political calculation. During the red scares, brazen political self-interest fed the frenzy.

In spring 1947, the Republicans seized control of Congress after sixteen years in the New Deal wilderness. The new speaker, Joseph Martin, promptly warned about "subversionists high up in the government." The House Un-American Activities Committee (HUAC), organized in the 1930s to keep an eye on Nazis, now went after leftists. It began with an attack on Hollywood. Shooting at the stars guaranteed a boxoffice smash.

Why the movies? Ronald Reagan later explained. "We had a weekly audience of about 500,000 souls." Transforming this enormous plant "into a Communist grist mill . . . would have been a magnificent coup for our enemies." Hollywood had become highly political—Communists, leftists, and liberals had worked together since 1935, united by depression, idealism, and loyalty to FDR. But they never really influenced the product. The idea, comments Michael Rogin, was nothing short of delusional. What Hollywood really represented was the New Deal—left-leaning labor militants with loose morals. The committee members stood, in contrast, for old-fashioned, small-town, conservative American values. The Jeremiahs got right down to the familiar business of blasting the media for corrupting our principles.[29]

Eric Johnson, the new president of the Motion Picture Producers Association, championed the committee's vision of the American Way: "We'll have no more *Grapes of Wrath*. We'll have no more films that show the seamy side of American life. We'll have no pictures that deal with labor strikes [or] . . . the banker as villain." Writer Ayn Rand pitched in with new cinema guidelines. Don't smear the free enterprise system, don't deify the common man. The cultural counterrevolutionaries saw pink everywhere. Take *The Best Years of Our Lives* (which won the Oscar for best film in 1946); the protagonist, played by Fredric March, attacks bankers for not lending money to servicemen—a nasty, Communistic attitude toward our free-enterprise banking system, charged the rising critics.[30]

National anxiety gave the culture war its force. "The Communist menace in America is no myth," said HUAC chairman J. Parnell Thomas. "This [is a] Moscow directed fifth column. This [is a] foreign conspiracy." The committee tore into its witnesses. Were they Communists? Left-leaning fellow travelers? Had they ever been? As with the original Salem Village witch-hunt, you could help yourself by confessing and naming names. Hidden enemies always put a premium on baring all and betraying others.[31]

Some stars—Ronald Reagan, Gary Cooper, Ayn Rand, Elia Kazan—came forward eagerly, pointing fingers. Kazan made the classic witch-hunt submission. He repudiated his leftist past, proclaimed his shame, and sold out his friends. Many others resisted. Arthur Miller confessed his own sins but stayed mum about others'. In 1953 he wrote *The Crucible*, a parable of the red scare set during the Salem witch trials. Under pressure from the relentless magistrate, Miller's agonized protagonist refuses to save his life by naming names:

"I speak my own sins; I cannot judge another. I have no tongue for it. . . . I have three children, how may I teach them to walk like men in the world, and I sold my friends?" Humphrey Bogart, sporting a dapper bow tie, led a delegation of dissenters, including Lauren Bacall, Danny Kaye, Jane Wyatt, and Ira Gershwin. The investigation, they argued, violated the First Amendment. The liberals stood up for the New Deal. More important, they made the case that lasted: HUAC's assault on dissenters seemed—seems—more un-American than anything their victims ever did.[32]

But the panic grew. Popular support for Bogart and free speech got shaken by hostile Hollywood witnesses who refused to answer questions. Some argued bitterly with committee members. Hollywood activists skulking behind the Fifth Amendment made headlines. The movie industry developed its notorious "blacklist"—repudiating a long roll of men and women who refused to testify or would not name names or got cited for contempt or ended up splattered with mud as the hearings went on. Frightened moviemakers drove some 500 colleagues out of the business. Many never got back in.

On one level, HUAC's cultural assault succeeded. The red scare chilled leftist thinking and writing for a decade. Many celebrated writers and artists ran into trouble: Charlie Chaplin, Zero Mostel, Ring Lardner, Jr., Leonard Bernstein, Aaron Copland, Orson Welles, Frank Capra, Paul Robeson. I watched, writes publisher André Schiffrin, the "near disappearance from American life of dissident and progressive points of view." In 1962, eight years after the purge had ended, Schiffrin proposed publishing a book by liberal journalist I. F. Stone. As Schiffrin tells the story, his colleagues nervously squirmed before bleating, "We could never take on anything so controversial."[33]

Hollywood was just the start of the search for Communists. The Chamber of Commerce pitched in with its "campaign to oust reds in U.S. Posts." Francis Cardinal Spellman, archbishop of New York, warned his flock of "Communist conquest and annihilation" by "sinister, scheming . . . pseudo Americans." The Catholic church had truly broken through the old nativism, comments David Bennett, when it could so comfortably glide to the right side of the us-them barrier.

The Truman administration jumped into the action, queasy about getting branded soft on Communists. The administration organized a Loyalty Review Board (in 1946), which investigated 4 million government employees in the next five years. Hundreds got dismissed, thousands resigned. The agents uncovered plenty of "unsuitables"—alcoholics, adulterers, and homosexuals— but scarcely a Communist in the bunch. A shoeblack working in the State Department basement faced repeated interviews because he had sent $10 to a defense fund for the "Scottsboro boys," a celebrated cause featuring young black men dubiously accused of the usual southern atrocity. Undeterred, Democratic Attorney General J. Howard McGrath tossed fuel onto the fire: "Today there are many Communists in America . . . they are everywhere . . . in factories, offices, butcher shops, street corners, in private businesses." He sounded like Cotton Mather describing the devils in Salem Village: "they swarm about us like the frogs of Egypt."[34]

Investigations, loyalty oaths, and blacklists spread. Administrators trained the spotlight on the classroom. The State Regents gave University of California faculty two months to sign a loyalty oath or quit. Intellectuals like Albert Einstein urged the teachers to stand up for free speech. About a fifth of the faculty anguished between their jobs and their convictions, but most submitted. In New York, school administrators fired more than three hundred teachers and fifty-eight college professors. The trauma of the assault on free speech and free thinking—especially in institutions dedicated to speech and thought—eventually yielded an ironic consequence: fervent, even moralistic, support for the tenure system.[35]

States put anti-red laws on the books. Thirty-nine states prohibited residents from advocating the violent overthrow of the government. Texas made membership in the Communist party a felony punishable by up to twenty years in jail. One town required a loyalty oath for a fishing license. Indiana required oaths of allegiance from professional wrestlers. Professional associations—for lawyers, physicians, teachers—proposed political tests for members.

The red scare compounded anxiety about America's moral strength. When investigations turned up "unsuitable" gays, the inquisitors expanded the scope of their outrage. "Sexual perverts . . . have infiltrated our government," wrote the Republican national chairman to his workers, and they are "perhaps as dangerous as the actual communists." Senator Kenneth Wherry called for a full investigation. "You can't hardly separate homosexuals from subversives. . . . A man of low morality is a menace in the government." Wherry called for strong action to secure "seaports and major cities" against the "conspiracy of subversives and moral perverts." The *New York Daily News* warned about the "all-powerful, super-secret, inner circle of highly educated . . . sexual misfits in the State Department . . . all highly susceptible to blandishments by homosexuals in foreign nations." Billy Graham praised the vigilant Americans who were busy "exposing the pinks, the lavenders, and the reds who have sought refuge beneath the wings of the American Eagle."[36]

In April 1953, an executive order barred gay men and lesbians from federal jobs. Many towns and cities also cracked down, flourishing variations of the "perverts subvert our character" motif. The sexual subversives menaced family and country by neutering American males. The skulking Communist and the stealthy pervert ran together—both spread their contagions. One "prancing minion of the Moscow party line"—like a single rotten apple—could spoil a whole office. The image of the gay man stood as the antipode of the strong American male holding the line against foreign danger.[37]

The Red Scare got really hot in early 1950. Bad news buffeted the United States. China had fallen to Communists in August 1949. The Soviets had tested the atomic bomb in September. In February 1950, a scientist who had worked on the Manhattan Project confessed to passing secrets. He named names. Only days later, North Korea attacked the south. The nation had already felt besieged, and now this extraordinary collection of troubles came crashing in.

Right on cue, Senator Joe McCarthy barged onto the jittery national scene. On February 9, 1950, the disheveled, disorganized, canny, crude, tough, boozy Wisconsin senator addressed the Republican Women's Club of Wheeling, West Virginia. Talking out there in the political wilderness, McCarthy began with the obvious. Things looked bad. Six years ago the Soviet orbit had 180 million people; our side counted 1.6 billion. "Today, only six years later, there are 800 million under the absolute domination of Soviet Russia. . . . In less than six years the odds have changed from nine to one in our favor to eight to five against us." Why had we fallen to such "impotency"? Simple. Rich boys, "with silver spoons in their mouths," had sold us out. And then McCarthy dropped his bomb: "I have in my hand 205 cases of individuals who would appear to be either card-carrying members or certainly loyal to the communist party who nevertheless are still helping to shape our foreign policy."[38]

McCarthy never got the number straight. The next day, 205 turned to 57. Later to 81. Or was it just 4? Reporters clamored for a single number or a name. He never actually showed anyone any lists, but he roiled the political scene with charges. McCarthy ripped through "Truman's iron curtain of secrecy." He shook up the "privileged, sissified, State Department," full of "egg-sucking phony liberals" who "hold sacrosanct those Communists and queers." And that went double for the guys at the top, like Secretary Dean Acheson, the "Red Dean of Fashion," with his "lace handkerchief, silk glove, and . . . Harvard accent." Anti-Communists flocked to McCarthy's side, sharing information, dossiers, files, and rumors. When critics pressed him for details, he plucked names out of the files and revealed the "spies," "stooges," or "masterminds." McCarthy slid from charge to charge, airily referring to "classified" secrets. He got into a fistfight with columnist Drew Person (broken up by that righteous Quaker Richard Nixon). He outraged liberals. "The sewers of our public life burst," railed columnist Joseph Alsop, "and the accumulated filth was flowing in the streets." McCarthy did not mind rough handling. He gave as good as he got, amplifying the fervent American cry against Communist corruption. "If you want to be against McCarthy, boys," he told the news hounds, "you've got to be either a Communist or a cocksucker."[39]

The Democrats had won back control of Congress in the 1948 election. They quickly tried to pin McCarthy. Senator Millard Tydings (D-Maryland) used his subcommittee of the Senate Foreign Relations Committee to investigate McCarthy's allegations. Acid proceedings yielded a blistering report: "We have seen the character of private citizens and government employees virtually destroyed by public condemnation on the basis of gossip, hearsay and deliberate untruths." They called McCarthy a "fraud" and a "hoax." Seven Republicans signed a declaration repudiating his "political exploitation of fear, bigotry, ignorance and intolerance," which posed the true threat to the "American way of life." But McCarthy rolled over the critics, sowing accusations and reaping headlines. Sympathetic newspapers scorned the "Tydings Report Whitewash." Another "green light to the Red Fifth Column in the United States," crowed the senator. McCarthy got the last word on this tormenter. He raised money and went to Maryland to campaign against Tydings. McCarthy circulated a faked photograph that made Tydings look like pals with former Communist Party leader Earl Browder. When Tydings lost his seat, McCarthy claimed the credit. Did he really make the difference? No matter. His colleagues became more chary about taking him on.

Raw partisan interest ran through the attacks. Robert Taft, the conservative Republican leader, advised McCarthy to keep talking. "If one case doesn't work out, proceed with another." Senator John Bricker urged on McCarthy with flattering guy talk: "You're a dirty son of a bitch, but there are times when you need a son of a bitch around and this is one of them." When the Republicans won back both Congress and the White House, in 1952, they no longer needed dirt on government officials—they now controlled the political establishment. The new majority shunted their son of a bitch to a nice boring committee. McCarthy rebelled: "We've only scratched the surface of Communism." He wrangled himself a permanent subcommittee from which to hunt for reds and then went too far. McCarthy hired a committee staff member who had unearthed the "largest single group supporting the Communist apparatus in the United States"—the Protestant clergy. The charge is often described as half mad; however, it actually reflected a hard-right critique of the Social Gospel preachers and the leftist implications of their creed. Still, no one heard the justifications. Public outrage buried his staff member, and Joe McCarthy moved on to even bigger game.[40]

McCarthy's subcommittee launched into its probe of the U.S. Army. "You're shielding communist conspirators," he told one brigadier general. "You are not fit to wear that uniform." The Army eventually shot back. It accused McCarthy of trying to win special treatment for David Schine, a young hotel heir who served as an unpaid consultant to McCarthy's committee. His own subcommittee now investigated its erstwhile chairman. A national television audience watched 188 hours of McCarthy's nasal, "points of order" and bare-knuckled attacks. "I'm glad we're on television," he sneered at Democrat Stuart Symington, so "millions of people . . . can see how low an alleged man can sink." Under stress, unshaven, drinking heavily, and perhaps not savvy about this new mass medium, McCarthy looked a mess and played a bully. *Time* magazine immediately picked out the decisive moment and correctly predicted that it would long be "remembered as the most memorable scene." As army counsel Joseph Welch doggedly pursued his case, McCarthy played his usual ace. Interrupting with a point of order, he suddenly went after a young col-league back at Welch's Boston law firm, Hale and Dorr; Fred Fisher had been a member of the National Lawyers' Guild, the "legal bulwark of the Communist Party." Welch had his famous answer prepared and smoothly drove it home. *Time* recounted the scene with all the flourishes of a mythic moment.

> Welsh slowly and with great sadness spoke up: "Until this moment, Senator, I think I never really gauged your cruelty and your recklessness. . . . Let us assas-sinate this lad no further. You have done enough. Have you no sense of decency, sir? At long last have you no sense of decency? If there is a God in heaven, it will do neither you nor your cause any good. . . ."
>
> There was a moment of profound silence, then a roll of thunderous ap-plause. . . . When the uproar had subsided, Joe Welsh, face drained white, rose from the committee table, silently walked past McCarthy and out into a corri-dor where he stood alone, dabbing at his eyes with a handkerchief.[41]

Joe McCarthy was through, the red scare over. Congress served up Mc-Carthy—voting to censure—as the anticommunist demagogue who had gone too far. But the scare had been going strong before he had bolted onto the scene. It stretched far beyond McCarthy or his party or Congress or Washing-ton, D.C. What, in the end, had this national trauma been about?

Early analysts saw an irrational American lynch mob. McCarthy had taken legitimate security concerns and blown them into a full-fledged witch-hunt. And the American public had fallen for it. Later, political scientists pointed at the political winners. Republicans had played astutely on the nation's fears, they said. McCarthy had effectively done their dirty work. Democrats would face taunts of being soft on communism for the next forty years.[42]

Still, the red paroxysm offered something deeper—a gut-level outcry against the New Deal, against the whole labor-friendly, leftist Social Gospel. How do you attack something as entrenched as the New Deal policy regime?

Every chapter of American moral politics yields the same answer: find an enemy. The HUAC attack began on Hollywood leftists and then rapidly spread. Americans once again found immoral others at the bottom of their anxieties. The lethal Communist idea—godless, perfidious, un-American—replaced the dissolute race or the dangerous ethnic group.

The red scare took an honest fear—there *were* Communists, and the Soviet Union *was* an implacable enemy—and pushed it into the rhetorical frame of the Puritan jeremiad. Echoing the old sermons, the red scare imagined a "horrible army of devils" swarming across the land (not to mention the State Department). Once again, the deeper problem lay not in hidden demons and traitors but in the ordinary men and women whose low morals hastened the Good Nation's decline. The postwar trouble ran to those spoiled, flabby, weak-willed Americans. Conservatives like Ayn Rand homed right in on the fountainhead of our troubles—the New Deal Social Gospel. The "virtue of the little people" looked like the "drooling of weaklings." Forget Roosevelt's harping about the Sermon on the Mount. Blessed are the peacemakers? The meek shall inherit the earth? Not a chance. The nation needed strong, virtuous, two-fisted citizens. Ultimately, the anti-Communists tried to wrench aside Roosevelt's nurturing moral vision and replace it with a stern conservative morality.

The New Deal survived. Its social welfare institutions held firm, and the Social Gospel prospered through the 1960s. In fact, the red scare stimulated its own opposite: an emphasis on personal rights. That roster of injured celebrities passed into popular culture as emblems of a national trauma, victims of a witch-hunt. Individual rights proliferated, almost as if piling on legal protections might blunt the angry mobs next time they set out to immolate American intellectual life.

Back in the 1690s, Cotton Mather had defended the Salem trials. After the delirium had passed, however, he diagnosed the underlying trouble: Invisible others make poor enemies. An uncertain them does not help unify an us. Instead, wrote Mather, we found ourselves "plunged into a blind man's buffet . . . hotly and madly mauling one another in the dark." That's the peril in every witch-hunt—that frenzied buffeting when fearful people turn on one another. Like the Salem Village original, this witch-hunt violated our principles of justice, ruined innocent lives, and spilled out into an ever-widening circle—from Communists to liberals to gays to Protestant ministers to the U.S. Army.

Still, each modern panic leaves behind institutional footprints. We watched the FBI get its big break from the white slave epidemic. Now the red scare consolidated the bureau's power. The agency penetrated deep into American society as it searched for Communists. Director J. Edgar Hoover managed an enormous network of informants—college students bullied into reporting on their classmates or Catholic leaders cooperating in the fight against Communism. "We want no Gestapo or secret police," complained President Truman privately, and "the FBI is tending in that direction. They are dabbling in sex life scandals and plain blackmail." The United States had entered World War II with relatively weak intelligence organizations; it emerged from the red scare with an extensive national security state. The cold war put a premium on intelligence gathering. The panic turned the spotlight inward. The urge to scrutinize government employees and shadow potential dissenters required large, strong operations. Those institutions helped define the cold-war nation as they snooped on the citizens.[43]

The cold-war security state grew till it balanced the New Deal welfare state. Each emerged as a pillar of the Washington establishment. In effect, both left and right had a powerful government establishment at the center of their political agendas. On the surface, both the welfare state and the security state looked like moral operations—intrusive, personal, judgmental. The FBI kept those detailed files on private behavior; the welfare department sent its minions out to check for illicit boyfriends before mailing child support checks.

But the United States remained a long way from the Comstock era. Fervent calls for purity failed to gain traction. On the contrary, the country appeared to be hurtling in precisely the opposite direction. The old sins—especially sex—had wormed their way into the popular culture.

Self-Control Meets Sexual Revolution

Censorship and Pornography

Congress revisited smut throughout the 1950s. The postal service fought the good fight, still reckoning its victories via the Comstock method: within the past ten days, Postmaster General Arthur Summerfield told an appreciative congressional committee in 1959, his men had seized "fifteen tons of films, slides, photographs and trashy literature." Familiar charges echoed through the congressional hearings. Smut peddlers were "corrupting children" and "sensationalizing sin." They mock wholesome married life, complained Representative John Dowdy (Texas), and call it "'for the birds or 'square' or whatever the current jive expression is."

Congressional testimony linked pornography with the "most vicious crimes . . . in recent history." Smut "weakened the moral fiber of the future leaders of our country." And—that 1950s clincher—it threatened national security. The testimony gathered cumulative force as a parade of witnesses told horror stories—undercut, occasionally, by a censorship fool. The U.S. mails should not "distribute and glamorize" sinful books like *Lady Chatterley's Lover*, which goes a "long way down the road to immorality and perversion." Well, no, admitted Congressman Dowdy, he had not actually read D. H. Lawrence, but he had heard . . .[44]

And how about comic books? Youngsters were getting hooked on this "marijuana of the nursery," warned crusading psychiatrist Frederic Wertham. By the time they turned sixteen, children had absorbed 18,000 beatings, shootings, stranglings, and blood puddles. When Wertham asked one lad what he wanted to be when he grew up, "the child replied enthusiastically, 'I want to be a sex maniac.'" The experts all reached the same conclusion: profit mongers were "poisoning the well of childhood."[45]

The condemnations echo Anthony Comstock at almost every turn—whole passages in the *Congressional Record* could have been lifted from *Traps for the Young*. However, the purity reformers of the fifties ran into problems Comstock never faced. The bulwarks of Victorian morality had crumbled. Almost every witness at the congressional hearings blasted the courts. "Freedom of the press seems to have been expanded to include freedom to debase and corrupt the moral standards of American youth and adult alike." The courts kept striking down censorship efforts, making it ever more difficult—eventually, almost impossible—to ban obscenity. But the moral guardians faced an even greater trouble: society itself had changed.

During World War II the military tossed aside the old illusions about purity in the ranks. American bombers flew into combat with naughty pin-up girls painted on the fuselage. The Army gave its boys eight condoms a week and almost included servicewomen in the condom rations. The victory celebrations offer a remarkable commentary on the fading purity ideal. Alfred Eisenstaedt snapped his famous photo of a celebrating sailor gaudily kissing a nurse in Times Square. That kiss was just one of many; *Life* ran it in a feature titled "The Men of War Kiss From Coast to Coast." Still another story pictured scores of servicemen kissing Hawaiian women before heading home. Women jumped into the celebration. *Life* pictured "two nude blondes who left their clothes and inhibitions in a waiting taxi" as they frolicked in a San Francisco lily pond while GIs "lustily cheered." "Churches were open and full," commented the editors (who did not bother with pictures of praying), "but so were the bars and nightclubs." You can see the baby boom bursting right out of the magazine.[46]

By the time House members had gotten around to denouncing D. H. Lawrence, Hugh Hefner had launched *Playboy* (in 1953). The first issue ran that brazen centerfold of a nude Marilyn Monroe posing confidently against a scarlet background. The photo would become an icon of the fifties. By 1960 *Playboy* was selling more than a million copies an issue. Something important had changed. As John D'Emilio and Estelle Freedman put it in *Intimate Mat-*

13.2. Fuselage pin-ups like Shady Lady were common. Crews proudly posed in front of their "girls." In this photo, from 1944, the exuberant art has faded into the background of everyday military life. (Courtesy of the National Archives [Photo No. 342-FH-3A45736])

13.3. *Life* celebrated victory in World War II with a special feature entitled, "The Men of War Kiss From Coast to Coast." This rough kiss, taken by Alfred Eisenstaedt, became the most celebrated . . .

13.4. . . . and this one the oddest. A whole squadron, coming home, stops in Hawaii for a feast and some necking. Behind a rope, more soldiers look on at the sexy fun. (Photos used by permission)

13.5. Hugh Hefner posed as a cool, jet-set sophisticate. Here he flies to a party given by
Ella Fitzgerald for the winners of the Playboy Jazz Poll. That's February Playmate Cynthia
Maddox at Hefner's side. January 1962. (Copyright Bettmann/CORBIS)

ters, "Pornography had moved from a dark side street into the most respectable neighborhoods." Here, after all, sat a peppy collegian, posing cheerfully with his girly magazine and promising to coach young men in the suave, modern social graces. His dirty pictures offered little fodder for moral panic. Panics erupt best around strangers—Jewish white slavers or Irish priests. In contrast, Hefner posed as clean-cut and cool.

The greatest blow to the Comstocks of the 1950s, however, came not from slick magazines but from boring science. A shy, cautious, unprepossessing workaholic named Alfred Kinsey (his colleagues at the Institute for Sex Research called him the Mother Superior) published a study of American sexual habits under the inflated title *Sexual Behavior in the Human Male* (1948). Indiana University's president anticipated the popular reaction when he asked Kinsey not to release his results while the state legislature was in session. The publishers had planned to print 10,000 copies; they shipped 186,000 in ten days. Five years later a second and more controversial book appeared: *Sexual Behavior in the Human Female.* Kinsey became a household name thanks to both his style and his blockbuster findings.

The books each ran more than eight hundred pages and were crammed with charts, tables, long footnotes, and spare scientific prose. Kinsey rolled through an exhaustive recitation of American sexual behavior, never raising an eyebrow. Even today the findings seem extraordinary: 85 percent of the white male population had premarital sex, 30 percent had reached at least one orgasm through homosexual contact, 50 percent had committed adultery, and one out of six farm boys had copulated with the animals. The *Sexual Behavior in the Female* reported less sex but seemed more shocking: one wife out of four had committed adultery; one of two had sexual relations before marriage; 62 percent of the married women regularly masturbated—higher frequency correlated directly with more education. In all, 19 out of every 20 Americans had broken a law having sex. Each section ends with a review of the relevant moral codes. Biblical commandments got treated as just another data set. ("Ancient codes [a footnote lists Middle Assyrian, Neo-Babylonian, and Hittite laws] ignored the possibilities of females having sexual contacts with animals.")[47]

The reports became cultural landmarks. "Hotter than the Kinsey report," they used to say in the 1950s. "Is there a Mrs. Kinsey?" asks the dubious wife in a Peter Arno cartoon. The *New York Times* refused an advertisement for the first book, then had to print the title as it shot up the best-seller list. Kinsey opened a Pandora's box—ostensibly scientific proof of widespread sexual experience among Americans. Never mind Hugh Hefner and Marilyn Monroe, Kinsey published shockers about the neighbors. Other sex scholars had been hinting about this or that for decades. But no one had ever laid out so much data from such a large sample in such unblinking detail. Moral champions in the early 1950s faced 1,600 pages of best-selling sexual science.[48]

Religious leaders did not take it quietly. Even liberals criticized the "absence of spontaneous ethical revulsion from the premises of the study." The report on women left them furious. "It is impossible to estimate the damage that this book will do to the already deteriorating morals of America," warned Billy Graham when the second study came out. Henry Pitney Van Dusen, the head of Union Theological Seminary in New York, took it even harder. The report pictured a "prevailing degradation in American morality approximating the worst decadence of the Roman empire." The archdiocese of Indiana released the standard salvo: Kinsey had helped "pave the way for people to believe in communism." Meanwhile, many secular reviewers treated the books with respect. Kinsey made the cover of *Time*. A positive story in *Look* genuflected to modern science. "For the first time data on human sex is entirely separated from questions of philosophy, moral values and social customs"—precisely what infuriated the moral guardians.[49]

The courts just kept getting looser. U.S. Supreme Court Justice William Brennan finally knocked over the last tottering bulwarks of censorship in the celebrated Fanny Hill case (1966): "A book cannot be proscribed unless it is found to be *utterly* without redeeming social value." To be ruled obscene, a work had to flunk all three court tests: it had to possess a "prurient appeal," it had to be "patently offensive." And as songwriter Tom Lehrer gleefully reworded the final test: "As the judge remarked the day that he / Acquitted my Aunt Hortense / To be smut it must be ut-terly / Without redeeming social importance." For a time, the court found almost nothing that missed the bar. It struck the "obscene" tag from everything that came before it.[50]

The courts also began to pull back on the minor religious establishments of the Eisenhower years. In one of its most unpopular decisions, the Supreme Court struck down a school prayer that the children in New York had been reciting (*Engel v. Vitale*, 1962). "It is no part of the business of government," wrote Hugo Black for a 6–1 majority, "to compose official prayers for any group of American people to recite." Senator Robert Bird (D-West Virginia) got to the microphones first: "Somebody is tampering with America's soul." The vitriol poured in—it is still pouring in, four decades later—from almost every direction: the decision "challenge[s] the fundamental concept of the American way of life," it "spits in the face of history," and it "sacrifices [American values] to appease a few agnostics and atheists." A letter to the plaintiffs flourished a standard cold-war taunt, "Communist kikes, why don't you go back to Russia?" Critics were flabbergasted at the court's reading of the First

Amendment: the same session that rejected the prayers restored postal privileges to three gay magazines.[51]

Birth Control

Science dealt another challenge to traditional sexual order when the Food and Drug Administration approved the birth control pill in 1960. Within three years, more than 2 million women were taking oral contraceptives. "Modern woman is at last free as a man is free," exulted Clare Boothe Luce, "free to dispose of her own body, to earn her living, to pursue the improvement of her mind, to try a successful career." The middle-class media played it pretty much the same way. A *Time* cover story called it the "miraculous tablet." The *Saturday Evening Post* added, "American women have gained what for eons was denied the daughters of Eve—a secure means of planning the birth of their child." "The modern temper" had married science and produced "magic," a "godsend," "freedom from fear," "liberated sex and family life," "strengthened love between husband and wife," and, just ahead, according to many experts, an opportunity to "defuse the population explosion" and "go far in eliminating hunger, want and ignorance from the world." Once upon a time, the newsmagazines told their readers, this sort of thing would have been "scorned and despised." Now "almost the whole nation has changed its mind." Underscore "almost."[52]

The celebrations came with whispers of trouble. First, who would get the birth control pill? It required a prescription. A Brown University student set off a national storm when she claimed that the campus physician had given her a "tentative prescription." "No way," responded the university's Dr. Rosewell Johnson. A student under twenty-one could get pills only with a note from her parents. How about students over twenty-one? That depends, said the doctor. "I want to feel I'm contributing to a good solid relationship and not to promiscuity." Physicians had slipped back into the role of moral gatekeeper. Many health care clinics added another twist. Young women who had already gotten pregnant outside marriage—that is, "sexual delinquents"—got hustled into family planning before they ran into more trouble. The pill turned personal morality into a professional question. The physician balanced parental consent, promiscuity, and the threat of pregnancy. How would Johnson and his university tell the "good relationship" from the promiscuous one? How would the medical clinics distinguish the good kid from the sexual delinquent? Once upon a time the government had been there to bar the door to these troubling questions. Now the decisions were thrown to the private sphere—to physicians or families or the women themselves.

Moreover, the pill fiddled with the American dream. As Clare Boothe Luce had predicted, women got to talking just like the guys. *Time* magazine quoted one young woman: "When I got married, I was still in college and I wanted to be certain that I finished. Now we want to buy a home and it's going to be possible a lot sooner if I teach. With the pill, I know I can keep earning money." *Time* blessed this Protestant ethos. "To these women, the pill spells freedom from fear." With one in three women working, the issue hit close to a lot of homes.[53]

In the old Victorian view, private lives carried profound consequences for the public good. The Victorians had organized a purity regime to guide citizens and families. Women belonged in that private sphere, building moral families. Social conservatives throughout the 1950s and '60s lamented the new freedoms—couples planning families, women launching careers. But the secular political trend was running away from government controls over sexual morals. Never mind the red scare about flabby morals, the courts kept right on dismantling the old purity laws.

In *Griswold v. Connecticut* (1965) the court struck down an 1879 Connecticut act—a "little Comstock law"—that made it a crime to use contraceptives or abet anyone trying to do so. Punishment had run up to a year in jail. In deciding *Griswold*, the court suddenly discovered a dramatic new constitutional right: privacy. "The first Amendment has a penumbra where privacy is protected from government intrusion." There were also "emanations" from other constitutional rights. Writing for the majority, Justice William Douglas summed it up with a famous question. "Would we allow the police to search the sacred precincts of marital bedrooms for telltale signs of the use of contraceptives?" He answered in the spirit of the day: "The very idea is repulsive to the notions of the privacy surrounding the marriage relationship." In 1972 the court extended the privacy right to unmarried couples (in *Eizenstadt v. Baird*), though it would stop short of applying the right to same-sex couples (in *Bowers v. Hardwick*, 1986).[54]

Commentators roasted the court for the way it had mysteriously found this constitutional right to privacy. But Douglas had put his finger precisely on the difference between moralizing politics (with its constant worry over private mischief) and classic liberalism. Liberalism draws its sharp line between private and public, between affairs of state and those of the bedroom. With an almost heroic constitutional exegesis—penumbra? emanations?—the court leaped onto solid liberal ground.

The Two American States

Two different government establishments emerged from the 1950s. On the one side, the New Deal welfare state flourished. By the 1950s supporters had won disability insurance and were pushing for Medicare. The cold war actually fostered Social Gospel visions. "The eyes of all people" really did seem to be upon the Americans, and all the attention spurred (cynics said shamed) the nation to new rounds of social justice. The communal vision would inspire another great burst of reform in the 1960s.

On the other side, the cold war built a formidable national security state. A network of government agencies rose up to protect the nation at home and abroad. This side of the state also honed new skills, gathered constituents, and lobbied for more. The security state offered a congenial institutional base for conservatives fighting for traditional virtues: patriotism, moral strength, self-reliance. The quest for virtue now operated in a new organizational frame. While the courts were dismantling the Victorian sexual control regime, the cold war nourished crime fighters—national, state, and local. The FBI outgrew the white slave business; the Prohibition precedents outlasted the bootleggers. Once the Social Gospel era finally passed—sometime in the 1970s—new calls for moral control would build on those foundations.

Both sides of the new American state sprang out of Roosevelt's four freedoms. Freedom from want summed up the aspiration of the social welfare state; freedom from fear called up a national security state. As the United States entered the sixties these two sides looked to be part of the same communal destiny. However, the next decade would split them apart. We'll see each offer a hard institutional context for one strain of the American moral vision—the Social Gospel filtered through social welfare politics while new Victorians called for less coddling and more discipline.

Chapter 14
The Sixties

NO era agitates Americans quite like the sixties—ground zero for the contemporary culture war. In their heyday, the sixties conjured up a dreamy Woodstock nation reaching for social justice. The civil rights crusade spilled out of the churches and into the streets. Even the hippies "evoked the early Christians," declared Episcopal Bishop James Pike, when they celebrated peace, love, Jesus, Buddha, and the Hobbit. Popular magazines kept rolling out the same adjectives to describe a nation of young activists: gentle, idealistic, nonviolent, utopian, all-American. In startling contrast, recent critics recall a decade of demons. The revised sixties plunged the nation into a spiritual abyss. Idealists? The destructive little nihilists razed our standards and trashed the culture. Peace and love? Richard Nixon served up the antidote. "To erase the grim legacy of Woodstock, we need a total war against drugs."[1]

Why demonize the decade? Because it stands for an undiluted version of the Social Gospel. The 1960s activists followed the Rauschenbusch recipe for reform. They blithely tossed aside taboos on "intemperance" or "unchastity" and aimed their jeremiads at "injustice" and "oppression." American Puritanism imploded. Critics still fume over the long roster of sins: drugs, sex, homosexuality, hedonism, feminism—the list goes on. The public bulwarks of private virtue—purity laws, obscenity standards, decency groups, television norms, dormitory rules—all tumbled down. As moral order seemed to collapse in the private realm, moralizing flooded into politics. "Morality in America threatens to engulf us all," complained political scientist Alexander Bickel. Out on the streets, they gauged laws and conventions by a higher standard; activists attacked everything that failed to measure up—segregated lunch counters, American foreign policy, and the gray corporate culture.[2]

Beneath our contemporary fight over the sixties lies a conflict between two

American moral traditions. Conservatives struggle to restore the Victorian virtues—buried, they think, somewhere around Woodstock. Meanwhile, progressives look back wistfully at the faded Social Gospel ideals; the great campaigns against racism, poverty, and injustice are what got buried, they believe, in the angry backlash against their glory days.

What made the period so intense? The sixties fits the pattern of evangelical great awakenings. Each awakening roused mobs, rattled institutions, and reorganized the culture. People flocked out of organizations that had once bound together their society. They reordered their world by simply leaving—walking out of the Congregational churches, "coming out" of any organization tainted by slavery, or questioning every authority in view. "What a fertility of projects for the salvation of the world!" exclaimed Emerson about the nineteenth-century reformers. The "din of opinion and debate" had brought a "keener scrutiny of institutions . . . than any we had ever known." Ditto the sixties.[3]

The upheavals yield chaos and social mobility. "What has been the effect," cried Charles Chauncey about the First Awakening in 1740, "but the people running wild?" Old hierarchies crumbled. Illiterate lads, Negroes, and women had bolted from their appointed places. It's the same thing every time. Previously excluded people surge forward. Class, race, and gender roles go up for grabs. The world turns upside down—fishmongers preach to proper clerics, college students lecture their professors. Today's sixties-haters echo their conservative predecessors. In the tumult, the irresponsible rebels pull down precious norms and hierarchies.

Worst of all, each awakening heralds a sexual revolution. Churchmen in the 1740s fretted about "brutish kisses" and "wives in common." Emerson scored the reformers who "attack the institution of marriage as the fountain of social evils." The storms expose the implicit public bulwarks that frame our private lives: the personal had been political all along. Shifting norms—in families, gender roles, and social manners—always provoke the hottest politics.[4]

Finally, the eighteenth- and nineteenth-century awakenings raised millennial hopes. God would return to his New Israel or—in the African revision—redeem his captive people. During the 1960s, however, the old millennial dream went terribly wrong. The United States began the decade moving to meet its manifest destiny. Suddenly its world-saving mission sank into the fury over the war in Vietnam. The march toward racial equality bogged down in race riots and recriminations. We'll see Lyndon Johnson bet the American mission itself on racial justice. The result seemed to be a sour generation of skeptics. The most radical cynics—Black Panthers, Yippies, Weathermen—would seize the language of apocalypse and use it to mock the nation. The gentle, Arcadian sixties seemed to break into days of rage. But when we stop reading the sixties' social movements as primarily male events, they end in something close to triumph. Americans transformed both race relations and gender roles. This awakening also changed the world.

In this chapter I follow four movements across the sixties (defined loosely as the mid-fifties to the early seventies): church reforms, the civil rights crusade, the student movement, and second-wave feminism. Each movement came on reverberating with moral power. Each left an important legacy for American moral politics. And all stoke a furious backlash that continues to the present day.

The Catholics' Revival

"Students are often hostile to the religious establishment," wrote one activist in 1962. If religion wants its young people back, "it must be made relevant to them." Religion tried. One bracing theological movement took its name from a Nietzschean epigram—act as if "God is dead." The true and only heaven lies in what we make of ourselves and our communities. However, the secular urge did not fill the church pews. Liberal Protestants saw their congregations dwindle; Methodists declined 10 percent between 1965 and 1975, Episcopalians 17 percent. In contrast, the unadulterated Southern Baptists surged 17 percent; the largest Protestant denomination began turning back from the cultural fringes. But no religion experienced the sixties quite like the nation's largest, the Roman Catholic church. The kids wanted relevance? For a time, the church delivered.[5]

Vatican II

The Second Vatican Council met in three sessions between 1962 and 1965. Pope John XXIII charged the assembly of bishops with adapting ancient truths to modern times. The bishops leaped to the task. By the end of the first Vatican session they had transformed Catholicism. The old church had propounded an exquisitely calibrated calculus of sin. Catholics knew precisely what was expected—and what forbidden—at every moment. Now conscience became the guide to salvation; the bishops emphasized a "growth of understanding" in the search for immutable truths. That opened the door to arguments, to moral discourse. All of a sudden, the people were invited to talk back.[6]

Moreover, the council introduced a "new humanism." Men and women shared responsibility for one another. The Vatican Council had found its own version of the old Protestant Social Gospel. The church launched an ecumenical ministry stressing good works. Priests might be instructing the people on "integrating their neighborhoods," reported *Newsweek,* rather than "on what book to read or avoid." The Vatican council sealed its reformation by shaking up church rituals. In the old days, the priest said mass in Latin, served by altar boys who mumbled ritual responses (the little slackers often faked the Latin), all with their backs turned to the people who had fasted since midnight if they wanted to take communion. Now the priest faced the congregation, prayed in English, and worked handshakes (the sign of peace, no less) into the Mass.[7]

Even bigger changes seemed to be coming. When I was in high school I visited a seminary at Villanova University. The young men studying to be priests talked enthusiastically about reformations stretching into a distant democratic future. Priests would soon be permitted to marry, they told me. Women might even be ordained. The men and women of the new church would go out into the world. Rather than snatching up converts from other faiths they would somehow—the particulars were a bit foggy—improve the world. The seminarians bubbled with reformist fervor.

While the Catholic Church remade itself, pharmacies were stocking the pill and the Supreme Court was striking down bans on birth control. What would the pope say to that? In the traditional catechism, all sexuality had to be open to procreation. The American church had sometimes slipped into the political sphere to fight for the old Comstock laws against selling condoms. Now the laity lobbied for lightening up. "What do Catholics gain by fighting to uphold birth control laws?" asked one churchman. "Little but the antagonism of non-Catholics." "It seems likely," reported *Newsweek,* that the church's "rules on divorce, birth control and other social obligations [will be] modified to fit the mores of modern society."

The pope faced the question in the new way. He appointed a commission of laypeople and clerics. They overwhelmingly (53 to 4) advised against the old ban on contraceptives. But by the time they delivered the report, Pope Paul VI had stepped into the papacy. He responded by stacking the commission with bishops and theologians and asking for a second look. Again the panel rejected the argument that contraceptives violate natural law (the theologians went four to one for reform). Effective contraceptives would "support conjugal love and marital chastity."[8]

In July 1968, the Vatican released its bombshell of an encyclical, *Humanae Vitae.* The birth control question would be settled the old-fashioned way, "by Ourself." The church would not budge on birth control. "Persuasion had failed," comments Garry Wills, so Paul VI tried "sheer church authority." That did not work either. A firestorm followed. "A few frightened, uninformed, and ambitious counselors around the Pope," speculated *Newsweek,* had egged him on.[9]

Catholics found themselves caught between their culture and their church.

One priest turned his protest into a best seller. In *A Modern Priest Looks at His Outdated Church*, James Kavanaugh described what it felt like to sit in a confessional as his most devout parishioners file in, feeling confused and guilty. A man steps into the booth; he already has six children—three courtesy of slips in that Catholic conjugal roulette, the rhythm method. He just can't afford any more kids. And I'm supposed to tell this man, wrote Kavanaugh, that "he is living in mortal sin. He could die and go to hell." This is rubbish. "He is among the best men I know." But if we pump up the volume on sex and sin we might wreck his marriage. Kavanaugh went to his colleagues for advice. The old ones recall sainted mothers who raised ten children, the young ones laugh and tell him to ignore the church policy.[10]

Father Charles Curran, a theologian at Catholic University in Washington, D.C., put the complaint more formally. In 1969 he published an analysis challenging the pope's logic about contraceptives. More than 600 scholars and clerics signed the statement. The issue spiraled rapidly from sexual ethics to the right to dissent and then on to church authority itself. The university eventually suspended Curran—who promptly took the administrators to court. Future historians, comments sociologist Father Andrew Greeley, "will judge *Humanae Vitae* to be one of the worst mistakes in the history of Catholic Christianity."[11]

We have seen this pattern. Debates about sexuality open into disputes about the social order. Outlaw sexuality threatens to break the traditional family, gender roles, and lines of moral authority. The Puritans fought battles over the issue—recall Winthrop's furious sermon about submission, or the 1679 synod on how the root of all problems lay in lax families. The pope's struggle to keep the ban on contraceptives turned into the same larger conflict over his own authority.

Catholics responded by ignoring the church leaders. At the start of the 1960s, most Catholics disapproved of birth control; twenty years later they had overwhelmingly changed their minds. In fact, Roman Catholics were more likely to use contraceptives than the rest of the nation. American Catholics took up the spirit of Vatican II—in fact, the spirit of mainstream American Protestantism: they followed their conscience. Many churchmen condemned the "cafeteria-style" religion—picking and choosing among church doctrines. But the sturdy old immutable faith had vanished. Most commentaries suggest that declining discipline was inevitable. American Catholics had moved up; they were well educated and well off. Hard constraints on personal freedom, writes Michael Cuneo, now seemed downright un-American. Still, the United States keeps refuting the standard expectation that modernity erodes faith.[12]

The tumult produced a deeper problem. A census taken shortly before I visited that seminary in Villanova counted almost 50,000 seminarians training for the priesthood in the United States. Today, the number has dwindled to 5,000. The decline in vocations among women is even steeper. The median age among Catholic nuns is seventy. Entire orders vanish, along with their economic base. Enforcing sexual orthodoxy on a tightly organized church put enormous strains on the institution itself. The laity made its own independent judgments; the clergy bore the tensions between church policy and societal norms.[13]

The Catholic perplexity reflects the basic trajectory of activism in the sixties. As Kavanaugh put it in the preface to his rant, he wrote his book "in the light" and the "hope" shed by Vatican II. A powerful, reforming, even utopian impulse had swept through the church. The changes fostered idealism, open debate, and an urge to use the gospel to engage the world. Once the ferment began it proved difficult to arrest. Quite suddenly, *Humanae Vitae* tried to slam the door on all that. The church hierarchy seemed out of touch with modern mores, with its own people, with the fervent idealism sweeping the world.[14]

Still, the reforms ended up fundamentally revising the institution. The rituals changed. Laypeople took up important new roles, and the American church adapted itself to a newly independent faithful who listened politely, then did—does—pretty much what it wants. The hidebound old structures, laying down tough norms, evaporated in the intoxicating, reformist moment—the essential sixties. The *New Yorker* poked at the dizzy evolution of Catholic sin with a little cartoon of hell. A puzzled devil asks his boss, "What do we do with all the guys who ate meat on Friday?"[15]

We'll see variations of the same pattern in every sixties social movement. Dreams of change stir the idealists. They then mobilize. Think big. Rattle the old institutions. Jim Crow laws tumble down, women win new opportunities, and universities scrape some ivy off their ancient ways. Then the backlash hits. The reforms never quite live up to the reformers' aspirations. The whirlwind passes, but it leaves behind deep changes. Great Awakenings never produce the Second Coming, but they generally manage to turn society upside-down.

Backlash

Conservatives hated the changes. "What in the name of God is going on in the Catholic Church?" implored a special issue of William F. Buckley's *National Review*. The traditional, immutable faith now glittered with unwelcome innovations. The new Mass was the worst of all. Condemnations poured in: "modernized," "demythologized," "deflated," "schismatic, sacrilegious, heretical and possibly invalid." An anonymous Wisconsin wit put the lament to rhyme:

Latin's gone, peace is too;
Singin' and shoutin' from every pew.
Altar's turned around, priest is too;
Commentators yellin' "page 22" . . .
Rosary's out, psalms are in;
Hardly ever hear a word against sin.[16]

A fiercer critique blasted the liberal ideas animating American religions. In a fire-breathing, anti-Communist bestseller, John Stormer warned that the "revolution in religion" was "subverting our . . . heritage" and draining our churches of any decent "effect on man and his life." Stormer fingered the "shrewd" theologian beneath America's moral troubles: Walter Rauschenbusch and his Social Gospel. Cut through the fancy language, charged Stormer, and what you get "is basically a restatement of the Marxian dogma." For Rauschenbusch, "religion was only a means toward achieving socialism." Stormer slips into hard right paranoia: seven thousand ministers were Communist dupes, the National Council of Churches practically a Communist front. But alongside the John Birch Society loopiness (picked up briefly by Senator Joe McCarthy) lies a deft statement of the conservative brief against the Social Gospel.

Stormer precisely identifies the core liberal heresy by quoting Rauschenbusch: "We differ from many Christian men and women who believe if only men are personally converted, wrong and injustice will gradually disappear from the construction of society." That passage—a fair statement of the Social Gospel premise—disparages the central evangelical tenet. In fact, it runs down the central premise of the Victorian vision of virtue. Stormer calls the very idea Communist, a melancholy reminder of how red-baiters bullied American moral discourse. Still, there's an important point in the hard right critique. Even moderates agreed with Stormer that something important had gotten lost in the effort to make American religion relevant. The heady, optimistic Social Gospel of the 1960s drained the hellfire and the miracles—the soaring transcendence—right out of religion.

During the First Great Awakening, the rebels had stood on the other side, with the Stormers of the day. They charged their old faith with going soft and getting enlightened. The people wanted their old-time gospels back. In the sixties, the Awakeners came from the other—liberal, secular—side. This time it would be the counterrevolutionaries who drew on the old fundamentals. Stormer clinches his brief against liberal heresy by describing the ultimate outrage. When the modernists sought to update their translation of the Old Testament, he writes, they took "Behold a virgin shall conceive and bear a son" and turned it into "Behold a young woman shall conceive and bear a son." The liberals messed with a fundamental truth: they denied the virgin birth of Christ.

Throughout American history the traditional sexual iconography stood for order, purity, submission, and hierarchy—everything the Social Gospel liberals threatened to overturn. Most Protestant denominations could not impose policies on their ministers the way the Catholics could. The conservative Protestants turned, instead, to the political realm, where their backlash gathered force. It came on so strong, in the following decades, because it tapped the ancient, often angry Calvinist moral vision that had been waiting in the American political wings since the 1920s.[17]

Race

In a nation made by moral crusades, the civil rights movement holds a special place. Here lies the very heart of the sixties. Everything revolved around the black struggle; the student movement stepped directly out of southern protests, the modern women's movement won its great legal breakthrough in a sarcastic twist to the Civil Rights Act of 1964. A whole people rose up, convulsed the country, ended 350 years of apartheid, broke through barriers, created a template for winning rights in every sphere, and, finally, fell short of its high-flying aspirations.[18]

Let Justice Flow Down Like Water

The battle against apartheid gathered speed during and after World War II. Fears of a black march on Washington pushed Franklin Roosevelt into his executive order banning discrimination. Japanese propaganda embarrassed the Justice Department into investigating lynch murders. The NAACP won a series of court victories on the fringes of segregation. Finally, in May 1954, the Supreme Court announced its ruling in *Brown v. Board of Education*. The mainstream media cheered. *Time* called it "another vital chapter in the greatest success story the world has ever known: the American Negro's rise from slavery."

A generation later some scholars cut off the applause. In *The Hollow Hope*, Gerald Rosenberg waves away the court's breakthrough. The justices could not deliver social change; worse, *Brown* misled social activists by luring them into court. I steer a course between the celebration and the criticism. The court changed the legal rules. Black Americans—brandishing legal judgments and orders—then rose up and won the rights that the courts had tried to proffer. Yes, the Supreme Court enabled the victories; and no, it did not guarantee much. The crucial dynamic lay in the interplay between the civil rights movement and government institutions—courts, Congress, the governors, and the presidents.[19]

At first glance, the *Brown* opinion seems dull and technical. Legal commentaries often focus on a footnote listing social science studies—talk about dry. But look again at where *Brown* trains its spotlight.

> Education . . . is the very foundation of good citizenship. Today it is a principal instrument in awakening the child to cultural values, in preparing him for later professional training, and in helping him adjust normally to his environment. In these days it is doubtful that any child may reasonably be expected to succeed in life if he is denied the opportunity of an education.
>
> Does segregation of children in public schools solely on the basis of race . . . deprive the children of the minority group of equal educational opportunities? We believe it does.[20]

Here is the most familiar image in American moral politics: the vulnerable child. The focus on children pushes aside the scornful underclass images that had plagued African Americans for seventy-five years. Instead, the court conjured up a Norman Rockwell picture. The innocent white children sleeping, "free from fear," in their Vermont village now became innocent black children stripped of the promises of American life—"citizenship," "cultural values," and "opportunity." The ruling springs directly from a Social Gospel vision: a cruel system squeezes good people; it is the source of their troubles. The court's moral image—imperiled innocents—would get burned onto the national retina by the pictures that flashed around the world from Little Rock, Arkansas, in September 1957: nine terrified black children tentatively walking up to Central High while a mob of white adults screams, spits, curses, and jeers.

The civil rights movement mobilized powerful images of innocent suffering in its long, hard fight against segregation. It began in Montgomery, Alabama, on December 1, 1955. Rosa Parks, a forty-two-year-old department store seamstress, was riding the bus home from work. She sat with three other black people in a row just behind the section reserved for white riders. The white section filled up and the driver told the four that a white man needed their row. State law and city ordinance both required bus companies to segregate the races—since the black section was also full, the whole row would have to stand. Three black riders got up. But Parks made the most famous decision in mass transit history. She said no. The bus driver pulled over and called the cops. Word of her arrest spread through a black population that was already roiling. When E. A. Nixon, the former president of the local NAACP, arrived to post bail he found hundreds of angry people milling around the jail. Montgomery's black leaders called for a boycott of the city buses and hastily invited twenty-six-year-old Martin Luther King, Jr., to head the campaign.

Just hours after being appointed, King rose at a public meeting in the Holt

Street Baptist Church. Some ten thousand people crowded the church and thronged the streets. Consider the context: A Baptist minister rises to preach to the people packed into a church, still the most durable institution in the black community. Loudspeakers amplify the voice in the pulpit for the people in the streets.

No one ever preached the Social Gospel like Martin Luther King did. In that first rally, far from the national spotlight (the *New York Times* tucked a notice of the boycott on page 31) and with only twenty minutes to prepare, King delivered a lyrical address that practically sums up the early civil rights movement. King pointed to the cold war, promised Christian nonviolence, and professed the black jeremiad.[21]

"If we were trapped in the dungeon of a totalitarian regime," King said, "we could not do this. But the great glory of American democracy is the right to protest." The cold war forms the crucial context for the entire movement. Those proud American postal ambassadors were flying their message—"In God We Trust"—around the world. Colonies were breaking free across Africa and Asia, poised between communism and capitalism. At every step of the civil rights campaign Americans would remind one another how this must look to the rest of the world. Headlines blared: Russia "stress[es] U.S. race relation abroad," Communist China "exploit[s] racial strife for propaganda," "Red press gloats over Little Rock," and Italian Communists "point to events in the South." Each black protest, each harsh white reaction, and each congressional dither provoked another round from the cold-war chorus: this looked like hell to people in other countries. "The eyes of all people upon us"—exactly what pushed the Roosevelt administration to move against lynching—profoundly framed the civil rights movement.[22]

Americans still honor Martin Luther King for his second theme, nonviolent passive resistance. "I want it to be known . . . throughout the nation that we are a Christian people," said King to the Holt Street throng. "The only weapon we have in our hand . . . is the weapon of protest." There will be "no crosses burned at any bus stops," "no white persons pulled out of their homes and taken on some distant road and murdered." Unearned suffering, King would keep saying, redeems us. Later, King pinpointed his inspiration: "It was the Sermon on the Mount . . . that initially inspired the Negroes of Montgomery to dignified social action." Taylor Branch described the ecstatic response to King's sermon as a great cloud of noise that shook the church and went on and on in waves, refusing to diminish. But the preacher himself heard something more specific. "The people had been as enthusiastic when I urged them to love as they were when I urged them to protest." The descriptions of King in the mainstream press would marvel at the peaceful resistance—eventually they would see the spirit of Mohandas Gandhi marching across the American South. A year later *Time* magazine did a cover story on King; the editors wanted to strike a description of the protesters opening their Holt Street meeting with the hymn *Onward Christian Soldiers*—too warlike, thought the editors, for this peace-loving movement.[23]

Alongside King's nonviolence lay an edgy black jeremiad with roots that reached way beyond *Onward Christian Soldiers*. "If we are wrong," roared King over shouts and amens from the throng, "God almighty is wrong. If we are wrong, Jesus of Nazareth was merely a utopian dreamer. . . . If we are wrong, justice is a lie." That sure sounds like blasphemy, but King's audience understood perfectly well: God could not be wrong nor justice lie. Redemption would come—God had promised it, Jesus died for it, justice demanded it. King capped the jeremiad with one of his favorite lines: "We are determined, here in Montgomery, to work and fight until justice rolls down like water, and righteousness like a mighty stream." He repeated the quotation in his most famous speech, "I Have a Dream." In that setting, justice running down like water seemed a soothing contrast to the "sweltering heat" of injustice and oppression. But the biblical allusion is a bit more complex than it seems. It comes from Amos, a short, angry Old Testament jeremiad describing the lord's wrath over injustice. "Woe to them that . . . are not grieved for the affliction of Joseph"— Joseph, of course, had also been sold into bondage. "Woe unto you. . . . Wailing shall be in all the streets." In fact, what flows down like water in Amos is not precisely justice but God's judgment and punishment. King artfully negotiated the great racial antinomy—reaching out to a nervous white nation with the soaring promise of justice, harmony, and nonviolence while connecting his black listeners to their faith in divine judgment and redemption.

King's Social Gospel, like Franklin Roosevelt's, was radical by contemporary standards. It begins, modestly enough, by bringing religion down to earth. But it goes on to embrace that other Puritan ideal: the people collectively share moral responsibility for their community. Roosevelt had repeatedly urged the collective idea, but it runs deepest in the black spiritual tradition. The communal faith does not fit easily with a competitive, highly individualistic America. As the long black jeremiad illustrates, the Social Gospel pivots on a tough-minded moral critique—not of individual sinners but of the political economy that pins people in poverty and pushes them toward vice. That steely part of King's message usually slips from sight. "We do not honor the critic of capitalism or the pacifist," muses Julian Bond. Progressives look to King for inspiration; they love the prophetic call to social justice. But they conveniently forget how the moral gospel came with an ardent critique of the injustice built into our political economy.[24]

For all the soaring rhetoric and rosy memories, the Montgomery campaign turned long, discouraging, violent, and scary. The black community organized an elaborate car pool—up to 350 cars a day. But its resources stretched thin. Where would they find replacement vehicles? Many black people defiantly walked to work, some went miles. How long could they keep that up? Meanwhile, the strikers faced fierce opposition. White people mocked their black employees and raved in white supremacy rallies. All three city commissioners joined the White Citizens' Council, the "uptown Klan." By late January the boycott's leadership sued for a compromise: How about voluntary segregation, with blacks moving backward and whites moving forward as seats opened up? The city scornfully rejected that plan. Whites move for Negroes? No chance. After two months the boycott leaders turned to the federal courts. King explained the legal suit to another packed church meeting. In the middle of the gathering his friend Ralph Abernathy interrupted with the whispered news that King's house had just been bombed. King rushed out. He found his wife, Coretta, and baby daughter frightened but unhurt. He calmed his distraught father and then quieted a black crowd on the verge of violence. Legend has it that the next day a white cop went around town saying, "I would sure enough be dead if it hadn't been for that nigger preacher."

The cops cracked down. They arrested the boycott's leaders and harassed the car-pool drivers. They nabbed King as he picked up riders, charged him with speeding, and drove off with him. King later admitted feeling terror as his own line rattled around in his head: "no white persons pulled out of their homes and taken on some distant road and murdered." What a relief, he reported, to actually arrive at the jail. King was arrested again and, in March, found guilty of leading an illegal boycott. But the city fathers had not reckoned on the growing audience. By now the national and international media had descended on Montgomery. Article after article repeated variations of the story: "King stresses the Christian basis of the protest" (as the *New York Times* put it in March 1956). The other side also got predictable coverage: "Montgomery Commissioners reject pleas."[25]

In November 1956, more than eleven months into the boycott, the city hauled King back into court. White leaders had finally hit on a winning maneuver: call the car pool an illegal business and shut it down. As Judge Eugene Carter prepared to lower the legal boom the courtroom began to buzz. The Supreme Court had affirmed the ruling of a three-judge panel striking down Alabama's state and local bus segregation laws. The race barrier on Montgomery buses finally fell on December 21, 1956.

Jubilation was quickly tempered by violence. A shotgun blast ripped into King's home, a gang of white men beat a fifteen-year-old black girl at a bus stop, people fired bullets into integrated buses (the city briefly suspended bus service for public safety), another wave of bombings terrorized the black community (four Baptist churches were hit in one night), and a local judge bitterly submitted to the Supreme Court's "evil construction."[26]

The Montgomery campaign illustrates the political trajectory of the early movement: the Supreme Court opened the door, mass action sprang up. National, then international, attention gathered around the protesters. Implacable whites resisted. And, finally, the court forced hostile segregationists to submit. Court rulings were not enough. A heroic movement won civil rights. But without the courts it is difficult to see how the protesters could have won.

Civil rights victories sprang from a dialectic between roused citizens marching in the streets and government institutions slowly responding. The courts sided with the marchers, though it took 382 days to renegotiate the seating on Montgomery buses. The civil rights protesters slowly nudged federal officials toward bolder action. Three administrations—Eisenhower's, Kennedy's, and Johnson's—each proposed increasingly tougher legislation. Congress eventually broke the southern filibusters. But each concession seemed too little, too late. That's because another impulse kept turning up the heat. The civil rights movement—in fact, the entire era—was profoundly shaped by the white resistance.

White Violence

Black Americans who tested race boundaries had always faced ferocious resistance. Now, civil rights agitation stirred up a new generation of terrorists. The most dramatic cases drew international attention. For example, in 1955, Emmett Till, a black fifteen-year-old from Chicago, was visiting relatives in Sumner Mississippi when he allegedly whistled at a white woman. Till was beaten and murdered. Although his uncle identified the killers, a white jury acquitted them in a bit more than an hour. In April 1959, a mob dragged Mack Parker from an unguarded cell—he left a trail of bloody handprints as he clawed at the jailhouse steps—then killed him and dumped his mangled body in the river. This time a large team of FBI agents arrived, gathered evidence, and got confessions from three members of the lynch mob. The grand jury refused to hear from the federal agents and then refused to indict members of the mob. Circuit Judge Sebe Dale pinned the blame for the lynching on that "board of sociology, sitting in Washington, garbed in judicial robes." In March 1956, four members of the Birmingham Ku Klux Klan seized a black handyman—picked at random—and castrated him as a message to all civil rights agitators.

The brutality went on and on. In September 1963, just weeks after the great march on Washington, a bomb blew up Birmingham's 16th Street Baptist Church. Four bodies—girls who had been downstairs changing into choir robes—were pulled from the rubble. Pastor John Cross rushed out and begged the gathering crowd to forgive; the police department put its faith in a six-wheel riot tank and buckshot. Officers shot and killed a black youth. Later that evening, white teens on a motorscooter buzzed past two black brothers on a bicycle and shot the thirteen-year-old dead. "And so six died on a Sunday in Birmingham," ended an unusually bitter report in *Time* magazine.[27]

What leaps out from the era, however, is not the dramatic and highly publicized murders but the constant, everyday violence. The White Citizens Council organized an attack on Nat "King" Cole when he came to Birmingham to sing to a "mixed" audience; Cole then called off concerts in Birmingham and Atlanta for fear of violence. Three women in Erath, Louisiana, beat up a colleague for teaching a mixed catechism class. The bishop briefly excommunicated two of the attackers but backed off when unrepentant church members warned him there would be more beatings unless he segregated the Sunday school. In Talladega County, members of the Klan seized three white men and "flogged" them for "associating with Negroes."[28]

Northerners enforced their own race line. On May 17, 1954—the same day as the *Brown* ruling—*Time* reported the final chapter of a nine-month saga on Chicago's South Side. Donald and Betty Howard had moved their family into a white housing project. How did the African American couple get a lease? The answer comes straight out of Gustave de Beaumont's racial balconies: the clerk did not realize that the light-skinned Mrs. Howard was a Negro. Mobs rectified the error. They gathered in front of the house, screamed, swore, heaved stones, set off stink bombs, hung the Howards in effigy, and burned nearby stores caught doing business with black people. After nine months, Chicago's finest prevailed on the Howards to move to a more suitable place.[29]

Southern leaders denounced the northern hypocrites. But the North did not offer the easy target of legal segregation; nor did its leaders hustle to the racial barricades with anything near the same bombast. "The South stands at Armageddon," announced Georgia Governor Marvin Griffin in December 1955. "The battle is joined. We cannot make the slightest concession to the enemy in this dark hour of struggle. . . . One break in the dike and the relentless seas will rush in and destroy us."

At that moment, the danger loomed from the University of Pittsburgh, Georgia Tech's opponent in the 1956 Sugar Bowl. Pitt had a black player, Bobby Grier, on its squad, and the university refused to leave him at home. Governor Griffin tried to cancel the game. Georgia Tech's president, Blake R. Van Leer, bluntly refused. When the president walked into his next faculty meeting, 800 faculty members rose and cheered him for more than five minutes. The students did their bit and hanged Griffin in effigy. The teams played and Georgia Tech won, 7–0.

A modest stream of racial tolerance seemed to be running alongside the terrorism. Look again at the preceding stories: The KKK flogged white people for consorting with blacks. A Louisiana archbishop meted out his church's strongest medicine for racial brutality. Mixed audiences bought tickets to see Cole perform. And the Georgia Tech faculty rose to applaud their president for defying the governor (though the students might have been cheering for football as much as race harmony).[30]

Might the furious southern race battles have turned out differently? Might enlightened leaders have kept the debate within the boundaries of decency? The prospect raises the underlying question: Where did all that hatred come from? Did politicians trolling for cheap votes provoke it? Or did it rise up from the white people gripping on to their status, their "wages of whiteness"? The answer seems irresistible: it came from both.

Leaders dashed to cash in on the bigotry. Arkansas governor Orville Faubus, a longtime moderate, discovered the political gold in racial epithets when he unexpectedly shut down the Little Rock schools rather than desegregate them in 1957. His tough line provoked harsh words—and federal paratroopers—from a reluctant President Eisenhower: "Our enemies are gloating over this incident and using it everywhere to misrepresent our whole nation." But hand-wringing in Washington, D.C., turned Faubus into a hero in Arkansas. He won a third term by a record-breaking margin. Political leaders throughout the South got the message.[31]

The Republican Party eventually caught on as well. It launched Operation Dixie, designed to break the Democratic grip on the South. Philip Klinkner and Rogers Smith summarize the spirit of the plan in a newspaper column written by Robert Novak. "A good many, perhaps a majority of the party's leaders, envisioned substantial political gold to be mined in the racial crisis by becoming, in fact, though not in name, 'the White Man's Party.' 'Remember,' one astute party worker said quietly . . . 'this isn't South Africa. The white man outnumbers the Negro 9 to 1 in this country.'"[32]

On the other hand, politicians who were slow to feed the beast got shoved aside by those who seized the chance. In 1958, George Wallace ran for governor of Alabama on a moderate platform of better schools and highways. He lost (to John Patterson in the Democratic primary) and drew a harsh lesson from his rival's chest-thumping segregation. Well, boys, said Wallace repeatedly, "no other son-of-a-bitch will ever out-nigger me again." Wallace won in 1962, breathing racial fire: "I draw the line in the dust and toss the gauntlet before the feet of tyranny and I say, segregation today, segregation tomorrow, segregation forever." He soon made a national reputation with his own Faubus moment when he refused to allow black students into the University of Alabama. Ministers, teachers, politicians, and judges who supported integration—who did not huff segregation with enough fire—soon found themselves pummeled by angry white citizens. Like the Salem witchcraft frenzy, the cry for blood seemed to rise up from the majority as much as it came down from bottom-feeding politicians.[33]

The segregationists kept trying to snatch the mantle of virtue away from the civil rights movement. They excoriated the villains who "attempted to overthrow the traditional American school system with its roots in Christian culture." They grew furious when the court struck down school prayer and censorship laws. Federal judges were promoting atheism, pushing porn, and pressing integration (still a synonym for miscegenation). But nothing posed so "violent" and "damaging" a "blow to Christian education" as the "hysterical attack of the racial integrationists." Somehow, mingling with black kids would subvert the morals of white children.[34]

We keep hearing this hard moral cry against black people. Slavery's defenders (in the 1830s) imagined that God had made them "stewards" of an inferior race. A half-century later, as they pushed their Jim Crow laws, southerners told a sympathetic nation that the immoral black tide had just not been ready for freedom; African Americans, they had said, endangered white women, children, and democracy. Now, in the 1950s and '60s, segregationists dusted off their trusty routine about southern morals and white innocents. They dredged up the old sex stories, now primly packaged as a fear of disease: "Little white girls" would become "highly susceptible to syphilis" if drinking fountains got integrated. It sounds ridiculous, but Virginia filed a brief to the Supreme Court challenging integration because "Negroes have a higher rate of infectious diseases than whites."[35]

This time, however, the old supremacist story flopped. Segregationists failed to pin the old moral stigma on black Americans. On the contrary, white segregationists turned into the moral villains; brutality and hate speech looked repugnant—both at home and abroad. Charismatic civil rights activists quoting Amos, Isaiah, and Lincoln proved far more persuasive as moral leaders. But the white demagogues left their terrible legacy. For a decade they fiercely resisted basic human rights. The hate-mongers forced the civil rights movement to spend its optimistic years fighting for the most basic rights: voting, riding buses, eating in restaurants, going to state schools, or playing in the Sugar Bowl. The long, hard fight bled away the patience—the long-suffering nonviolence—that might have been turned on harder problems, like economic injustice, racial animosity, and social inequality. What a different history southern leaders might have written if they had calmed the racial furies rather than leaping forward to inflame them.

The American Mission Revised

The political cycle kept repeating itself: protesters rose up and demanded basic rights only to meet appalling violence. The demonstrations—and the backlash—got hotter. Ugly pictures flashed around the world. The furor slowly pushed the president toward the activists in his administration. But each reform faced a long, loud, political gauntlet. By the time policies actually emerged they seemed behind the curve, inadequate for the fast-moving problem at hand. Even so, the painful process yielded monumental civil rights laws and memorable presidential statements about American morality. Let's look at the street storms that produced two great moral conversions and, eventually, American legal landmarks.

In February 1960, four African American undergraduates in Greensboro, North Carolina, sat down at a segregated lunch counter. They did not get any food, of course. But their strategy caught on, and sit-ins spread across the South. Jeering white toughs soon gathered, pouring Coke or ketchup on the people sitting at the counters, and holding lighters to the women's hair. Slowly—the original counter in Greensboro hung on for six months—the lunch counters integrated. The sit-ins blossomed into swim-ins for integrating pools, wade-ins for the beaches, pray-ins at churches, wait-ins at housing developments, and stand-ins before ticket booths. Almost 4,000 activists landed in jail within six months.[36]

In 1961, reformers turned to freedom rides. Blacks and whites got on buses and rode together across the South. Pictures of the ferocious reaction still seem hard to grasp: A Greyhound bus blazed in Annison, Alabama, after a posse of cars caught up to it. Mobs attacked freedom riders in Birmingham and Montgomery leaving some badly hurt. Montgomery's police commissioner offered the segregationists his benediction: "We have no intention of standing guard for a bunch of troublemakers coming into our city." J. Edgar Hoover agreed: "We simply can't wet nurse everybody who goes down to try to reform or re-educate the Negro population down South." Today, a romantic haze clings to the civil rights movement, but the photos and film clips jolt us back to the hard reality about the movement: it took extraordinary courage.[37]

Protests reached full boil in 1963, after King organized a campaign to desegregate Birmingham. The outgoing police chief—a glowering caricature of segregation named Bull Connor—became the international poster boy for white repression. The Birmingham campaign produced some of the most memorable images in recent American history. *Time* described the results:

14.1. The movement took extraordinary courage: A lunch counter sit-in, Jackson, Mississippi. (AP Photo/*Jackson Daily News*/Fred Blackwell)

Shocking news photos splashed across the pages of the world's press—of a young Negro sent sprawling by a jet of water, of a Negro woman pinned to the sidewalk with a cop's knee at her throat, of police dogs lunging at fleeing Negroes.

With that, millions of people—North and South, black and white—felt the fangs of segregation and at least in spirit, joined the protest movement.[38]

The Birmingham protests, concluded *Time*, were the "sparking point of the Negro revolution of 1963." A great wave swept the South and turned northward. The civil rights rebellion teetered on the edge of violence. Almost nine years had passed since the *Brown* decision. And what had come from all the marches and meetings, sermons and spirituals, beatings and bombings? Almost nothing. In the deep South, only a tiny number of schools—one sixth of one percent—had desegregated. Most black people still could not vote.

Prodded by the turbulence, President John Kennedy finally broke with southern Democrats and sponsored tough civil rights legislation in June 1963. His new bill would outlaw segregation in public places; it would even leverage

14.2. The first freedom bus to roll into the South. After a large posse of cars managed to force the bus of the road, someone threw a fire bomb through the window. The mob tried but failed to barricade the door to the burning bus, and the riders all got out. (Copyright, photo by the *Birmingham News*, 2001. All Rights Reserved. Reprinted with permission.)

the interstate commerce clause into a ban on racial discrimination by private business. Kennedy reached for the high ground. He called civil rights a "moral issue . . . as old as the scriptures and as clear as the American Constitution." *Time*'s headline snickered about the prospects: "Better at Moralizing than Legalizing." On the other side, Arthur Schlesinger, Jr., hailed Kennedy's address as a "magnificent speech" delivered in "burning language" about the "moral crisis that could not be quieted by token talk."[39]

Today scholars look past all the moral talk and instead stress the cold war and the hot cities that pushed Kennedy to action. Pictures of the strife in Birmingham flew around the world. Intelligence agencies tallied up the Soviet propaganda and announced that Birmingham had topped the charts with 1,420 Communist commentaries in two weeks (that's one every fifteen minutes). Back home, nervous moderates speculated about growing black violence. The older black leaders were practically sprinting to keep up with the angry young people in the streets.

Still, President Kennedy's moral language was more than rhetorical window dressing. The civil rights activists had put their cause in fundamentally moral terms as they pressed it onto the national agenda. Ironically, the white supremacists sealed the moral perspective by responding with such violence. Kennedy's rhetoric reflects the way the civil rights activists had framed the issue. And his moral rhetoric offered a way to justify the political cost. Everyone knew this was going to make a mess of the old Democratic coalition; the president had to reach for something larger than the usual political calculations. In context, echoing Martin Luther King and invoking a higher moral calculus seemed perfectly plausible. Finally, the moral framing acknowledges that the normal political give and take would not win this legislation. That "burning language" was a way of trying to wrench the debate beyond politics as usual.[40]

Since the Senate had not broken a filibuster in decades, even many liberals thought the Civil Rights Act a long shot. Success followed the extraordinary March on Washington (August 1963), the political recoil from President Kennedy's assassination (November 1963), and plenty of hard political work. President Johnson courted Republicans like Senator Everett Dirksen more assiduously, he later claimed, than he had courted his wife, Lady Bird.

Lyndon Johnson went through the same political wringer as Kennedy. His own transforming moral statement—introducing the Voting Rights Act of 1965—belongs on any short list of sermons about the American mission. All the familiar elements swirled around Johnson as he stuck his political neck out. This time, the uprising took place in Selma, Alabama, in March 1965. Again television cameras captured white savagery—state troopers and mounted volunteer posse members waded in and beat young marchers. Again the president looked over his shoulder at the rest of the world. By now, the racial crisis appeared to be spinning entirely out of control. The previous summer, riots had touched off in eight cities. The nation buzzed with edgy speculation about what was coming next—in fact, the shattering Watts riot in Los Angeles lay just ahead. In that context it is easy to shrug off Johnson's sermon. But take a second look at the president's extraordinary language.

> Rarely in any time does an issue lay bare the secret heart of America itself. Rarely are we met with a challenge, not to our growth or abundance, our welfare or our security but rather to the values and the purposes and the meaning of our beloved nation.
>
> The issue of equal rights for American Negroes is such an issue. And should we defeat every enemy, should we double our wealth and conquer the

stars, and still be unequal to this issue, then we will have failed as a people and as a nation.

For with a country, as with a person, "What is a man profited, if he shall gain the whole world, and lose his own soul?"[41]

Here is the city on a hill in a jarring new context. When Winthrop announced the errand in the American wilderness, he was vague about just what would count as success or failure. We've seen a long string of Americans imagine different missions for the world to see and emulate. But here's something different. Johnson waves aside wealth, the race for the stars, and even our cold-war Manifest Destiny. Redeeming the country's soul means getting beyond "poverty, disease, and ignorance," beyond bigotry and second-class citizenship. The city on a hill was inviting the world to measure it by the standards of racial equity. And to cover his bet, Johnson laid down the American mission itself: "We will have failed as a people and as a nation."

A whole generation grew up watching the wheel spin on that bet. If the 1960s ended in bitterness and anger, it was largely because the stakes had seemed so awesome and the hopes had run so high. Conventional wisdom traces American disenchantment to the Vietnam War and the Watergate scandal. But the real source lies right here, in the promise of racial equality.

Two decades earlier Gunnar Myrdal had described race as the quintessential American dilemma. He saw it as a fundamentally moral question, which perfectly suited the national temperament. When he first addressed the issue in 1944, Myrdal predicted success. He revisited the issue in 1962 and applauded the progress. The changes that Americans had already made, he wrote, rank among the "most rapid in the history of human relations." At this rate, he predicted, the prejudice between black and white will fade, by the end of the century, to nothing more severe than the mild prick between Catholics and Protestants. When LBJ stared into the TV monitors and evoked the city on a hill, just three years later, all that optimism was fast bleeding away. Even Myrdal had turned gloomy; he had not paid enough attention, he now said, to the hard economic inequality between the races.[42]

Three years after Johnson's call, Martin Luther King would be dead. The great dream of a nation beyond inequality, even beyond racial prejudice, would be over—written off as impossibly naive. At least for the generation that came of age in the late 1960s, Johnson's sad prophesy seemed to sum up the nation itself: we had gained the entire world and lost our soul. There would be other missions and other glorious evocations of the city on a hill. But somewhere around King's death the era of the American Social Gospel flickered out. There has been little sign of it since.

Beyond Morals, or "Look Out, Whitey! Black Power's Gon' Get Your Mama"

Martin Luther King struggled to keep the exploding movement in the Social Gospel frame. "I am many things to many people," he told an interviewer in 1965, "but in the quiet recesses of my heart, I am fundamentally a clergyman, a Baptist preacher. This is my being and my heritage for I am also the son of a Baptist preacher, the grandson of a Baptist preacher and the great-grandson of a Baptist preacher." The night before he died, King delivered a haunting sermon in which he transformed the Birmingham fire hoses into baptismal fonts: "Bull Conner didn't know history. There was a certain kind of fire that no water could put out. And we went before the fire hoses; we had known water. If we were Baptist . . . we had been immersed. If we were Methodist . . . we had been sprinkled, but we knew water."[43]

Another Baptist preacher's son offered a less soothing alternative. Malcolm X's father, Earl Little, had preached Marcus Garvey's Black Nationalist message. Though he was a large and fearless man, the KKK had managed to run Little out of Omaha, Nebraska. The family washed up in Lansing, Michigan, where town leaders pummeled Little for being an "uppity nigger." They warned him about his Black Nationalist preaching and finally—probably— murdered him. His son, Malcolm, would take the Black Nationalist message to the next generation.[44]

Elijah Muhammad's black Muslims found Malcolm X in prison. The Muslims recruited effectively in jails, preaching self-respect and strict discipline: no drugs, no liquor, no pork. Elijah Muhammad took an unblinking view of race relations. Why push integration with people who so clearly despise you? The Muslims scorned white people as corrupt, swine-eating devils. A mad scientist named Yakub had invented the white race, they said; Yakub was driven out of the Garden of Eden for his appalling sin. Muhammad warned black people to get away from the corrupt whites; when God returned he would smite the white oppressors and raise the black nation back to glory. The Yakub narrative masterfully flips—and parodies—the long line of racist Bible thumpers who found justification for racial oppression in their scriptures.

As Malcolm X moved further into public view he edged away from the tales of Yakub and emphasized, instead, Muhammad's Black Nationalism—black moral dignity and white responsibility for oppression. At Yale University, in 1962, he challenged his listeners with pure black jeremiad.

> Mr. Muhammad says that only after the American Negro's condition is corrected will Uncle Sam's health improve . . . for only then will Uncle Sam look healthy in the eyes of the fast-awakening dark world. . . .
>
> What will God's price be? What will God's solution be? Can America pay God's price? . . . Will America blindly reject God's Messenger, and in so doing bring on her own Divine Destruction?[45]

The judgment warnings, implicit in King's sermons, rushed straight to the surface of Malcolm's. Both preached in a fundamentally American idiom that stretches from Cotton Mather to Billy Graham. The African American variation translates Revelation's wrath and judgment into racial terms—the Yale sermon sounds for all the world like David Walker warning white America to repent of slavery before God lets loose His terrible judgment. Malcolm X, like Walker in 1830, cast the black jeremiad, just as the American racial universe appeared about to boil over.

Near the end of his life Malcolm broke with the black Muslims and moved beyond the raw rejection of all whites. The change came during his *hajj*, his pilgrimage to Mecca, when he discovered "brotherly love with many white-complexioned Muslims who never gave a single thought to . . . the complexion of another Muslim." In Mecca, marveled Malcolm, people did not seem to code, judge, or discriminate by skin color. His last writings, in 1964, stress what he learned there: "Black men and white men truly could be brothers." The moment he returned, however, Malcolm felt swallowed up by American racial fury. As the press crowded around him at a New York airport, he mused that a white man with a rifle is protected by the Constitution; a black man talking about guns is "ominous."[46]

"They called me 'the angriest Negro in America,' " he wrote. They accused me of "stirring up Negroes" during the "long hot summer of 1964." But, he stressed, "I'm not for wanton violence. I'm for justice." White observers had a hard time hearing the distinction. Black Nationalism seemed like fancy talk for urban violence.

In a horrified description of the Harlem riot, in July 1964, *Time* kept coming across Black Nationalists stirring up people with angry rhetoric and radical politics. Go back to the description today, however, and another narrative leaps out from the sounds of the riot. The ghetto fury was expressed largely through comparisons to southern violence: "Mississippi is here in New York." "I saw New York's night of Birmingham." "They walk all over me in Greenville, South Carolina, and they . . . run all over me here." The shouts and slogans and sermons—even the pleas for nonviolence—brim with southern references: to the KKK, to night riders, to lynch mobs, to mob rule. At the time, they all were so familiar that no one paid much attention. But today those references testify how the northern racial fire was stoked by the decade of brutality in the South.[47]

Black urban neighborhoods were poor and crowded. People were packed tight into Harlem—at that population density the entire American population would have fit into just three of New York City's boroughs. But the voices of the riots express a different anger. The decade of southern violence had burned into the urban mind. American culture reverberated with firebombs, fire hoses, filibusters, and all that fussing over Soviet propaganda. A real connection linked Martin Luther King, Malcolm X, and the young nihilists looting stores: they all bore the fierce sense of injustice stirred up by years of watching black Americans turn the other cheek just to get the vote or ride in the front of the bus.

By the mid-1960s, movement activists were turning defiantly away from moral politics altogether. In June 1966, James Meredith began a 220-mile pilgrimage from Memphis to Jackson, Mississippi; he hoped to embolden black voters. Two days out of Memphis a shotgun blast left him bleeding on the pavement. Civil rights activists flocked to the highway to carry on Meredith's trek. In Greenwood, Mississippi, the police went into their familiar routine and arrested three marchers; the "outside troublemakers" had pitched their tents on the grounds of a black elementary school—a nasty case of trespassing. When Stokely Carmichael got out of jail a few hours later, he went back to the marchers' rally and launched into a fierce speech: "This is the twenty-seventh time I've been arrested," he told a crowd of perhaps 3,000, "and I ain't going to jail no more." Carmichael then began his famous chant. The crowd soon got the call-and-response cadence down: "What do we want?" shouted Carmichael. "Black power!" screamed the crowd. "Say it again!" wailed Carmichael. "Black power!" roared the crowd. The liberal integrationist dream disappeared fast.[48]

Black power leaped outside the moral realm. Angry young men fused Black Nationalism to third-world revolutionary ideology. What did it mean? Stokely Carmichael and Charles Hamilton summed up: making our own decisions, celebrating black virtues, and protecting ourselves from the murderous whites. When police killed an unarmed black sixteen-year-old, Huey Newton and Bobby Seale organized the Black Panther Party for Self-Defense. The Panthers' platform did not mess around with biblical allusions or moral claims. Instead, it defined black community beyond white America. It laid out demands—housing, education, an end to policy brutality, and real justice (like juries of black peers). The Panthers demanded U.N.-sponsored elections in the black American "colonies." Then they launched into the really radical stuff—the first two sections of the Declaration of Independence: "When in the course of human events, it becomes necessary for one people to dissolve the political bands which have connected them with another. . . . " It sounded pretty hot coming from armed black men.[49]

Success?

The civil rights campaign unleashed one of the great moral movements in American history. The Supreme Court opened the door to fundamental change. Black Americans seized the opportunity by gathering in southern churches, marching in the streets, and challenging segregation everywhere they found it. In the process, leaders preached the American Social Gospel at its most eloquent. The civil rights movement eventually produced a national crisis—marked first by white violence and then by black riots. The tumult—like the politics in every chapter of this book—produced laws and institutions that changed the nation.

The Civil Rights Act of 1964 broke through a seventy-five-day filibuster and abolished segregation in public places, even if they were privately run— movie theaters, restaurants, hotels, gas stations. The law forbade discrimination in institutions that received federal funds. It barred discrimination by employers or unions. And it created an Equal Employment Opportunity Commission to oversee compliance. The following year the liberals broke another filibuster and passed what the *New York Times* called the strongest voting rights bill in American history.[50]

The civil rights ideal infused American politics. For example, in 1965, Congress passed Medicare. The officials who administered the program used federal funds to integrate southern hospitals. Segregated institutions survive to this day; but without any Medicare funds they are small and limited, stranded on the periphery of American medicine. In the mid-1960s the War on Poverty pushed "maximum feasible participation" on community agencies around the nation. Most people remember the agencies mainly for Daniel Patrick Moynihan's sneer: "maximum feasible misunderstanding." But the agencies had a terrific impact; they took a generation of young black leaders and gave them a vehicle through which to enter the urban political establishment.[51]

Meanwhile, far from the civil rights spotlight, another quiet barrier fell. Congress scrapped the 1920s national origins legislation. Developing nations received more generous limits; and, crucially, close relatives would be admitted above the quota. Almost no one noticed at the time, but the United States had once again flung open the door to foreign nations. A new generation of Americans began arriving, largely from Asia and Latin America; in the coming decades they would take their own turn at rewriting American culture. Would they push the United States beyond its insistent black-versus-white racial coding? Past immigrants had grabbed onto "whiteness." Perhaps a new generation would resist that American racial delirium.

By the time the civil rights movement had unraveled into rage, America was a different country. Sermons, marches, court victories, and legislation had turned a deeply segregated society into an essentially multicultural and integrated one. A half-century after *Brown*, Americans are still weighing the consequences—of the *Brown* decision itself, of the civil rights movement, of race in America.

Looking back on the sixties today, we pass too lightly over the struggle for civil rights. The soaring aspirations and the violent backlash framed everything that followed. The racial dialectic—hope and violence—was everywhere. It transformed American politics.

Even modern conservatism has roots in the racial gray zone. As conservatives enjoy success today, they celebrate the heroes who stood up to the Social Gospel tide. In the first circle of the pantheon stands Barry Goldwater, the Republican presidential candidate in 1964. Goldwater was a formidable character. He insisted on a single high principle: resist—and roll back—federal government incursions on American civic life. He inspired a conservative generation. But that principle looks more complicated in the context of the time. Goldwater made headlines, day after day, by opposing the Civil Rights Act. Only four other Senate Republicans (out of thirty-three) joined the fire-eating southern Democrats to fight civil rights. At the time, Republicans feared that siding with segregationists would lead them to an electoral thumping—which it did. But Goldwater pried the deep South from the Democrats once and (perhaps) for all. To be sure, by ferociously attacking the federal government— even when it pursued high moral ideals like civil rights—he sounded the call for modern conservatives. At the time, however, many of Goldwater's followers had something uglier in mind when they cheered his salvos against civil rights legislation. His cunning campaign slogan winked directly at the dark side: "In your heart you know he's right." Modern American conservatism emerged from this ambiguous moral zone: fighting off the federals— even on principle—meant marching shoulder to shoulder with the segregationists.

Decades later, many cultural conservatives train their fire on the 1960s. Often ignoring Martin Luther King, Malcolm X, and the shameful segregationist reaction, they focus instead on college students indulging themselves. Let's turn to the moral fiber of Woodstock nation.

The Student Movement

"Let the word go forth," declared President Kennedy in his inaugural address in 1961, "that the torch has been passed to a new generation of Americans." Kennedy wanted everyone to know that the United States "would pay any price" and "bear any burden" for "those human rights to which this nation has always been committed . . . at home and around the world." Four months later, young activists hopped onto their freedom buses and carried the word to Alabama. Young people signed up for the Peace Corps (more Harvard graduates had applied for the Peace Corps than for corporate jobs), volunteered for VISTA (the domestic equivalent), risked their skulls for civil rights, and organized their own social movement.[52]

Peace and Love

Black college students organized the Student Nonviolent Coordinating Committee (SNCC, pronounced "snick!") in 1960. It reverberated with the energy of the sit-ins. "We affirm the religious ideal of nonviolence as the foundation of our purpose," proclaimed SNCC's original statement of purpose. "Nonviolence as it grows from Judaic-Christian traditions seeks a social order of justice permeated by love." Love would vanish the bigotry. "Mutual regard cancels enmity. Justice for all overcomes injustice." The students rushed into the southern protests. SNCC took its mantra, "beloved community," and tied it to a prime directive—"Put your body on the line!"[53]

In 1962, Students for a Democratic Society (SDS) published its own manifesto, the Port Huron Statement. Against an uneasy backdrop—"the Southern struggle against racial bigotry" and "the cold war symbolized by the Bomb"—the mainly white students proclaimed an edgy American romanticism: "We regard men as infinitely precious and possessed of unfulfilled capacities for reason, freedom and love." They challenged a society that depersonalized, standardized, and controlled; SDS would celebrate the people's "unrealized potential for self cultivation." Everyone would "participate in decision making" over their own lives. The manifesto's dreams would eventually spring to life in the movement's most successful offshoot: the movement feminists.[54]

At the heart of the Port Huron ideal lay the powerful American urge to organize communal life around direct citizen participation. That wish stretches back to the New England town meeting and the Puritan congregation. In the last chapter we saw the democratic image polished up and presented as Norman Rockwell's *Freedom of Speech*. In the 1960s, efforts at participatory democracy ran into every crevice of politics—poverty agencies, school boards, and student organizations.

The young people who organized SNCC and wrote the Port Huron Statement imagined a gentler, kinder, more peaceful politics. Historian William McLoughlin still clung to the hope even after the tide had passed: today's counterculture strives to be "tolerant, soft spoken, respectful of the feelings and opinions of others; it frowns on the aggressive, defensive, hostile, and possessive attitudes of the cultural past; it likes what men and women have in common." This gentle spirit, concluded McLoughlin, turned youth politics toward oppressed races, prisoners, battered spouses, and endangered species. "For the first time," repeated *Newsweek*, "men and women are becoming friends." The language of kindness—of love—got used so often it became a cliché. Looking backward, it is easy to ignore. But at the time, it lay at the very core of the youth movement. It was all over the Port Huron Statement, the sit-ins, the freedom rides, and, indeed, Woodstock's Aquarian Exposition of Peace and Music.[55]

Even the silliest side of the youth movement, the hippies, seemed at first to promote the same soft values. The hippies "live joyously, creatively, [and] . . . close to God," decided *Newsweek*. With their peace and honesty, agreed *Time*, hippies lead considerably more virtuous lives than the great majority of their fellow citizens." "The hippies are beautiful," conceded an essay in the *Nation*. "They know a lot of things that the squares don't." Like what? "That it is health[y] to be spontaneous, communal and tolerant." Of course they did trample the rules, "most notably those prohibiting the use of drugs." But their gentle virtue "helps explain why so many people in authority, from cops to judges to ministers, tend to treat them gently and with a measure of respect."[56]

We have seen all this before. The more romantic abolitionists also rejected hard-hearted "Anglo-Saxon" traits, like the aggressive drive to get ahead. Instead, they honored the gentle, nurturing Christian spirit that they thought they saw in African Americans and women—just the groups, incidentally, who would win fundamental changes in the 1960s. This time those virtues sprang directly from the civil rights campaign. The student movement was deeply influenced by the black rebels pouring out of their churches and threatening to wear down their enemies with love. Some white student leaders had been there; the rest had seen or heard. Martin Luther King and the southern civil rights movement created a template for every reformist voice raised in the early 1960s.

Great Awakenings never seem normal. Participants reject business as usual. Their movements seem, somehow, to dissolve the lines between science and magic, between politics and poetry. They are "moments of madness," as Aristide Zolberg put it after watching the students run through the streets of Paris: Everything seems possible, everything within reach. Something transformative seemed to be stirring. The Puritans had felt the same spirit and recognized it for the millennium—Jesus returning to redeem the world. When the black abolitionists heard the thunder two centuries later, they knew their own redemption must be at hand. The youth movement imagined something just as big. And once again the political madness was racing around the world. Developing nations shook off colonial masters and groped toward self-government and freedom. Demonstrations shook western Europe: In Prague enormous processions celebrated the remarkable spring of the people's free will. In

Madrid and Barcelona people chanted "Death to Francisco Franco." In Rome demonstrators demanded the passage of a university reform bill, and in Paris they condemned sociology as a capitalist fraud. Everywhere young people imagined a new, more democratic, more socially responsible order. Among the things they challenged—out there on the streets—were the spies, the armies, and the bombs of the cold-war state.[57]

Hell No, We Won't Go

The civil rights movement had inspired American young people, white and black. By the mid-1960s, however, that crusade had imploded into frustrated factions. Loving your enemies looked like yesterday's strategy—timid, cautious, old. Young African Americans turned to black power. They spurned white alliances. The fight for racial justice faded from the white youths' agenda. A new moral issue loomed before them.

The war in Vietnam convulsed America because it got trapped by the deep changes in America's mission to the world. We saw the cold war filter into every feature of American life during the early 1950s. At the start of the sixties the fight was still vital—that's what Kennedy really had in mind with his trumpet call to the struggle. Of course cold-war nags like George Kennan and Reinhold Niebuhr kept chiding Americans about dividing the world into stark Manichean zones, a good us versus the wicked them. Don't get blinded by too much confidence in our own virtue, warned Niebuhr; moral illusions would trap our foreign policy. Niebuhr's danger caught up to American leaders in Southeast Asia.[58]

The old image—of a virtuous nation fighting tyrants to protect liberty—ran headlong into the postcolonial paradigm. The rising new nations in Africa and Asia were constantly in the news; they had just won their freedom, sometimes despite the imperialists who did not want to let go. Back home the civil rights movement also reached for freedom. Martin Luther King invoked Gandhi's heroic nonviolence. The ferocious reaction in the American South provoked a heretical thought: maybe the United States was not so innocent. Cold warriors only undercut their own perspective by attacking the civil rights leaders as communists and fellow travelers. J. Edgar Hoover, in particular, loudly mistrusted the protesters. He bristled with contempt, kept elaborate files on the leaders, and forced King to break with close (but "un-American") colleagues. When King won the Nobel Peace Prize in 1964, Hoover called reporters into his office and stunned them by blasting the "notorious" Martin King. King defended Hoover and then delivered a dazzling sermon in Oslo. The audience inside the auditorium interrupted him with cheers while hundreds of college students held torches outside in the snow. For young people, attacks like Hoover's only boomeranged on the cold-war paradigm itself. The new spirit of the era ran from the students in Oslo saluting the brave marchers in Birmingham who, in turn, invoked the nonviolent rebels in India, themselves a symbol of the rising anticolonial era. They were all fighting for liberty. Next to them, cold warriors like Hoover looked lost in time—dirty hands, closed minds, and tired fears.[59]

By the mid-1960s the whole notion of a Communist monolith was slipping away. Russia and China seemed as likely to fight one another as to turn on the United States. Evil menace drained away from Communism, and international morality ran to gray. President Richard Nixon would soon underscore the change by opening diplomatic doors to Russia and China. The old urge to demonize enemies now showed its flip side: who wants to "bear any burden" or "pay any price" to fight an ambiguous foe? Even worse, from the postcolonial perspective, the United States looked suspiciously like a stand-in for defeated colonial power in Vietnam. Protesters turned Kennedy's inaugural address inside out: the American cop—so it seemed—resisted freedom both at home and abroad.

The white student movement, pushed out of civil rights, poured its protests into the war. Demonstrations grew and spread. The public had once supported military action in Vietnam. Now the polls turned. Student leaders kept notching up their fury: "The war in Vietnam . . . has finally severed the last vestiges of illusion that morality and democracy are the guiding principles of American foreign policy." The critique turned from the war itself to "the system" that drove "good men to make decisions that lead . . . to mutilation and death of thousands." The epigrams of peace flowed through youth culture. You could not get far on campus without hearing from Herbert Marcuse: "Obscene is not the picture of a naked woman who exposes her pubic hair but a fully clothed general who exposes his medals rewarded in war of aggression; obscene is not the ritual of the hippies but the declaration of a high dignitary of the church that war is necessary for peace."[60]

No one put the antiwar case more ardently than King himself. He offered a rousing call for nonviolence when he accepted his Nobel Prize. "One day mankind will bow before the altars of God and be crowned triumphant over war and bloodshed. . . . 'And the lion and the lamb shall lie down together and every man shall sit under his own vine and none shall be afraid.'" By 1967, King had turned up the volume and gotten specific. "When I see our country mutilating hundreds of thousands of Vietnamese children with napalm, burning villages and rice fields at random, painting the valleys of that small Asian country red with human blood, leaving broken bodies in countless ditches and sending home half-men, mutilated mentally and physically. . . . then I tremble for the world." But the worst of it was what the war had done to the United States. "A few years ago, there was a shining moment," preached King in 1967. "It seemed as if there was a real promise of hope for the poor—both black and white—through the poverty program. . . . Then came the buildup in Vietnam and I watched the program broken as if it were some idle political plaything of a society gone mad on war, and I knew that America would never invest the necessary funds or energies in rehabilitation of its poor so long as adventures like Vietnam continued to draw men and skills and money like some demoniacal destructive suction tube."[61]

To be sure, the other side fought back. Conservatives were beside themselves. Explain the war, they begged first President Johnson then Nixon. Not in abstractions. Rally the people. Escalate. Fight to win. "To what conceivable purpose do we leash our military?" anguished an article in *National Review* (June 28, 1966). Frustrated, they sometimes got carried away. "The United States has not had . . . a better occasion for using nuclear weapons."

In the best traditions of the city on a hill, both sides agreed that this was a moral issue. Each made its case by furiously spinning moral images of the North Vietnamese. Cold warriors saw the enemy as the latest brand of Communist monster. When Paul Goodman, a left-leaning intellectual, called a convention of defense contractors "obscene," the meeting's chairman snapped back. "Your remark about our committing genocide in Vietnam is obscene. What is really intolerable there, the Viet Cong single out college graduates for extermination." On the other side, the left saw a liberation struggle rather than Communist aggression. They turned the cold warrior's ogres into brave democratic people fighting imperialists for their homeland. Tom Hayden visited Hanoi and caught the image with almost perfect postcolonial pitch. "We identify with the poor and oppressed. So do they."[62]

Conservatives are still arguing thirty years later: we could have won. The Communists were oppressive, even evil. The antiwar movement was the spasm of a spoiled generation afraid to fight. But the revisionist case works only if the arguments are plucked out of time. Back in the sixties, the battle rose out of a clash of paradigms. The old anti-Communists lost their public with a great lurch in the international zeitgeist. International communism seemed less dangerous. Civil rights at home seemed connected with third-world nationalism; some cold warriors damaged their own cause when they hogged headlines resisting both. As to the claim that the kids were chicken, student anti-war protests were every bit as furious in London and Paris and Berlin. To understand the sixties, take its moral dreams seriously. If the past is any guide, they will be back.

Still, resisting the war proved frustrating. Foreign policy cannot easily be reshaped from the streets or the college campuses. With time, the joyous madness drained right out of the student movement. In fact, the students had to hustle just to keep up with the culture's cynicism. The unhinged general in Stanley Kubrick's *Dr. Strangelove* (1964) conserves his precious bodily fluids when he orders the big strike on the Ruskies; his sane colleague avoids the woman waiting for him (in a bikini) by sticking to the President's side and not so secretly cheering on the plane which will destroy the planet—an acid vision of Armageddon. Joseph Heller's novel *Catch-22* (1961) mocked military thinking so deftly that everyone became familiar with the eponymous catch: if you're willing to fly into combat you are nuts and deserve an immediate medical discharge; but you can't get the discharge unless you ask for it, and by asking for it you've proved your sanity—no discharge for you.

The sarcastic spirit spread. After a week of protests in Washington, D.C., in October 1967, one youthful battalion marched on the Pentagon. Norman Mailer described this army of the night: garbed as hippies, the protesters "assembled from all the intersections between history and the comic books, between legend and television, the Biblical archetypes and the movies." When they got to the Pentagon, the peace legion tried to "levitate" it. They planned to spin the evil spirits right out of the building. Something went wrong with the magic, apparently, because the Pentagon remained solidly on the ground. The early 1960s optimism faded. Eventually the youth movement shattered. The attention focused on the angry young men (mainly) who spun into nihilistic rage.[63]

You Don't Need a Weatherman

"America is the place Utopias are put into practice," wrote one historian pondering the 1670s, "only to discover that they're not practical." The 1960s youth movement may have been even less practical than most Arcadian dreamers. Joan Didion turned her cool, make-no-judgments writing on the hippies in San Francisco's Haight-Ashbury. She buried the dreamy stories about groovy alternative life styles in a picture of irresponsible squalor: "Sue Ann's three-year-old Michael started a fire this morning before anyone was up, but Don got it out before much damage was done. Michael burned his arm though, which is probably why Sue Ann was so jumpy when she happened to see him chewing on an electric cord. 'You'll fry like rice,' she screams." No one else in the commune notices. They're too busy trying to retrieve the fine Moroccan hash which slipped through a floorboard damaged in the fire. Didion's postcards from California injected an ominous alarm into the fun. Buzzing through her head, in the late 1960s, ran that menacing question at the end of William Butler Yeats's "The Second Coming": "What rough beast, its hour come round at last, slouches toward Bethlehem to be born?" Yeats became the hook for the cynical revision read back onto the whole generation—by the mid-1990s, Robert Bork tagged it the most quoted poem of our time.[64]

Bob Dylan had warned the old generation that they'd better start swimming or they'd sink like a stone. But institutions don't sink, they evolve. Slowly. When Tom Hayden went before the House Un-American Activities Committee (HUAC), each side seemed genuinely baffled by the other. Don't you believe in the democratic system? they asked him. "You have destroyed the American democratic system, by the existence of a committee of this kind," he responded. They just shook their heads. "You have indeed a very strange philosophy, sir," summed up a congressman from Michigan.

How could Hayden explain the Port Huron dream of a radical new society to a congressional committee hunting down un-American activists? Grassroots dreamers usually shake up the old order more effectively than they launch a new one. The movement—and the sixties—certainly shook up American politics. But mere reforms seemed to pale next to the original dream. Again Hayden offered the most famous epitaph: "We ended a war, toppled two presidents, desegregated the south, broke other barriers of discrimination. How could we accomplish so much and have so little in the end?"[65]

The usual story lingers on how it all came to a bitter finish. In the developing world the heady liberation moment passed; new nations lost their cold-war leverage and sank into debt and poverty. At home the civil rights movement ended in blood and bitterness. The Vietnam War absorbed international protests and ground on. Forget the radical rethinking of national values, the movement couldn't shift a single unpopular foreign policy. And how could anyone claim to be radical when Black Panthers took up guns, Cuban guerillas spread revolution, heroic Vietnamese fought for freedom (so it seemed), and Prague dissidents stood up to Soviet tanks?

A small group within the movement tried to keep up by pushing out to the radical edge. The ferocious SDS convention in June 1969 watched an intimidating visit from armed Black Panthers before splintering. One faction, led by Bernadine Dohrn, took its name from Bob Dylan's raucous *Subterranean Homesick Blues:* "You don't need a weatherman to know which way the wind blows" (an acid retort to Dylan's own *Blowin' in the Wind*). The Weathermen bolted the convention, full of rage and destruction. For a time, the highest toll from their revolution fell on the radicals themselves—blown up making their bombs.[66]

The establishment faced its own troubles. The unredeemed promise of civil rights and the tumult of the Vietnam War ran into an economic downturn and produced what historian James Patterson labels a sour political era. In 1974, after a long legal fight, President Nixon finally released his secret recordings of White House conversations. Suddenly, after months of denial, the president could be heard directing a sleazy coverup just six days after the ludicrous burglary of Democratic Party headquarters. On tape after tape and page after transcribed page the tormented man battled his weird demons: "I don't give a shit what happens. I want you all to stonewall it, let them plead the Fifth Amendment, cover-up or anything else." The gutter language poured out of the president; the torrent of "expletive deleted" clogging the transcripts seems jolting even now. Politics never was a branch of the Sunday school business, as a nineteenth-century spoilsman warned a gang of reformers. But the Nixon tapes really let it all hang out. That profanity—and all that came with it—transformed the relationship between the presidency and the press.[67]

Feminism

The sixties' story comes with another ending. The Port Huron Statement's real legacy lies with the women who took those nebulous values of peace and social justice and infused them with meaning. They joined a larger social movement that grew stronger as the decade went on.

When we last looked at the "woman problem," *Life* magazine was fretting about Mom: "The family is in special trouble," thanks to a "dominating" and "joyless" generation of mothers. In 1963, Betty Friedan turned that discussion inside out in *The Feminine Mystique*. Friedan, told a story about women who nourished dreams that they could neither fulfill nor forget. Instead, they felt trapped in their social roles—housewife, mother—and by a stifling "feminine mystique." Friedan voiced an inchoate middle-class feminine sensibility. The book found an enormous audience.

The political vanguard was already active. Between 1960 and 1966, Congress considered over 400 pieces of legislation on women's rights. However, the great breakthrough—the feminist equivalent of *Brown v. Board of Education*—came with the Civil Rights Act of 1964. Congressman Howard Smith, an ardent segregationist from Virginia, rose during the legislative battle and proposed an amendment: prohibit employers from discriminating by sex as well as by race, religion, or national origin. Though the National Women's Party had lobbied Smith for the amendment, he had an ulterior motive. Smith hoped to turn the proposed law into a farce and give northern representatives cover for rejecting the whole thing. "Now I am very serious about this," insisted Smith, as he regaled the House with a letter from a woman who could not snag a husband. "I just want to remind you," he chortled, "that in this election year, it is pretty nearly half of the voters that are affected so you had better sit up and take notice."

The Johnson administration and most congressional liberals nervously opposed Smith's amendment. With a filibuster hanging over the Senate, they did
not want to jeopardize black rights by tossing gender into the law. Emanuel
Celler of New York led the opposition in the House. Since he was about to celebrate his fiftieth wedding anniversary, joshed Celler, he could let everyone in
on his connubial secret: in every discussion, "I usually have the last two words,
and those words are 'yes dear.'" When they finally stopped chuckling, the
southern congressmen went into their cavalier routine: "Never let it be said
that a southern gentleman would . . . discriminate against women," expounded
Congressman J. Russell Tuten. "It is incredible to me that the authors of this
monstrosity," proclaimed Representative L. Mendel Rivers of South Carolina,
"would deprive the white woman of mostly Anglo-Saxon or Christian heritage
equal opportunity before the employer."

Somewhere between the merriment and the bombast, an earnest voice entered the debate. Eleven of the twelve women in Congress broke with the official liberal line and supported the gender provision. "White women and Negroes occupied the same position in American society," said Representative
Martha Griffiths (quoting Gunnar Myrdal). She also commented on all the
fun the boys were having. "If there had been any necessity of pointing out that
women were a second-class sex, the laughter would have proved it." Howard
Smith's gender amendment passed, and, two days later, the entire civil rights
bill went through the House. Every man who spoke up for barring sex discrimination voted against the Civil Rights Act.[68]

The Equal Employment Opportunity Commission (EEOC), charged
with monitoring compliance, largely ignored the gender provision. The agency
put out only the mildest regulations. But even liberals hooted at the effort.
"Why should a mischievous joke perpetrated on the floor of the House of Representatives be treated [seriously] by a responsible administrative body?" asked
the *New Republic*. The *Wall Street Journal* ran an article full of huffing execu-
tives. An airline representative illustrated the absurdity of the new law: "What
are we going to do now when a gal walks into our office, demands a job as an
airline pilot and has the credentials to qualify?" The members of the EEOC
agreed; they took such a soft approach that Representative Griffiths reminded
them about their "oath to uphold the [entire] law, not just the part of it that
they are interested in."[69]

We have seen race and gender equality run together through American history. In fighting to strike off the slave's chains, wrote abolitionist Abbey Kelley
Foster, "we found most surely that we were manacled ourselves." Frederick
Douglass had asked the women to put all that aside. "The slave's cause is already too heavily laden." The same word circulated after the Civil War: getting
black men their political rights would be tough enough, and radical women's

proposals might sink the whole effort. Fifty years later, during the Progressive Era, getting realistic ran the other way. Racial equality? Lynching legislation? The South would never stand for it. Winning women's rights would be tough enough without throwing racial reform into the mix. Now, in the sixties, the "unrealistic" burden shifted back onto women. They had been on the line during the sit-ins, marches, and SNCC rallies; but only a southern segregationist tactic gave women enough votes for a place in the civil rights legislation. And the hard part still lay ahead. As the Supreme Court decision in *Brown* had shown, reformers would have to mobilize to bring their legal protections to life.[70]

A network of activists began to meet and plan. The National Organization for Women (NOW) formally organized in 1966. The goal seemed simple: "the hallmark of American democracy—equality, no more, no less." But getting there required rethinking the most basic social categories: responsibility in the family, opportunity in society, the cultural expectations about sex and gender.[71]

How do you even think about such fundamental categories? The questions—if not the answers—had already been posed by the student movements. The Port Huron Statement had groped toward new human values. The statement stood on "unfulfilled capacities for reason, freedom and love" and on "the potential for self-cultivation, self-direction, self-understanding, and creativity." Its goals ran to a meaningful life, an escape from powerlessness, and generosity to others. And the kids had defined independence with a line that sounds like a cross between Virginia Woolf and Betty Friedan: "not to have one's way so much as . . . to have a way that is one's own." The students in the civil rights movement came at it from a different direction: the Christian vision of "beloved community." Black women, organizing SNCC from the start, had drawn on their church notions; they had articulated the beloved community as clearly as anyone in the movement.

By the mid-1960s, both SNCC and the SDS were groping for new directions and identities. Segregationist violence had exhausted them. The black students, in particular, suffered from a kind of combat fatigue. All the jeers and jailings, savagery and shooting took a terrible toll, the forgotten feature of the early 1960s. In their search for a new way, each student group met, talked, delivered speeches, and issued statements. Neither organization found its new direction. And what everyone remembers today is the turn to rage: SNCC and black power, SDS and the Weathermen. But something profoundly radical came out of all those efforts to rethink. Slowly, women began to gather separately and assess their own role in the movement. In the SDS they thought hard about their subordination; about male egos, power plays, and gender roles. Women in SNCC confronted their own double bind—they faced precisely the same paternalism and condescension from the men in SNCC as black people faced in society as a whole.

The women ran up against the stubborn disconnection between the movement's freedom goals and its female roles. Radical men acted more or less like the straights in Congress. Most found women's stuff silly. Some became abusive. Activist Shulamith Firestone recalled getting up on stage during a Nixon counter-inauguration; as she tried to address women's issues, one man got annoyed by the distraction and screamed, "Take her off the stage and fuck her." Over at SNCC, Stokely Carmichael had proved a charismatic and popular leader. But during one of his long, funny riffs, an inside joke got a laugh and became a Carmichael staple: "The only position for a woman in SNCC is prone." To some, the paternalism felt even worse than the abuse. A women's caucus fought to get its resolution before a national conference for new politics in 1967. The conference finally, reluctantly agreed. When the issue came up the group immediately approved the caucus resolution—with plenty of catcalls but not a word of serious discussion. Jo Freeman, who had come forward to lead the discussion, recalled being stunned by the indifference. And then stung by condescension: "Move on, little girl," said the moderator, "we have more important issues to talk about here than women's liberation."[72]

Women's groups broke away and rapidly began developing their own political theory. The new approach ranged from the political to the personal, from employment discrimination to marriage and motherhood. From this perspective the Port Huron Statement can be reread not as an ironic herald of the Weathermen but as a set of intuitions (the personal as political) that the women's branch of the movement would push in increasingly sophisticated ways. When we stop reading the movement—the 1960s reformers, back and white—as a story about men, the sixties end very differently. The movement won extraordinary change. That snorting airline spokesman had glimpsed the future: gals started flying the planes.

The Sixties

The long Social Gospel swing ended in a dazzling awakening. A heroic civil rights generation beat the violence. Black Americans did not win full racial justice, but they ended lynch law, desegregated American society, and buried the deep taboos on interracial . . . well, almost everything.

At the same time, women began to rethink gender roles. They won their place in the public sphere and remade basic expectations about American domestic life. Here's a marker of change: back in 1964 the men in Congress thought that banning sexual discrimination was a hilarious idea. Today the men's bathroom in every mall includes a diaper-changing station. Congressman Celler would not have had a clue.

The sixties finally buried the old Victorian purity laws. The courts discovered a constitutional right to privacy and dismantled the last Comstock bans on birth control. This rethinking of privacy reached beyond the traditional family. The gay rights movement began—we can fix an exact date—on June 27, 1969. Police conducted a routine raid on a gay bar in Greenwich Village, and gays and lesbians surprised everyone by fighting back. "Gay power" sprang up, and the Gay Liberation Front was organized. The culture of the day offered gays plenty of protest marches to join. A new social movement swiftly emerged. NOW endorsed gay rights in 1973, the American Psychiatric Association removed homosexuality from its roster of mental disorders in 1974, and the U.S. Civil Service Commission lifted the Truman-era ban on gays and lesbians in 1975.[73]

The high tide for liberalism and privacy came with *Roe v. Wade* in 1973, when the Supreme Court struck down state laws forbidding abortion. *Roe* overthrew the whole legal network that went back to Horatio Robinson Storer and the AMA campaigns to outlaw abortion. With *Roe* the court had almost fully dismantled the Victorian sexual regime—and roused a completely new era of hellfire politics. The long socially progressive swing ended, and the political pendulum headed back toward the politics of personal morality.

The Social Gospel era offers an alternative moral vision—one I never expected to find. This moral impulse reverses the usual urge: rather than blaming bad people for society's troubles, society takes responsibility for all its people. The concept goes back to the Puritans: God made His covenant with the entire community, and divine praise or punishment would fall on everyone. The radical abolitionists resurrected the idea in the nineteenth century. But no one ever pushed the collective theory—we are our neighbors' keepers—quite like the social democrats did during the four decades following the 1932 election. A look at the most eloquent Social Gospel preachers—Franklin Roosevelt and Martin Luther King, Jr.—yields an arresting conclusion: by contemporary standards, they sound like radicals. Both blamed the social economic system for people's troubles. Both insisted that society has an obligation to every member. Their sermons—their entire perspective—rested on an important implicit story: the poorest and weakest in our society are good, honest people. The cold war got Americans marketing that conclusion to the entire world.

The Social Gospel half-century revisited every moral issue back to the Salem witch trials. It reversed many of the limits that had been constructed to keep the immoral others in their place: it repealed Prohibition, revoked Jim Crow laws, reversed the purity codes, reopened the borders to immigrants, rejected the anti-Darwin laws (in the Scopes II trial), and profoundly revised women's roles. Congress eventually got around to amending the Mann Act—you may now cross state lines with perfectly dirty thoughts as long as your partner is old enough and like-minded.

In the 1970s the tide started running the other way. The Social Gospel underpinnings—honoring the poor—collapsed, and Victorian morals rushed back in. Generations of snickering about Victorian moralists began to fade. Politics barged right back toward the "sacred precincts of the marital bedroom." In the next election Jimmy Carter would run for office flaunting his Baptist roots; after winning he would hector his young employees about living in sin and push them to get married. *Playboy* could no longer posture as the national guide to cool.[74]

Moral conservatives launched their backlash against the wide-ranging policies of the Social Gospel decades: abortion, gay rights, affirmative action, and poverty were now spun back into sins. The poor became a lazy underclass again. A new generation of moralists blamed bad behavior for every manner of social problem: crime, alcoholism, drug abuse, bastards, rude kids, pornography, and a menacing underclass. Today, a full generation after the sixties, those certainly look like individual sins. Sex? Drink? Drugs? Stop whining about underprivilege and just say no! It takes a great imaginative leap to even remember the vibrant Social Gospel: We all share moral fates. We are our neighbors' keepers. We are responsible for the whole community. For further details, as FDR used to tell the preachers, go back to the Sermon on the Mount.

We'll meet the new Victorians in the next chapter. They launched their counterattack against the Social Gospel with a red-hot assault on "the sixties." Their version of the decade sometimes seems to boil down to little more than draft dodgers, Weathermen, free love, and irresponsible hippies. The preceding pages describe a very different time. At the heart of the decade—organizing and inspiring everything else—stands the extraordinary quest for racial equality. The villainy in the sixties—and the repressed memory of our own time—lies in the ferocious violence that fought black Americans and their moral crusade. The crucible of racial hate and fire profoundly shaped the downside of this great awakening—the drift and rage of the late 1960s.

The assault on the sixties has succeeded brilliantly. Even progressives apologize for the period. But no apologies are necessary. The Social Gospel half-century made the United States a far more decent place. At its height, men and women stood up courageously for the American dream. They won dignity and rights for minorities, women, poor people, and the elderly that Americans across the political spectrum now take for granted. The movement's victories—America's democratic legacies—came at great sacrifice and with enormous courage.

PART V

The Puritans Roar Again

Top Disciplinary Problems in School

1940
1. Talking out of turn
2. Chewing gum
3. Making noise
4. Running in the halls
5. Cutting in line

1990
1. Drug abuse
2. Alcohol abuse
3. Pregnancy
4. Suicide
5. Rape

THIS often-repeated list is a contemporary legend, leaping from one jeremiad to another. Turns out the original was the brainchild of a born-again fundamentalist who wrote it in 1982. What it captures is not a crisis in the schools so much as that ancient Puritan anguish: we are declining, we are going to hell—just look at what's happened to the kids.[1]

Chapter 15
Modern Morals

I N 1997 the Southern Baptist Convention voted to boycott Walt Disney. Mickey, Minnie, and Bambi had morphed into a media conglomerate chasing profits by trashing American morals. "Gays have 25 or 30 characters on TV shows," complained one boycott leader, "and every last one of them is positive." Disney sponsored hot television like *NYPD Blue* (through its ABC affiliates), produced the heretical *Priest* (through its Miramax subsidiary), and permitted "gay days" at Disney World. The boycott got great press—then flopped. Prime time went from bad to worse. No sooner had the conservatives organized, for example, than *Ally McBeal* served up a famous primetime episode. Two high-priced lawyers, both women, are working late. Suddenly, Ally and Lucy Liu fall into each other's arms, kissing. That one scene racked up a culture war trifecta: women in power suits, an Asian American corporate lawyer, and casual gay sex.[1]

There are plenty of ways to read modern American culture, but the Jeremiahs have been roaring loudest. They find moral trouble at every turn: the pill, legal abortions, and welfare payments team up to break the connection between sex and families. Unmarried couples set up house. Married couples cheat and split. Forty percent of our children live apart from their dad. Vermont began blessing gay unions in 2000. Eleven million people smoked pot last month. A New Yorker gets murdered every fourteen hours. And just look at what's happening in the schools. The moral critics—some proudly declare themselves new Victorians—have effectively spread their alarm.[2]

These new Victorians scorn the Social Gospel reflex that blames the system. Individuals, they insist, are responsible for their own behavior—and for our common problems. The Christian Coalition deftly summed up the shifting moral paradigms in its *Contract with the American Family:* Progressives "generally argue that crime results from . . . poor education, economic deprivation, racism and low esteem. Their prescription, quite naturally, takes the form of early government intervention with a multitude of programs aimed at job creation." Frances Willard, Franklin Roosevelt, and Martin Luther King could not have put their own views more tidily. Social Gospel liberals, continued the *Contract*, focus on the "external circumstances" that foster drug abuse or crime or despair. In contrast, conservatives train the moral spotlight directly on the vicious. "Criminals, not society, are responsible for crime. Crime results from a lack of moral restraint." And whom do we blame for that? The *Contract* lined right up behind the synod of 1679 and its "defects as to family governance": "The lack of moral restraint typically follows from the absence of nurturing parents and their constant discipline. When families fail, government must be ready to deliver a firm message."[3]

Traditionalists complain that the message barely seems to have dented the popular culture. But in many ways their perspective triumphed. American politics roils with tough love: drug wars, in-your-face crime fighting, zero tolerance, a jail-building boom, federally funded abstinence education, and a deep rethinking of New Deal welfare entitlements. President Franklin Roosevelt condemned self-interest as poor economics and false ethics. But conventional wisdom now runs the other way. Social Gospel fancies about sharing the wealth get ticked down as bad economics and worse morals—tired political flotsam from long ago. Charity breeds sloth, social programs bring inefficiencies. We're almost all the way back to Henry Ward Beecher: "No man in this land suffers from poverty unless it be more than his fault—unless it be his *sin*." Only a few leftover leftists demur as inequality grows.[4]

Progressives offer an entirely different picture of the nation. The ostensibly slack 1960s, they say, have nothing to do with our troubles. Rather, vibrant global capitalism hums with choices your grandparents never imagined: French country bread, National Public Radio, vacations in Katmandu, and dirty internet pictures right on your desktop. Walt Disney was only playing by the new rules: grow, merge, and acquire—or perish. The wired globe delivers choices, opportunities, and nerve-racking uncertainty. Lifelong work for a single company fades into history. The stable family in which Dad brought home the paycheck is long gone. Necessity pushed many woman to work—the minimum wage won't lift an individual (much less a family) out of poverty. And the new economy rewards Mom a lot more often than the old economy did. Reliable birth control, protected by the Constitution's "penumbra," frees women to face the same professional choices—and pressures and anxieties—that were once reserved for men. Forget the *Playboy* philosophy, the book on this society is *The Overworked American*. While cultural conservatives lament lax morals, progressives see relentless pressure on hard-working men and women; where the right frets over a lazy welfare class, the left finds poor people struggling to get by—blending government assistance, low-wage jobs, and helping hands (like emergency housing) from family and friends.[5]

Progressives call for programs that can help families cope with the rush of pressures from job and home. The agenda is familiar: day care for children, reproductive health services for all women, a living wage for every worker, universal health insurance, and good schools in every neighborhood. We've starved the public sphere, they argue; 40 million people have no health insurance, and American teachers' salaries rank twenty-second among the industrial democracies. But these ideas have found scant support in recent years. Their last great moment, President Bill Clinton's national health insurance proposal (1994), plunged from 70 percent approval to big-government debacle in less than a year.[6]

With their programs off the political agenda, progressives lament the political culture almost as loudly as conservatives. Each side gravitates to an entirely different political model. Social conservatives see policy through the familiar moral lens—private vice and virtue shape our common fate. In contrast, progressives have abandoned their Social Gospel morality for classical liberalism (partially a legacy of the abortion wars). They insist on a strong line between public and private spheres; they protect personal rights and privacy. The liberal frame offers strong ground for fighting off government—protecting reproductive rights or free speech, for example. But it does not easily rally Americans to a positive agenda, to programs that require more government and higher taxes. The Social Gospel cries for social justice; liberalism serves the thinner gruel of new rights (a "patient's bill of rights") or technocratic fiddling (Clinton-care: lower costs with wider access).

The conservative crusade—crackling with moral verve—peaked in the mid-1990s. After the impeachment of President Clinton the entire culture war cooled down. But the new Victorians had set the political agenda. Their assumptions dominated the national discourse. And, most important, they inspired a vast institutional infrastructure that continues to grind on after the strongest passions faded.

The new Victorian surge revised the classic American sins—violence, substance abuse, sex, and sloth. In many cases the pendulum has swung from the old Social Gospel dreams of shared responsibility to the new Victorian fear of bad people and social decline. But every sin—each policy realm—is different. Each reflects past policies as much as present politics. Reformers more easily meet success when they build within an existing institutional framework.

When crime soared, for example, crime warriors could build on the sprawling criminal justice network. When the crack panic swept the nation, Prohibition-era legal rules offered tough-minded politicians a foundation from which to launch a drug war. In contrast, the courts had dismantled the Comstock sexual regime; neo-Puritans found few organizational foundations on which to build it back. The 1990s saw ferocious sexual politics—Americans impeached a president and brawled over abortion; but, ironically, social conservatives won their strongest gender victories in the framework of that thoroughly progressive construction, the welfare state. Why? Because that's where they found the organizational leverage for social change.[7]

The Old Jeremiads Ring Out Again

In the late 1970s a delegation of evangelical preachers visited President Jimmy Carter. The meeting went terribly. Carter would not fight abortion or the Equal Rights Amendment. As the Reverend Tim LaHaye left the president's office he bowed his head and prayed: "God, we have got to get this man out of the White House and get someone in here who will be aggressive about bringing back traditional moral values." The Reverend Jerry Falwell wrote it down with more fire: "Satan had mobilized his forces to destroy America. . . . God needed voices raised to save the nation from inward moral decay." In June 1979, Falwell, LaHaye, and others organized the Moral Majority and plunged conservative Christians back into the political fray (they had withdrawn after the Scopes trial and the fall of Prohibition). The Moral Majority pronounced itself "pro-life, pro-traditional family, pro-moral and pro-American." A year later, they cheered (and claimed lots of credit) as Ronald Reagan won the prize.[8]

Two months after taking office, President Reagan rose before the National Association of Evangelicals and ran through Cotton Mather's Puritan inventory: looming apocalypse, satanic enemies, and backsliding saints. The special people are embattled, said the president; foes loom abroad and at home. The foreign enemy, of course, was Communism, the "focus of evil in the modern world." With genial self-confidence the president waved aside the grays and the bitterness of the 1960s and plunked the nation back into 1950s black and white. Communism again became what *Life* magazine had once tagged a "form of Satan in action." At home, danger whirled around "modern-day secularism." In evangelical writing, secularism is the great temptation—LaHaye called it the "invisible enemy threatening our society." Secularists honor "pluralism and tolerance and relative values," explained the Reverend Pat Robertson. President Reagan touched all these evangelical keys and lingered over the political ramifications. He scorned the Social Gospel and its political progeny—the New Deal, the Great Society. Don't blame society, he would repeat, blame the sinner.[9]

The Christian conservatives got extraordinary press. They were organized, passionate, and brash. When Falwell's Moral Majority faltered, Robertson snapped up the banner with his Christian Coalition (in 1989). The activists sometimes got carried away. Randall Terry, the hotheaded founder of an anti-abortion group called Operation Rescue, launched a glowering sermon in 1993: "We are called by God to conquer this country. I want you to let a wave of hatred wash over you. . . . Those who love God must hate sin." Terry sounded like Billy Sunday on a hot day. "I've had it," he said, with "namby pamby so called Christian pantywaists who preach tolerance of others' beliefs. . . . If a Christian voted for Bill Clinton he sinned against God. It's that simple." Pat Robertson went even further while resisting equal rights legislation in Iowa: "The feminist agenda is not about equal rights for women. It is a socialist, anti-family political movement that encourages women to leave their husbands, kill their children, practice witchcraft, destroy capitalism and become lesbians."[10] The occasional assault on classical liberal rights—voting choice, divorce, secular values—sometimes made the preachers look extreme, even fringe.

Despite all the noise, the missionary right remained a relatively small band. National surveys never registered a Christian army rising up to vote Republican. Though millions of conservatives proclaimed their faith in Jesus, most of them did not sound like Randall Terry or Pat Robertson. In fact, African Americans remained the most churched demographic group in the country; they professed—they profess—more conservative social values than any Christian bloc. And they vote reliably Democratic.[11]

The fundamentalists played a crucial role in framing the American moral debate. But many voices—from almost every political quarter—amplified the sermons about spiritual decline. The New Democrats at *Washington Monthly*, for example, called on readers to open their minds: "American evangelicals have a message we all need to hear," announced one headline. "Shame!" blasted a *Newsweek* cover; the subtitle summed up the story. "Intolerance has gotten a bad rap in recent years, but there should be a way to condemn behavior that's socially destructive." Prestigious academics, popular magazines, and plenty of politicians all converged on moral decay. Together they composed a narrative about American politics and culture. Good people clung to their morals in the face of a secular tide. Now, wrote historian Gertrude Himmelfarb, virtuous people were apologizing for being "obsessively puritanical." People scorned honorable virtues like chastity and fidelity. Meanwhile, vice grew shameless and went public. The tone varied from tart irony to raw outrage—the latter for public schools that bought condoms and barred Christ. The chroniclers of moral decline gathered strength and resonance throughout the 1980s and early 1990s. The message boiled down to this: our society has abandoned the morals that once guided us. And there will be hell to pay.[12]

In short, the call to moral arms got organized and articulated in the Carter years (the late 1970s), gathered velocity with Reagan in the bully pulpit (1981–1989), and consolidated its political power with the stunning midterm election of 1994. In that election, the Republicans took control of both House and Senate in Washington, captured both houses of the state legislature in eleven *new* states, and took fifteen *new* governorships (between 1993 and 1996). The Republicans surged from minority to majority at every level of government. That one election cycle, exulted Christian Coalition director Ralph Reed, "signaled the largest single transfer of power from a majority party to a minority party in the twentieth century."[13]

The new Victorian message rewrote American public policy in one area after another. It filtered into local communities across the nation. A suburban Colorado principal was briefly suspended for permitting junior high school students to taste a "thimbleful" of wine during a three-hour meal in France ("They tasted wine," said a spokesman for the school. "They may have ingested alcohol.") Zero tolerance brings back that old Victorian trick, making pledges. The White Cross (purity) and the teetotal (alcohol) vows are back. Schoolchildren pledge sexual abstinence before marriage. Here in rural New Hampshire, a local high school asks parents to "pledge to supervise all parties in their homes" and to "welcome calls from other parents about the whereabouts of the kids."

The efforts to restore responsibility come with the familiar Victorian dark side. We stand firm, stay sober, control our kids, and sign pledges; but thanks to the recalcitrants all around us, our society goes to hell. In Newport, New Hampshire, the weekly *Argus Champion* bemoaned the paltry response to the call for parental pledges. "Yikes, that's not how we remember our teenage years. The parents we knew didn't need anyone to tell them that unsupervised house parties weren't a good idea." Even in Norman Rockwell villages, it's the virtuous us versus a slack and irresponsible them.[14]

Crime War

The most startling neo-Puritan product is the army of Americans in jail. In fact, it may be the most startling fact about American society. Despite a decade of falling crime (by 2000, our murder rate was the same as the murder rate back in 1911), the United States has more than 6 million citizens in jail or prison, under probation, or on parole. Our incarceration rate runs up to five times higher than that of other industrialized democracies. We may prize the picture of an unbridled cowboy culture, but the United States tolerates a lot less deviance than many other western countries. Could it be our racial and ethnic divisions?

For most of the century, we jailed about 100 people out of every 100,000. Other nations stick to roughly that rate—97 per 100,000 in England, 111 in Canada, 177 in Venezuela. But the American rate took off during the Reagan years and kept rising: 313 (per 100,000 adults) by 1985 and 648 by 1997. Zero in on black men and the incarceration rate flies up to 6,838 out of every 100,000. The prison population tripled between 1985 and 1997—and 70 percent of the new inmates were black or Hispanic. Our bitter racial history poses hard questions about the lopsided data.[15]

The crime numbers challenge the standard view of Americans as champion state-bashers. Only an unusually muscular state could push 3 percent of the adult population into its criminal justice system.

Roots

How did we get here? For starters, those dubious old constructions about white and black leaped back into play. Images of virtue rubbed against fears of them and kindled a political storm. In 1977, *Time* magazine replayed DeWitt Talmage and the nineteenth-century tracts about the nightmare metropolis. "Behind the [ghetto's] crumbling walls lives a large group of people who are more intractable, more socially alien and more hostile than almost anyone had imagined. They are the unreachables: The American underclass." This group, reported *Time,* could be recognized by its complete lack of values. They were delinquents, drug addicts, welfare mothers, and worse. Ken Auletta made the term famous in his book *The Underclass.* "As Jacob Riis warned more than a century ago," wrote Auletta, "a 'few generations of slum life might produce monsters.'" To members of the underclass, "upward mobility is a lie and organized society is the enemy." Talk about the "other." These tales of ghetto depravity all stress the same gloomy point—the underclass had almost nothing in common with middle-class America.[16]

Social critics cut straight to the hellfire. "The root cause of crime today," concluded one widely quoted analysis, is "moral poverty." The age-old script applied: evil people were threatening us. James Q. Wilson famously filled in the detail: "We are terrified by the prospect of . . . being gunned down at random, without warning and almost without motive, by youngsters who afterwards show us the blank, unremorseful faces of seemingly feral, pre-social beings." The demonic images buried old sixties fancies about inequality, lack of opportunity, discrimination, or despair. The government swung into action to protect us from them.[17]

President Reagan, drawing on many sources (like New York's harsh drug laws and the Nixon administration's tough talk) launched the national effort. Scary underclass images permitted him to scoff at lingering traces of Social Gospel compassion. Reagan "utterly rejected [the] utopian presumption about human nature that sees man as primarily a creature of his material environment." That kind of talk just fed the illusion that government can "permanently change man and usher in an era of prosperity and virtue." Instead, Reagan promised just punishment and hard time. The tough talk spread. *Time* magazine caught what it called the national "shared unconscious" with a screaming cover in 1994: "Lock 'Em up and Throw Away the Key: Outrage Over Crime Has America Talking Tough."[18]

The familiar American racial alchemy made the underclass—with its blank-faced teen-age gunmen—an icon for crime, for declining American morals, and (in some corners) for black America. The early magazine reports described an underclass made up "mostly of impoverished urban blacks who suffer from the heritage of slavery." The popular images multiplied: the super-predator was black, crazy with crack, and bred in violence. This hazy view gave the real crime problem a vivid racial cast. *Time*'s original underclass had been only a "minority within a minority." But the danger rippled out to every black person on the street. The stereotypes invited people to shrug off racial biases, which seeped deep into the gears of criminal justice. Again.

More sympathetic eyes see entirely different urban communities. Carol Stack's lyrical *Call to Home* portrays profoundly stable family networks stretching across generations. She pictures communities of sophisticated city folks and their rural kin struggling with wisdom and patience against poverty and racism. They work hard to make ends meet. Yes, the black death rate is high— the numbers look like those from poor, developing nations. Yes, violence and drug abuse plague poor black communities (they plague all poor communities). But it is not simply the gun and the needle. The *New England Journal of Medicine* recently listed the leading scourges in black neighborhoods: "unrelenting stress," "cardiovascular disease," "cancer," and "untreated medical conditions" topped the list. Real people with real needs (remember national health insurance?) get buried in the racial cartoons.[19]

Rising Crime

But what about crime itself? After all, underclass fears did not spring out of nowhere. Crime really did soar. Figure 15.1 tells the murder story (murder offers more reliable historical data because it is much harder to sweep under the

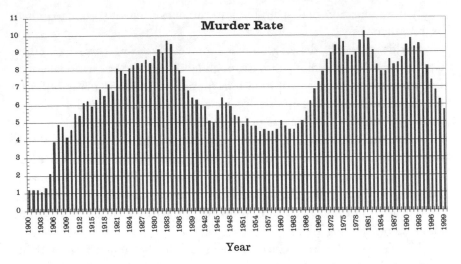

15.1. The U.S. murder rate in the twentieth century. The figures show the number of murders per 100,000 people in the population. Note how the rate at the end of the century is down to the same level as the early 1910s.

statistical rug than, say, spouse abuse). First of all, we do not face unprecedented crime rates. The murder rate shot up in the first three decades of the twentieth century, peaked in 1933, then fell till the mid-1950s. After that it began rising again and peaked (just above that 1933 level) in 1974, 1980, and 1991. For two decades the United States confronted a seething crime problem. The overall murder rate doubled. It looked even worse on the city streets. New York saw 390 murders in 1960; thirty years later, in 1990, the toll stood at 2,245. People had good reason to be frightened. Then the murder rate plunged again. It fell straight through the 1990s. By the end of the decade the murder rate was lower than it had been in any year between 1912 and 1942. Getting back to New York, the number of killings fell from 2,245 to 633. In short, twentieth-century America endured two murder booms, each lasting about thirty years and peaking at roughly the same level. Each peak was followed by a dramatic drop in homicides. Other crimes follow roughly the same pattern. For contemporary policy, the key point is simple: crime plunged during the 1990s.

Did getting tough make a difference? Yes. Locking away the most violent criminals had a real impact; one widely cited analysis credits the rise in jailing with a quarter of the fall in crime. But incarceration does not fully explain the startling drop.

Demographics also made a big difference. Young males commit most crimes. The 1950s had the smallest percentage of young adults (aged 15 to 24) of the century—and the lowest crime rates. As baby boom generations move into their high-crime years, crime generally rises; as they age out, crime tends to fall. Second, a rising economy (after both 1933 and 1991) reduced the crime rate. Jobs get young people off the streets and into work. And don't forget substance abuse. In the 1933, Americans repealed Prohibition; in the 1990s, crack use declined and the illegal drug market stabilized. Gun control efforts may also have slowed crime. Finally, police departments claim credit for their law enforcement methods; surely they made a difference—though early analyses suggest that crime fell in almost every city, regardless of police tactics.[20]

The jail numbers go deeper than the rise and fall of crime itself. Americans lap the industrial world in homicides (Finland comes in a distant second at half our rate), but we rank relatively low on most other offenses. Even back in 1995 the typical American was less likely to be touched by crime than were citizens in England, Holland, Switzerland, Scotland, Canada, or France. New York had only about three-fifths as much theft and burglary as London. There's more to our prison rates than crime. The urge to incarcerate springs from crime, fear, high moral expectations, and the deep social trenches that cross our cities.

The crime war roars on despite falling crime rates. By now, most prisoners are doing time for nonviolent crimes. (Perpetrators of violent crimes account for 48 percent of state inmates, and just 13 percent of those in the federal penitentiaries.) Even former hardliners have begun calling for peace. "We have maxed out on jail," argues John DiIulio. Two million prisoners are more than enough. In fact, locking people up at these rates may begin to exacerbate crime—many criminologists warn that there is a tipping point (perhaps 1 percent of the community), after which each prison sentence leads to more crime. Stuffing the jails and prisons disrupts families and communities. Getting small offenders behind bars cuts them off from civil society. Parents and siblings vanish; doing time becomes a normal expectation; and the line between law-abiding and criminal blurs and seems arbitrary.

But even with the crime hawks suing for peace, we keep locking them up. "Defying gravity," reported the *New York Times* in 1998, "the inmate count climbs again." The paper ran the same story the following year. And the year after that—although in 2000, arrests on the state and local levels finally declined by a whisker (a rise in federal prison populations slightly offset the decline). Why does the jail count keep rising even though crime rates have not been this low since *Father Knows Best* ran in primetime?[21]

Perhaps the crime-fighting simply lags behind the crime reality. In the 1930s, the incarceration rate peaked five years after crime did, and then rapidly fell. The current crime war has rolled on for a full decade after the peak, but incarceration finally appears to be running into resistance.

Or perhaps the numbers keep climbing because Americans remain fright-ened. After all, people don't study crime tables, they watch television. And what they see is murder and mayhem. Washington and Wall Street shut down by 5 P.M., get covered on the evening news, and turn stale by primetime. As every TV producer knows, the late local news serves up fresh material follow-ing a simple formula: "If it bleeds, it leads." Many Americans go to bed with pictures of the latest local atrocity—body bags, weeping spouses, grim cops— all fresh in their mind. Despite the data, the crime epidemic still seems to be going strong.[22]

Moreover, a series of numbing crimes have projected a sense of horror onto the national culture. An angry man blows up a federal building in Oklahoma City (in 1995). Two boys go on a murderous rampage at a high school in Col-orado (1999). The footage, endlessly repeated, reinforces the conventional wis-dom: we face a rising tide of moral depravity and violent dangers.

The video images provoke a spate of laws and policies. But the terrible pic-ture can deceive. No one can deny the depravity and anguish behind the mur-ders. And yet the quiet statistical reality showed that schools, for example, were safe (less than 1 percent of child homicides occurred in school) and getting safer. Even with the tragedy in Colorado, school deaths fell through the 1990s.[23]

Not surprisingly, getting tough makes popular politics. Legislatures write mandatory sentences. Politicians blast the courts for turning soft. Uproars greet parole boards who turn lenient. The tough attitude runs through the system— federal authority, local police, prison authorities, parole officers, and juvenile justice systems. Every state now permits youngsters to be tried as adults.

Moreover, twenty years of fighting crime have built up powerful institu-tions with their own vested interest in tough justice. Americans constructed a thousand new jails and prisons in the past two decades—by the late 1990s, we were cutting the ribbon on a new facility about once a week. California watched its inmate population rise from 19,700 in 1977 to 159,000 by 1997. Even so, the backlog of arrest warrants—not served because there is just no place to stuff the offenders—has reached 2.6 million, according to one Califor-nia commission. The Corrections Corporation of America announced that it would build three prisons in California entirely on speculation. "If you build it in the right place," announced a company executive, "the prisoners will come."[24]

All those jails add up to a private-public network invested in the crime war—a kind of "prison-industrial complex." The Reagan, Bush, and Clinton administrations all advertised themselves as tough on crime; each encouraged the investor-owned chains. The companies now take their place at the crime-policy bargaining table where they find plenty of allies. Rural areas lobby hard for their own facilities, hoping for good jobs. A great network of federal, state, and local crime agencies is all part of the politics of criminal justice. (The Department of Justice draws on data from 9,500 agencies to tabulate its annual arrest tables.) Industry lobbyists, cities and counties, crime control professionals, and law-and-order politicians form a powerful political establishment invested in fighting crime and filling jails. Only a stiff fiscal crisis in the states finally applied the brakes in the early 2000s.

Mark Mauer, an ardent critic of the jail boom, reports getting an unexpected phone call. An eager entrepreneur wanted help gauging the size of potential inmate markets in various nations where his prison corporation could expand. "Prisoners have been thought of as sinners, deviants, or members of an oppressed class," muses Mauer. "Now, they've become a commodity pursued by global entrepreneurs." As the prison business grows, it sucks resources away from other spending priorities. And it eagerly offers a solution to all kinds of problems. When the stock market collapsed amid accounting scandals in 2002, the George W. Bush administration had its answer ready: lock up the bad apples.[25]

Overwhelming Force

The crime war landed hard on city streets. A new police regime sprang from a theory known as "broken windows." According to this theory, small crimes and shabby neighborhoods erode respect and civility. Instead of letting the little things go, police are urged to draw a firm line from the start. No more drinking beer on the sidewalk, peeing into the gutter, or pilfering from the corner store. Authorities assert zero tolerance for misbehavior. Police take back the streets; the courts and jails mete out tough justice that sends a strong message.

Vigorous policing comes with formidable firepower. Starting in Los Angeles, cities geared for riots with paramilitary units called SWAT teams. (The tough-sounding acronym originally stood for special weapons attack team.) When crack hit the cities, in the late 1980s, the SWAT teams turned their focus from riot control to drug war. The military approach spread to midsize and small cities till the nation bristled with 30,000 heavily armed SWAT teams. Even the little Cape Cod town of Harwich, Massachusetts (population 11,000), boasts a ten-person team. SWAT team members wear fatigues, helmets, and flak vests. In just two years the Department of Defense sent local SWAT teams more than 1 million pieces of military hardware, including 73 grenade launchers and 112 armored personnel carriers. For serious operations the teams call in helicopters.

Some SWAT teams have become part of routine policing. They roll into

15.2. A SWAT team on patrol in Meriden, Connecticut, 1999. (Keith Meyers, *The New York Times*)

high-crime neighborhoods and assert the law with overwhelming force. From Fresno, California, to Champaign, Illinois, SWAT teams serve drug warrants, patrol streets, and launch nightly raids. In a handful of cases (as in Fresno), the paramilitary police patrol the streets—with armored vehicles, submachine guns, helicopters, and dogs—seven days a week. Toward the end of the decade, as crime fell and budgets pinched, some cities finally began to deploy their squads less often.[26]

The idea of a military police transforms law enforcement. Militaries occupy foreign soil, writes Christian Parenti. That is precisely the logic—the feel—of these heavily armed units. Poor neighborhoods and dangerous classes get a face full of the state's raw muscle.[27]

All that power and intimidation come down powerfully on the black community. Loose talk about predators and monsters takes its terrible toll. A fast sample of recent findings might include the following: Among kids who land in court, black kids are 6 times more likely to go to jail and 48 times more likely to get sentenced for drug offenses; they draw an average jail term that is 61 days longer than white youths charged with the same offense. One New York study found that 84 percent of the motorists stopped by police were black or Hispanic (the two groups make up only half the city's population). In one white neighborhood, nine out of ten stops involved minorities. In Royal Oaks, Michigan, the national news carried a story that has become emblematic of the biases in the entire crime-fighting enterprise. Police pulled Dennis Archer out of his Jeep Grand Cherokee; they handcuffed him, stuck a shotgun in his face, and interrogated him. Archer is a lawyer, and his father is the mayor of Detroit. In the sardonic urban jest, Archer got caught DWB—driving while black.[28]

Racism? Not always. Sociologist Jerome Skolnick illustrates how it works by simply listing the arrests he has witnessed. "A group of men gather on the sidewalk in Manhattan, listen to a boom box and disturb the neighbors." The result: a $75 citation. Police swoop down on a young man drinking beer outside his apartment on a hot summer night, on a youth smoking a joint on the street, on a couple driving with a broken taillight. These cases were not driven by racial animus. Suburbanites and rural people just don't get into as many scrapes with police because their little lapses take place in more private settings. But in poor city neighborhoods, vigorous policing mixes with life lived on the streets and pushes the law in your face. Add the images of a predatory underclass, and the results are a pervasive bias shot through American crime policy. Arrest enough people and the relations between police and people grow tense, the fabric of the community unravels (2 percent of our kids now have a parent in jail), and jail time becomes just another feature of life in the neighborhood.

The Pattern of Moral Politics

We have followed the same panic-policy cycle throughout American history. This time the danger was real. Crime rose, fast and frightening. Politicians jockeyed to sponsor tougher rules—mandatory sentences, life in jail after three offenses, and beefier police tactics. The United States built a vast web of crime-fighting institutions, public and private. As the problem receded, the machinery kept on churning, deeply invested in a war that it had largely won.

This mobilization comes to the same disheartening conclusion as past efforts. Tough policies rush toward the people on the margins of power. Two million people pile up behind bars. An extraordinary 7 percent of American black men are behind bars today. The racial bias in jail time goes far beyond anything that might be justified by the crime rates. What we are developing looks vaguely like the old segregationist establishment. In fact, ten states (five in deep Dixie) bar more than 20 percent of their black men from voting because of criminal convictions.[29]

Why no backlash? The answer lies in the endless jeremiad about American moral decline. Genuine difficulties—crime, drug addiction—grow into something more than policy problems; they become markers of national depravity. Fears of rampant immorality obscure concern about common sense or fairness. Once again, moral alarms organize institutions that crack down on the least powerful. Every new sermon about bad behavior carries this melancholy dark side.

There is an alternative, of course. We have traced long swings in American morals across the past 150 years. By now—more than two decades after the Reagan administration recast American political morality—it is difficult to even remember the other side. It begins with a radical thought: the fear of decline is an old myth. Just look at the crime data. We face problems, not moral meltdown. In that context, we bear obligations to one another—and especially to the poorest and least powerful. The pendulum has swung entirely away from those old calls to community and mutual aid. They sound like soft leftovers from the sixties. The crime war's rising toll brilliantly illuminates what happens when Victorian tough love swamps the Social Gospel.

The crime picture changed in a sick instant on September 11, 2001. Terrorists hijacked planes and plowed them into New York's World Trade Center and Washington's Pentagon. They murdered thousands of people in a stroke. Suddenly, danger—hard, real, undeniable—entered the nation from abroad. It felt like the cold war as Americans mobilized to meet the threat. We've seen the Americans face a long string of foreign enemies. From the Pequots (in 1636) to the Communists (circa 1956), they all seemed to embody "a form of Satan in action." Like a long line of leaders before him, President George W. Bush insistently pointed to "the evil ones."

Past struggles with foreign evil serve us a vivid warning. The threats from abroad have a way of rebounding on groups at home; tarred by association with the latest army of foreign devils, the accused faced deep bias and injustice. World War I made life miserable for "hyphenated Americans"; after the war, a red scare routed leftists and foreigners; World War II inspired the Japanese-American internment camps; the cold war set off the great red scare.

The search for dangerous agents hidden in the good society always raises the specter of the witch-hunt. The caution offered by the Puritan ministers remains relevant for every generation: "The proceedings [should] be managed with an exceeding tenderness towards those that may be complained of"—don't forget due process. What turns an episode into a witch-hunt is not the witches; it is the rush to toss aside our norms and standards of justice as we chase after them. Give in to that temptation and the hunters—not the witches—harm the community most.[30]

Drug War

We have been here before. Liquor Prohibition served up all the classic ingredients: Dangerous un-Americans. An evil industry. Innocent children. Intimations of national decline. The dreamy faith that if we ban this substance our worst problems evaporate. And—the match that ignites the mix—ferocious worries about the crumbling boundaries between a good us and a malicious them. Drug policies faithfully follow the classic Prohibition plot. If anything, they deliver an even greater racial jolt.

Roots

The link between race fear and drug wars goes all the way back. Early controls on opium swept in on fears about Chinese immigrants. "Opium destroys the Chinaman far less surely, quickly, and completely," reported one popular tract, "than [it destroys] the Caucasian [and] Americans in particular." Worse, Chinese men used the drug to enslave "white girls, hardly grown to womanhood." A whole genre of lurid exposés touted the Chinese danger to our innocent white daughters. "They are a constant and terrible menace to society," warned reformer Jacob Riis. "The harshest repressive measures are justifiable in Chinatown." Driven by racial anxiety, eleven states banned opium smoking between 1877 and 1900; national prohibition followed in 1907. Other forms of opium and morphine yielded more balanced debates and remained available longer.[31]

Another racial alarm produced cocaine prohibitions. Just after southern majorities pushed their Jim Crow laws into place (at the turn of the past century), wild stories about drug-crazed black men hit the news. Now that state prohibitions had dried up southern whiskey, "Negro cocaine fiends" started running through the white imagination. The addicts allegedly committed "seventy percent of all the crimes in Atlanta" and, inevitably, "most of the attacks upon white women in the South." *Good Housekeeping* magazine warned mothers about "old colored men" who hid cocaine in their pushcarts and spread the poison through the cities. And it got worse. The drug gave African American men superhuman strength: "bullets fired into vital parts that would drop a sane man in his tracks," warned the *New York Times*, "fail to check the fiend, fail to stop his rush or weaken his attack." Not even a .32 caliber bullet through the heart could arrest a black drug fiend. These racial phantasms proved so potent that southern delegates tabled their speeches about states' rights and voted for federal action. The Harrison Act (1914) organized the first major federal anti-narcotic law. Meanwhile, police forces around the nation upped the caliber of their firearms.[32]

During the Great Depression, a western panic roiled around Mexican Americans high on marijuana. "If I could show you what a small marijuana cigarette can do to one of our degenerate Spanish speaking residents . . . ," puffed a Colorado newspaper editorial. Marijuana provoked them to "delirious rage," "sexual assault," and the "greatest percentage of our crimes." As usual, the plague endangered American innocents: "Mexican peddlers have been caught distributing sample marijuana cigarettes to school children." While the political agenda was set by anti-Mexican organizations, other voices spoke out. Marijuana releases inhibitions, reported Dr. Walter Bromberg to the American Psychiatric Association, and "acts as a sexual stimulant [particularly to] overt homosexuals." At congressional hearings, in spring 1937, the American Medical Association advised putting off federal restrictions till more studies could explore the drug's effects. But for calming the nativists, only total prohibition would do. The Marijuana Tax Act outlawed the drug in October 1937. The Federal Bureau of Narcotics had not been eager for the new job; however, they quickly put aside hints that perhaps marijuana was not so dangerous.[33]

The marijuana scare hit during the film era. *Reefer Madness,* a propaganda movie from the 1930s, had turned into low undergraduate camp by the 1960s. However, the underlying racial realities—these drug fears imagined a Mexican menace to "our" women and children—got lost in the transition from panic to parody.

Race Again

America's tangle with drugs, writes David Musto, swings between too much tolerance and too much punishment. The key—in every generation—lies in the popular picture of the user: We are sophisticated or foolish or ill; if necessary, we get help. They are immoral and dangerous; it is imperative that they be punished.

By the 1970s marijuana had developed middle-class resonance as a drug for college kids rather than Chicano farmers or black musicians. By 1977 eight states had reduced penalties for possession to simple fines. The Carter administration proposed doing the same under federal law—till columnist Jack Anderson charged the administration's drug policy director with snorting cocaine at a Washington party. The charge sounded plausible. Cocaine was chic. "Among hostesses in the smart sets of Los Angeles and New York," postured *Newsweek,* "a little cocaine, like Dom Perignon and beluga caviar, is now *de rigueur.* . . . The user experiences a feeling of potency, of confidence, of energy." *Time* had used precisely the same food metaphor to describe the hippie drug culture: "Grass is their staple and LSD their caviar." Novelist Jay McInerney painted a more ambiguous picture in the first scene of his urban noir, *Bright Lights, Big City* (1984). "All might become clear if you could just slip in to the bathroom and do a little more Bolivian Marching Powder," reports the protagonist at the start of the book. "Then again, it might not." Maybe cocaine was not such a good thing, implied McInerney, but it sure seemed to be everywhere.[34]

Tolerance came to a sudden end in the early 1980s. Both Nixon (who called for war on drugs) and Carter had defined drug abuse as illness and put their money into treatment; Reagan recast drug use as a crime and called out the cops. The president and Mrs. Reagan stood together on national television while Nancy Reagan delivered a drug war homily: "There is no middle ground. Indifference is not an option. . . . For the sake of our children I implore each of you to be unyielding and inflexible in your opposition to drugs."[35]

Right on cue, crack roared into the cities. Crack is cocaine prepared for smoking—it delivers a fast, intense, very brief high. Users had been smoking (or freebasing) cocaine for a decade. Now some outlaw whiz had a marketing brainstorm: sell crack in individual doses. Cocaine suddenly went downtown. A fancy trade to people who could afford $100 a gram turned into a traffic for poor folks. Crack turned cocaine ominous, poor, and black.

What followed perfectly illustrates the recurring tangle—drug abuse, race, panic, and tough justice. Crack was dangerous. Its intense highs left users itching for more. Poor people took greater risks—and had fewer safety nets—than the wealthy freebasers. And rival suppliers unleashed a slaughter on American streets as they battled for a share of the lucrative new market.

The drug problem blew into an all-out panic. In 1986, more than one thousand crack stories appeared in the press. NBC alone aired more than four hundred reports; over at CBS, news anchor Dan Rather announced a special "two hours of hands-on horror" in the crack "war zone." *Newsweek* and *Time* each splashed crack across the cover of five issues that year. The number of Americans who identified drugs as the "number one problem facing the nation today" jumped from under 1 percent in 1985 to 54 percent in 1989.[36]

All the usual images fed the panic. This time, the innocent child came onto the scene as a crack baby. Irresponsible junkie mothers were poisoning their little kids. The black underclass—now familiar after a full decade of media attention—had plunged to new depths of depravity.

The pandemic seemed to have no boundaries. In 1986, the world champion Boston Celtics drafted Len Bias, a terrific basketball player and heir apparent to Boston superstar Larry Bird. The young man celebrated his good fortune with crack and alcohol. "It chilled everyone," reported the *Washington Post*, "when Len's six feet eight inch body of granite keeled over and died." The drug appeared poised to touch everyone. "We thought crack use was going to grow and take over society," recalls one research analyst.

Public officials rushed to respond. The Anti-Drug Abuse Act of 1986 appropriated $1.7 billion for a stiff, take-lots-of-prisoners program. The House of Representatives, in Democratic Party hands, called for death to drug dealers; the Republican Senate would not go that far, but it stuffed plenty of harsh penalties into the crime package. Congress ramped up punishment on a range of illegal drugs. But nothing got jail time like crack—it became the only drug to carry a mandatory sentence for a first offense of simple possession. In contrast, first possession of heroin or powdered cocaine is a misdemeanor. Some penalties for crack—drafted in mid-panic—are one hundred times harsher than punishments for other forms of cocaine: five grams of crack and five hundred grams of cocaine powder each net five years in prison.[37]

The panic ran its inevitable course. The violence waned once suppliers secured their turf. The crack-baby horrors turned out to be exaggerations. Tough penalties limited the spread of the drug. Less than 2 percent of the crack-related deaths could be attributed directly to the drug's effect on users. When the hyperbole waned, public health officials began to get crack in context: "For every one cocaine-related death in the United States in 1987," reported Reinarman and Levine, there were approximately 300 tobacco related deaths and 100 alcohol related deaths.

As the crack panic receded it left behind sick addicts, sparse compassion, severe penalties, and an army of crime-busters eager for business. In the cold post-panic light, the glaring racial bias came into focus. The harsh crack penalties fell almost entirely on African Americans. One Los Angeles study discovered that no whites had been prosecuted under the crack laws between 1994 and 1998 even though whites made up about a third of the city's frequent crack users. A national report revealed that black people got 88.3 percent of the convictions for crack and 27 percent of those for powdered cocaine. And crack is the most dramatic part of a deep racial bias that runs through the entire drug war.[38]

Racial biases show up at every turn. Working with FBI statistics, Kenneth Meier counted twenty-three states with a racial disparity in drug arrests of more than five to one—five black arrests for every non-black arrest. Yet the data also consistently show African Americans using illegal drugs at about the same rates as whites. Even *USA Today* got into the story with a front-page headline: "Is the Drug War Racist? Disparities Suggest the Answer Is Yes." The small print explained why: "Blacks are four times as likely as whites to be arrested on drug charges—even though the two groups use drugs at almost the same rate." The data keep piling up: arrests correlate more with race than with drug abuse.[39]

Arrest is only the first stage of bias. The National Institute on Drug Abuse tracked the racial differences through the judicial process: blacks make up 13 percent of monthly drug users; they face 35 percent of all arrests (for possession), 55 percent of all convictions, and a whopping 74 percent of all prison sentences. Put bluntly, blacks go to jail in huge numbers, far beyond anything justified by the crime numbers. We've already seen the many reasons why: Race panics wrote the drug laws. The city trade is out on the open street rather than behind closed suburban doors. Police focus on poor black neighborhoods.

Drug warriors target black people for closer inspection. The criminal justice system tilts against defendants who are poor and black. The list runs on.

We have transformed disease into crime, warns physician David Lewis. We've built a national apparatus that incarcerates the addicts we ought to be treating. The drug war feeds the crime war, accounting for roughly one-third of the new inmates. It grinds on with a fierce racial bias, sweeping the city streets of young black men. This is a campaign that promises us generations of trouble.[40]

The Black Response

Black leaders wrestle uncomfortably with the politics of morality. After all, they still rise through the pulpits, and their churched communities tend to be socially conservative. But black people have long faced trumped-up charges of moral poverty—we've heard that slur from slaveholders, temperance leaders, early family planners, white supremacists, and segregationists. Now drugs bring together two familiar troubles: the very real damage created by substance abuse in poor communities and a state policy that appears deeply biased against black men and women. The African American community fights on both fronts.

On one side, black leaders take a forceful line on drugs. A close reading of American culture yields constant small-gauge efforts. In Hammond, Indiana, the Mount Zion Baptist church sponsors marches to "reclaim the community" from drug dealers. In Dallas a young Methodist minister leads his congregation to the shooting galleries where they sing hymns and chant: "Shame! Shame!" Like temperance women praying before saloons or purity crusaders gathering in the red-light districts, black congregations take to the streets hoping to prod local police into action against crack houses and dope dealers. In 1998 the Congressional Black Caucus announced a drug agenda that included getting tough on major dealers, expanding treatment programs, and launching an aggressive new round of drug education.

On the other side, black leaders constantly face the unhappy consequences of government policy. The drug war—seen as unjust and oppressive—gets as much black press as the drug problem. The founder of Houston Ministers Against Crime put it poignantly: "If the police are called in, I try to get them to not arrest all of [the kids]. I try to remind them to be human." The Black Caucus's drug agenda gives equal time to this ugly side of the drug dilemma: it calls for justice when drug warriors violate the law, demands an end to the sentencing disparities for crack, and pushes for a serious investigation into allegations of drug dealing by the federal government. That last issue—the fed as pusher—vividly captures the black fury at government bias.[41]

Simmering resentment against the state broke open when the *San Jose*

Mercury News published Gary Webb's sensational three-part series charging that the CIA had flooded central Los Angeles with crack as part of a tangled scheme to fund the Contra rebels in Nicaragua. Senator Arlen Specter (R-Pennsylvania) convened Senate hearings. CIA director John Deutch appeared before a raucous Los Angeles audience in November 1996; Deutch denied all, then promised an investigation. Most observers thought Webb's article wildly exaggerated (the *Mercury News* itself backed down). From a broader historical perspective, however, the furor captures the bitter legacy of police action in minority communities. For a moment the cultural icons of corruption got flipped—the familiar stigma surrounding a black underclass turned into charges of a corrupt and racist state that bends rules, breaks down doors, and wastes entire black neighborhoods.[42]

A more sustained backlash against the drug war latches onto the 100-to-1 disparity between crack and powdered cocaine. In 1995, the U.S. Sentencing Commission (a nonpartisan agency that advises on sentencing policy) published a report "strongly recommending" revision of the sentencing guidelines. The Minnesota Supreme Court struck down a state law (fourteen states had passed laws that mirrored the federal disparity); the state court argued that almost all (97 percent) of the crack defendants in Minnesota were African Americans, whereas most powdered cocaine defendants were white. Federal courts took up the issue when defendants in a California trial argued that the state prosecuted only blacks for crack and filed a motion for discovery—they asked to look at the government's files in order to prove the racial bias. The district court granted the motion and, when the prosecutors refused to turn over the information, dismissed the case. A divided circuit court upheld the ruling.[43]

These intimations of change were eventually rebuffed by every branch of the federal government. The Supreme Court overruled the California decision (8–1). Only Justice John Paul Stevens dissented, pointing to the "extraordinary severity of the imposed penalties and the troubling pattern of enforcement." Over at the White House, the Democrats ducked. The Clinton administration had worked hard to seize the crime issue from the Republicans. Yet each election cycle brought new charges about an administration grown soft on drugs. In 1996, *Newsweek* pronounced drugs "one of the few issues where [Republican candidate] Bob Dole has found some traction." In 2000, George W. Bush blasted the Clinton-Gore drug policy as "one of the worst public policy failures of the '90s." Back off the drug war? Not near an election year. In his final week in office, as movers were carting the Democratic furniture out of the White House, Bill Clinton announced strong support for a change in the sentencing laws. Much too little, far too late.[44]

The Republican Congress flatly rejected the Sentencing Commission's call for new guidelines. Members reauthorized the old penalties, then instructed the commission to reexamine its findings. The issue remains contested; the Sentencing Commission bounced right back the following year with another report urging Congress to close the gap. Congress showed no inclination to do so. "No member of Congress is going to lose a vote because they're tough on drugs," commented a congressional staffer who had helped draft a reform proposal. But the matter goes deeper than simple partisan calculations.[45]

Drug law reformers keep confronting the same brute cultural fact. Prohibitions rise out of social constructions about us and them. Race images ushered in the 100 to 1 ratio. Racial cartoons keep them locked in place. After Congress rebuffed another effort to lighten the crack disparity, one discouraged activist summed up the problem: "When you mention crack cocaine, their minds immediately jump to an image of a young black man with gold chains and a gun in his pocket." Just the sort of image that nourishes every prohibition.[46]

Cross the race and class lines and the picture changes. High-tone advertisements in fashion magazines flaunt models with a look the *New York Times* tags "heroin chic." *Vanity Fair* ran a cover story about the search for a real opium den: "It is the perfect drug, the most delicately exquisite of intoxicants," reported Nick Tosches after finding one. Yes, he admits, opium is terribly addictive. "How could the taste of paradise be otherwise?" Poor communities reverberate with sermons and SWAT teams. Meanwhile, like Prohibition-era college boys flaunting their flasks, swank magazines flirt with naughty drug romances.[47]

Medical Marijuana

In at least one corner of drug policy, the stigma has slipped off the user. A spate of medical marijuana proposals has put aside the crack addict for a grandmother with glaucoma or a person with AIDS. The shifting user makes all the difference.

In 1996, California asked its voters whether "seriously ill Californians have the right to . . . use marijuana for medical purposes where . . . recommended by a physician." Arizona offered voters marijuana, LSD, heroin, and other drugs if two physicians found a scientific basis for the prescription. Opponents charged that this was a thinly disguised wedge for legalization; illegal drugs, they insisted, are wrong and harmful. Here is a variation of an old pattern: progressives turn sins into illness and moral problems into medical ones. We've watched that switch on liquor and even poverty (which Franklin Roosevelt redefined as a public health issue). But medical marijuana adds a new variation: the sinful substance becomes a health cure.

Both propositions won easily. They were followed by a wave of medical marijuana referenda—all winners. By 2001, Alaska, Nevada, Oregon, Washington, Maine, and the District of Columbia had all voted yes. Hawaii became the first state to approve through legislation.[48]

Drug hawks reacted furiously. "I am extraordinarily embarrassed," confessed Senator John Kyle (R-Arizona) when his state fell. He concluded that the sponsors had "deliberately deceived" the voters. Others blamed currency trader George Soros for lavishly funding the medical marijuana propositions; that charge, however, drifted into the treacherous waters of campaign finance. Critics soon tacked back to more reliable criticism. "Marijuana remains illegal under federal law," proclaimed Representative Bob Barr (R-Georgia), "and it would send a terrible message to America's young people to allow these laws to be openly flouted." Barr blocked Washington, D.C., from counting its referendum votes till a federal court intervened (another landslide—68.6 percent—for medical marijuana). Federal officials—Democrats and Republicans, the courts, Congress, and the president—keep denouncing the medical marijuana proposals, resisting their implementation, and warning about the opening wedge to legalization.[49]

Medical marijuana forces squirming drug hawks to face the oldest lesson in prohibition: moral bans lose power as the dangerous villains fade—precisely what happened to alcohol six decades ago. Today's drug warriors acquiesced in popular stereotypes and drew political capital from public anxieties about the user. Now medical marijuana shifts those pictures. The rejoinders just don't carry the same symbolic force as that "young black man with . . . a gun in his pocket."

Do the referenda bode a less harsh drug policy? Or will complete prohibition hold? For the first time since the 1970s, the debate is back on.

What Next? Tomorrow's Drug Policy

The referenda can easily be exaggerated. The drug war roars ahead. By the late 1990s the United States was racking up 1.5 million drug arrests a year—almost half for marijuana. But actually winning this prohibition seems no more likely than winning the last one. Drug use fell between the late 1970s and the late 1980s, especially among casual users; then it leveled out (cocaine) or rose (heroin). By 1998 the United States had an estimated 3.3 million hard-core cocaine users (one in four on crack) and about 980,000 heroin addicts. Perhaps 11 million people smoked pot last month.

Despite vigorous efforts to stop the flow, illegal drugs remain plentiful. Spending on drug interdiction jumped from $5 million (in 1982) to $1.27 billion a decade later. American borders bristle with Navy warships, Air Force fighters, AWAC radar systems, and border guards. They are not enough. The world is too wide, American borders too big, the national appetite too high. Spray the fields in one poor nation and another leaps into the coca leaf or poppy business. Drug smugglers cross into the United States alongside more than 500,000 planes, 118 million cars, and 422 million people a year; meanwhile, the entire national demand for cocaine can be met by four jumbo jets or 13 trailer trucks packed with powder. Border controls pick off about 1 percent of the contraband. A kilo of cocaine wholesales ten times higher in Miami than in the Andes; big profits and large bounties ensure the supply despite strenuous efforts to curtail it.[50]

Is there an alternative? Yes. Drug policy owls are claiming the territory between the legalization doves and the drug war hawks. Treat drug addiction like alcoholism, they urge. After all, many users are suffering from what amounts to a disease. Past waves of drug use—heroin in the 1970s, crack in the 1980s— have left seriously addicted people; rather than hunt them as criminals, treat them for an illness. "We have 5 million people chronically addicted to drugs," admitted General Barry McCaffrey, the Clinton administration drug czar. "They are a total mess. They are in misery." The owls argue that treatment would do far more to reduce drug use than anything else—if (a large if) addicts could get immediate access to care rather than face the long waiting lists that mark our underfunded programs. Today most addicts (some 57 percent) get no medical attention at all.

The most ambitious owls move beyond medical thinking and focus on the texture of people's lives. Nothing beats drug addiction, they say, like decent jobs, stable lives, genuine opportunity, and a hopeful future. They would link drug treatment to job training, job placement, family support, and housing advocacy. Push "treatment," they say, all the way down to the root causes of addiction.[51]

The public health approach would take a more realistic perspective on saying no: lower penalties for lighter drugs like marijuana, prevention programs with less furious railing about the first puff. Owls would lose the hard edge of zero tolerance. They tout their own buzz phrase, "harm reduction." They would reduce the harmful side effects of drug abuse—provide clean needles, offer more treatment, stop filling the prisons with users, and step down the drug wars. Even hawks acknowledge that backing off might very well result in "less crime," "fewer gangs," and a "more straightforward public health approach."

The media has begun to play up this side of the drug war. Stories focus on a different kind of criminal. An addicted mother of two gets arrested three times— jail for life, thanks to the Kansas three-strikes law. A mother of four with no criminal record makes $40 by mailing a dubious package for a dangerous friend—ten years courtesy of mandatory crack sentences. Both stories run with pictures of the women clutching their photogenic children. Similarly, a *New York Times* story on harm reduction comes illustrated with a photo of a woman charged with drug possession; she hugs her little girl, who stares solemnly at the photographer and us. The pictures summarize a thousand owl analyses. These moms are not the super predators that launched the drug wars. They are neighbors—black and white—who became addicted or made foolish mistakes. Look at their attractive children. What happens to those kids if we lock their mothers away for years? What happens to a society piling mothers and fathers—2 million people—into prisons and jails?[52]

In some states, the moderate owl analyses have begun to filter into policy. In 2000, California voters overwhelmingly (61 percent) approved a program shunting first- and second-time nonviolent drug offenders into treatment rather than jail (despite opposition from most law enforcement officials and many healthcare professionals). New York state courts also began turning drug offenders from jail to treatment. The policy shift grows from the sense that too many small violators have gotten caught in the gears of justice. In its early years, for example, the California three-strikes law locked away twice as many pot smokers (and suppliers) as murderers, rapists, and kidnappers combined.[53]

These remain weak policy straws in a strong wind. The vigorous neo-Puritan view still dominates the debates: Drugs are wrong. Users destroy their own lives, damage their children, and subvert our values. Even if calling off the drug war means less social trouble, as James Q. Wilson wrote in *Drugs and Crime,* the "government has the obligation to form and sustain the character of the citizenry." Or, recalling *The Contract with the American Family,* when parents fail to inculcate moral values, "government must be ready to deliver a firm message."

When the Clinton administration proposed expanding drug treatment in 1994, a Democratic congressional majority refused and budgeted no increase at all. Five years later, a Republican Congress responded to the calls for moderation with hearings entitled "The Pros and Cons of Drug Legalization, Decriminalization, and Harm Reduction." Most members spoke vigorously against the progressive fancies. But even robust rhetoric did not fend off conservative scorn. "We do not have hearings on 'The Pros and Cons of Rape,'" jabbed Congressman Mark Souder (R-Indiana). The classic moral view still stands, without apologies: Drug users are criminals, just like rapists. Chase them down and punish them.

During the harm reduction hearing, a lone voice from Brooklyn imagined an alternative America. "The solution is that we have a humane society so people don't grow up feeling they have to do these things," said Edolphus Towns (D-New York). "And when they do these things," he continued in unabashedly

15.3. The *New York Times*, February 1999. Intimations of a new drug policy? A young woman hugs her child while she waits her turn in court. She is accused of simple possession of cocaine. Thanks to a new California initiative, she is about to get treatment rather than jail time. That little girl with the big eyes makes an eloquent, silent plea against harsh drug-war penalties that would lock up her mother. (AP Photo/Rich Pedroncelli)

Social Gospel mode, "they need appropriate treatment." Towns's sentiments fall outside today's dominant paradigm—a communal vision in a Victorian era. For the time being, at least, the emphasis on a humane society will get a predictable reception: "soft," "unrealistic" and "out-of touch."[54]

Beneath all the policy back and forth lies hard organizational self-interest. The drug and crime wars now run deep in the American criminal justice system. Police forces have reorganized themselves for the new prohibition. Forfeiture laws permit them to seize assets like cars, boats, planes, and cash. Some agencies have gotten hooked on the proceeds. The same goes for the whole network of agencies and bureaus that makes its living from the free-flowing drug-fighting funds.

Echoes of liquor prohibition reverberate: Popular calls for lighter laws (light beer, medical marijuana) get dismissed by Washington hardliners. States legislate more lenient policies that federal courts strike down. States hold referenda that do not count. Enforcement tensions strain across national, state, and local jurisdictions. A giant quasi-military apparatus remakes American law enforcement. Jails overflow. Racial divisions and ethnic stereotypes lie at the heart of the enterprise. Civil liberties get renegotiated. The state disrupts entire communities. Violent criminal gangs spring up, amass wealth and power, and get romanticized in some neighborhoods.

Finally, for all the troubles they introduced, both liquor and drug prohibitions developed fervent support. Sophisticates derided the "noble experiment" of the 1920s—they called it unjust, corrupt, and violent; but prohibitions gathered support among the pious. Outcries about the waning respect for authority met countercalls that the government must make a firm moral statement.

But there is an obvious difference between prohibitions, and it raises the big questions. Liquor prohibition fell. Tobacco—another dangerous drug—remains legal. In contrast, the drug war grinds on. Why? Why do some habits shift from private vice to public danger? How do common vices become crimes? How do they run back the other way and turn legal again?

We've followed the same pattern across American time: A band of true believers discovers a problem and pushes prohibition. Two crucial steps win allies and get them through the checks and balances of American politics: the right enemies and a good panic.

The enemies are familiar—dangerous users. These sinners lie at the heart of our prohibition—that's why race and ethnic fears play such crucial roles. In most cases, a second villain eventually appears: the suppliers peddle their poison for profits—the city saloons, the drug pusher, the Colombian cartel. Contemporary tobacco wars have, so far, yielded only the second villain—perfidious corporate suppliers.

Panics or crises push the prohibition through the political process. It's a moral classic: Dangerous people threaten our innocents. Prohibitions generally rise up the political agenda with gothic stories about the first sip, puff, or snort. The bad companion lures foolish youngsters to their terrible fate. The weak-willed fail to stand firm (to just say "no!"). The pattern goes back to the essential Puritans' warning: anyone could fall to the level of the lustful savages.

Once the restrictions win, four distinct political forces lock the prohibitions into place: a group of activists rallies around a moral ideal; fears of a dangerous them draw allies to the cause; the enforcers have their own organizational self-interest in maintaining the prohibition; and political inertia is designed into our system of checks and balances.

The collapse of liquor prohibition played the preceding factors in reverse. The dangerous characters faded from political view. New immigrants stopped arriving, and the second generation moved into the middle class. The dangerous industry—the breweries and the saloons—had vanished. Interestingly, local prohibition lingered longest precisely where the dangerous other remained in place; southern states continued to pin black populations. (That is not, of course, the full story of southern prohibition, but the pattern is striking.)

True believers continued to back Prohibition, but as the fears faded, they lost their allies. Even so, waning zeal would not have been enough to overthrow the Prohibition establishment; the Hoover administration was bulking up enforcement till the end. Rather, the Great Depression, and the Democratic tidal wave that came with it, broke through organizational self-interest and political inertia.

Today, a change in drug policy—never mind legalization—faces the same barriers. And, as with every prohibition, the debate begins with the image of the user. Do we face the crack head "with gold chains and a gun in his pocket" (race coding not subtle)? Or the hurting addict who is, as Clinton drug czar Barry McCaffrey put it, "in misery" and a "total mess"? The different pictures come embedded in different moral philosophies and social systems. Once again, it is sinners versus sick people, punishment versus treatment, new Puritans versus the Social Gospel, a dangerous them versus one of us.

Sex

Sex always raises the fiercest moral conflicts. However, the institutional framework for this fight is very different from that of the crime wars. We watched the courts dismantle the Victorian sexual regime one case at a time. In 1933, Judge

John Woolsey scuttled the bans on James Joyce's *Ulysses* with a blithe shrug: "His locale was Celtic and his season spring." Thirty years later Justice Brennan wrote the epitaph for the Comstock censors: "A book cannot be proscribed unless it is found to be utterly without redeeming social value." The court replaced Victorian controls with privacy rights. The state could not rush into the bedroom—into the citizen's personal space—and ration birth control (1965) or outlaw abortion (1973). Stern moral revisions might rewrite criminal justice and launch drug wars. But it made far slower progress in—to describe it from both sides—restoring family values or breaking down the door to the bedroom.

Today most progressives gather along a battle line defined by *Roe v. Wade*. Privacy rights deflect government meddling in personal lives. Classical liberalism—separating public from private—yields the same answer to a full spectrum of sexual questions. Homosexuality, divorce, abortion, promiscuity, and sex in the Oval Office all produce the same political wisdom: it is none of your business.[55] On the other side, conservatives see a hedonist culture swamping all our virtues. The moral collapse of the American family bodes deep trouble for American society. The Victorian wave that has remade other policy areas also pounds at this one.

The sex debate appears to bubble into every cranny of the culture. But today's hot political conflicts rage around the same matters that made for hot political conflicts back in the Victorian era: lust, the proper family, gender roles, and an irresponsible them. And, once again, abortion roils all the gender themes together—it defines contemporary sexual politics, perhaps moral politics altogether. And it appears to offer the sexual counterrevolution its big chance.

Lust

"The spirit of the sixties," wrote Robert Bork in 1996, "brought us at last to Bill and Hillary Clinton, the very personifications of the sixties generation." The president embodied the lost self-control that plagued the entire nation. Bork sounded moderate in the swarm of exposés that covered Clinton—salacious details darted into public view right from the start of the administration.

For example, Gary Aldrich, a retired FBI agent who had been assigned to the White House, scorched the Clintons in his jeering bestseller, *Unlimited Access*. Aldrich helped decorate the Clintons' Christmas tree—they chose the twelve days of Christmas as the theme. Hillary seized the chance to "celebrate sex, drugs, and rock and roll," reports Aldrich. Twelve lords a-leaping all sported large erections. And the five golden rings turned out to be "sex toys knows as 'cock rings.'" (Aldrich would not have known, of course, but one of the chuckling "male florists"—nudge, wink—filled him in on the joke.) Crack pipes and condoms helped round out the Clinton idea of Christmas. "Why," moaned the White House staffers, "why is Hillary so hostile to families?" Aldrich fondly remembered Barbara Bush and her lovely needlepoint. The more dramatic episodes in the book would be exposed as flat-out fiction. No matter, *Unlimited Access* flew out of the bookstores. And, true or false, the details fed the anti-Clinton rage. What would anyone expect from these avatars of the 1960s except crack pipes and cock rings hanging from America's Christmas tree?[56]

The Monica Lewinsky scandal confirmed all the worst suspicions. For the men and women eager to impeach, the crisis ran deeper than a self-indulgent public official caught in the act. Conservatives could repeal the old liberal programs and redefine the policy mood. But nothing in their political kit—crimefighting, drug war, welfare reform, tax cuts, or even the 1996 Defense of Marriage Act—seemed to staunch the low mores that had oozed out of the sixties.

When the scandal broke, even many moderates insisted that it was not just about sex. After all, whispers about infidelity had swirled around more than a third of his predecessors. No, said the critics, Bill Clinton had lied—in court, to the public, on television. This baby boomer constantly violated the prime Puritan directive: control thyself. He stood for a whole generation that, as the Puritans had charged the antinomians in 1637, would not crucifie the lusts of the flesh. William Bennett laid out the charges most systematically. The president would not check his "unruly appetites" and "passions." He was "out of control" and "incorrigible." But the gravest danger, warned Bennett, radiated from Clinton's defenders and their toxic catcalls: "It's only sex, get over it" or "This is the real world, not *The Sound of Music*." All that nonchalance bodes deep trouble for the United States, warned Bennett. "Morality is central to our politics and attitudes in a way that is not the case in Europe." In fact, "our moral streak is what is best about us." That moral streak saved the world from communism and fascism. We lose our special strength if the liberals—"worldly wise" and "sophisticated"—manage to turn us "European."[57]

Below the high-flying principles ran gutter politics. A string of bruising sex scandals littered the 1990s Washington scene: Clarence Thomas (had he rented pornographic videos?), Anita Hill (one pit-bull journalist called her a "little bit slutty"), Republican majority leader Bob Livingston (extramarital affair), and presidential advisor Dick Morris (foot fetish with a prostitute).

Everything got broadcast. Voracious tabloids left no rumor out of bounds; respectable news outlets faithfully reported the latest shockers from their tabloid cousins. Larry Flint, the publisher of a violently pornographic magazine, turned the tables and offered bounties for dirt on Republicans. An independent investigator (the Democrats had stoutly defended the concept till it turned on them) outdid them all and documented every nuzzle of the Lewinsky affair in unblinking clinical detail: "In the hallway by the study, the President and Ms. Lewinsky kissed. On this occasion, according to Ms. Lewinsky, 'he focused on me pretty exclusively,' kissing her bare breasts and fondling her genitals. At one point, the President inserted a cigar into Ms. Lewinsky's vagina, then put the cigar in his mouth and said: 'It tastes good.'"

Perhaps the investigators thought the particulars would shame the president out of office. Or set off an indignant storm that shoved him out. But the report only hardened the sides. Each saw something entirely different in the inquiry—and, ultimately, in President Clinton himself.

To his critics, Clinton came from that dangerous tribe, the 1960s hedonists. In effect, the anti-Clinton press restored the tropes and terrors of the old nativist tracts: those people will subvert American values. As the critics saw it, Clinton blundered into office promising to turn the military over to the gays, then—in the face of the moral thunder—retreated to that distinctly self-revealing policy, "don't ask, don't tell." Next he tried to turn the entire healthcare system over to government bureaucrats. The White House had become a sixties shambles: undisciplined and unorganized, hashing out ultra-liberal policies in all-night bull sessions.

Clinton's defenders saw an entirely different man—too eager to please and too ready to compromise. A sixties radical? "We wish," lamented the progressives. Clinton served the Democrats all kinds of policy spinach: deficit reduction, free trade (NAFTA came before health care), welfare revisions, and a vigorous war on crime (he incessantly touted his 100,000 new cops on the streets). From this perspective the Lewinsky scandal seemed simple: the man had an affair and tried to hide it. The more frightening problem lay in the right-wing firestorm that had rained down on Clinton from the day he took office. The president's defenders scorched Special Prosecutor Kenneth Starr as head witch-hunter, dispensing Puritan pieties and pornographic details. Al Goldstein, a publisher who had managed to get himself arrested for obscenity nineteen times, summed up the backlash against Starr with wicked delight: "Even with my creative mind and [my] staff of sleazy satirists, I could not have managed a porn story as creative as [the Starr report]." Clinton's behavior may have been indefensible and stupid, said the left; but his enemies were scary.[58]

When Clinton got away, some religious conservatives began to talk about retreating to the private sphere and minding their own business. If Americans would not rise up in outrage after seeing what this man had done, they said, what hope could there be for the nation? Clinton mirrored a slack people. Conservative Christians would repudiate politics and rely on their faith to heal the nation.[59]

And yet a closer look reveals something weirdly puritanical running right through even the hottest scenes of the Starr Report. During their first encounter, Clinton told Lewinsky to stop the oral sex. Lewinsky responded that she wanted to complete the act, but he demurred. "He said that he needed to wait until he trusted me more." The same thing happened the next time. "Once again, he stopped her before he ejaculated because, Ms. Lewinsky testified, 'he didn't know me well enough.' " Here's Bill Clinton drawing some bizarre moral line. He "trusted" her enough to unzip his fly and, well, so on; but not enough to orgasm. Much earlier, Clinton had set off derisive hoots by claiming that he had tried marijuana but did not inhale. In his own way, he was struggling with limits and boundaries. It is not what Cotton Mather might have imagined. But it sure looks like the classic struggle between a Puritan battling temptation (he is a Baptist, after all) and a man succumbing to sin. Clinton's ethical compass is not as unusual or as amoral or as un-American as his critics imagined.

International surveys keep discovering the same Puritan tension in the general population. The *American Journal of Public Health* compared sexual behavior in Britain and the United States. The survey, reported with fanfare in the English press, revealed that American men and women engage in a lot more premarital sex: they are "roughly twice as likely as their British counterparts to have 21 or more sexual partners in their lifetime." At the same time, Americans are more apt to condemn promiscuity. Twenty-five percent of all American men call premarital sex "always wrong"—more than three times the number of Englishmen. The colonists have stuck to the old Puritan spirit, chortled the *Economist* (May 9, 1998). And they pay a price. American public policies must be carefully steered between sin and censure. When AIDS hit, for example, the more tolerant and abstemious Europeans went straight into forceful public health campaigns—leaflets, television advertisements, needle exchanges, and so forth. Across the Atlantic, Americans delayed their own effort while they squabbled over the exact moral nuance of the message, "particularly the degree of emphasis that should be placed on abstinence." The American incidence of AIDS soon measured ten times higher than Britain's. Our public health troubles, concluded the *American Journal of Public Health*, may be the price we pay for our dogmatic Puritanism. Precisely the same tension—education versus abstinence—haunts other public health campaigns, like the battle over teen pregnancy or the war on drugs.

Public health, education, family law, and even the presidency all are entangled in the American dialectic between morals and privacy, punishment and permissiveness, crime fighting and harm reduction. The fierce arguments mark us—despite everything—deeply moralistic.

The Family

Define America by its morals, and families immediately become the crucibles of national destiny. After all, the city remains up there on the hill only if each generation passes on its legacy, its special virtue. We've traced the battle over family values past the Victorians (with their generation of lambs menaced by wolves) to the Puritans and the mainspring of all their troubles, "defects as to family government." Today the family remains ground zero in the struggle for a good society. "We may build cities of gold and silver," writes William Bennett, "but if the family fails, fewer and fewer of our children will ever learn to walk in justice and virtue." At least in some minds, nothing less than civilization itself hangs in the balance. This time the Jeremiahs back up their warnings with reams of gloomy data. Forty percent of our marriages end in divorce. One out of three kids lives with just one parent, usually the mother; the number jumps to 60 percent for black children. More than 5 million people cohabit rather than marry. Even the Catholic Church sanctions some 60,000 annulments a year.[60]

Conservatives blame the sixties and its sexual revolution. Marriage became "old fashioned, beleaguered, even quaint," writes David Blankenhorn, "a way of life primarily suited to older people or boring people." *U.S. News and World Report* boiled down one story to a young woman's lament: "I used to complain to my mother how my boyfriends seemed commitment shy and she would say, 'Well, why buy the cow when the milk is free?'" Even marriage offers only fleeting commitment. In this culture, writes Blankenhorn, divorce is cool. And, thanks to legal changes, it is easy.

How to fix the family? Traditionalists gather up their sticks and carrots: rewrite the tax laws, get parents to recite pledges, reanimate the stigmas that once marked divorce and bastardy, beef up the Defense of Marriage Act (which draws the line against same-sex marriages), and make divorce harder to get. Louisiana pioneered a marriage innovation; couples choose between the standard form (with its easy, no-fault divorce) or a Covenant marriage (which makes divorce very difficult). "We're trying to slow down the hemorrhaging of the American family," explained one Louisiana legislator. "Pretty small beer," sighs the *Economist* in an otherwise approving survey of the proposals. The gloomy data runs right across the Western world. Maybe a fiery religious movement would bring people back to the Victorian family values, muses Francis Fukuyama.[61]

Not everyone buys the problem. Progressives maintain the classical liberal line: leave people to their private lives. Better yet, help them cope with the global forces that stress families across the industrial world. Socioeconomic troubles require socioeconomic solutions. Family policies ought to push economic justice. Mend our communities. Strengthen the public and private services that support parents struggling to make ends meet. Win a living wage for every worker.

The negotiable dispute about where to place the accent—about whether the divorce rate stems from individual pleasure or institutional pressure—masks a deeper difference: the revolution in sex roles. From the progressive perspective, that divorce rate is not entirely bad news. When nineteenth-century feminists denounced spouse abuse they were hushed as radicals; when they pressed on and called for more liberal divorce laws, they learned that legal changes were meaningless till "woman got her own purse." Those golden days of stable marriage featured dependent women with few options about either career or motherhood. Today, 60 percent of all American women participate in the labor force (the figure stands at 75 percent for men). Reproductive rights, financial independence, and demands for equality add up to fundamental social change. Many women have won control over their own lives. Their independence remakes the whole debate about this "cornerstone of civilized society." Restoring the family runs directly into the issue of just what a family ought to look like in the first place. The range of contemporary views is extraordinary. And each comes packaged with its own primer on the woman's proper place.[62]

The National Organization for Women (NOW) wrote one view right into its organizing statement. "A true partnership between the sexes demands a different concept of marriage, an equitable sharing of responsibilities of home and children and economic burdens." NOW soon made the message gender neutral: two monogamous adults share the job of making money, keeping house, and raising kids.

That opens the door to "cosmopolitan, world-beat, feminist and democratic family rhythms." You can get an idea what that means from the insouciant chapter headings in Judith Stacey's *In the Name of the Family*. "The Family Is Dead, Long Live Our Families" and "All Our Families Are Queer; Let's Get Used to It!" Pamela Paul writes lightly about the rise of "starter marriages"—unions among twenty-somethings that don't last a year. And Carol Tavris rubs it in with a description of her stepson's postmodern marriage ceremony: "The groom, in his toast, warmly acknowledged the bride's ex-husband (the father of her son), who was there with his longtime partner, who sat next to a lesbian couple with their new baby."[63]

At the other end of the culture, men don't wash dishes and women don't go to work. "The ladies have proven their mettle," purrs the Reverend Pat Robertson. "Women can write, produce, legislate, administrate, and sell as well as [men]. Thirty years ago few believed in their ability, now few doubt it." But to save the nation, a woman—Everywoman—must become "a wife, a mother, and a homemaker." The lost income might pinch. But as the Reverend Jerry Falwell puts it, "God intends the husband to be the decision maker. Wives and children want to follow."[64]

The Southern Baptist Convention grabbed national headlines with its 1998 declaration on biblical marriage: a husband should "provide for, protect and lead his family," and a wife is to "submit graciously to the servant leadership of her husband." The submission of wives may seem "strange to the secular world," commented one church leader, "but it is clearly revealed in scriptures. . . . Southern Baptists experience family trouble like everyone else but at least they know how God intended to order the family." Christian broadcasters make the theme an airwave staple. Visions of "gracious submission" reverberate across traditional religions and leap into more secular corners. In New Hampshire, for example, the unapologetically conservative *Manchester Union Leader* cheered: "The Southern Baptists, God bless 'em, decline to be swept away by the current fads and fashions of modernity. [They] took a stand for the traditional family."[65]

The rest of the media jumped in on all sides of this fray. "Should Hubby Be the Boss?" yowled a cover of the *National Examiner,* a supermarket tabloid. For the answer they turned to television actress Della Reese. "'The word submit is all wrong,' says the 66-year-old actress, who is also an ordained minister with her own congregation." She went on to announce, "I've been married three times and I know that being submissive never works." Married three times? Some moralists might call Reese part of the problem. Yet there she is on the cover, speaking to millions—and a minister for good measure.[66]

The traditional family remains elusive—perhaps even chimerical—in a society where the "submissive wife" meets working women with rights, abilities, and paychecks equal to their husbands'. Gender conflicts are nothing new. We saw the Puritans in 1637 and the Victorians in the 1870s devise family regimes that fit a larger political economy. In both cases social leaders defeated what we'd now call a feminist challenge to their authority. Today's new Victorians, on the other hand, operate in a more hostile setting. Women work. They hold the technology and, at least for now, the right to control reproduction. The paternalistic employer is gone. The tight, stable American community is going. The government guards privacy rights, sues employers for gender discrimination, and, in at least one state, blesses gay unions. Politics, economics, and society all reinforce modern marriages built on "equal partnership."

The conflict rages on. To the critics, the decline of the traditional family is nothing less than America's tragedy. The arguments leveled at Bill Clinton and his supporters—nonchalance about the president's misbehavior marked the end of America's special morality—apply to the whole nation. Many of these critics point out that broken families harm children and impoverish women. But the central jeremiad runs deeper. The essential building block of the good society—of traditional America, of what made us us—is imperiled. Our families have crumbled in a single generation.

Progressives see a more complicated moral universe. For many, the brave new world of families means independence and fulfillment. They stand alongside teary families at Vermont civil unions and call the anti-gay broadsides pinched and mean. In a larger context, the changing family reflects the contemporary wired universe. Fifty years ago, tightly bounded communities offered men and women limited options, for both better and worse. Today a new global economy—marked by instant communication, vast information, constant motion, and almost unlimited consumer choices—drives a social revolution in the industrial world and beyond. The new markets challenge plenty of social and political institutions. From this perspective, the real challenge lies in getting beyond a simple defense of privacy and restoring that largely forgotten moral call: make sure no one gets left too far behind in the scramble for wealth and status.

Conservative reformers, stymied in their effort to restore traditional society, have discovered one set of institutions that enables their social reconstructions. Ironically, it is the welfare state. Like the crime-control state, the welfare establishment offers reformers real institutional levers. Of course, the programs come with an obvious limitation—they touch mainly poor people.

Them

On the surface, welfare programs turn the rhetoric toward another classic sin—sloth. For decades conservatives pictured a bloated federal government passing cash to the shiftless. The welfare queen became the powerful symbol of Social Gospel folly; resentment against her grew almost legendary. By 1994 pollsters were telling Republican Party officials that one in five Americans identified welfare as the "largest program in the federal budget." (Aid to Families with Dependent Children—usually described as welfare—did not quite scrape up to 2 percent of federal spending.) When the rancor burst out and helped propel the Republicans to power in 1994, Senator Phil Gramm (R-Texas) wrote the headlines: the 40 million people who had been getting a free ride would now "get out of the welfare cart and help the rest of us push." President Clinton had tried to manage the discontent by promising to "end welfare as we know it." The new Republican majority made him keep that promise.[67]

Congress gave welfare reform a hard moral twist. The free ride fostered immorality. Once upon a time, reasoned the reformers, a pregnant woman had no choice but to marry the baby's father; he in turn faced up to his responsibility and supported the family. Like it or not, sex had real consequences. Then the government blundered in and gave that mother her financial independence. She no longer needs the man; she may not even want him around. "What welfare reform is really about," reported William Tucker in the *American Spectator,* "is illegitimacy. The ultimate goal . . . is to promote marriage and family formation." Conservatives touted the idea across Washington. True welfare reform, Robert Rector told the Senate Finance Committee, had to aim at "reducing illegitimacy and fostering moral . . . renewal." Here lay one solution to the family chaos—at least for the poor Americans at the bottom of so much social pathology.[68]

The Republican Congress buried the old welfare program, Aid to Families with Dependent Children. The press immediately began counting the people who filtered from welfare to work. But that, say many conservative analysts, was never really the point. What difference does it make, asked Charles Murray, "if single mothers go to work"? None. In fact, it is probably bad for the kids. The reform was not designed to turn the single mother into a viable economic unit, agreed William Tucker. It is probably not possible and surely not desirable. Rather, we stop writing federal checks so that "underclass men and women will start forming families again." Low-income women will need husbands, mothers will need to stick with fathers. Lawmakers repeated the new welfare policy mantra: "Encourage the formation of two-parent families." Look again at the legislation's title: the Personal Responsibility and Work Opportunity Act—reforming the personal comes before the prospect of a job.[69]

The legislation took sexual responsibility all the way to grade school by funding abstinence education. The program is mandated and overseen in Washington, designed by the states, and carefully monitored by private groups (which grade the states on their effort). Despite chuckles from the left, the virginity campaign hit the field with no apologies about traditional values: "A monogamous relationship in the context of marriage is the expected standard of human sexual activity," read one program guideline. Sponsors shrugged off gay protests and moved onto their next controversial demand. Teach only abstinence; never dilute the message with sex education. The message must be unequivocal: wait till marriage. Youngsters who gave in ought to get the full blast of old-fashioned stigma. The surgeon general sternly reminded abstinence warriors about the importance of both tolerance (gay-bashing is a real peril, he said) and sex education (which leads, he reported, not to more sex but to greater safety). Abstinence advocates remained unmoved. They gather virginity pledges, resist sex education, and condemn all sexual activity outside marriage.[70]

The effort to refurbish stigma falls into the long, troubling heritage of race bias in our moral reformations. Although most welfare recipients are white, the images run black. Welfare's "cultural destruction," announced the *American Spectator* (October 1996) "has been [largely] limited to black America." The debate turns on the provocative racial picture of children having children. In the 1990s, the unwed black teen mother replaced the black welfare queen as the icon of social pathology. The teen pregnancy rate is much higher among black teens than among white teens. A more careful look, however, yields a surprise. Between 1970 and 1997 (that is, from the end of the dreaded '60s to the implementation of welfare reform) the black teen birth rate fell 20 percent—the largest drop of any group. The black teen rate has declined (more or less) steadily for decades. Now, the virginity warriors barge in talking zero tolerance and slamming down stigmas. Up go the old lines between us and them, between good kids and bad. Forget the cheerful progress; harsh images and tough love keep coming down on the usual heads—school kids, their welfare moms, their criminal dads.

The progressives respond with the familiar alarm. Most poor people—on or off welfare, black or white—work extraordinarily hard to make ends meet. They struggle in the face of a changing economy that rewards high education and special skills. The full range of social pathologies rises and falls with the economy, with the job (and life) prospects of the poor. If those pictures capture even a partial truth, the entire policy attitude—"cultural destruction," "free ride," "lazy"—is misguided, even cruel. Cutting off benefits and dredging up old stigma will just turn hard lives even harder.

Classic pictures of good people surrounded by sinners reverberate through American public policy. Never mind that crime, teen pregnancy, and drug use are all way down. Funds flow to prisons rather than to public universities, to police rather than health programs, to marriage sermons rather than food stamps. Notions of willful evil blot out the problems that fester in poor neighborhoods: the stress of poverty, the location and funding of hospitals, the struggle for decent jobs, and the lingering whispers of racism. Who remembers the real urban killers—high blood pressure, stress, heart disease—when the blockbuster political images are so easily at hand: fatherless kids with high-power weapons.

Abortion

Abortion brings all the gender issues to full boil. In *Roe v. Wade* (January 1973) the Supreme Court ruled that a woman's constitutional right to privacy prohibited the government from interfering with abortion in the first trimester.

In a single stroke, the court struck down every abortion restriction in the United States. Historians scrambled for big metaphors: "No decision since *Dred Scott* . . . created quite such a storm." "No decision [ever] would create as big a rift in the nation." *Roe* set off "the nation's most divisive cultural issue since Prohibition." The decision, and the fight that followed, redefined American morality politics.[71]

A large and angry coalition converged around abortion. Christian fundamentalists swallowed their animosity toward Roman Catholics (who had owned the issue) and swept back into politics for the first time since the 1920s. This was as evil as slavery, wrote Jerry Falwell; it was another Holocaust. The pro-life movement placed the fetus in the long American line of endangered innocents. Christopher Hitchens stunned his left-leaning colleagues at the *Nation* by flaunting the gory details: "In order to terminate a pregnancy, you have to still a heartbeat, switch off a developing brain, . . . break some bones and rupture some organs." "If abortion had nothing to do with stilling heartbeats and brains," added a piece in *Atlantic Monthly*, "there would be no controversy." One after another, activists repeat the movement's mantra: 40 million dead babies.[72]

The attack on abortion twists the culture of easy sexuality into a cult of mass murder. It transforms post-sixties feminism—and the whole family-planning regime—into the slaughter of the innocents. Fighting abortion offers a way to resist hedonism, eroding family values, and changing gender roles. Rejecting abortion would restore the link between sex and families and return women to motherhood. Here, in short, lies a rejoinder to the sexual revolution. Bill Kristol, the editor of the influential *Weekly Standard*, puts it bluntly: "Abortion is today the bloody crossroads of American politics. It is where judicial liberation (from the Constitution), sexual liberation (from traditional mores) and women's liberation (from natural distinctions) come together. It is the focal point of liberalism's simultaneous assault on self-government, morals and nature." Moral fervor infused the pro-life movement, then spread to other issues and causes. As Stephen Carter puts it, public religious appeals became—"all at once and quite thunderously"—the sole property of conservative causes. Meanwhile, moral claims and Social Gospel drained quietly out of the political left.[73]

Moral rage regularly lands anti-abortion activists in hot water. After the terrorist attack on the World Trade Center and the Pentagon, for example, Jerry Falwell gave a television audience an earful (with Pat Robertson at his side, nodding in agreement): "The abortionists have got to bear some burden for this because God will not be mocked. And when we destroy 40 million little innocent babies, we make God mad. . . . I point the finger in their face and say, 'You helped this happen.' " An outraged backlash pushed both ministers to retreat and apologize. But months later, the Operation Rescue homepage still pictured a bloody fetus, a blazing World Trade Center, and a brazen caption that advised America to "connect the dots!" Such hot rhetoric only sends moderates scurrying for the firewall between the sacred and the secular—precisely the line the Supreme Court constructed in *Roe v. Wade*.

The court framed *Roe* on classic liberal ground: the state may not meddle in private affairs. Many progressives—perhaps prodded by the anti-abortion hellfire—embraced the court's logic. They defended the private realm, denounced religious politics, and drew on science (which makes its own distinction between private values and objective facts). Progressives turned *Roe* into a public health epic. "Legalizing abortions was a public health triumph that for pregnant women ranked with the advent of antisepsis and antibiotics," wrote Katha Pollitt. In New York, maternal mortality plunged 45 percent in the year following decriminalization.[74]

Some pro-choice theorists cast about for ways to beef up *Roe*'s liberal logic. For example, the court had noted the fierce disagreement on the crucial matter of when, exactly, life begins. The majority ducked the issue and simply protected abortions in the first trimester when the fetus was not viable outside the womb (which left abortion rights hostage to scientific progress). Critics of *Roe* responded by trying to muster up legislation declaring that life begins at conception. Ronald Dworkin advised the court to declare the entire definition of life's beginning a "matter of religious faith," thereby lodging abortion rights more securely in the private realm, beyond the political reach of meddling moralizers. Other observers, especially on the political left, feel queasy about the privacy framework. Hitchens taunted his pro-choice colleagues for turning into selfish individualists. "The majority of feminists and their allies have stuck to the dead ground of 'Me Decade' possessive individualism, an ideology that has more in common than it admits with the prehistoric right."[75]

Many feminists also criticized the privacy argument. That logic protects existing power relations. What about marital coercion? Or marital rape? Privacy abandons women to fend for themselves. More than a century ago, Victoria Woodhull and Elizabeth Cady Stanton tried to call attention to harsh marital relations—till Comstock laws shut them up; today, argue many feminists, the division between private and public is no more gender neutral than it was a century ago. Marriages can still be oppressive and violent. Instead, feminist theorists propose a more robust basis for abortion rights: the equal protection of the laws guaranteed by the Fourteenth Amendment. In the real world women cannot always say no to sex, and mothers are usually responsible for children, both before and after birth. A woman's success—work, career, promotion—rests on her power to control reproduction, to control the number and timing of her children. Gender equality itself rests partially on abortion rights.[76]

Moreover, privacy offers only negative protection—it stops the state from interfering but does not confer abortion rights. That leaves poor women no grounds for getting public funding. Deborah McFarlane and Kenneth Meier analyzed the restrictions that state governments have piled onto abortions (after the Supreme Court gave states limited license in *Planned Parenthood of Southeastern Pennsylvania v. Casey*, 1992). Despite plenty of political thunder, every legal limitation had a negligible effect on abortion rates—at least in the short run—except one: prohibitions on public funding. It's the same story in every policy area, from crime control to family planning; American politics and policies look entirely different from the economic bottom.[77]

The abortion debate makes many social scientists squirm. The issue does not seem to fit the normal logic of American politics—wheeling and dealing, logrolling and compromise. As one analysis ruefully put it, fertility issues seem to be about morality rather than policy analysis. That may not look like politics as usual, but it reflects what might just be our oldest political legacy. The really big battles are rarely about compromising differences or fine-tuning policies. Instead, they define who we are—often by invoking visions of good and evil.

The very first social conflict in the English colonies, the trial of Anne Hutchinson in 1637, raised early variations of the questions. Hutchinson challenged gender roles (with behavior "not fitting for her sex"), questioned authority relations ("disparaged all our ministers"), and promoted indecency (by refusing to "crucifie the lusts of the flesh"). That fight, too, turned on feverish images of deformed fetuses and defined the Puritan way for the next half-century. Birthing, gender roles, and social authority got tangled together right from the Puritan-American start.

Today, political observers across the political spectrum urge abortion activists to soften their voices and seek middle ground. Many decent people grope for a way to calm the furies. But past moral conflicts—slavery, purity, the rise and fall of liquor prohibition—rarely got resolved by splitting differences. The partisans stuck to their sides. Instead, shifts in the larger political economy pushed the old debate into a new framework. The changing context moved the political bystanders. For example, Prohibition swept to victory amid the patriotic furor of World War I ("Patriotism spells Prohibition"). It collapsed when the Great Depression remade American politics and buried the Hoover Republicans and all their works. Abolitionists stormed at slavery for a generation; the issue caught fire when the free labor Republicans (largely unsympathetic to abolitionist radicals) reframed the slavery issue by fusing race and morals with a powerful economic vision. In each case, the larger political framework swept new activists into the debate, shifted the question, and reshaped the lines of conflict. What larger issues frame the abortion debate? Perhaps the role of women. Today, most women work, they have "their own purse." The entire social framework—law, education, economics, sports, politics—seems to push toward gender equality.

The abortion conflict turns on the role of women in contemporary society. The dispute is so passionate and hard fought, comments Kristen Luker, "because it is a referendum on the place and meaning of motherhood." Outlawing abortion would drive women back to their traditional roles. Feminists fix on precisely the same data that enrages the anti-abortion activists: one out of two American women has an abortion sometime during her life; abortions terminate one out of four pregnancies. From this side, however, the prevalence of the procedure signals its importance. Feminists look at the numbers and see nothing less than a bulwark for equality.[78]

Moreover, it is extremely difficult to forbid a common activity—a dramatic lesson from alcohol prohibition. On the other hand, restrictions and limitations generally prove easier to apply than total prohibition. Opponents build barriers and slowly push discouraged providers out of entire areas (precisely what liquor's opponent's managed before national prohibition). Those kinds of limits go furthest against poor people, for they raise costs. Past prohibition campaigns suggest a distinctly mixed prospect for this one: deep-rooted gender equality for wealthier and better-educated Americans, who are likely to maintain some access to family planning. On the other hand, abortions may very well grow increasingly difficult for poor women to procure.[79]

For progressive politics, that underscores the trouble with the liberal approach in the first place. The more powerful defend the gender rights won over the past four decades. Those gains have become more precarious for low-income women. It is the outcome that runs through every aspect of modern morality. Limits of every sort—inspired by the crime war, drug war, welfare reform, and the constant urge to teach moral lessons—coil around poor people. Abortion politics pushes the same old story into another realm. Can progressives reverse that long list of biases? The historic way to mobilize support for big changes lies in a Social Gospel that was discarded and has lain largely dormant for a generation—in fact, since right around the time of the *Roe* decision in 1973.

In that sense, *Roe v. Wade* extracted a heavy price from American progressives. The left has ceded its moral politics to conservatives—across the full range of American politics. Many factors propelled the change—after all, the

Social Gospel always had a strong secular streak. But *Roe* helped define the alternative—privacy—and the roar of abortion politics hastened the trend. Each unadulterated Puritan blast—announcing that the latest plague or pestilence was God's righteous wrath against us—only reinforces the left's retreat from moral politics. However, privacy rights work only for people who wield power in their personal lives. It leaves others to fend for themselves against the odds. What progressives have lost is the moral fervor that fights to rally the country.

Liberalism protects our people from dangerous impulses, from discrimination and hate crimes. But it does not rouse people to win new rights, wider justice, and greater social equity. It does not dream big dreams about a better society.

Epilogue

AT first glance, the United States looks like a nation of shoppers—a land of malls, Sam's Clubs, and stock tips. Americans ardently preach capitalism while they scatter McDonald's and Starbucks across the planet.

The Shoppers' Nation—political scientists call it liberalism—tolerates plenty of poverty. The United States always ranks near the top when industrial countries count poor people or infant mortality rates. But that has always been part of the plan—success and failure lie in your own hands. The Puritans read wealth and poverty as divine hints about salvation and perdition. Lincoln saw the honest, sober, and industrious irresistibly rising; his colleagues drew the harsh implications when they told the poor they had only themselves to blame. And Ted Turner spoke for the most recent generation of go-getters with this infamous quip: "Money is how we keep score in life."

Until the markets crash. Then entrepreneurs turn into the villains who rigged the system and took advantage of vulnerable people. The poor become innocent victims. "The practices of the unscrupulous money changers stand indicted in the court of public opinion, rejected by the hearts and minds of men," declared Franklin Roosevelt in his first inaugural address. Back in 1933, the "moral stimulation of work" had become more important than the "mad chase of evanescent profits," and our deepest destiny was to "minister . . . to our fellow man." Seventy years later, after another stock market crash, the chairman of the Federal Reserve Board condemned "infectious greed" for the latest chase after evanescent profits. When times turn hard, the policy winds shift and politicians damn the wealthy.[1]

Boom or bust, we cram moral lessons into our economics. It's not only about money, but about good and bad people. Vice and virtue sneak into most of the big questions. Morals constantly leak into the secular sphere—they define our problems and imply solutions.

The first Muslim invocation in the U.S. House of Representatives (in June 1991) hints at why: "Do you not know, O people, that I have made you into tribes and nations that you may know each other." The verse from the Qur'an calls for pluralism while it injects still another tribe into the American cultural chaos. Here's a wide-open society that imagines itself an exemplar for the entire world. Each new group at the gate, every shift in race relations or gender roles, each economic transformation raises the same unsettling question—what does this mean for our Manifest Destiny? What will *those* people do to the virtues that got us where we are?[2]

The critical moral boundaries run between us and them, between virtuous and vicious. But American politics constantly spins the categories. At times, the entire framework shifts—embarrassing preachers who are slow to adjust. Two days after terrorists destroyed the World Trade Center, the Reverend Jerry Falwell appeared on a television show (Pat Robertson's *700 Club*) and blamed "the pagans and the abortionists and the feminists and the gays and the lesbians." They're responsible, agreed Pat Robertson, for "God lifting his protection over this nation." The men were applying the age-old Puritan jeremiad: lust and disordered families have explained God's wrath back to the first New England Indian Wars.

This time the backlash was so intense that Falwell hustled onto CBS's *Good Morning America* to apologize. He had "missed the mark," he said. In reality, the mark—the entire national zeitgeist—had lurched away from religious extremes. The United States was under attack. Before long, "Taliban" became a cultural code word for any religious fanatic, at home or abroad.[3]

Where does that leave American moral politics today? In the same old place: up for grabs. The two venerable traditions face off in a new era.

The New Victorians

The redeemer nation is back. Once again American leaders rally the good people against a "calculated, malignant, devastating evil," an "axis of evil" that girds the globe. Again the nation hears about its "Manifest Duty" to the rest of the world. "The United States and only the United States can see this effort through to victory," said Vice President Dick Cheney in 2002.[4]

The nation gets reorganized by its enemies. A rapid mobilization forges a vast new security apparatus—new bureaucracies, new laws, new regulations, and, inevitably, new judicial rulings and precedents. How long will the terrorist threat last? No one knows. But its permanent legacy is assured in the institutions rising around the concept of homeland security.

The domestic implications are complicated because they simultaneously unify and divide. During the cold war Americans showed no patience for minor cultural differences. As President Eisenhower put it, "Our government makes no sense unless it is founded on a deeply held religious faith—and I don't care what it is." The good people, standing up against communist evil, were not going to squabble about their religious differences—arguments about, say, teaching evolution were luxuries for a less dangerous day. A Manichean world reduces politics to black or white. Even most historians writing during the cold war put aside old interpretations based on class and conflict. Instead, they found Americans sharing a creed, a deep consensus about the basic values, long prized at home and now proclaimed to the world.

But sometimes the good people become leery about the weak links in their society. Agents of the enemy seem to take advantage of our liberties. We've watched that cry go up against witches, Roman Catholics, foreigners (from Jews to Japanese), reds, gays, and all kinds of others. Witch-hunts don't always chase imaginary dangers—there often *are* witches or communists. Rather, we call them witch-hunts when the fears of hidden enemies goad people into violating their principles of justice. The results include an ever-widening circle of suspects, scarred communities, and ruined innocents. Sometimes old-fashioned political interests lie at the bottom of the trouble. But Cotton Mather's epitaph on Salem Village still offers the best summation: we found ourselves "plunged into a blind man's buffet . . . hotly and madly mauling one another in the dark."

Who might it be this time? Moslems? Arab Americans? Critics of the patriotic majority? Dissenters of every sort? At least the talk about witch-hunts—and there has been a great deal—suggests a serious concern for civil liberties and an urge to learn from past convulsions.

But the contemporary war on terror—in fact, any prolonged international crisis—bears a deeper political implication than the danger of a witch-hunt. The past generation built a formidable war on crime with a vast organizational apparatus that shows no tolerance for misbehavior or deviance. Now, Americans pile on new rules and institutions that extend the political logic of the past two decades. Even with every due process in place, the result is a more formidable security state, a zero-tolerance society.

The rising organizations may well renew the national commitment to the Victorian ideals—we are only as good, and as strong, as our people and their families. When individuals slip, the state must be ready to step in with discipline. The basic moral message, already flying high, now gains another boost—with calls for inculcating strength, patriotism, manliness. This is no time to tolerate any weakness that subverts national resolve, that gives comfort to our enemies. The focus on good and bad individuals grows stronger. The dynamics of the last chapter tighten their grip on American politics and culture. Or might the quest for security be balanced by a completely different moral vision?

A New Social Gospel?

The alternative moral tradition shifts the focus from individual conduct to communal responsibility. Drug wars give way to national health insurance, unfettered markets to a living wage. The Social Gospel may finally be stirring after a generation in the political wilderness. To see why, take another look at two familiar images.

When the planes struck the World Trade Center and the Pentagon, people rushed to help one another. Ordinary men and women refused to abandon strangers as they made the long flight to safety. Firefighters and medical personnel ran directly into harm's way. Long lines gathered at the hospitals as New Yorkers offered to donate blood, to volunteer, to help in any way. Others came from around the nation to pitch in. The many stories all testify to a deep, shared community, to powerful bonds running (as Lincoln put it in a different context) "from every . . . patriot grave, to every heart and hearthstone all over this broad land." The images from that terrible day construct a formidable sense of us.

Craven memories balance the heroic ones. Every economic boom ends with charges of villainy—the stock market bust of the early 2000s proved no exception. Corporations admitted to a long roll of brazen financial tricks. Perhaps their crimes seemed more egregious for sharing the television screen with the working-class heroism of the World Trade Center. Together the pictures get us almost all the way back to Franklin Roosevelt: "If I read the temper of our people correctly, we now realize as we have never realized before our interdependence on each other." Politics change when rich sinners replace poor ones. That shift raises subversive questions about the bias of the system and the basis of wealth and poverty. People begin to "realize their interdependence."[5]

Of course, political images can be spun many ways. The terrorist attacks stir cries of revenge as well as calls to community. Corporate misbehavior launches an old jeremiad about rotten apples as well as reflections about social justice. But the powerful political jolts put a new focus on our collective lives. What would it take to make the leap into a resurgent Social Gospel era? For starters, a generation of leaders committed to deep changes in the tone and meaning of our politics. The Victorian revival has plenty of preachers. The social gospel may be stirring—but it still faces the first political test: champions who are willing to stand up for a new social justice rooted in moral conviction.

When leaders revive an old moral vision, they stake their political claims on visions of virtue, on right and wrong. But on a deeper level, moral arguments construct a simple explanation of the times. They pinpoint the source of our problems (God's wrath? Lazy people? A new global economy?) and suggest solutions (More discipline? More assistance?). In short, moral visions tell us how we got here and where we ought to go next.

We've watched two great moral paradigms develop and duel across American history. Of course they grow, change, and overlap, but each offers Americans a distinctive political logic. The Victorian view rose to dominate the last generation. Deftly championed by Ronald Reagan in the 1980s, it won support from across the political spectrum by the 1990s (and moved an unlikely cast of characters to lecture Americans about personal responsibility). The Victorian claims fit neatly into the high times of a shopping nation: Sober, honest, and industrious people rise and prosper. The failures have only themselves to blame.

What next? A manifest American destiny that saves the world from evil? More tough love for recalcitrants at home? Or a revival from the other side of the Puritan legacy—a new Social Gospel era committed to social justice? With 2 million people in jail and new intimations of community stirring, perhaps we have reached the limits of the Victorian model. We may be ready to renew our faded sense of collective responsibility. Or perhaps the Victorians have only just begun.

Whatever lies ahead, the past offers one final lesson. When the established faiths—political, social, religious—begin to grow stale, there is always another hot American revival in the wings. Americans play many roles and believe many different things. But after more than three and a half centuries—for better and for worse—we remain Puritans all.

Notes

INTRODUCTION

1. Alexis de Tocqueville, *De la Démocratie en Amérique* (1835; Paris: Flammarion, 1981), vol. 1: 398. My translation.

G. K. Chesterton, "On American Morals," in *The Man Who Was Chesterton: The Best Essays, Stories, Poems and Writings of G. K. Chesterton* (New York: Dodd, Mead, 1937), 54.

Gunnar Myrdal, *An American Dilemma* (New York: Pantheon, 1944), vol. 1: lxviii.

2. James Madison or Alexander Hamilton, *Federalist* No. 51. For Hamilton's probably apocryphal remark, see Gordon S. Wood, "Evangelical America and Early Mormonism," *New York History*, October 1980, p 360.

3. Tocqueville, *De la Démocratie en Amérique,* vol. 2: 130. On capital and work, vol. 1: 382–383. (*Democracy in America,* George Lawrence, trans. [Garden City, N.Y.: Doubleday, 1969]). The famous, controversial update of this argument is Louis Hartz, *The Liberal Tradition in America* (New York: Harcourt, Brace and World, 1955). J. David Greenstone refurbished Hartz and put him in Puritan context: "Political Culture and American Political Development: Liberty, Union and the Liberal Bipolarity," *Studies in American Political Development* 1 (1986): 1–49.

4. John Locke, *A Letter Concerning Toleration* (1689; Amherst, N.Y.: Prometheus, 1990); Nancy Rosenblum, *Liberalism and the Moral Life* (Cambridge, Mass.: Harvard University Press, 1989); Steven Holmes, *Anatomy of Antiliberalism* (Cambridge, Mass.: Harvard University Press, 1992), and "The Liberal Idea," *American Prospect* 7 (Fall 1991): 81–96. Ira Katznelson, *Liberalism's Crooked Circle: Letters to Adam Michnik* (Princeton: Princeton University Press, 1996).

5. Andrew Johnson, "First Annual Message" (December 4, 1865), James Richardson, ed., *Messages and Papers of the Presidents* (Washington, D.C.: Bureau of National Literature, 1911), vol. 5: 3559; Alexander Saxton, *The Rise and Fall of the White Republic* (New York: Verso, 1990), 256–257.

6. J. David Greenstone, *The Lincoln Persuasion: Remaking American Liberalism* (Princeton: Princeton University Press, 1993), Webster cited on 226; for a vivid contemporary example of this debate see Theodore R. Marmor, *The Politics of Medicare* (New York: Aldine, 2000), esp. part 1.

7. See Michael Sandel, *Democracy's Discontent: America in Search of a Public Philosophy* (Cambridge, Mass.: Harvard University Press, 1996), Laurel Thatcher Ulrich, *Good Wives: Image and Reality in the Lives of Women in Northern New England* (New York: Knopf, 1982). Gordon S. Wood, *The Creation of the American Republic, 1776–1789* (Chapel Hill: University of North Carolina Press, 1969), esp. chap 2; Amitai Etzioni, *The New Golden Rule: Community and Morality in a Democratic Society* (New York: Basic Books, 1996). Robert N. Bellah et. al, *Habits of the Heart: Individualism and Commitment in American Life* (Berkeley: University of California Press, 1985).

The most exciting recent report from this front is Robert Putnam, *Bowling Alone: The Collapse and Revival of American Community* (New York: Simon and Schuster, 2000).

8. The wonderful term "imagined community" comes from Benedict Anderson, *Imagined Communities: Reflections on the Origin and Spread of Nationalism* (New York: Verso, 1983).

9. William Carlos Williams, *In the American Grain* (1925; New York: New Directions, 1956), 208; Rogers M. Smith, *Civic Ideals: Conflicting Visions of Citizenship in U.S. History* (New Haven: Yale University Press, 1997).

10. Parts I and II detail the claim. See also Barry Alan Shain, *The Myth of American Individualism* (Princeton: Princeton University Press, 1994); Laurel Thatcher Ulrich, *A Midwife's Tale* (New York: Knopf, 1990).

11. Tocqueville, *De la Démocratie en Amérique*, vol. 1: 382. (*Democracy in America*, 278); Thomas Shepherd, "The Parable of the Ten Virgins" (1636), in Alan Heimert and Andrew Delbanco, eds., *The Puritans in America: A Narrative Anthology* (Cambridge, Mass.: Harvard University Press, 1985), 172.

12. The half-way covenant allowed the baptism of children whose parents had not yet demonstrated their own salvation. We'll see why it mattered in Chapter 1.

13. Cotton Mather, *Magnalia Christi Americana, or The Ecclesiastical History of New England* (1702; Hartford, Conn.: Silas Andrus and Son, 1855), vol. 2: 552 (Indian wars), 508 (antinomians); Mather, *Wonders of the Invisible World* (December 1692; London: John Russell Smith, 1862), 13, 14 ("horrible army").

14. John Winthrop, "A Modell of Christian Charity," in *Winthrop Papers* (Boston: Massachusetts Historical Society, 1931), vol. 3: 294–295. The image of the city on a hill comes from Matthew 5:14 (Sermon on the Mount).

15. Sacvan Berkovitch, *The American Jeremiad* (Madison: University of Wisconsin Press, 1978), 11 (Canadian immigrant).

16. See Andrew Delbanco, *The Real American Dream* (Cambridge, Mass.: Harvard University Press, 1999), 16–17.

17. Peter Berkowitz, *Virtue and the Making of Modern Liberalism* (Princeton: Princeton University Press, 1999); John Tomasi, *Liberalism Beyond Justice* (Princeton: Princeton University Press, 2001); Stephen Macedo, *Liberal Virtues: Citizenship, Virtue, and Community* (Oxford: Oxford University Press, 1990); Amy Guttman, *Democracy and Disagreement* (Cambridge, Mass.: Harvard University Press, 1996). Robert Horwitz, *The Moral Foundations of the American Republic* (Charlottesville: University Press of Virginia, 1986).

18. John Stuart Mill, *On Liberty* (London: Longmans, Green, 1884), 6.

19. See Klaus J. Bade, "Immigration and Social Peace in United Germany," *Daedalus* 123, no. 1 (Winter 1994): 85–106; and Thomas Faist, "How to Define a Foreigner? The Symbolic Politics of Immigration in German Partisan Discourse, 1978–1992," ZeS Arbeitspapier Nr 12/1993, Zentrum für Sozialpolitik, Universitat Bremen (Bremen, Germany).

20. Figures from U.S. Department of Justice, Bureau of Justice Statistics, *Sourcebook of Criminal Justice Statistics, 1999* (Washington, D.C.: U.S. Department of Justice, 2000), 484 (table 6.1) and 497 (table 6.20); "Serious Crimes Fall for Eighth Consecutive Year," *New York Times*, May 8, 2000, p A21. For a splendid reflection on American culture and institutionalizing deviance, see David J. Rothman, *The Discovery of the Asylum* (Boston: Little, Brown, 1990), and "The Crime of Punishment," *New York Review of Books*, February 17, 1994, pp 34–38.

21. Elders and Messengers of the Churches Assembled in Synod, *The Necessity of Reformation* (Boston: John Foster, 1679), 5 ("defects") and passim.

22. Benjamin Franklin, "Letter to James Parker," in Archibald Kennedy, *The Importance of Gaining and Preserving the Friendship of the Indians to the British Interest Considered* (London: E. Cave, 1752), 43–45. These are Franklin's reflections on an advance copy of Kennedy's book, printed at the end of the text as a kind of eighteenth-century blurb.

23. Max Weber, *The Protestant Ethic and the Sprit of Capitalism* (1904–1905; New York: Scribner's, 1958), chap 2. Weber described Benjamin Franklin, with all his maxims about striving and scrimping, as the embodiment of the Protestant ethos in America.

24. On the Irish, see Maria Monk, *The Awful Disclosures of Maria Monk . . . of Five Years as a*

Novice and Two Years as a Black Nun, in the Hotel Dieu Nunnery in Montreal (1836; Salem, N.H.: Ayer Reprints, 1992); Jacob Riis, *How the Other Half Lives* (New York: Charles Scribner's Sons, 1890), 92.

25. E. A. Ross, *The Old World in the New* (New York: Century, 1913), 293 ("morally below"), 303 (William and Tonio), 294 ("selfish"), 300 ("like pigs"), 154 (Jews), 223 ("coarse peasant philosophy"), 223 (depraved tastes), 244 ("avaricious"), 287 ("sugar loaf heads"), 237 (endangering womanhood), 302 (race suicide).

26. Beecher quoted in Sidney E. Ahlstrom, *A Religious History of the American People* (New Haven: Yale University Press, 1972), 789 (emphasis in original).

27. Anthony Comstock, *Traps for the Young* (1883; Cambridge, Mass.: Harvard University Press, 1967); James Q. Wilson, "What To Do About Crime" *Commentary* 98 (September 1994): 25–34.

28. Walter Rauschenbusch, *Christianity and the Social Crisis* (New York: Macmillan, 1907), 278; Jane Addams, *A New Conscience and an Ancient Evil* (New York: Macmillan, 1912); Frances Willard, *Glimpses of Fifty Years: The Autobiography of an American Woman* (Chicago: H. J. Smith/Women's Temperance Publication Association, 1889), 423–424.

29. "The Philosophy of Social Justice Through Social Action," Detroit, October 2, 1932. *The Public Papers and Addressees of Franklin D. Roosevelt* (New York: Random House, 1938), vol. 2 (1932): 771–780.

30. Ida Joyce Jackson, "Do Negroes Constitute a Race of Criminals?" *Colored American Magazine* 12, no. 4 (April 1907): 252–255 and no. 5 (May 1907): 352–357.

31. Abraham Lincoln, Speech at Peoria, October 16, 1854, *The Collected Works of Abraham Lincoln*, ed. Roy P. Basler (New Brunswick, N.J.: Rutgers University Press, 1953), vol. 2: 255.

Joshua Giddings, House of Representatives, February 13, 1843 (on the motion to reconsider the vote taken on final passage of the Bill for Relief of the Owner of Slaves Lost From on Board the Comet and Encomium).

Martin Van Buren, Second Annual Message, in Richardson, *Messages and Papers of the Presidents*, vol. 3: 1715. Van Buren was talking about that other racial matter, the Democrats' policy toward Native Americans.

Gustave de Beaumont, *Marie, or Slavery in the United States*, Barbara Chapman, trans. (1835; Baltimore: Johns Hopkins University Press, 1999), 202.

32. See James A. Morone, *The Democratic Wish: Popular Participation and the Limits of American Government* (New Haven: Yale University Press, 1998), 204.

33. Seymour Martin Lipset, *American Exceptionalism: A Double-Edged Sword* (New York: Norton, 1996), 131. For a summary of the optimistic view, see Stephan Thernstrom and Abigail Thernstrom, *America in Black and White: One Nation, Indivisible* (New York: Simon and Schuster, 1997).

34. For a nice review of the data—optimistic, pessimistic, and in between—see Jennifer Hochschild, *Living Up to the American Dream* (Princeton: Princeton University Press, 1995), chap 2. For challenges to the optimistic view, see Andrew Hacker, *Two Nations: Black and White, Separate, Hostile, Unequal* (New York: Ballantine, 1995), and Ellis Cose, *The Rage of a Privileged Class* (New York: HarperCollins, 1993).

35. Dinesh D'Souza, *The End of Racism* (New York: Free Press, 1996).

36. Frederick Douglass, *My Bondage and Freedom* (August 1855; New York: Library of America, 1994), 374–375. Douglass published three autobiographies. The first, *Narrative of the Life of Frederick Douglass, An American Slave* is the best known; it ends shortly after his escape to freedom. *My Bondage and Freedom* is the second. The third, *The Life and Times of Frederick Douglass*, was published in 1881 and later revised and expanded. For a nice reflection on the revisions, see Eric J. Sundquist, *To Wake the Nations: Race in the Making of American Literature* (Cambridge, Mass.: Harvard University Press, 1993): 83–93.

37. Cornel West, *Race Matters* (New York: Random House, 1994), xv.

38. James Q. Wilson, *The Moral Sense* (New York: Free Press, 1993), vii; Gertrude Himmelfarb, *The De-Moralization of Society: From Victorian Virtues to Modern Values* (New York: Knopf, 1995), 257; Stephen Carter, *The Culture of Disbelief: How American Law and Politics Trivializes*

Religious Devotion (New York: Basic Books, 1993), 7; the Stoppard play is *Jumpers.* Jay Tolson, "Academia's Getting Its Religion Back," *U.S. News and World Report,* August 28, 2000, p 52. See also A. James Reichley, *The Values Connection* (New York: Rowman and Littlefield, 2001), chap 1.

39. Richard John Neuhaus, ed., *Unsecular America* (Grand Rapids, Mich.: William Erdman, 1986), statistical appendix, pp 119, 124. See also Barry Kosmin and Seymour Lachman, *One Nation Under God* (New York: Harmony, 1993). A caveat: Americans appear to exaggerate their own piety when talking to pollsters—that exaggeration might even be read as still another, more roundabout indicator of religion's place in the culture.

40. Joseph R. Gusfield, *Symbolic Crusade: Status Politics and the American Temperance Movement* (Urbana: University of Illinois Press, 1963 and 1986), 1 ("silly"), 9–10.

41. Jerry Falwell, *Strength for the Journey* (New York: Simon and Schuster, 1987), 360; Tim F. LaHaye, *The Battle for the Mind* (Old Tappan, N.J.: Power Books, 1980), 88; Robert H. Bork, *Slouching to Gomorrah: Modern Liberalism and American Decline* (New York: Regan Books/HarperCollins, 1996). We'll turn to contemporary morals in Chapter 15.

42. This section speaks to the large and exciting literature focused on American state-building. In particular, I draw on Theda Skocpol, *Protecting Soldiers and Mothers: The Political Origins of Social Policy in the United States* (Cambridge, Mass.: Harvard University Press, 1992), esp. 1–66. Skocpol forcefully makes the point, developed below, that public policies spawn interest groups, as well as the other way around. See also Stephen Skowronek and Karen Orren, *The Search for American Political Development* (New York: Norton, forthcoming).

43. Bertram Wyatt-Brown, "Prelude to Abolitionism: Sabbatarian Politics and the Rise of the Second Party System," *Journal of American History* 58 (1971): 316–341. For a rich description of the protest, see Richard John, *Spreading the News* (Cambridge, Mass.: Harvard University Press, 1995), chap 5, esp. 204–205. When we get to the details, we'll see, as John points out, that the mobilization actually helped revive Sabbath observance.

44. See Daniel Carpenter, *The Forging of Bureaucratic Autonomy: Reputation, Networks, and Policy Innovation in Executive Agencies, 1862–1928* (Princeton: Princeton University Press, 2001).

45. Between 1905 and 1910 the United States received almost 6 million immigrants. After that the average declined, though individual years bounced around: 4.7 million (between 1911 and 1916), just over 2 million (1917–1922), and just 255,000 (by 1931–1936). We'll see just how and why in Chapter 11. Calculated from *The Statistical History of the United States* (New York: Basic Books, 1976) (Prepared by the U.S. Bureau of the Census), 105.

PART I

1. Dinner reported in John Winthrop, *Winthrop's Journal: History of New England,* ed. James Kendall Hosmer (New York: Charles Scribner's Sons, 1908), 49 (Saturday, June 12, 1630). For a fine recent edition of Winthrop's indispensable journal, see Richard S. Dunn, James Savage, and Latitia Yeandle, eds., *The Journal of John Winthrop, 1630–1649* (Cambridge, Mass.: Harvard University Press, 1996).

Population calculated from *The Statistical History of the United States* (New York: Basic Books, 1976), 1168. The population numbers for this period are estimates. By 1640 there were two other colonies of some size: Virginia, with more than 10,000 settlers; and New York, with 1,472.

2. Gordon S. Wood, "Struggle over the Puritans," *New York Review of Books,* November 9, 1989, p 26. Bernard Bailyn, *On the Teaching and Writing of History* (Hanover, N.H.: University Press of New England, 1994), 30; Edmund S. Morgan quoted by Wood, "Struggle over the Puritans," 26. Donald Hall adds that the term Puritanism is so vague that he tries to do without it altogether. See *Worlds of Wonder, Days of Judgment: Popular Religious Belief in Early New England* (Cambridge, Mass.: Harvard University Press, 1989), 256fn1.

3. Thomas Shepard, "The Parable of the Ten Virgins," in *The Puritans in America: A Narrative Anthology,* Alan Heimert and Andrew Delbanco, eds. (Cambridge, Mass.: Harvard University Press, 1985), 182.

4. For a splendid account of the enemies as definers of New England boundaries, see Kai T.

Erikson, *Wayward Puritans: A Study in the Sociology of Deviance* (New York: Wiley, 1966); for a more recent version, see Andrew Delbanco, *The Puritan Ordeal* (Cambridge, Mass.: Harvard University Press, 1989), esp. 13–14.

CHAPTER 1. *Us: The City on a Hill*

1. Nathaniel Hawthorne, *The Scarlet Letter* (Boston: Houghton Mifflin, 1892), 16, 17, 263. Vernon Louis Parrington, *Main Currents in American Thought: The Colonial Mind* (New York: Harcourt Brace, 1927), vol. 1: 13, 14, 15. James Truslow Adams, *The March of Democracy* (New York: Scribner's, 1932), vol. 1: 19–20. J. Hillis Miller, "Presidential Address 1986: The Triumph of Theory, the Resistance to Reading, and the Question of the Material Base," *PMLA* 102, no. 3: 282.

2. Richard Hofstadter, *Anti-Intellectualism in American Life* (New York: Knopf, 1962), 59; Samuel Eliot Morison, *The Builders of the Bay Colony* (New York: Houghton Mifflin, 1930), preface. Morison is discussed in Richard Shlatter, "The Puritan Strain," in John Higham, ed., *The Reconstruction of American History* (New York: Harper and Brothers, 1962), 9–45.

3. John Winthrop, "A Modell of Christian Charity," *The Winthrop Papers* (Boston: Massachusetts Historical Society, 1931), vol. 2: 282–295, quoted at 294, 293.

4. Winthrop, "Modell of Christian Charity," vol. 2: 282–295, quoted at 282, 283, 294, 295. Winthrop, *Journal*, in *Winthrop Papers*, vol. 2 (1645): 239 ("murmur and oppose").

5. Winthrop, "Modell of Christian Charity," 294–295.

6. Sacvan Bercovitch, *The American Jeremiad* (Madison: University of Wisconsin Press, 1978); Conrad Cherry, *God's New Israel: Religious Interpretations of American Destiny* (Englewood Cliffs, N.J.: Prentice Hall, 1971); Ernest Tuveson, *Redeemer Nation: The Idea of America's Millennial Role* (Chicago: University of Chicago Press, 1968); Robert Bellah, *The Broken Covenant: American Civil Religion in Time of Trial* (Chicago: University of Chicago Press, 1992).

7. Recently, historians have suggested that the idea of a mission became more powerful in the following decade; this has since been read back into Winthrop's sermon. In any case, the idea of a mission certainly developed quickly and sustained itself. See, for a recent variation, Philip A. Klinkner with Rogers M. Smith, *The Unsteady March* (Chicago: University of Chicago Press, 1999), which argues that great racial reforms came about largely thanks to American concern over international reaction to our practices.

8. See Edmund S. Morgan, *Visible Saints: The History of a Puritan Idea* (Ithaca, N.Y.: Cornell University Press, 1963), chap 1. Jon Butler, *Awash in a Sea of Faith: Christianizing the American People* (Cambridge, Mass.: Harvard University Press, 1990), 20 ("sharp shitting").

9. Sydney Ahlstrom, *A Religious History of the American People* (New Haven: Yale University Press, 1972), 124, 125.

10. Kai T. Erikson, *Wayward Puritans: A Study in the Sociology of Deviance* (New York: Wiley, 1966), 41. In formal church parlance, this branch of Puritans was made up of nonseparating Congregationalists.

11. John Winthrop, *Winthrop's Journal: History of New England,* ed. James Kendall Hosmer (New York: Charles Scribner's Sons, 1908), vol. 1: 309.

12. Perry Miller, *Errand in the Wilderness* (Cambridge, Mass.: Harvard University Press, 1956), 13, 14, 15. Miller is exaggerating for effect. New England did not do "everything that Winthrop demanded." Quite the contrary. It seemed forever embroiled in controversy. As we shall see, while civil war was breaking out in England, Boston was in an uproar over a stolen pig.

13. Bercovitch, *American Jeremiad*, 14, 17, 18. Perry Miller, *The New England Mind: The Seventeenth Century*, 2nd ed. (Cambridge, Mass.: Harvard University Press, 1954), 434, 522–523 (note 1); Samuel Danforth, "A Brief Recognition of New England's Errand into the Wilderness," in Giles Gunn, ed., *Early American Writing* (New York: Penguin, 1994), 198–207, quoted at 206.

14. The great description of the Puritan covenant is in Miller, *Errand in the Wilderness*, 48–98. The argument of the following three paragraphs is derived from Miller. Thomas Shepherd, "The Covenant of Grace" (1651), in Gunn, *Early American Writing*, 73.

15. See "Robert Browne's Statement of Congregational Principles" (1582), in Williston Walker, ed., *The Creeds and Platforms of Congregationalism* (New York: Charles Scribner and Sons, 1893), 18–27, esp. 19.

16. Perry Miller and Thomas Johnson, eds., *The Puritans* (New York: Harper, 1963), vol. 1: 53 (on modern terms); Miller, *Errand in the Wilderness,* 74 ("coils"). On the Anglican opposition, see Miller, *New England Mind,* 435ff.

17. Genesis 9:8–17 (Noah); Genesis 17 (Abraham). For an exploration of the Bible and the idea of covenants, see Daniel Elazar, "The Political Theory of Covenant: Biblical Origins and Modern Developments," *Publius* 10, no. 4 (Fall 1980): 3–30. Elazar counts seven sorts of "paradigmatic covenants" in the Bible, each relevant to political life in a different way.

18. Michael Walzer, *The Revolution of the Saints: A Study in the Origins of Radical Politics* (Cambridge, Mass.: Harvard University Press, 1965), 6 (foot and head), 301 ("human bond").

19. See J. David Greenstone, *The Lincoln Persuasion* (Princeton: Princeton University Press, 1993), 268.

20. "The Charlestown-Boston Covenant," in Walker, *Creeds and Platforms,* 131 ("sweet"), 130.

21. Dedham covenant quoted by Kenneth Lockridge, *A New England Town: The First Hundred Years* (New York: Norton, 1970), 5.

22. Kenneth Wald, *Religion and Politics in the United States* (New York: St. Martin's, 1987), 40–41. See also Louis Hartz and his "cult of constitution worship" and "America's constitutional fetishism," *The Liberal Tradition in America* (New York: Harcourt, Brace and World, 1955), 9.

23. Greenstone, *Lincoln Persuasion,* 285.

24. Elders and Messengers of the Churches Assembled in Synod, *The Necessity of Reformation* (Boston: John Foster, 1679), 1 ("controversy," "desolations"); General Court of Massachusetts, "Provoking Evils" (1675) in Edmund S. Morgan, ed., *Puritan Political Ideas, 1558-1794* (Indianapolis: Bobbs-Merrill, 1965), 228 ("damnable heresies"), 226 ("heathens," "rods").

25. Michael Wigglesworth, "God's Controversy with New England: Written in the Time of the Great Drought, 1662," Alan Heimert and Andrew Delbanco, eds., *The Puritans in America* (Cambridge, Mass.: Harvard University Press, 1985), 235.

26. Synod of 1679, *Necessity of Reformation,* 5. We'll get to Metacom's war later.

27. Synod of 1679, *Necessity of Reformation,* quoted on 2 (apparel), 5 ("defects"), 6 (naked), 1 (mission, "perishing"). The synod gathered up and repeated many prior inventories of iniquity. For instance, the General Court, cited above, covered some of the juiciest ground four years before the synod in "Provoking Evils." *The Necessity of Reformation,* in turn, was widely circulated and studied. It would be repeated from the New England pulpits for years.

28. Genesis 9:1, God's instruction to Noah; see also Genesis 17:2, where it is part of God's promise (rather than an instruction) to Abraham.

29. John Cotton's sermon and Robert Keayne's controversial trial reported by Winthrop, *Winthrop's Journal* (November 1639), vol. 1: 315–318. Synod, *Necessity of Reformation,* 2.

Elsewhere Winthrop reports a delightful instance of a serving-man's insolence (as Winthrop saw it). Goodman Rowley had to sell his oxen to pay his servant, then told the servant he could no longer afford to keep him. The servant replied that he would accept Rowley's cattle as payment. "But how shall I do (saith the master) when all my cattle are gone? The servant replied, you shall then serve me, and so you may have your cattle again" (vol. 2: 228).

30. John Cotton, "Christian Calling," Miller and Johnson, *Puritans,* 319–327, quoted on 320. See also Perry Miller, *The New England Mind: From Colony to Province* (Cambridge, Mass.: Harvard University Press, 1953), chap 3; and Stephen Innes, *Creating the Commonwealth: The Economic Culture of Puritan New England* (New York: Norton, 1995), 25–33.

31. Covenants quoted in Walker, *Creeds and Platforms,* 131 (Boston), 117 (Salem), and Lockridge, *New England Town,* 5 (Dedham).

32. Synod, *Necessity of Reformation,* epistle dedicatory, 1; Cotton Mather, *The Wonders of the Invisible World* (1692; London: John Russell Smith, 1862), 14.

33. John Cotton quoted by Cotton Mather, *Magnalia Christi Americana, or The Ecclesiastical*

History of New England (1702; Hartford, Conn.: Silas Andrus and Son, 1855), vol. 1: 325; Paul Boyer, *When Time Shall Be No More* (Cambridge, Mass.: Harvard University Press, 1992), 71, 226.

34. Jonathan Edwards, "Some Thoughts Concerning the Present Revival of Religion in New England," ed. C. C. Goen, in *The Works of Jonathan Edwards* (New Haven: Yale University Press, 1972), vol. 4: 353–358. For additional context, see Boyer, *When Time Shall Be No More,* 71.

35. Bercovitch, *American Jeremiad,* 16, 9, 23.

36. See Nathan O. Hatch, *The Sacred Cause of Liberty* (New Haven: Yale University Press, 1977).

37. Andrew Delbanco, *The Puritan Ordeal* (Cambridge, Mass.: Harvard University Press, 1989), 16.

38. Puritan church offices were limited to a pastor, a teacher, ruling elders, deacons (to care for temporal things), and ancient widows (to give succor to the sick). For a description, see "The Cambridge Platform (1648)," chaps 6–9, in Walker, *Creeds and Platforms,* 210–214.

39. For a general description of the process, see Morgan, *Visible Saints,* 69–73, 88–91; the conversion stages are on 72. See Lockridge, *New England Town,* chap 2, for a picture of the process at its most utopian.

40. Critique of membership number in Letter from Robert Stansby (to John Winthrop), *Winthrop Papers,* vol. 2: 390. See the discussion in Morgan, *Visible Saints,* 106–108.

There is a guarded discussion of Hooker's leniency in Mather, *Magnalia,* vol. 1: 349–350. On Williams, see Winthrop, *Journal,* vol. 1: 309.

Church membership calculated from Robert Emmet Wall, *Massachusetts Bay: The Crucial Decade, 1640–1650* (New Haven: Yale University Press, 1972), 39–40; the number was 47.5 percent. See also Lockridge, *New England Town,* 31ff.

41. Winthrop, *Journal,* vol. 1 (August 6, 1637), 230 (drowning infant), (February 6, 1637), 210 (Weymouth man). Edwards, *Works of Jonathan Edwards,* vol. 4: 206, 109–110 (Hawley). All three of these famous cases took place amid religious upheaval.

42. Patricia Caldwell, *The Puritan Conversion Narrative: The Beginnings of American Expression* (New York: Cambridge University Press, 1983), 26.

43. As I discuss below, the franchise had a far more limited meaning to the Puritans than it does to modern-day democrats. Still, who voted was a constant work in progress. Church members voted beginning in 1631; in 1635, church membership was required for local elections as well. Rules were loosened in 1647 (when non–church members started voting in local elections). When Charles II demanded a wider franchise, Massachusetts deviously opened the franchise to any one who paid ten shillings' tax (not 3 in 100, says Perry Miller), or any churchman. Eventually, William III cut out all church requirements and pegged the property requirements to 40 shillings.

44. Synod of 1679, *Necessity of Reformation,* 10; statistics taken from Richard Bushman, *From Puritan to Yankee: Character and the Social Order in Connecticut* (Cambridge, Mass.: Harvard University Press, 1967), 158, quoted 160.

45. The second president of Harvard, Henry Dunster, refused to baptize his child (Baptist "heretics" did not baptize anyone till after the conversion experience). His colleagues could, as Cotton Mather delicately put it, "provide him a successor" at Harvard. Dunster moved to the more accommodating congregation at Scituate (in Plymouth), which embraced him in his error. Mather, *Magnalia,* vol. 2: 406.

46. Lockridge, *New England Town,* 90.

47. Lockridge, *New England Town,* 33–34.

On gender and conversions, see Mary Maples Dunn, "Saints and Sisters: Congregational and Quaker Women in the Early Colonial Period," *American Quarterly* 30 (1978): 582–601, 591, table 1.

48. "The Answer of the Elders and Other Messengers of the Churches, Assembled at Boston in the Year 1662," in Walker, *Creeds and Platforms,* 313–339, quoted on 314. For a discussion of the politics that followed, see Robert G. Pope, *The Half-Way Covenant: Church Membership in Puritan New England* (Princeton: Princeton University Press, 1969).

49. Connecticut formally organized supra-congregational appeals boards (consociations) de-

signed to shore up church discipline and strengthen ministerial authority. Massachusetts resisted demands for such standing committees, but its ministers also managed to centralize church authority. The changes were introduced by the Saybrook Platform of 1708. See "The Saybrook Meeting and Articles" in Walker, *Creeds and Platforms,* 502–506.

50. Lockridge, *New England Town,* 42 (on Dedham); Wall, *Massachusetts Bay,* 25 (Salem and Boston; the figures go up to 1647); Patricia Tracy, *Jonathan Edwards, Pastor: Religion and Society in Eighteenth-Century Northampton* (New York: Hill and Wang, 1979), 148–149.

51. Winthrop, *Journal,* vol. 1: 78 (May 1, 1632).

52. Winthrop, *Journal,* vol. 2, 238 (July 5, 1645). Compare the quite similar theme that Thomas Hooker preached at the first Connecticut election in 1638, "Hartford Election Sermon," Perry Miller, ed., *The American Puritans* (Garden City, N.Y.: Doubleday, 1956), 88–89.

53. Winthrop, *Journal,* vol. 2: 239 (July 5, 1645). See also the more formal "Discourse on Arbitrary Government," *Winthrop Papers,* vol. 4: 468–488. To the contemporary sensibility, the gender angle overwhelms everything else in Winthrop's text (which may be why the first part of the text is quoted so much more often than the second). We'll get to the gender story in the next chapter.

54. Winthrop, *Journal,* vol. 1: 74–75.

55. The cries for suffrage quoted in this paragraph came from members of the Hingham militia arguing about who was their proper captain. This is the issue that got Winthrop accused. Winthrop, *Journal,* vol. 2: 230 (May 14, 1645). See the splendid account of the lesser gentry in Wall, *Massachusetts Bay,* chap 1.

56. Winthrop, Letter on Richard Saltonstall's Treatise on the Standing Council, ca. May 1642, *Winthrop Papers,* vol. 4: 347 (on murder conspiracy); Winthrop, Letter to the Elders of the Massachusetts Churches, ibid., 360.

57. Winthrop, *Journal,* 2: 64–66, 116–120 (quoted at 65). For the General Court's summary ("digesting the sow business," as Winthrop put it when the case entered its second year), see "John Winthrop's Summary of the Case Between Richard Sherman and Robert Keayne," *Winthrop Papers,* vol. 4: 349–352.

58. "Summary of the Case Between Richard Sherman and Robert Keayne," *Winthrop Papers,* vol. 4: 349–352. This solution (actually suggested by John Cotton) was not a new one.

59. "The Federal Convention: Madison's Notes on the Debates," in Winton Solberg, ed., *The Federal Convention and the Formation of the American States* (New York: Bobbs-Merrill, 1958), May 31, 84 (Gerry), 85 (Wilson).

CHAPTER 2. *Them: Heretic, Heathen, and Witch*

1. Cotton Mather, *Magnalia Christi Americana, or The Ecclesiastical History of New England* (1702; Hartford, Conn.: Silas Andrus and Son, 1855), vol. 1: 246; Mather's great work is a wonderful introduction to the Puritans. He simply swallows other Puritan texts (though he usually spices up the language). As a result, *Magnalia* reads like a massive, biased, semi-edited collection of Puritan writing. Williams quoted by Edmund S. Morgan, *The Puritan Dilemma* (Boston: Little, Brown, 1958), 135.

2. John Cotton, "The Way of Congregational Churches Cleared" (1648), in David Hall, ed., *The Antinomian Controversy, 1636–1638: A Documentary History* (Middletown, Conn.: Wesleyan University Press, 1968), 412.

3. Hutchinson left behind no writings. Her views are described by her enemies in Winthrop, *Journal,* vol. 1: 195–196, and Mather, *Magnalia,* vol. 2: 517. John Cotton, on the other hand, left a voluminous record; see his exchange of letters with fellow ministers Thomas Shepard and Peter Bulkeley in Hall, *Antinomian Controversy,* 24–42.

4. John Cotton, "Way of Congregational Churches Cleared," in Hall, *Antinomian Controversy,* 412 (works); Winthrop, *Winthrop Papers,* vol. 3: 344.

5. Perry Miller, *The New England Mind: From Colony to Province* (Cambridge, Mass.: Harvard University Press, 1953), 54.

6. Assembly of Churches meeting in New Town [Cambridge], August 30, 1637, "Cata-

logue of Erroneous Opinions," included in John Winthrop, "A Short Story of the Rise, Reign, and Ruine of the Antinomians, Familists, and Libertines" (London: Ralph Smith, 1644), reprinted in Hall, *Antinomian Controversy*, 245 ("If I be holy," "If Christ"), 246 ("crucified my lusts"), 264 ("indevour"); Morgan, *Puritan Dilemma*, 140.

7. Assembly of Churches, "Catalogue of Erroneous Opinions," included in Winthrop, "Short Story," 245. This passage is commonly cited, as it is here, as a prime instance of Hutchinson's aspiration. But note that it was published by her enemies, who were refuting her views. On the quest for certainty, see David D. Hall, *Worlds of Wonder, Days of Judgment* (Cambridge, Mass.: Harvard University Press, 1989), 140–141.

8. Religious historians often make this point. See Morgan, *Puritan Dilemma*, 136; Sidney Ahlstrom, *A Religious History of the American People* (New Haven: Yale University Press, 1972), 153–154.

9. Cotton, "The Way of Congregational Churches Cleared," in Hall, *Antinomian Controversy*, 413. Wheelwright was Hutchinson's brother-in-law.

10. Winthrop, *Journal*, vol. 1: 196–197.

11. Winthrop, *Journal*, vol. 1: 209, 207 (Pequot war).

12. John Wheelwright, "A Fast Day Sermon," in Hall, *Antinomian Controversy*, 152–172, quoted at 158, 163. Wheelwright was quoting from Psalms 2:9 and Hosea 6:5, 6:7–11.

13. Winthrop, *Journal*, vol. 1: 212.

14. John Winthrop, "A Declaration in Defense of an Order of Court" (May 1637), in Edmund S. Morgan, ed., *Puritan Political Ideas* (Indianapolis: Bobbs-Merrill, 1965), 143–149, quoted at 146. The immigration restriction is cited in chap 1, note 5. What the General Court was worried about were the followers of Roger Brierly of Grindleton Chapel, whose views were similar to those of Anne Hutchinson.

15. Assembly of Churches, "Catalogue of Erroneous Opinions," from Winthrop, "Short Story," 219–247.

John Wheelwright recanted in 1643, admitting he had been "dazzled by the buffetings of Satan." The court rescinded his punishment. See *Winthrop Papers*, vol. 4: 414–415.

16. "The Examination of Mrs. Anne Hutchinson at the Court at Newton" [Cambridge], November 1637, in Hall, *Antinomian Controversy*, 314, 315, 316, 318. Morgan, *Puritan Dilemma*, 148.

17. "Examination of Mrs. Anne Hutchinson," 312, 318. The charge of violating the Fifth Commandment was not unusual.

18. "Examination of Mrs. Anne Hutchinson," 314–315.

19. Winthrop, "Short Story," 268–269. The complications of trial by Bible are vivid as the principals turn over the meanings of each passage. The passage in Titus does indeed call on aged women to teach young women, but the curriculum is also provided: "teach them to be sober, to love their husbands, to love their children" (Titus 2:4). This, charges Winthrop, is not exactly what you were doing. On the other side, Winthrop cites I Timothy (2:12), "I permit not a woman to teach," and Hutchinson responds, "That is meant of teaching men." The full passage: "But I suffer not a woman to teach, nor to usurp authority over man, but to be in silence."

20. "Examination of Mrs. Anne Hutchinson," 329ff.

21. Winthrop, "Short Story," 273–275. See also "Examination of Mrs. Anne Hutchinson," 348.

22. On Cotton, see the letters between Thomas Shepard and John Cotton and the exchange between Peter Bulkeley and John Cotton in Hall, *Antinomian Controversy*, 24–42. Thomas Hooker, "Dangers of Desertion," in Alan Heimert and Andrew Delbanco, eds., *The Puritans in America* (Cambridge, Mass.: Harvard University Press, 1985), 68. Delbanco also points to Hooker's sermon as a context for Hutchinson's remarks; see his *Puritan Ordeal* (Cambridge, Mass.: Harvard University Press, 1989), 118–119, 135–137. See also Kai T. Erikson, *Wayward Puritans: A Study in the Sociology of Deviance* (New York: Wiley, 1966), for the argument that the trial crystallized the new Puritan orthodoxy.

23. Winthrop, *Journal*, vol. 2: 225.

24. "Examination of Mrs. Anne Hutchinson," 312, 314, 316.

25. Hall, *Antinomian Controversy*, 205–206.

26. Mather, *Magnalia,* vol. 2: 516, 517, 518.

27. Mather, *Magnalia,* vol. 2: 519.

28. Mather, *Magnalia,* vol. 2: 519, 518.

29. Winthrop, "Short Story," 214; see also Winthrop, *Journal,* vol. 1: 267; Mather, *Magnalia,* vol. 2: 519.

30. Mather, *Magnalia,* vol. 2: 519; Winthrop, "Short Story," 281.

31. For the evidence of witchcraft, see Mather, *Magnalia,* vol. 2: 519–520.

32. Ben Barker-Benfield, "Anne Hutchinson and the Puritan Attitude Toward Women," *Feminist Studies* 1 (Fall 1972): 65–93. Quoted on 85.

33. Edmund S. Morgan, *The Puritan Family* (New York: Harper and Row, 1966), chaps 1, 7. See his list of metaphors on p. 166. See also Barker-Benfield, "Anne Hutchinson and the Puritan Attitude Toward Women," 72–74. "Nursing Fathers" in Winthrop, "Short Story," 250; also, in Synod of 1679, *Necessity of Reformation,* 11.

34. Miller, *New England Mind,* 63.

35. This formulation reflects James David Hunter, *Culture Wars* (New York: Basic Books, 1991). He calls the opposing traditions orthodox and progressive. See also George Lakoff, *Moral Politics* (Chicago: University of Chicago Press, 1996).

36. See the flamboyant description in Brooks Adams, *The Emancipation of Massachusetts* (1887; Boston: Houghton Mifflin, 1962), 313–314. Adams was a ferocious Puritan basher. Though often quoted (and a great read), he is unreliable, for he regularly embellished his Puritan quotations to make them sound nastier. For a description of the Quakers' treatment, see also David Lovejoy, *Religious Enthusiasms in the New World* (Cambridge, Mass.: Harvard University Press), 117.

37. Adams, *Emancipation of Massachusetts,* 273; Miller, *New England Mind,* 11.

38. Erikson, *Wayward Puritans,* 113. Erikson argues that the Quaker incident redefined the boundaries of acceptable behavior in Puritan New England by identifying what was and was not deviant.

39. Mather, *Magnalia,* vol. 2: 526 ("shoemaker"); Ahlstrom, *Religious History of the American People,* 177 (Fox quotation).

40. See Hall, *Worlds of Wonder,* 62–68, quoted at 64 ("mouldy books").

41. Lovejoy, *Enthusiasms,* 118 ("teach doctrines"); Mather, *Magnalia,* vol. 2: 526; Roger Williams, *The Complete Writings of Roger Williams* (New York: Russell and Russell, 1963), vol. 5: 72.

42. "The Trial of Margaret Brewster" (August 4, 1677), in H. Shelton Smith, Robert Handy, and Lefferts A. Loetscher, eds., *American Christianity: An Historical Interpretation with Representative Documents* (New York: Charles Scribner's Sons, 1960), vol. 1: 175–180, quoted at 177. The trial transcript is a wonderful tug-of-war between an unbowed and disrespectful Brewster and an exasperated magistrate struggling to maintain control (if not dignity). Brewster was the last woman to be whipped for being a Quaker.

43. Roger Williams, *George Fox Digg'd out of His Burrowes* (Boston: John Foster, 1676), 9.

44. Mather, *Magnalia,* vol. 2: 644–645. A number of Quakers made this point. See, for example, Edward Wharton, *New England's Present Suffering Under Their Cruel Neighboring Indians* (London: B. Clarke, 1675), esp. p 4, which includes a similar passage.

45. "Quaker Resolution Against Slavery," February 18, 1688, reprinted in Smith, Handy, and Loetscher, *American Christianity,* vol. 1: 180–182.

46. The General Court of Massachusetts, "Provoking Evils," in Morgan, *Puritan Political Ideas,* 228; Williams, *Complete Writings of Roger Williams,* vol. 5: 72; Mather, *Magnalia,* vol. 2: 522 (see also 522–526 and 644–647).

47. The legislation is described in George Bishope, *New England Judged, Not by Man's, but the Spirit of the Lord . . .* (London: Robert Wilson, 1661), 50. Bishop's ardent anti-Puritan tract would be reprinted in the nineteenth century; it remains widely cited today. For a discussion, see Erikson, *Wayward Puritans,* 116–118. See also Adams, *Emancipation of Massachusetts,* 311ff (pro-Quaker), and Mather, *Magnalia,* vol. 2: 525–526 (anti-Quaker).

48. Erikson, *Wayward Puritans,* 119.

49. On the execution liturgy, see Karen Halttunen, "Early American Murder Narratives," in Richard Wightman Fox and T. J. Jackson Lears, eds., *The Power of Culture* (Chicago: University of Chicago Press, 1993), 67–101; Hall, *Worlds of Wonder,* 188–189.

50. "The Trial of Margaret Brewster" (August 4, 1677), in Smith, Handy, and Loetscher, *American Christianity,* vol. 1: 175.

51. Bishope, *New England Judged, Not by Man's, but the Spirit of the Lord,* 52.

52. Mather, *Magnalia,* vol. 2: 525. The hospital of St. Mary of Bethlehem in London was used as a hospital for lunatics (the original Bedlam).

53. Erikson, *Wayward Puritans,* 126–136; Miller, *New England Mind,* 125.

54. See Winthrop Jordan, *White Over Black: American Attitudes Toward the Negro, 1550–1812* (Chapel Hill: University of North Carolina Press, 1968), 20–25.

55. Mather, *Magnalia,* vol. 2: 552 ("devil worship," epic contest), 620 ("hellish conjurors").

56. Captaine John Underhill, *Newwes from America, Or, A New And Experimental Discoverie of New England* (London: Peter Cole, 1638), 22; Mary Rowlandson, "Sovereignty and Goodness of God," in Alden Vaughan and Edward Clark, eds., *Puritans Among the Indians: Accounts of Captivity and Redemption, 1630–1692* (Cambridge, Mass.: Harvard University Press, 1981), 36.

57. Mather, *Magnalia,* vol. 2: 400 ("indulgent"); see also Synod of 1679, *Necessity of Reformation,* 5 (discussed at note 35). On kinship patterns, see William Simmons, "Cultural Bias in the New England Puritans' Perception of Indians," *William and Mary Quarterly* 38 (1981): 56–72, Roger Williams quoted on 62.

58. For discussions of sexual mores, see Simmons, "Cultural Bias," 62, 63 ("whoredoms"). On both sex and cannibalism myths, see Richard Slotkin's splendid *Regeneration Through Violence: The Mythology of the American Frontier, 1600–1860* (New York: HarperCollins, 1996), chap 2, esp. pp 47ff.

59. Increase Mather was especially sharp on the matter of elbow room. See the Synod of 1679, *Necessity of Reformation,* 6. On ranging up and down, see William Bradford, *Bradford's History "of Plimouth Plantation"* (Boston: Wright and Potter, 1898), 32–33. On premarital sex rates, see Daniel Scott Smith and Michael S. Hindus, "Premarital Pregnancy in America, 1640–1971: An Overview and Interpretation," *Journal of Interdisciplinary History* 5, no. 4 (1975): 537–570.

60. Increase Mather, *A Brief History of the Warr with the Indians in New England (From June 24, 1675 when the First Englishman Was Murdered by the Indians, to August 12, 1676, when Philip, alias Metacomet, the Principal Author and Beginner of the Warr, was Slain)* (Boston: John Foster, 1676), 20; John Williams, "The Redeemed Captive Returning to Zion," in Vaughan and Clark, *Puritans Among the Indians,* 189, 209. For aggregate data on the fate of Indian captives, see Slotkin, *Regeneration Through Violence,* 97–98.

61. Mather, *Magnalia,* vol. 2: 400.

62. Synod of 1679, *Necessity of Reformation,* 5; see also Mather, *Magnalia,* vol. 2: 431. The seal of the Massachusetts Bay Company depicted an Indian standing on the shore seeking European help. See Francis Bremer, *The Puritan Experiment* (Hanover, N.H.: University Press of New England, 1995), 199.

63. Lockridge, *New England Town,* 84; Mather, *Magnalia,* vol. 2: 577 (Maine); Boston lynch mob in Slotkin, *Regeneration Through Violence,* 82. The praying Indians had to be moved onto islands in Boston harbor and guarded to protect them from angry residents.

64. Mather, *Magnalia,* vol. 2: 552 ("take alarum"), 553 ("division"). Michael Wigglesworth, "God's Controversy with New England: Written in the Time of the Great Drought, 1662" in Heimert and Delbanco, *Puritans in America,* 231–232 (space).

65. Alfred Cave, *The Pequot War* (Amherst: University of Massachusetts Press, 1996), 46.

66. For John Winthrop's description of the causes, see *Winthrop's Journal,* vol. 1: 183–190; John Higginson to John Winthrop, May 1637, *Winthrop Papers,* vol. 3: 404–405, 407–408.

67. This story is constantly repeated. The version quoted here is from Woodrow Wilson, *A History of the American People* (New York: Harper Brothers, 1908), vol. 1: 154.

68. Underhill, *Newwes from America,* 9.

69. Cave, *Pequot War,* 8.

70. Mather, *Magnalia,* vol. 2: 555. See also Underhill, *Newwes from America,* 38–40. He puts the dead in the fort at 400.

71. Underhill, *Newwes from America,* 39–40.

72. Bradford, *History "of Plimouth Plantation,"* book 2: 425–426.

73. Mather, *Magnalia,* vol. 2: 556.

74. Underhill, *Newwes from America,* 40. Only two years after the war, the Puritans are already defensive about their action. I altered Underhill's punctuation.

75. Underhill, *Newwes from America,* 43 ("furious"), 40–41 ("seven men").

76. Bradford, *History "of Plimoth Plantation,"* book 2: 197, 198.

77. Glenn LaFantasie, ed., *The Correspondence of Roger Williams* (Hanover, N.H.: Brown University Press/University Press of New England, 1988), 102–103. Biblical quotation, II Kings 14:6. On Puritan doctrine about killing war prisoners, see Morgan, *Puritan Family,* 110.

78. Edward Wharton, *New England's Present Sufferings, Under Their Cruel Neighboring Indians: Represented in Two Letters, Lately Written from Boston to London* (London: B. Clarke, 1675), 4.

79. See Francis Jennings, *The Invasion of America* (Chapel Hill: University of North Carolina Press, 1975). Gary Nash, *Red, White, and Black: The Peoples of Early North America* (Englewood Cliffs, N.J.: Prentice Hall, 1992). Ann Kibbey, *The Interpretation of Material Shapes in Puritanism: A Study of Rhetoric, Prejudice, and Violence* (New Haven: Yale University Press, 1986).

80. For example, in 1631 Winthrop reported that an Indian woman and her husband complained that a young man solicited her to incontinency. The man was whipped, reports Winthrop, and the Indians were very well satisfied. Winthrop, *Journal,* vol. 1: 67.

81. Alden Vaughan, *New England Frontier: Puritans and Indians, 1620–1657,* 3rd ed. (Norman: University of Oklahoma Press, 1995), xxvii (on blame), xlvii (comparison to other colonies).

82. Cave, *Pequot War,* chap 5.

83. Cave, *Pequot War,* chap 5.

84. For a fine account of this war and its meaning, see Jill Lepore, *The Name of War: King Philip's War and the Origins of American Identity* (New York: Knopf, 1998).

85. Mather, *Magnalia,* vol. 1: 88; data from Nash, *Red, White, and Black,* 121–123; and Bremer, *Puritan Experiment,* 168–171.

86. Increase Mather, *History of the Warr with the Indians,* 21.

87. On intermarriage, see Daniel Mandell, *Behind the Frontier* (Lincoln: University of Nebraska Press, 1996), chap 6.

88. Cotton Mather, *The Wonders of the Invisible World* (1693; London: John Russell Smith, 1862), 14 (preternatural), 43 (buffet).

89. The standard disclaimer to this view is Perry Miller's dictum (plucked out of context): "The most curious of all the facts in that welter we call Salem witchcraft is this: . . . The intellectual history of New England *up to 1720* can be written as though no such thing ever happened. It had no effect on the ecclesiastical or political situation" (emphasis added). First of all, that "up to 1720" is crucial: Miller argues that the effect was delayed—but devastating. Miller's actual analysis runs like this: although "at that moment, nobody quite heard the crash, a central pillar of the jeremiad . . . tumbled to earth." In the end, the "real effect of the tragedy is not to be traced in the field of politics or society, but in the intangible area of federal theory, and in the still more intangible region of self esteem." For, though the ministry "desperately concealed" it for a time, the episode exposed a "flaw in the very foundation of the covenant conception." The entire covenant scaffolding was left "dangerously shaken and out of kilter." It would be another generation, argues Miller, before the Salem Village chickens would fully come home to roost. But the damage had been done. Miller, *New England Mind,* 191, 195, 207, 192.

90. For sheer volume, nobody beats Adams, *Emancipation of Massachusetts.* See also Samuel G. Drake, ed., *The Witchcraft Delusion in New England* (Roxbury, Mass.: W. Elliot Woodward, 1866), vol. 1, which reprints Mather's *Wonders of the Invisible World* with an acid commentary in footnotes that run the length of the text.

91. Estimates of the number of people executed as witches vary enormously. On Germany, see Pennethorne Hughes, *Witchcraft* (Harmondsworth, Eng.: Penguin, 1971), 63. On England,

see Thomas Rogers Forbes, *The Midwife and the Witch* (New Haven: Yale University Press, 1966), 113 ("30,000"). See also Alan Macfarlane, *Witchcraft in Tudor and Stuart England* (London, 1970), and C. L. Ewen, *Witch Hunting and Witch Trials* (London, 1929). For a New England critique of English witch-hunts, see Mather, *Magnalia,* vol. 2: 477. For really eye-popping estimates, see Andrea Dworkin, *Women Hating* (New York: Penguin, 1974), chap 7.

92. On the rates of execution, see John Putnam Demos, *Entertaining Satan: Witchcraft and the Culture of Early New England* (New York: Oxford University Press, 1982), 11–13. On early American episodes, see David Hall, ed., *Witch-Hunting in Seventeenth-Century New England: A Documentary History* (Boston: Northeastern University Press, 1991), 147–163, and Mather, *Magnalia,* vol. 2: 448. For an overview of the cases before Salem, see Carol Karlsen's splendid *The Devil in the Shape of a Woman: Witchcraft in Colonial New England* (New York: Vintage, 1989), chap 1.

93. "Petition of the Salem Farmers About the Military Watch," in Paul Boyer and Stephen Nissenbaum, eds., *Salem-Village Witchcraft: A Documentary Record of Local Conflict in Colonial New England* (Boston: Northeastern University Press, 1993), 229–232. For a general portrait of Salem Village and its troubles, see Paul Boyer and Stephen Nissenbaum, *Salem Possessed: The Social Origins of Witchcraft* (Cambridge, Mass.: Harvard University Press, 1974), chaps 2 and 3. For an elaboration on the geographic theme, see James Lemon, "Spatial Order: Households in Local Communities and Regions," in Jack Greene and J. R. Pole, eds., *Colonial British America* (Baltimore: Johns Hopkins University Press, 1984), esp. 99–100.

94. The description of the girl's looking glass is often repeated. The original source is a rather opaque second-hand account in John Hale, *A Modest Inquiry into the Nature of Witchcraft, and How Persons Guilty of the Crime May Be Convicted* (Boston: B. Green and F. Allen, 1702), quoted on 132 ("tampered") and 133 ("spectre"). For a good discussion, see Chadwick Hansen, *Witchcraft at Salem* (New York: George Braziller, 1969), 30ff. Mather, *Magnalia,* vol 2: 471–472 ("tormented").

95. Deodat Lawson, "A True Narrative of Some Remarkable Passages Relating to Sundry Persons Afflicted by Witchcraft at Salem Village . . . ," reprinted in Mather, *Wonders of the Invisible World,* sermon interruptions quoted at 202–203.

96. Of the 43 formally diagnosed as afflicted, 38 were women, 35 were younger than twenty-one years old. Calculated from Richard Weisman, *Witchcraft, Magic, and Religion in Seventeenth-Century Massachusetts* (Amherst: University of Massachusetts Press, 1984), appendix F, 222–223; and Lawson, "True Narrative," 201–210.

97. Boyer and Nissenbaum, *Salem Possessed,* 26–28.

98. Increase Mather, *Remarkable Providences Illustrative of the Earlier Days of American Colonisation* (1684; London: Reeves and Turner, 1890), chap 6. And Increase Mather, *Cases of Conscience Concerning Evil Spirits Personating Men* (1692), in Mather, *Wonders of the Invisible World,* 222.

For an extended discussion of the possession theme, see David Harley, "Explaining Salem: Calvinist Psychology and the Diagnosis of Possession," *American Historical Review* 101, no. 2 (April 1996): 307–330.

99. This point is often made. Perry Miller calls witchcraft in the seventeenth century "not only plausible but scientifically rational." *New England Mind,* 191. See also Karlsen, *Devil in the Shape of a Woman,* 133.

100. Mather, *Magnalia,* vol. 2: 479 ("obtained an ability"). Hale, *Modest Inquiry,* 132 (door).

101. See Richard Goodbeer, *The Devil's Dominion: Magic and Religion in Early New England* (New York: Cambridge University Press, 1992), countermagic discussed on 42–46. On magic generally see also Hall, *Worlds of Wonder;* Weisman, *Witchcraft, Magic, and Religion;* Jon Butler, *Awash in a Sea of Faith: Christianizing the American People* (Cambridge, Mass.: Harvard University Press, 1990), chap 3.

102. Mather, *Magnalia,* vol. 2: 471. The section on Salem is an extended quote from John Hale, *Modest Inquiry.* Samuel Parris, "Statement on the Witchcraft Outbreak," in Boyer and Nissenbaum, *Salem-Village Witchcraft,* 278.

103. Mather, *Wonders of the Invisible World,* in Drake, *Witchcraft Delusion,* 57. Deodat Law-

son, "Christ's Fidelity the Only Shield Against Satan's Malignity," a sermon preached at Salem Village, March 24, 1692, in Boyer and Nissenbaum, *Salem-Village Witchcraft*, 124–128.

104. Mather, *Wonders of the Invisible World*, 13–14.

105. *Records of Salem Witchcraft* (Roxbury, Mass.: W. Elliot Woodward, 1864), vol. 2: 112 (on George Jacobs); Demos, *Entertaining Satan*, 179–180 ("secret parts").

106. Adams, *Emancipation of Massachusetts*, 393.

107. "The Return of Several Ministers consulted by his Excellency, and the Honourable Council upon the Present Witchcrafts in Salem Village," Boston, June 15, 1692, in Mather, *Wonders of the Invisible World*, 290.

108. *Records of Salem Witchcraft*, vol. 1, 17–21. Also in Boyer and Nissenbaum, *Salem-Village Witchcraft*, 5–7. Lack of residence, Boyer and Nissenbaum, *Salem Possessed*, map 1.

109. *Records of Salem Witchcraft*, vol. 1: 19.

110. See Elaine G. Breslaw, *Tituba, Reluctant Witch of Salem: Devilish Indians and Puritan Fantasies* (New York: New York University Press, 1996), chap 1 and pp 188–197 (transcripts). A less complete set of transcripts is in *Records of Salem Witchcraft* vol. 1: 43–48.

111. Breslaw, *Tituba*, 117–122. The numbers vary slightly from source to source. For a summary of cases prior to Salem, see Demos, *Entertaining Satan*, 402–409; for a summary of Salem cases, see Weisman, *Witchcraft, Magic, and Religion*, appendices C–F. A useful revision of Weisman's list on Salem can be found in Breslaw, *Tituba*, 183–187.

112. Lawson, "True Narrative," in Mather, *Wonders of the Invisible World*, 203–205. See also *Records of Salem Witchcraft*, vol. 1: 50–60, esp. 59.

113. Lawson, "True Narrative," 209–210; *Records of Salem Witchcraft*, vol. 1: 75–76.

114. *Records of Salem Witchcraft*, vol. 1: 212–213.

115. *Records of Salem Witchcraft*, vol. 1: 214 (Jarvis), 226 (Downer). Karlsen, *Devil in the Shape of a Woman*, 138.

116. Boyer and Nissenbaum, *Salem-Village Witchcraft*, 73–80; *Records of Salem Witchcraft*, vol. 2: 109–128.

117. Account given by Mr. Nathaniel Cary in Robert Calef, *More Wonders of the Invisible World* (London: Nath. Hillar, 1700). Facsimile edition, Chadwick Hansen, ed. (New York: York Mail-Print, 1972), 95–98.

118. "Return of Several Ministers," in Mather, *Wonders of the Invisible World*, 290.

119. Calef, *More Wonders of the Invisible World*, 102 (Good), 106 (Corey). On Giles Corey, see Samuel Sewall, *The Diary of Samuel Sewall: 1674–1729*, M. Halsey Thomas, ed. (New York: Farrar, Straus and Giroux, 1973), vol. 1: 295. The traditional story is that Giles Cory was protecting his estate by refusing to plead, but this is now disputed as a nineteenth-century invention. See the discussion in Bernard Rosenthal, *Salem Story: Reading the Witch Trials of 1692* (New York: Cambridge University Press, 1995), 163–165.

120. Calef, *More Wonders of the Invisible World*, 103–104. Calef was Mather's great tormenter and certainly might have embellished the story. But the sober Samuel Sewall confirms the basic details. See Sewall, *Diary of Samuel Sewall*, vol. 1: 294.

121. "The Petition of Mary Easty," *Records of Salem Witchcraft*, vol. 2: 44.

122. Cotton Mather, *Magnalia*, vol. 2: 477.

123. Increase Mather, *Cases of Conscience*, 283; the fake disclaimer is in the postscript, 285–288. Perry Miller writes that the postscript turns a "bold stroke" into a "miserable species of doubletalk." Miller, *New England Mind*, 199.

124. Boyer and Nissenbaum, *Salem Possessed*, 34 (map 1), chap 2.

125. Samuel Huntington, *Political Order in Changing Societies* (New Haven: Yale University Press, 1968), 5, 460–461.

126. Miller, *New England Mind*, 195.

127. Thomas Brattle, "Copy of a MS. Letter, Giving a Full and Candid Account of the Delusion Called Witchcraft, Which Prevailed In New England" (October 8, 1692), *Collections of the Massachusetts Historical Society for the Year MDCCXCVIII* (Boston: Samuel Hall, 1798), 61–80, quoted at 66–67, 65, 72, 79.

128. Calef, *More Wonders of the Invisible World,* 13–14. See the discussion of Calef in Andrew Delbanco, *The Death of Satan* (New York: Farrar, Straus and Giroux, 1995), 63–64.

129. Calef, *More Wonders of the Invisible World,* 21.

130. See Demos, *Entertaining Satan,* 60–64, appendix 1; for Salem Village numbers, see Breslaw, *Tituba,* appendix A.

131. Heinrich Institoris and James Sprenger, *The Malleus Maleficarum* (New York: Dover, 1971), 41, 47; see, generally, Question VI. The Puritans would not normally read a Roman Catholic text, but *Malleus* sets out the basic logic of the old world witch-hunt. See the discussion in Karlsen, *Devil in the Shape of a Women,* 156ff.

132. Karlsen, *Devil in the Shape of a Woman,* 116; on widows (or "relicts" as they were known), see Laurel Thatcher Ulrich, *Good Wives: Image and Reality in the Lives of Women in Northern New England* (New York: Knopf, 1982), 7–8.

133. See Barbara Ehrenreich and Deirdre English, *Witches, Midwives, and Nurses: A History of Women Healers* (Old Westbury, N.Y.: Feminist Press, 1973), 10–13. Ehrenreich and English also emphasize competition with the medical profession, which came later in the United States. Institoris and Sprenger offered the old world perspective: "Midwives surpass all others in wickedness." *Malleus Maleficarum,* 41. On New England numbers, see Karlsen, *Devil in the Shape of a Woman,* 142.

134. Institoris and Sprenger, *Malleus Maleficarum,* 41; Karlsen, *Devil in the Shape of a Woman,* 138; Mather, *Wonders of the Invisible World,* 33.

135. See Karlsen, *Devil in the Shape of a Woman,* epilogue; Ulrich, *Good Wives,* 103–105; Christine Stansell, *City of Women* (Urbana: University of Illinois Press, 1987).

136. See Chadwick Hansen, "The Metamorphosis of Tituba, Or Why American Intellectuals Can't Tell an Indian Witch from a Negro," *New England Quarterly* (March 1974): 3–12.

CHAPTER 3. *The Puritans Become America*

1. For wonderful descriptions of the religious frenzy, see Jonathan Edwards, *Some Thoughts Concerning the Present Revival in New-England* (1742), ed. C. C. Goen, in *Works of Jonathan Edwards* (New Haven: Yale University Press, 1972), vol. 4: 331–347, quoted on 332 ("exultation"). For an attack on the outlandish behavior, see The Querists, "A Short Reply to Mr. Whitefield's Letter," in Alan Heimert and Perry Miller, eds., *The Great Awakening: Documents Illustrating the Crisis and Its Consequences* (Indianapolis: Bobbs-Merrill, 1967), esp. 138.

2. "No single issue in all of American history," writes Nathan O. Hatch, "has attracted more talent than that of linking the Great Awakening and the Revolution." Hatch made the comment partially in response to a great caveat that hangs over the entire literature on the Great Awakening: Jon Butler's bold assertion that the whole episode is an "interpretive fiction." Butler's tossed gauntlet has not led to a wholesale revision (he first made the challenge in 1982). But it had a large effect: writing became far more cautious. The revival did not sweep through every region or all colonies. It operated differently in different places. It reflected local concerns and conditions.

Still, the New Englanders discussed below—both enthusiasts and critics—all thought something big was happening. In New England at least, the consequences were wide and deep. Butler acknowledges this, but he meets the objection by arguing—along with many historians—that New England is overemphasized.

This too is a topic of much discussion. One simple bit of context can be found in the population statistics. By 1740, Massachusetts was the second largest colony, Connecticut the fourth. Together, they made up 26.6 percent of the entire (estimated) colonial population.

Nathan O. Hatch, *The Democratization of American Christianity* (New Haven: Yale University Press, 1989), 221. Jon Butler, "Enthusiasm Described and Decried: The Great Awakening as Interpretive Fiction," *Journal of American History* 69, no. 2 (September 1982): 305–325. And Jon Butler's terrific *Awash in a Sea of Faith: Christianizing the American People* (Cambridge, Mass.: Harvard University Press, 1990), chap 6. Population estimates calculated from U.S. Bureau of the Census, *The Statistical History of the United States: From Colonial Times to the Present* (New York: Basic Books, 1976), 1168.

3. See Jonathan Edwards, *A Faithful Narrative of the Surprising Work of God in the Conversion of Many Hundred Souls* (1736), ed. C. C. Goen, *Works of Jonathan Edwards*, vol. 4: 146 ("dullness," "taverns"), 149, 150; see also *The Distinguishing Marks of a Work of the Spirit of God*, a discourse delivered in New Haven, September 10, 1741, ed. Goen, ibid., vol. 4: 268, 265 ("perverseness"); "Letter to Benjamin Colman" (May 30, 1735), ibid., 104; George Whitefield, *Journals* (1740), in Richard Bushman, ed., *The Great Awakening: Documents on the Revival of Religion, 1740–1745* (New York: Athenaeum, 1970), 30–31 ("dead men" preach).

4. Edwards, *Thoughts Concerning the Present Revival*, and *Faithful Narrative*, ed. Goen, in *Works of Jonathan Edwards*, vol. 4: 387–388 ("heat"), 146; the idea of soul "harvest" came from the formidable Solomon Stoddard, Edwards's grandfather, who had presided over five such revivals.

5. Jonathan Edwards, "Sinners in the Hands of an Angry God," in Giles Gunn, ed., *Early American Writing* (New York: Penguin, 1994), 325. This is surely the most famous sermon of the era—justly so. It was delivered in Enfield, Connecticut, in July 1741. For a rhetorical analysis, see Ernest Bormann, *The Force of Fantasy* (Carbondale: Southern Illinois University Press, 1985), 60–68.

6. Edwards, "Sinners in the Hands of an Angry God," 232–233.

7. Edwards kept returning to descriptions of the suicide. See his "Letter to Benjamin Colman" (May 30, 1735), ed. Goen, in *Works of Jonathan Edwards*, vol. 4: 109–110. The story of the German woman is attributed to Henry Melchior Muhlenberg, an evangelical Lutheran. See the account in David Lovejoy, *Religious Enthusiasm in the New World: Heresy to Revolution* (Cambridge, Mass.: Harvard University Press, 1985), 185.

8. Charles Chauncy, "Letter to George Wishart," in Bushman, *Great Awakening*, 116. George Whitefield, *Journals* (1740), in Bushman, *Great Awakening*, 30–31. For a discussion of the turnout, see Gary Nash, *The Urban Crucible* (Cambridge, Mass.: Harvard University Press, 1979), 480 n 38.

9. Whitefield, *Journals*, in Bushman, *Great Awakening* 31.

10. *New England Weekly Journal*, December 4, 1739, in Bushman, *Great Awakening*, 22.

11. Gilbert Tennent, "The Danger of an Unconverted Ministry" (1741), in Heimert and Miller, *Great Awakening*, 78, 79, 80, 86, 89, 95. When Whitefield's journal was published, it revealed precisely the same views. Even while enjoying the hospitality of the Boston clergy Whitefield had been scribbling the same sharp judgments: his colleagues were "dead men," mere "pharisees" talking of an "unknown, unfelt Christ." The official reception was decidedly more frosty on his next New England visit.

12. Charles Chauncy, *Seasonable Thoughts on the State of Religion in New England* (Boston: Rogers and Fowle, 1743), 55.

13. There is a large literature sorting out the class implications. Local studies find variations in different communities. See the survey of local studies in C. C. Goen, *Revivalism and Separatism in New England, 1740–1800* (Middletown, Conn.: Wesleyan University Press, 1987), "Introduction to the Wesleyan Edition." See also Nash, *Urban Crucible*, 208–212. William Cooper, Preface to Edwards, *The Distinguishing Marks of a Work of the Spirit of God* (originally preached September 10, 1741), ed. Goen, in *Works of Jonathan Edwards*, vol. 4: 219.

14. "Religious Excess at New London," *Boston Weekly Post-Boy*, March 28, 1743, in Bushman, *Great Awakening*, 51–53. J. M. Bumsted and John E. Van De Wetering, *What Must I Do to Be Saved? The Great Awakening in Colonial America* (Hinsdale, Ill.: Dryden, 1976), 90 ("bare-arsed"). Nash, *Urban Crucible*, 209.

15. *Boston Weekly Post-Boy*, March 28, 1743 ("wild"), in Bushman, *Great Awakening*, 52, 121; Chauncy, "Letter to Wishart" (August 1742), in Bushman, *Great Awakening*, 121. For a discussion of the class implications of the Davenport revivals, see Harry S. Stout and Peter Onuf, "James Davenport and the Great Awakening in New London," *Journal of American History* 70 (1983–1984): 557–578.

16. Stout and Onuf, "James Davenport and the Great Awakening," 567 (hay); Chauncy, *Seasonable Thoughts*, 370 ("unfit for the services"); Chauncy, "Letter to Wishart," in Heimert and Miller, *Great Awakening*, 117; Alan Heimert, *Religion and the American Mind* (Cambridge,

Mass.: Harvard University Press, 1966), 53 ("religion of labor," "idle visions," "deluded trades-men").

17. Edwards, *Thoughts Concerning the Present Revival*, in *Works of Jonathan Edwards*, vol. 4: 396–397; see also *Faithful Narrative*, vol. 4: 150.

18. Nash, *Urban Crucible*, 208 ("anarchy"); Heimert, *Religion and the American Mind*, 12 ("mobbish"); and Chauncy, *Seasonable Thoughts*, 372–373.

19. Chauncy, "Letter to Wishart," in Bushman, *Great Awakening*, 119 ("lads"); and Charles Chauncy, "Enthusiasm Described and Caution'd Against," in Heimert and Miller, *Great Awakening*, 241.

20. Chauncy, "Enthusiasm Described and Caution'd Against," 243 (wives); Chauncy, "A Letter from a Gentleman in Boston," in Bushman, *Great Awakening*, 116–117 ("Females"). The cartoon is in Butler, *Awash in a Sea of Faith*, 189. For a fine analysis of the sexual angle, see Susan Juster, *Disorderly Women: Sexual Politics and Evangelicalism in Revolutionary New England* (Ithaca, N.Y.: Cornell University Press, 1994).

21. Edwards, *Some Thoughts Concerning the Present Revival of Religion*, in *Works of Jonathan Edwards*, vol. 4: 468–469; Lovejoy, *Religious Enthusiasm*, 197; Perry Miller, *Errand in the Wilderness* (Cambridge, Mass.: Harvard University Press, 1956), 154.

22. Cooper, Preface to Edwards, *Distinguishing Marks*, in *Works of Jonathan Edwards*, vol. 4: 220.

23. Edwards, "Sinners in the Hands of Angry God," *Early American Writing*, 333 ("gathering"); Lovejoy, *Religious Enthusiasm*, 180 ("anvil").

24. Edwards, *Thoughts Concerning the Present Revival*, in *Works of Jonathan Edwards*, vol. 4: 353–358, quoted at 358, 353, 354. The clergy's manifesto is described in Paul Boyer, *When Time Shall Be No More: Prophecy Belief in Modern American Culture* (Cambridge, Mass.: Harvard University Press, 1994), 70. "The dawn of the glorious work of God . . . [in] America," retorted Chauncy, is "uncertain conjecture" based "upon evidence absolutely precarious." *Seasonable Thoughts*, 372.

25. Aristide Zolberg, "Moments of Madness," *Politics and Society* 2, no. 2 (1972): 183–207.

26. William McLoughlin, "Enthusiasm for Liberty: The Great Awakening as the Key to the Revolution," *Proceedings of the American Antiquarian Society* 87 (1977): 69–95, esp. 73. See also note 3 above.

27. Cooper, Preface to Edwards, *Distinguishing Marks*, in *Works of Jonathan Edwards*, vol. 4: 219–220 ("most ignorant"); "The Separates in Norwich, Connecticut," in Bushman, *Great Awakening*, 102 ("lowly preaching"), 103 ("covenant"); John Winthrop, *Winthrop's Journal: History of New England* (New York: Charles Scribner's Sons, 1908), vol. 2: 238.

28. Harry S. Stout, *The New England Soul* (New York: Oxford University Press, 1986), 217.

29. On the Baptists, see William McLoughlin's magisterial *New England Dissent: 1630–1833* (Cambridge, Mass.: Harvard University Press, 1971). Baptist census from Sydney E. Ahlstrom, *A Religious History of the American People* (New Haven: Yale University Press, 1974), 292–293; the population of the six New England states rose from 579,000 in 1770 to 1,233,000 in 1800. Calculated from *Historical Statistics of the United States*, 24–35, 1168.

30. Quoted by Richard Bushman, *From Puritan to Yankee: Character and the Social Order of Connecticut, 1690–1765* (Cambridge, Mass.: Harvard University Press, 1967), 253. See, generally, the vivid description of Connecticut politics in part 5. On Virginia, see Wesley M. Gewehr, *The Great Awakening in Virginia, 1740–1790* (Gloucester, Mass.: Peter Smith, 1965), quoted at 89.

31. Bushman, *From Puritan to Yankee*, 260ff, quoted on 262.

32. See James A. Morone, *The Democratic Wish: Popular Participation and the Limits of American Government* (New Haven: Yale University Press, 1998).

33. E. P. Thompson, *The Making of the English Working Class* (New York: Vintage, 1963), 388, 390–391. On upper-class anxiety and missionary activity, see Stedman Jones, *Languages of Class: Studies in English Working Class History* (Cambridge: Cambridge University Press, 1983), 188ff.

The English Methodists (evangelical Anglicans) were exuberant, irrepressible missionaries: by the early nineteenth century, their annual report listed 872 traveling preachers spread from Ceylon to Canada. "Foreign Articles: Report on 74th Annual Conference of the Methodists of the United Kingdom," *Niles Register,* October 11, 1817, 110.

34. Eric Hobsbawm, *Workers* (New York: Pantheon, 1984), 33. See also Hobsbawm, *The Age of Revolution* (New York: Random House, 1962), chap 12, and, for a slightly earlier period, Thompson, *English Working Class,* chap 11. On reactionary revivals, see Sandra Halperin, *In the Mirror of the Third World: Capitalist Development in Modern Europe* (Ithaca, N.Y.: Cornell University Press, 1997), 105–113; Hobsbawm, *Age of Revolution,* chap 12, quoted at 229 ("compulsive").

35. Quoted by Gaetano Cingari, *Brigantaggio, Proprietari e Contadini nel Sud: 1799–1900* (Reggio Calabria: Editori Meridionali Riuniti, 1976), 38. Translated by my dad, James A. Morone. The passage is discussed in Hobsbawm, *Workers,* 34.

36. On Boston, see Nash, *Urban Crucible,* 221–222. On New York's horrible racial savagery, see Joel Tyler Headley, *The Great Riots of New York* (New York: E. B. Treat, 1873), chap 2, and Lovejoy, *Religious Enthusiasm,* 201–206.

37. Louis Hartz begins his classic analysis of the liberal tradition with "the story book truth about American history: that America was settled by men who fled from the feudal and clerical oppressions of the Old World." *The Liberal Tradition in America* (New York: Harcourt, Brace and World, 1955), 3.

The classic account of the link between central authority and religion is Sidney Mead, "The Rise of the Evangelical Conception of the Ministry in America," in H. Richard Niebuhr and Daniel D. Williams, eds., *The Ministry in Historical Perspectives* (New York, pub. 1956). For a more recent analysis, see John Markoff, *The Abolition of Feudalism* (University Park: Pennsylvania State University Press, 1996). For wonderful descriptions of the religious frenzy, see Jonathan Edwards, *Thoughts Concerning the Present Revival,* in *Works of Jonathan Edwards,* vol. 4: 331–347. For an attack on the outlandish behavior, see The Querists, "A Short Reply to Mr. Whitefield's Letter," in Heimert and Miller, *Great Awakening,* esp. 138.

PART II

1. Gustave de Beaumont, *Marie or Slavery in the United States,* Barbara Chapman, trans. (1835; Stanford, Calif.: Stanford University Press, 1958), 4–5.

2. Arthur Schlesinger, Jr., wrote the classic version of this story, *The Age of Jackson* (Boston: Little, Brown, 1945). See Lee Benson, *The Concept of Jacksonian Democracy* (Princeton: Princeton University Press, 1961), chap 15. For my own version of the age of Jackson, see James A. Morone, *The Democratic Wish: Popular Participation and the Limits of American Government* (New Haven: Yale University Press, 1998), chap 2.

On the economy, see, especially, Sean Wilentz, *Chants Democratic* (New York: Oxford University Press, 1984), and Edward Pessen, *Riches, Class, and Power Before the Civil War* (Lexington, Mass.: D. C. Heath, 1973). On the rise of parties, see John Aldrich, *Why Parties?* (Chicago: University of Chicago Press, 1996).

On achieving the American dream, see Samuel Huntington, *American Politics: The Promise of Disharmony* (Cambridge, Mass.: Harvard University Press, 1981), 224. Voter turnout reached 80.2 percent in 1840 and 81.2 percent in 1860.

3. Abraham Lincoln, "Address to the Young Men's Lyceum of Springfield," January 27, 1837, in *The Writings of Abraham Lincoln,* Arthur Brooks Lapsley, ed. (New York: Putnam, 1905), vol. 1: 149, 150, 151. On the Anglo-Saxon celebrations, see Reginald Horsman, *Race and Manifest Destiny: The Origins of Racial Anglo-Saxonism* (Cambridge, Mass.: Harvard University Press, 1981).

4. Rogers M. Smith, *Civic Ideals: Conflicting Visions of Citizenship in U.S. History* (New Haven: Yale University Press, 1997), 201.

5. Donald Mathews, "The Second Great Awakening as an Organizing Process, 1780–1830: An Hypothesis," *American Quarterly* 21, no. 1 (Spring 1969): 42; J. K. Paulding, *Slavery in the United States* (New York: Harper and Brothers, 1836), 310 ("mulattoes").

6. John Calhoun, Speech on the Reception of Abolition Petitions, delivered in the Senate, February 6, 1837, *The Works of John Calhoun,* Richard Cralle, ed. (New York: D. Appleton, 1860), vol. 2: 626–627.

7. Frederick Douglass, "The Anti-Slavery Movement," 1855, in Philip Foner, ed., *The Life and Writings of Frederick Douglass* (New York: International Publishers, 1950), vol. 2.

CHAPTER 4. *The Wrath of God in Black and White*

1. The link between religious revivals and abolitionist reformers was first made by Gilbert Hobbs Barnes, *The Anti-Slavery Impulse: 1830–1844* (New York: Harcourt, Brace and World, 1933). Barnes focused on the role of Theodore Dwight Weld, whose letters he had edited. Weld's letters from the 1820s and early 1830s make the connection between revival and abolition quite vivid. See *Letters of Theodore Dwight Weld, Angelina Grimké Weld, and Sarah Grimké,* Gilbert Barnes and Dwight Dumond, eds. (New York: Appleton-Century, 1934), vol. 1: 3–184.

2. Laurel Thatcher Ulrich offers a marvelous illustration in her description of a midwife's life in Maine. The glories of the revolution and the Washington administration touched the woman's life mainly by inspiring names for her grandsons—George, Samuel Adams, and De Lafayette. In contrast, her diary is full of religious references—sermons, local religious divisions, prayers, pieties. Ulrich, *A Midwife's Tale* (New York: Knopf, 1990), 31, 107, and passim.

3. On the scope and impact of the revivals, see Gordon S. Wood, *The Radicalism of the American Revolution* (New York: Knopf, 1992), 332; Nathan O. Hatch, *The Democratization of American Christianity* (New Haven: Yale University Press, 1989), 34–35 and passim; Perry Miller, *The Life of the Mind in America: From the Revolution to the Civil War* (New York: Harcourt, Brace and World, 1965), 7.

4. This section heading comes from preacher Lorenzo Dow's song "Zion's Desolation and Recovery," in *History of Cosmpolite, The Four Volumes of Lorenzo Dow's Journal* (Wheeling, Va.: Joshua Martin, 1848), 574. For a terrific description of the revivals, see Hatch, *Democratization of American Christianity,* chap 2, quoted at 21 ("Mother Hutchinson"), and Alice Felt Tyler, *Freedom's Ferment* (Minneapolis: University of Minnesota Press, 1944), 37; on black preachers and white converts, see Albert J. Raboteau, "The Black Experience in American Evangelicalism," in Timothy Fulop and Albert J. Raboteau, eds., *African American Religion* (New York: Routledge, 1997), 94.

5. James B. Finley, *The Autobiography of James B. Finley: Or Pioneer Life in the West,* W. P. Strickland, ed. (Cincinnati: Printed at the Methodist Book Concern for the Author, E. P. Thompson, Printer, 1853), 166–169. Upon seeing this, writes Finley, "my hair rose up on my head . . . and I thought I was going to die." Off he went to the nearest tavern for a dram of brandy—half a mile from the revival, the tavern was also doing a booming business.

6. Dow, *History of Cosmpolite,* 593. Dow's volcano of a journal offers a vivid account of the life of an itinerant preacher. There are fascinating similarities and contrasts between Dow's defense of revivals and the one written by Jonathan Edwards in 1742 (see Chapter 3). In many places, Dow's defense closely follows Edwards's—for instance, concerning the charge that too much time is lost in revival meetings. The greatest difference in emphasis is this: Dow's main concern is refuting criticism about the active participation of commoners and women; the ax he grinds is about religious leveling.

7. See Robert Abzug, *Cosmos Crumbling: American Reform and the Religious Imagination* (New York: Oxford University Press, 1994), chap. 4; Donald Mathews, "The Second Great Awakening as an Organizing Process," *American Quarterly* 21, no. 1 (Spring 1969): 23–43. The Methodist numbers are from Hatch, *Democratization of American Christianity,* 220.

8. Lyman Beecher, *Beecher's Works* (Boston: John P. Jewett, 1852), vol. 1: 118 ("inequality"), 119–120 ("desolation"), and, generally, 114–115; Lyman Beecher, *A Plea for the West,* 2nd ed. (Cincinnati: Truman and Smith, 1835), 7–40. See also Conrad Cherry, ed., *God's New Israel: Religious Interpretations of American Destiny* (Englewood Cliffs, N.J.: Prentice Hall, 1971), quoted at 127 ("reckless mass").

9. For descriptions of the benevolent societies in action, see Clifford Griffin, *Their Brother's*

Keeper: Moral Stewardship in the United States, 1800–1865 (New Brunswick, N.J.: Rutgers University Press, 1960). Paul Boyer, *Urban Masses and Moral Order in America: 1820–1920* (Cambridge, Mass.: Harvard University Press, 1978), part 1. For the link between evangelicals and reform that went far beyond formal religion, see Abzug, *Cosmos Crumbling*, esp. parts 2 and 3.

10. Beecher, *Beecher's Works*, vol. 1: 66; Timothy Dwight quoted in Hatch, *Democratization of American Christianity*, 19. The cheesemonger was the influential Republican John Leland. He presented President Thomas Jefferson with a 1,235-pound cheese in 1802; Jefferson invited him to address Congress. The real problem lay in Leland's Republican faith and strong support for religious freedom. Cutler was a Congregational clergyman who served two terms in Congress. Quoted in Hatch, *Democratization of American Christianity*, 96.

11. Beecher, *Beecher's Works*, vol. 1: 66–69; Beecher claimed that he was merely restoring the true Calvinist doctrine of the American Puritan fathers. Dow, *History of Cosmopolite*, 351 ("A-double-L), 365 ("damned if you do").

12. Wood, *Radicalism of the American Revolution*, 333; on the divisions over slavery, see Sidney E. Ahlstrom, *A Religious History of the American People* (New Haven: Yale University Press, 1972), chap 40.

13. Charles Finney, letter to Theodore Dwight Weld, March 30, 1831, in *Letters of Theodore Dwight Weld, Angelina Grimké Weld, and Sarah Grimké*, vol. 1: 45. For a description of the vernacular in the revivals, see Hatch, *Democratization of American Christianity*, chap 1.

14. The "moral police" in the 1830s mills gave the factory girls strict instructions: "All persons in the employ of the Company are required . . . to evince on all occasions . . . a laudable regard for temperance, virtue and their moral obligations. . . . No person may be employed . . . whose known habits are . . . dissolute, indolent, dishonest, or intemperate, or who habitually absent themselves from public worship." This kind of regulation also reassured families back home: factory work would be morally safe for young women.

15. Paul Johnson, *A Shopkeeper's Millennium: Society and Revivals in Rochester, New York, 1815–1837* (New York: Hill and Wang, 1978).

16. For a description of the dispute, see Daniel Walker Howe, *The Political Culture of the American Whigs* (Chicago: University of Chicago Press, 1979), 160–161. The acrimony did not last long. A year after the failed meeting they issued a joint statement (ignoring the gender issue), and Beecher eventually invited Finney to preach in Boston. Dow, *History of Cosmopolite*, 592.

17. See *Letters of Theodore Dwight Weld*, vol. 1: 137–201; for an overview, see Howe, *Political Culture of the American Whigs*, 164–165.

18. Lyman Beecher, *A Plea for the West*, 2nd ed. (Cincinnati: Truman and Smith, 1835), 7–40. Lorenzo Dow, "Hints on the Fulfillment of Prophesy," in *History of Cosmopolite*, 525, 526. Finney described in Johnson, *Shopkeeper's Millennium*, 3–4.

19. Revelation 20:4. The passage reads: "I saw the souls of them . . . which had not worshipped the beast, neither his image, neither had received his mark upon their forehead . . . ; and they lived and reigned with Christ a thousand years."

The shift from pre- to post-millennialism is often linked to Jonathan Edwards and the First Great Awakening. Sacvan Berkovitch argues that the shift was not so neat, that the New England Puritans were mixing the two right from the start. See *American Jeremiad* (Madison: University of Wisconsin Press, 1978), chap 4. Berkovitch's view neatly reflects the whole framework of the Puritan covenants: they stood somewhere between the inscrutable force of Calvin's God and the human agency that emerged during the course of the revivals and became explicit in the early nineteenth century.

20. Beecher, *Beecher's Works*, vol. 1: 317–322, 325. Compare Dow, *History of Cosmopolite*, "Hints on the Fulfillment of Prophecy," 525–542, which describes almost precisely the same reforms as those required for fulfilling the scriptures.

For a general discussion of millennial reform in America, see Howe, *Political Culture of the American Whigs*, 150–157, and Hatch, *Democratization of American Christianity*, 30–34.

21. Haven's sermon came later than the other millennial visions quoted here. But the themes are the classics for the entire period. See Gilbert Haven, "Armageddon and After," in John Thomas, ed., *Slavery Attacked* (Englewood Cliffs, N.J.: Prentice Hall, 1965), 172–174.

22. Ralph Waldo Emerson, "New England Reformers," in *Essays* (Cambridge, Mass.: Riverside Press, 1903), 253.

There is an enormous literature on the antebellum reformers. See especially Ronald Walters, *American Reformers: 1815–1860* (New York: Hill and Wang, 1978), and Abzug, *Cosmos Crumbling*.

23. Figures on temperance from Ahlstrom, *Religious History*, 426; Boyer, *Moral Order and the City*, 23–24 (Bibles).

24. Footnote: The section's title comes from the old spiritual "Steal Away, Jesus":

> My Lord He calls me, He calls me by the thunder,
> The Trumpet sounds with-a my soul,
> I ain't got long to stay here.

Reprinted in Deirdre Mullane, ed., *Crossing the Water: Three Hundred Years of African-American Writing* (New York: Doubleday, 1993), n.p.

25. The classic argument on religion as submission comes from Benjamin Mays, *The Negro's God as Reflected in His Literature* (Boston: Chapman and Grimes, 1938), and E. Franklin Frazier, *The Negro Church* (New York: Schocken, 1963). See also Orlando Patterson, *Slavery and Social Death* (Cambridge, Mass.: Harvard University Press), 71–76.

For discussions of the contrasting views, see the essays by William Becker, Vincent Harding, and Albert J. Raboteau in Fulop and Raboteau, *African American Religion*. See also Eric Lincoln and Lawrence Mamiya, *The Black Church in the African American Experience* (Durham, N.C.: Duke University Press, 1990).

26. Albert J. Raboteau, *Slave Religion: The Invisible Institution in the Ante-Bellum South* (New York: Oxford University Press, 1978), 144 (Asbury), 145 ("better"), 161 ("judicious"); Hatch, *Democratization of American Christianity*, 105.

27. Frederick Douglass, *Life and Times of Frederick Douglass* (1881; New York: The Library of America, 1994), 534; blues quoted from Eric J. Sundquist, *To Wake the Nations: Race in the Making of American Literature* (Cambridge, Mass.: Harvard University Press, 1993), 57.

28. Harriet Beecher Stowe, *Uncle Tom's Cabin* (1852; New York: Norton, 1994), 262; for commentary on Christian passivity, see W. E. B. Du Bois, *Soul of Black Folk* (1903; New York: Penguin, 1982), 218; Harding, "Religion and Resistance Among Ante-Bellum Slaves," in Fulop and Raboteau, *African American Religion*, 110; Raboteau, *Slave Religion*, 164–165; and Eugene Genovese, *Roll, Jordan, Roll: The World the Slaves Made* (New York: Random House, 1972), 162–164.

29. For a typical romantic account of a plantation mission, see W. W. Sleigh, *Abolition Exposed! Proving That the Principles of Abolitionism Are Injurious to the Slaves Themselves . . .* (Philadelphia: D. Shneck, 1838), 56–59, quoted at 57. Randy Sparks, *On Jordan's Stormy Banks: Evangelicalism in Mississippi, 1773–1876* (Athens: University of Georgia Press, 1994), 123 ("yours—wholly yours").

Slavery may have most closely approached European feudalism in this repressive nexus of gentry and minister. See John Markoff, *Abolition of Feudalism* (University Park: Pennsylvania State University Press, 1997), 48.

30. Genesis 9:25 (Noah's curse of Ham—the progenitor, in the white southern imagination, of Canaan and of all black people); Leviticus, 25:44; Ephesians, 6:5. See Sparks, *On Jordan's Stormy Banks*, 123.

31. Stowe, *Uncle Tom's Cabin*, 28; Frederick Douglass, *Narrative of the Life of Frederick Douglass, An American Slave, Written by Himself* (1845; New York: Norton, 1997), 53, 75.

32. Richard Allen, *The Life Experience and Gospel Labors of the Rt. Rev. Richard Allen* (1833; New York: Abingdon, 1960), 25; William Becker, "The Black Church: Manhood and Mission" in Fulop and Raboteau, *African American Religion*, 182 (freedom march). Du Bois, *Soul of Black Folk*, 217. See also Hatch, *Democratization of American Christianity*, 104–110.

33. Du Bois, *Soul of Black Folk*, 211.

34. Albert J. Raboteau, "Turning to Exodus," *Common Quest* 2, no. 2 (Summer 1997): 17; Du Bois, *Soul of Black Folk*, 220–221.

35. David Walker, *Appeal to the Coloured Citizens of the World* (1829; New York: Hill and

Wang, 1965), 40, 43, 39. Walker was found dead in his shop on June 28, 1830—two days before the third edition of the *Appeal* hit the streets.

36. Henry Highland Garnet, "An Address to the Slaves of the United States" (1843), reprinted in Garnet, *A Memorial Discussion by the Reverend Henry Highland Garnet Delivered in the Hall of the House of Representatives* (Philadelphia: Joseph M. Wilson, 1865), and in John Bracey, August Meier, and Elliot Rudwick, *Black Nationalism in America* (Indianapolis: Bobbs-Merrill, 1970), 73. Douglass, *Narrative of the Life of Frederick Douglass*, 78. The quotation is from Jeremiah 5:29.

37. For a brief description, see Raboteau, *Slave Religion*, 147, 163.

38. *The Confessions of Nat Turner and Related Documents* (November 1831), Kenneth Greenberg, ed. (Boston: Bedford Books/St. Martin's, 1996), 46.

39. Governor John Floyd, "Letter to James Hamilton," November 19, 1831, reprinted in Greenberg, *Confessions of Nat Turner*, 109–111. James Hamilton, Jr., was the governor of South Carolina.

40. Floyd, "Letter to James Hamilton," 110.

41. Harriet A. Jacobs, *Incidents in the Life of a Slave Girl Written By Herself* (1861), Jean Fagan Yellin, ed.(Cambridge, Mass.: Harvard University Press, 1987), 66, 67. Similarly, Frederick Douglass describes a mob breaking up a Sunday school he was trying to teach and warning Douglass that he'd end up like Nat Turner if he didn't look out. Douglass, *Life and Times*, 559.

42. Genovese, *Roll, Jordan, Roll*, 257 (quoted) and, generally, 232–280.

43. William Lloyd Garrison, "The Insurrection," *Liberator*, September 3, 1831, p 143.

44. The debate was reported and analyzed by Thomas Dew (a professor of law at William and Mary) in his *Abolition of Negro Slavery*, first published in *American Quarterly Review* 12 (September and December 1832): 189–205. An expanded version appeared as *Review of the Debate in the Virginia Legislature of 1831–'32* (Richmond, Va.: T. W. White, 1832). The longer version was included in the most celebrated compendium of pro-slavery thought, *The Pro-Slavery Argument; As Maintained by the Most Distinguished Writers of the Southern States* (Richmond, Va.: Walker, Richards, 1852), 282–490, quoted at 290.

45. Lincoln, in Roy Basler, ed., *The Collected Works of Abraham Lincoln* (New Brunswick, N.J.: Rutgers University Press, 1953), vol. 2: 409, 132; *Niles Weekly Register*, November 8, 1817, p 165.

46. Lincoln, in Basler, *Collected Works of Abraham Lincoln*, vol. 2: 132; on black nationalism and its roots, see the collection of essays by Wilson Jeremiah Moses, ed., *Classical Black Nationalism: From the American Revolution to Marcus Garvey* (New York: New York University Press, 1996).

47. *Niles Weekly Register*, March 11, 1826, p 18. At first, this Democratic paper responded very skeptically to the colonization scheme. The cost was prohibitive. And, in harsh (bigoted) language, the editor predicted that the colonists would not make a go of it. See *Niles Weekly Register*, October 4, 1817, 82–83, and November 15, 1817, 177–181.

48. Douglass, *Narrative of the Life of Frederick Douglass*, 62.

49. Thomas Jefferson, "Notes on Virginia, Query XIV," *The Life and Selected Writings of Thomas Jefferson*, Adrienne Kock and William Peden, eds. (New York: Random House, 1944), 262, 256; for David Walker's heated response, see *Appeal*, 10–17: "After having reduced us to the deplorable condition of slaves under their feet, [they] held us up as descending originally from the tribes of Monkeys or Orang-utans. I appeal to every man of feeling. . . . Is it not heaping the most gross insult upon our miseries?" For a typical example of the use of this ugly trope, see J. H. Van Evrie, M.D., *Negroes and Negro "Slavery": The First and Inferior Race—The Latter Its Normal Condition* (Baltimore: John D. Toy, 1853), 10. Van Evrie was an important proponent of slavery—the title neatly sums up his views.

50. Winthrop Jordan, *White Over Black: American Attitudes Toward The Negro, 1550–1812* (Chapel Hill: University of North Carolina Press, 1968), 543 ("sex"), 544 (Henry); Lincoln, "Speech at Springfield," in Basler, *Collected Works of Abraham Lincoln*, vol. 2: 409.

51. George Fredrickson, *The Black Image in the White Mind: The Debate on Afro-American Character and Destiny, 1817–1914* (1971; Hanover, N.H.: Wesleyan University Press/Published

by University Press of New England, 1987), 17; Lincoln, "Address on Colonization to a Deputation of Negroes," in Basler, *Collected Works of Abraham Lincoln,* vol. 5: 371.

52. "Protest and remonstrance of the people of color of the city and county of Philadelphia, against the plan of colonizing free people of color," *Niles Register,* November 27, 1819, pp 201–202; Pittsburgh resolution in William H. Pease and Jane H. Pease, eds., *The Antislavery Argument* (Indianapolis: Bobbs-Merrill, 1965), 36–38; Walker, *Appeal,* 70, 60 ("tears"). For a general discussion, see Benjamin Quarles, *Black Abolitionists* (New York: Oxford University Press, 1969), chap 1.

53. Peter Williams, "A Discourse, Delivered on the Death of Capt. Paul Cuffee Before the New York African Institution in the African Methodist Zion Church," October 21, 1817 (New York: B. Young, 1817), 16.

54. William L. Garrison, letter to Henry Benson (July 30, 1831) ("antipathy"); "Letter to the Board of Managers of the New England Anti-Slavery Society" (July 1, 1833) ("cursed"). *The Letters of William Lloyd Garrison,* Walter Merrill, ed. (Cambridge, Mass.: Harvard University Press, 1971), vol. 1: 124, 245.

Garrison acknowledged his debt to the African American critics of colonization who came before him (and reprinted many of their pieces).

55. Dew, "Professor Dew on Slavery," in *Pro-Slavery Argument,* 292–293. Federal revenue from Ben Wattenberg, *The Statistical History of the United States,* Prepared by the United States Bureau of the Census (New York: Basic Books, 1976), 1104.

56. Garrison, "To the Editor of the London Patriot," *Letters of William Lloyd Garrison,* vol. 1: 253; Alexis de Tocqueville, *De la Démocratie en Amérique* (1835; Paris: G. F. Flammarion, 1981), vol. 1: 476 [*Democracy in America,* George Lawrence, trans. (Garden City, N.Y.: Doubleday/Anchor Books, 1969), 359].

57. Lincoln, Preliminary Emancipation Proclamation, September 22, 1862, in Basler, *Collected Works of Abraham Lincoln,* vol. 5: 434.

On Exodus metaphor and colonization, "Eulogy on Henry Clay," July 6, 1852, vol. 2: 132, and "Speech at Springfield," June 26, 1857, vol. 2: 409 ("out of Egyptian bondage"). In Basler, ibid.

By the 1860s, Lincoln's colonies were not in Africa but in Central America—Honduras, Nicaragua, and Costa Rica all protested the plan (hinting that force might be used to repel any settlers).

58. [No author], *American Review* 5 (March 1847): 231–239, quoted at 231, 239.

59. W. Gilmore Simms, Esq., *The Morals of Slavery* (1837), in *Pro-Slavery Argument,* 270–271.

The Reverend Henry Highland Garnet laid into the slave colonizers with particular flair: "The Pharaohs are on both sides of the blood red waters . . . The propagators of American slavery are spending their blood and treasure, that they may plant the black flag in the heart of Mexico and riot in the halls of Montezuma." From "A Memorial Discourse by Reverend Henry Highland Garnet," in Bracey et al., *Black Nationalism,* 73.

60. Van Evrie, *Negroes and Negro "Slavery,"* 18 (on Spanish America). Reginald Horsman, *Race and Manifest Destiny* (Cambridge, Mass.: Harvard University Press, 1981), 280 ("perishing center") 281 (Maury quoted).

61. Quotations from Eric Foner, *Free Soil, Free Labor, Free Men,* 2nd ed. (New York: Oxford University Press, 1995), 273 (quoting the *Albany Evening Journal* in 1857).

62. John Calhoun, *Works of John C. Calhoun* (New York: Appleton, 1860), vol. 4: 410–411.

CHAPTER 5. *Abolition!*

1. Otis quoted by Horace Greely, *The American Conflict: A History of the Great Rebellion* (Hartford, Conn.: O. D. Case, 1865), vol. 1: 122; see also Wendell Phillips and Francis Jackson Garrison, *William Lloyd Garrison, 1805–1879: The Story of His Life Told by His Children* (Boston: Houghton Mifflin, 1885–1889), vol. 1: 244–245.

Even in 1833, after Garrison had hit the headlines, abolitionist Theodore Dwight Weld would sheepishly admit to Garrison that he had not heard of his organization. "Letter to William

Lloyd Garrison," January 2, 1833, *Letters of Theodore Dwight Weld, Angelina Grimké Weld and Sarah Grimké,* edited by Gilbert Barnes and Dwight Dumond (New York: Appleton-Century, 1934), vol. 1: 98.

For predecessors to Garrison, see the Reverend George Bourne of Virginia, *The Book and Slavery Irreconcilable* (1816); James Duncan of Kentucky, *Treatise on Slavery* (1824); and Garrison's earlier collaborator, Benjamin Lundy, editor of the *Genius of Universal Emancipation.*

2. William Lloyd Garrison, "To the Public," *Liberator,* January 1, 1831, emphasis in original. Robert Abzug, *Cosmos Crumbling* (New York: Oxford University Press, 1994), 135.

3. For a description of the come-outers, see Louis Filler, *Crusade Against Slavery* (Algonac, Mich.: Reference Publications, 1986), 147ff. Filler's book is a fine overview of the abolitionist movement. See also Ronald Walters, *The Antislavery Appeal* (New York: Norton, 1978), 47–48, and Bertram Wyatt-Brown, *Lewis Tappan and the Evangelical War Against Slavery* (Cleveland: Case Western Reserve University Press, 1969), 321–322.

4. James G. Birney, *Letters of James Gillespie Birney,* Dwight L. Dumond, ed. (New York: Appleton-Century, 1938), vol. 1: 129; Lydia Maria Child, *Lydia Maria Child: Selected Letters,* Milton Meltzer and Patricia Holland, eds. (Amherst: University of Massachusetts Press, 1982), 207; see also 186–187 (Child footnote).

5. Theodore Weld, *American Slavery As It Is: Testimony of a Thousand Witnesses* (New York: American Anti-Slavery Society, 1839), 62–63 (floggings), 77 (brandings). The work was put together with Angelina and Sarah Grimké.

6. Weld, *American Slavery As It Is,* 27–44; Frederick Douglass, *A Narrative of the Life of Frederick Douglass, An American Slave, Written by Himself* (1845; New York: Norton 1997), 26. See also Robert William Fogel and Stanley L. Engerman, *Time on the Cross,* 2nd ed. (New York: Norton, 1989), 270. While Fogel and Engerman challenge many of the abolitionist claims, they do suggest that malnutrition affected children in slave communities.

7. Douglass, *Narrative of the Life of Frederick Douglass,* 16; see also Weld, *American Slavery As It Is,* 27–44.

8. William Weld, Letter to Garrison, January 2, 1833, *Letters of Theodore Dwight Weld,* vol. 1: 98; Hannah Johnson, July 31, 1863, in Ira Berlin et al., eds., *Free at Last: A Documentary History of Slavery, Freedom, and the Civil War* (New York: New Press, 1992), 449 (punctuation altered).

9. Lydia Maria Child, *Anti-Slavery Catechism* (Newburyport, Mass., 1839), quoted in John Thomas, ed., *Slavery Attacked: The Abolitionist Crusade* (Englewood Cliffs, N.J.: Prentice Hall, 1965), 67–68.

10. Anne Norton, *Alternative Americas: A Reading of Antebellum Political Culture* (Chicago: University of Chicago Press, 1986), 75–76.

11. Weld, *American Slavery As It Is,* 115; Douglass, *Narrative of the Life of Frederick Douglass,* 29. Lyman Beecher, "The Remedy of Intemperance," *Beecher's Works* (Boston : J. P. Jewett, 1852–53), vol. 1: 398–399. For Beecher, intemperance was even worse than slavery, for the soul's loss would be eternal. See also Walters, *Antislavery Appeal,* 71.

12. Jack Blocker, *American Temperance Movement* (Boston: Twayne, 1989), 26–27 (pledges). William Lloyd Garrison, William Weld, and James Birney are all reformers who got into abolition via temperance.

13. Herman Humphrey, "Terrible Parallel Between Intemperance and the Slave Trade: An Address Delivered at Amherst College," July 4, 1828 (Amherst, Mass.: Amherst and Adams, 1828). W. J. Rorabaugh, *The Alcoholic Republic: An American Tradition* (New York: Oxford University Press, 1979), 214–215; on slaves' drinking, see Douglass, *Narrative of the Life of Frederick Douglass,* 52, and Harriet A. Jacobs, *Incidents in the Life of a Slave Girl, Written by Herself,* Jean Fagan Yellin, ed. (1861; Cambridge, Mass: Harvard University Press, 1987), 119. On Legree's drinking, see Harriet Beecher Stowe, *Uncle Tom's Cabin* (1852; New York: Norton, 1994), 297, 323, 326, 352, 355.

14. Charles Loring Brace, founder of the Children's Aid Society, quoted by Paul Boyer, *Urban Masses and Moral Order in America, 1820–1920* (Cambridge, Mass: Harvard University Press, 1978), 98.

15. *The Education of Henry Adams,* Ernest Samuels, ed. (Boston: Houghton Mifflin, 1973), 47, 558.

16. "Why Do We Meddle with Slavery," *New York Daily Times,* May 16, 1857.

17. Child, *Anti-Slavery Catechism,* 66–67. Despite my use of this passage as an example of ineffectual argument, Child was one of the most elegant and modern of the abolitionist writers.

18. Reverend William Ellery Channing quoted in the Senate by Benjamin Leigh, *Gales and Seaton's Register of Debates in Congress,* January 19, 1836, p 199; see also William Ellery Channing, *Slavery* (Boston: J. Munroe, 1835); Frederick Douglass, *Narrative of the Life of Frederick Douglass,* 13 ("desires").

19. Jacobs, *Incidents in the Life of a Slave Girl,* 51–52 (gifts), 35 (eleven children).

20. Jacobs, *Incidents in the Life of a Slave Girl,* 51–52 ("meanest slave"), 35.

21. Channing, *Slavery,* quoted and attacked by William Leigh on the Senate floor; James A. Thome, Speech of James A. Thome of Kentucky, Delivered at the Annual Meeting of the American Anti-Slavery Society, May 6, 1834, in William H. Pease and Jane H. Pease, eds., *The Antislavery Argument* (Indianapolis: Bobbs-Merrill, 1965), 91–93.

22. Walters, *Antislavery Appeal,* 74 and chap 5.

23. Walters, *Antislavery Appeal,* 74 (quoting an abolitionist with the appropriate pseudonym Puritan). Comments on white women quoted in Martha Hodes, "Wartime Dialogues on Illicit Sex: White Women and Black Men," in Catherine Clinton and Nina Silber, *Divided Houses: Gender and the Civil War* (New York: Oxford University Press, 1992), 238.

24. Thome, "Speech," in Pease and Pease, *Antislavery Argument,* 92–93.

25. Senator Benjamin Leigh, *Gales and Seaton's Register,* January 19, 1836, p 200; William Harper, "Harper's Memoir on Slavery," 41, and W. Gilmore Simms, "The Morals of Slavery," 229, both in *The Pro-Slavery Argument; As Maintained by the Most Distinguished Writers of the Southern States* (Richmond, Va.: Walker, Richards, 1852).

26. *Mary Chesnut's Civil War,* ed. C. Vann Woodward (New Haven: Yale University Press, 1981), 29–31, 54, 168. The entries are from March, April, and August 1861.

27. Winthrop Jordan, *White over Black: American Attitudes Toward the Negro, 1550–1812* (Chapel Hill: University of North Carolina Press, 1968), 137 and chap 4. Fogel and Engerman, *Time on the Cross,* 126–138; one interesting result of their quantification is the moral question it raises: At what point—at just what number—should we be outraged? They themselves concede that the issue of moral outrage over slavery is the one point on which the first edition of their book was flat-footed. See "Afterword 1989," 272–275. Catherine Clinton, *The Plantation Mistress* (New York: Pantheon, 1982), 222.

28. Lydia Maria Child, *An Appeal in Favor of That Class of Americans Called Africans* (1833; Amherst: University of Massachusetts Press, 1996), 186 (emphasis in original). For a description of abolitionist views toward free African Americans, see George Fredrickson, *The Black Image in the White Mind: The Debate on Afro-American Character and Destiny, 1817–1914* (1971; Hanover, N.H.: Wesleyan University Press/Published by University Press of New England, 1987), chap 1, Tocqueville quoted on 22.

29. William Lloyd Garrison, *Thoughts on African Colonization* (Boston: Garrison and Gnapp, 1832), 33; the other quotes are taken from Fredrickson's survey of abolitionist writing, *Black Image in the White Mind,* 4, 8, 33. See also Jane H. Pease and William H. Pease, *They Who Would Be Free: Blacks' Search for Freedom, 1830–1861* (New York: Atheneum, 1974), 3–5.

30. Filler, *Crusade Against Slavery,* 32–33.

31. The argument is developed in Fredrickson, *Black Image in the White Mind,* chap 4. My description draws heavily on Fredrickson. Wilson Jeremiah Moses, *Black Messiahs and Uncle Toms: Social and Literary Manipulations of a Religious Myth* (University Park: Pennsylvania State University Press, 1993), locates the romantic racialist line of thought in the traditions of black nationalism.

32. T. R. Sullivan, *Letters About the Immediate Abolition of Slavery* (Boston: Hilliard, Gray, 1835), 3, 2.

33. Alexander Kinmont, A. M., *Twelve Lectures on the Natural History of Man and the Rise and Progress of Philosophy* (Cincinnati: U. P. James, 1839), 193, 191.

34. Kinmont, *Natural History of Man*, 191, 195

35. See Fredrickson, *Black Image in the White Mind*, for a list of abolitionist variations on the romantic racialism theme. Quoted at 107, 106.

36. Stowe, *Uncle Tom's Cabin*, 375, 156.

37. Jane P. Tompkins, *Sensational Designs: The Cultural Work of American Fiction* (New York: Oxford University Press, 1985), chap 5.

38. *Liberator*, March 26, 1852, in William Cain, ed., *William Lloyd Garrison and the Fight Against Slavery: Selections from The Liberator* (Boston: Bedford Books/St. Martin's, 1995), 129, 131 (emphasis in original). Garrison conceded the power of the novel—he even admitted shedding the "scalding tear" for Uncle Tom.

39. Harriet Beecher Stowe, *Dred: A Tale of the Great Dismal Swamp* (Boston: Phillips, Sampson, 1856), iv. Stowe included excerpts from *The Confession of Nat Turner* in an appendix. Stowe, *Uncle Tom's Cabin*, 388 (wrath). For an interesting contrast between the two Stowe novels, see T. R. Hovet, "Christian Revolution: Harriet Beecher Stowe's Response to Slavery and the Civil War," *New England Quarterly* 47, no. 4 (December 1974): 535–549.

40. Moses, *Black Messiahs and Uncle Toms*, 50–51.

41. Fredrickson, *Black Image in the White Mind*, 125–129.

42. For a fabulous string of sappy examples, see Walters, *Antislavery Appeal*, 91–106, quoted ("bliss") at 91. On the family and romantic reform, see John Thomas's splendid "Romantic Reform in America," *American Quarterly* 17, no. 4 (Winter 1965): 667, 677.

43. Walters, *Antislavery Appeal*, 105 (both quotes).

44. *Letters of Theodore Dwight Weld*, vol. 1: 175. Antislavery Society quoted in Keith Melder, "Abby Kelley and the Process of Liberation," in Jean Fagan Yellin and John C. Van Horne, eds., *The Abolitionist Sisterhood* (Ithaca, N.Y.: Cornell University Press, 1994), 234.

45. Child, *Appeal in Favor of That Class of Americans Called Africans*, 22.

46. Susan B. Anthony, "Letter to the Readers of the National Anti-Slavery Standard" (February 22, 1859), *The Selected Papers of Elizabeth Cady Stanton and Susan B. Anthony*, vol. 1, ed. Ann B. Gordon (New Brunswick, N.J.: Rutgers University Press, 1997), 385–386.

47. William Lee Miller, *Arguing About Slavery: The Great Battle in the United States Congress* (New York: Knopf, 1997), 32–33 and passim.

48. Lydia Maria Child, "To the Legislature of Massachusetts," March 30, 1839, in *Lydia Maria Child: Selected Letters*, 111. For a description of the case, see Louis Ruchames, "Race, Marriage, and Abolition in Massachusetts," *Journal of Negro History* 40 (1955): 251–273, quoted at 255 ("a man"), 257 ("virtuous," "Othello").

49. Paula Giddings, *When and Where I Enter: The Impact of Black Women on Race and Sex in America* (New York: Bantam, 1984), 49–55.

50. William Lloyd Garrison, "To Mrs. Sarah Benson," Boston, May 19, 1838, *Letters of William Lloyd Garrison*, vol. 2: 362–364. Two days earlier Grimké had married abolitionist Theodore Dwight Weld. See the *Letters of Theodore Dwight Weld*, vol. 2: 701–702.

51. Philip Hone, *The Diary of Philip Hone*, Allan Nevins, ed. (New York: Dodd, Mead, 1927), vol. 1: 327–328.

52. James Kirke Paulding, *Slavery in the United States* (New York: Harper and Brothers, 1836), 310. Paulding had written critically of slavery in 1816; now the criticism was gone from Paulding's pages. He became Van Buren's Secretary of the Navy in 1838.

53. Ruchames, "Race, Marriage, and Abolition," 251.

54. Garrison, March 8, 1834, *Letters of William Lloyd Garrison*, vol. 1: 289–290.

55. Yellin and Horne, *Abolitionist Sisterhood*, 9–10; Congressman Benjamin Howard (Maryland), quoted by Miller, *Arguing About Slavery*, 317 ("rush into").

56. Sullivan, *Letters Against the Immediate Abolition of Slavery*, 18; Aileen Kraditor, *Means and Ends in American Abolitionism: Garrison and His Critics on Strategy and Tactics, 1834-1850* (New York: Vintage, 1969), 43.

57. Child, *Lydia Maria Child: Selected Letters*, 119–124, quoted at 123.

58. Abby Kelley married Stephen Foster (Garrison's printer) in 1845. In descriptions of this convention her name appears both with and without the Foster. Lewis Tappan to Weld, May 26,

1840, *Letters of Theodore Dwight Weld,* vol. 2: 836 (emphasis in original). For a description of the conflict, see Wyatt-Brown, *Lewis Tappan and the Evangelical War Against Slavery,* 197–199.

59. The revisionist perspective is beautifully laid out in Kraditor, *Means and Ends in American Abolitionism,* chap 3, sorcerer's apprentice quoted at 47. For the rest of Child's argument, see Lydia Maria Child, "To Abolitionists," May 20, 1841, *A Lydia Maria Child Reader,* Carolyn Karcher, ed. (Durham, N.C.: Duke University Press, 1997), 192–199, quoted at 195 ("Stop," "gush").

60. Child, "To Abolitionists," *Lydia Maria Child Reader,* 194, 195; Susan B. Anthony, "From the Diary of Susan B. Anthony, November, 1853," *Selected Papers of Elizabeth Cady Stanton and Susan B. Anthony,* vol. 1: 230. On legal independence, see Lydia Maria Child, "To Ellis Gray Loring," February 24, 1856, *Letters of Lydia Maria Child,* 279.

61. Abby Kelley Foster quoted by Benjamin Quarles, *Black Abolitionists* (New York: Oxford University Press, 1969), 248 (emphasis in original).

62. The difference between the eras is nicely laid out in Kraditor, *Means and Ends in American Abolitionism,* 39–40; Douglass, *Life and Times of Frederick Douglass,* 667, 905; Douglass quoted in Peggy Cooper Davis, *Neglected Stories* (New York: Hill and Wang, 1997), 24–25 ("how beautiful").

63. The critic was Leonard Bacon, the pastor of the First Congregational church and, later, a professor at Yale Divinity School. See *The Letters of James Gillespie Birney: 1831–1857* (New York: Appleton-Century, 1938), vol. 1: 480–481 (emphasis in original).

64. *The Statistical History of the United States* (New York: Basic Books, 1976), 49. On the changing nature of the family, see Walters, *Antislavery Appeal,* chap 6.

CHAPTER 6. *South: The Pro-Slavery Argument*

1. James Henry Hammond, "Hammond's Letters on Slavery," *The Pro-Slavery Argument; as Maintained by the Most Distinguished Writers of the Southern States* (Richmond, Va.: Walker, Richards, 1852), 109–110. Hammond represented South Carolina in the House of Representatives (1835–1836), in the Senate (1857–1861), and as governor (1842–1844); William Harper, "Memoir on Slavery," in *Pro-Slavery Argument,* 5–8; W. Gilmore Simms, "The Morals of Slavery," in *Pro-Slavery Argument,* 251; George Fitzhugh, *Cannibals All! or Slaves Without Masters* (1857; Cambridge, Mass.: Harvard University Press, 1988), 135. See also John Calhoun, *The Works of John C. Calhoun* (New York: Appleton, 1860), vol. 1: 55–57.

2. Louis Hartz, *The Liberal Tradition in America* (New York: Harcourt, Brace, and World, 1955). The terms quoted are all plucked from chapter 6.

3. Calhoun, "Speech on the Reception of Abolition Petitions," delivered in the Senate, February 6, 1837, *Works,* vol. 2: 630. For examples of the Burkean view, see Thomas Dew, "Review of the Debate in the Virginia Legislature," *Pro-Slavery Argument,* 355; Fitzhugh, *Cannibals All!* 71.

4. Simms, "Morals of Slavery," 273 (cannibalism). The piece was originally in *Southern Literary Messenger* 3 (November 1837): 641–657. The essay itself is organized as a long critique of an anti-slavery book by Harriet Martineau. Simms was a novelist with a lushly romantic view of the South. He was elected to Congress in 1844 and defeated in 1846.

Calhoun, *Works,* vol. 2: 630; J. H. Van Evrie, M.D., *Negroes and Negro "Slavery": The First an Inferior Race, the Latter Its Normal Condition* (Baltimore: John D. Toy, 1853), 30 (emphasis in original). We'll return to Van Evrie, a New Yorker living in Washington, D.C.—even in this crowd, Van Evrie stands out in his tooth-rattling racism.

On the moral steward theme, see Drew Gilpin Faust, *Southern Stories: Slaveholders in Peace and War* (Columbia: University of Missouri Press, 1992), chap 1.

5. Simms, "Morals of Slavery," 274 (emphasis in original).

6. Harper, "Memoir on Slavery," 14.

7. Harper, "Memoir on Slavery," 34; Simms, "Morals of Slavery," 265.

8. Thomas Dew, "Professor Dew on Slavery," *Pro-Slavery Argument,* 444–445.

9. James Kirke Paulding, *Slavery in the United States* (New York: Harper and Brothers, 1836), 57–61.

10. Simms, "Morals of Slavery," 269, 270; on the original draft, see Clement Eaton, *The Mind of the Old South* (Baton Rouge: Louisiana State University Press, 1964), 195.

11. Josiah Nott, *Two Lectures on the Connection Between the Biblical and Physical History of Man. Delivered, by Invitation, from the Chair of Political Economy in the Louisiana University* (Mobile, Ala.: Bartlett and Welford, 1848), 13, 41; Van Evrie, *Negroes and Negro "Slavery,"* 2, 10, 30–31.

12. Thorton Stringfellow, "A Brief Examination of Scripture Testimony on the Institution of Slavery," in Drew Gilpin Faust, ed., *The Ideology of Slavery* (Baton Rouge: Louisiana State University Press, 1981), 136–167, quoted at 140. For the curse of Canaan, see Genesis 9:21–27.

13. Stephen Jay Gould, *The Mismeasure of Man* (New York: Norton, 1981), 69–72.

14. South Carolina Governor George McDuffie introduced the term in 1836. See Hammond, "Letter on Slavery," *Pro-Slavery Argument*, 109–111; George Fredrickson, *Black Image in the White Mind: The Debate on Afro-American Character and Destiny* (1971; Hanover, N.H.: University Press of New England, 1987), 64 (Stephens). See also Faust, *Southern Stories*, 211.

15. See *Secret and Sacred: The Diaries of James Henry Hammond, a Southern Slaveholder*, Carol Bleser, ed. (New York: Oxford University Press, 1988), 272–273; the speech is discussed in George Fredrickson, *The Arrogance of Race: Historical Perspectives on Slavery, Racism, and Social Inequality* (Hanover, N.H.: University Press of New England, 1988), 22; Harper, "Memoir on Slavery," 51–53.

16. Thomas Dew, *Pro-Slavery Argument*, 336–339.

17. On the real world of the plantation household, see Catherine Clinton, *The Plantation Mistress* (New York: Random House, 1982); on gender in yeomen households, see Stephanie McCurry, "Politics of Yeomen Households," in Catherine Clinton and Nina Silber, eds., *Divided Houses* (New York: Oxford University Press, 1992), 23–41, quoted at 29.

18. Harper, "Memoir on Slavery," 40, 41; Simms, "Morals of Slavery," 230.

19. Harper, "Memoir on Slavery," 42–44.

20. Harper, "Memoir on Slavery," 43, 44, 45.

21. On the critique of falling in love with the master, see Clinton, *Plantation Mistress*, 212. "The slave female, for example, could not give herself 'freely' for she did not have herself to give. . . . To imagine that falling in love might be a decisive element in the formula is a sentimental . . . assessment of such interracial unions."

22. Simms, "Morals of Slavery," 244; Hammond, "Letters on Slavery," 111; Stephens quoted by Fredrickson, *Black Image in the White Mind*, 64.

23. Hammond, "Letters on Slavery," 111.

24. W. E. B. Du Bois, *Black Reconstruction in America, 1860–1880* (1935; New York: Atheneum, 1992), esp. 700–708. See also the splendid elaboration by David R. Roediger, *The Wages of Whiteness* (New York: Verso, 1991).

25. The contrasting views are nicely summarized by Richard Ellis, "Legitimating Slavery in the Old South," *Studies in American Political Development* 5, no. 2 (Fall 1991): 340–351. Eugene Genovese, *Roll, Jordan, Roll: The World the Slaves Made* (New York: Random House, 1972), has a fine portrait of the paternalists' view. Fredrickson, *Black Image in the White Mind*, chap 2, defines the Herrenvolk and puts the distinction front and center. See also *The Arrogance of Race*, chap 1. The Herrenvolk are also described (though not referred to as such) in James Oates, *The Ruling Class* (New York: Norton, 1998), chap 5. The distinction between schools is critiqued by Faust, *Southern Stories*, 216; their differences seem to me to be about emphasis and shading.

26. Dew, "Thomas Dew on Slavery," 436, and Hammond, "Letters on Slavery," 110–111.

27. Dew, "Thomas Dew on Slavery," 462.

28. Fitzhugh, *Cannibals All!* 155 (emphasis in original).

29. Fitzhugh, *Cannibals All!* 16–17.

30. Fitzhugh, *Cannibals All!* 201.

31. Fredrickson, *Black Image in the White Mind*, 69–70.

32. Van Evrie, *Negroes and Negro "Slavery,"* 31 (on Jackson); Yancey quoted by Fredrickson, *Black Image in the White Mind*, 61.

33. Cobb quoted in Fredrickson, *Black Image in the White Mind*, 62.

34. Van Evrie, *Negroes and Negro "Slavery,"* 11.

35. Fitzhugh, *Cannibals All!* 194, 196, 198, 191, and 254 ("free love"), 192 ("Madame hen").

36. Van Evrie, *Negroes and Negro "Slavery,"* 18; Senator Benjamin Leigh, "Slavery in the District of Columbia," *Gales and Seaton's Register: Senate*, January 19, 1836, 202.

CHAPTER 7. *North: The Ragged Chorus of the Union*

1. James Gordon Bennet, "State of the Country," *New York Herald,* September 1, 1835, p 1; "Chorus of the union" from Abraham Lincoln, "First Inaugural Address," March 4, 1861, in *The Collected Works of Abraham Lincoln,* Roy P. Basler and Christian O. Basler, eds. (New Brunswick, N.J.: Rutgers University Press, 1953), vol. 4, 262–271.

2. President Andrew Jackson, "Seventh Annual Message," December 7, 1835, James Richardson, ed., *Messages and Papers of the Presidents* (Washington, D.C.: Bureau of National Literature, 1911), vol. 2: 1394.

3. Leonard Richards tabulated the riots in *Gentlemen of Property and Standing* (New York: Oxford University Press, 1970), 10–19; Lydia Maria Child, Letter to Louisa Loring, *Lydia Maria Child, Selected Letters,* Milton Meltzer and Patricia Holland, eds. (Amherst: University of Massachusetts Press, 1982), 31; Abraham Lincoln, "Address Before the Young Men's Lyceum of Springfield Illinois," *Collected Works,* vol. 1: 108–115; William Lloyd Garrison, *Liberator, Extra,* November 7, 1835 ($100 bounty).

4. Garrison, *Liberator,* November 7, 1835; Garrison's account shares the page with a feisty letter from Thompson. See also William Lloyd Garrison, *The Letters of William Lloyd Garrison,* Louis Ruchames, ed. (Cambridge, Mass.: Harvard University Press, 1971), vol. 1: 542.

5. Garrison, *Liberator,* November 7, 1835. A terrific biography of Garrison describes this incident in more detail. See Henry Mayer, *All on Fire: William Lloyd Garrison and the Abolition of Slavery* (New York: St. Martin's, 1998).

6. *Niles Register,* November 6, 1824, p 160. A close look at this case suggests something more serious than the *Niles* dispatch lets on. A group of whites attacked a black neighborhood in Providence, Rhode Island, and destroyed some twenty homes. See Howard Chudacoff and Theodore Hirt, "Social Turmoil and Government Reform in Providence," *Rhode Island History* 31 (1972): 21–33.

7. James Kirke Paulding, *Slavery in the United States* (New York: Harper and Brothers, 1836), 7–8.

8. Paulding, *Slavery in the United States,* 109–110 (despots); J. H. Van Evrie, M.D., *Negroes and Negro "Slavery": The First an Inferior Race—The Latter Its Normal Condition* (Baltimore: John D. Toy, 1853), 12.

9. T. R. Sullivan, *Letters Against the Immediate Abolition of Slavery* (Boston: Hilliard, Gray, 1835), 10–13; Andrew Jackson, in Richardson, *Messages and Papers of the Presidents,* vol. 2: 1394. Theodore Weld to James Birney, *Letters of James Gillespie Birney,* Dwight Dumond, ed. (New York: Appleton-Century, 1938), vol. 1: 136 (boarding house); Richards, *Gentlemen of Property and Standing,* 63–64 (Concord, Lynn).

10. Gustave de Beaumont, *Marie* (1835; Baltimore: Johns Hopkins University Press, 1999), 202.

11. Sullivan, *Letters Against the Immediate Abolition of Slavery,* 21; Richards, *Gentlemen of Property and Standing,* 60–61. The poems ran along the following lines: "You are very young 'tis true / But there's much that you can do / Even you can plead with men / that they buy not slaves again . . . " (from the abolition collection, John Hay Library, Brown University).

12. Paulding, *Slavery in the United States,* 288.

13. Andrew Jackson, "Annual Address," Richardson, *Messages of the Presidents,* vol. 2: 1394; for the definitive (and myth-deflating) account of this event, see Richard R. John, *Spreading the News: The American Postal Service from Franklin to Morse* (Cambridge, Mass.: Harvard University Press, 1995), chap 7, esp. 260–277. Kendall is also quoted in Richards, *Gentlemen of Property and Standing,* 74.

14. The idea of private organizations "fitting" with government agencies comes from Theda Skocpol, *Protecting Soldiers and Mothers* (Cambridge, Mass.: Harvard University Press, 1992), chap 1.

15. Bertram Wyatt-Brown, "Prelude to Abolitionism: Sabbatarian Politics and the Rise of the Second Party System," *Journal of American History* 58 (1971): 316–341; John, *Spreading the News,* chap 5.

16. Garrison, *Liberator, Extra:* November 7, 1835 (emphasis in original).

17. Philip Hone, *Diary of Philip Hone,* Allan Nevins, ed. (New York: Dodd, Mead, 1927), vol. 1: 171.

18. The New York riots of July 1834 are described by Beaumont, *Marie,* appendix L—the riot is the pivotal event of the novel. See also Joel Tyler Headley, *The Great Riots of New York* (1873; New York: Bobbs-Merrill, 1970), chaps 5 and 6. Linda Kerber, "Abolitionists and Amalgamators: The New York City Race Riots of 1834," *New York History,* January 1967, pp 28–39.

19. John Runcie, "'Hunting the Nigs' in Philadelphia: The Race Riot of August 1834," *Pennsylvania History* 39, no. 2 (April 1972): 187–218, quoted 215 (newspaper); Noel Ignatiev, *How the Irish Became White* (New York: Routledge, 1996), 125–128.

20. Figures for 1820s and 1830s are annual averages for the decade. In the decade following 1845, 2,944,833 immigrants arrived (peaking in 1854, with 427,833). That total was 14.6 percent of the resident population in 1845 (figures include slaves). Calculated from *Historical Statistics of the United States:* 8, 106, 118. Quotation from Elizabeth Cady Stanton, *The Selected Papers of Elizabeth Cady Stanton and Susan B. Anthony,* Ann Gordon, ed. (New Brunswick, N.J.: Rutgers University Press, 1997), vol. 1: 594.

21. Child, *Selected Letters,* 169–170 ("dogs"), 383 (drunkenness).

22. The Catholics did not change the American Protestant emphasis on individual conscience. The conversion went the other way. In the United States, the Catholic church became distinctly American; members inherited the tradition of active congregations and individual conscience. American Catholicism lost the ascriptive quality that marks the European church. Instead, Catholics took to measuring their Catholicism against their conscience—producing the concept of "lapsed Catholics" and promoting the American penchant for questioning church policy. I am grateful to Gordon Wood for pointing out the irony.

23. Samuel C. Busey, *Immigration: Its Evils and Consequences* (New York: Dewitt and Davenport, 1856), 108–110, 116–117; Eric Foner, *Free Soil, Free Labor, Free Men,* 2nd ed. (New York: Oxford University Press, 1995), 232 (Yankee spirit).

24. James Blaine, "Chinese Immigration," February 21, 1879, in *Political Discussions: 1856–1886* (Norwich, Conn.: Henry Bill, 1887), 239.

25. "Emigrants and Intemperance," *American Protestant* 4 (February 1849): 271–273. Joseph Gusfield, *Symbolic Crusade* (Urbana: University of Illinois Press, 1986).

26. Lyman Beecher, "The Evils of Intemperance," *Beecher's Works* (Boston: J. P. Jewett, 1852–1853), vol. 1: 383; this was the third lecture of his famous six lectures on intemperance. Rufus Clark, "More Destructive to Human Life Than War, Famine, Pestilence, and Fire," in Joel H. Silbey, *Transformation of American Politics, 1840–1860* (Englewood Cliffs, N.J.: Prentice Hall, 1967), 59. James King, *Facing the Twentieth Century: Our Country, Its Power and Its Peril* (New York: American Union League Society, 1899), 414–415 ("almshouse").

27. Hone, *Diary,* 122–123 (1834); see also, for example, 336–337 (July 1838), 596 (April 1842). Child, *Selected Letters of Lydia Maria Child,* 170. On the early riots, see Paul Gilje, *Road to Mobocracy: Popular Disorder in New York City, 1763–1834* (Chapel Hill: University of North Carolina Press, 1987), chap 5. On crime in early New York, see Charles Christian, *A Brief Treatise on the Police of the City of New York* (New York: Southwick and Pelsue, 1812).

28. Anne Norton, *Alternative Americas: A Reading of Antebellum Political Culture* (Chicago: University of Chicago Press, 1986), 71. Rufus Clark, "More Destructive to Human Life Than War, Famine, Pestilence and Fire," quoted in Silbey, *Transformation of American Politics,* 59.

29. *New York Independent* quoted in Ronald Takaki, *Iron Cages: Race and Culture in Nineteenth-Century America* (New York: Oxford, 1979), 116. See also David Roediger, *The Wages of Whiteness: Race and the Making of the American Working Class* (New York: Verso, 1991), 153.

30. Maria Monk, *The Awful Disclosures . . . of the Hotel Dieu Nunnery in Montreal* (New York: Maria Monk, 1836), 47 ("criminal intercourse"); Richard Delisser, *Pope or President? Startling Disclosures of Romanism as Revealed By Its Own Writers* (New York: Delisser, 1859 113 ("veil")); William Hogan, *Popery! As It Was and As It Is,* quoted and discussed in Norton, *Alternative Americas,* 69–70.

31. For a description, see Gustavus Myers, *History of Bigotry in the United States* (New York:

Random House, 1943), chap 9. Ray Allen Billington, *The Protestant Crusade* (Chicago: Quadrangle, 1964), chap 3, and Charles Morris, *American Catholic* (New York: Random House, 1997), 54–58. On confinement and flagellations, see Monk, *Awful Disclosures*, 47, and Delisser, *Pope or President*, 102–103. On Beecher's role, see Daniel Walker Howe, *The Political Culture of the American Whigs* (Chicago: University of Chicago Press, 1979), 164. See also Rogers M. Smith, *Civic Ideals: Conflicting Visions of Citizenship in U.S. History* (New Haven: Yale University Press, 1997), 211.

32. Richard Hofstadter, *The Paranoid Style of American Politics* (New York: Random House, 1952), 21. In *Ulysses,* James Joyce sends Bloom to a pornographic bookstore where he is offered, among other things, Maria Monk's *Awful Disclosures.*

33. Norton, *Alternative Americas,* 70.

34. The list of adjectives is from Ronald Takaki, *A Different Mirror* (Boston: Little, Brown, 1993), 149. See also Roediger, *Wages of Whiteness,* 133; and, especially, Ignatiev, *How the Irish Became White.*

35. Leon Litwack, *North of Slavery: The Negro in the Free States, 1790–1860* (Chicago: University of Chicago Press, 1961).

36. Frederick Douglass, *My Bondage and My Freedom* (1855; New York: Library of America, 1994), appendix, "The Slavery Party," 443; Smith, *Civic Ideals,* 210 ("whack"). The Irish flight to whiteness is beautifully described by Ignatiev, *How the Irish Became White.*

The German story, incidentally, is entirely different. The Germans arrived in North America far more sympathetic to abolition—if anything, the American context sometimes eroded their support for black freedom.

37. Anonymous [David Croly], *Miscegenation: The Theory of the Blending of Races Applied to the American White and Negro* (New York: H. Dexter Hamilton, 1864), 39–40. Croly's son, Herbert, would found the *New Republic* and become the foremost theorist of the Progressive era.

38. Litwack, *North of Slavery,* 164–165.

39. Litwack, *North of Slavery,* 74–93.

40. For a fine account of the Know-Nothings, see Tyler Anbinder, *Nativism and Slavery* (New York: Oxford, 1992).

41. Anbinder, *Nativism and Slavery,* 252–268.

42. George Templeton Strong, *Diary,* Allan Nevins and Milton Halsey Thomas, eds. (New York: Macmillan, 1952), vol. 2: 196; Anbinder, *Nativism and Slavery,* 84.

43. Abraham Lincoln, Letter to Joshua Speed, August 24, 1855, in *Collected Works,* vol. 2: 323.

44. William Bean, "An Aspect of Know-Nothingism—The Immigrant and Slavery," *Southern Atlantic Quarterly* 23 (October 1924): 319–333; Harry Carmen and Reinhard Luthin, "Some Aspects of the Know-Nothing Movement Reconsidered," *Southern Atlantic Quarterly* 39 (1940): 213–234; Anbinder, *Nativism and Slavery,* 86. Garrison jeered Fillmore as the "supple tool of the slave oligarchy." See his Letter to James Miller McKim, *Letters,* vol. 4: 407.

45. The Massachusetts law divides historians. Joel Silbey wrote that the law "stands as a climactic example of the association of nativist sentiment within the republican party." Eric Foner argues, on the contrary, that the passage of only a two-year waiting period "revealed how weak nativism had become in a state where it had been all powerful just a few years before." Anbinder finds truth on both sides: nativism had greatly diminished by 1859, but it continued to influence Massachusetts Republicans. Silbey, *Transformation of American Politics,* 14–15; Foner, *Free Soil,* 250; Anbinder, *Nativism and Slavery,* 252. For the California resolution, see Silbey, *Transformation of American Politics,* 69.

46. George Fitzhugh, *Cannibals All!: or Slaves Without Masters* (1857; Cambridge, Mass.: Harvard University Press, 1988), 15, 18.

On the northern view of work more generally, see Gordon S. Wood, *The Radicalism of the American Revolution* (New York: Knopf, 1992), 277; on the southern view, see William Harper, "Memoir on Slavery," in *The Pro-slavery Argument; as Maintained by the Most Distinguished Writers of the Southern States* (Richmond, Va.: Walker, Richards, 1852), 19–20.

47. The women in the mills put the same thing more poetically:

> Oh isn't it a pity
> That such a pretty girl as I
> Should be sent to the factory to pine away and die?
> Oh I cannot be a slave
> Oh I will not be a slave
> For I am so fond of liberty
> That I cannot be a slave.

David Roediger and Philip Foner, *Our Own Time: A History of the Working Day* (New York: Verso, 1989), 47.

Orestes A. Brownson, "The Laboring Classes," *Boston Quarterly Review* 3 (July 1840): 370 ("cunning device"), 362ff (England); Brownson edited the *Review.*

48. For a sympathetic portrait of Brownson, see Arthur M. Schlesinger, Jr., *Orestes A. Brownson: A Pilgrim's Progress* (Boston: Little, Brown, 1939). On the morning dram, see W. J. Rorabaugh, *The Alcoholic Republic: An American Tradition* (New York: Oxford University Press, 1979), 132.

49. Lincoln, *Collected Works,* vol. 2: 364 ("man who labored"); 3: 462 (no permanent class); 3: 478 ("mudsill class"); 3: 468, 479 (virtues).

50. Lincoln, *Collected Works,* vol. 2: 379.

51. Horace Greeley, *Hints Toward Reforms* (New York: Harper and Brothers, 1850), 17, 16, 33, 328. It was, incidentally, often the profligate wives who hounded weak men into ruin (329–330). Greeley was the editor of the *New York Tribune,* an anti-slavery paper that attained considerable influence in the North in the 1850s.

52. Paul Boyer, *Urban Masses and Moral Order in America, 1820–1920* (Cambridge, Mass.: Harvard University Press, 1978), 53 ("almshouses"); Foner, *Free Soil,* 24–25 (*Chicago Press and Tribune*); Greeley, *Hints Toward Reforms,* 359ff.

53. Brownson, "Laboring Classes," 369–370.

54. President Andrew Johnson, "First Annual Message," Richardson, *Messages and Papers of the Presidents,* vol. 5: 3559.

55. On the frontier and the battle over slavery, see Richard Slotkin, *The Fatal Environment* (Middletown, Conn.: Wesleyan University Press, 1985), chap 10. On winning over poor whites with the dream of holding slaves, see William Freehling, *The Reintegration of American History: Slavery and the Civil War* (New York: Oxford University Press, 1994), 125–137.

56. Garrison, *Letters,* vol. 3: 473–474; Foner, *Free Soil,* 267 (Wilmot), 266 ("free white men"). The Senate, evenly split between slave and free states, blocked the Wilmot Proviso.

57. Litwack, *North of Slavery,* 70–75; Bernard Bailyn, David Brion Davis, David Herbert Donald, John Thomas, Robert Wiebe, and Gordon S. Wood, *The Great Republic* (Boston: Little, Brown, 1977), 617–618 (on California).

58. Litwack, *North of Slavery,* 70–71.

59. Litwack, *North of Slavery,* 72–73. Ohio was the one state that repealed some of its black laws after abolitionist and free soiler agitation.

60. See Alexis de Tocqueville, *Démocratie en Amérique* (1835, Paris: Flammarion, 1981), vol. 1: 458; *Democracy in America,* 344, 343. Beaumont, *Marie,* 245.

61. James Pike, "What Shall We Do with the Negro?" *New York Tribune,* March 13, 1860, p 6. Pike would become Lincoln's minister to the Netherlands.

62. Pike was not unusual. Observers often speculated about the survival of black Americans, sometimes drawing an analogy to the fate of the American Indians. Tocqueville mused that if whites remained united, blacks were destined to succumb—"either under sword or from misery." His bleak alternatives fit the regional differences in antebellum race politics—the sword of southern violence, economic misery in northern labor markets. Tocqueville, *Démocratie en Amérique,* vol. 1: 474; *Democracy in America,* 357–358.

63. See Andrew Johnson, "First Annual Message" (December 4, 1865), Richardson, *Messages of the Presidents,* vol. 5: 3559; the passage is discussed in the Introduction.

64. The Compromise of 1850 cobbled together the following elements: California entered as a free state, even though it was south of the old Missouri Compromise line dividing slave and free states (Southerners were pushing to extend that line to the Pacific). The rest of the territory taken from Mexico—the Utah and New Mexico territories—would determine slavery for itself by "popular sovereignty," a vague and eventually explosive alternative to the Wilmot Proviso (which was being pushed by many northerners). The compromise officially ended the slave trade (but not slavery) in Washington, D.C., settled a boundary dispute on the Texas border, and made it simpler to snatch back fugitive slaves. Each part of the package attracted a different coalition, making for a distinctly unstable whole.

The debate raised a momentous question: Could the federal government rule out slavery in the territories? The compromise rested on the assumption that it could (the premise behind popular sovereignty); but Congress invited critics to put the question to the courts. They got their answer with the *Dred Scott* decision.

65. Horace Greeley, *The American Conflict* (Hartford, Conn.: O. D. Case, 1865), vol. 1: 216; W. E. B. Du Bois, *Black Reconstruction in America, 1860–1880* (1935; New York: Atheneum, 1992), 20.

66. Gary Collison, *Shadrach Minkins* (Cambridge, Mass.: Harvard University Press, 1997).

67. Albert J. Von Frank, *The Trial of Anthony Burns* (Cambridge, Mass.: Harvard University Press, 1998), xiii.

68. Deuteronomy 27: 15–26; Isaiah (28:15), discussed above. See *Liberator,* July 7, 1854; for a nice description of this familiar rally, see Mayer, *All on Fire,* 443–445.

69. *Dred Scott v. Sandford* 60 US (19 How.) 393 (1857).

70. *Dred Scott v. Sandford* 60 US (19 How.) 393 (1857).

71. Lincoln, *Collected Works,* vol. 2: 408.

72. *The Lincoln-Douglas Debates: The First Complete, Unexpurgated Text,* ed. Harold Holzer (New York: HarperCollins, 1993), 110, 143.

73. *Lincoln-Douglas Debates,* 189, 254, 190, 63. See also Lincoln, *Collected Works,* vol. 2: 405. See Exodus 12:37.

74. Lincoln, *Collected Works,* vol. 2: 409.

75. Lincoln, "First Inaugural Address," *Collected Works,* vol.4: 263. Edward A. Pollard, *Southern History of the War* (1866; New York: Fairfax, 1977), 48, 51; Douglass quoted in Du Bois, *Reconstruction,* 61.

76. C. Vann Woodward, *The Burden of Southern History,* 3rd ed. (Baton Rouge: Louisiana State University Press, 1993), 72 and, generally, chap. 4.

77. *New York Times,* June 11, 1863, pp 4, 8. James M. McPherson, *The Negro's Civil War* (New York: Ballantine, 1991), 187–190.

78. Thomas Wentworth Higginson, *Army Life in a Black Regiment* (1870; New York: Penguin, 1997), 206; Dudley Taylor Cornish, *The Sable Arm: Negro Troops in the Union Army, 1861–5* (New York: Longmans, Green, 1956), 288 (figures) 290 (Butler). Lincoln, "Public Letter to James Conkling," in *Collected Works,* August 26, 1863, vol. 6: 243.

79. Leon Litwack, *Been in the Storm So Long* (New York: Vintage, 1979), 125–131; Iver Bernstein, *The New York City Draft Riots* (New York: Oxford University Press, 1990).

Edward Ayers suggests that the gloomy race view expressed in this paragraph has been all but buried in the triumphal, self-congratulatory view of the Civil War as the great redeeming struggle and suggests that it is time to begin seeing the war as "vindictive, hateful, and destructive" and the peace as a period "that nullified much that the war claimed to have won." Ayers, "Worrying About the Civil War," in *Moral Problems in American Life,* Karen Halttunen and Lewis Perry, eds. (Ithaca, N.Y.: Cornell University Press, 1998), 149–165, quoted at 159. See also David Brion Davis, "The Enduring Legacy of the South's Civil War Victory," *New York Times,* August 26, 2001.

80. Revelation, 14:19 and 20:11–12. For an extended discussion of Revelation and "The Battle Hymn of the Republic"—which makes these connections, passage by passage—see Garry Wills, *Under God* (New York: Simon and Schuster, 1990), chap 19, and Ernest Tuveson, *Redeemer Nation: The Idea of America's Millennial Role* (Chicago: University of Chicago Press, 1969), 197–202.

81. Du Bois, *Black Reconstruction in America,* chap. 5; Higginson, *Army Life in a Black Regiment,* 197.

82. See Wills, *Under God,* 218.

PART III

1. T. DeWitt Talmage, *Social Dynamite, or the Wickedness of Modern Society* (Philadelphia: C. R. Parish, 1888), 48–49, 142; Louis Albert Banks, ed., *T. DeWitt Talmage: His Life and Work* (Philadelphia: John C. Winston, 1902), 77–78. For other celebrated examples of the urban exposés, see Matthew Hale Smith, *Sunshine and Shadow in New York* (Hartford: J. B. Burr, 1870); Helen Campbell, *Darkness and Daylight: Lights and Shadows of New York Life* (Hartford: A. D. Worthington, 1897); John Gough, *Sunlight and Shadow* (Hartford: A. D. Worthington, 1881); James Bryce, *The American Commonwealth* (London: Macmillan, 1888), vol. 2: 281.

2. That Michigan physician was J. J. Mulheron, "Foeticide," *Peninsular Journal of Medicine* 10 (September 1874): 385–391. For the context, see James Mohr, *Abortion in America* (New York: Oxford, 1978).

3. Horatio Robinson Storer, *Why Not? A Book for Every Woman* (Boston: Lee and Shepard, 1866), 85.

4. Howard Grose, *Aliens or Americans* (New York: American Baptist Home Mission Society, 1906), 241.

CHAPTER 8. *Purity and the Woman's Sphere*

1. Courtland Palmer, "A Liberal on Postal Laws to Prevent the Transmission of Indecent Literature in the Mails," *New York Observer,* April 26, 1883. The article is reprinted in its entirety in Anthony Comstock, *Traps for the Young* (New York: Funk and Wagnalls, 1883), chap 13.

2. On the public-private line, see Daniel Scott Smith, "Family Limitation, Sexual Control, and Domestic Feminism in Victorian America," in Nancy Cott and Elizabeth Pleck, *A Heritage of Her Own* (New York: Simon and Schuster, 1979). See also John D'Emilio and Estelle B. Freedman, *Intimate Matters: A History of Sexuality in America* (New York: Harper and Row, 1988), 55–57. D'Emilio and Freedman's book is, for my money, the best single overview of sexual politics in America.

3. Nicholas Francis Cooke, *Satan in Society: By a Physician* (Cincinnati: Vent, 1872), 826; Horatio Robinson Storer, *Is It I? A Book for Every Man* (Boston: Lee and Shepard, 1867), 89–90.

4. Cooke, *Satan in Society,* 41 ("puny"); L. B. Coles, *Philosophy of Health: Natural Principles of Health and Cure* (Boston: Ticknor, Reed and Fields, 1853), 155 ("mental exertion"); D'Emilio and Freedman, *Intimate Matters* 190 ("castrated," "incompetents"); Carroll Smith-Rosenberg, *Disorderly Conduct* (New York: Oxford University Press, 1985), 258 ("grammarian"); Comstock, *Traps for the Young,* 245 ("duty").

5. "Shopping," *New York Times,* June 13, 1881, p 4. See Nicola Beisel's splendid *Imperiled Innocents* (Princeton: Princeton University Press, 1997). Beisel quotes the same article.

6. J. H. Carstens, "Education as a Factor in the Prevention of Criminal Abortion and Illegitimacy," *Journal of the American Medical Association* 47, no. 23 (December 8, 1906): 1889 ("puts on too much style"); Reverend Hollis Read, *The Footprints of Satan* (New York: Treat, 1874), 468; Frances Willard, *Glimpses of Fifty Years* (Chicago: Woman's Temperance Publication Association, 1889), 677.

7. Horace Greeley, *Hints Toward Reforms* (New York: Harper Brothers, 1850), 326–330.

8. Smith-Rosenberg, *Disorderly Conduct,* 224–225.

9. Elizabeth Cady Stanton, "The Solitude of Self" (January 18, 1892) in Ellen Carol DuBois, ed., *The Elizabeth Cady Stanton–Susan B. Anthony Reader* (Boston: Northeastern University Press, 1992). Nesbett quoted in D'Emilio and Freedman, *Intimate Matters,* 62.

10. Smith-Rosenberg, *Disorderly Conduct,* 225.

11. Cooke, *Satan in Society,* 143 ("innocent"); Storer, *Is It I?* 140–141. For a discussion of the power implications, see Nancy Cott, "Passionlessness: An Interpretation of Victorian Sexual Ideology," in Cott and Pleck, *Heritage of Her Own.*

12. See, for example, William Lee Howard, M.D., "The Protection of the Innocent," *Journal of the American Medical Association* 47, no. 23 (December 8, 1906): 1891–1894 (quoted at 1893).

13. See, for example, J. H. Kellogg, *Plain Facts for Old and Young* (Burlington, Iowa: Segner, 1889), 158–160. Kellogg scorches both "the men of the world" and the physicians who warn against sexual abstinence.

14. During the Civil War, General Joseph Hooker found the number of prostitutes in Washington, D.C., a nuisance for his Army of the Potomac. He designated a district for the women, who promptly became known as "Hooker's legions," then as hookers. A variation of the story suggests that Fighting Joe Hooker was not just a regulator but an eager client.

See D'Emilio and Freedman, *Intimate Matters*, figure 15.

15. Coles, *Philosophy of Health*, 154. The advice is ubiquitous in both the medical and the moral tracts following the war.

16. Kellogg, *Plain Facts*, 465–466; Cooke, *Satan in Society*, 150 ("thrice a month").

17. Kellogg, *Plain Facts*, 502–503; Samuel Smiles, *Character* (Chicago: Belford, Clarke, 1883), 178.

18. Cooke, *Satan in Society*, 146 (violence); Victoria Woodhull, "A Speech on the Principles of Social Freedom" (delivered November 20, 1871), in Madeleine Stern, ed., *The Victoria Woodhull Reader* (Weston, Mass.: M & S, 1974), 17; Stanton, "Speech to the McFarland-Richardson Protest Meeting" (delivered May 1869), DuBois, *Stanton-Anthony Reader*, 127.

19. Sex in the tenements was a popular theme. See, for example, W. Travis Gibb, "Criminal Aspects of Venereal Diseases in Children," *Transactions of the American Society for Sanitary and Moral Prophylaxis* 2 (1908): 26; Jacob Riis, *How the Other Half Lives: Studies Among the Tenements of New York* (New York: Scribner's, 1890), 92.

20. On the YMCA, see Beisel, *Imperiled Innocents*, 49–53. Beisel computes that a quarter of the members of the Society for the Suppression of Vice were either millionaires or in the Social Register. For a general description of the Y, see Paul Boyer, *Urban Masses and Moral Order in America: 1820–1920* (Cambridge, Mass.: Harvard University Press, 1978), 112–121.

21. Comstock, *Traps for the Young*, 6. For a biography of Comstock, see Heywood Broun and Margaret Leech, *Anthony Comstock: Roundsman of the Lord* (New York: Albert and Charles Boni, 1927). The army experience is described on 45–58. Broun and Leech quote extensively from Comstock's private journals. When the book was published, Comstock's colleagues—fellow censors—promptly destroyed the journals. Poetic justice, perhaps, but a terrible loss nevertheless.

22. Merriam's speech reprinted in "Obscene Literature," *New York Times*, March 15, 1873, p 1.

23. "Obscene Literature," p 4. The article, like Merriam's speech, looks as if it were written by Comstock himself. Compare Comstock, *Traps for the Young*, preface.

24. *Congressional Globe*, 42nd Congress, 3rd Sess., II (March 1, 1873): 2004–2005.

25. *Congressional Globe*, 42nd Congress, 3rd Sess., II (March 1, 1873): 2005.

26. On the numbers, see Anna Louise Bates, *Weeder in the Garden of the Lord* (New York: University Press of America, 1995), 13.

27. Quotes from Kellogg, *Plain Facts*, 162, 163, 231. Minor variations on the theme can be found in any Victorian advice manuals—the main difference lies only in how explicitly they picture the horrors.

28. These examples come from Cooke, *Satan in Society*, 111–113, and Kellogg, *Plain Facts*, 248–261. This was one of the most popular themes of the Victorian advice books.

29. Comstock, *Traps for the Young*, 139, 132–133; Reverend Louis Banks, *T. DeWitt Talmage: His Life and Work* (Philadelphia: Winston, 1902), 195; Coles, *Philosophy of Health*, 154 ("ruining the race"); Cooke, *Satan in Society*, 97–98. Cooke presumably had seen a patient with advanced syphilis and ascribed the suffering to masturbation. See also Kellogg, *Plain Facts*, 233.

30. Kellogg, *Plain Facts*, 181 ("evil men"), 239 ("cut the throats"); compare Comstock, *Traps for the Young*, 133, 245.

31. Nicola Beisel, "Constructing a Shifting Moral Boundary: Literature and Obscenity in Nineteenth-Century America," in Michele Lamont and Marcel Fournier, eds., *Cultivating Differences: Symbolic Boundaries and the Making of Inequality* (Chicago: University of Chicago Press, 1992), 112, 114.

32. The emphasis on children and class is explored in detail in Beisel, *Imperiled Innocence*.

33. Comstock, *Traps for the Young*, chap 3—in this long list of horrors, Comstock stops just long enough to take a shot at T. DeWitt Talmage. The comments about dime museums are from Elbridge Gerry, founder of the New York Society for the Prevention of Cruelty to Children, quoted in Timothy Gilfoyle, *City of Eros* (New York: Norton, 1992), 190.

34. James Monroe Buckley, in Comstock, *Traps for the Young*, 2. Buckley was the vice president of the New York Association for the Suppression of Vice.

35. Roger Shattuck, "When Evil Is Cool," *Atlantic Monthly*, January 1999, 73–78.

36. Comstock, *Traps for the Young*, chaps 10 and 13.

37. E. H. Heywood, *Cupid's Yokes or The Binding Forces of Conjugal Life* (Princeton, Mass.: Co-operative, 1877), 4, 5, 22.

38. Victoria C. Woodhull, "A Speech on the Principles of Social Freedom," delivered in Steinway Hall (November 20, 1871) (New York: Woodhull, Claflin, 1871), 14, 19; on her congressional testimony, see Victoria Woodhull, "The Memorial of Victoria C. Woodhull" in Paulina Davis, ed., *A History of the National Woman's Rights Movement: From 1850 to 1870* (1871; New York: Kraus, 1971), 95. See also Linda Gordon, *Woman's Body, Woman's Right* (New York: Viking, 1976), 104.

39. Elizabeth Cady Stanton, "Speech to the McFarland-Richardson Protest Meeting" (1869) and "Home Life" (1875), in DuBois, *Stanton–Anthony Reader*, 129, 133.

40. Stanton, "Speech to the McFarland Richardson Protest Meeting" (May 1869), in DuBois, *Stanton–Anthony Reader*, 126–127; Storer, *Is It I?* 108.

41. For Comstock's melodramatic account, see *Traps for the Young*, chap 10; for balance, see Broun and Leech, *Anthony Comstock*, chap 12.

42. The best description of the case is in Beisel, *Imperiled Innocence*, 89–95.

43. Victoria Woodhull became embroiled in one of the great scandals of the era. Frustrated by the stifling double standard, she published the sordid details of a spectacular adultery between one of the most celebrated preachers of the era, the Reverend Henry Ward Beecher, and Elizabeth Tilton—the wife of Beecher's friend and protégé, Theodore Tilton. Beecher sailed through the scandal; Woodhull got pummeled, sued, and ruined. She eventually wound up in England, married nobility, denied her past, and embraced conservative ways. It didn't work. Polite society gossiped, backbit, and shunned her.

On Woodhull, see Barbara Goldsmith, *Other Powers: The Age of Suffrage, Spiritualism, and the Scandalous Victoria Woodhull* (New York: Knopf, 1998). On Stanton's lectures, see Elizabeth Pleck, *Domestic Tyranny* (New York: Oxford University Press, 1987), 65–66.

44. The phrase is often quoted. See Broun and Leech, *Anthony Comstock*, 89.

45. Gilfoyle, *City of Eros*, 188 ("vigilance"). On the post office, see Daniel Carpenter, *The Forging of Bureaucratic Autonomy* (Princeton: Princeton University Press, 2001).

46. For the connection to urban philanthropy, see Paul Boyer, *Purity in Print* (New York: Scribners, 1968), 8–10, 13. On Comstock and the Women's Christian Temperance Union, see Frances Willard, *Glimpses of Fifty Years: The Autobiography of an American Woman* (Chicago: Woman's Temperance Publication Association 1889), 420.

47. Beisel, *Imperiled Innocents*, 85–87. See Comstock's acid rejoinder in *Traps for the Young*, chap 12.

48. *Life*, July 24, 1884, p 1, and July 31, 1884, p 62; David Pivar, *Purity Crusade: Sexual Morality and Social Control, 1868–1900* (Westport Conn.: Greenwood, 1973), 233 ("Half-Holiday"). On public amusements, see D'Emilio and Freedman, *Intimate Matters*, 195–200.

49. "Who's Bernard Shaw? Asks Mr. Comstock," *New York Times*, September 28, 1905, p 9 ("smut dealer"); George Bernard Shaw, *Bernard Shaw: Collected Letters*, ed. Dan H. Laurence (London: Reinhard, 1972), 559–562 ("Comstockery"); Boyer, *Purity in Print*, 29 (on *New Republic*). The cartoon first appeared in *The Masses*, September 1915, p 19. It appears in almost every book on Comstock.

50. Upton Sinclair, "Poor Me and Poor Boston," *Nation*, June 29, 1927; Shaw, *Collected Letters*, 559.

51. Bates, *Weeder in the Garden of the Lord*, vii.

52. Bates, *Weeder in the Garden of the Lord*; Gilfoyle, *City of Eros*, 188 ("mercy").

53. Gordon, *Woman's Body, Woman's Rights*, 103–105.

54. Kate Sanborn, "Frances E. Willard," in *Our Famous Women: An Authorized Record by Twenty Eminent Authors* (Hartford: A. D. Worthington, 1884); Sidney Ahlstrom, *A Religious History of the American People* (New Haven: Yale University Press, 1972), 870. Ahlstrom calls Willard the "single most impressive reformer to have worked within the context of the evangelical churches."

55. Willard, *Glimpses of Fifty Years*, 426–427 ("puffing"), 418 ("inflamed"). *Women's Journal*, December 8, 1894 ("football").

56. My next-door neighbor, half a mile up the dirt road from where I am writing, still has that portrait of Frances Willard (now ignominiously relegated to the closet). Eighty-year-old Yorrick Hurd and his brother Al dimly remember their great-grandmother beginning the Lempster (N.H.) WCTU meetings with a solemn pledge made facing the portrait. The women of the Lempster WCTU were a social force to be reckoned with.

For a terrific description of Willard's politics, see Suzanne Marilley, *Woman Suffrage and the Origins of Liberal Feminism in the United States* (Cambridge, Mass.: Harvard University Press, 1996), chaps 4–6, statistics at 101.

57. Willard, *Glimpses of Fifty Years*, 419–420; for an excellent description, see Pivar, *Purity Crusade*, 110–117.

58. Pivar, *Purity Crusade*, 114.

59. Talmage, *Social Dynamite*, 140.

Susan B. Anthony had addressed the women's temperance organization when it was first formed in 1874. She had been skeptical about a women's do-good organization and pointedly warned them about the political side that they were overlooking in their moral enthusiasm.

> I am always glad to welcome every association of women for any good purpose, because I know that they will quickly learn the impossibility of accomplishing any substantial end . . . without political power. . . .
>   Frederick Douglass used to tell how, when he was a Maryland slave . . . he would go into the far corner of the tobacco field and pray to God to bring him liberty; but God never answered his prayers until he prayed with his heels. And so, dear friends, He never will answer yours for the suppression of the liquor traffic until you are able to pray with your ballots.

By 1881, President Willard was championing suffrage and the WCTU had opened a Franchise Department.

60. For a slightly different shading, see Marilley, *Woman Suffrage*. She describes the first campaign (Anthony, Stanton, and Davis) as the feminism of rights, the second (Willard) as the feminism of fear.

61. Willard, *Glimpses of Fifty Years*, 423–424; Barbara Leslie Epstein, *The Politics of Domesticity* (Middletown, Conn.: Wesleyan University Press, 1981), 137–146.

62. Charles Sheldon, *In His Steps: What Would Jesus Do?* (Chicago: Advance, 1897), 65, 78. Due to a copyright error, many editions of the book sprang up—all quotes are taken from chap 4 (pagination varies).

I use Sheldon as a bit of straw man. His real focus was not on the poor but on the social responsibility of the upper classes—*In His Steps* was originally read chapter by chapter to rouse his congregation and its social conscience.

63. Ida B. Wells-Barnett, *A Red Record: Lynchings in the United States* (1895; Salem, N.H.: Ayer, 1987), 80, 81; on the South, see, among many examples, Willard, *Glimpses of Fifty Years*, 562–568.

64. Wells-Barnett, *Red Record*, 83.

65. Frederick Douglass, "Why Is the Negro Lynched?" *The Lesson of the Hour* (1894), in Philip S. Foner, *The Life and Writings of Frederick Douglass* (New York: International Publishers, 1955), vol. 4: 491; quoted by Wells-Barnett, *Red Record*, 59.

66. Douglass, *Life and Writings*, vol. 4: 503; Wells-Barnett, *Red Record*, 88; see the discussion in Angela Davis, *Women, Race, and Class* (New York: Random House, 1983), chap 11.

67. Pivar, *Purity Crusade*, 139–146. The author has compiled an extremely useful chart showing changes in the age of consent in every state. Pivar endorses the rising new moral stan-

dard; compare D'Emilio and Freedman, *Intimate Matters,* who see in them another restriction on the working class.

68. Mary E. Odem, *Delinquent Daughters: Protecting and Policing Adolescent Female Sexuality in the United States, 1885–1920* (Chapel Hill: University of North Carolina Press, 1995), 81 (traps).

69. Odem, *Delinquent Daughters,* 79–81.

70. Kellogg, *Plain Facts,* 489; Cooke, *Satan in Society,* 151; Storer, *Is It I?* 105, 137. On birth control prices after the Civil War, see D'Emilio and Freedman, *Intimate Matters,* 60–61.

71. Broun and Leech, *Anthony Comstock,* 153.

72. Cooke, *Satan in Society,* 152 ("national vice," "Onan"), 162 ("smile").

73. The nineteenth-century battles over abortion draw a huge commentary. The definitive account is in James Mohr, *Abortion in America* (New York: Oxford University Press, 1978). For the emphasis on male identity as a factor, see G. J. Barker-Benfield, *Horrors of the Half-Known Life* (New York: Harper and Row, 1976). For an emphasis on power relations, see Carroll Smith-Rosenberg, *Disorderly Conduct,* 217–244.

74. For a fascinating review of the available techniques, see Mohr, *Abortion in America,* chap 1.

75. Mohr, *Abortion in America,* 151 ("rare"); estimates of frequency from Catherine Clinton, *The Other Civil War: American Women in the Nineteenth Century* (New York: Hill and Wang, 1999), 157. Smith-Rosenberg, *Disorderly Conduct.*

76. Cooke, *Satan in Society,* 119–123.

77. Horatio Robinson Storer, *Why Not? A Book for Every Woman* (Boston: Lee and Shepard, 1866). Mohr, *Abortion in America,* 157; the most famous analysis of the AMA's power came from the editors of the *Yale Law Journal,* "The American Medical Association: Power, Purpose, and Politics in Organized Medicine," *Yale Law Journal* 63 (May 1954): 933–1022.

78. *New York Times,* April 2, 1878, p 1 ("nefarious"), August 23, 1871, p 6 ("Evil"). On the *Police Gazette,* see Smith-Rosenberg, *Disorderly Conduct,* 226; D'Emilio and Freedman, *Intimate Matters,* figure 8.

79. Mohr, *Abortion in America,* 196–197.

80. "End of a Criminal Life," *New York Times,* April 2, 1878, pp 1–2; Mohr, *Abortion in America,* 199, 303.

81. For a full account of the AMA's motivation, see Mohr, *Abortion in America,* 160–170 and 152 ("mother").

82. On rivals, see Paul Starr, *The Social Transformation of American Medicine* (New York: Basic Books, 1984), 96–99 and part 1, passim. Mohr, *Abortion in America,* 161 ("one sex or another").

83. Mohr, *Abortion in America,* 161.

84. Storer, *Why Not?* 822.

85. Storer, *Why Not?* 64 (Catholics), 63 (foreign birth); Mohr, *Abortion in America,* 167 ("low lived"); J. J. Mulheron, "Foeticide," *Peninsular Journal of Medicine* 10 (September 1874): 390–391.

86. Quotes from Smith-Rosenberg, *Disorderly Conduct,* 237–238; for the link to women's rights, see Barker-Benfield, *Horrors of the Half-Known Life.*

87. Storer, *Why Not?* 81 ("boast"), 82 ("holiest"); Storer, *Is It I?* 9 ("fashion").

88. Willard, *Glimpses of Fifty Years,* 614.

89. Carstens, "Education as a Factor," 1889–1891, quoted at 1890. Lares and Penates were the Roman household gods and meant one's household effects.

CHAPTER 9. *White Slaves and the Modern Witch-Hunt*

1. Frances Willard, *Glimpses of Fifty Years* (Chicago: H. J. Smith for the Women's Temperance Publication Association, 1889), 422; *The Social Evil: With Special Reference to Conditions Existing in the City of New York, A Report Prepared Under the Direction of the Committee of Fifteen* (New York: Putnam, 1902), chap. 7. For a fine discussion of the regulation effort, see David Pivar, *Purity Crusade: Sexual Morality and Social Control, 1868–1900* (Westport, Conn.: Greenwood, 1973), chap 2.

2. Dr. G. Frank Lydston, quoted by Allan M. Brandt, *No Magic Bullet* (New York: Oxford, 1987), 36. Brandt's book is the classic account of venereal disease and American politics.

3. Albert Burr, "The Guarantee of Safety in the Marriage Contract," *Journal of the American Medical Association* 47 (no. 23): 1887–1888; Brandt, *No Magic Bullet,* 12–13 (quoting Morrow).

4. Brandt, *No Magic Bullet,* 20 ("degenerate"); Burr, "Guarantee of Safety in the Marriage Contract," 1888 (malaria). For the same analogy, see Jane Addams, *A New Conscience and an Ancient Evil* (New York: Macmillan, 1912).

5. W. Travis Gibb, "Criminal Aspect of Venereal Diseases in Children," *Transactions of the American Society of Sanitary and Moral Prophylaxis* 2 (1908): 25 ("foreign ideas").

6. Brandt, *No Magic Bullet,* 23 ("poorest to richest").

7. L. C. Allen, *American Journal of Public Health* 5 (1915): 194–203, 196.

8. It was still not entirely polite to discuss the disease in public. Progressives like Prince Morrow pushed the dangers into the open. Physicians congratulated one another for holding symposia on subjects that had been taboo a quarter-century earlier. And yet when the *Ladies Home Journal* published a series on venereal disease in 1906, it lost a reported 75,000 subscribers. When *Damaged Goods,* a play about the VD epidemic, hit Broadway, the *New York Times* primly described it as work dealing with a rare blood disorder.

9. George Kibbe Turner, "The Daughters of the Poor: A Plain Story of the Development of New York City as a Leading Center of the White Slave Trade of the World under Tammany Hall," *McClure's* 34 (November 1909): 45–61. This was the second and more dramatic of two stories Turner wrote for *McClure's.* Ernest A. Bell, *Fighting the Traffic in Young Girls, or War on the White Slave Trade* (n.p.: G. S. Bell, 1910), 261 ("dumps").

10. Turner, "Daughters of the Poor," 47.

11. "To Curb White Slaver," *New York Times,* November 25, 1909, p 7 ("startling"); William Howard Taft, First Annual Message, December 7, 1909, in James Richardson, *Papers and Messages of the Presidents* (Washington, D.C.: Bureau of National Literature, 1911), vol. 10: 7818.

12. *New York Times,* October 24, 1909, p 12 (editorial on Turner article), October 25, 1909, p 2 (a Murphy denial), October 26, 1909, p 3 (reward); October 28, 1909, p 3 (Jewish denial).

13. Bell, *Fighting the Traffic in Young Girls,* 130, 131, 71 ("fruit stores"); for a variation on precisely the same themes, see Clifford Roe, *The Great War on White Slavery: Or Fighting for the Protection of Our Girls* (n.p.: Clifford Roe, 1911), 106–107. Both books continued the "wicked city" tradition by promising (and delivering) "striking pictures."

14. Charles Nelson Crittenton, "The Traffic in Girls," 132–133 (wedding stories, barred doors); Clifford Losh, "The Destruction of the Vice District in Los Angeles," 450, both in Bell, *Fighting the Traffic in Young Girls.*

15. Crittenton, "Traffic in Girls," 132 (sins); *New York Times,* May 5, 1910, p 10 ("five years").

16. *The Statistical History of the United States: From Colonial Times to the Present* (New York: Basic Books, 1976), 716; David Langum, *Crossing the Line* (Chicago: University of Chicago Press, 1994), 130 (Allen quip).

17. The Reverend Charles H. Parkhurst, *Our Fight with Tammany* (New York: Scribners, 1895), 155 ("enticing"), 161 ("Turkey").

18. Frederick Grittner, *White Slavery: Myth, Ideology, and American Law* (New York: Garland, 1990), 90, 104; Bell, *Fighting the Traffic in Young Girls,* 260, 262.

19. Bell, *Fighting the Traffic in Young Girls,* 260.

20. "To Curb White Slaver," *New York Times,* November 25, 1909, p 7; "Oppose White Slave Bill," *New York Times,* December 16, 1909.

21. Langum, *Crossing the Line,* 42, 43; Langum's book is a wonderful account of the Mann Act.

22. Langum, *Crossing the Line,* 49–59.

23. Langum, *Crossing the Line,* 70.

24. "White House Slave Debate Stirs a Row in House," *New York Times,* July 30, 1913, p 2; Langum, *Crossing the Line,* 70–75.

25. Langum, *Crossing the Line,* chaps 5–6; motor vehicles numbers from *Historical Statistics,* 716.

26. Langum, *Crossing the Line*, 179–186. See also "Jack Johnson and White Women: The National Impact," *Journal of Negro History* 58 (January 1973).

27. George J. Kneeland, *Commercialized Prostitution in New York City* (New York: Century, 1913), and *Social Evil in Chicago: A Study of Existing Conditions* (Chicago: Vice Commission of Chicago, 1911); "Is White Slavery Nothing More Than a Myth?" *Current Opinion* 55 (November 1913): 348 ("fifteen thousand").

28. Kneeland, *Commercialized Prostitution*, 104, 103, 105.

29. Kneeland, *Commercialized Prostitution*, 100–106. On the reformers' reactions, see, for example, Kneeland, "Is White Slavery Nothing More Than a Myth?" 348; "Popular Gullibility as Exhibited in the New White Slavery Hysteria," *Current Opinion* 56 (February 1914): 129.

30. Turner quoted in "Defends White Slavery Story," *New York Times*, July 2, 1910: 2; Kneeland, *Commercial Prostitution*, 107 (prostitutes' age).

31. Turner criticized in "White Slave Story False, Says Guide," *New York Times*, October 28, 1909, p 3.

32. Addams, *New Conscience*, 45 (Sims), 49 (Roe), 145 (Roe). Walter Reckless, *Vice in Chicago* (Chicago: University of Chicago Press, 1933), 36–39; see also Grittner, *White Slavery*, chap 3. It gets even more complicated. Contemporary social scientists quote Jane Addams's white slave stories (again, picked up from Roe and Sims) to suggest that it was not only the panic-mongers spreading wild stories. See Ruth Rosen, *The Lost Sisterhood: Prostitution in America, 1900–1918* (Baltimore: Johns Hopkins University Press, 1982).

33. In 1910, 14.6 percent of the population had been born abroad. Calculated from *Historical Statistics*, 8, 117.

34. Lucie Cheng Hirata, "Free, Indentured, Enslaved: Chinese Prostitutes in Nineteenth-Century America, *Signs: Journal of Women in Culture and Society* 5, no. 1 (Autumn 1979): 3–29.

35. Kneeland, *Commercialized Prostitution*, 105–106.

36. Jane Addams, *A New Conscience*, 82 ("dissolute father"), 76 ("shoes"). On the minimum wage, see Ruth Rosen, *Lost Sisterhood*, 26–27.

The battle for a minimum wage was a part of a larger contest regulating women and work. The whole issue was treated differently for men and women. See Theda Skocpol, *Protecting Soldiers and Mothers* (Cambridge, Mass.: Harvard University Press, 1992), especially chaps 4 and 7.

37. "The Futility of White Slave Agitation as Brand Whitlock Sees It," *Current Opinion* 56 (1914): 287–288. Whitlock succeeded Golden Rule Jones as mayor of Toledo and, in 1914, became the U.S. ambassador to Belgium. See also Rosen, *Lost Sisterhood*, 31–32.

38. Lawrence Friedman, *Crime and Punishment in American History* (New York: Basic Books, 1993), 328–332. Rosen, *Lost Sisterhood*, 27–33.

39. "Futility of White Slave Agitation,"287–288. Friedman, *Crime and Punishment in American History*, 330–331.

40. On continuing violence, see Rosen, *Lost Sisterhood*, 32; Friedman, *Crime and Punishment in American History*, 331 (Chicago); "Futility of White Slave Agitation," 287; Freedman and D'Emilio, *Intimate Matters*, 213.

41. Theodore Dreiser, "Foreword: The Early Adventures of Sister Carrie," *Sister Carrie* (New York: Random House/Modern Library, 1927), v–vii.

42. Theodore Roosevelt, *Presidential Addresses and State Papers* (New York: Review of Reviews, 1910), vol. 2: 509.

43. Theodore Roosevelt, "Race Decadence," *Outlook*, April, 8, 1911, pp 763–769, quoted at 764, 766, 767; "The Negro in America," *Outlook*, June 4, 1910, pp 241–244. See also "A Premium on Race Suicide, *Outlook*, September 27, 1913, pp 163–164; Thomas Dyer, *Theodore Roosevelt and the Idea of Race* (Baton Rouge: Louisiana State University Press, 1980), 139–140 (Chinese, Filipinos), 147 (Italians), 149 ("battle for the cradle").

44. Heywood Broun and Margaret Leech, *Anthony Comstock: Roundsman of the Lord* (New York: Albert and Charles Boni, 1927), 248–249; Linda Gordon, *Women's Body, Women's Right* (New York: Viking, 1970), 249–259.

45. Gordon, *Woman's Body, Woman's Right*, 279, 281, 282; Ellen Chesler, *Woman of Valor: Margaret Sanger and the Birth Control Movement in America* (New York: Simon and Schuster, 1992), 217, 287.

46. Michael Guyer, *Being Well Born: An Introduction to Eugenics* (Indianapolis: Bobbs-Merrill, 1920). The text was extremely popular and can still be found in school libraries. For a discussion of feminism, race suicide, and eugenics, see Gordon, *Woman's Body, Woman's Right,* chaps 6, 7 and passim; for a lively overview, see Friedman, *Crime and Punishment in American History,* 335–359.

47. Guyer, *Being Well Born,* 281 (prostitutes), 283 ("criminals"), 298 ("worthless").

48. The tabulation was made by a presidential task force in 1933, reported by John Hingham, *Strangers in the Land: Patterns of American Nativism* (New York: Athenaeum, 1971), 150–151; Guyer, *On Being Well Born,* 301 ("sympathetic man").

49. Friedman, *Crime and Punishment in American History,* 335–336; Odem, *Delinquent Daughters,* 98. The contemporary "three strikes" programs jails for life men and women convicted of three felonies.

50. *Buck v. Bell,* 274 U.S. 205–207 (1927); for discussion, see Rand Rosenblatt, Sylvia Law, and Sara Rosenbaum, *Law and the American Health Care System* (Westbury, N.Y.: Foundation, 1997), 1329–1333; on Nevada and Indiana, see Friedman, *Crime and Punishment in American History,* 337.

51. Paul Lombardo, "Three Generations, No Imbeciles: New Light on *Buck v. Bell,*" *N.Y.U. Law Review* 60 (1985): 30, 61; Stephen Jay Gould, *The Mismeasure of Man* (New York: Norton, 1981).

52. For a terrific description of the cases, see Langum, *Crossing the Line,* 61–56, quoted at 63.

53. One great exception illustrates the rule. The archetypal moral villain did not skulk about on the fringes. Rather, slaveholders had stood at the brilliant center of antebellum society. But recall the abolitionists' response—they imagined the slaveholders right out of the nation. Radicals shunned any act (like voting) that implied community with slavery. Garrison kept insisting: "no union with slaveholders." The fanciful mental gymnastics conceived the slaveholders outside—beyond the social fringe. Normally it does not take so much effort. The villains are usually the weak, the poor, the strangers, the other.

54. See Jane Addams, *Twenty Years at Hull-House* (1910; Urbana: University of Illinois Press, 1990), especially chap 8.

55. Quoted in Aileen S. Kraditor, *The Ideas of the Woman Suffrage Movement, 1890–1920* (New York: Norton, 1981), 119.

56. D'Emilio and Freedman, *Intimate Matters,* 213–214.

57. Quotes from D'Emilo and Freedman, *Intimate Matters,* 209.

CHAPTER 10. *Temperance: Crucible of Race and Gender*

1. The most effective proponent of Prohibition as success is John Burnham. See his "New Perspectives on the Prohibition Experiment of the 1920s," *Journal of Social History* 2 (1968): 51–68, and, more generally, *Paths into American Culture* (Philadelphia: Temple University Press, 1988). Data from United States Alcohol Epidemiological Data Reference Manual, vol. 1 (Rockville, Md.: U.S. Department of Health and Human Services, Public Health Service, Alcohol, Drug Abuse, and Mental Health Administration, National Institute on Alcohol Abuse and Alcoholism, 1985), 6.

2. William Howard Taft, "Is Prohibition a Blow to Personal Liberty?" *Ladies Home Journal,* May 1919, 31; Will Rogers, *The Cowboy Philosopher on Prohibition* (New York: Harper Brothers, 1919), 7, x; Richard Hofstadter, *The Age of Reform* (New York: Knopf, 1955), 289; Upton Sinclair, *The Wet Parade* (New York: Farrar and Rinehart, 1931), vii–viii. On wowsers, see Sinclair's pro-Prohibition novel.

3. Franklin Adams, *New York World,* quoted by David Kyvig, *Repealing National Prohibition* (Chicago: University of Chicago Press, 1979), 114.

4. Tin-eared temperance advocates cheered Russia for going "absolutely dry" while opponents like Samuel Gompers warned Congress that this was the American road to Bolshevism. See the *New York Times,* December 12, 1920 (Russia dry); July 4, 1919 (Gompers); August 7, 1921; and Fabian Franklin, *What Prohibition Has Done to America* (New York: Harcourt, Brace, 1922), chap 10.

5. Jack Blocker, *American Temperance Movements: Cycles of Reform* (Boston: Twayne, 1989), 3 ("all the time"); W. J. Rorabaugh, *The Alcoholic Republic* (New York: Oxford, 1979), 14, 26 (auctions), 27 (southerner); Sean Wilentz, *Chants Democratic* (New York: Oxford, 1984), 146 (shoe merchant); Thomas Pegram, *Battling Demon Rum* (Chicago: Ivan Dee, 1998), 8, 9 (Adams, estimates of consumption). That's a high estimate of per capita consumption; Rorabaugh pegs it at more than five gallons per capita (p 8). My wine estimate assumes 15 percent alcohol content.

6. William Bradford, "Of Plimoth Plantation" (1620–1647; Boston: Wright and Potter, 1898), 33; Andrew Barr, *Drink: A Social History of America* (New York: Carroll and Graff, 1999), 36–38. Rorabaugh, *Alcoholic Republic*, 95–97.

7. On frames, see Joseph Gusfield, "The Culture of Public Problems," in Allan Brandt and Paul Rozin, eds., *Morality and Health* (New York: Routledge, 1997), 201–230. Rorabaugh, *Alcoholic Republic*, 30, 11. The famous quote about "good creature of God" comes from Increase Mather. But the source is reassuringly puritanical: *Wo to Drunkards* (Cambridge, 1673), 4.

8. Wilentz, *Chants Democratic*, 306–314.

9. Gough stayed in the preaching business, offering a positively rococo story to explain his shame. See John Gough, *Autobiography and Personal Recollection of John B. Gough* (Springfield, Mass.: Bill, Nichols, 1869), 201–205.

10. See James A. Morone, "Enemies of the People," *Journal of Health Politics, Policy and Law* 22 (August 1997): 1006.

11. Neal Dow, *The Reminiscences of Neal Dow* (Portland, Me.: Evening Express, 1898), 543 (disarming a drunk), chap 14 (Maine law), chap 18 (touring). See also Dow's entry in *The Cyclopaedia of Temperance and Prohibition* (New York: Funk and Wagnalls, 1891), 411–412.

Frances Willard called Dow the "frosty . . . immortal father of prohibition." *Glimpses of Fifty Years: The Autobiography of an American Woman* (Chicago: Woman's Temperance Publication Association, 1889), 458.

12. Tyler Abinder, *Nativism and Slavery: The Northern Know-Nothings and the Politics of the 1850s* (New York: Oxford University Press, 1992), 141–144.

13. Dow, *Reminiscences of Neal Dow*, 531–539.

14. Benjamin Andrews, *The History of the Last Quarter Century in the United States: 1970–1895* (New York: Scribners, 1896), 293–295. There were lots of different versions of this sly buffoon. See him in his beer garden ("peer garten"), for example, in W. H. Daniels, *The Temperance Reform and Its Great Reformers* (New York: Phillips and Hunt, 1879), 256–258. For the outstanding contemporary description, see Jack S. Blocker, Jr., *"Give to the Winds Thy Fears": The Women's Temperance Crusade, 1873–4* (Westport, Conn.: Greenwood, 1985).

15. The anti-slavery parallel is everywhere. See *Cyclopaedia of Temperance and Prohibition*, 30–33, for some farfetched examples. "National evil" from the WCTU publication *Union Signal*, quoted by Richard Hamm, *Shaping the Eighteenth Amendment* (Chapel Hill: University of North Carolina Press, 1995), 26.

16. Willard, *Glimpses of Fifty Years*, 460.

17. Jack London, *John Barleycorn* (New York: Century, 1913), 4; "A moral substitute," *New York Times*, September 29, 1918. Women had also won full suffrage in Michigan and New York.

18. Peter Odegard, *Pressure Politics: The Story of the Anti-Saloon League* (New York: Columbia University Press, 1928), vii; Lincoln Steffens, *The Autobiography of Lincoln Steffens* (New York: Literary Guild, 1931), 860.

19. Sinclair, *Wet Parade*, 97. The image went back to before the Civil War. But Sinclair breathed life into the old melodrama as late as 1931.

20. The phrase originates with Rayford Logan, *The Negro in American Life and Thought* (New York: Dial, 1954), quoted at 52.

21. The flags fly in Andrews, *Last Quarter Century*, vol. 2: 373. The quotes about white resistance come from James Truslow Adams, *The March of Democracy* (New York: Charles Scribner's Sons, 1933), vol. 2: 132; William A. Dunning, *Reconstruction: Political and Economic* (New York: Harper Brothers, 1907), 117; and Andrews, *Last Quarter Century*, vol. 2: 375. The same story—in the same language—also floats through the novels described in the following paragraph.

22. Thomas Dixon, Jr., *The Leopard's Spots: A Romance of the White Man's Burden* (New York: A. Wessels, 1902), 125–127.

23. Eric Foner, *Reconstruction: America's Unfinished Revolution* (New York: Harper and Row, 1988), xxv, 147.

24. Frederick Hoffman, *Race Traits of the American Negro* (New York: Macmillan, 1896), 328–329. (The book was sponsored by the American Economics Association.) For discussion, see James Morone, "The Corrosive Politics of Virtue," *American Prospect*, May–June 1996. I am grateful to Deborah Stone for this source.

25. Representative Edward Pou (D-N.C.), in *Congressional Record*, 63rd Congress, 3rd session, vol. 52, part 1. December 22, 1914: 507. Philadelphia newspaper quoted by Andrews, *Last Quarter Century*, vol. 2: 155.

26. Lynching statistics from *The Statistical History of the United States: From Colonial Times to the Present* (New York: Basic Books, 1976), 422. Roberta Smith, "An Ugly Legacy Lives On," *New York Times*, January 13, 2000. For recent analyses, see Jacquelyn Dowd Hall, *Revolt Against Chivalry* (New York: Columbia University Press, 1993); W. Fitzhugh Brundage, *Lynching in the New South* (Chicago: University of Illinois Press, 1993); Glenda Elizabeth Gilmore, *Gender and Jim Crow* (Chapel Hill: University of North Carolina Press, 1996); and Leon Litwack, *Trouble in Mind* (New York: Knopf, 1998).

27. On Ida B. Wells, see *The Memphis Diary of Ida B. Wells*, Miriam DeCosta-Willis, ed. (Boston: Beacon, 1995). The newspaperman, John Temple Graves, quoted in Hall, *Revolt Against Chivalry*, 147.

28. Ida Joyce Jackson, "Do Negroes Constitute a Race of Criminals?" *Colored American Magazine* 12 (April 1907), no. 4: 252 (and no. 5: 357).

29. Litwack, *Trouble in Mind*, 348. Evelyn Brooks Higginbotham, *Righteous Discontent: The Women in the Black Baptist Church, 1880–1920* (Cambridge, Mass.: Harvard University Press, 1993), 226–227.

30. J. C. Price, "Negroes," in *Cyclopaedia of Temperance and Prohibition*, 450–451.

31. John Corrigan, "The Prohibition Wave in the South," *American Review of Reviews*, September 1907, pp 328–334, quoted at 329, 330; see also Frank Foxcroft, "Prohibition in the South," *Atlantic Monthly*, May 1908, 627–634.

32. *Crisis* 2, no. 5 (September 1911): 196; Price, *Cyclopaedia of Temperance and Prohibition*, 451; Edward L. Ayers, *The Promise of the New South: Life After Reconstruction* (New York: Oxford University Press, 1992), 180.

33. The argument from the last two paragraphs is taken from Ayers, *Promise of the New South*, 178–182, quoted at 180. The classic source on race trends and Prohibition on the county level is Leonard Blakey, *Sale of Liquor in the South* (New York: N.p., 1912).

34. "The Promotion of Prejudice," *Crisis* 2, no. 5 (September 1911): 196; Price, *Cyclopaedia of Temperance and Prohibition*, 451.

35. "The Promotion of Prejudice," 196.

36. Reverend John E. White, "Prohibition: The New Task and Opportunity of the South," *South Atlantic Quarterly* 7 (1908): 130–142, quoted at 136. Andrews, *Last Quarter Century*, vol. 2: 376.

37. Quoted by Denise Herd, "Prohibition, Racism, and Class Politics in the Post Reconstruction South," *Journal of Drug Issues* 13, no. 1 (Winter 1983): 81.

38. James Timberlake, *Prohibition and the Progressive Movement, 1900–1920* (New York: Atheneum, 1970), 120–124.

39. Will Irwin, "The American Saloon, VI: The Model License League," *Colliers* 41, no. 8 (May 16, 1908), and "More About Nigger Gin," *Colliers* 41, no. 21 (August 15, 1908).

40. Irwin, "More About Nigger Gin," 28, 30; Irwin, "Who Killed Margaret Lear?" *Colliers*, 41, no. 8 (May 16, 1908): 11; Hamm, *Shaping the Eighteenth Amendment*, 238.

41. For a description of the riot, see David Levering Lewis, *W. E. B. DuBois: Biography of a Race* (New York: Henry Holt, 1993), 333–337; and Ayers, *Promise of the New South*, 435–436.

42. "Prohibition."

43. *Congressional Record*, 63rd Congress, 3rd session, vol. 52. December 22, 1914: 507 (Pou),

542 (coach laws). This debate, on the Webb-Kenyon Act described below, is the longest sustained congressional debate on liquor and Prohibition.

44. Haskell quoted in "Beer Test Appeal May Be Filed Today," *New York Times,* May 26, 1919; Fabian Franklin, *What Prohibition Has Done to the Constitution* (New York: Harcourt, Brace, 1922), 73. See a similar sentiment in Sinclair, *Wet Parade,* 108.

45. Between 1905 and 1915, America received 10 million immigrants.

46. Howard Grose, *Aliens or Americans? A Forward Mission Study Course* (New York: American Baptist Home Mission Society, 1906), 159. E. A. Ross, *The Old World in the New* (New York: Century, 1913), 280–290 (ugliness, Jews); Madison Grant, *The Passing of the Great Race* (New York: Scribners, 1920), 18.

47. Josiah Strong, *Our Country* (1886; Cambridge, Mass.: Harvard University Press, 1963), 54–55 ("liquor traffic"); Ross, *Old World in the New,* 274–275; Jacob Riis, *How the Other Half Lives* (New York: Scribners, 1890), 211 (rum shops).

48. Riis, *How the Other Half Lives,* 210 and, generally, chap 18; Howard Grose, *Aliens or Americans?* 216–217; "Dry Law Violators Here Mostly Aliens," *New York Times,* June 12, 1923.

49. Cited in Sidney Ahlstrom, *A Religious History of the American People* (New Haven: Yale University Press), 871–872.

50. Strong, *Our Country,* 55 ("appetites"); Ross, *Old World in the New,* 303.

51. Sinclair, *Wet Parade,* 245; E. A. Ross, "Prohibition as the Sociologist Sees It," *Harper's,* January 1921, pp 186–192, quoted at 187; London, *John Barleycorn,* 75, 61, 54. London's novel is a fascinating book of barroom boasts and bravado by a man struggling with alcohol. He wants an end to it through Prohibition, for he cannot control himself.

52. Grant, *Passing of the Great Race,* 55; Ross, "Prohibition as the Sociologist Sees It," 188–189.

53. Roy Haynes, *Prohibition Inside Out* (New York: Doubleday, Page, 1923), 308.

54. William Howard Taft, "Is Prohibition a Blow at Personal Liberty?" *Ladies' Home Journal,* May 1919, p 31. Taft had opposed Prohibition. In this article he explains why, then calls for Americans to support Prohibition, which had just been ratified by the states. The article, however, became enormously influential and would often be cited by wets.

55. Joseph Gusfield, *Symbolic Crusade* (Urbana: University of Illinois Press, 1986). Though often criticized, Gusfield's book remains one of the most important (and imaginative) accounts of the American obsession.

56. Alan P. Grimes, *The Puritan Ethic and Woman Suffrage* (New York: Oxford University Press, 1967), 115–116.

57. Theodore Dreiser, *Sister Carrie* (1900; New York: Modern Library, n.d.), 48.

58. Riis, *How the Other Half Lives,* 211; *Prohibition: Its Relation to Temperance, Good Morals and Sound Government,* compiled by Joseph Debar (Cincinnati: Joseph Debar, n.d.), 306, 307 (Germans, clubs). This is a useful collection of anti-Prohibition sentiments from the state-level debates. Madelon Powers, *Faces Along the Bar* (Chicago: University of Chicago Press, 1999), 6.

59. Niles Carpenter, "Immigrants and Their Children: A Study Based on Census Statistics," Department of Commerce, Bureau of the Census (Washington, D.C.: Government Printing Office, 1927), 151, 164, and chap 4; Jon Kingsdale, "The Poor Man's Club: Social Functions of the Urban Working-Class Saloon," *American Quarterly* 25 (October 1973): 472–505.

60. Paul Boyer, *Urban Masses and Moral Order* (Cambridge, Mass.: Harvard University Press, 1978), 196; Strong, *Our Country,* 126.

61. *Congressional Record,* 63rd congress, 3rd session, vol. 52. December 22, 1914, 500.

62. Rogers, *Cowboy Philosopher on Prohibition,* 14.

63. For a fine description of prohibition and interstate commerce, see Hamm, *Shaping the Eighteenth Amendment,* chap 7.

64. Peter Odegard, *Pressure Politics,* 143.

65. In fact, Taft was right. In April 1919 the Supreme Court ruled that liquor in transit from one state to another could not be seized, even if both states were dry. But by then it did not matter—the states had already ratified Prohibition. See *New York Times,* April 16, 1919.

66. *Congressional Record*, 63rd Congress, 3rd session, vol. 52. December 22, 1914, 495–620. These 125 pages offer one of the best overviews of the prohibition issue.

67. *Congressional Record*, 63rd Congress, 3rd session, vol. 52. December 22, 1914, 612.

68. *Congressional Record*, 63rd Congress, 3rd session, vol. 52, December 22, 1914 (quoted at 513, 514, 604, 605, 606).

69. *Congressional Record*, 63rd congress, 3rd session, vol. 52, December 22, 1914, 500, 510, 540 (on states' rights), 581 ("dope"). Taft repeated the argument he had made in "Is Prohibition a Blow to Personal Liberty?" 78.

70. See Norman Clark, *Deliver Us From Evil* (New York: Norton, 1966), 124, for a skeptical view of the dry majority.

71. The co-sponsor was Charles Randall, the only member of the House from the Prohibitionist Party who once sponsored a bill to outlaw any American from drinking anywhere—even China. To get a good taste of James Reed, see his "The Pestilence of Fanaticism," *American Mercury* 5, no. 17 (May 1925): 1–7. Reed attacks moral fanatics who push Prohibition, female suffrage, the Mothers' Bureau (staffed by "spinsters beyond the period of hope"), and other schemes, "half bolshevistic, half idiotic."

72. For a good account, see Stephen Skowronek, *Building a New American State* (New York: Cambridge University Press, 1982). See also James A. Morone, *The Democratic Wish: Popular Participation and the Limits of American Government* (New Haven: Yale University Press, 1998), chap 3.

73. Allan Brandt, *No Magic Bullet* (New York: Oxford University Press, 1987), chap 2, quoted at 66 (heretofore), 72 (liquor).

74. "Patriotism Spells Prohibition," *New York Times*, June 18, 1917, p 8.

75. *New York Times*, November 3, 1918.

76. Thomas Pegram, *Battling Demon Rum* (Chicago: Ivan Dee, 1998), 145; on German backlash, see Eric Foner, *The Story of Freedom* (New York: Norton, 1999), 178.

77. *New York Times*, May 1, 1917. The *Times* ran other articles on this theme on April 22, April 23, April 26, May 3, and May 15.

78. Rogers, *Cowboy Philosopher on Prohibition*, 7; Reed, "Pestilence of Fanaticism," *American Mercury* 3, no. 6. "Gompers warns house judiciary committee that growth of bolshevism and other forms of radicalism is due to oppressive legislation," *New York Times*, July 4, 1919; for a similar story, see *New York Times*, June 15, 1919; Italians quoted in "Anti-Dry Men Tell of Wide Support," *New York Times*, January 25, 1919.

79. "Referendum Elections Will Be Sought in 14 States," *New York Times*, February 19, 1919; "Nebraska District Court Holds Ratification Non Binding," *New York Times*, August 19, 1919. For a good description of the Ohio imbroglio, see David Kyvig, *Repealing National Prohibition* (Chicago: University of Chicago Press, 1979), chap 1. See also Rogers, *Cowboy Philosopher on Prohibition*, 22.

80. The idea of organizational fit is described in Theda Skocpol, *Protecting Soldiers and Mothers* (Cambridge, Mass.: Harvard University Press, 1992), chap 1.

CHAPTER 11. *Prohibition and the Rise of Big Government*

1. This chapter is based, in part, on a reading of every *New York Times* article on Prohibition published between 1916 and repeal. I've balanced the *Times* view with partisans on both sides of the issue.

See *New York Times*, April 24, 1919, May 24, 1919 (scientific affidavits), June 2, 1919 (Penn students), June 15 1919 (labor rally). On the definition of "intoxicating," see H.R. 6810 Title II, Sec I. (Title I deals with wartime prohibition, still in effect.)

2. National Prohibition Act, Preface, Title II: Sec 3, and II: Sec 21 (illegal to possess); Title II: Sec 35 (private dwellings); Title II: Sec. 25 (no search warrants).

3. National Prohibition Act, Title II: Sec. 29 (juice). The warning label from David Kyvig, *Repealing National Prohibition* (Chicago: University of Chicago Press, 1979), 21.

4. *New York Times*, May 7, 1930 (Supreme Court); May 29, 1930 (brewing illegal); July 25,

1920 (ban lifted); June 9, 1930 (La Guardia); September 28, 1930 ("immune"). *Daily News* quoted by Edward Behr, *Prohibition: Thirteen Years That Changed America* (New York: Arcade, 1996), 79. Historian Lizbeth Cohen describes raids on immigrant homes in Illinois; the New York newspaper described thousands of raids in the New York area, but not on private homes. See Cohen, *Making a New Deal: Industrial Workers in Chicago, 1919–1939* (New York: Cambridge University Press, 1990), 211.

5. Kenneth Murchison, *Federal Criminal Law Doctrines: The Forgotten Influence of National Prohibition* (Durham, N.C.: Duke University Press, 1994), 16; Justice Holmes was right about the Eighteenth Amendment but not about the Volstead Act.

6. Wayne Wheeler, "The Success and Failure of Prohibition," *Current Opinion* 70 (January 1921): 35–38, quoted at 37. Fish and game figure from Richard Hamm, *Shaping the Eighteenth Amendment* (Chapel Hill: University of North Carolina Press, 1995), 267.

7. *New York Times*, June 10, 1923 (Ford); June 26, 1923 (Harding); January 25, 1926 (Mellon). Andrew Mellon, *Collier's*, January 1926. Upton Sinclair, *The Wet Parade* (New York: Farrar and Rinehart, 1931), 431 (emphasis in original).

8. *New York Times*, June 12, 1923 (arrests).

9. For a fascinating description, see Hamm, *Shaping the Eighteenth Amendment*.

10. *New York Times*, October 16, 1919.

11. See *New York Times*, November 28, 1926; December 2, 1926. (The Prohibition unit went under civil service in 1927.)

12. Everyone quotes this one. For a good context, see Harry Gene Levine, "The Alcohol Problem in America: From Temperance to Alcoholism," *British Journal of Addiction* 79 (March 1984): 110.

13. Herbert Asbury, "When Prohibition Was in Flower," *American Mercury* 63 (July 1946): 40–47.

14. See *New York Times*, January 17, 18, 20, 22, 23, 25, 29; February, 3, 7, 14, 15, 18; March 3, 4, 7, 19, 27 (all 1920).

15. Fabian Franklin, *What Prohibition Has Done to America* (New York: Harcourt, Brace, 1922), 58.

16. *New York Times*, January 1, 1930 (dispute); February 16, 1930 (1,360); February 24, 1930 (61 dead); June 15, 1929 (La Guardia). See also Michael Woodiwiss, *Crime, Crusaders, and Corruption* (New York: Barnes and Noble, 1988), 18–19 (*Tribune, Herald*).

17. *New York Times*, January 19, 1930 (*Congressional Record*); April 27, 28, 30, 1929 (applause); May 10, 1930 (college student).

18. Murder rates calculated from *Historical Statistics*, 414, and U.S. Census Bureau, *Statistical Abstract of the United States: 1999*, 119th ed. (Washington, D.C., 1999).

19. For a description of Remus, see Behr, *Prohibition*, chap 7.

20. Frederick Lewis Allen, *Only Yesterday: An Informal History of the 1920s* (New York: Harper and Brothers, 1931), 259–269, quoted at 261. Graft estimate from Woodiwiss, *Crime, Crusaders, and Corruption*, 73.

21. James Reed, "The Pestilence of Fanaticism," *American Mercury* 5 (May 1925): 3; Kai Erikson, *Wayward Puritans* (New York: Macmillan, 1966), 20.

22. Elton Raymond Shaw, *Prohibition Coming or Going?* (Berwyn, Ill.: Shaw, 1924), 250, 251. Shaw had been the executive secretary of a Prohibition Association. *New York Times*, January 10, 1921 (woodshed).

23. Murchison, *Federal Criminal Law Doctrines*, 72.

24. *New York Times*, January 4, 1930 (attorney general); February 29, 1930 (jury trial). Murchison, *Federal Criminal Law Doctrines*, 154–157, 187, 72.

25. See Paul M. Murphy, "Societal Morality and Individual Freedom," in David Kyvig, ed., *Law, Alcohol, and Order: Perspectives on National Prohibition* (Westport, Conn.: Greenwood, 1985), 73–75; Murchison, *Federal Criminal Law Doctrines*, 54–55.

26. For a colorful description of the case, see Behr, *Prohibition*, 137–139; Murchison, *Federal Criminal Law Doctrines*, 65–68.

27. Murphy, "Societal Morality," 76–77. Murchison, *Federal Criminal Law Doctrines*, 67–68.

28. Murphy, "Societal Morality," 76; Kenneth Rose, *American Women and the Repeal of Prohibition* (New York: New York University Press), 66.

29. Clarence Darrow, "The Ordeal of Prohibition," *American Mercury* 4 (August 1924): 419; for context, see Kyvig, *Repealing National Prohibition*, chap 4.

30. Franklin, *What Prohibition Has Done to America*, 27–28; organizing letter quoted by Kyvig, *Repealing National Prohibition*, 46.

31. The cries about crime appeared with increasing frequency and anger. See, for a small sample, *New York Times*, January 18, 1930; March 9, 1930; April 17, 1930 (stressing juvenile delinquency); May 2, 1930.

32. Franklin, *What Prohibition Has Done to America*, 55–57; the Supreme Court summarized in Murchison, *Federal Criminal Law Doctrines*, and Murphy, "Societal Morality."

33. Alan Grimes, *The Puritan Ethic and Women Suffrage* (New York: Oxford University Press, 1967), 116 (German newspaper); Robert Wesser, "Women Suffrage, Prohibition, and the New York Experience," Milton Plesur, ed., *An American Historian: Essays to Honor Selig Adler* (Buffalo: State University of New York, 1980), 140–148. This was not entirely new—back in 1890, Susan B. Anthony had urged an alliance with wets in the larger cause of suffrage; see Aileen S. Kraditor, *The Ideas of the Woman Suffrage Movement, 1890–1920* (New York: Norton, 1981), 57–58.

34. Rose, *Women and the Repeal*, quoted at 10, 11; Kyvig, *Repealing National Prohibition*, 119, 120.

35. The amusing *Vogue* spread is reproduced in Rose, *Women and the Repeal*, plate 16.

36. E. A. Ross, "Prohibition as the Sociologist Sees It," *Harper's*, January 1921, p 192.

37. Wayne Wheeler, "The Success and Failure of Prohibition," *Current Opinion* 70 (January 1921): 37.

38. Reed, "Pestilence of Fanaticism, 4.

39. *New York Times*, December 28, 1926 (holiday deaths), December 30, 1926 (suicide), December 30, 1930 (editorial). See also, for example, January 18 and 22, 1930.

40. Richard Hofstadter, preface, Andrew Sinclair, *Era of Excess* (New York: Harper, 1955), vii–viii.

41. Edward Larson, *Summer for the Gods: The Scopes Trial and America's Continuing Debate Over Science and Religion* (Cambridge, Mass.: Harvard University Press, 1997), 35–37; Sidney Ahlstrom, *A Religious History of the American People* (New Haven: Yale University Press, 1972), 902–903.

42. Homer Rodeheaver, *Twenty Years with Billy Sunday* (Winona Lake, Ind.: Rodeheaver Hall-Mack, 1936), 69.

43. For a terrific account of the trial, see Larson, *Summer for the Gods;* for an overview of the fundamentalists, see Paul Boyer, *When Time Shall Be No More* (Cambridge, Mass.: Harvard University Press, 1992); Clyde Wilcox, *Onward Christian Soldiers?* (New York: Westview, 2000); Ahlstrom, *Religious History*, 912–915.

44. Klansman's Manual (Knights of the Ku Klux Klan, 1924), 17. On the new Klan, see Nancy MacLean, *Behind the Mask of Chivalry* (New York: Oxford, 1994), esp. chap 5.

45. Leonard Moore, *Citizen Klansmen: The Ku Klux Klan in Indiana, 1921–1928* (Chapel Hill: University of North Carolina Press, 1991), 171, 191; Nancy MacLean, *Behind the Mask*, 104–105 (anti-vice campaign); Rose, *Women and the Repeal*, 66.

46. MacLean, *Behind the Mask*, introduction.

47. For a splendid account of American immigration policy, see Daniel Tichenor, *Dividing Lines: The Politics of Immigration Control in America* (Princeton: Princeton University Press, 2002).

48. Mae M. Ngai, "The Architecture of Race in American Immigration Law: A Reexamination of the Immigration Act of 1924," *Journal of American History* 86 (June 1999) 1: 67–92, esp. 68–69; James Davis, *Selective Immigration* (St. Paul: Scott Mitchell, 1925), 206.

49. Behr, *Prohibition*, 227–228 (Smith speech).

50. See the description in Kyvig, *Repealing Prohibition*, 98–102.

51. Kyvig, *Repealing Prohibition*, 103; Gustavus Myers, *History of Bigotry in the United States*, 2nd ed. (New York: Capricorn, 1964), 270–271 (Bob Jones); Robert Moats Miller, *American Protestantism and Social Issues* (Chapel Hill: University of North Carolina Press, 1958), 51.

52. For the bleak wet denials, see *New York Times,* November 7, 1928.

53. *New York Times,* February 19, 1929 (advertising); February 15, 1929; May 12, 1929; September 9, 1929 (Cherrington of the ASL on insurance); October 16, 1928 (handsome). Ernest Cherrington, *Current Opinion,* January 1921, p 36.

That last idea—making the men more handsome—made an odd motif across the long Victorian moral swing: the crusaders thought virtue actually shined out of people's faces. Remember, for example, how Horatio Storer thought contraception left his generation of women less attractive. The immigrant bashers wouldn't stop about the ugliness of the newcomers. Here, Prohibition made the guys better looking.

54. For a nice description, see Kyvig, *Repealing National Prohibition,* 111–114.

55. *Public Papers and Addresses of Franklin D. Roosevelt* (New York: Random House, 1938), 1933 vol.: 66, 204.

56. Kyvig, *Repealing National Prohibition,* chap 9.

57. *New York Times,* July 20, 2000.

PART IV

1. Edmund Wilson, *The Shores of Light* (New York: Farrar Straus and Young, 1952), 492–499. Michael Denning, *The Cultural Front* (New York: Verso, 1997), 163ff, Franklin Roosevelt quoted from one of his most celebrated speeches, Campaign Address on Progressive Government at the Commonwealth Club, San Francisco, September 23, 1932, in *The Public Papers and Addresses of Franklin D. Roosevelt* (New York: Random House, 1938), vol. 1 (1932): 756.

2. Billy Sunday, "Food for a Hungry World," in Charles Clayton Morrison, ed., *The American Pulpit* (New York: Macmillan, 1925), 331–339. The original story, which is closer to Sunday's first version, is in Matthew 14:16 –21.

3. "Sunday in Manhattan," *Time,* January 15, 1934, p 58; Sunday, "Food for a Hungry World."

4. Walter Rauschenbusch, especially his *Christianity and the Social Crisis* (New York: Macmillan, 1907), quoted at 67, 66, 68. The Social Gospel usually refers to thinkers and activists working mainly between 1885 and 1920. However, the basic Social Gospel precepts leap out at you from Roosevelt's speeches; and, it seems to me, they infuse American cold war thinking as well as the 1960s movements. Of course, plenty of historians had gotten there long before I did. See especially William McLoughlin, *Revivals, Awakenings, and Reform* (Chicago: University of Chicago Press, 1978), and Sidney E. Ahlstrom, *A Religious History of the American People* (New Haven: Yale University Press, 1972).

CHAPTER 12. *The New Deal Call to Alms*

1. Campaign Address on Progressive Government at the Commonwealth Club, San Francisco, September 23, 1932, in *The Public Papers and Addresses of Franklin D. Roosevelt* (New York: Random House, 1938), 1932 vol.: 742–756. For a splendid analysis, see Sidney Milkis, *The President and the Parties* (New York: Oxford, 1993), esp. 38–46.

2. "The Philosophy of Social Justice Through Social Action," Detroit, Mich., October 2, 1932. *Public Papers and Addresses of Franklin D. Roosevelt,* 1932 vol.: 771–780.

3. "Campaign Address on Prohibition," Sea Girt, New Jersey, August 27, 1932. *Public Papers and Addresses of Franklin D. Roosevelt,* 1932 vol.: 684–692.

4. *Time,* October 28, 1935, pp 9–10. The angry quotes came back when Roosevelt sent a letter to churchmen asking for advice. *Time* ran a full page of hot ones. "See Church Losing Power in Politics," *New York Times,* January 12, 1933 (Yearbook of American Churches).

5. Sidney Ahlstrom, *A Religious History of the American People* (New Haven: Yale University Press, 1972), 921–922 (youth pledge); "President Extols Methodist Council," *New York Times,* February 4, 1938; "Churches to Fight for Recovery Program; Leaders of All Faiths Asked to Aid Drive," *New York Times,* July 13, 1933; "Dr. Coffin Advises Clergy: Preach on Gospel, Not Social

Issues," *New York Times,* July 6, 1938. For an extended liberal statement, see Benson Landis, *The Third American Revolution* (New York: Association Press, 1933), esp. 128ff.

6. "Weakening of Religious Faith of College Students," *New York Times,* January 22, 1933.

7. *Time,* November 9, 1936, 14; "President Extols Methodist Council," *New York Times,* February 4, 1938; Matthew 5–7.

8. Second Inaugural Address, January 20, 1937, *Public Papers and Addresses of Franklin D. Roosevelt,* 1937 vol.: 1–6; "President Extols Methodist Council," *New York Times,* February 4, 1938.

9. Informal Remarks to Visiting Protestant Ministers, January 31, 1938, *Papers and Addresses of Franklin D. Roosevelt,* 1938 vol.: 74–75.

10. Roosevelt quoted in "To Put the People Back to Work: Presidential Statement on N.I.R.A., June 16, 1933," in *Public Papers and Addresses of Franklin D. Roosevelt,* 1933 vol.: 251–255; I tell the story in *The Democratic Wish: Popular Participation and the Limits of American Government* (New Haven: Yale University Press, 1998), chap 5, esp. 156–159.

11. Senator Robert Wagner (R-New York) pushed labor's participation past the opposition in both Congress and the administration. Wagner was there, in the first place, thanks to Prohibition. He won his Senate seat in 1926, knocking off the Republican incumbent James Wadsworth. Wadsworth had not been quite dry enough for the Anti-Saloon League, which ran its own candidate, split the conservative vote, and almost certainly won Judge Wagner his Senate seat. Wadsworth offered the perfect political epitaph for the prohibitionists' brand of morals: "We shall continue to suffer just so long as 'thou shalt not' is in the constitution." By the 1930s, Wadsworth was back in Congress, a rising Republican star in the House of Representatives. See David Kvyig, *Repealing National Prohibition* (Chicago: University of Chicago, 1979), 77; *Time,* January 15, 1934, p 23.

12. The Wagner Act is the familiar name for the National Labor Relations Act. See David Plotke, *Building a Democratic Political Order* (New York: Cambridge University Press, 1996).

13. For the first version of "Share the Wealth," and a revealing self-portrait, see Huey P. Long, *Every Man a King: The Autobiography of Huey Long* (New Orleans: National, 1933), esp. 338–340. He shows the changing media coverage by contrasting two stories in *Collier's,* both by the same author: "unconquerable confidence" becomes the "burning eye of fanaticism" (320). For a lively description, see Alan Brinkley, *Voices of Protest: Huey Long, Father Coughlin, and the Great Depression* (New York: Knopf, 1982), 71ff; the bathroom brawl is described at 65. See Hodding Carter, "Kingfish to Crawfish," *New Republic* 77 (1934): 302–305.

14. John Steinbeck, *The Grapes of Wrath* (1939; New York: Penguin, 1992), 11.

15. Ira Katznelson, *The Long 1940s,* manuscript, Columbia University.

16. See Robert Lieberman's splendid *Shifting the Color Line* (Cambridge, Mass.: Harvard University Press, 1998), chap 2. See also Theda Skocpol, "African Americans in U.S. Social Policy," in Paul Peterson, ed., *Classifying by Race* (Princeton: Princeton University Press, 1995); and Jill Quadango, *The Transformation of Old Age Security* (Chicago: University of Chicago Press, 1988); Alice Kessler-Harris, "Designing Women and Old Fools," in Linda Kerber, Alice Kessler-Harris, and Kathryn Kish Sklar, eds., *U.S. History as Women's History* (Chapel Hill: University of North Carolina Press, 1995), 87–106. Kessler-Harris quotes Harlem's Adam Clayton Powell, Jr.

17. Gwendolyn Mink, "The Lady and the Tramp," in Linda Gordon, ed., *Women, the State, and Welfare* (Madison: University of Wisconsin, 1990), 111 ("suitability"); Lieberman, *Shifting the Color Line,* 51 ("decency").

18. *The Statistical History of the United States* (New York: Basic Books, 1976), 422; W. Fitzhugh Brundage, *Lynching in the New South* (Urbana: University of Illinois Press, 1993), epilogue.

19. Brundage, *Lynching in the New South;* Jacquelyn Dowd Hall, *Revolt Against Chivalry: Jessie Daniel Ames and the Women's Campaign Against Lynching* (New York: Columbia University Press, 1993), 169.

20. Suzanne Mettler, *Dividing Citizens: Gender and Federalism in New Deal Public Policy* (Ithaca: Cornell University Press, 1998); Kessler-Harris, "Designing Women and Old Fools," 105 (family wage).

21. Kessler-Harris, "Designing Women and Old Fools," 88 (grandfather).

22. Mink, "Lady and the Tramp," 111ff.

23. Paul Boyer, *Purity in Print* (New York: Scribners, 1968), 84–85 (Joyce), 252 (Will Rogers), 253, 258.

24. Woolsey quoted at length in Robert Haney, *Comstockery in America* (Boston: Beacon, 1960), 27–28; Lawrence Friedman, *Crime and Punishment in America* (New York: Basic Books, 1993), 350–352. See also John D'Emilio and Estelle Freedman, *Intimate Matters* (New York: Harper and Row, 1988), 279–280.

25. Cole Porter, *Anything Goes*—listen to Ella Fitzgerald's recording with the Buddy Bregman Orchestra (February 1956, Capital Studios, Los Angeles). D'Emilio and Freedman, *Intimate Matters,* 280 (they also quote Cole Porter); Haney, *Comstockery in America,* 26–30.

26. D'Emilio and Freedman, *Intimate Matters,* 278–280.

27. Malcolm X, *The Autobiography of Malcolm X,* as told to Alex Haley (New York: Ballantine, 1973), 48; D'Emilio and Freedman, *Intimate Matters,* 245.

28. Frank Walsh, *Sin and Censorship: The Catholic Church and the Motion Picture Industry* (New Haven: Yale University Press, 1996), 79–81.

29. *Time,* July 16, 1934, p 28.

30. James R. Peterson, *The Century of Sex* (New York: Grove, 1999), 116–121. This is a partisan anticensorship view with splendid descriptions of the censored films. Walsh, *Sin and Censorship,* 83–85; Haney, *Comstockery in America,* chap 9; D'Emilio and Freedman, *Intimate Matters,* 280–282.

31. Gregory Black, *The Catholic Crusade Against the Movies* (New York: Cambridge University Press, 1998), chap 3; *United States v. Paramount Pictures* (334 U.S. 131); *Joseph Burstyn, Inc. v. Wilson,* quoted in Haney, *Comstockery in America,* 122.

32. The pledge is often reprinted; see Haney, *Comstockery in America.*

33. Franklin Roosevelt, Annual Message to the Congress, January 6, 1941, *Public Papers and Addresses of Franklin D. Roosevelt,* 1940 vol.: 663–672.

34. Henry R. Luce, "The American Century," *Life,* February 17, 1941.

35. Henry R. Luce, "America's War and America's Peace," *Life,* February 16, 1942.

36. Bruce Bliven, "This Is Where I Came In," *New Republic,* January 5, 1938, 245.

37. Jonathan Daniels, "Pearl Harbor Sunday: The End of an Era," in Isabel Leighton, ed., *The Aspirin Age: 1919–1941* (New York: Simon and Schuster, 1949), 481 (Daniels was Roosevelt's press secretary in 1942–1943). "Editorial: America Goes to War," *Life,* December 22, 1941. See also Henry R. Luce, "America's War and America's Peace," *Life,* February 16, 1942; the ditty is quoted in Robert Dallek, *The American Style of Foreign Policy* (New York: Knopf, 1983), 131.

38. See Robert Westbrook, "Fighting for the American Family," in Richard Wrightman Fox and T. J. Lears, eds., *The Power of Culture* (Chicago: University of Chicago Press, 1993), 195–221; Warren Susman, *Culture as History* (New York: Pantheon, 1984), 194; Norman Rockwell, *My Adventures as an Illustrator* (Garden City, N.Y.: Doubleday, 1960). Stuart Murray and James McCabe, *Norman Rockwell's Four Freedoms: Images that Inspire a Nation* (Stockbridge, Mass.: Berkshire House, 1993).

39. Freda Kirchwey, "Luce Thinking," *Nation,* February 28, 1942.

40. Ruth Benedict, *Race: Science and Politics* (New York: Modern Age, 1940), 220–221; a series of anti-racist resolutions and manifestos is reprinted in an appendix. "The Negro: His Future in America—A Special Section," *New Republic,* October 18, 1943, p 539. David Bennett, *The Party of Fear* (New York: Vintage, 1990), 284–285.

41. Wendell Willkie, *One World* (New York: Simon and Schuster, 1943), chap 13.

42. Eric Foner, *The Story of American Freedom* (New York: Norton, 1998), 239. Peter Biskind, *Seeing Is Believing* (New York: Pantheon, 1983), 59–60.

43. Foner, *Story of American Freedom,* 242; "The Negro: His Future in America," 539.

44. Dan Tichenor, *Dividing Lines: The Politics of Immigration Control in America* (Princeton: Princeton University Press, 2002), chap 6; I. F. Stone, "For the Jews—Life or Death," *Nation,* June 10, 1944; *Public Papers of Franklin D. Roosevelt,* 1938 vol.: "The United States Moves to Help

Refugees from Germany," March 24, 1938, pp 169–175, and "The 501st Press Conference," November 18, 1938, pp 602–604. *Historical Statistics of the United States,* 105. For a general description, see Peter Novick, *The Holocaust in American Life* (Boston: Houghton Mifflin, 1999).

45. "America Goes to War," *Life,* December 22, 1941 ("slant-eyed"); Carey McWilliams, *New Republic,* March 2, 1942, 295–297 ("Yellow Peril," "look alike"); John P. Diggins, *The Proud Decades: America in War and Peace, 1941–1960* (New York: Norton 1988), 32–34 ("rats"); Eugene Rostow, "Our Worst Wartime Mistake," *Harper's,* September 1945, pp 193–201; Howard Zinn, *A People's History of the United States* (New York: Harper and Row, 1980).

46. Carey McWilliams, "The Zoot-Suit Riots," *New Republic,* June 21, 1943, pp 818–820.

47. Walter White, *A Man Called White* (New York: Viking, 1948).

48. Philip A. Klinkner with Rogers M. Smith, *The Unsteady March* (Chicago: University of Chicago Press, 1999), 173; Dominic Capeci, "The Lynching of Cleo Wright," *Journal of American History* 72 (March 1986).

CHAPTER 13. *Manifest Destiny and the Cold War*

1. Reported by Ronald Takaki, *A Different Mirror* (Boston: Little, Brown, 1993), 377. The story was recorded at a reunion of the regiment and the inmates. John Patrick Diggins, *The Proud Decades* (New York: Norton, 1988), 34. On the liberation of the camps, see Peter Novick, *The Holocaust in American Life* (Boston: Houghton Mifflin, 1999), chap 4.

2. See "Protestant Architect," *Time,* April 19, 1954, pp 62–66; Matthew 5:14, 16.

3. U.S. Brewer's Foundation, 1951 (from a series entitled "Home Life in America"); *Life,* January 29, 1951, p 22 (Macy's); February 11, 1957, p 38 (Kasmir); January 1, 1951, pp 89–96.

4. "Communist Power in France," *Life,* January 29, 1951, pp 90–107.

5. Art Buchwald, "New York, C'est Formidable," *Saturday Review,* April 17, 1954.

6. Dulles quoted in "Foreign Aid and Our Moral Credo," *Life,* April 22, 1957, p 42; Diggins, *Proud Decades,* 159; James Patterson, *Grand Expectations* (New York: Oxford, 1996), 282–284 ("dull, duller"). For a similar description cast in the language of mission and covenant, see Anders Stepanson, *Manifest Destiny* (New York: Hill and Wang, 1995), 124; George Jessup, "The World, the Flesh, and the Devil," *Life,* December 16, 1955 ("Satan"); R. Ronald Oakley, *God's Country: America in the Fifties* (New York: Dembner, 1990), 208–209 ("roundhead").

7. George Kennan, *American Diplomacy* (1951; Chicago: University of Chicago Press, 1984), 100–101.

8. *New York Times,* May 22, 1954; *Time,* August 18, 1947, pp 76–77; Reinhold Niebuhr, *The Irony of American History* (New York: Scribners, 1962), 174; for a description of neo-orthodoxy, see Sidney Ahlstrom, *A Religious History of the American People* (New Haven: Yale University Press, 1972), chap 55.

9. *Time,* April 19, 1954, p 62 ("wiseacres"). Will Herberg, *Protestant, Catholic, Jew: An Essay in American Religious Sociology* (Garden City, N.Y.: Doubleday, 1960), 46–47.

10. Eisenhower quoted in Patterson, *Grand Expectations,* 329. Foreign observers were a bit more skeptical about the nationalist streak in the American revival. "American Christianity looks rather earthbound," commented Norwegian Bishop Eivind Berggrav, as if it is "expecting the fulfillment of God's Kingdom here on earth—one might even say expecting its realization in the U.S.A." *Time,* April 19, 1954, p 62.

11. "Big Issue in D.C.: The Oath of Allegiance," *New York Times,* May 23, 1954.

12. *New York Times,* May 23, 1954.

13. *New York Times,* June 15, 1954.

14. "President Hails Revised Pledge," *New York Times,* June 15, 1954.

15. *New York Times,* April 4, 1954.

16. "Emergency in Florida," *New York Times,* June 9, 1954.

17. John K. Jessup, "The World, the Flesh and the Devil," *Life,* December 26, 1955.

18. "Great American Churches," *Life,* January 1, 1951, pp 80–87, quoted at 83.

19. *Time,* October 24, 1954, 54, 58–59; William Packard, *Evangelism in America* (New York: Paragon House, 1996), 156 ("Western Union").

20. *Life,* May 27, 1957, pp 20–27. *Time,* May 31, 1954, pp 58–59 (grateful clergy); and October 25, 1954, 54–60. William Martin, *With God on Our Side* (New York: Broadway Books, 1996), 29 (on communism).

21. *New York Times,* May 7, 1960, p 26 (on the heal-off); *Life,* May 27, 1957, 21 (Catholics); Richard Wrightman Fox, "Experience and Explanation in Twentieth-Century American Religious History," in Harry Stout and D. G. Hart, eds., *New Directions in American Religious History* (New York: Oxford University Press, 1997), 394–412, quoted at 400. For Graham's version, see Billy Graham, *Just As I Am* (San Francisco: HarperSanFranciso, 1997), quoted at 301.

22. Michael Rogin, *Ronald Reagan, the Movie* (Berkeley: University of California Press, 1987), 243, 252; Biskind, *Seeing Is Believing: How Hollywood Taught Us to Stop Worrying and Love the Fifties* (New York: Pantheon, 1983), 137.

23. Biskind, *Seeing Is Believing,* 162–182.

24. Brand Names Foundation, *Life,* January 29, 1951, p 103.

25. Philip Wylie, *Generation of Vipers,* 2nd ed. (New York: Holt, Rinehart and Winston, 1955), 198–199, 65. The book was originally published in 1942; the revised edition takes on the cold war through elaborate footnotes. There is a great deal of commentary on Wylie. See Molly Ladd-Taylor and Lauri Umansky, *"Bad" Mothers: The Politics of Blame in Twentieth-Century America* (New York: New York University Press, 1998).

26. *Life,* December 24, 1956; J. Edgar Hoover, "The Twin Enemies of Freedom: Crime and Communism," delivered before the 28th annual convention of the National Council of Catholic Women, Chicago, November 9, 1956. *Vital Speeches of the Day,* vol. 23 (1956–1957): 104–107.

27. Ruth Rosen, *The World Split Open* (New York: Viking, 200), chap 1, quoted at 14–15 (Spock).

28. Robert Wiebe, "Modernizing the Republic," in Bernard Bailyn et al., *The Great Republic* (Boston: Little, Brown, 1977), 1120–1121.

29. Rogin, *Ronald Reagan,* 27–28.

30. Larry May, "Movie Star Politics," in Larry May, ed., *Recasting America,* 145–146; Frank Walsh, *Sin and Censorship: The Catholic Church and the Motion Picture Industry* (New Haven: Yale University Press, 1996), 194.

31. David Bennett, *The Party of Fear: From Nativist Movements to the New Right in Americana History* (Chapel Hill: University of North Carolina Press, 1988), 287 ("fifth column").

32. Arthur Miller, *The Crucible* (New York: Penguin, 1952), 131–132; Biskind, *Seeing Is Believing,* 169–170; Diggins, *Proud Decade,* 163–165.

33. André Schiffrin, *The Business of Books* (New York: Verso, 2000), 38–39.

34. Bennett, *Party of Fear,* 286–290. Cotton Mather, *Wonders of the Invisible World,* in Samuel G. Drake, ed., *The Witchcraft Delusion in New England* (Roxbury, Mass.: W. Elliot Woodward, 1866), vol. 1.

35. Diggins, *Proud Decade,* 166–167.

36. K. A. Cuordileone, "Politics in an Age of Anxiety: Cold War Political Culture and the Crisis in American Masculinity, 1949–1960," *Journal of American History* 87 (September 2, 2000): 515–545, quoted at 532–533 (Wherry, *News,* Graham); D'Emilio and Freedman, *Intimate Matters,* 292–293.

37. Patterson, *Grand Expectations,* 190; D'Emilio and Freedman, *Intimate Matters,* 293–295.

38. Bennett, *Party of Fear,* 294; David Halberstam, *The Fifties* (New York: Villard, 1993), chap 3.

39. Joseph Alsop, *I've Seen the Best of It* (New York: Norton, 1992), 326; Cuordileone, "Politics in an Age of Anxiety," 521 (queers, Dean Acheson); Halberstam, *The Fifties,* 54 ("against McCarthy").

40. Bennett, *Party of Fear,* 293–305, quoted at 298; Oakley, *God's Country,* 64.

41. *Time,* June 15, 1954, pp 21–22.

42. See Richard Hofstadter, *The Paranoid Style in American Politics* (New York: Random House, 1967); Daniel Bell, ed., *The Radical Right* (Garden City, N.Y.: Doubleday 1964), esp. chap 14; Michael Rogin, *McCarthy and the Intellectuals* (Cambridge, Mass.: MIT Press, 1967); Nelson Polsby, "Toward an Explanation of McCarthyism," *Political Studies* 8 (October 1960): 250–271; Bennett, *Party of Fear,* 310–315.

43. Patterson, *Grand Expectations,* 188 (Gestapo).

44. "Obscene Matter Sent Through the Mail," hearing before the Subcommittee of Postal Operations of the Committee on Post Office and Civil Service, House of Representatives, 86th Congress, First Session, April 23, May 18, 22, 1959 (Washington, D.C.: U.S. Government Printing Office, 1959), 5, 14, 36, 38.

45. Frederic Wertham, M.D., "The Comics . . . Very Funny!" *Saturday Review,* May 29, 1948.

46. *Life,* August 27, 1945, pp 21, 23, 24, 26, 27, 103–109. The *Enola Gay,* which dropped the atomic bomb on Hiroshima, was named after the pilot's mother—still another turn on Wylie's twisted momism.

47. Staff of the Institute for Sex Research, *Sexual Behavior in the Human Female* (Philadelphia: W. B. Saunders, 1953), and *Sexual Behavior in the Human Male* (Philadelphia: W. B. Saunders, 1947).

48. *Time,* January 15, 1934, p 38; Halberstam, *The Fifties,* chap 20; D'Emilio and Freedman, *Intimate Matters,* 285–287.

49. Halberstam, *The Fifties,* chap 20; Patterson, *Grand Expectations,* 355–358. D'Emilio and Freedman, *Intimate Matters,* 286 (quoting *Look*). There is still disagreement over Kinsey's data. One often-mentioned criticism points to the bias introduced by using jail inmates in the large sample (they interviewed more than 18,000 people). For an example of earlier forays into sex research, see "Scholars on Sex," *Time,* July 16, 1934, pp 38–40.

50. Fanny Hill was the heroine of John Cleland's 1750 underground classic *Memoirs of a Woman of Pleasure.* The Supreme Court struck down a Massachusetts ban of a reprint. *A Book Named "John Cleland's Memoirs of a Woman of Pleasure" et al. v. Attorney General of Massachusetts,* 383 U.S. 413, 419 [1966]. See D'Emilio and Freedman, *Intimate Matters,* 287. See also Lawrence Friedman, *Crime and Punishment in American History* (New York: Basic Books, 1993), 352–353.

51. *Newsweek,* July 9, 1962, pp 43–45.

52. *Time,* April 7, 1967, pp 78–83; *Saturday Evening Post,* January 15, 1966, pp 21–25, 66–70. Halberstam, *The Fifties,* 605–606 (Luce).

53. *Time,* April 6, 1967, p 79.

54. *Griswold v. Connecticut,* 381 U.S. 479, 85 S.Ct 1678, 14 L.Ed.2d 510 (1965).

CHAPTER 14. *The Sixties*

1. *Time,* July 7, 1967, pp 18–22 (Pike); Robert Bork, *Slouching Towards Gomorrah* (New York: HarperCollins, 1996), chaps 1–2; Richard Nixon, *In the Arena* (New York: Simon and Schuster, 1990), chap 11. Bishop James Pike was an iconoclastic and controversial figure; see James Pike, *If This Be Heresy* (New York: Harper and Row, 1967).

2. Samuel Huntington, *American Politics: The Promise of Disharmony* (Cambridge, Mass.: Harvard University Press, 1981), 178 (quoting Bickel).

3. For a reading of the sixties as a Great Awakening, see William McLoughlin, *Revivals, Awakenings, and Reform: An Essay on Religion and Social Change in America, 1607–1977* (Chicago: University of Chicago Press, 1978).

4. Ralph Waldo Emerson, "New England Reformers," a lecture read March 3, 1844, in *The Complete Works of Ralph Waldo Emerson* (Cambridge: Riverside, 1903), vol. 3: 253.

5. Philip Altbach, "The Student and Religious Commitment" (1962), in Mitchell Cohen and Dennis Hale, eds., *The New Student Left* (Boston: Beacon, 1966), 22–26; Maurice Isserman and Michael Kazin, *America Divided* (New York: Oxford, 2000), 245 (religious data).

6. For a splendid description of Vatican II and the reactions to it, see Michael Cuneo, *The Smoke of Satan* (Baltimore: Johns Hopkins University Press, 1999), 10–20. I paraphrase Cuneo in the contrast between old and new Catholicism. For original documents, see Walter Abbott, S.J., ed., *The Documents of Vatican II* (London: Geoffrey Chapman, 1966).

7. "How U.S. Catholics View Their Church," *Newsweek,* March 20, 1967, pp 68–75.

8. *Newsweek,* July 26, 1960, p 70; *Newsweek,* July 4, 1960, p 77. Steven Spencer, "The Birth Control Revolution," *Saturday Evening Post,* January 15, 1966, p 67.

9. *Newsweek,* May 1, 1967. Garry Wills, *Under God* (New York: Simon and Schuster, 1990), chap 27.

10. James Kavanaugh, *A Modern Priest Looks at His Outdated Church* (New York: Simon and Schuster, 1967), chap 10.

11. *Newsweek,* May 1, 1967. Chester Gillis, *Roman Catholicism in America* (New York: Columbia University Press, 1999), 108–110.

12. Andrew Greeley, *The American Catholic: A Social Portrait* (New York: Basic Books, 1977); Cuneo, *Smoke of Satan,* 18–19.

13. Figures from Gillis, *Roman Catholicism in America,* chap 4.

14. Kavanaugh, *Modern Priest,* xiii.

15. Cartoon reprinted in *Newsweek,* March 20, 1967, p 70.

16. *National Review,* May 4, 1965 ("modernized"); Cuneo, *Smoke of Satan,* 22–23 ("schismatic"); Isserman and Kazin, *America Divided,* 250 ("Latin's gone").

17. John Stormer, *None Dare Call It Treason* (Forlissant, Mo.: Liberty Bell, 1964), 124–128. The publisher claimed to have run through 15 printings and 3.4 million books in seven months.

18. For a more extended treatment of the civil rights movement, see James A. Morone, *The Democratic Wish: Private Power and American Democracy* (New Haven: Yale University Press, 1998), 186–252.

19. "To All on Equal Terms," *Time,* May 24, 1954, pp 24–25; Gerald Rosenberg, *The Hollow Hope: Can Courts Bring About Social Change?* (Chicago: University of Chicago Press, 1991).

20. *Brown v. Board of Education of Topeka,* 347 Supreme Court Reporter 483 (1954).

21. Martin Luther King, Jr., *Stride Toward Freedom: The Montgomery Story* (New York: Harper and Row, 1958). An even fuller description of King's address appears in Taylor Branch's extraordinary *Parting the Waters: America in the King Years* (New York: Simon and Schuster, 1988), 128ff, 138–142.
A hostile police force officially estimated the crowd at five thousand (the number reported without comment by the press). Later reconstructions estimate the crowd at between 10,000 and 15,000 people. See *New York Times,* December 6, 1955.

22. *New York Times,* March 24, 1956; June 3, 1963; September 26, 1957; February 27, 1956; April 4, 1955; May 27, 1963. Italian communists in Branch, *Parting the Waters,* 203.

23. King, *Stride Toward Freedom,* chap 5; Branch, *Parting the Waters,* 203.

24. Martin Luther King, "Letter from a Birmingham Jail," "I See the Promised Land," both in James Melvin Washington, ed., *I Have a Dream: The Essential Writings and Speeches of Martin Luther King* (San Francisco: HarperSanFranciso, 1986), 96, 284. Martin Walker, *American Reborn* (New York: Knopf, 2000), 328 (Bond).

25. *New York Times,* March 20, 1956; March 23; March 26; April 3.

26. *New York Times,* December 22, 1956 (integrated buses); December 25, 1956 (beating); December 27, 1956; December 28, 1956, and December 30, 1956 (gunfire). See also King, *Stride for Freedom,* chap 9.

27. For a dramatic and bitter description of the church bombing, see *Time,* September 27, 1963, p 17; the castration is described in Dan Carter, *From George Wallace to Newt Gingrich* (Baton Rouge: Louisiana State University, 1996), 2.

28. *New York Times,* December 24, 1955 (terror); April 11, 1956; April 18, 1956 (Cole); November 28, 1955 (beating); May 24, 1961 (flogging).

29. *Time,* March 1, 1954, p 19; May 17, 1954, pp 33–34.

30. *New York Times,* December 3, 1955; December 6, 1955; December 7, 1955 (faculty applause).

31. Eisenhower quoted in Morone, *Democratic Wish,* 203–204.

32. Philip A. Klinkner with Rogers M. Smith, *The Unsteady March: The Rise and Decline of Racial Equality in America* (Chicago: University of Chicago, 1999), 262–263.

33. *Time,* September 27, 1963, p 19. Carter, *George Wallace to Newt Gingrich,* 2.

34. *New York Times,* February 26, 1954 (growth of councils). White Citizens Council, "How Can We Educate Our Children," Irwin Unger and Debi Unger, eds., *The Times Were a Changin': The Sixties Reader* (New York: Three Rivers, 1998), 124–127. The Alabama White Citizens Coun-

cil split over the issue of whether to permit non-Christians to join their fight for segregation, *New York Times*, March 6, 1956.

35. White Citizens Council cited in Wyn Craig Wade, *The Fiery Cross* (New York: Simon and Schuster, 1988), 299 (syphilis). *New York Times*, April 10, 1955 (Virginia).

36. The sit-ins fast became part of the culture. When students at Clemson College (South Carolina) taunted their first black student, Harvey Gantt, he had a ready answer: "If you don't cut it out, I'll have lunch with you." *Time*, August 30, 1963, 12.

37. *Time*, August 30, 1963, pp 9–14; Howard Sitcoff, *The Struggle for Black Equality* (New York: Hill and Wang, 1981), 105 ("troublemakers"). *Newsweek*, November 30, 1964, p 29 (Hoover).

38. *Time*, August 30, 1963, p 12.

39. Morone, *Democratic Wish*, 210–212.

40. *New York Times*, June 20, 1963. *Time*, July 12, 1963, pp 19–20. For analysis, see Philip A. Klinkner and Rogers M. Smith, *Unsteady March* (Chicago: University of Chicago Press, 1999), 268. Arthur Schlesinger, Jr., *A Thousand Days* (Boston: Houghton Mifflin, 1965), 880–881.

41. Lyndon Baines Johnson, "Special Message to Congress: The American Promise," March 15, 1965, in *Public Papers of the Presidents of the United States: Lyndon Baines Johnson* (Washington, D.C.: Government Printing Office, 1965), vol. 1: 281–287.

42. Gunnar Myrdal, *An American Dilemma* (New York: Harper and Row, 1944), vol. 1: lxviii–lxix. Myrdal is usually seen as a consensus liberal, celebrating the American creed. But from the start, he also emphasizes the power of American moralism.

43. *Ebony*, August 1965, p 76; King, "I See the Promised Land," Washington, *Essential Writings and Speeches of Martin Luther King, Jr.*, 281.

44. *The Autobiography of Malcolm X*, as told to Alex Haley (New York: Ballantine, 1964), chap 1.

45. Quoted in Wilson Jeremiah Moses, *Black Messiahs and Uncle Toms: Social and Literary Manipulations of a Religious Myth* (University Park, Pa.: Pennsylvania State University Press, 1993), 213–214. See also Louis Lomax, *The Negro Revolt* (New York: New American Library, 1962), 184–187, for the transcript of an interview with Malcolm X about white devils.

46. *Autobiography of Malcolm X*, 364–368.

47. *Time*, July 31, 1964, pp 9–16; *Autobiography of Malcolm X*, 366.

48. David Garrow, *Bearing the Cross* (New York: Random House, 1986), 481; James T. Patterson, *Grand Expectations: The United States, 1945–1974* (New York: Oxford University Press, 1997), 656; John Dittmer, *Local People: The Struggle for Civil Rights in Mississippi* (Urbana: University of Illinois Press, 1994), 396.

49. "What We Want, What We Believe: Black Panther Party Platform," in William L. Van Deburg, ed., *Modern Black Nationalism: From Marcus Garvey to Louis Farrakhan* (New York: New York University Press, 1997), 249–251. Stokely Carmichael and Charles Hamilton, *Black Power* (New York: Random House, 1967), 47; Julius Lester, *Look Out, Whitey! Black Power's Gon' Get Your Mama!* (New York: Grove, 1968).

50. *New York Times*, June 11, 1964.

51. See Morone, *Democratic Wish*, 218–252.

52. John F. Kennedy, "Inaugural Address," January 20, 1961. For the claim about Harvard graduates, see Jack Newfield, "One Cheer for the Hippies," *Nation*, June 26, 1967.

53. SNCC statement quoted by Sara Evans, *Personal Politics* (New York: Vintage, 1980), 36. Tom Hayden vividly described SNCC in "SNCC in Action" (1961), in *The New Student Left* (Boston: Beacon, 1966), 75–86.

54. Port Huron Statement, drafted June 11–15, 1962. Reprinted in the appendix of James Miller's splendid *Democracy Is in the Streets: From Port Huron to the Siege of Chicago* (New York: Simon and Schuster, 1987), appendix. The following two paragraphs draw on Miller, 146–147.

55. McLoughlin, *Revivals, Awakenings, and Reform*, 216. "Dropouts with a Mission;" *Newsweek*, February 6, 1967, pp 92–95.

56. "The Hippies," *Time*, July 7, 1967, pp 18–22; Newfield, "One Cheer for the Hippies."

57. Aristide Zolberg, "Moments of Madness," in *Politics and Society* 2, no. 2 (1972): 183–207; McLoughlin, *Revivals, Awakenings, and Reform,* 205.

58. Reinhold Niebuhr, *The Irony of American History* (New York: Scribner's, 1962), 16, 42.

59. *Newsweek,* November 30, 1964, pp 29–30 (Hoover's blast); December 21, 1964 (Nobel Prize).

60. Paul Potter, "The Incredible War," speech at Washington antiwar march, April 17, 1965, in Massimo Teodori, ed., *The New Left: A Documentary History* (New York: Bobbs-Merrill, 1968), 246–248. Herbert Marcuse, *An Essay on Liberation* (Boston: Beacon, 1969), 7–8.

61. "Nobel Prize Acceptance Speech," December 10, 1964, 224–226 (lion and lamb), and *Where Do We Go from Here: Chaos or Community?* 627 (napalm), both in *Testament of Hope: Writings and Speeches of Martin Luther King;* "Beyond Vietnam," April 4, 1967, reprinted in *Lyndon Johnson and American Liberalism,* 208–212 ("shining moment").

62. James Burnham, "What Is the President Waiting For?" *National Review,* June 28, 1966, p 612; Paul Goodman, "A Causerie at the Military Industrial Complex," *New York Review of Books,* November 23, 1967. Miller, *Democracy Is in the Streets,* 260.

63. Norman Mailer, *Armies of the Night: History as a Novel, the Novel as History* (New York: New American Library, 1968).

64. Joan Didion, *Slouching Towards Bethlehem* (1968; New York: Modern Library, 2000), 113; Kenneth Lockridge, *A New England Town* (New York: Norton, 1985), 90; Robert Bork, *Slouching Towards Gomorrah,* epigraph.

65. Miller, *Democracy Is in the Streets,* 306 (congressional committee); *Time,* August 15, 1977.

66. Thanks to my colleague Beth Kilbreth for an account of the 1969 SDS convention.

67. Patterson, *Grand Expectations,* chap 25.

68. *Congressional Record—House,* February 8, 1964 (Washington, D.C.: U.S. Government Printing Office, 1964), vol. 110, part 2: 2577, 2578, 2583. For a fine overview of the legislative wrangling, see Cynthia Harrison, *On Account of Sex: The Politics of Women's Issues 1945–1968* (Berkeley: University of California Press, 1988), chap 9.

69. Harrison, *On Account of Sex,* 189; Ruth Rosen, *The World Split Open* (New York: Viking, 2000), 73.

70. On race and gender reform in the nineteenth century, see Chapter 5, above.

71. See Rosen, *World Split Open,* 74–81.

72. D'Emilio and Freedman, *Intimate Matters,* 310–311 (Firestone); Rosen, *World Split Open,* 128–129 (Freeman); Evans, *Personal Politics,* 86–89 and, generally, chap 4.

73. D'Emilio and Freedman, *Intimate Matters,* 324.

74. The giddy media high point of the 1976 election campaign came when Jimmy Carter, the Democratic nominee, tried to reassure readers of *Playboy* (broad moral trends develop slowly) that he was not a latter-day Cotton Mather come to hang witches. "I've looked on a lot of women with lust. I've committed adultery in my heart many times. This is something that God recognizes I will do—and I have done it—and God forgives me for it." The point he was trying to make—that his God would forgive a human foible—was entirely lost in the media's glee about this Baptist with "lust in his heart." The interview appeared in *Playboy,* November 1976.

PART V

1. See Barry O'Neil, "The History of a Hoax," *New York Times Magazine,* March 6, 1994, 46–49. For a classic variation, see William Bennett, *The Index of Cultural Indicators* (New York: Simon and Schuster, 1994), 83.

CHAPTER 15. *Modern Morals*

1. Mark Fisher, "Religious Right Baits a Mousetrap, Disney Boycott Expands," *Washington Post,* August 28, 1997. The boycott's sponsors also included such culturally conservative groups as the Catholic League and James Dobson's Focus on the Family.

2. On the "new Victorians," see Gertrude Himmelfarb, *The Demoralization of Society: From Victorian Virtues to Modern Values* (New York: Knopf, 1994), 3. Himmelfarb begins the book by quoting Prime Minister Margaret Thatcher's enthusiastic response when a reporter sarcastically asked her if her values weren't "Victorian." "Oh, exactly. Very much so. Those were the values when our country became great."

3. *Contract with the American Family: A Bold Plan by the Christian Coalition to Strengthen the Family and Restore Common Sense Values* (Nashville: Moorings/Ballantine, 1995), 122–123. This was a companion to Newt Gingrich's celebrated book *Contract with America*.

4. Andrew Sullivan, "The Scolds," *New York Times Magazine,* October 11, 1998, p 54; "Modern Morality," *Wall Street Journal,* editorial, June 11, 1997; Robert H. Bork, *Slouching Towards Gomorrah: Modern Liberalism and American Decline* (New York: HarperCollins, 1996).

5. Juliet B. Schor, *The Overworked American: The Unexpected Decline of Leisure* (New York: Basic Books, 1991).

6. Education data from Jodi Wilgoren, "Education Study Finds U.S. Falling Short," *New York Times,* June 13, 2001.

7. In the 1960s, the courts did impose limits on police and asserted new rights for defendants. But, in contrast to purity politics, they did not fundamentally reshape crime-fighting organizations and their interests.

8. Jerry Falwell, *Strength for the Journey: An Autobiography* (New York: Simon and Schuster, 1987), 362–365; William Martin, *With God on Our Side: The Rise of the Religious Right in America* (New York: Broadway Books, 1996), 189 (quoting LaHaye). Tim LaHaye is a formidable and prolific evangelical—49 books written, 26 million sold. His latest—and enormously popular—series (written with Jerry Jenkins) offers a blow-by-blow account of the premillennial apocalypse. See, esp., the first book in the series: LaHaye and Jenkins, *Left Behind* (Wheaton, Ill.: Tindale, 1995).

9. "Reverend Reagan," *New Republic,* April 4, 1983, pp 7–9; Tim LaHaye, *The Battle for the Mind* (Old Tappan, N.J.: Revell, 1980), chap 4; Pat Robertson, *The Collected Works of Pat Robertson* (New York: Inspirational Press, 1990), 63.

10. Falwell, *Strength for the Journey,* 360; Terry reported in "Terry Preaches Theocratic Rule: No More Mr. Nice Christian," *News Sentinel* (Fort Wayne, Ind.), August 16, 1993; "Equal Rights Amendment in Iowa Attacked," *Washington Post,* August 23, 1992; Maralee Schwartz and Kenneth Cooper, "Equal Rights Initiative in Iowa Attacked," *Washington Post,* August 23, 1992 (Robertson); I first saw the Robertson quote in Judith Stacey, *In the Name of the Family* (Boston: Beacon, 1996), 1.

11. On the data behind the hype, see Richard Berke, "Christian Right Defies Categories: Survey Discloses Diversity in Politics and Religion," *New York Times,* July 22, 1996; on black Christians, see Clyde Wilcox, *Onward Christian Soldiers? The Religious Right in American Politics* (Boulder: Westview, 2000), 54–57.

12. The material in the previous two paragraphs is from James Morone, "The Corrosive Politics of Virtue, *American Prospect,* May–June 1996, p 31. LaHaye, *Battle for the Mind,* 88. For outstanding examples of the moral case, see James Q. Wilson, *The Moral Sense* (New York: Free Press, 1993), x; Himmelfarb, *Demoralization of Society,* 15, 222. William Bennett, *The Death of Outrage* (New York: Free Press, 1998). Jon Meacham, "What the Religious Right Can Teach the New Democrats," *Washington Monthly,* April 1993, pp 42–46.

13. Ralph Reed, "The Christian Coalition and an Agenda for the New Congress," Remarks to the Detroit Economic Club, January 17, 1995. The Republicans controlled both chambers in the state legislature in just six states in 1990, with the Democrats in control of 30 and 13 split. After the 1994 election, the Republicans controlled 19, the Democrats 19, and 12 were divided.

14. James Brooke, "School Spreads Alcohol Policy to Wine Sips in Paris," *New York Times,* May 31, 1998. "Pledges," *Argus Champion* (Newport, N.H.), January 3, 2001.

15. Figures from U.S. Department of Justice, Bureau of Justice Statistics, *Sourcebook of Criminal Justice Statistics, 1999* (Washington, D.C.: U.S. Department of Justice, 2000), 484 (table 6.1), and 497 (table 6.20); Fox Butterfield, "Serious Crimes Fall for Eighth Consecutive Year,"

New York Times, May 8, 2000, and "Number in Prison Grows Despite Crime Reduction," *New York Times,* August 10, 2000. By 1999 the rate was up to 690 prisoners per 100,000. On Latinos, see Cindy Rodriguez, "Latin Prison Count Called Inaccurate," *Boston Globe,* June 7, 2001.

16. For a splendid overview, see Michael Katz, ed., *The Underclass Debate* (Princeton: Princeton University Press, 1993), esp. the introduction; "The American Underclass," *Time,* August 29, 1977, pp 14–15; Ken Auletta, *The Underclass* (New York: Random House, 1982), 50.

17. William Bennett, John DiIulio, and John Walters, *Body Count: Moral Poverty and How to Win America's War Against Crime and Drugs* (New York: Simon and Schuster, 1996); James Q. Wilson, "What to Do About Crime," *Commentary* 98 (September 1994): 25–34; Jerome Skolnick, "Tough Guys," *American Prospect,* January–February 1997, pp 86–91.

18. *Time,* February 7, 1994.

19. Arline Geronimus et al., "Excess Mortality Among Blacks and Whites in the United States," *New England Journal of Medicine* 1996, no. 335, pp 1552–1558. Arline Geronimus, "To Mitigate, Resist or Undo: Addressing Structural Influences on the Health of Urban Populations," *American Journal of Public Health* 90, no. 68 (June 2000): 867–872; Carol B. Stack, *Call to Home: African Americans Reclaim the Rural South* (New York: Basic Books, 1996); Kathryn Edin and Laura Lein, *Making Ends Meet: How Single Mothers Survive Welfare and Low-Wage Work* (New York: Sage, 1997).

20. See Alfred Blumstein and Joel Wallman, eds., *The Crime Drop in America* (New York: Cambridge University Press, 2000).

21. Crime data from U.S. Federal Bureau of Investigation, reported in U.S. Department of Commerce, *Statistical Abstract of the United States: 1999,* 119th ed. (Washington D.C., 1999). See Blumstein and Wallman, *Crime Drop in America,* esp. chaps 1, 4, 9. For population estimates by age, see U.S. Bureau of the Census, *Statistical History of the United States* (New York: Basic Books, 1976), 10. Marc Mauer, *Race to Incarcerate* (New York: New Press, 1999), 27 (international comparisons), 35–36 (inmates by offense, numbers slightly different than statistical abstract); Clifford Krauss, "How Low Can Crime go?" *New York Times,* January 28, 1996; John D. DiIulio, "Two Million Prisoners Are Enough," *Wall Street Journal,* March 12, 1999. Fox Butterfield, "Defying Gravity, Inmate Population Climbs," *New York Times,* January 19, 1998, and "Number of People in State Prisons Declines Slightly," *New York Times,* August 13, 2001.

22. Mauer, *Race to Incarcerate,* 172.

23. School crime data from *1999 Annual Report on School Safety,* a joint report prepared by the U.S. Department of Education and the U.S. Department of Justice (Washington D.C., 2000), chap 1.

24. This paragraph and the next draw on Eric Schlosser's chilling "Prison Industrial Complex," *Atlantic Monthly,* December 1998, pp 51–77.

25. Mauer, *Race to Incarcerate,* xiv; Mary Zdanowicz, "Mentally Ill at Rikers," *New York Times,* July 24, 2000 (Letters).

26. Christian Parenti, *Lockdown America: Police and Prisons in the Age of Crisis* (New York: Verso, 1999), 137; Timothy Egan, "Soldiers of the Drug War Remain on Duty," *New York Times,* March 1, 1999, and "War on Crack Retreats, Still Taking Prisoners," *New York Times,* February 28, 1999.

27. See Michel Foucault, *Discipline and Punish* (New York: Vintage, 1979), 30, 138–140; Parenti, *Lockdown America,* 133, 137.

28. Fox Butterfield, "Racial Disparities Seen as Pervasive in Juvenile Justice," *New York Times,* April 26, 2000; Robyn Meredith, "Near Detroit, a Familiar Sting in Being a Black Driver," *New York Times,* July 16, 1999; Louise Palmer, "Number of Blacks in Prison Soars: Some Blame Police for Widening Disparity," *Boston Globe,* February 28, 1999; Michael Fletcher, "Criminal Justice Disparities Cited," *Washington Post,* March 4, 2000.

29. Voting reported in "13% of Black Men Won't Be Voting," *Boston Globe,* October 23, 1998.

30. I described four features of the witch-hunt: First, the hunters violate their own society's norms. Second, the boundary between guilt and innocence blurs. Third, people ascribe setbacks

not to a messy real world but to the malice of the neighborhood witch. Finally, buried in the panic glints cold political calculation.

31. Helen Campbell, *Darkness and Daylight: Or Lights and Shadows of New York Life* (Hartford: Worthington, 1900), 573; Jacob Riis, *How the Other Half Lives* (New York: Scribners, 1890), 96, 102; Douglas Kinder, "Shutting Out the Evil: Nativism and Narcotics Control in the United States," *Journal of Policy History* 3, no. 4 (1991): 473.

32. Dr. Edward Williams, "Negro Cocaine Fiends Are a New Southern Menace," *New York Times,* February 8, 1914; David Musto, *The American Disease: The Origins of Narcotics Control* (New York: Oxford, 1987), 282–283.

33. Musto, *American Disease,* 220–228.

34. Elaine Sharp, *The Dilemma of Drug Policy* (New York: HarperCollins, 1994), chap 3; Jay McInerney, *Bright Lights, Big City* (New York: Vintage, 1984), 1; *Time,* July 7, 1967. Musto, *American Disease.*

35. Excerpts from the President's Address, *New York Times,* September 15, 1986.

36. Data from the United States Sentencing Commission, *Special Report to the Congress: Cocaine and Federal Sentencing Policy* (Washington, D.C.: U.S. Government Printing Office, 1995), 122 (on the panic), 1–2 (disparities). For public opinion data—and a terrific overview of the entire scare—see Craig Reinarman and Harry Levine, "Crack in Context: Politics and Media in the Making of a Drug Scare," *Contemporary Drug Problems* 16 (Winter 1989): 535–577. On crack, see Mark Kleiman, *Against Excess: Drug Policy for Results* (New York: Basic Books, 1992), 295–302. For a nicely balanced view, see Dan Waldorf, Craig Reinarman, and Sheigla Murphy, *Cocaine Changes: The Experience of Using and Quitting* (Philadelphia: Temple, 1991).

37. Michael Wibon, "Year After Bias Death, Some Unlearned Lessons," *Washington Post,* June 19, 1987; Egan, "War on Crack Retreats" ("take over"); U.S. Sentencing Commission, *Special Report to the Congress: Cocaine and Federal Sentencing Policy,* 1–2 (disparities).

38. Reinarman and Levine, "Crack in Context," 545. David Lewis and Eric Klineberg, "Taking a Measure of U.S. Drug Policy" (manuscript), 5 (crack deaths); *New York Times,* November 20, 1996; *Washington Post,* May 4, 200.

39. Kenneth Meier, *The Politics of Sin* (Armonk, N.Y.: Sharpe, 1994), 119–121; "Is the Drug War Racist?" *USA Today,* July 23–25, 1993.

40. David Lewis has written extensively on the need to treat rather than jail. See "Medical and Health Perspectives on Failing U.S. Drug Policy," *Daedalus* 121, no. 3 (1992): 165–194. On race and incarceration, see Fox Butterfield, "More Blacks in Their 20s Have Trouble with the Law," *New York Times,* November 5, 1995, and "Defying Gravity, Inmate Population Climbs," *New York Times,* January 11, 1998; David Rothman, "The Crime of Punishment," *New York Review of Books,* February 17, 1994, pp 34–38.

41. On morals and black leaders, see Cathy Cohen, *The Boundaries of Blackness: AIDS and the Breakdown of Black Politics* (Chicago: University of Chicago Press, 1999); D. Hatchett, "Crackin' Down on Crack and Crime," *Crisis* 102 (1995): 18–20 ("be human"); "Church Groups Use Pressure Tactics in Drug Fight," *New York Times,* June 23, 1997 (Indiana). The Texas case comes from interviews I did in Dallas: "Beyond Legalization: New Ideas for Ending the War on Drugs," *Nation,* September 20, 1999, pp 15–16 (congressional caucus).

42. D. B. Ayres, "CIA Director Goes to Watts to Deny Rumors of a Crack Conspiracy," *New York Times,* November 16, 1996; Gary Webb, *Dark Alliance: The CIA, the Contras, and the Crack Cocaine Explosion* (San Francisco: Seven Stories Press, 1999).

43. *New York Times,* November 20, 1996.

44. *U.S. v. Armstrong,* 116 S.Ct. 1490 (1996), 1487, 1494; D. Klaidman, "Here's the Straight Dope," *Newsweek,* October 21, 1996, p 37; Alison Mitchell, "Bush Says the Clinton Administration Waged a Lackluster War on Illegal Drugs," *New York Times,* October 7, 2000.

45. Christopher Wren, "The Opposing Camps Square off at Congressional Hearing," *New York Times,* June 20, 1999 (votes); Laurie Asseo, "Panel Calls for Closing Gap in Cocaine Sentence Standards," *Boston Globe,* April 30, 1997.

46. "Less Disparity Urged in Cocaine Sentencing," *New York Times,* November 20, 1996 (gun).

47. Nick Tosches, "Confessions of an Opium Seeker, *Vanity Fair,* September 2000, p 238.

48. California Proposition 215, section 11362.5 (b), (1), (A).

49. "Senate Tackles Propositions Allowing Illegal Drugs," *New York Times,* December 3, 1996. Irvin Molotsky, "Washington Backs Medical Use of Marijuana, Late Tally Shows," *New York Times,* September 21, 1999; Christopher Wren, "Opposing Camps Square Off," *New York Times,* June 20, 1999.

50. Eva Bertram, Morris Blachman, Kenneth Sharpe, and Peter Andreas, *Drug War Politics: The Price of Denial* (Berkeley: University of California Press, 1996), chap 2, quoted 20–21. Mathea Flaco, "Foreign Drugs, Foreign Wars," *Daedelus* 121, no. 3 (Summer 1992): 1–14.

51. For a splendid and sustained version of this approach, see Bertram et al., *Drug War Politics;* Peter Reuter, "Hawks Ascendant: The Punitive Trend in American Drug Policy," *Daedalus* 121, no. 3 (Summer 1992): 15–52. McCaffrey quoted in John Donelly, "Report Points to U.S. Youth Drug Use," *Boston Globe,* January 2, 2000. On the most ambitious view, see Elliot Currie, "Yes, Treatment. But . . . " *Nation,* September 20, 1999, pp 18–19.

52. The pictures are in Egan, "War on Crack Retreats."

53. Evelyn Nieves, "California Gets Set to Shift on Sentencing Drug Users," *New York Times,* November 10, 2000. Skolnick, "Tough Guys," 86–91 (three strikes).

54. Christopher Wren, *New York Times,* June 20, 1999. Those adjectives are not confined to conservatives. They run through the left-leaning magazines. See the special issue of *Nation,* "Beyond Legalization: New Ideas for Ending the War on Drugs," September 20, 1999.

55. Or recall Justice Brandeis (on wiretaps): "the right to be left alone—the most comprehensive of rights and the right most valued by civilized men."

56. Bork, *Slouching Towards Gomorrah,* 2. Gary Aldrich, *Unlimited Access: An FBI Agent Inside the Clinton White House,* rev. ed. (Washington, D.C.: Regnery, 1998), chap 6.

57. Bennett, *Death of Outrage,* 14–18.

58. The Starr Report: Referral to the U.S. House of Representatives to Title 28, U.S. Code 595(c), Submitted by the Office of Independent Counsel, September 9, 1998, quoted at footnote 274 (cigar), 164, 195. Al Goldstein, "Starr: The New Porn King," *Philadelphia Inquirer,* October 3, 1998.

59. For a heartfelt reflection on this theme, see Cal Thomas and Ed Dobson, "Blinded by Might: The Problem with Heaven and Earth," in E. J. Dionne, Jr., and John J. DiIulio, Jr., eds., *What's God Got to Do with the American Experiment?* (Washington, D.C.: Brookings Institution, 2000), 51–55. The renewed popularity of millennial themes may be an example of the same principle; the premillennial apocalypse emphasizes preparing yourself—there is no saving the nation from the wrath of the last days.

60. U.S. Department of Commerce, *Statistical Abstract, 1999,* table 76. The family data is slippery with politics. William J. Bennett, *The Broken Hearth: Reversing the Moral Collapse of the Family* (New York: Doubleday, 2001), 12 ("gold," "civilization").

61. David Whitman, "The Trouble with Premarital Sex," *U.S. News and World Report,* May 19, 1997, 58 (free milk); David Blankenhorn, *Fatherless America* (New York: Basic Books, 1995), 223–225 ("boring people"). "America's Family Crisis," *Economist,* April 8, 1995, p 79. Francis Fukuyama, "The Great Disruption," *Atlantic Monthly,* May 1999, pp 55–78. Kevin Sack, "Louisiana Approves Measure to Tighten Marriage Bonds," *New York Times,* June 24, 1997.

62. Judith Stacey, "The Family Values Fable," in Stephanie Coontz, ed., *American Families: A Multicultural Reader* (New York: Routledge, 1999), 488, and *The Way We Never Were* (New York: Basic, 1992); U.S. Department of Commerce, *Statistical Abstract, 1999,* tables 654, 651. Morone, "Corrosive Politics of Virtue."

63. Judith Stacey, *In the Name of the Family: Rethinking Family Values in a Postmodern Age* (Boston: Beacon, 1996), 13, 38, 105; Pamela Paul, *I Do . . . for Now: Starter Marriages and the Future of Marriage in America* (New York: Villard, 2001). Carol Tavris, "Goodbye, Ozzie and Harriet," *New York Times Book Review,* September 22, 1996, p 27.

64. Pat Robertson, *The Turning Tide* (Dallas: Word, 1995), 163, 166; Falwell, *Strength for the Journey.*

65. Liberal theologians offer a rival interpretation of the key biblical passage in St. Paul's Letter to the Ephesians, 5:22–31. Gustav Niebuhr, "Southern Baptists Declare Wife Should

Submit to Her Husband," *New York Times,* June 10, 1998; the Baptist official quoted is R. Albert Mohler, Jr., president of the Southern Baptist Theological Seminary in Louisville ("strange"), and Mohler, "Against an Immoral Tide," *New York Times,* June 19, 2000 ("family trouble"). Diego Ribadeneira, "Southern Baptists Trumpet a Victory," *Boston Globe,* June 14, 1998; for another strong statement along the same lines, see Minister Stephen Farish, Council of Biblical Manhood and Womanhood, "Sermon Notes for October 13, 1996" (www.cbmw.org/html/farish_1.htm); for a liberal rejoinder, see A. N. Wilson, "The Good Book of Few Answers," *New York Times,* June 16, 1998; "Biblical Baptists," *Manchester Union Leader* (N.H.), June 12, 1998.

66. "Della Joins Bible Battle: Should the Hubby Be the Boss?" *National Examiner,* July 7, 1998, p 17.

67. *USA Today,* November 9, 1994. See James Morone, "Nativism, Hollow Corporations, and Managed Care: Why the Clinton Health Reform Failed," *Journal of Health Politics, Policy, and Law* 20, no. 2 (Summer 1995): 391–399.

68. William Tucker, "The Moral of the Story," *American Spectator,* October 1996, pp 21–25; Robert Rector, Hearing Before the Committee on Finance, U.S. Senate, 104th Congress, March 9, 1996.

69. Charles Murray, "And Now for the Bad News," *Wall Street Journal,* February 2, 1999; Laura Meckler, "Marriage to Be Welfare Focus: Conservatives Seek Changes in '96 Law Urging Poor to Wed," *Boston Globe,* February 21, 2001.

70. See Sandra Vergari, "Morality Politics and the Implementation of Abstinence-Only Sex Education," in Christopher Z. Mooney, ed., *The Public Clash of Private Values* (New York: Chatham House, 2001), 201–210. Diana Jean Schemo, "Virginity Pledges by Teenagers Can Be Effective, Federal Study Finds," *New York Times,* January 4, 2001, and "Surgeon General's Report Calls for Sex Education Beyond Abstinence Courses," *New York Times,* June 29, 2001.

71. Lawrence M. Friedman, *A History of American Law* (New York: Simon and Schuster, 1986), 671 (Dred Scott); Martin, *With God on Our Side,* 192; Leo Ribuffo, *Right, Center, Left: Essays in American History* (New Brunswick, N.J.: Rutgers University Press, 1992), 68 (Prohibition).

72. Falwell, *Strength for the Journey,* 336; George McKenna, "On Abortion: A Lincolnian Position," *Atlantic Monthly,* September 1995.

73. Kristol quoted in Andrew Sullivan, "The Scolds," *New York Times Magazine,* October 11, 1998, p 50; Stephen L. Carter, *The Culture of Disbelief: How American Law and Politics Trivialize Religious Devotion* (New York: Basic Books, 1993), 58.

74. Katha Pollitt, "Abortion in American History," *Atlantic Monthly,* May 1977.

75. Ronald Dworkin, *Life's Dominion: An Argument About Abortion, Euthanasia, and Individual Freedom* (New York: Knopf, 1993). Hitchens cited in McKenna, "On Abortion."

76. Mary Jo Frug, *Women and the Law* (Westbury, N.Y.: Foundation Press, 1992), 432–499; Catherine A. MacKinnon, *Feminism Unmodified: Discourses of Life and Law* (Cambridge, Mass.: Harvard University Press, 1987); Eileen L. McDonagh, *Breaking the Abortion Deadlock: From Choice to Consent* (New York: Oxford University Press, 1996).

77. Deborah R. McFarlane and Kenneth J. Meier, *The Politics of Fertility Control* (New York: Chatham House, 2001), chap 6. In the long run, limits and other forms of pressure seem to drive away abortion providers, making abortions harder to get. For an analysis of abortion rights in a larger social policy context, see Jean Reith Schroedel, *Is the Fetus a Person?* (Ithaca: Cornell University Press, 2000).

78. Kristen Luker, *Abortion and the Politics of Motherhood* (Berkeley: University of California Press, 1984).

79. Abortion figures calculated from U.S. Department of Commerce, *Statistical Abstract,* table 114, p 123. Data from 1996—which had the lowest abortion rate in two decades. Calculations do not include fetal losses.

EPILOGUE

1. Franklin Roosevelt, Inaugural Address, March 4, 1933, *The Public Papers and Addresses of Franklin D. Roosevelt* (New York: Random House, 1938), vol. 2: 11–16.

2. Invocation quoted in Diana Eck, *A New Religious America: How a "Christian Country" Has Become the World's Most Religiously Diverse Nation* (San Francisco: HarperSanFrancisco, 2001), 222.

3. For the quotes and a good analysis, see Michael Naparstek, "Falwell and Robertson Stumble," *Religion in the News* 4 (Fall 2001): 5, 27.

4. Robert Worth, "A Nation Defined by Its Enemies," *New York Times*, February 24, 2002. Quoting Attorney General Ashcroft ("malignant"), President George W. Bush ("axis"), and Vice President Dick Cheney.

5. Roosevelt, "Inaugural Address."

Index

Abernathy, Ralph, 418

abolition movement, 120–122; and African American stereotypes, 156–159; and anti-abolition mobs, 183–186; evangelical roots of, 123–128, 131, 144–145; factions of, 145; as foreign conspiracy, 185; and gender issue, 121, 165, 186; pamphlets and propaganda for, 186–189; and sexual stereotypes, 149–155

abortion: and morality politics, 453, 487–492; and *Roe v. Wade,* 444, 478, 487–488, 489, 491–492; and Victorian moral reform, 219, 250–256

abstinence: sexual behavior and, 225, 481, 486; and temperance movement, 284

Addams, Jane, 18, 269, 270, 279

affirmative action, 205

African Americans: and abolitionism, 157, 190, 205–215; and American crime policy, 456–457, 462–463; and black jeremiads, 134, 428–430, 435; church affiliation of, 454; as Civil War soldiers, 212–213; colonization and, 136, 137–142, 209, 212; and drug war, 465, 468, 469–471; as immoral "others," 227–228; incarceration rate of, 456, 468; and Irish racism, 196–198; as "mud-sill" class, 169, 174, 180; and Prohibition, 297–302, 310; and racial divisions, in U.S., 20–22; racial eugenics and, 274–275; racial stereotypes of, 155–159, 205–215, 245–247, 293, 294, 487; and religious revivalism, 131–137; sexual stereotypes of, 97, 153, 155, 245–247, 259–260, 294, 422; slaveholder stewardship and, 172–173; Social Security program and, 358; voting

rights for, 208, 295, 301–302; and welfare system, 487; white violence against, and civil rights movement, 419–423; and World War II, 372, 374–375. *See also* amalgamation; lynching

African Methodist Episcopal Church, 133

AIDS: and homosexuals as "others," 97–98; public health response to, 481

Aid to Families with Dependent Children, 358, 485, 486

alcohol consumption: by immigrants, 193, 302–308; and Prohibition cycle, 283–287; racial stereotypes and, 292–302, 305; Social Gospel views of, 19, 308; and temperance movement, 287–292

Allen, Richard, 133, 138–139

amalgamation: and colonization, 138; and Dred Scott decision, 207–208; fears of, and abolition movement, 149–150, 155, 161–162, 163, 164, 167, 171; Irish views of, 196; and "race suicide," 273–277; and sexual stereotypes, 155; Victorian morality and, 227–228, 255

"America First" Committee, 367

American Anti-Slavery Society, 121, 162, 165, 184, 186

American Bible Society, 126, 130

American Colonization Society, 136, 137, 138

American (Know-Nothing) Party, 198–199, 203, 207

American Medical Association (AMA): and abortion, 249, 251, 253, 254, 273, 444; and marijuana, 466

American Revolution, and Great Awakening, 108–112